D0537057

The Days of
H. L. MENCKEN

Happy Days
Newspaper Days
Heathen Days

THE DAYS OF
H. L. MENCKEN

Happy Days

Newspaper Days

Heathen Days

DORSET PRESS   *NEW YORK*

THE DAYS OF H. L. MENCKEN *was first published separately in
three volumes as follows:*
HAPPY DAYS   *Published January 22, 1940*
NEWSPAPER DAYS   *Published October 20, 1941*
HEATHEN DAYS   *Published March 1, 1943*

This edition published by Dorset Press
a division of Marboro Books Corporation,
by arrangement with Alfred A. Knopf, Inc.
1989 Dorset Press

ISBN 0-88029-417-5

Printed in the United States of America
M 9 8 7 6 5 4 3 2 1

Author's Note

THE HISTORY of the three books here brought together is told in their prefaces, and there is little to add save the hope that putting them into one volume will be as convenient to the reader as it has been to the printer, the binder and the publisher. This volume is issued at a time when printing costs have risen so dizzily that every separate book is a furious headache to all concerned in its production. The amalgamation abates that headache by nearly two-thirds, and can be offered at a price considerably less than the price that would have to be asked for separate reprints of the three original volumes. All of them have been published since I reached the perhaps indelicate age of sixty, and I am naturally glad to be able to report that they have sold very well, and brought me a great many agreeable letters from readers. Indeed, they have sold better than any of my other books save " The American Language " and its supplement, and the letters that have come in have been far more friendly than those that the others ever produced. Nearly everyone seems to be pleased, and it follows without saying that I am pleased myself.

One of the things that has most interested me in this correspondence is the fact that many letters have come from women, and that most of them, especially those relating to " Happy Days," have said, in substance, " I had precisely the same experience." It never occurred to me in my youth, or to any other normal American boy of the time, that creatures in skirts and pigtails saw the world as we did. Yet it seems to have been the case, and I am glad of it, for it means that many grandmothers of today, like their husbands and brothers, cherish memories of an era when the world was a great deal more comfortable and amusing than it is today. We were lucky to have been born so soon. As the shadows close in we can at least recall that there was a time when people could spend weeks, months and even years without being badgered, bilked or alarmed. Much of the tang we sensed, of course, was a mere function of youth, but there was also a good deal, I believe, in things themselves. The human race had not yet succumbed to the political and other scoundrels who have been undertaking of late to save it, to its infinite cost and degradation. It had a better time in the days when I was a boy, and also in the days when I was a young newspaper reporter, and some of that better time even slopped over into the first half of the space between the two World Wars. I enjoyed myself immensely, and all I try to do here is to convey some of my joy to the nobility and gentry of this once great and happy Republic, now only a dismal burlesque of its former self.

H. L. M.

Baltimore, 1947.

Contents

HAPPY DAYS

CONTENTS

NEWSPAPER DAYS

CONTENTS

HEATHEN DAYS

HAPPY

DAYS

1880-1892

H. L. MENCKEN

NOTE

Some of these chapters have appeared, either wholly or in part, in the *New Yorker*. The author offers his thanks to the editors of that magazine for permission to reprint them.

Preface

THESE casual and somewhat chaotic memoirs of
days long past are not offered to the nobility and
gentry as coldly objective history. They are, on
the contrary, excessively subjective, and the record of an event is no doubt often bedizened and
adulterated by my response to it. I have made a
reasonably honest effort to stick to the cardinal
facts, however disgraceful to either the quick or
the dead, but no one is better aware than I am of
the fallibility of human recollection. Fortunately,
I have been able to resort, at many points, to contemporary inscriptions, for my people have lived
in one house in Baltimore since 1883, and when I
returned to it in 1936, after five years of absence,
and began to explore it systematically, I found its
cupboards and odd corners full of family memo-
rabilia. My mother, who died in 1925, was one of
those old-fashioned housewives who never threw

anything away, and in the years following her death my sister apparently made only slow progress in excavating and carting off her interminable accumulations. Moreover, I found that my father, ordinarily no cherisher of archives, had nevertheless preserved, for some reason unknown, a file of household bills running from the year of his marriage to the early nineties — not a complete file, by any means, but still one showing many well-chosen and instructive specimens.

I have mined this file diligently, and found a number of surprises in it. One is the discovery that my memory was grossly at fault, for nearly half a century, on a salient point of my education. For all those years I boasted that I could read music at the age of six at the latest — indeed, I boasted that I could read it so far back in my nonage that it was impossible for me to recall the time when I couldn't. These boasts turned out, on reference to the bill file, to be mere sound and hooey, signifying nothing. Therein, as plain as day, was a receipt showing beyond cavil that there was no piano in the house until my *eighth* year — or, to be precise, until I was seven years, four months and one day old. This disconcerting experience caused me to check and re-check the whole saga of my infant recollections, partly by the same bill file, partly by the countless other documents, glyphs and cave-drawings in the house, and partly by the memories of surviving contemporaries. I unearthed many other

PREFACE

errors, but none so gross as the one about my genesis as a *Tonkünstler*, and on the whole I made a
pretty good average score. As Huck Finn said of
" Tom Sawyer," there are no doubt some stretchers
in this book, but mainly it is fact.

It has, so far as I can make out, no psychological,
sociological or politico-economic significance. My
early life was placid, secure, uneventful and happy.
I remember, of course, some griefs and alarms, but
they were all trivial, and vanished quickly. There
was never an instant in my childhood when I
doubted my father's capacity to resolve any difficulty that menaced me, or to beat off any danger.
He was always the center of his small world, and
in my eyes a man of illimitable puissance and resourcefulness. If we needed anything he got it
forthwith, and usually he threw in something that
we didn't really need, but only wanted. I never
heard of him being ill-treated by a wicked sweat
shop owner, or underpaid, or pursued by rent-col-
lectors, or exploited by the Interests, or badgered
by the police. My mother, like any normal woman,
formulated a large programme of desirable improvements in him, and not infrequently labored
it at the family hearth, but on the whole their marriage, which had been a love match, was a marked
and durable success, and neither of them ever neglected for an instant their duties to their children.
We were encapsulated in affection, and kept fat,
saucy and contented. Thus I got through my non-

age without acquiring an inferiority complex, and the present chronicle, both in its materials and in its point of view, must needs fall out of the current fashion, which seems to favor tales of dirty tenements, wage cuts, lay-offs, lockouts, voracious landlords, mine police, foreclosed mortgages, evictions, rickets, prostitution, larceny, grafting cops, anti-Semitism, Bryanism, Hell-fire, droughts, xenophobia, and other such horrors. I was a larva of the comfortable and complacent bourgeoisie, though I was quite unaware of the fact until I was along in my teens, and had begun to read indignant books. To belong to that great order of mankind is vaguely discreditable today, but I still maintain my dues-paying membership in it, and continue to believe that it was and is authentically human, and therefore worthy of the attention of philosophers, at least to the extent that the Mayans, Hittites, Kallikuks and so on are worthy of it.

How, on one of its levels, it lived and had its being in a great American city in the penultimate decade of the last century is my theme, in so far as there is any theme here at all. I shut down my narrative with the year 1892, which saw my twelfth birthday. I was then at the brink of the terrible teens, and existence began inevitably to take on a new and more sinister aspect. It may be that I'll resume the story later on, but that is not certain, for on the whole I am more interested in what is going on now than in what befell me (or anyone

else) in the past. My days of work have been
mainly spent, in fact, in recording the current
scene, usually in a far from acquiescent spirit. But
I must confess, with sixty only around the corner,
that I have found existence on this meanest of plan-
ets extremely amusing, and, taking one day with
another, perfectly satisfactory. If I had my life to
live over again I don't think I'd change it in any
particular of the slightest consequence. I'd choose
the same parents, the same birthplace, the same education (with maybe a few improvements here,
chiefly in the direction of foreign languages), the
same trade, the same jobs, the same income, the
same politics, the same metaphysic, the same wife,
the same friends, and (even though it may sound
like a mere effort to shock humanity), the same relatives to the last known degree of consanguinity,
including those in-law. The Gaseous Vertebrata
who own, operate and afflict the universe have
treated me with excessive politeness, and when I
mount the gallows at last I may well say with the
Psalmist (putting it, of course, into the prudent
past tense) : The lines have fallen unto me in pleasant places.

Roaring Gap, N. C., 1939.   H. L. M.

I

INTRODUCTION TO THE

𝕌niverse

At the instant I first became aware of the cosmos
we all infest I was sitting in my mother's lap and
blinking at a great burst of lights, some of them
red and others green, but most of them only the
bright yellow of flaring gas. The time: the evening
of Thursday, September 13, 1883, which was the
day after my third birthday. The place: a ledge
outside the second-story front windows of my father's cigar factory at 368 Baltimore street, Baltimore, Maryland, U. S. A., fenced off from space
and disaster by a sign bearing the majestic legend:
AUG. MENCKEN & BRO. The occasion: the
third and last annual Summer Nights' Carnival of
the Order of Orioles, a society that adjourned *sine
die*, with a thumping deficit, the very next morning,

3

and has since been forgotten by the whole human race.

At that larval stage of my life, of course, I knew nothing whatever about the Order of Orioles, just as I knew nothing whatever about the United States, though I had been born to their liberties, and was entitled to the protection of their army and navy. All I was aware of, emerging from the unfathomable abyss of nonentity, was the fact that the world I had just burst into seemed to be very brilliant, and that peeping at it over my father's sign was somewhat hard on my still gelatinous bones. So I made signals of distress to my mother and was duly hauled into her lap, where I first dozed and then snored away until the lights went out, and the family buggy wafted me home, still asleep.

The latter details, you will understand, I learned subsequently from historians, but I remember the lights with great clarity, and entirely on my own. They constitute not only the earliest of all my earthly recollections, but also one of my most vivid, and I take no stock in the theories of psychologists who teach that events experienced so early in life are never really recalled, but only reconstructed from family gossip. To be sure, there is a dead line beyond which even the most grasping memory does not reach, but I am sure that in my own case it must have run with my third birthday. Ask me if I recall the occasion, probably before my sec-

ond, when I was initiated into the game of I-spy by
a neighbor boy, and went to hide behind a wire
screen, and was astonished when he detected me —
ask me about that, and I'll admit freely that I recall nothing of it whatever, but only the ensuing
anecdote, which my poor mother was so fond of telling that in the end I hid in the cellar every time she
started it. Nor do I remember anything on my own
about my baptism (at which ceremonial my father,
so I have heard, made efforts to get the rector
tight, and was hoist by his own petard), for I was
then but a few months old. But not all the psychologists on earth, working in shifts like coal-miners,
will ever convince me that I don't remember those
lights, and wholly under my own steam.

They made their flash and then went out, and the
fog again closed down. I don't recall moving to the
new house in Hollins street that was to be my home
for so many years, though we took possession of it
only a few weeks later. I don't recall going into
pants at about a quarter to four years, though it
must have been a colossal experience, full of pride
and glory. But gradually, as my consciousness
jelled, my days began to be speckled with other
events that, for one reason or another, stuck. I recall, though only somewhat vaguely, the deck of an
excursion-boat, *circa* 1885, its deafening siren, and
the wide, gray waters of Chesapeake Bay. I recall
very clearly being taken by my father to a clothing-
store bright with arc-lights, then a novelty in the

world, and seeing great piles of elegant Sunday suits, and coming home with one that was tight across the stern. I recall a straw hat with flowing ribbons, a cat named Pinkie, and my brother Charlie, then still a brat in long clothes, howling like a catamount one hot Summer night, while my mother dosed him with the whole pharmacopoeia of the house, and frisked him for outlaw pins. I recall, again, my introduction to the wonderland of science, with an earthworm (*Lumbricus terrestris*) as my first subject, and the experiment directed toward finding out how long it would take him, laid out in the sun on the backyard walk, to fry to death. And I recall my mother reading to me, on a dark Winter afternoon, out of a book describing the adventures of the Simple Simon who went to a fair, the while she sipped a cup of tea that smelled very cheerful, and I glued my nose to the frosty window pane, watching a lamplighter light the lamps in Union Square across the street and wondering what a fair might be. It was a charming, colorful, Kate Greenaway world that her reading took me into, and to this day I can shut my eyes and still see its little timbered houses, its boys and girls gamboling on village greens, and its unclouded skies of pale blue.

I was on the fattish side as an infant, with a scow-like beam and noticeable jowls. Dr. C. L. Buddenbohn, who fetched me into sentience at 9 p.m., precisely, of Sunday, September 12, 1880, apparently made a good (though, as I hear, somewhat rough) job of it, despite the fact that his surviving bill, dated October 2, shows that all he charged " to one confinement " was ten dollars. The science of infant feeding, in those days, was as rudimentary as bacteriology or social justice, but there can be no doubt that I got plenty of calories and vitamins, and probably even an overdose. There is a photograph of me at eighteen months which looks like the pictures the milk companies print in the rotogravure sections of the Sunday papers, whooping up the zeal of their cows. If cannibalism had not been abolished in Maryland some years before my birth I'd have butchered beautifully.

My mother used to tell me years afterward that my bulk often attracted public notice, especially when it was set off dramatically against her own lack of it, for she was of slight frame and less than average height, and looked, in her blue-eyed blondness, to be even younger than she actually was. Once, hauling me somewhere by horse-car, she was confronted by an old man who gaped at her and me for a while with senile impertinence, and then burst out: " Good God, girl, is that baby *yours?* " This adiposity passed off as I began to run about, and from the age of six onward I was rather skinny, but toward the end of my twenties my cross-section again became a circle, and at thirty I was taking one of the first of the anti-fat cures, and beating it by sly resorts to malt liquor.

My gradually accumulating and clarifying memories of infancy have to do chiefly with the backyard in Hollins street, which had the unusual length, for a yard in a city block, of a hundred feet. Along with my brother Charlie, who followed me into this vale when I was but twenty months old, I spent most of my pre-school leisure in it, and found it a strange, wild land of endless discoveries and enchantments. Even in the dead of Winter we were pastured in it almost daily, bundled up in the thick, scratchy coats, overcoats, mittens, leggings, caps, shirts, over-shirts and under-drawers that the young then wore. We wallowed in the snow whenever there was any to wallow in, and piled it up into crude houses, forts and snow-men, and inscribed it with wavering scrolls and devices by the method followed by infant males since the Würm Glaciation. In Spring we dug worms and watched for robins, in Summer we chased butterflies and stoned sparrows, and in Autumn we made bonfires of the falling leaves. At all times from March to October we made a Dust Bowl of my mother's garden.

The Hollins street neighborhood, in the eighties, was still almost rural, for there were plenty of vacant lots nearby, and the open country began only a few blocks away. Across the street from our house was the wide green of Union Square, with a fishpond, a cast-iron Greek temple housing a drinking-fountain, and a little brick office and tool-house for the square-keeper, looking almost small enough to have been designed by Chick Sale. A block to the westward, and well within range of our upstairs windows, was the vast, mysterious compound of the House of the Good Shepherd, with nuns in flapping habits flitting along its paths and alleys, and a high stone wall shutting it in from the world. In our backyard itself there were a peach tree, a cherry tree, a plum tree, and a pear tree. The pear tree survives to this day, and is still as lush and vigorous as it was in 1883, beside being thirty feet higher and so large around the waist that its branches bulge into the neighboring yards. My brother and I used to begin on the cherries when they were still only pellets of hard green, and had got through three or four powerful bellyaches before the earliest of them was ripe. The peaches, pears and plums came later in the year, but while we were waiting for them we chewed the gum that oozed from the peach-tree trunk, and practised spitting the imbedded flies and June bugs at Pinkie the cat.

There was also a grape-arbor arching the brick walk, with six vines that flourished amazingly, and produced in the Autumn a huge crop of sweet Concord grapes. My brother and I applied ourselves to them diligently from the moment the first blush of color showed on them, and all the sparrows of West Baltimore helped, but there was always

9

INTRODUCTION TO THE UNIVERSE

enough in the end to fill a couple of large dishpans, and my mother and the hired girl spent a hot after-noon boiling them down, and storing them away in glass tumblers with tin tops. My brother and I, for some reason or other, had no fancy for the grape jelly thus produced with so much travail, but we had to eat it all Winter, for it was supposed, like camomile tea, to be good for us. I don't recall any like embalming of the peaches, plums and pears; in all probability we got them all down before there were any ripe enough to preserve. The grapes es-caped simply because some of them hung high, as in the fable of the fox. In later years we collared these high ones by steeple-jacking, and so paid for escape from the jelly with a few additional belly-aches.

But the show-piece of the yard was not the grape-arbor, nor even the fruit-trees; it was the Summer-house, a rococo structure ten feet by ten in area, with a high, pointed roof covered with tin, a wooden floor, an ornate railing, and jig-saw spi-rals wherever two of its members came together. This Summer-house had been designed and exe-cuted by my mother's father, our Grandfather Ab-hau, who was a very skillful cabinet-maker, and had also made some of the furniture of the house. Everything of his construction was built to last, and when, far on in the Twentieth Century, I hired a gang of house-wreckers to demolish the Summer-house, they sweated half a day with their crowbars and pickaxes. In the eighties it was the throne-room and justice-seat of the household, at least in Summer. There, on fair Sunday mornings, my father and his brother Henry, who lived next door, met to drink beer, try out new combinations of tobacco for their cigar factory, and discuss the credit of customers and the infamies of labor agitators. And there, on his periodical visitations as head of the family, my Grandfather Mencken sat to determine all the delicate questions within his jurisdiction.

My mother was an active gardener, and during her forty-two years in Hollins street must have pulled at least a million weeds. For this business, as I first recall her, she had a uniform consisting of a long gingham apron and an old-time slat-bonnet — a head-dress that went out with the Nineteenth Century. Apron and slat-bonnet hung on nails behind the kitchen door, and on a shelf adjoining were her trowels, shears and other such tools, including always a huge ball of twine. My brother Charlie and I, as we got on toward school age, were drafted to help with the weeding, but neither of us could ever make out any difference between weeds and non-weeds, so we were presently transferred to the front of the house, where every plant that came up between the cobblestones of Hollins street was indubitably verminous. The crop there was always large, and keeping it within bounds was not an easy job. We usually tackled it with broken kitchen knives, and often cut our hands. We disliked it so much that it finally became convict labor. That is to say, it was saved up for use as punishment. I recall only that the maximum penalty was one hour, and that this was reserved for such grave offenses as stealing ginger-snaps, climbing in the pear-tree, hanging up the cat by its hind leg, or telling lies in a gross and obvious manner.

Charlie was somewhat sturdier than I, and a good deal fiercer. During most of our childhood he could lick me in anything approximating a fair fight, or, at all events, stall me. Civil war was forbidden in Hollins street, but my Grandfather Mencken, who lived in Fayette street, only three blocks away, had no apparent objection to it, save of course when he was taking his afternoon nap. I remember a glorious day when eight or ten head of his grandchildren called on him at once, and began raising hell at once. The affair started as a more or less decorous pillow-fight, but proceeded quickly to much more formidable weapons, including even bed-slats. It ranged all over the house, and must have done a considerable damage to the bric-a-brac, which was all in the Middle Bismarck mode. My grandmother and Aunt Pauline, fixed by my grandfather's pale blue eye, pretended to be amused by it for a while, but when a large china thunder-mug came bouncing down the third-story stairs and a black hair-cloth sofa in the parlor lost a leg they horned in with loud shrieks and lengths of stove-wood, and my grandfather called time.

Charlie and I were very fond of Aunt Pauline, who was immensely hospitable, and the best dough-nut cook in all the Baltimores. When the creative urge seized her, which was pretty often, she would make enough doughnuts to fill a large tin wash-boiler, and then send word down to Hollins street that there was a surprise waiting in Fayette street. It was uphill all the way, but Charlie and I always took it on the run, holding hands and pretending that we were miraculously dashing car-horses. We returned home an hour or so later much more slowly, and never had any appetite for supper. The immemorial tendency of mankind to concoct rituals showed itself in these feasts. After Charlie had got down his first half dozen doughnuts, and was taking time out to catch his breath and scrape the grease and sugar off his face, Aunt Pauline would always ask " How do they taste? " and he would always answer " They taste like more." Whether this catechism was original with the high contracting parties or had been borrowed from some patent-medicine almanac or other reference-work I don't know, but it never varied and it was never forgotten.

There were no kindergartens, playgrounds or other such Devil's Islands for infants in those in-nocent days, and my brother and I roved and ram-paged at will until we were ready for school. Hol-lins street was quite safe for children, for there was little traffic on it, and that little was slow-moving, and a cart approaching over the cobblestones could be heard a block away. The backyard was enough for us during our earliest years, with the cellar in reserve for rainy days, but we gradually worked our way into the street and then across it to Union Square, and there we picked up all the games then prevailing. A few years ago, happening to cross the square, I encountered a ma'm in horn-rimmed spectacles teaching a gang of little girls ring-around-a-rosy. The sight filled me suddenly with so black an indignation that I was tempted to grab the ma'm and heave her into the goldfish pond. In the days of my own youth no bossy female on the public payroll was needed to teach games to little girls. They taught one another — as they had been doing since the days of Neanderthal Man.

Nevertheless, there was a constant accretion of novelty, at least in detail. When we boys chased Indians we were only following the Sumerian boys who chased Akkadians, but the use of hatchets was certainly new, and so was the ceremony of scalping; moreover, our fiends in human form, Sitting Bull and Rain-in-the-Face, had been as unknown and unimagined to the Sumerian boys as Henry Ward Beecher or John L. Sullivan. The group songs we sang were mainly of English provenance, but they had all degenerated with the years. Here, precisely, is what we made of " King William " in Hollins street, *circa* 1885:

King William was King James's son;
Upon a ri' a race he won;
Upon his breast he wore a star,
The which was called the life of war.

What a *ri'* was we never knew and never inquired, nor did we attach any rational concept to
the life of war. A favorite boys' game, called
" Playing Se*bast*apool " (with a heavy accent on
the *bast*), must have been no older in its outward
form than the Crimean War, for Sebastapool was
plainly Sevastopol, but in its essence it no doubt
came down from Roman times. It could be played
only when building or paving was going on in the
neighborhood, and a pile of sand lay conveniently
near. We would fashion this sand into circular
ramparts in some friendly gutter, and then bristle
the ramparts with gaudy tissue-paper flags, always
home-made. Their poles were slivers of firewood,
and their tissue-paper came from Newton's toy-
store at Baltimore and Calhoun streets, which
served the boys and girls of West Baltimore for
seventy years, and did not shut down at last until
the Spring of 1939. The hired girls of the block
cooked flour paste to fasten the paper to the poles.

To the garrison of a Sebastapool all the smaller
boys contributed tin soldiers, including Indians.
These soldiers stood in close and peaceful ranks,
for there was never any attempt at attack or defense. They were taken in at night by their own-
ers, but the flags remained until rain washed the

15

Sebastapool away, or the milkman's early morning horse squashed it. There were sometimes two or three in a block. Girls took a hand in making the flags, but they were not allowed to pat the ramparts into shape, or to touch the tin soldiers. Indeed, for a little girl of that era to show any interest in military affairs would have been as indecorous as for her to play leap-frog or chew tobacco. The older boys also kept rather aloof, though they stood ready to defend a Sebastapool against raiders. Tin soldiers were only for the very young. The more elderly were beyond such inert and puerile simulacra, which ranked with rag dolls and paper boats. These elders fought in person, and went armed.

In the sacred rubbish of the family there is a specimen of my handwriting dated 1883 — two signatures on a sheet of paper now turned a dismal brown, the one small and rather neat and the other large and ornamented with flourishes. They seem somehow fraudulent, for I was then but three years old, but there they are, and the date, which is in my mother's hand, is very clear. Maybe she guided my stubby fingers. In the same collection there is another specimen dated January 1, 1887. It shows a beginning ease with the pen, though hardly much elegance. My mother also taught me many other humble crafts — for example, how to drive a nail, how to make paper boats, and how to sharpen a lead pencil. She even taught me how to thread a needle, and for a time I hoped to take over darning my own stockings and patching the seats of my own pants, but I never managed to master the use of the thimble, and so I had to give up. Tying knots was another art that stumped me. To this day I can't tie a bow tie, though I have taken lessons over and over again from eminent masters, including such wizards as Joe Hergesheimer and Paul Patterson. When I go to a party someone has to tie my tie for me. Not infrequently I arrive with the ends hanging, and must appeal to my hostess.

This incapacity for minor dexterities has pursued me all my life, often to my considerable embarrassment. In school I could never learn to hold a pen in the orthodox manner: my handwriting satisfied the professors, but my stance outraged them, and I suffered some rough handling until they finally resigned me to my own devices. In later life I learned bricklaying, and also got some fluency in rough carpentering, but I could never do anything verging upon cabinet-work. Thus I inherited nothing of the skill of my Grandfather Abhau. All my genes in that field came from my father, who was probably the most incompetent man with his hands ever seen on earth. I can't recall him teaching me anything in my infancy, not even marbles. He would sometimes brag of his youthful virtuosity at all the customary boys' games, but he always added that he had grown so old (he was thirty-one when I was six) and suffered so much

17

from dead beats, noisy children and ungrateful cigarmakers, drummers and bookkeepers that he had lost it. Nor could he match the endless stories that my mother told me in the years before I could read, or the many songs. The only song I ever heard him sing was this one:

> Rain forty days,
> Rain forty nights,
> Sauerkraut sticking out the smokestack.

Apparently there were additional words, but if so he never sang them. The only *Märchen* in his répertoire had to do with a man who built a tin bridge. I recall nothing of this tale save the fact that the bridge was of tin, which astonished my brother and me all over again every time we heard of it. We tried to figure out how such a thing was possible, for the mention of tin naturally made us think of tomato-cans. But we never learned.

II

THE

Caves of Learning

My first day in school I have forgotten as I have forgotten my first day on earth, but my second I remember very well, for I etched it on my cortex by getting lost, along with my cousin Pauline, who lived next door in Hollins street.

Pauline and I were of an age, and hence entered the caves of learning together. They were situate in the very heart of old Baltimore, a good mile and a half from Hollins street, and the business of getting to them involved a long journey by the Baltimore-street horse-car, with a two-block walk to follow. On the first day we were taken over the route by Pauline's father, my uncle Henry, who gave us careful sailing directions along the way, pointing out all salient lights and landfalls — the City Hall dome, the *Sun* Iron Building, Oehm's Acme Hall (which specialized in boys' pants with double seats), and so on. On the second day, launched on our own, we recalled enough of this instruction to board the horse-car going in the right direction, and even enough to get off correctly at Holliday street, but after that our faculties failed us, and we set out afoot toward the right instead of the left.

The result was that we presently found ourselves in Pratt street, an inferno of carts and trucks, with the sluggish Back Basin, which smelled like the canals of Venice, confronting us on the far side. The Basin looked immense to us, and unmistakably sinister. Over its dark, greasy waters a score of Chesapeake Bay packets were in motion, churning up the slime with their paddles and blowing their sirens ferociously. It was a fascinating spectacle, but terrifying, and in a little while we began to blubber, and a crowd of Aframerican dock-wallopers gathered around us, and a cop was soon pushing his way through it, inquiring belligerently what in hell the trouble was now. We must have managed to tell him the name of our school, though that part of it is a blank, for he delivered us only a few minutes late to the principal and proprietor thereof, Professor Friedrich Knapp, and got a shot of Boonekamp bitters for his pains.

This was my introduction (barring that obliterated first day) to F. Knapp's Institute, a seminary that catered to the boys and girls of the Bal-

timore bourgeoisie for more than sixty years. It
was already beginning, in 1886, to feel the competition of the public schools, but Professor Knapp
was not alarmed, for he believed firmly, and often
predicted, that the public schools would collapse
soon or late under the weight of their own inher-
ent and incurable infamy. They were fit, he argued
freely, only for dealing with boys too stupid, too
lazy, too sassy or too dirty to be admitted to such
academies as his own, and it was their well-deserved
destiny to be shut down eventually by the police, if
not by actual public violence. As for sending girls
to them, he simply could not imagine it; as well
shame and degrade the poor little angels by cutting
off their pigtails or putting them into pants.

The professor discoursed on the obscene subject
very often, and with special heat whenever another
boy left him to tackle the new and cheaper learning.
He always hinted that he had really kicked the
traitor out, and sometimes he followed with a homily on parents who neglected the upbringing of
their children, and so bred forgers, footpads and
assassins. The worst punishment he ever threatened against a boy who came to school with his hair
uncombed, or supernormal shadows behind his ears,
was expulsion with a certificate so unfavorable that
only the public schools would take him. Every
time there was a hanging at the city jail (which was
pretty often in those days when psychiatrists still
confined themselves to running madhouses), he re-

ferred to the departed, not by his crime but by his
education, which was invariably in the public
schools. No authentic graduate of F. Knapp's Institute, he let it be known, had ever finished on the
gallows.

Otherwise, the professor was a very mild and
even amiable man, and much more diligent at praise
than at blame. He was a Suabian who had come to
Baltimore in 1850, and he still wore, nearly forty
years afterward, the classical uniform of a German
schoolmaster — a long-tailed coat of black alpaca,
a boiled shirt with somewhat fringey cuffs, and a
white lawn necktie. The front of his coat was dusty
with chalk, and his hands were so caked with it that
he had to blow it off every time he took snuff. He
was of small stature but large diameter, and wore
closely-clipped mutton-chop whiskers. His hands
had the curious softness so often observed in pedagogues, barbers, and Y.M.C.A. secretaries. This
impressed itself on me the first time he noticed me
wiggling a loose milk-tooth with my tongue, and
called me up to have it out. He watched for such
manifestations sharply, and pulled, I should say,
an average of six teeth a week. It was etiquette in
the school for boys to bear this barbarity in silence.
The girls could yell, but not the boys. Both, however, were free to howl under the bastinado, which
was naturally applied to the girls much more
lightly and less often than to the boys.

The professor viewed the pedagogical art with

great pride, and was a man of some eminence in the town. He was on easy terms with the Mayor, General Ferdinand C. Latrobe, who once got us an hour's release from learning by dropping in from the City Hall across the street to harangue us darkly on civic virtue. The old professor, in the days when I knew him, had begun to restrict his personal teaching to a few extra abstruse subjects, *e.g.*, fractions, but he always lined up all the boys for inspection in the morning, and he led both boys and girls in the singing that opened every day's session. For this last purpose all hands crowded into the largest classroom. The professor conducted with his violin, and his daughter Bertha helped out at a parlor organ. The songs, as I recall them, were chiefly German favorites of his youth — "Goldene Abend Sonne," "Winter, Adieu!," "Fuchs, du hast die Gans gestohlen," "Hurrah, Hurrah, Hurra-la-la-la-la!," and so on. Most of the pupils knew very little German, though they were taught it fiercely, but they all managed to sing the songs.

As I have said, the institute had already begun to wither around the edges when I first knew it. In 1879 (so I gather from a faded announcement in an old Baltimore directory) it had had a teaching staff of twelve savants, and offered instruction in French, Latin and Hebrew, not to mention German and English, but by my time the staff had evaporated down to six or seven, and French and Latin had been abandoned. There was still, however, a class in Hebrew for the accommodation of a dozen or more Jewish boys, and I sat in on its proceedings (which went on in the same classroom with less exotic proceedings) long enough to learn the Hebrew alphabet. This must have been in my ninth year. By the time I left Knapp's for the Polytechnic the class had been shut down, and I had forgotten all the letters save *aleph*, *beth*, *vav*, *yodh* and *resh*. These I retain more or less to the present day, and whenever I find myself in the society of an orthodox rabbi I always show them off. On other Jews I do not waste them, for other Jews seldom recognize them.

There was no enmity between the Chosen and the *Goyim* in the old professor's establishment, and no sense of difference in his treatment of them, though he was in the habit, on bursting into a classroom that was disorderly, to denounce it violently as a *Judenschule*. He used this word, not because it was invidious, but simply because it described precisely the thing he complained of, and was sound colloquial German. He was also fond of using a number of Hebrew loan-words, for example, *tokos* (backside), *schlemihl* (oaf), *kosher* (clean) and *mashuggah* (crazy), most of which have since come into American. The Jewish boys of Baltimore, in that innocent era, were still palpably and unashamedly Jews, with Hittite noses, curly hair, and such given names as Aaron, Leon, Samuel and

Isaac. I never encountered one named Irving, Sidney, Malcolm or Wesley, nor even Charles or William. The old professor and his aides labored hard to teach these reluctant Yiddo-Americans the principles of their sacred tongue, but apparently with very little success, for the only textbook I ever saw in use was an elementary *Fibel*, with letters almost as large as those in the top line of an oculist's chart. All its victims were of German-Jewish origin, and came of well-to-do families, for in those days Eastern Jews were still rare in Baltimore, and whenever we boys passed one on the street we went Bzzzzzzzz in satirical homage to his beard. I must add in sorrow that the Jewish boys at Knapp's were unanimously *Chazirfresser*.

There was also in the school a group of students, all male, from Latin America, chiefly Cubans and Demerarans. I recall that their handkerchiefs were always well doused with perfume, and that they willingly paid tops, marbles and slate-pencils for the seats nearest the stove in Winter. There was one Cuban whose father had been captured by brigands and carved in a dreadful manner: his detailed description of the paternal wounds was very graphic, and made him something of a hero. For the rest, the student-body included German-Americans, Irish-Americans, French-Americans, Italian-Americans and even a few American-Americans. There was never any centrifugence on racial lines, and the only pupil I can remember who had a nickname hinting at anything of the sort was a husky German girl, lately arrived in the Republic, who went under the style or appellation of Germany-On-Wheels. She had a fist like a pig's foot and was not above clouting any boy who annoyed her. Moreover, she was a mistress of all the German declensions, and hence unpopular. The old professor treated these diverse tribes and species with uniform but benevolent suspicion — all, that is, save the American-Americans, whom he plainly regarded as intellectually underprivileged, to say the least. I also heard him hint more than once that their fathers were behind with their tuition fees.

The Institute, in its heyday, had specialized in German, but by my time all its teaching was in English. I must have learned some German in it, for to this day I can rattle off the German alphabet in par, and reading the Gothic type of a German newspaper is almost as easy to me as reading the Lateinisch. Also, I retain a few declensions in poll-parrot fashion, and can recite them with fearful fluency, especially under malt-and-hops power. Again, I can still write a very fair German script, though reading the script of actual Germans often stumps me. Yet again, I always get the curious feeling, hearing German spoken, that it is not really a foreign language, for all its sounds seem quite natural to me, including even the *ch* of *ich*. But the professor and his goons certainly never taught me to speak German, or even to read it with any ease. They tried to ram it into their pupils as they rammed in the multiplication table — by endless repetition, usually in chorus. To this day I know the conjugation of *haben* down to *Sie würden gehabt haben*, though I couldn't write even a brief note in Hoch Deutsch without resort to a grammar and a dictionary. What little of the language I actually acquired in my youth I picked up mainly from the German hired girls who traipsed through the Hollins street kitchen during the eighties — corralled at the Norddeutscher-Lloyd pier at Locust Point by my father (who spoke next to no German, but knew the chief inspector of immigrants), and then snatched away, after a year or so, by some amorous ice-man, beer-man or ash-man. One actually married a saloonkeeper, learned bartending, survived him, and died rich. My mother complained bitterly that these husky Kunigundas, Käthes, Ottilies and Charlöttchens were hardly house-broken before they flitted away, but some of them, and especially the Bavarians, were prime cooks, and all of them were ready to feed my brother Charlie and me at any moment, and to lie us out of scrapes.

My father, whose mother had been British-born, had a firm grasp upon only the more indecorous expletives of German, so the language was not used in the house. But my mother knew it well enough to palaver with the hired girls, and with the German marketmen, plumbers, tinners, beermen and grocery boys who were always in and out. When her father dropped in he would speak to her in German, but she would usually talk back, for some reason that I never learned, in English. Such bilingual dialogues sometimes went on for hours, to the fascination of my brother and me. We tried to figure out what the old man had said on the basis of what my mother answered. Maybe this taught us some German, but probably not much. One of the family anecdotes has to do with my efforts as a small child to dredge out of this grandfather an explanation of the puzzling differences between his language and ours. " Grandpa," I asked him, " if the German for *kiss* is *Kuss*, why isn't the German for *fish Fush?* " He knew English well enough, but this mystery he could not explain. My brother and I concocted a dreadful dialect for communicating with the German hired girls in their pre-English stages. Its groundwork was a crudely simplified English, but it included many pseudo-German words based on such false analogies as the one I have just mentioned, for example, *Monig* for *money* (from *Honig-honey*) and *Ratz* for *rat* (from *Katz-cat*). How we arrived at *Roch* for (*cock*)*roach* (pronounced in the German manner, to rhyme with *Loch*) I can't tell you: it must have been a sheer inspiration. To this day, alas, my

German is dreadful (though not quite as bad as my Sanskrit and Old Church Slavonic), and it always amuses me to encounter the assumption that I am a master of it, and even a scholar.

Professor Knapp, to return to him, spent most of his day moseying in and out of his classrooms at the institute, observing the technic of his agents and doing drum-head justice on boys of an evil nature. He was a virtuoso with the rattan, and chose his tool for a given caning with apparent care. He had an arsenal as large as a golfer's bag of clubs, and carried it with him from class to class. But the routine of the operation was always the same, and every boy knew it as familiarly as he knew the rules of run-a-mile or catty. The condemned would be beckoned politely to the place of execution beside the teacher's desk, and at the word *Eins* from the professor he would hold up his hands. At *Zwei* he would lower them until they stuck out straight from his shoulders, and at *Drei* he would bend over until his finger-tips touched his ankles. The punitive swooshes *a posteriori* would follow — sometimes two, three or even four, but more often only one. As I have said, it was etiquette for the condemned to make an outcry. He was also allowed and even expected to massage his *gluteus maximus* violently as he pranced back to his bench. This always led the professor to remark sagely: " You can't rub it out." Criminal girls were punished more gently, with smacks from a ruler on the open palm. They consoled themselves by hugging the insulted hand under the opposite arm.

The professor showed very little moral indignation when he carried on such exercises, and I never heard of a victim denouncing them as unjust. Whenever they took place the whole class seemed to be convinced that they were sound in law and equity, and necessary to peace and civilization. No doubt this was because the professor always took much more visible delight in rewards than in punishments. When, listening in on a recitation, he noted a boy or girl who did well, he grinned like a Santa Claus, and halted the proceedings long enough to give the worthy one a " merit." A merit was simply a card inscribed with the date and the recipient's name, and signed by the professor. Teachers could also award them, but we naturally liked the professor's best. A pupil who accumulated fifty in the course of a year received a book at the close of school, with his parents present to swell with pride. I received my first on June 28, 1888. It was a copy of Grimms' Fairy Tales, horribly translated by a lady of the name of Mrs. H. B. Paull. I got it, as the inscription notifies, " for industry and good deportment." I have it still, and would not part with it for gold and frankincense.

These merits were not plain cards, but works of art in the *Gartenlaube* manner, and very elegant in our eyes. They were lithographed in full color, and

commonly showed a spray of flowers, a cat playing
with a ball of wool, or a Winter scene in the Black
Forest, with the snow represented by powdered
mica. Sometimes the art took the form of a separate hand, embossed as well as colored. The hand
was anchored to the card at the cuff, which was always laced, and one got at the inscription by
turning back the fingers. Merits with hands were
especially esteemed, though they had no greater exchange value than the plain ones. One of them
still survives as a bookmark in the copy of Grimms'
Fairy Tales aforesaid. On my withdrawal from
these scenes it will go to the League of Nations.

There were teachers at the institute who came
and went mysteriously and have been forgotten,
but I remember very clearly all the members of the
permanent staff — the old professor's daughter,
Miss Bertha; his niece, Miss Elvina; his son, Mr.
Willie; his chief-of-staff, Mr. Fox; and his slave,
Mr. Paul. Mr. Paul was a tall, smooth-shaven,
saturnine German who always wore a long black
coat, and was greatly given to scenting himself with
Kölnischeswasser. There was no science of ven-
tilation in those days, and schoolrooms were kept
hermetically sealed. Mr. Paul's powerful aroma
thus served admirably as a disinfectant, but toward the end of a laborious day it sometimes made
us more or less giddy. He lived at the school, taking part of his emolument in board and lodging,
and I heard years later, from a fellow pupil who

31

was a great hand at the keyhole, that his maximum salary in cash was never above $10 a week.

This fact was no doubt responsible for his generally subversive frame of mind, which led him to an unhappy false step in 1888 or thereabout, almost fatal to his career. It took the form of an address to his class advocating the eight-hour day, then an anarchistic novelty in the world, and almost as alarming to the bourgeoisie as the downright confiscation of tax-free securities would be today. Worse, he recited a slogan in support of it, running as follows:

> Eight hours for work;
> Eight hours for sleep;
> Eight hours for what you will.

The boys could make nothing of his argument, but quickly learned the slogan. I did so myself and one evening recited it proudly to my father, looking confidently for his applause. Instead, he leaped from his chair, turned pale, and began to swear and splutter in a fearful manner. I made off in alarm, and it was years afterward before I learned from him why he was so indignant, and what followed from his dudgeon.

It appeared then that he had been convinced in conscience, and was still convinced in conscience, that the eight-hour day was a project of foreign nihilists to undermine and wreck the American Republic. In his own cigar factory nearly all work

was piece-work, so he really didn't care how long
his men kept at it, but he conceived it to be his duty
to holler against the heresy in the interest of other
employers. This he did, it appeared, on the very
next day, and to Professor Knapp. The professor,
who had also heard from other fathers, was much
upset, and had Mr. Paul on the carpet. From that
time on we heard nothing more of the subject.
Mr. Paul applied himself with undivided diligence
to his chosen branches — penmanship, free-hand
drawing, mathematics up to the multiplication table, and deportment — and discreetly avoided all
politico-economic speculations.

He was a kindly man, with some gifts as a drafts-
man. He taught me to draw complicated, fantastic, incredible flowers with both pen and pencil, and
on lazy afternoons he would often suspend his
teaching and entertain the boys and girls by covering the blackboard with images of birds carrying letters in their bills, and their plumage bulging out into elaborate curlicues. This art, now in
decay, was greatly esteemed in those days. In penmanship Mr. Paul followed classical models. Every downstroke had to be good and thick, and every
upstroke as thin as a spider's web.

At Christmas time all the boys and girls were
put to writing canned letters of filial duty to their
parents. Fancy four-page blanks were provided
for this purpose, with the first page lithographed
in full color. The text was written on the black-

board, all inkwells were cleaned and refilled, and new pens of great fineness were provided. The first boy who made a blot tasted the rattan, and after that everyone was very careful. As I recall it, the business of concocting these letters occupied the better part of a day. The professor himself dropped in from time to time to praise the young penmen who were doing well, and to pull the ears of those who were making messes. When an error was detected his son, Mr. Willie, was sent for to scratch it out with a sharp penknife. Too many errors caused the whole blank to be condemned and torn up, and the offender had to buy another at a cost of ten cents. We were always glad when this agony was over.

Mr. Willie, when I first knew him, was in his middle thirties. He was short and stocky, wore the silky mustache of the period, and combed his hair in oyster-shell style. He was much more worldly than Mr. Paul, and often entertained us with tales of his adventures. One of his favorite stories recounted his observations and sensations on seeing a surgeon cut off a man's leg. This happened somewhere in the West, where he had served for a year or two as a disbursing agent of the General Land Office. The boys liked the story, and encouraged him to improve its horrors, but the girls clapped their hands over their ears whenever he began it, and professed to shiver. He was also fond of telling about the hazards of navigating the Missouri

river, which he had traversed during the seventies
to the southern frontier of what is now South Da-
kota. In one of his stories he told how the river-
packets of the time, when they ran aground on a
sandbar, put out stilts operated by steam, and
lifted themselves over it. Not a boy in the school
believed this story, and I myself was nearly forty
years old before I discovered that it was really
true. But one of Mr. Willie's actual stretchers I
swallowed without a shadow of doubt. He was discoursing one day on the immense number of books
in the world, and their infinite variety. " On the
single subject of the eye of the dog," he said,
" enough has been written to fill this classroom."
We all believed that one.

The dean or first mate of F. Knapp's Institute
was Mr. Fox, a tall Pennsylvanian with a goatish
beard, greatly resembling the late Admiral Winfield Scott Schley. He ran the school store, and
carried it about with him in a large black dispatch-
box. The boys believed that he made a large income selling them pens, slate-pencils, pads of
scratch-paper, and other such supplies. They also
believed that he made a great deal of additional
money by serving as the secretary of a lodge of
Freemasons. The business of this lodge occupied
him on dull afternoons, when recitations degenerated into singsong, and there was no rattaning to
be done. He would spend hours addressing postcards to the members, notifying them of initiations,

oyster-roasts, funerals, and the like. While he plugged away he would solemnly chew his beard. We boys marvelled that it never grew any shorter.

Mr. Fox assisted the old professor as lord high executioner, and did most of the minor fanning of the wicked. He employed a frayed rattan of small percussive powers, and was but little feared. One day in 1889 I saw demonstrated before him the truth of Oscar Wilde's saying that nature always imitates art. The comic papers of the time had among their stock characters a boy who put a slate, a shingle or a book in his pants to protect himself from justice. This was actually done in my sight by a very small boy whose name, as I recall it, was Johnnie Horlamus. When Mr. Fox turned him over, the seat of his pants bulged out into an incredible square, and Mr. Fox halted the proceedings to investigate. His search produced a third grade geography-book. When he pulled it out the whole class roared, and he had to bite his beard hard to keep from roaring himself. He let Johnnie off with a single very gentle clout.

Mr. Fox was no virtuoso like the professor. He rattaned conscientiously, but without any noticeable style. The professor not only adorned the science, but made a notable contribution to it. This was the invention of mass caning, the use of which was confined to his morning inspection in the schoolyard. It often happened that he would detect three, four or even five boys with unshined shoes or unwashed ears. He would order them to step forward a few paces, and then line them up very precisely. When they had all got into the position called for by his command of *Drei* he would try to fetch their fundaments simultaneously with one swoop of an extra-long rattan. Sometimes he succeeded, and sometimes he failed. The favorite spot in the line was naturally the one nearest him, for the boy who had it got the thick part of the rattan, swinging through a small arc, and was hence but little hurt. The boy at the far end got the thin and poisonous tip, swinging over an orbit long enough to give it the speed of a baseball and the bite of an adder's fang.

The professor believed that he was responsible for the policing and sanitation of his pupils from the time they left home in the morning until they returned there safely in the afternoon. It was a felony by the school code for a boy to hook a ride on a horse-truck. Culprits were detected by the simple fact that such trucks, being dirty, commonly left marks on the knees of stockings or seats of pants or both, but the boys preferred to believe that they were betrayed by stooges among the girls. Many an innocent girl had her pigtail severely yanked on that charge. This yanking was itself a felony, but the victim seldom complained, for if she did so her pigtail would be surely yanked again, and with a yo-heave-ho so hearty that it just fell short of scalping her.

The most serious of all crimes, of course, was fighting on the streets. When detected, it not only brought a Class A rattaning, but also a formal threat of banishment to the Gehenna of the public schools. But the institute's statutes, like the canon law of Holy Church, always provided for exceptions and dispensations. In this case the pummeling, clubbing and even (if it could be imaginably achieved) strangling and dismemberment of a boy from Scheib's School was dismissed as venial. Scheib's was so close to F. Knapp's that the two were separated only by the narrow channel of Orange alley. Professor Knapp and Pastor Scheib were ostensibly on the most fraternal footing, and always spoke of each other in flattering terms, but there was a great deal of pupil-snatching to and fro, and deep down in their chalky pedagogical hearts they were a Guelph and a Ghibelline.

III

RECOLLECTIONS OF

𝔄𝔠𝔞𝔡𝔢𝔪𝔦𝔠 𝔒𝔯𝔤𝔦𝔢𝔰

SOME time ago I read in the New York papers
about the death of an Irishman who had been
esteemed and honored in life as the inventor of
the hot-dog. The papers themselves appeared to
believe that he had deserved this veneration, for
they gave his peaceful exitus almost as much space
as they commonly give to the terminal deliriums
of a movie star or United States Senator. They
said that he had made his epochal invention in the
year 1900 or thereabout, and that it had been first
marketed as consumers' goods at the Polo Grounds.

All this made me smile in a sly way, for I devoured hot-dogs in Baltimore 'way back in 1886,
and they were then very far from new-fangled.
They differed from the hot-dogs of today in one

detail only, and that one was hardly of statistical significance. They contained precisely the same rubbery, indigestible pseudo-sausages that millions of Americans now eat, and they leaked the same flabby, puerile mustard. Their single point of difference lay in the fact that their covers were honest German *Wecke* made of wheat-flour baked to crispness, and not the soggy rolls prevailing today, of ground acorns, plaster-of-Paris, flecks of bath-sponge, and atmospheric air all compact.

The name hot-dog, of course, was then still buried in the womb of time: we called them *Weckers*, being ignorant that the true plural of *Weck* was *Wecke*, or in one of the exceptional situations so common in German grammar, *Wecken*. They were on sale at the Baltimore baseball-grounds in the primeval days before even Muggsy McGraw had come to town, and they were also sold at all picnics. In particular, I recall wolfing them at the annual picnic of F. Knapp's Institute. One year I got down six in a row, and suffered a considerable bellyache thereafter, which five bottles of sarsaparilla did not cure. My brother Charlie did even better. He knocked off eight *Wecke*, and then went strutting about with no bellyache at all. But Charlie, in those days, had a gizzard like a concrete-mixer, and I well recall the morning when he ate eighteen buckwheat cakes for breakfast, and gave up even then only because the hired girl had run out of batter.

The annual picnic of F. Knapp's Institute, always holden in early June, was the great event
of the school year, and the older pupils began
chattering about it soon after Christmas. Tickets
were twenty-five cents each, but every pupil could
buy them at five for a dollar, and the extra quarter
was his profit. It was clearly understood that the
money thus amassed was undividedly his own, and
that the way he spent it was nobody's damned
business. It was not etiquette for the teachers of
the institute, or even his parents, to molest him
when he set out to clean up the *Wecke*, pretzels,
doughnuts and other delicatessen that were on
sale on the grounds, or tried to stretch his skin
over ten or a dozen bottles of sarsaparilla. If he
collapsed there were benches for him to lie on, and
a bottle of paregoric to medicate him.

The picnic was always held at Darley Park, a
pleasant grove adjoining a suburban brewery. It
was outfitted in the stark, Philistine style of the
period, with all the trees whitewashed up to a
height of six feet. Scattered about were a couple
of dozen plain board tables, each outfitted with
hard benches. In the middle of the grove was a
small pavilion, with a senile excursion-boat piano
in the center of it. Along one boundary ran a long
brick building, and somewhere within it was a bar.
The *Weck*, crab-cake, pretzel, doughnut and sarsaparilla vendors circled about, howling their
wares. In a far corner was a portable carrousel

with four horses, operated by what was then always called jackass-power. That is to say, it was kept going by a sweating Aframerican turning a crank. He turned it steadily from 10 a.m. to 4 p.m., and there were always plenty of girls and baby-class boys waiting in line. We more elderly roués spent all our money on food and drink. Sarsaparilla had a sharp bite, and, like opium, produced an appetite for itself. So did *Wecke*.

When the great day arrived all the pupils of the institute piled into a string of Gay-street horse-cars and proceeded to Darley Park at high speed. Professor Knapp always traveled by the first car, and took up at once the police duties of the day. He never carried his battery of rattans along, but he had sharp eyes and a good memory, and any boy who pulled too many of the girls' pigtails, or engaged in fisticuffs with another boy, or indulged himself in sassing a teacher was sure to go on trial the next morning, with two or three swooshes to rearward following. But crime was relatively rare at those picnics, and I remember one (I should add in frankness that it was considered exceptional) which didn't produce a single culprit. We played the immemorial games of the schoolyard, but mainly we played follow-your-leader. Sometimes as many as forty boys would be in line, and the course would include hurdles over all the benches in the park, and even up into the pavilion and over the excursion-boat piano. One year the leader, a large, gaunt boy who was generally regarded as feebleminded, led the gang out of the park and into an adjoining brickyard, and there took it through a series of puddles bottomed with red clay. When the procession returned and the professor saw the boys' shoes, he got into a dreadful lather, and soon after sunrise the next morning he broke a rattan over the half-wit's caboose.

At noon or thereabout parents began to arrive, usually in buggies. They were received formally by the whole faculty of the school, and the mothers proceeded at once to track down and inspect their offspring, looking (in the case of boys) for dirty hands, holes in stockings and skinned shins, and (in the case of girls) for torn skirts and lost hair-ribbons. Sometimes a black-hearted boy would sneak into the adjacent brickyard, which was covered in large part with Jimson weeds, plantains and other such vegetable outlaws, and return with a large ball of nigger-lice.[1] One of these nigger-lice, on being thrown at a girl, would stick to her dress. If it hit her hair, getting it out would be a tedious and even painful business. Indeed, it was generally believed by the boys of Baltimore that a nigger-louse lodged in the wool of an actual Negro girl could not be removed without shaving her head. When nigger-lice began to fly about at a school picnic the whole faculty would mobilize instantly, and in a little while the marks-

[1] The burrs of the common burdock (*Arctium minus*).

men would be detected and disarmed, and next morning they would get hearty fannings from the professor.

While the mothers of the pupils were inspecting them, their fathers, following custom, would invite the male pedagogues to the bar, and there ply them with beer. My father always had a low opinion of the Baltimore beers, and complained bitterly whenever he had to drink them. He concocted an elaborate legend about one of the worst of them, to the effect that it was made of the ammoniacal liquor discharged from the Baltimore gasworks, with mill-feed for malt and picric acid for hops. Once, when I was still a small boy, I was riding proudly with him on the platform of a horse-car, when he encountered a *Todsäufer* [2] belonging to the brewery that made it, and proceeded to warn him solemnly that drinking his own goods would wreck his kidneys and bring him to an early grave. To my astonishment, the *Todsäufer* admitted it freely, but explained that he

---

[2] A *Todsäufer* (literally, dead-drinker) was, and is a sort of brewer's customers' man. He is commonly called a collector, but his duties go far beyond collecting the bills owed to breweries by saloonkeepers. He is supposed to stand a general treat in the bar whenever he calls, to go to all weddings, birthday parties and funerals in the families of saloonkeepers, and to cultivate their wives and children with frequent presents. When a saloonkeeper himself dies the *Todsäufer* is the principal mourner *ex officio,* and is expected to weep copiously. He is also one of the brewery's political agents, and must handle all the license difficulties of his clients. He belongs to all the clubs and societies that will admit him, including always, if there is one, the town press-club.

owed $2000 to a building association on a house he had bought, and wanted to work off the debt before returning to his former and less remunerative trade of soft-drink drummer. My father thereupon offered him a job as a cigar salesman, but they couldn't come to terms. He must have actually died soon afterward, for I remember my father citing him as a tragic example of what men will do and suffer for money.

But the pedagogues appeared to stand the Darley Park beer very well, and indeed plainly liked it. As father after father dropped in, and schooner after schooner was dispatched, the gogues apparently gave glowing accounts of the diligence and scholarship of their pupils, for it was not uncommon for a father, coming out for air, to give his boy an extra ten cents. Mr. Fox, a man of quasi-military bearing, usually swayed ever so gently as the session in the bar ended, and he made his way to the pavilion for the closing ceremonies of the day. As for Mr. Paul, he emerged mopping his face solemnly with his cologne-scented handkerchief, and burping surreptitiously under it. I never detected any such signs in Mr. Willie, but that was probably because he was something of an *eleganto*, and always called for small beers. His hair was plastered down with plenty of soap, and not a strand of it was ever out of place. The old professor, being a Suabian, was immune to all the ordinary effects of alcohol. Toward the close of the ceremonies in the pavilion he always fell into a doze, but he did the same thing every afternoon of his life, whether he had been consuming malt liquor or well water.

The ceremonies themselves tended to be banal, for everybody was tired by then. They began with some songs by the massed pupils, accompanied by Miss Bertha on the excursion-boat piano, and they moved through the classical répertoire of recitations. I was once chosen to do " The Wreck of the Hesperus," but blew up in the second stanza. Elocution, indeed, has always been a closed art to me, for I have never been able to memorize even the shortest piece, whether in prose or verse. At the time of my first and only appearance as an actor on the public stage (it was after I had left F. Knapp's Institute) I forgot both of my two lines. My brother Charlie was called for to pinch hit for me when " The Wreck of the Hesperus " went phooey, but he did not respond, and a quick and quiet search found him hiding under the pavilion. There was always a little girl with a piano solo, but she was invariably drowned out by a freight-train of the Pennsylvania Railroad, which ran only a few blocks away.

If there were any politicoes present, which was usually the case, they arose to expound the issues of the hour. General Ferdinand C. Latrobe, Mayor of Baltimore for seven terms, always showed up, and always made a speech. Inasmuch as the pro-

fessor was a German, the general devoted himself
courteously to whooping up the unparalleled scientific, aesthetic and moral gifts of the German
people, and to revealing all over again the fact that
he was partly of German blood himself, despite
his French-sounding name. He made exactly similar speeches at all gatherings of predominantly
non-Anglo-Saxon Baltimoreans, omitting only the
Aframericans and the Chinese. In his later years
(I had by then become a newspaper reporter) I
heard him claim not only Irish, Scotch, Welsh,
Dutch and other such relatively plausible bloods,
but also Polish, Bohemian, Italian, Lithuanian,
Swedish, Danish, Greek, Spanish and even Jewish.
Once I actually heard him hint that he was remotely an Armenian. Unable by the current *mores*
to boast of African ancestry, he consoled his colored
customers by speaking in high terms of Abraham
Lincoln, whom he described as a Republican with
a Democratic heart. The best he could do for the
Chinese, who were then very few in Baltimore, was
to quote some passages from the Analects of Confucius, which he had studied through the medium
of a secretary.

When the last politico shut down the professor
called off the proceedings, and we all started home.
My father drove the family buggy, and I sat between him and my mother, with my brother roost-
ing on a hassock on the floor. We kept to the horse-
car tracks as much as possible, for the cobblestones

of Baltimore, in those days, were world-famous
for their roughness. Whenever we had to turn out
on them my brother bounced off his hassock, and
had to be derricked back. He and I were pretty
well used up by the time we got home, and after
a meager supper were ordered to bed. We slept
as profoundly as convicts in the death-house, for
it was not until the next morning that the chigger-
bites picked up in the brickyard began to make
themselves manifest. Half the boys scratched violently for three or four days thereafter, but none
of the girls. The old professor always dropped in
to point the moral. The boys, being naturally
vicious, had disobeyed orders and explored the
brickyard, which was a resort of noxious insects
and human desperadoes, but the girls, being virtuous and law-abiding, had stayed on the right
side of the fence. Hence their immunity.

There were plenty of other gala days during the
school year, but none so stupendous as the day of
the annual picnic, save maybe the day of the circus parade. All parades in Baltimore passed within
hearing of F. Knapp's Institute, for the City Hall
was only across the street, and its portico was the
customary reviewing-stand. The most brutal punishment that could be imagined by a Knapp boy,
or indeed any Baltimore schoolboy, was to be confined to barracks when a circus parade was under
way. So far as I can recall, it never actually happened in our school, though it was often threatened.

We always turned out in command of Mr. Fox and
Mr. Paul, each of them armed with a rattan, and
the cops made room for us along the curb. If any
of the loafers who hung about the City Hall refused to move, the cops fell upon them with fists
and night-sticks, at the same time denouncing them
as low characters, fit only for penal servitude.

I remember of these circus parades only the
patient tramp of the elephants, the loudness of the
music, and the unearthly beauty of the lady bare-
back-riders, with their yellow wigs, dazzling span-
gles and pink tights. They seemed to us boys to
be even more beautiful than Miss Bertha and Miss
Elvina, who were our everyday paragons of female loveliness. The parade consumed most of the
morning, and those boys whose fathers were taking
them to the actual circus also escaped for the afternoon. They returned next day full of astounding
tales and in a low state of health, for pink lemonade
in that era was actually pink, and four or five
glasses of it left the gall-bladder considerably fevered. There was a memorable year when two circuses came to town, and another when the circus
was followed by Buffalo Bill's Wild West Show.
We admired Buffalo Bill and shivered at the sight
of his bloodthirsty Indians, but the general feeling
was that the circus was better. Certainly the lady
sharpshooters and Indian squaws had nothing on
the bareback riders.

Now and then the old professor and his staff

would shepherd the whole student body to some other public show, usually of a painfully cultural character. I remember clearly only one such expedition. It was an exhibit of Mexican arts and handicrafts at a hall in Charles street. The squat pottery, gaudy blankets, crude jewelry and other such stuff left me cold; indeed, I dislike all Mexican fancy-goods to this day, and regard even the masterpieces of Diego Rivera as trash. But I remember very brilliantly a sort of side-show, for it consisted of two human skeletons, the first I had ever seen. One was the skeleton of a peon who had been shot by a bandit, with the bullet hole plainly visible in the center of his forehead. The other was the skeleton of the bandit who had shot him, with one of the cervical vertebrae dislocated to show the effect of the rope that had punished the crime.

These ghastly relics were displayed in two long boxes covered with black cloth, and set up at an angle of sixty degrees. My brother and I, at first sight of them, turned quickly and slunk away, but things that are horrible are always fascinating to boys, and so we came back every now and then for another look, and by the end of the afternoon we had got massive eyefuls. That night (we slept together) we pulled the quilt over our heads and dreamed dreadful dreams of shootings, stabbings, scalpings, hangings, graveyards and dissecting-rooms, with herds of bleeding ghosts all over the place. I have encountered a great many skeletons since, and got upon easy terms with some of them, but whenever I shut my eyes and ponder upon mortality I always see the poor bones of those forlorn and anonymous Mexicans, bounced into Heaven in a far country and so long ago.

The crown and consummation of the year at Knapp's was the annual exhibition in June, following soon after the picnic. For this sombre event the largest schoolroom was chosen, and chairs for the parents of the pupils were arranged on the two sides of the teacher's desk. The programme followed classical models, stretching back, I suppose, to the times of Tiglath-pileser. First the whole school would sing, with Miss Bertha at the organ and the old professor leading with his violin; then the prizes (always books) won by diligent and docile pupils would be presented to them by Mr. Fox, who was an eminent Freemason and hence accustomed to public speaking; and then Mr. Willie would call up, one by one, all those who were not downright idiotic, and show off their learning. Some recited, some spelled hard words, some bounded Caroline county, Maryland, or Ohio, or Spain, some parsed all the components of such sentences as " The dog ate the bone," and some read in high-pitched, staccato, somewhat panicky voices out of the McGuffey Readers.

My own contribution to this symposium never took the form of a recitation, for, as I have said, I was born incapable of remembering anything longer than a limerick. Once, in term, Mr. Paul gave me a German poem of two brief stanzas to memorize, and I made such heavy weather of trying to get it that my father had to rescue me with a note to the old professor, desiring him to instruct Mr. Paul to lay off such infernal nonsense. (In those days, parents who patronized private schools had some voice in what their children were taught. On another occasion my father was full of indignation when I brought home the news that Mr. Paul believed and was teaching that the first *a* in *national* should be pronounced exactly like the first *a* in *nation*. Indeed, he was so upset that he made a call on the old professor the next morning, and was closeted with him for an hour. Mr. Paul, so far as I know, never formally recanted, but he at least went so far as to avoid the word thereafter.)

My own contribution to the annual exhibition usually took the form of a mathematical demonstration at the blackboard, say the multiplication of 75.876593 by 1129.654, or the division of 17/39ths by 71/163rds. I had no interest whatever in figures, but my father was a violent fan for them, so it gave him a great kick if I came out with an error of no more than plus-or-minus ten per cent., and when we got home he handed me a nickel, which in those days would buy a grab-bag containing at least half a pound of broken taffy and a ring or stickpin set with a large ruby.

My cousin Pauline, who was a very good reader, went through McGuffey at high speed, and my brother Charlie usually gave a more or less creditable performance at spelling, especially when the words lined out happened to be of less than two syllables. The other boys and girls displayed their various gifts one by one, and so the long morning wore on, with Mr. Willie sweating away doggedly, the boys scraping their feet on the floor and squirming in their chairs, and the parents (save when their own progeny were up) yawning dismally and rubbing themselves. As for the old professor, he invariably fell into a quiet doze, with his gold-rimmed spectacles shoved up on his forehead. When the City Hall bell struck twelve and the noon whistles began to blow he awoke suddenly and half rose to his feet.

" Villie," he would say, " daash ish genook."

At all events, that is how it sounded to me, and how I recall it today. He was, as I have noted, a Suabian, and reverted to the dialect of his native *Dorf* whenever his faculties were dimmed. Mr. Willie understood him to say " Das ist genug," which, in English, is " That's enough," and so the proceedings terminated.

The boys always piled out leaping and howling like early Christian martyrs delivered by angels from the stake, for next day was the beginning of the Summer vacation.

IV

THE BALTIMORE OF

the Eighties

THE CITY into which I was born in 1880 had a reputation all over for what the English, in their real-estate advertising, are fond of calling the amenities. So far as I have been able to discover by a labored search of contemporary travel-books, no literary tourist, however waspish he may have been about Washington, Niagara Falls, the prairies of the West, or even Boston and New York, ever gave Baltimore a bad notice. They all agreed, often with lubricious gloats and gurgles, (*a*) that its indigenous victualry was unsurpassed in the Republic, (*b*) that its native Caucasian females of all ages up to thirty-five were of incomparable pulchritude, and as amiable as they were lovely, and (*c*) that its home-life was spacious, charming,

54

full of creature comforts, and highly conducive
to the facile and orderly propagation of the species.
There was some truth in all these articles, but
not, I regret to have to add, too much. Perhaps the
one that came closest to meeting scientific tests was
the first. Baltimore lay very near the immense protein factory of Chesapeake Bay, and out of the
bay it ate divinely. I well recall the time when
prime hard crabs of the channel species, blue in
color, at least eight inches in length along the shell,
and with snow-white meat almost as firm as soap,
were hawked in Hollins street of Summer mornings
at ten cents a dozen. The supply seemed to be almost unlimited, even in the polluted waters of the
Patapsco river, which stretched up fourteen miles
from the bay to engulf the slops of the Baltimore
canneries and fertilizer factories. Any poor man
could go down to the banks of the river, armed with
no more than a length of stout cord, a home-made
net on a pole, and a chunk of cat's meat, and come
home in a couple of hours with enough crabs to
feed his family for two days. Soft crabs, of course,
were scarcer and harder to snare, and hence higher
in price, but not much. More than once, hiding
behind my mother's apron, I helped her to buy
them at the door for two-and-a-twelfth cents apiece.
And there blazes in my memory like a comet the
day when she came home from Hollins market complaining with strange and bitter indignation that
the fishmongers there — including old Harris, her

favorite — had begun to *sell* shad roe. Hitherto, stretching back to the first settlement of Baltimore Town, they had always thrown it in with the fish. Worse, she reported that they had now entered upon an illegal combination to lift the price of the standard shad of twenty inches — enough for the average family, and to spare — from forty cents to half a dollar. When my father came home for lunch and heard this incredible news, he predicted formally that the Republic would never survive the Nineteenth Century.

Terrapin was not common eating in those days, any more than it is in these, but that was mainly because few women liked it, just as few like it today. It was then assumed that their distaste was due to the fact that its consumption involved a considerable lavage with fortified wines, but they still show no honest enthusiasm for it, though Prohibition converted many of them into very adept and eager boozers. It was not, in my infancy, within the reach of the proletariat, but it was certainly not beyond the bourgeoisie. My mother, until well past the turn of the century, used to buy pint jars of the picked meat in Hollins market, with plenty of rich, golden eggs scattered through it, for a dollar a jar. For the same price it was possible to obtain *two* wild ducks of respectable if not royal species — and the open season ran gloriously from the instant the first birds wandered in from Labrador to the time the last stragglers set sail for Brazil.

So far as I can remember, my mother never bought any of these ducks, but that was only because the guns, dogs and eagle eye of my uncle Henry, who lived next door, kept us oversupplied all Winter.

Garden-truck was correspondingly cheap, and so was fruit in season. Out of season we seldom saw it at all. Oranges, which cost sixty cents a dozen, came in at Christmas, and not before. We had to wait until May for strawberries, asparagus, fresh peas, carrots, and even radishes. But when the huge, fragrant strawberries of Anne Arundel county (pronounced Ann'ran'l) appeared at last they went for only five cents a box. All Spring the streets swarmed with hucksters selling such things: they called themselves, not hucksters, but Arabs (with the first *a* as in *day*), and announced their wares with loud, raucous, unintelligible cries, much worn down by phonetic decay. In Winter the principal howling was done by colored men selling shucked oysters out of huge cans. In the dark backward and abysm of time their cry must have been simply " Oysters! ", but generations of Aframerican larynxes had debased it to " Awn-eeeeeee! ", with the final *e*'s prolonged until the vendor got out of breath. He always wore a blue-and-white checked apron, and that apron was also the uniform of the colored butlers of the Baltimore gentry when engaged upon their morning work — sweeping the sidewalk, scouring the white marble front steps, polishing up the handle of the big front door, and bragging about their white folks to their colleagues to port and starboard.

Oysters were not too much esteemed in the Baltimore of my youth, nor are they in the Baltimore of today. They were eaten, of course, but not often, for serving them raw at the table was beyond the usual domestic technic of the time, and it was difficult to cook them in any fashion that made them consonant with contemporary ideas of elegance. Fried, they were fit only to be devoured at church oyster-suppers, or gobbled in oyster-bays by drunks wandering home from scenes of revelry. The more celebrated oyster-houses of Baltimore — for example, Kelly's in Eutaw street — were patronized largely by such lamentable characters. It was their playful custom to challenge foolish-looking strangers to wash down a dozen raw Chincoteagues with half a tumbler of Maryland rye: the town belief was that this combination was so deleterious as to be equal to the kick of a mule. If the stranger survived, they tried to inveigle him into eating another dozen with sugar sprinkled on them: this dose was supposed to be almost certainly fatal. I grew up believing that the only man in history who had ever actually swallowed it and lived was John L. Sullivan.

There is a saying in Baltimore that crabs may be prepared in fifty ways and that all of them are good. The range of oyster dishes is much narrower, and they are much less attractive. Fried oysters I have just mentioned. Stewed, they are undoubtedly edible, but only in the sorry sense that oatmeal or boiled rice is edible. Certainly no Baltimorean not insane would argue that an oyster stew has any of the noble qualities of the two great crab soups — shore style (with vegetables) and bisque (with cream). Both of these masterpieces were on tap in the old Rennert Hotel when I lunched there daily (years after the term of the present narrative) and both were magnificent. The Rennert also offered an oyster pot-pie that had its points, but the late Jeff Davis, manager of the hotel (and the last public virtuoso of Maryland cookery), once confessed to me that its flavor was really due to a sly use of garlic. Such concoctions as panned and scalloped oysters have never been eaten in my time by connoisseurs, and oyster fritters (always called flitters in Baltimore) are to be had only at free-for-all oyster-roasts and along the wharves. A roasted oyster, if it be hauled off the fire at the exact instant the shell opens, is not to be sniffed at, but getting it down is a troublesome business, for the shell is too hot to be handled without mittens. Despite this inconvenience, there are still oyster-roasts in Baltimore on Winter Sunday afternoons, and since the collapse of Prohibition they have been drawing pretty good houses. When the Elks give one they hire a militia armory, lay in a thousand kegs of beer, engage 200 waiters, and prepare for a mob. But the mob is not attracted by the oysters alone; it comes mainly to eat hot-dogs, barbecued beef and sauerkraut and to wash down these lowly victuals with the beer.

The greatest crab cook of the days I remember was Tom McNulty, originally a whiskey drummer but in the end sheriff of Baltimore, and the most venerated oyster cook was a cop named Fred. Tom's specialty was made by spearing a slice of bacon on a large fork, jamming a soft crab down on it, holding the two over a charcoal brazier until the bacon had melted over the crab, and then slapping both upon a slice of hot toast. This titbit had its points, I assure you, and I never think of it without deploring Tom's too early translation to bliss eternal. Fred devoted himself mainly to oyster flitters. The other cops rolled and snuffled in his masterpieces like cats in catnip, but I never could see much virtue in them. It was always my impression, perhaps in error, that he fried them in curve grease borrowed from the street railways. He was an old-time Model T flat-foot, not much taller than a fire-plug, but as big around the middle as a load of hay. At the end of a busy afternoon he would be spattered from head to foot with blobs of flitter batter and wild grease.

It was the opinion of my father, as I have recorded, that all the Baltimore beers were poisonous, but he nevertheless kept a supply of them in the house for visiting plumbers, tinners, cellar-inspectors, tax-assessors and so on, and for Class D social callers. I find by his bill file that he paid $1.20 for a case of twenty-four bottles. His own favorite malt liquor was Anheuser-Busch, but he also made occasional experiments with the other brands that were then beginning to find a national market: some of them to survive to this day, but the most perished under Prohibition. His same bill file shows that on December 27, 1883, he paid Courtney, Fairall & Company, then the favorite fancy grocers of Baltimore, $4 for a gallon of Monticello whiskey. It retails now for from $3 to $3.50 a *quart*. In those days it was always straight, for the old-time Baltimoreans regarded blends with great suspicion, though many of the widely-advertised brands of Maryland rye were of that character. They drank straight whiskey straight, disdaining both diluents and chasers. I don't recall ever seeing my father drink a high-ball; the thing must have existed in his day, for he lived on to 1899, but he probably regarded its use as unmanly and ignoble. Before every meal, including breakfast, he ducked into the cupboard in the diningroom and poured out a substantial hooker of rye, and when he emerged he was always sucking in a great whiff of air to cool off his tonsils. He regarded this appetizer as necessary to his well-being. He said that it was the best medicine he had ever found for toning up his stomach.

How the stomachs of Baltimore survived at all in those days is a pathological mystery. The

standard evening meal tended to be light, but the
other two were terrific. The repertoire for breakfast, beside all the known varieties of pancake and
porridge, included such things as ham and eggs,
broiled mackerel, fried smelts, beef hash, pork
chops, country sausage, and even — God help us
all! — what would now be called Welsh rabbit.
My father, save when we were in the country,
usually came home for lunch, and on Saturdays,
with no school, my brother Charlie and I sat in.
Our favorite Winter lunch was typical of the time.
Its main dishes were a huge platter of Norfolk
spots or other pan-fish, and a Himalaya of corn-
cakes. Along with this combination went succo-
tash, buttered beets, baked potatoes, string beans,
and other such hearty vegetables. When oranges
and bananas were obtainable they followed for
dessert — sliced, and with a heavy dressing of
grated cocoanut. The calorie content of two or
three helpings of such powerful aliments probably
ran to 3000. We'd all be somewhat subdued afterward, and my father always stretched out on the
dining-room lounge for a nap. In the evening he
seldom had much appetite, and would usually complain that cooking was fast going downhill in
Baltimore, in accord with the general decay of
human society. Worse, he would warn Charlie and
me against eating too much, and often he undertook to ration us. We beat this sanitary policing
by laying in a sufficiency in the kitchen before

sitting down to table. As a reserve against emergencies we kept a supply of ginger snaps, mushroom crackers, all-day suckers, dried apricots and solferino taffy in a cigar-box in our bedroom. In fear that it might spoil, or that mice might sneak up from the cellar to raid it, we devoured this stock at frequent intervals, and it had to be renewed.

The Baltimoreans of those days were complacent beyond the ordinary, and agreed with their envious visitors that life in their town was swell. I can't recall ever hearing anyone complain of the fact that there was a great epidemic of typhoid fever every Summer, and a wave of malaria every Autumn, and more than a scattering of smallpox, especially among the colored folk in the alleys, every Winter. Spring, indeed, was the only season free from serious pestilence, and in Spring the communal laying off of heavy woolen underwear was always followed by an epidemic of colds. Our house in Hollins street, as I first remember it, was heated by Latrobe stoves, the invention of a Baltimore engineer. They had mica windows (always called isinglass) that made a cheery glow, but though it was warm enough within the range of that glow on even the coldest Winter days, their flues had little heat to spare for the rooms upstairs. My brother and I slept in Canton-flannel nightdrawers with feathers above us and underneath, but that didn't help us much on January mornings when all the windows were so heavily frosted that we couldn't see outside. My father put in a steam-heating plant toward the end of the eighties — the first ever seen in Hollins street —, but such things were rare until well into the new century. The favorite central heating device for many years was a hot-air furnace that was even more inefficient than the Latrobe stove. The only heat in our bath-room was supplied from the kitchen, which meant that there was none at all until the hired girl began to function below. Thus my brother and I were never harassed by suggestions of morning baths, at least in Winter. Whenever it was decided that we had reached an intolerable degree of grime, and measures were taken to hound us to the bathroom, we went into the vast old zinc-lined tub together, and beguiled the pains of getting clean by taking toy boats along. Once we also took a couple of goldfish, but the soap killed them almost instantly.

At intervals of not more than a month in Winter a water-pipe froze and burst, and the whole house was cold and clammy until the plumbers got through their slow-moving hocus-pocus. Nothing, in those days, seemed to work. All the house ma-chinery was constantly out of order. The roof sprang a leak at least three times a year, and I recall a day when the cellar was flooded by a broken water-main in Hollins street, and my brother and I had a grand time navigating it in wooden wash-tubs. No one, up to that time, had ever thought

of outfitting windows with fly-screens. Flies over-
ran and devoured us in Summer, immense swarms
of mosquitoes were often blown in from the swamps
to the southwest, and a miscellany of fantastic
moths, gnats, June-bugs, beetles, and other insects, some of them of formidable size and pug-
nacity, buzzed around the gas-lights at night.

We slept under mosquito canopies, but they were
of flimsy netting and there were always holes in
them, so that when a mosquito or fly once got in
he had us all to himself, and made the most of it.
It was not uncommon, in Summer, for a bat to
follow the procession. When this happened my
brother and I turned out with brooms, baseball bats
and other weapons, and pursued the hunt to a kill.
The carcass was always nailed to the backyard
fence the next morning, with the wings stretched
out as far as possible, and boys would come from
blocks around to measure and admire it. Whenever an insect of unfamiliar species showed up we
tried to capture it, and if we succeeded we kept it
alive in a pill-box or baking-powder can. Our
favorite among pill-boxes was the one that held
Wright's Indian Vegetable Pills (which my father
swallowed every time he got into a low state), for
it was made of thin sheets of wood veneer, and was
thus more durable than the druggists' usual cardboard boxes.

Every public place in Baltimore was so furiously
beset by bugs of all sorts that communal gather-

ings were impossible on hot nights. The very cops
on the street corners spent a large part of their
time slapping mosquitoes and catching flies. Our
pony Frank had a fly-net, but it operated only
when he was in motion; in his leisure he was as
badly used as the cops. When arc-lights began
to light the streets, along about 1885, they attracted so many beetles of gigantic size that their
glare was actually obscured. These beetles at once
acquired the name of electric-light bugs, and it
was believed that the arc carbons produced them
by a kind of spontaneous generation, and that their
bite was as dangerous as that of a tarantula. But
no Baltimorean would ever admit categorically that
this Congo-like plague of flying things, taking one
day with another, was really serious, or indeed a
plague at all. Many a time I have seen my mother
leap up from the dinner-table to engage the swarming flies with an improvised punkah, and heard her
rejoice and give humble thanks simultaneously that
Baltimore was not the sinkhole that Washington
was.

These flies gave no concern to my brother Charlie
and me; they seemed to be innocuous and even
friendly compared to the chiggers, bumble-bees
and hornets that occasionally beset us. Indeed,
they were a source of pleasant recreation to us,
for very often, on hot Summer evenings, we would
retire to the kitchen, stretch out flat on our backs
on the table, and pop away at them with sling-

shots as they roosted in dense clumps upon the ceiling. Our favorite projectile was a square of lemon-peel, roasted by the hired girl. Thus prepared, it was tough enough to shoot straight and kill certainly, but when it bounced back it did not hurt us. The hired girl, when she was in an amiable mood, prepared us enough of these missiles for an hour's brisk shooting, and in the morning she had the Red Cross job of sweeping the dead flies off the ceiling. Sometimes there were hundreds of them, lying dead in sticky windrows. When there were horse-flies from the back alley among them, which was not infrequently, they leaked red mammalian blood, which was an extra satisfaction to us. The stables that lined the far side of the alley were vast hatcheries of such flies, some of which reached a gigantic size. When we caught one we pulled off its wings and watched it try idiotically to escape on foot, or removed its legs and listened while it buzzed in a loud and futile manner. The theory taught in those days was that creatures below the warm-blooded level had no feelings whatever, and in fact rather enjoyed being mutilated. Thus it was an innocent and instructive matter to cut a worm into two halves, and watch them wriggle off in opposite directions. Once my brother and I caught a turtle, chopped off its head, and were amazed to see it march away headless. That experience, in truth, was so astonishing as to be alarming, and we never monkeyed with turtles thereafter. But we got a good deal of pleasure, first and last, out of chasing and butchering toads, though we were always careful to avoid taking them in our hands, for the juice of their kidneys was supposed to cause warts.

At the first smell of hot weather there was a tremendous revolution in Hollins street. All the Brussels carpets in the house were jimmied up and replaced by sleazy Chinese matting, all the hair-cloth furniture was covered with linen covers, and every picture, mirror, gas bracket and Rogers group was draped in fly netting. The carpets were wheelbarrowed out to Steuart's hill by professional carpet beaters of the African race, and there flogged and flayed until the heaviest lick yielded no more dust. Before the mattings could be laid all the floors had to be scrubbed, and every picture and mirror had to be taken down and polished. Also, the lace curtains had to come down, and the ivory-colored Holland shades that hung in Winter had to be changed to blue ones, to filter out the Summer sun. The lace curtains were always laundered before being put away — a formidable operation involving stretching them on huge frameworks set up on trestles in the backyard. All this uproar was repeated in reverse at the ides of September. The mattings came up, the carpets went down, the furniture was stripped of its covers, the pictures, mirrors and gas brackets lost their netting, and the blue Holland shades were displaced by the ivory ones. It always turned out, of course, that the flies of Summer had got through the nettings with ease, and left every picture peppered with their calling cards. The large pier mirror between the two windows of the parlor usually got a double dose, and it took the hired girl half a day to renovate it, climbing up and down a ladder in the clumsy manner of a policeman getting over a fence, and dropping soap, washrags, hairpins and other gear on the floor.

The legend seems to prevail that there were no sewers in Baltimore until after the World War, but that is something of an exaggeration. Our house in Hollins street was connected with a private sewer down the alley in the rear as early as I have any recollection of it, and so were many other houses, especially in the newer parts of the town. But I should add that we also had a powder-room in the backyard for the accommodation of laundresses, whitewashers and other visiting members of the domestic faculty, and that there was a shallow sink under it that inspired my brother and me with considerable dread. Every now and then some child in West Baltimore fell into such a sink, and had to be hauled out, besmeared and howling, by the cops. The one in our yard was pumped out and fumigated every Spring by a gang of colored men who arrived on a wagon that was called an O.E.A. — *i.e.*, odorless excavating apparatus. They discharged this social-minded duty with great fervor and dispatch, and achieved non-odoriferousness, in the innocent Aframerican way, by burning buckets of rosin and tar. The whole neighborhood choked on the black, greasy, pungent smoke for hours afterward. It was thought to be an effective preventive of cholera, smallpox and tuberculosis.

All the sewers of Baltimore, whether private or public, emptied into the Back Basin in those days, just as all those of Manhattan empty into the North and East rivers to this day. But I should add that there was a difference, for the North and East rivers have swift tidal currents, whereas the Back Basin, distant 170 miles from the Chesapeake capes, had only the most lethargic. As a result it began to acquire a powerful aroma every Spring, and by August smelled like a billion polecats. This stench radiated all over downtown Baltimore, though in Hollins street we hardly ever detected it. Perhaps that was due to the fact that West Baltimore had rival perfumes of its own — for example, the emanation from the Wilkins hair factory in the Frederick road, a mile or so from Union Square. When a breeze from the southwest, bouncing its way over the Wilkins factory, reached Hollins street the effect was almost that of poison gas. It happened only seldom, but when it happened it was surely memorable. The householders of the vicinage always swarmed down to the City Hall the next day and raised blue hell, but they

never got anything save promises. In fact, it was
not until the Wilkinses went into the red and shut
down their factory that the abomination abated
— and its place was then taken, for an unhappy
year or two, by the degenerate cosmic rays projected from a glue factory lying in the same general direction. No one, so far as I know, ever argued that these mephitic blasts were salubrious,
but it is a sober fact that town opinion held that
the bouquet of the Back Basin was. In proof
thereof it was pointed out that the clerks who
sweated all Summer in the little coops of offices
along the Light street and Pratt street wharves
were so remarkably long-lived that many of them
appeared to be at least 100 years old, and that
the colored stevedores who loaded and unloaded
the Bay packets were the strongest, toughest,
drunkenest and most thieving in the whole port.

The Baltimore of the eighties was a noisy town,
for the impact of iron wagon tires on hard cobble-
stone was almost like that of a hammer on an anvil.
To be sure, there was a dirt road down the middle
of every street, kept in repair by the accumulated
sweepings of the sidewalks, but this cushioned track
was patronized only by hay-wagons from the
country and like occasional traffic: milk-men, grocery deliverymen and other such regulars kept to
the areas where the cobbles were naked, and so
made a fearful clatter. In every way, in fact, city
life was much noiser then than it is now. Children

at play were not incarcerated in playgrounds and
policed by hired ma'ms, but roved the open streets,
and most of their games involved singing or yelling. At Christmas time they began to blow horns
at least a week before the great day, and kept it
up until all the horns were disabled, and in Summer
they began celebrating the Fourth far back in
June and were still exploding fire-crackers at the
end of July. Nearly every house had a dog in it,
and nearly all the dogs barked more or less con-
tinuously from 4 a.m. until after midnight. It
was still lawful to keep chickens in backyards, and
many householders did so. All within ear range of
Hollins street appeared to divide them as to sex
in the proportion of a hundred crowing roosters
to one clucking hen. My grandfather Mencken
once laid in a coop of Guineas, unquestionably the
noisiest species of *Aves* known to science. But his
wife, my step-grandmother, had got in a colored
clergyman to steal them before the neighbors arrived with the police.

In retired by-streets grass grew between the
cobblestones to almost incredible heights, and it
was not uncommon for colored rag-and-bone men
to pasture their undernourished horses on it. On
the steep hill making eastward from the Washington Monument, in the very heart of Baltimore,
some comedian once sowed wheat, and it kept on
coming up for years thereafter. Every Spring the
Baltimore newspapers would report on the pros-

pects of the crop, and visitors to the city were
taken to see it. Most Baltimoreans of that era, in
fact, took a fierce, defiant pride in the bucolic as-
pects of their city. They would boast that it was
the only great seaport on earth in which dandelions
grew in the streets in Spring. They believed that
all such vegetation was healthful, and kept down
chills and fever. I myself once had proof that the
excess of litter in the streets was not without its
value to mankind. I was riding the pony Frank
when a wild thought suddenly seized him, and he
bucked me out of the saddle in the best manner of
a Buffalo Bill bronco. Unfortunately, my left foot
was stuck in the stirrup, and so I was dragged
behind him as he galloped off. He had gone at
least a block before a couple of colored boys stopped
him. If the cobblestones of Stricker street had been
bare I'd not be with you today. As it was, I got
no worse damage than a series of harsh scourings
running from my neck to my heels. The colored
boys took me to Reveille's livery-stable, and
stopped the bloodshed with large gobs of spider
web. It was the hemostatic of choice in Baltimore
when I was young. If, perchance, it spread a little
tetanus, then the Baltimoreans blamed the mercies
of God.

V

𝕽𝖚𝖗𝖆𝖑 𝔇𝖊𝖑𝖎𝖌𝖍𝖙𝖘

THOUGH the bourgeoisie of Baltimore, in the days
I write of, always denied fiercely that the town
was an inferno in Summer, they nevertheless
cleared out whenever they could — and usually
they could. The nether moiety of them — mainly
bachelors and young married couples — went to
boarding houses in the hills that fenced in the town
to westward and northward, the middle section
rented cottages in the same cool and sanitary regions, and the relatively well-heeled bought or
built Summer homes of their own. Some of these
Summer homes still stand as monuments to the
unearthly taste of the Chester A. Arthur or Cast
Iron era, though most of them have lost the towers
and cupolas that were once their chief flaunts of
elegance, and nearly all the jig-saw rails and braces
of their wide-flung porches have been replaced by
less elaborate millinery.

74

People now live in them the year round, shuttling in and out of town by motor-car. Efficient oil-heaters keep them snug in Winter, and the telephone and radio bring them all the great boons and usufructs of our Christian civilization. In the days I write of they were vastly more remote; in fact, they were so remote that the women and children in them, having once undergone the ordeal of being moved out, stayed put for the rest of the Summer. The head of each house, of course, had to come to town every day to look after his business, for it was not usual, at that time, for males with any sense of responsibility to take holidays, but no one ever mistook this round trip for a pleasure jaunt; on the contrary, it was regarded as heroic, and mentioned with praise. The only feasible way to get to our first Summer retreat in Howard county, Maryland, was by Baltimore & Ohio train to the ancient village of Ellicott City, and then up a steep zigzag road in the village hack. My father and my uncle Henry, whose family shared the house with us, made the round trip every day, but its second half always left them hot, dusty and worn-out, and I doubt that they could have endured it if the ground rules had not allowed them a couple of mint juleps when they finally reached the front porch. The luxurious day-coaches that now distinguish the Baltimore & Ohio were unheard of in those primitive days. The Main Line local to Ellicott City was made up of creaky wooden cars that had all seen heroic service in the Civil War, and in the fifteen-mile run (it took nearly an hour) they shipped enough cinders to set all their passengers to strangling.

From our house in Hollins street to Ellicott City was but ten miles by the old National pike, but the road had no surface save bare rock and there were four or five toll-gates and six or seven immense hills along the way, so no one ever drove it if the business could be avoided. One of the hills was so steep and so full of hair-pin bends that it was called the Devil's Elbow. A hay-wagon coming up would take half a day to cover the mile and a half from bottom to top, and sometimes a Conestoga wagon from Western Maryland (there were still plenty of them left in the eighties) got stuck altogether, and had to be rescued by the plow-horses of the adjacent farmers. At intervals of a mile or so along the road there were old-time coaching inns, and they were still doing a brisk trade in 25-cent country dinners and 5-cent whiskey.

The one nearest to town, kept by a German named Adam Dietrich, actually survived until the great catastrophe of Prohibition. Its ancient wagon-yard hugged the townward side of Loudon Park Cemetery, and in my youth it was believed that all experienced hack horses, on starting home from a funeral, turned in automatically to give the pallbearers a whack at old Adam's beer, which sold for five cents, came in glasses as large as gas masks, and carried a crab-cake or two fried oysters as *lagniappe*. It was no fun in those days to go to a funeral in Loudon Park. The outward trip, at the solemn pace funerals then affected, took a full hour. But the trip homeward, once the pallbearers had wiped their mustaches, was naturally much quicker, for most of it was downhill and the hack horses knew that oats were ahead. The hay-wagon drivers who made the long and arduous trek from Howard and Frederick counties did not patronize Adam, but preferred the specialists in 5-cent whiskey. Having imbibed, they would take their seats on boards which jutted out from the sides of their lumbering wagons, between the fore and hind wheels, and from that perch they undertook to work the brakes. Very often a jolt knocked one of them off, and the hind wheels converted him into an angel, or into the two halves of an angel. For many years this mishap was one of the principal causes of death among Maryland farmers, and it was not until hay-wagons began to disappear that anyone thought of putting the driver's seat in a safer place.

The house above Ellicott City was a double one, with a hall down the middle. We occupied one side, and the family of my uncle Henry had the other. It had been built by a German named Reus, a winegrower from the Rhineland, and he had chosen the site because the hillside that swept down to the upper Patapsco, there a placid country stream,

seemed perfect for vineyards. In the eighties his
terraces were still visible, but their vines were in a
sad state of decay, for Mr. Reus had discovered too
late that Americans were not wine drinkers. He
was now dead, and the place, which was still called
the Vineyard, was owned by his widow, whose elder
son had married my father's half-sister. She had
two more sons, somewhat older than my brother
Charlie and I, but still young enough to be polite to us. They were very pleasant fellows, and
the two Summers that we spent with them were full
of delight. When the big house was rented they
lived with their mother and a sister in a tenant-
house, and on the place there was also a farmhouse
inhabited by a German *Bauer* named Darsch, of
whom more anon. From the big house there was a
superb view of the valley of the Patapsco — a
winding gorge with wooded heights on both sides.
Many years later, standing on the hill at Richmond
in England and enjoying the famous prospect of
the Thames, I was struck by the fact that it was
completely familiar. Suddenly I recalled that the
view from the Vineyard was almost precisely the
same, though on a smaller scale.

The impact of such lovely country upon a city
boy barely eight years old was really stupendous.
Nothing in this life has ever given me a more thrilling series of surprises and felicities. Everything
was new to me, and not only new but romantic, for
the most I had learned of green things was what

was to be discovered in our backyard in Hollins
street, and here was everything from wide and smiling fields to deep, dense woods of ancient trees, and
from the turbulent and exciting life of the barnyard to the hidden peace of woodland brooks. The
whole panorama of nature seemed to take on a new
and larger scale. The sky stretched further in every direction, and was full of stately, piled up
clouds that I had never seen before, and on every
side there were trees and flowers that were as
strange to me as the flora of the Coal Age. When
a thunder-storm rolled over the hills it was incom-
parably grander and more violent than any city
storm. The clouds were blacker and towered
higher, the thunder was louder, and the lightning
was ten times as blinding. I made acquaintance
with cows, pigs and all the fowl of the barnyard.
I followed, like a spectator at a play, the immemorial drama of plowing, harrowing, planting and
reaping. Guided by the Reus boys, who had been
born on the place, I learned the names of dozens
of strange trees and stranger birds. With them I
roved the woods day after day, enchanted by the
huge aisles between the oaks, the spookish, Grimms'
Fairy Tale thickets, and the cool and singing little
streams. There was something new every minute,
and that something was always amazing and beautiful.

I recall with special vividness the charm of early
morning in the country. We all turned out at an

hour that would have seemed unearthly in the city, for my father and my uncle had to stagger down the crooked road to Ellicott City and catch the eight o'clock train for Baltimore. After breakfast, and sometimes before, I would go for a walk in the fields, still wet with the dew. They radiated a fragrance that far surpassed that of Mr. Paul's cologne water, and even that of the Jockey Club and New-Mown Hay of our hired girls. I'd lie on my belly watching the grasshoppers, crickets and other such saucy fellows at work around the roots of the grass — and picking up a supply of chiggers that was renewed daily, and kept me scratching all Summer. I also liked the hot calm of July and August afternoons. The whole country would pass into a sort of cataleptic state, with no sound breaking the silence save the drone of bees along the hedge-rows and the far-off clang of the blacksmith's hammer down in the village. The cows, clearing out of the fields, drowsed under the trees, the barnyard fowl dozed in the shadows of strawstack and manure-pile, and the wild birds all seemed to vanish. Darsch the farmer was always busy somewhere along the slope, but he was a silent man, and seldom spoke to the laborious son at his side, or even to his horse.

There was a brook down in the woods, called the Sucker branch, that seemed to me to encompass the whole substance and diameter of romantic adventure. My brother and I waded in it, dammed it, leaped over it, and searched under its stones for crayfish and worms. It rose in a distant field, ran down through the deepest part of the Vineyard woods, and disappeared toward the Patapsco in a thicket so dense and forbidding that my brother and I never ventured into it. Where the path from the house came to the brook there were the ruins of an old grist-mill, dating back to the first years of the century and maybe even beyond, but with its dam and the better part of its wooden wheel still surviving. Under the wheel there was a little pool that seemed infinitely deep to my brother and me: we would heave stones into it, and were always sure that we could never hear them strike the bottom. My father and uncle once undertook, on a Summer afternoon, to go swimming in it, but it was too small to give them elbow-room, and they quickly clambered out, shivering with the cold of the spring water. The Reus boys preferred a swimming-hole in the Patapsco itself, at the foot of the long hill stretching down from our house. They reported it to be full of bottomless pits and treacherous undertows, and refused loftily to let my brother and me come along.

The trees along the brook belonged to the original forest, and some of them were immense. Great vines clung to their trunks, and between them was a jungle of saplings and shrubs. There we made acquaintance with brambles and poison oak, and learned to detect the tracks of possums, coons and

foxes, though we never saw any in the flesh. The
Reus boys, inspired by our willingness to learn,
also showed us the tracks of wolves, mountain lions,
bears, and even tigers and elephants, but here we
remained skeptical. This region was our Wild
West, our Darkest Africa, our Ultima Thule. It
even had its anthropophagus — a half-grown yahoo who was supposed to hunt little boys over the
countryside, and to inflict mysterious indignities
upon them when captured. What these indignities
were we could never make out, and the Reus boys
also appeared to be uncertain, but whenever there
was a noise in the underbrush across Sucker branch
one of them would shriek the yahoo's name, and
all of us would make for home at a gallop. Our
cousin John Henry was always a member of these
expeditions. He was somewhat older than my
brother Charlie and somewhat younger than I, and
he was commonly called Little Harry to distinguish
him from me, though in later years he grew tall
enough to look over my head.

I had caught butterflies in the backyard at Hollins street, but at the Vineyard they were enormously more numerous. My mother made me a new
net, and in few weeks I had a fine collection, all of
them poniarded to cards with pins. My brother
and I also captured a great many lizards, and often
came home of a late afternoon with a bird fallen
from the nest, or a can of minnows from the brook,
or a grasshopper leaking his tobacco-juice all over

our hands, or maybe the skull of a rabbit come to
death and dissolution in the woods. The Reus boys
taught us many of the ancient arts and crafts of
country boys — how to make whistles of willow
twigs, how to climb trees, how to detect poison-oak,
how to cut off a chicken's head, and so on. They
even tried to teach us how to milk a cow, but the
switching of the creature's tail disturbed us so
much that we were unable to concentrate. One day
they announced proudly that they were squiring
the family cow to a farm up Merrick's lane for a
necessary biological purpose, and we pleaded to be
taken along. They were willing enough and promised an instructive exhibition, but the project was
overruled by higher authority.

My uncle Henry, unable to go out for ducks in
Summer, kept his eagle eye in trim by shooting
such chickens as were needed for the table. He
would go down to the barnyard on Sunday morning, draw a bead upon a strutting cockerel, and lift
off its head with the ease of a laryngologist fetching an adenoid. We boys greatly admired his technic, and so did Darsch the farmer. At dawn one
Sunday morning there was a loud explosion in the
direction of the barnyard, followed by a series of
grisly, despairing yells, as of an archbishop collared by Satan. My father and uncle turned out in
their night-shirts, and made for the scene with slippers flapping. They returned in a few moments
with Darsch, and my mother and aunt spent the

next half hour bandaging him with strips of bed-sheet. Never in this life have I seen a more luxuri-ant hemorrhage, though I have sat at the ringside through many a high-toned exhibition of scientific boxing. It appeared that Darsch, panting to emu-late my uncle, had unearthed a fowling-piece brought from Germany in 1857, loaded it to the muzzle, and loosed it at an old rooster. When the barrel exploded the rooster suffered nothing worse than shock, but Darsch himself was dreadfully chewed up. But it is almost impossible to kill a German *Bauer* with anything short of siege artil-lery, and in a week he was back at the plow and see-ing out of both eyes.

Some time after this, on a Sunday afternoon, while my father and his brother were sitting on the verandah drinking mint juleps, Darsch passed along the roadway in front of the big house, driv-ing a calf. My uncle stopped him to inquire how his wounds were getting on, and then offered him the hospitality of a julep. The drink was a new one to Darsch, who had been to Baltimore only twice in nine years, and it appeared at once that he re-garded it with approbation. Indeed, he not only liked it, but said so with unprecedented loquacity, and was soon chattering in a care-free and aimless manner, with swinging gestures. This exhilaration suggested something to my uncle, who was a man, like my father, of predominantly anti-social hu-mor. Reaching for an old-time tin shaker that stood on the table, he poured three or four fingers of rye into it, and then offered to give Darsch's julep another shake. This, he explained, was a necessary process, designed to keep the julep from going flat. Darsch handed up his glass, got it back reinforced, took a long pull of it, and began babbling louder and faster than ever before. His calf wandered off, but he did not notice it. The second time my uncle made it five or six fingers, and the third time he emptied what was left of the bottle. Suddenly Darsch drained the glass with a great gulp, mint and all, leaped high into the air, let off a single explosive whoop, and started down the roadway at a gallop. My uncle and father set out after him, hoping to capture and calm him before he could do himself any harm, but he was too fast for them, and by the time they got to the barnyard he was disappearing through the door of the old bank-barn. They found him presently in the stable below, threshing around in the litter behind the cow. He had taken a header through the hatchway. They hauled him home and his wife put him to bed, and the next day he was down with what was described as malaria. I recall my uncle observing afterward that it was an agreeable and instructive episode, but that it had pretty well emptied a prime bottle of Maryland rye, and was thus rather expensive.

Housekeeping at the Vineyard must have been something of an ordeal for my mother and my aunt,

who fed their flocks separately. The best cook-
stoves available were poor things that burned kero-
sene, and they were set out in a sort of arbor behind
the house. Down in the village there was a butcher
whose family had carried on in one of the old stone
houses along the main (and only) street for the better part of a century, but I can recall no baker,
and all the bread we ate was baked at home. Vegetables and fruits, such as they were, came from
Darsch's market-garden, and fowl came from his
barnyard. There must have been ice in the house,
for I can't imagine my father drinking warm beer
without alarming symptoms, and he and his brother
often made mint juleps, especially when company
took the long trail out from the city of a Sunday.
But there were times when ice ran short, for I recall a Sunday afternoon when, after an overdose
of Seckel pears, filched from Darsch's sclerotic
trees, I developed a case of 1000-volt cholera morbus, and a colored boy had to be dispatched to the
village on horseback to fetch a cake. When he arrived he had it in a gunnysack lashed to his horse.
My father cracked it with a hatchet that he found
in the cellar, cutting himself two or three times, and
my mother fed it to me with a kitchen spoon. It
seemed to work, for by Tuesday I was back at the
Seckel pears.

The road down to the village was steep and
rough, and the trip up was full of tribulation. It
started off the main street at what must have been

at least a ten per cent. grade, passed the county
jail (bowered in flowers, and always showing a sad
blackamoor or two at its barred windows), skirted
a curious old house called the Château (it had
towers and battlements, and clung to a steep crag
overhanging the Patapsco), went by the columned
portico of the Patapsco Female Institute, and finally brought up at our gate. One day my mother
sent me down to the village for a can of lard and
a sack of flour, and on my painful way home I was
overtaken by a colored man driving a large, empty
wagon. I accepted his offer of a lift with sincere
thanks, and climbed in with my burden. Unhappily, he had but lately delivered a load of coal,
and his wagon was still black with its remains, so
when his horses started up the rough road and the
wagon began to jolt and bounce, the dust almost
smothered me. I got home with my face and hands
black, my clothes ruined, the lard covered with a
foul, bituminous scum, and the flour turned to a
depressing gray. I was washed with kitchen soap,
arrayed in a fresh outfit, and sent back to the village for another cargo, and this time I toted it
home on foot.

We were at the Vineyard only two Summers, but
it made so powerful an impression on me that I remember every detail of the place to this day — the
wonderful adventures in the woods and along the
brook, the fascinating life of beasts and birds,
the daily miracles of the farm, and above all, the

gay songs of the Reus boys of an evening, to the accompaniment of their sister Carrie's pre-Beethoven piano. If I am able today to distinguish between an oak tree and a locust, a goose and a duck, a potato vine and a tomato plant, it is because I acquired those valuable knacks on that happy hill. Some time ago my brother August and I drove up to it on a Sunday morning, and found Carrie and her husband living in the big house. The main terraces of the vineyard had been converted into roads, the roads were lined with bungalows, and in the field that I roved for butterflies there were more bungalows and worse ones, but the woods down by the brook had not changed at all, save that the trees were now almost as large in fact as they seemed to me as a boy. The old barnyard was also still there, with a sow and her pigs snuffling about. But Darsch the farmer was gone, and so was his diligent son, and the last Seckel-pear tree had long since yielded to human progress.

Early in 1892, at the close of the period covered by this record, my father bought a country house of his own at Mt. Washington, to the north of Baltimore, and at the same time my uncle Henry bought one at Relay, half way to Ellicott City. Mt. Washington was then a remote and beautiful place, and in Spring and Autumn I went to school in the city by train, but it was already mainly given over to the Summer homes of city people, and in a little while it began to attract the malignant notice of real-estate developers. We lived there every Summer until my father's death, but Baltimore was creeping out block by block, year by year. First a trolley line penetrated to Roland Park, half a mile or more away, and then another thrust itself along the Falls road, only a few hundred feet from our house. Today that southern part of Mt. Washington is only a shabby suburb of the city, with a filling-station where a one-room country school used to be, and traffic lights at every corner.

Nevertheless, a part of it has been fortuitously preserved, and remains today substantially as it was in 1892. This is a stretch of perhaps half a mile of wild woodland, running up a steep hill from the east bank of Jones' falls, south of Belvedere avenue. The land there is too steep to encourage realtors, and so it continues almost untouched. Even hikers from the city avoid it, for the old mill-road that used to lead into it has long since washed away, and there are no other paths. My brother Charlie and I roved it for many happy Summers, setting traps for rabbits in the woods (and never catching any), fishing and gigging eels in the stream, and trying to dam it at every shallow. An old carp of huge size lived in a pool under the Belvedere avenue bridge, and we used to spend hours throwing stones at him as he basked just under the surface, and never hitting him. He was finally fetched by a wicked boy who lifted a stick of dynamite from a trolley construction camp, and let him have it from the bridge. The roar brought a rush of game wardens from all directions, but by that time we were safe in the woods. The carp either made off for Europe or was blown to bits, for no sign of him was ever seen thereafter.

This bridge, which still stands, was also the scene of my own first experience as a target. The line of the Northern Central Railway ran along the west bank of Jones' falls, and the freight trains that came down from the north began to slow up there for the entrance to the Baltimore yards. The same wicked boy who assassinated the carp invented the game of dropping horse apples and other such waggish missiles upon the brakemen who rode on top of the box-cars, working the old hand brakes. The trick was to fire the shot just as the car emerged below the bridge, and then hide behind the heavy wooden stringpiece. Unfortunately, the brakemen, in their dudgeon and alarm, mistook the horse apples for rocks, and conceived the theory that they were being beset by homicidal tramps. On a memorable afternoon one of them was waiting for us, and as the first apples fell he yanked out his revolver and let go. I can still hear the whistle of that lead. Some of it came so near to my head that I could actually feel its heat.

VI

THE

Head of the House

My grandfather Mencken, in the days when I first became aware of him, was approaching sixty, and hence seemed to me to be a very old man. But there was certainly nothing decrepit about him, even though a broken leg dating from the Civil War era had left him with a slight limp, for he threw back his shoulders in a quasi-military fashion, he had a piercing eye of a peculiarly vivid blue, and he presented to the world what I can only describe as a generally confident and even somewhat cocky aspect. His bald head rose in a Shakespearean dome, and the hair that survived over his ears was brushed forward stiffly. His cheeks were shaven down to the neck, but he wore a mustache of no particular kind, and allowed his

beard to sprout and hang down within the meridi-
ans of longitude marked off by his eyes. Whiskers
of such irrational design were not uncommon in
that age, which was immensely more hairy than
the present glorious day. Many of the extant generals of the Civil War had sets of them, and so did
many German forty-eighters. My grandfather, in
a way of speaking, was a forty-eighter himself, for
he shoved off for these shores from his native Saxony at almost the precise moment the German
Vorparlament met at Frankfort-on-Main. But
that was as far as his connection with democratic
idealism ever went. In his later life he used to hint
that he had left Germany, not to embrace the boons
of democracy in this great Republic, but to escape
a threatened overdose at home. In world affairs
he was a faithful customer of Bismarck, and in his
capacity of patriotic American he inclined toward
the ironically misnamed Democratic party, which
had fought a long war to save slavery and was still
generally disreputable. His two sons, who were
high tariff Republicans, finally managed, I believe,
to induce him to vote against Grover Cleveland in
1884, but my father told me years later that they
viewed his politics with some distrust to the end of
his days.

I recall him best on his visitations to our house
in Hollins street, which, though not very frequent,
were carried out with considerable ceremonial. He
lived in Fayette street, only a few blocks away, and

usually arrived on foot. When the stomp-stomp of his tremendous shillelagh of a cane was heard, and he heaved into sight in his long-tailed black coat, his Gladstonian collar and his old-fashioned black cravat, a hush fell upon the house, my mother and father put on their best party manners, and my brother Charlie and I were given a last nervous inspection and cautioned to be good on penalty of the knout. Arrived, he deposited his hat on the floor beside his chair, mopped his dome meditatively, and let it be known that he was ready for the business of the day, whatever it might turn out to be, and however difficult and onerous. It covered, first and last, an immense range, running from infant feeding and the choice of wallpaper at one extreme to marriage settlements and the intricacies of dogmatic theology at the other. No man on this earth ever believed more innocently and passionately in the importance of the family as the basic unit of human society, or had a higher sense of duty to his own. As undisputed head of the American branch of the Menckenii he took jurisdiction over all its thirty members — his two sons, his three daughters, his two daughters-in-law, his three sons-in-law, and his twenty grandchildren — with his wife, my step-grandmother, thrown in as a sort of friendly alien. There was never, so far as I could learn afterward, any serious challenge of his authority, nor, I must add, did he ever exercise it in a harsh and offensive manner. He simply assumed as a matter of course — indeed, as an axiom so self-evident that the human mind could not conceive a caveat to it — that he was charged by virtue of his status and office with a long list of responsibilities, and he met them in the amiable and assured fashion of a man who knew his work in the world, and was ready to do it though the heavens fell.

My mother, in the years after his death, always defended the justice of his decisions, or, at all events, their strict legality, though more than once, by her own account, they went counter to her own judgment and desire. There was, for example, the matter of the christening of my younger brother, born in 1889. For some reason that I never learned she wanted to call him Albert, and for months that was actually his studio or stable name. Even my father, who was prejudiced against the name because the only Albert he knew was a dead-beat who owed him a bill of $135, nevertheless acquiesced, and all the cups, rattles, knitted jackets, belly-bands and velvet caps that came in for the baby were so engraved or embroidered. But my father yet hesitated strangely to send for a clergyman and have the business over, and one day the reason therefor appeared. It was a beautiful Sunday in early Spring and my grandfather chose it to set up his Court of King's Bench in the Summer-house in our backyard. Without any time-consuming preliminaries, he announced simply that the baby

would have to be called August — plain August
and nothing else, with no compromise on a second
name that might convert him eventually into A.
Albert, A. Bernard, A. Clarence . . . . . . or A.
Zoroaster. August had been the name of his own
father, and was the name of his first-born son, my
father. It was a proud and (to his ears) mellif-
luous name, ancient in the Mencken family and
going back, in one form or other, to the dawn of
civilization. Since this erstwhile Albert was my
mother's fourth child, and in all human probability
would be her last, it was of paramount necessity,
as a matter of family decency and decorum, that
he should be August. And August he was, and is.

Why the name hadn't been given to me I don't
know, and the fact that it wasn't shows a touch
of the mysterious, for I was the *Stammhalter* and
hence the object of my grandfather's special concern and solicitude. As the eldest son of his eldest
son I'd someday enjoy, in the course of nature, the
high dignities of head of the family, and it goes
without saying that he must have given a great
deal of consideration to my labeling. His reasons
for deciding that I was to be named after his second
son, my uncle Henry, I have never been able to discover, and for many years I wondered what source
had provided my incongruous middle name of
Louis. Then I learned that my grandfather's first
wife and my own grandmother, Harriet McClel-
lan, had borne and lost a son in 1862, and died

herself a few months later, and that this ill-starred and forgotten infant had been named Louis after one of her uncles. The old man never ceased to mourn his poor Harriet. They had married when she was but sixteen, and had been happy together in years of hard struggle. My mother once told me that he used to make surreptitious afternoon visits to Hollins street in his declining years, to talk about his lost love. His undying thought of her greatly touched my mother, and was probably mainly responsible for the affection and respect that she always seemed to have for him. His judicial decisions as head of the house had more than once gone against her, but she was nevertheless staunchly for him, and liked to tell me about him.

One of his judgments I recall very clearly, though it must have been handed down not later than 1886. It had to do with the hairdressing of my brother Charlie and me. We had been patronizing a neighborhood barber of the name of Lehnert, and we liked him very much, for he cut our hair in not more than three minutes by the clock, and always gave us a horse-doctor's dose of highly perfumed hair-oil. When we got back from his atelier we let the admiring hired girl smell our heads, which continued to radiate a suffocating scent for days afterward. But my grandfather objected to Lehnert's free and far from well-considered use of the clippers, and one day issued an order that he was to be notified the next time our

hair needed cutting. When the time came word
was duly sent to him, and he appeared in Hollins
street the following Sunday morning. My father
vanished discreetly but my mother stood by for
the operation, which was carried out in the side-
yard. What I chiefly recall of it is that Charlie
and I sat in a kitchen chair and were swathed in a
bed-sheet, and that it seemed to us to take a dreadfully long while. Lehnert could have clipped a
whole herd of boys in the same time. When the
job was done at last my mother professed politely
to admire the result, but there was very little enthusiasm in her tone. The next day my father took
us both downtown, and had my grandfather's zigzag shear marks smoothed out by the head barber
at the Eutaw House, a majestic man of color who
claimed to have serviced not only all the principal
generals of the Civil War, but also every Governor
of Maryland back to colonial days. But when the
time came to return to Lehnert for another clip
he was warned to follow the model before him, and
this he always did thereafter, to the relief and satisfaction of all concerned.

My grandfather, as I have said, wore a Gladstonian collar and a stock-like cravat of archaic
design. Both had disappeared from the marts of
commerce before my time, but my aunt Pauline
had plans and specifications for them, and so enjoyed the honor of making them. She was the
châtelaine of my grandfather's big house in Fay-

THE HEAD OF THE HOUSE

ette street, for his wife, my step-grandmother, was
in indifferent health. Aunt Pauline was already
married, with two children of her own, but she
never forgot her filial duty to her father, nor did
he. When he arrived home for dinner, which was
at about 2 p.m., the soup had to be ready to go on
the table at the precise instant he hung up his
hat in the hall. He had copious and complicated
ideas about cooking and household management,
as he had about medicine, law, moral theology,
economics, interior decoration and the use of the
spheres, and his public spirit, though it was not
strong, nevertheless forbade him to keep them to
himself. In his backyard in Fayette street he carried on extensive horticultural experiments, virtually all of which, I believe, failed. What I chiefly
remember of them is his recurrent reports that
cats had rolled in and ruined his strawberries, or
that a storm had blown down his lima-beans, or
that some other act of God had wrecked his effort
to produce a strain of tobacco resistant to worms,
high winds, and the irrational fluctuations of the
market. But he seems to have had some luck with
the *Curcurbitaceae*, for every year he presented all
his daughters and daughters-in-law with gourds
for use in darning stockings. Inasmuch as these
gourds, though very light, had surfaces as hard as
iron, they did not wear out, and so my mother,
who never threw anything away if room could be
found for it in the house, accumulated a large bat-

tery. Sometimes, when she was out shopping, my brother Charlie and I fought with them in the cellar, for when one of them collided with a human skull it made a loud, hollow, satisfying report, and yet did not cause death or even unconsciousness.

There is a document in the family archives, headed grandly " Halte im Gedächtniss Jesum Christum! ", which certifies that my grandfather submitted to the rite of confirmation as a Christian of the Protestant sub-species in the church at Borna, Saxony, on March 20, 1842, but he had apparently lost his confidence in Jahveh by the time I became acquainted with him. Indeed, it would not be going too far to say that he was an outright infidel, though he always got on well with the rev. clergy, and permitted his three daughters to commune freely with the Protestant Episcopal Church, the American agency of his first wife's Church of England. It was in his character of skeptic that he subscribed toward the Baltimore crematorium in 1889, and ordered his two sons to subscribe too — so far as I know, the only example of overt social-mindedness that he ever showed. He belonged to no organization save a lodge of Freemasons, and held himself diligently aloof from the German societies that swarmed in Baltimore in the eighties. Their singing he regarded as a public disturbance, and their *Turnerei* as insane. Most of the German business men of Baltimore, in those days, had come from the Hansa towns, and as a

Saxon he was compelled to disdain them as *Platt-deutschen*, though his own remote forbears had been traders in Oldenburg. I somehow gathered the impression, even as a boy, that he was a rather lonely man, and my mother told me years later that she was of the same opinion. Left a widower at thirty-four, with four small children to care for and his roots in America still shaky, he had seen some hard and bitter years, and they had left their marks upon him. He showed none of the expansive amiability of his two sons, but was extremely reserved.

By the time I knew him his days of struggle were over and he was in easy waters, but he still kept a good deal to himself, and when he took me of an afternoon, as a small boy, on one of his headlong buggy-rides, he seldom paid a visit to anyone save the Xaverian Brothers at St. Mary's Industrial School, a bastile for problem boys about two miles from Hollins street. These holy men tried to teach their charges trades, and one of the trades they offered was that of the cigarmaker. My grandfather, who dealt in Pennsylvania leaf tobacco, sold them their raw materials, and my father and uncle undertook to market their output — in the end, an impossible matter, for the cheroots that the boys made were as hard as so many railroad spikes, and no one could smoke them. When my grandfather called upon the Xaverians the tobacco business was quickly disposed of, and he and they sat down to drink beer and debate theology. These discussions, as I recall them, seemed to last for hours, and while they were going on I had to sit in a gloomy hallway hung with gory religious paintings — saints being burned, broken on the wheel and disemboweled, the Flood drowning scores of cows, horses, camels and sheep, the Crucifixion against a background of hair-raising lightnings, and so on. I was too young, of course, to follow the argument; moreover, it was often carried on in German. Nevertheless, I gathered that it neither resulted in agreement nor left any hard feelings. The Xaverians must have put in two or three years trying to rescue my grandfather from his lamentable heresies, but they made no more impression upon him than if they had addressed a clothing-store dummy, though it was plain that he respected and enjoyed their effort. On his part, he failed just as dismally to seduce them from their oaths of chastity, poverty and obedience. I met some of them years afterward, and found that they still remembered him with affection, though he had turned their pastoral teeth.

The buggy that he used for his movements about town was an extraordinarily stout vehicle, and it had need to be, for when he got under way he paid no attention to the fact that the cobblestones of Baltimore were very rough. Where we went when I was aboard I didn't always know, for the top

was always up and we elder grandchildren rode
standing in the space between the seat and the back
curtain. Sometimes he would jam in four or five
of us, with a couple of juniors on the seat beside
him and two or three more on hassocks on the
floor. When, in his wild career over the cobbles,
he struck one of the stepping-stones that used
to run across the roadway at street corners, we
all took a leap into the air, and came down somewhat mixed up. But somehow it never hurt us,
and in the end we got so used to it that we rather
liked it. In the last years of his life, after my
brother Charlie and I had acquired a pony, my
grandfather would drive out with us of an afternoon — he in his caterpillar-tread buggy and we
in our cart. Once, proceeding out the Franklin
road, we came in sight of a tollgate, and he ordered
us to drive ahead of him. When the tollkeeper
asked for his money we were to point to the buggy
following, and say that the old man in it would pay
for us. We did so as ordered, but when he came
up he denied that he knew us. By that time, of
course, we were out of the tollkeeper's reach. The
old man thought it was a swell joke, and told my
father and uncle about it as if expecting applause,
but they failed to be amused. The next time we
drove out the Franklin road the tollkeeper charged
ten cents instead of five, and he kept on charging
us ten cents instead of five until his professional
wounds were healed.

My grandfather made frequent trips to Pennsylvania to buy tobacco, and was full of anecdotes of the singular innocence of the Pennsylvania Germans, whose ghastly dialect he had picked up. His favorite tale concerned a yokel of Lancaster county from whom he had bought a crop of tobacco for future delivery, offering a three-months' note in payment. The yokel declined the note on the ground that he needed nothing to help his memory: he would be on hand without fail when the time came to settle. " Keep it yourself," he said, " so you won't forget to pay me." My grandfather traded with these ill-assimilated *Bauern* for many years in complete amity, and had a high regard for them. He sold their tobacco all over. Some of it actually went to Key West, which was then assumed by most Americans to be foreign territory, using only Havana leaf in its celebrated cigars. In deference to the visitors who sometimes dropped in at the factories, the Pennsylvania leaf sent to them was repacked in empty Havana tobacco bales. My grandfather, as a moral theologian, admitted that there was something irregular about this transaction, but he consoled himself by saying that Key West was full of swindlers escaped from Cuba and points south, and that it was impossible to do any business with them at all without yielding something to their peculiar ethics.

The house in Fayette street was a wonderland

to us youngsters of Hollins street, for grandchildren are always indulged more than children,
and we had privileges in it that were unknown at
home. I have described in Chapter I a pillow-
fight that almost wrecked it. We always made a
formal call on Christmas morning — my brother
Charlie and I representing the Augustine line of
the family, and my cousins Pauline and John
Henry representing the Henrician. Ostensibly, of
course, our mission was to offer our duty to our
grandparents, but actually, we glowed with other
expectations. They were never disappointed. The
parlor in Fayette street had a much higher ceiling
than those in Hollins street, and so the Christmas
tree that flamed and coruscated there was larger
and more splendid. At its foot were piles of toys,
and among them there was always an express-
wagon — to haul the other things home. One year
this wagon was for my cousin John Henry, the
next it was for Charlie, the next it was for me, and
so *da capo*. After taking aboard a suitable refreshment of *Pfeffernüsse*, *Springele*, *Lebkuchen*
and other carbohydrates, and stuffing our pockets
with almonds, butternuts, walnuts, candy and
fruit, we loaded our cargo and started home at a
run, yelling and cavorting along the way. Christmas in those days was a gaudy festival, and my
Grandmother Mencken (or maybe it was my Aunt
Pauline) had a singular facility for choosing good
Christmas presents. Down to the middle of my

teens she always managed to find something for me that really delighted me, and many of the books that provided my earliest reading were her selections — including the " Chatterbox " that took me through my first full-length story. But of this, more hereafter.

VII

MEMORIALS OF

Gormandizing

My brother Charlie and I, in the days of our nonage, were allowed officially to eat all that we could hold but twice a year. The first of our two debauches came in the early Spring, the occasion being the annual picnic of F. Knapp's Institute, already described in Chapter III; the second was at Christmas, beginning for the same on the morning of the great day itself and continuing doggedly until our gizzards gave out at last, and Dr. Z. K. Wiley, the family doctor, arrived to look at our tongues and ply us with *oleum ricini*.

Our running time, in the average year, was about thirty-six hours, with eight hours out for uneasy sleep, making a net of twenty-eight. When we came leaping downstairs in our flannel nightdrawers on Christmas morning there was not only a blazing tree to dazzle us, and a pile of gifts to surprise us (of course only in theory, for we knew the cupboard where such things were kept, and always investigated it in advance and at length), but also a table loaded with candies, cakes, raisins, citrons and other refreshments of the season, on all of which, and to any amount we could endure, we were free to work our wicked will.

At other times things of that sort were doled out to us in a very cautious and almost niggardly way, for the medical science of the era taught that an excess of sweets would ruin the teeth. But at Christmas, under the prevailing booziness and goodwill to men, this danger was ignored, and we were permitted to proceed *ad libitum,* not only at home, but also on our morning visit to our Grandfather Mencken's house in Fayette street. Thus we worked away all of Christmas day, keeping our pockets full and grabbing another load every time we came within arm-reach of the reserves. When we were ordered to bed at last, for a night of pathological dreams, we went only reluctantly, and immediately after breakfast on Christmas Monday we resumed operations. It was in the early evening of that day that Dr. Wiley drove up in his buggy, hitched his horse to the ring in the marble horse-block out front, and came in to do his duty.

He was a tall, spare Georgian with a close-cropped head and a military goatee. He had been a surgeon in the Confederate army, and was thus appreciably older than my father, who was a boy of seven when the Civil War began, but the two were nevertheless very good friends, and whenever the doctor made one of his regular calls he and my father investigated the demijohns parked in the dining-room cupboard, and discussed at length the evils of the times. The doctor was a humane and understanding man, and so he never introduced the subject of succoring my brother and me until we had had a dozen or more last whacks at the stuff on the table. Then he would suddenly fix us with his cold gray eye, call for a tablespoon, and proceed to view our tongues. His verdict, of course, was always the same. Indeed, my mother invariably anticipated it by fetching the castor-oil bottle while he pondered it. Two horrible doses from the same spoon, and we were packed off to bed. Christmas was over, though the tree still stood, and some of the toys were yet unbroken. We never had much appetite the day following.

Dr. Wiley had a low opinion of the Yankees, and was full of anecdotes of their treachery in the war. His accounts of surgical practice in the Confederate army were so gruesome that my mother always retired when he introduced them, but my brother and I enjoyed them, as boys always enjoy tales that raise the hair. But his best stories had to do with his professional exploits as dean of one of the Baltimore medical colleges in the seventies.

There was then no Anatomy Act in Maryland, and in consequence the students suffered a dearth of cadavers. The only way to get a supply was to lift them from colored graveyards, and in this scientific *Arbeit* Dr. Wiley, by virtue of his office, necessarily had some hand, though not, of course, as an actual field worker.

He liked to tell how he had figured out a way to beat the Baltimore cops when they took to searching wagons driving in the Annapolis road late at night. His scheme, he said, was to prop up the carcass between the two students who manned every wagon. When a cop heaved in sight, they would steady the late lamented, and if he wobbled nevertheless they would explain to the cop that he was a friend in his cups. The Baltimore police, of course, were eager to stretch every probability in favor of the young doctors, and so they usually overlooked the singularity of a pair of Caucasians taking so much trouble with a drunken Aframerican and the even greater unusualness of an Aframerican going on a jag in his best Sunday clothes and a white choker collar.

Whether or not Dr. Wiley really invented this device to liberate anatomy from the imbecility of the law I don't know: it was claimed, as I learned much later, by every dean of a Baltimore medical school, and in those days there were eight or ten of them. But he liked to tell the story, and my brother and I never got tired of it, though our delight in it was always punished by fearful dreams. We greatly admired the doctor, despite the fact that his standard treatment for a sore throat was mopping it with *tinctura ferri chloridi*, which had a taste like a mixture of stove polish and tabasco. I am informed that medicine has made considerable progress since his day, but all the same he had a great deal of natural talent for his trade, and his clinical experience was so enormous that he was seldom at a loss.

Twice, with scarlet fever in the house, he pulled the patients through, and somehow managed to quarantine the rest of us. Of the four Mencken children, he eased three into this slough of misery, all of them sound and howling, and from time to time he dealt successfully with such universal pests as chicken-pox, measles, whooping-cough, quinsy and cholera morbus. He cured me, in my teens, of malaria, and his instruction that the milk used in the house be boiled probably saved us all from typhoid. When he performed the rite of vaccination there was a scar like a volcanic crater to show for it. In her old age my mother gave him at least five per cent. of the credit for the fact that all her children had reached maturity with straight limbs, powerful digestions, and no cross-eyes.

His order that the household milk be boiled was a source of minor but continuous gustatory delight to my brother and me. The milk was brought in the morning by a milkman who had it in a huge can with a shiny brass spigot, and when he rang his bell the hired girl went out to his wagon, and fetched it in in a pitcher. In its raw state it foamed like beer, and was full of cow hairs, small twigs and other such adulterations. She got rid of them by straining it through a cloth, and then boiled it in a large saucepan. The smell of the boiling always reached my brother and me, and we waited impatiently until it was over. Then the hired girl poured the milk back into the pitcher, and made a mark with a knife across the bottom of the saucepan, which was covered with a gummy precipitate, brown underneath and reeking with incomparable flavors. One side of the mark was my brother's territory, and the other was mine. We fell to with spoons, and had the saucepan clean in a minute.

In those days ice-cream was still something of a novelty in the world, and the nearest store that sold it, an old-fashioned confectioner's, was six or eight blocks from Hollins street. Thus getting it in was a nuisance, and sometimes also a vanity, for on a hot Summer day it would melt on the way. My father accordingly bought a freezer, and announced grandly that we could now feast like Belshazzar whenever the mood was on us. But that was as far as he ever went in the matter, for his gusto for physical labor was even less than his skill at the mechanic arts, so he always avoided diligently the usual chores of a householder. This left the operation of the freezer to the hired girl, with

111

such help as my mother and my brother and I could give her. It was not much. The first time we tackled the job it took nearly an hour, and all of us were worn out. Worse, the ice-cream came out of the machine in large, irregular hunks, frozen solid in their middles and slushy at their edges. Yet worse, some of the crushed rock-salt that was mixed with the ice had got into the cream.

My father ordered it condemned as probably poisonous, but my brother and I followed it back to the kitchen, and devoured it there during the afternoon. Dr. Wiley came that night, looked at our tongues as usual, and prescribed his standard remedy. For a month or so thereafter nothing was heard about the ice-cream freezer, but then it began to appear that the hired girl had been experimenting with it on the sly, and mastering its technic. One Sunday the first fruits of her researches came upon the table — a very passable imitation of boughten ice-cream, with large segments of peach (including slivers of kernel) imbedded in it. After that we had ice-cream every Sunday, and then twice a week, and then three times, and then almost every day ; indeed, we had it so often that even my brother and I began to sicken of it, and to this day I always think of it as next door in unappetizingness to chain-store bread and fruit salad, and seldom eat it save in politeness.

The only member of the family who never got enough was the pony Frank, who had been ac-

quired in 1890 or thereabout, and lived in a tiny
stable at the lower end of the backyard. One Sunday he broke out of his imprisonment and trotted
up to the sideyard that ran along the dining-room.
The window being open, he stuck in his head in his
usual blarneying manner and began to sniff. It
occurred to someone that he smelled the ice-cream,
and a gob of it in a kitchen pan was set on the sill,
to see what he would make of it. He downed it with
happy snuffles, and whinnied for more. After that
he got his share whenever ice-cream was on the bill-
of-fare, and eventually he was eating as much as
all the rest of us put together. My father made an
end to this by issuing a formal injunction, supported by an oral opinion. Feeding ice-cream to
horses, he declared, was as insane a waste of money
as shooting at clay pigeons or contributing to
foreign missions. Frank repined somewhat, but
was placated with an occasional half-peck of raw
carrots, which he liked even better than ice-cream.
So, in fact, did I — and so I do now.

There was another delicacy that delighted my
brother and me almost as much as the rubbery
lining of the milk saucepan, but we could enjoy it,
unfortunately, only in Summer, when we were in
the country. It consisted of stewed blackberries,
spread while still warm on home-made bread, also
still warm. To this day I can taste it at the moments when an aging man's memory searches
through his lost youth for bursts of complete felic-

ity. It had a heavenly flavor, and an even more
heavenly smell. My brother and I would start out
of an afternoon with a couple of lard pails and
pluck the berries along the edge of some nearby
wood. If there was a shortage of ripe ones we'd
turn to the adjacent fields and hunt for dewberries.
The job cost us a good many chigger bites and now
and then a bee sting, but who cared?

When the cans were full we hurried back to the
house, and emptied them on a newspaper spread
out on the kitchen table. The hired girl would then
go through the crop, rejecting the contaminating
gravel, twigs, dead grasshoppers and wild flowers,
and when the cleaning was done it would be raked
into a saucepan along with a handful of sugar. The
stewing took only a little while, but it seemed pretty
long to my brother and me. When it was finished
the fragrant berries were spread upon large slices
of the home-made bread, and we fell to. The hired
girl had strict orders to give us no more than two
slices apiece, but we had ways of blackmailing her.
One was to agree to return the copy of the *Fireside
Companion* that we had lifted and hidden as a
device of pressure politics. Another was to promise
to pull harder the next time she had a day off, and
needed help with the lacing of her stays. The hired
girls of those days were built like airplane-carriers,
but always bought corsets designed for Marguerite
Gautier. I recall one, of Irish extraction and
heavily muscle-bound, who squeezed and pulled

herself into such brief compass that she fainted dead away, and had to be revived with a stiff shot of Monticello. The whiskey made her dizzy and set her to weeping, and in a little while she had a full-fledged and alarming attack of what were then called hystics.

This gobbling of stewed blackberries was policed only defectively, but nevertheless it was policed. The house statutes, as I have said, limited us to two slices of bread, and there was a rider to the effect that they must not be too thick. If law enforcement was knowingly slack — and I have no doubt that my mother knew of and condoned our violations, for hired girls always blabbed — it was because there was a theory in those days that all stewed fruits were good for children. In the raw state even apples were regarded with suspicion, but when stewed they took on all the virtues of spinach, rhubarb and sulphur-and-molasses. At F. Knapp's Institute the boarding pupils were fed apple-butter every day, not only because it was cheap, but also because it was supposed to tone up the system, inure them to the perfect Baltimore climate, and prevent boils.

But my brother and I had no fancy for stewed apples, nor for stewed pears, peaches, cherries, plums, apricots, bananas, grapes, pineapples, oranges or what not. Our sole passion was for stewed blackberries (including, of course, dewberries, which are their brothers) ; we even excluded

115

stewed raspberries, huckleberries and strawberries. But for all raw fruits, since they were regarded as deleterious, we naturally had a great liking, and stuffed them down at every chance. On the hilltop above Ellicott City where we spent two Summers there were the remains of a large orchard. The fruit had not been sprayed for thirty years, and was thus in a state of extreme senescence. I recall especially that the Seckel (always pronounced *sickle*) pears had skins of the thickness and consistency of tin-foil, and were almost coal black. We were warned that they were dangerous to life and limb, and had even floored hogs, but the warning only urged us to follow the suicidal pattern of boys by eating more and more. Nothing happened save an occasional bellyache, sometimes rising to the virulence of cholera morbus. We ate until the compulsion wore off, and then simply stopped.

Many other eatables, in those days, were thought to be injurious to the young, or even fatal. One of them was cheese. When a boy was allowed to eat it at all it was a sign that he was almost well enough along.to be intrusted with horses, edged tools and firearms, and even so he was always introduced to it by slow stages, with many cautious halts. His first dose was a very thin slice, and he was watched carefully for symptoms of spasms. If he appeared to turn a shade pale he was at once given a jigger of ipecac and put to bed, with the blankets piled a foot high, Winter or Summer.

My brother and I had little confidence in such notions, and one day we made off with a heel of cheese that had been laid aside by the hired girl for her mouse-traps. We divided it evenly and ate it boldly, defying Jahveh, Dr. Wiley or anyone else it might concern to do his worst. Once more, nothing much happened. The taste was dreadful — indeed, so dreadful that we pitied the poor mice. But apart from a few sharp twinges in the gastric region, maybe of psychic origin, we suffered no damage.

Pork was another article of diet that was thought in that age to be unfriendly to the young. We were never permitted to eat it at night, for at night all foods, including even such generally salubrious things as raw carrots, were believed to take on virulence. My brother and I, ever eager for scientific experiment, dispatched at least a pound of cold roast pork one night when our parents were at the theatre, and suffered no evil that we could detect with the crude methods then available. If we slept a little uneasily, it was probably only conscience, for even boys of six and eight are afflicted by that curse of mankind. Another night we ate the better part of a prime *Cervelatwurst*, and heard the hired girl accused the next morning of feeding it to a suitor who had waited on her before our raid. She was stupid beyond the general, and defended herself by declaring that she had given him only four or five ham sandwiches, half a pie, a cup of coffee, and six bottles of Class D Baltimore beer. Under cover of the ensuing uproar we slipped off to school.

Thus we gradually accumulated a profound distrust of the dietetic science of the day, and ate anything we could collar, and in any amount, whenever constabulary backs were turned. There were plenty of days when, though we radiated innocence, we actually got down almost as many calories as we were allowed on the glorious day of F. Knapp's annual picnic. But such licentiousness, of course, gradually diminished as we gathered years and wisdom, and we got a boost along the road every time Dr. Wiley dropped in to do his dismal duty. It was not really the castor oil that alarmed us, for every boy of ordinary vanity, in those days, liked to boast that he could swallow it in any quantity, and without gagging. What scared us was the doctor's inspection of our tongues — always long drawn out, and done in sinister silence. We trembled lest he discover signs of sore throat, and get out his dreadful bottle of chloride of iron and his ancient and scratchy mop.

VIII

THE TRAINING OF A

Gangster

THE BALTIMORE of the eighties had lately got over an evil (but proud) name for what the insurance policies call civil commotion. Down to the Civil War and even beyond its gangs were of such enterprise and ferocity that many connoisseurs ranked them as the professional equals, if not actually the superiors, of the gangs of New York, Marseilles and Port Said. It was nothing for them to kidnap a police sergeant, scuttle a tugboat in the harbor, or set fire to a church, an orphan asylum or a brewery. Once a mob made up of the massed gangs of the town broke into the jail and undertook to butcher a party of military gentlemen who had sought refuge there after a vain effort to save an unpopular newspaper from pillage. One of these gentlemen, a doddering veteran of the Revolution named General James M. Lingan, was done to death with great barbarity, and another, General Light Horse Harry Lee, father of the immortal Robert E. Lee, was so badly used that he was never the same again.

At the opening of the Civil War, as every schoolboy knows, another Baltimore mob attacked a Massachusetts regiment passing through the city on its way to save democracy at Bull Run, and gave it such a lacing that what it got in that battle three months later seemed almost voluptuous by comparison. This was in April, 1861. Before the end of the year the town proletariat had switched from the Confederate theology to the Federal, and devoted itself to tarring and feathering Southern sympathizers, and wrecking their houses. The war over, it continued its idealistic exercises until the seventies, and at the time I was born Baltimore was still often called Mob Town, though by then the honorific had begun to be only retrospective.

Thus it was necessary for every self-respecting boy of my generation to belong to a gang. No one, in fact, ever asked him if he wanted to join or not join; he was simply taken in when he came to the right ripeness, which was normally between the ages of eight and nine. There was, of course, some difference between the gangs of the proletariat and those of the more tender bourgeoisie. The former tried to preserve, at least to some extent, the grand tradition. They had quarters in empty houses or stable lofts, smoked clay pipes, rushed the can, carried lethal weapons, and devoted themselves largely to stoning cops and breaking into and looting the freight cars of the Baltimore & Ohio Railroad. The latter were a great deal milder and more elegant. They carried only clubs, and then only in times of danger; they never got any further along the road to debauchery than reading dime-novels and smoking cigarettes; and the only thing they ever stole (save, of course, ash-barrels and garbage-boxes on election night) was an occasional half-peck of apples, potatoes or turnips. These victuals were snatched on the run from the baskets that corner-grocers then set outside their stores, along with bundles of brooms, stacks of wooden kitchen-pails, and hog carcasses hanging from hooks.

I attained, by the age of eight, to a considerable proficiency in this larceny, and so did my brother Charlie. Our victim was usually Mr. Thiernau, a stout, bustling, sideburned man who operated a grocery-and-meat store at Gilmor and Baltimore streets, less than a block from our back gate. He wore invariably what was then the uniform of his calling — a long white apron stained with blood, a Cardigan jacket, and large cuffs made of some sort of straw. Around the little finger of his left hand ran a signet ring, and behind his right ear he carried his pencil. So far as I can remember, he never made any attempt to pursue the boys who looted him; in truth, I suspect that his baskets were set out as a kind of accommodation to them, with the aim of gaining their favor. Not infrequently they were delegated to buy supplies for their mothers, and on such occasions they always chose Mr. Thiernau's store, not that of the Knoops across the street. The Knoops, two brothers and a cousin, appear to have leaned toward Levirate ideas, for when the cousin died one of the brothers married his widow. They were Germans of large girth, gloomy aloofness and high commercial acumen, and they accumulated among them a considerable estate, but they never exposed anything that was edible on the sidewalk, and so the boys of the neighborhood were against them. Even Mr. Thiernau, I believe, kept his best vegetables to be sold inside his store, not stolen in front of it.

One day, after my brother Charlie and I had made a fine haul of sweet potatoes, my father came home unexpectedly and caught us roasting them on a fire in the backyard. He demanded to know where we had got them from, and our guilty looks betrayed us. He thereupon made a great uproar, declaring that he would drown us, ship us to the Indian country or even hand us over to the child-stealers rather than see us grow up criminals. I put all the blame on Charlie, for he had actually made the snatch while I bossed the job and watched, and my father ordered him to return the potatoes to Mr. Thiernau at once, half burned as they were. Charlie set off boo-hooing, threw the potatoes into a garbage-box in the alley, and came home prepared to report that Mr. Thiernau had taken them back with polite thanks. But he delayed on the way to watch the Thiernau colored driver unload a cargo of dead hogs, and by the time he returned my father had apparently forgotten the matter, for we heard no more from him about it. We discovered the next day, however, that the hired girl had orders to supply us with potatoes whenever the roasting fever was on us, and for a week or so we patronized her. But her stock never seemed to have the right flavor, though it came from the same Thiernau's, and we eventually resumed our larcenies. They were terminated a year or so later by Mr. Thiernau's sudden death, which was a great shock to us, and naturally turned us to moral considerations and made us uneasily Hell-minded.

The Hollins street gang functioned as a unit only on occasions of public ceremonial — for instance, at election time. It began lifting boxes and barrels for the election night bonfire two or three weeks before the great day, usually under command of a large, roomy boy named Barrel Fairbanks, and they were commonly stored in the stable behind his house. If we managed to collar a paint barrel it was a feat that cheered us, for paint barrels burned with a fierce flame and made a great deal of smoke. The grocerymen and feed dealers of the neighborhood, knowing that we were on the prowl, tried to save their good boxes and barrels by setting out their decrepit ones, and we always accepted the suggested arrangement. It was only when there was a real famine in fuel that we resorted to taking back gates off their hinges, and even then we confined ourselves to gates that were ready to fall off of their own motion.

The first election night bonfire that I remember was built on the evening of that day in November, 1888, which saw the stuffings of Cleveland and Thurman knocked out of them by Harrison and Morton. The returns were published from the portico of a Democratic ward club at Lombard and Stricker streets, across Union Square from our house, and the fire was kindled at the crossing of Hollins and Stricker streets. As the sad news dribbled along the Democrats fell into a low state of mind, and some of them actually went home before the kegs of beer that they had laid in were empty; but my father rejoiced, for as a high-tariff Republican he was bound in conscience to regard Cleveland as a fiend in human form. I recall him coming down to the corner to see and applaud the fire, which blazed higher than the houses along Hollins street. The cops offered no objection to it, though in those days they were all Democrats, for the flames did no damage to the solid Baltimore cobblestones that underlay them, and if they singed a few trees it was only God's will. When the cobbles yielded to asphalt, long after I was a grown man, election-night bonfires were prohibited.

I recall one election night when the tough boys from the region of the Baltimore & Ohio repair-shops, having had bad luck in collecting material for their own fire, made an attempt to raid ours. They arrived just as it was kindled. They were armed with clubs, and made their attack from two sides, yelling like Indians. We of Hollins street were ordinarily no match for these ruffians, but that night there was an audience looking on, so we fought fiercely, and finally managed to drive them off. Some of them, retreating, carried off blazing boxes, but not many. I got a clout across the arm that night, and nursed it proudly for a week. I was in hopes that Dr. Wiley would order the arm into a sling, but when he dropped in the next day he could find nothing save a large blue bruise. When he began to show signs of taking a routine look at my tongue, I slipped away quickly, pleading an important engagement.

Every Baltimore boy, in those days, had to be a partisan of some engine company, or, as the phrase ran, to go for it. The Hollins street boys went for No. 14, whose house was in Hollins street three blocks west of Union Square. Whenever an alarm came in a large bell on the roof of the engine-house broadcast it, and every boy within earshot reached into his hip-pocket for his directory of alarm-boxes. Such directories were given out as advertisements by druggists, horseshoers, saloon-keepers and so on, and every boy began to tote one as soon as he could read. If the fire was nearby, or seemed to be close to a livery-stable, a home for the aged, or any other establishment promising lively entertainment, all hands dropped whatever was afoot and set off for it at a gallop. It was usually out by the time we reached the scene, but sometimes we had better luck. Once we saw a blaze in a slaughter-house, with a drove of squealing hogs cremated in a pen, and another time we were entranced by a fire in the steeple of a Baptist church. Unhappily, this last ended as a dud, for the firemen quickly climbed up their high ladders and put it out.

The duties of a boy who went for an engine were not onerous. The main thing was simply to go for it. At an actual fire he could not distinguish between his own firemen and those of some other and altogether abhorrent company, for they all wore the same scoop-tailed helmets and the same black rubber coats. But he was expected nevertheless to go for them through thick and thin. If, venturing into a strange neighborhood, he was halted by the local pickets and asked to say what engine he went for, he always answered proudly and truthfully, even though the truth might cost him a black eye. I never heard of a boy failing to observe this obligation of honor. Even the scoundrels who went for No. 10, when we caught one of them in our territory, never tried to deceive us. The most they would do would be to retreat ten paces before letting off their clan cry. We would then proceed, as in duty bound, to hang them out, which is to say, to chase them off the soil of our Fatherland.

The frontiers of the various gangs in West Baltimore were known to all the boys denizened there, and it was not common for a boy to leave his own territory. If he did so, it was at the risk of being hung out, or maybe beaten. But fights between adjoining gangs were relatively rare, for the cops kept watch along the borders, and all hands avoided them diligently. Once the Hollins street gang, engaged in exploring Franklin Square, which was three blocks from Union Square, encountered a gang that went for No. 8 engine, and a battle was joined. But it had gone on for no more than a few minutes when a cop came lumbering up Calhoun street, and both armies at once fled northward, which is to say, into No. 8 territory. The No. 8 boys, though they were officially obliged to do us in at every chance, concealed us in their alleys until the cop gave up the chase, for in the presence of the common enemy gang differences sank to the level of the academic. Any boy in flight from a cop was sure of sanctuary anywhere. In fact, a favorite way of making a necessary journey through

hostile lines was to do it at a run, yelling " Cheese it!
The cops! " Boys respected this outcry even when
they knew it was fraudulent.

There was in West Baltimore a neutral territory
that all gangs save the ruffians from the region of
the B. & O. shops respected — and they seldom
invaded it, for.they had better hunting-grounds
nearer their base. It was a series of open lots
beginning at Fulton avenue and Baltimore street,
three blocks from Union Square, and running westward until it was lost in a wilderness of lime-kilns,
slaughter-houses and cemeteries. From east to
west it must have been a mile long, and from south
to north half a mile wide. It is now covered with
long rows of the red brick, marble trimmed two-
story houses that are so typical of Baltimore, but
in my nonage it was wild country, with room
enough for half a dozen baseball diamonds, not to
mention huge thickets of Jimson weeds, nigger-lice,
and other such nefarious flora. The lower end, at
Fulton avenue, was much frequented by the colored
men who made their livings beating carpets. They
would erect poles, string them with washlines, hang
the carpets, and then flog them by the hour, raising
great clouds of dust. A little further to the westward other colored men pursued the art and mystery of the sod-cutter. They would load their
rolled-up sods on wheelbarrows and push them
down into the city, to refresh and adorn the backyards of the resident bourgeoisie.

We Hollins street boys spent many a pleasant afternoon roving and exploring this territory, which had the name of Steuart's Hill. We liked to watch the operation of the lime-kilns, all of them burning oyster shells, and the work of the carpet-beaters and sod-cutters. But best of all we liked to visit the slaughter-houses at the far western end. There was a whole row of them, and their revolting slops drained down into a deep gully that we called the Canyon. This Canyon was the Wild West of West Baltimore, and the center of all its romance. Whenever a boy came to the age when it became incumbent on him to defy God, the laws of the land and his father by smoking his first cigarette, he went out there for the operation. It was commonly a considerable ceremony, with a ring of older boys observing and advising. If the neophyte got sick he was laid out on one of the lower shelves of the Canyon until he recovered. If he began crying for his mother he was pelted with nigger-lice and clods of lime.

The Canyon was also a favorite resort of boys who read dime novels. This practice was regarded with horror by the best moral opinion of the time, and a boy who indulged it openly was given up as lost beyond hope. The best thing expected of him was that he would run away from home and go west to fight the Indians; the worst was that he would end on the gallows. In the more elderly years of my infancy I tried a few dime novels, trembling like a virgin boarding an airship for Hollywood, but I found them so dull that I could scarcely get through them. There were other boys, however, who appeared to be able to bear them, and even to like them, and these addicts often took them out to the Canyon to read in peace. No cops ever showed themselves in that vicinity, which was probably, in fact, outside the city limits of Baltimore. It was an Alsatia without laws, and tolerated every sort of hellment. I have seen a dozen boys stretched on the grass within a circumference of fifty feet, all of them smoking cigarettes and reading dime novels. It was a scene of inspiring debauchery, even to the most craven spectator.

One afternoon, having been left behind when the Hollins street gang made a trip to the Canyon, I set out alone to overtake it. Just west of Fulton avenue, which is to say, in full sight of householders and passers-by along Baltimore street, I was held up with perfect technic by three boys of a strange gang. One of them aimed a cap pistol at my head and ordered me to stick up my hands, and the other two proceeded to frisk me. They found a pocket-knife, a couple of sea-shells, three or four nails, two cigarette pictures, a dozen chewing-tobacco tags, a cork, a slate pencil, an almost fossil handkerchief, and three cents in cash. I remember as clearly as if it were yesterday their debate over the three cents. They were sorely tempted, for it appeared that they were flat broke, and needed money badly. But in the end they decided primly that taking it would be stealing. The other things they took without qualm, for that was only hooking.

When they turned me loose at last I ran all the way to the Canyon, and sounded the alarm. The gentlemen of the Hollins street gang were pleasantly engaged in throwing stones into a pool of hog blood that had formed beneath the scuppers of one of the slaughter-houses, but when they heard my story they started for the scene of the outrage at once, scooping up rocks on the way. They got there, of course, too late to capture the bandits, but they patrolled the vicinity for the rest of the afternoon, and revisited it every day for a couple of weeks, hoping to make a collar, and get me back my handkerchief, nails, slate pencil, and chewing-tobacco tags. I may say at once that they were never recovered, nor did I ever see the robbers again. They must have come from some remote part of West Baltimore. Or perhaps they were prisoners escaped from the House of Refuge.

This bastile was a mile westward, on the banks of Gwynn's Falls. It was a harsh granite building surrounded by sepulchral trees, and all the boys of West Baltimore feared it mightily. Its population consisted of boys who had become so onery that their own fathers resigned them to the cops. The general belief was that a rascal who once entered its gates was as good as lost to the world. If he ever got out at all, which was supposed to be very unusual, the cops were waiting to grab him again, and thereafter he made quick progress to the scaffold. I knew only one boy who ever actually sat in its dungeons. He was a lout of fourteen whose father kept an oyster-bay in Frederick avenue. The passion of love having seized him prematurely, he got into a fight over a girl, and stabbed the other fellow with an oyster-knife. I well recall the day the cops dragged him through Union Square to the watch-house in Calhoun street, and then hurried back to haul his victim to the University of Maryland hospital in a grocery-wagon.

This affair caused a great sensation in Hollins street, for it was the introduction of many of us to the hazards and terrors of amour. We crowded around the watch-house a day or two later, waiting to hear the result of the cutthroat's trial, and slunk away in silence when a colored malefactor we knew came out and reported that he had been doomed to the House of Refuge, or, as we always called it, the Ref. We assumed as a matter of course that he had been sentenced for life. If he ever got out I didn't hear of it, and for all I can tell you he may be there yet, though the Ref was long ago transformed into a storehouse for the Baltimore sewer department. No member of the Hollins street gang ever entered its door. We had our faults, as I freely admit, but the immemorial timorousness of the bourgeoisie restrained us from downright felony. Two of the boys I chased cats with in 1888 drank

themselves to death in their later years, two others
went into politics, one became a champion bicycle
racer, three became millionaires, and one actually
died an English baronet, but none, to my knowledge, ever got to the death-house, or even to the
stonepile.

In those days the nicknames of boys ran according to an almost invariable pattern, though all
boys, of course, did not have them. The example
of Barrel Fairbanks I have mentioned: he was too
fat to be called simply Fats and not quite fat
enough to be worthy the satirical designation of
Skinny, so he took the middle label of Barrel. Any
boy who happened to be lame was called Hop, anyone who had lost an eye was One-eye, and anyone
who wore glasses (which was then very unusual)
was Four-eyes. If a boy had a head of uncommon
shape he was always called Eggy. The victims of
such cruel nicknames never, so far as I can recall,
objected to them; on the contrary, they appeared
to be proud of their distinctions. Many nicknames
were derived from the professions of their bearers'
fathers. Thus the eldest son of a doctor was always
Doc, and if a boy's father had the title of Captain
— whether ship captain, fire captain, police captain, or military captain, it was all one — he was
himself known as Cap. The eldest sons of all policemen above the grade of patrolmen took their father's titles as a matter of course. A block or two up
Hollins street lived a sergeant whose son was called

Sarge, and when the father was promoted to a lieutenancy the son became Loot. In case a boy's father had the military title of Major, which was not unusual in those days, for West Baltimore swarmed with householders who had been officers in the Civil War, he was called Major himself. I never knew a boy whose father was a colonel or general, but those to be found elsewhere in Baltimore undoubtedly followed the rule. The eldest sons of pedagogues were all called Professor, and if a boy's father was a professional gambler (there was such a boy in Hollins street) he was apt to be called either Colonel or Sport. Younger sons did not share in these hereditary honors, which went by primogeniture. The nicknames they bore, if they had any at all, were based upon their own peculiarities.

The latter-day custom of calling boys by their full given names was quite unknown. Every Charles was Charlie, every William was Willie, every Robert was Bob, every Richard was Dick and every Michael was Mike. I never heard a boy called Bill: the form was always Willie or Will. Bill was reserved for adults of the lower ranks, for example, ashcart drivers. My own stable-name, as I have noted, was Harry, and my immediate relatives so hail me to this day. My father's brother Henry, whose house was next door to ours in Hollins street, was Uncle Hen to us until the time of the World War, when the changing fashion converted him into the more decorous Uncle Henry. I had two uncles with the same given name of John: one was Uncle John to me and the other was Uncle Johnnie, though Uncle Johnnie was the elder. I had an uncle named William, but I still call him Uncle Will, though his son, more than forty years his junior, rates the formal William. My father was Gus to his wife and all his friends, though his sisters called him August, and his underlings called him Mr. August. My mother's given name was Anna, but my father always called her Annie, and she was Aunt Annie to the cousins next door. One of the rules of the time was that a boy named Albert was always called Buck, never Al. Only a boy with an unusual given name escaped these *Koseformen.* The name of Theodore, for example, which was seldom encountered in the pre-Roosevelt era, was never supplanted by Teddy or Ted, but always remained Theodore. There was a boy in Hollins street named Seymour, and he remained Seymour until he broke his leg, when he became Hop. But most boys were Eddie, Johnnie, Bob, Dick or Willie.

The humor of the young bourgeoisie males of Baltimore, in those days, was predominantly skatological, and there was no sign of the revolting sexual obsession that Freudians talk of. The favorite jocosities had to do with horse apples, O.E.A. wagons and small boys who lost control of their sphincters at parties or in Sunday-school;

when we began to spend our Summers in the country my brother and I also learned the comic possibilities of cow flops. Even in the city a popular ginger-and-cocoanut cake, round in contour and selling for a cent, was called a cow flop, and little girls were supposed to avoid it, at least in the presence of boys. Colored girls were fair game for any prowling white boy, but there was never anything carnal about hunting them; they were pursued simply because it was believed that a nigger-louse burr, entangled in their hair (we always kept stocks at hand in the season), could not be removed without shaving their heads. Otherwise, the relations between the races were very friendly, and it was not at all unusual for a colored boy from the alley behind Hollins street to be invited to join a game of one-two-three, or a raid on Mr. Thiernau's potatoes and turnips. Many of the cooks in our block were colored women, though our own were always Caucasians down to 1900 or thereabout. All surplus victuals and discarded clothes were handed as a matter of course to the neighboring blackamoors, and they were got in for all sorts of minor jobs. There have been no race riots in Baltimore to this day, though I am by no means easy about the future, for a great many anthropoid blacks from the South have come to town since the city dole began to rise above what they could hope to earn at home, and soon or late some effort may be made to chase them back. But if that time ever comes the uprising will probably be led, not by native Baltimoreans, but by the Anglo-Saxon baboons from the West Virginia mountains who have flocked in for the same reason, and are now competing with the blacks for the poorer sort of jobs.

The Baltimore Negroes of the eighties had not yet emerged into the once-fine neighborhoods they now inhabit; they still lived, in the main, in alleys, or in obscure side-streets. We boys believed in all the traditional Southern lore about them — for example, that the bite of one with blue gums was poisonous, that those of very light skin were treacherous and dangerous, that their passion for watermelon was at least as powerful as a cat's for catnip, and that no conceivable blow on the head could crack their skulls, whereas even a light tap on the shin would disable them. Mr. Thiernau once set me to tussling with a colored boy in his store, and I made desperate efforts to reach his shins with my heel, but he was too agile for me, and so he got the better of the bout. When I reached home my mother sniffed at me suspiciously, and then ordered me to take a bath and change my clothes from the skin out. The alley behind our house had some colored residents who had lived there for many years, but most of its inhabitants came and went rather frequently, with the rent-collector assisting them. He always appeared on Saturday evening, and if the rent was not ready he turned out his tenant at once, without bothering to resort to legal means. The furniture that he thus set out on the sidewalk was often in a fantastic state of dilapidation, but it always included some of the objects of art that poor blackamoors of that era esteemed — a blue glass cup with the handle off, a couple of hand-painted but excessively nicked dinner-plates, a china shepherdess without a head, and so on. These things had come out of trash-cans, but they were fondly cherished. Behind the alley in the rear of our house, cutting off the Negro cabins from the houses in Baltimore street, ran a blind and very narrow sub-alley, perhaps not more than three feet wide. It was considered a good joke to inveigle a strange boy into it, for it was full of fleas. There were many such blind alleys in West Baltimore. One of them, running off Gilmor street, a block or so from our house, was called Child-stealers' alley, and we avoided it whenever possible. It was supposed to be the den of a monster who stole little children and carried them off to unknown but undoubtedly dreadful dooms. Such criminals were never spoken of as kidnappers, but always as childstealers. So far as I can recall, none of them ever actually stole a child; indeed, none was ever seen in the flesh. But they were feared nevertheless.

Like all other boys, my brother Charlie and I were always in a condition of extreme insolvency. My mother had read an article in an early issue of

the *Ladies' Home Journal* [1] arguing that children
should not be given money freely but required to
earn it, and this became the rule of the house. My
brother and I alternated in shining our father's
Congress gaiters of a morning, and received five
cents for each shine, then the standard price in
Baltimore. For other chores we were paid on the
same scale, and in good weeks our joint income
reached sixty or seventy cents, and sometimes even
a dollar. But it was never enough, so we supple-
mented it by various forms of graft and embezzlement. When my mother sent me to Hollins market
with two or three dollars in hand and a list of supplies to be bought, I always knocked down at least
a nickel. My brother and I also got a little revenue
from Sunday-school collection money, for when we
were given dimes we put in only nickels, and when
we were given nickels we put in only pennies. All
the male scholars save a few milksops followed the
same system. The teachers must have been aware
of it, but they never did anything about it. We
picked up more money by walking to and from
school — a round trip of at least three miles —
and pocketing the three-cent fare each way. Sometimes, when a car was crowded we managed to elude
the conductor, and so rode without paying. On
some cars there was no conductor, and the driver

[1] She had subscribed for it from its first issue, and continued to do so until her death in 1925. Once, when she somehow let her subscription lapse, she got a letter from Edward
W. Bok, the editor, urging her not to desert him.

had to see to the fares. Inasmuch as he couldn't leave his horses, there were channels running down the sides of the car to carry to him the coins inserted by passengers. When a dozen boys got on a car together, it was usually possible for at least half of them to dodge paying fare. The driver always made a pother, but every boy swore that it was his money that had rolled down. The ensuing debate could be easily protracted until we were at our destination.

When all such devices failed, and Charlie and I faced actual bankruptcy, we had to resort to more desperate measures. Here, unhappily, we were cribbed, cabined and confined by the notions of dignity that prevailed among the West Baltimore bourgeoisie. We somehow understood without being told that it would be unseemly for us to run errands for Mr. Thiernau, or to carry the marketing of strange ladies returning home from Hollins market, or to shovel snow off sidewalks in Winter, or to help hostlers with their horses, or carriage-washers at their work. But there was one labor that, for some reason or other, was considered more or less elegant, though it was strictly forbidden by all parents, and that was selling newspapers. In 1889 or thereabout my brother Charlie and I undertook it in the hope of accumulating quickly enough funds to buy a cat-and-rat rifle. We had an air-rifle, but wanted a cat-and-rat rifle, which used real cartridges, and our father's harsh and profane prohibition of it only made us want it the more. So we hoofed down to the alley behind the old *Evening World* office in Calvert street — a good mile and a half from Hollins street — and laid in six *Worlds* at half a cent apiece. Leaping on horse-cars and howling " Paper! Paper! " was a grand adventure, but we soon found that a great many tougher, louder and more experienced boys were ahead of us, and when we counted up our profits at the end of two or three hours of hard work, and found that we had made but six cents between us, we decided that selling papers was far from what it had been cracked up to be. Incidentally, we never got that cat-and-rat rifle.

School took in in those days early in September, and ran on until the end of June. There were very few holidays save the Saturdays and Sundays, and boys had to depend for their major escapes from learning upon the appearance of measles or chicken-pox in the house. But there was one day that was always kept in Baltimore, and that was September 12, the anniversary of the Battle of North Point. This historic action was fought at the junction of the Chesapeake Bay and the Patapsco river in 1814, and as a result of it Baltimore escaped being burned by the British, as Washington was. Moreover, it produced two imperishable heroes in the shape of a pair of Baltimore boys, Wells and McComas, who hid in a tree and assassinated the British commander, General Robert

Ross. Yet more, Francis Scott Key, jugged on a British ship in Baltimore harbor, wrote "The Star-Spangled Banner" while the accompanying bombardment of Fort McHenry was going on. Thus September 12 was always celebrated in Baltimore, and all the boys got a day off from school, which was to me a matter of special rejoicing, for the day was my birthday. The last doddering veterans of the War of 1812 are dead now, and there is no longer a Defenders' Day parade, but September 12 remains a legal holiday in Maryland, and my birthday is still marked by blasts of patriotic rhetoric and artillery.

IX

Cops

AND THEIR WAYS

THE FIRST policeman I ever became acutely aware of on this earth was one Cookie, a short, panting fellow with the sagittal section of an archbishop. I was about six years old at the time, and along with my brother Charlie I was watching and admiring some older boys playing at par, which was the Baltimore name for leap-frog. This was on a hot Summer afternoon and at the corner of Hollins and Gilmor streets, not more than a hundred feet from our own front door. Suddenly one of the par-players stopped his play, turned pale, shook with a kind of palsy, pointed like a setter, and exclaimed "Cookie!" in a shrill, hysterical voice. The rest picked up the enemy at once. He was plodding along Gilmor street in the shadow of the high wall of the House of the Good Shepherd, stretching a whole block down to Lombard street.

The next thing I recall is being dragged along at a speed of what seemed to be at least a mile a minute by the obese Barrel Fairbanks, with my brother tagging behind in tow of a boy named Socks Cromwell. Why we were in such haste I didn't gather at the minute, for I was yet unaware of the dreadful nefariousness of the police. Infants of six were still ignorant in such matters. They gaped at cops as innocently as they gaped at letter-carriers, garbage-men and organ-grinders' monkeys. But now my brother and I had been accepted as licensed followers, though still very far from members, of the Hollins street gang, and the facts quickly soaked into us when its lawful leaders ordered a halt in Booth alley behind our house, to catch breath and consider strategy.

Some were in favor of running on to Reveille's livery-stable, two blocks away, and hiding in the hay. Others proposed making a long detour around Reveille's and laying a course by forced draft out Fayette street to Steuart's Hill. There were objections to both plans. The Reveille brothers were hospitable to boys whose fathers stabled buggies in their establishment (which let in my brother and me), but for boys in general they had only a sour welcome, and none at all for boys in gangs. As for Steuart's Hill, it was at least six blocks away by the route suggested, and most of that route was uphill. Moreover, the Hill was likely to be swarming, on a Summer afternoon, with boys from strange gangs, and if they were in a mood of aggression they might break the truce usually prevailing there, and make short work of the Hollins street gang, burdened, as it was, by such raw and loutish troops as my brother and I.

All this may sound like a long council, but it actually took no more than half a minute. Finally, some smart fellow suggested that we send a spy to the end of the alley to find out if Cookie was still lumbering down on us. No one volunteered for that office, so the smart fellow had to undertake it himself. He sneaked up to Gilmor street along the back-fences, according to the approved technic for scouts in the Indian country, and peeped cautiously around the stable at the corner. Returning in a moment, his caution gone, he reported that Cookie had anchored in a cool spot along the convent wall, and was engaged in mopping his bald head and biting off a chew of tobacco. The hunt was thus over, for Cookie's ordinary jurisdiction did not extend to Booth alley, and he would follow boys there, it appeared, only in the heat of pursuit. No such heat was visible.

But the time and place seemed opportune for the older boys to instruct my brother and me in the tricks and deviltries of cops, and this they did at length. It was never safe, they explained, to let a cop come within reach. There was no telling what infamy he might be up to. For one thing, he might grab a more or less innocent boy, accuse him of breaking a window-pane in a house six blocks away, and proceed to do justice upon him on the spot, with the thin leather thong that flowed from the end of every cop's espantoon, enabling him to swing it ostentatiously as he patrolled his beat. For another thing, he might rush upon boys playing catty and break up the game in sheer ill-nature, with no excuse save the labored one that a flying catty had hit a baby carriage, and scared the infant half to death. For a third thing, he was an incurable tattle-tale, and delighted in writing down the names of boys detected in chasing cats, or throwing nigger-lice at colored girls, or blowing spitballs at the Salvation Army, and then blabbing on them to their fathers.

In brief, a cop was a congenitally iniquitous character, an enemy to society, a master of all the slimy devices of espionage and betrayal. He was against all the manly sports of boys of normal mind and high metabolism. If they started a ball-game in the street he would take his stand behind a tree a block away, watching for some violation of his arbitrary and incomprehensible regulations, and spoiling all the fun. He objected to the harmless pulling of girls' pigtails, to making bonfires in alleys, to setting dogs to fighting in Union Square, to catching goldfish in the pond there, to overturning and emptying ash-boxes, to stealing rides on trucks or horse-cars, to hunting sparrows with air-rifles, to making game of cripples and idiots, to throwing horse-apples at aged or drunken men, to walking along the tops of backyard fences, to prodding mules with sticks, to pulling doorbells on Hallowe'en, to making sliding-places in the gutters in Winter, to scaring little girls with false-faces, to nailing up backyard gates, to putting on white pillow-slips after dark and terrorizing pious colored people, to yelling " Rats! " at Chinese laundrymen, to upsetting the wooden Indians in front of cigar-stores.

Himself an habitual snitcher of peanuts and Johnny-bread from poor Italians, he prohibited lifting a few cheap turnips or carrots from the baskets outside the stores of rich grocerymen. When there was a funeral and boys collected on the sidewalk to see the pallbearers in their plug hats, he spoiled it by heaving into sight, and setting the whole gang to flight. When there was a fire, he made watching it hazardous, and no fun. No boy of any sense would approach voluntarily within half a block of a cop. If one came ambling down the street the sidewalk would clear as swiftly as if he had been Sitting Bull himself. A boy who had occasion to enter a livery-stable always peeped first, to make sure that no cop was there before him. A boy who turned a corner and came face-to-face with one took to flight at once, yelling " Cheese it! " to warn all other boys. Even girls felt uneasy when they saw a blue uniform, though cops never molested them. But from the moment a boy made the first faltering step toward manhood they had it in for him, and he had it in for them.

The one thing to be said in favor of these ruffianly kill-joys was that they were heavy on their feet, and hence easy to out-run. There may have been lean and high-geared cops in other communities, but I never heard of one in the West Baltimore I grew up in. They all wore extraordinarily thick and uncomfortable-looking uniforms, in Summer as in Winter, squeaky shoes with soles as solid as slabs of oak, and domed helmets that always fell off when they attempted to run, scattering lead-pencils, peanuts, red bandana handkerchiefs and chewing-tobacco, and maybe a few cigars, oranges or bananas. A cop in pursuit of a boy had to hold on to his helmet with one hand, and with the other clutch his revolver, lest it go off in the holster flopping from his stern and shoot him in the leg. Any boy in the full possession of his faculties could beat such a mud-scow in a fair race. Even Barrel Fairbanks, fat as he was, could do it. It was only the boy collared by stratagem — always dirty — who was ever actually captured and switched.

So far as I can recall, this switching, when it was done, never brought out any hullabaloo from the victim's parents. His father continued to speak to the cop amicably, and his mother continued to threaten him with the cop when he failed to wash behind his ears. Even the boys themselves did not object to the switching *per se;* all they complained of was being switched by the object of their common contempt and execration — an insult rather than an injury. In those Mousterian days no one had yet formulated the theory that a few licks across the backside would convert a normal boy into a psychopathic personality, bursting with Freudian complexes and a rage against society. It was still universally considered that an occasional rataplan cleansed him of false ideas and softened his native boorishness. School-teachers whaled very freely, and with no more thought of tort than a dentist pulling a tooth, and so did parents. On a window-sill in the kitchen of our house in Hollins street lay a wooden ruler that certainly gathered no cobwebs. Once, having tasted it three times in a single morning, my brother Charlie sneaked it away and buried it in the yard, but the next day there was another in its place, and no questions asked.

I remember well the first time a cop actually came into the house: it must have been a year or so after our initiation into the infamy of Cookie. The time was a Sunday morning, an unusual one for callers, and when the doorbell rang Charlie and I peeped out of a third-story window to see who was there. When we saw the blue uniform we were almost paralyzed with fright — but not quite enough to keep us from piling into a cupboard in the rear room, pulling the door shut, and holding it tight. We stayed there until the bell rang for lunch, and even then we came down the stairs very gingerly, peeping over the banister to make sure that the monster had left. We gathered from my father's talk to my mother that he was one Lieutenant Smith, apparently a cop of great puissance. But we couldn't make out what he had come for, and we were too scared to ask. It was a great relief when we gathered that it was not for us.

Rather curiously, the most ferocious cop I ever knew was more tolerant of boys than the general, and enjoyed a kind of repute among them that was almost, though certainly not quite good. He was a huge Irishman of the name of Murphy, and he wore the heavy black mustache that went in those days with the allied sciences of copping and bartending. Murphy, I suspect, really wanted to be friends with the boys, but they never let him get near enough to them to show it. When we were playing ball in the street, he would come round the corner with a sort of ingratiating tread, much different from his standard plodding, and stand there rather wistfully as we yelled " Cheese it! " and galloped away.

Murphy reserved all his Berserker fury for the Aframericans who lived in Vincent alley, two blocks away. Our own dark neighbors in Booth alley were of a peaceful disposition, and the few ructions back there were almost always caused by visitors, but in Vincent alley the wars continued round the calendar, and were especially bloody on Saturday nights. I mean bloody in its literal sense. There were not many ladies of the Vincent alley set who had not been slashed more than once by the bucks they adored and supported, and I can recall no buck who had not had an ear bitten off, or a nostril slit, or a nose mashed. The alley began to buzz at 6 p.m. on Saturday, when such of its male inhabitants as worked at all came home with their pay, and by 8 o'clock Murphy was hard at it dragging the wounded out of its tenements and clubbing the felonious into insensibility.

There were in those days no patrol-wagons in Baltimore: a cop who made an arrest had to tool his prisoner to the nearest watch-house on foot, with such incidental help as he could get from friendly dray-drivers. Many's the time I have watched Murphy slide, shove and yank a frantic colored lady down the long path which ran obliquely (and still runs) through Union Square, with a huge gallery of white and black fans crowding after. The screams and contortions of such viragoes entertained us boys as neatly as a fire, and we learned a lot about anatomy and physiology from their remarks. Murphy never used his espantoon on females if he could help it, and when he couldn't he always bounced them gently — a tap just sufficient to cause a transient dizziness. He reserved his masterstrokes for males. One stupendous crack, and it was all over. If his customer revived before they got to the police-station it was so unusual as to amount to a marvel. When he applied himself seriously to a bad nigger there was one bad nigger less for a minimum of thirty days.

As I have said, this was before there were any patrol-wagons in Baltimore, or, at all events, in West Baltimore. When they came in at last, in the twilight of the eighties, Murphy seemed to lose form. It was only half a block from the hell-mouth of Vincent alley to the nearest box, and dragging his prisoners so short a distance, with help so quickly and easily obtainable, sapped his old pride of craftsmanship. More than once I observed him at the box looking baffled and foolish. When the wagon backed up he heaved his blackamoor aboard with a kind of resigned contempt, and barely spoke to the driver and footman. He belonged to the post-Civil War school of bare-hand cops, and was a fit match for Killer Williams of New York, though he never rose to any rank in his profession. In the end, if my recollection serves me, he was put on trial before the police commissioners on the charge of giving a bad nigger a clout of unnecessary violence. As I recall it, he was acquitted with honor, but the notion that anyone could imagine hitting a bad nigger too hard was beyond his comprehension, and he withdrew from the force. Baltimore, by 1890, was already fast degenerating, and so was civilization.

There were not only no patrol-wagons in service

in Murphy's heyday, but also no ambulances. The cops had to get the sick and injured to hospital as best they could, and more often than not their best consisted only in commandeering a one-horse truck or ash-cart. In the case of patients emanating from Vincent alley that made no great difficulty, for no colored West Baltimorean of that era, so long as he retained his wits, would let the cops or anyone else take him to hospital. The word always meant to him the old University of Maryland Hospital at Lombard and Greene streets, and every Aframerican knew that it swarmed with medical students who never had enough cadavers to supply their hellish orgies, and were not above replenishing their stock by sticking a knife into a patient's back, or holding his nose and forcing a drink out of the black bottle down his throat.

The ordinary wounded of Vincent alley were patched up at a drug-store nearby, or by one of the sporty doctors who hung about the neighborhood livery-stables. If their injuries turned out to be beyond the science of these quacks, getting them to hospital was a laborious business — that is, in case they were conscious, and hence able to resist. Their struggles against being arrested were, in the main, only formal, and it took only a stroke or two of Murphy's wand to subdue them, but going to hospital was something else again. Not infrequently, in fact, it couldn't be managed without beating them into a coma, even with three or four cops and half a dozen civilian volunteers on the job. Once a patient was on his way, his neighbors gave him up as dead, and his lady friend began looking for a new admirer. There were, of course, aberrant cases of Aframericans, even in Vincent alley, who had been dragged to Lombard and Greene streets and yet returned, but they were very rare and carried a spookish and suspicious aura. Indeed, any blackamoor who had so survived was avoided by his fellows thereafter. He was one who had come unscathed from a charnel-house, and there were certainly reasonable grounds for surmising that he had escaped only by entering into some more or less diabolical pact with the doctors. No one wanted him about. He made everyone uncomfortable.

I must have been at least ten or eleven years old before my fear of cops began to abate. It was probably laid at last by two circumstances. The first was the fact that a young cop named Tom O'Donnell made a headline in the Baltimore *Sunpaper* one morning by excavating a burglar from the cellar of my father's warehouse in Paca street. Tom went in after the fellow alone, bare-handed and in complete darkness, and after he had emerged with his prisoner and dragged him to the nearest watchhouse it was discovered that he had collared a desperate cop-hater with a long string of assaults and mayhems behind him. My father and his brother and the other business men of the vicinity thereupon waited on the police commissioners and demanded that Tom be promoted for his courage, and he was presently made a detective. He served in that office until only the other day, and I still see him on the streets occasionally, his eye continuing to oscillate for pickpockets, for an old cop never stops copping so long as he is on his legs. I got to know him very well in my days as a newspaper reporter, and spared no rhetoric when he made another dramatic collar, which was often. My father's high, astounding praise of him convinced my brother and me that there must be occasional cops who were not enemies of society, just as there were occasional Sunday-school teachers who were not idiots. It was disillusion and hence painful, but there was also some relief in it.

But what really shook us was the appearance in the next block of Hollins street of a boy who actually had a policeman for a father. It seemed wholly fantastic, but the evidence could not be gainsaid, for the boy admitted it himself, and we used to see his father coming home of an evening, exactly like any other father. He was a sergeant when he moved into Hollins street, but was presently promoted to a lieutenancy, and his son was thus known to us as Loot. We all liked him, and in his presence talk about the iniquity of cops had to be avoided. Gradually it fell off even when he wasn't present, and especially it fell off after he had invited us to his house to see his new steam-engine, and his father, in mufti, came down to the cellar and undertook to show us how to work it. He failed completely, as fathers always failed, and we began to realize that he was a human being almost like any other, at least when not in uniform. When the family moved away there was some recrudescence of cop-hating, but all the old steam was out of it.

Today the fear of cops seems to have departed teetotally from American boys, at least on the level of the bourgeoisie. I have seen innocents of eight or nine go up to one boldly, and speak to him as if he were anyone else. Some time ago the uplifters in Baltimore actually organized a school for Boy Scouts with cops as teachers, and it did a big trade until the cops themselves revolted. What happened was that those told off to instruct the Scouts in the rules of traffic, first aid, the operation of fire-alarm boxes, etiquette toward the aged and blind, the elements of criminal law and other such branches got so much kidding from their fellows that they were covered with shame, and in the end the police commissioner let out the academy *sine die*, and restored its faculty to more he duties.

X

LARVAL STAGE OF A

𝕭𝖔𝖔𝖐𝖜𝖔𝖗𝖒

THE FIRST long story I ever read was " The Moose Hunters," a tale of the adventures of four half-grown boys in the woods of Maine, published in *Chatterbox* for 1887. *Chatterbox,* which now seems to be pretty well forgotten, was an English annual that had a large sale, in those days, in the American colonies, and " The Moose Hunters " seems to have been printed as a sort of sop or compliment to that trade, just as an English novelist of today lards his narrative with such cheery native bait as " waal, pardner," " you betcha " and " geminy-crickets." The rest of the 1887 issue was made up of intensely English stuff ; indeed, it was so English that, reading it and looking at the woodcuts, I sucked in an immense mass of useless information about English history and the English scene, so that to this day I know more about Henry VIII and Lincoln Cathedral than I know about Millard Fillmore or the Mormon Temple at Salt Lake City.

" The Moose Hunters," which ran to the length of a full-length juvenile, was not printed in one gob, but spread through *Chatterbox* in instalments. This was an excellent device, for literary fans in the youngest brackets do their reading slowly and painfully, and like to come up frequently for air. But writing down to them is something else again, and that error the anonymous author of " The Moose Hunters " avoided diligently. Instead, he wrote in the best journalese of the era, and treated his sixteen-year-old heroes precisely as if they were grown men. So I liked his story very much, and stuck to it until, in a series of perhaps twenty sessions, I had got it down.

This was in the Summer of 1888 and during hot weather, for I remember sitting with the volume on the high marble front steps of our house in Hollins street, in the quiet of approaching dusk, and hearing my mother's warnings that reading by failing light would ruin my eyes. The neighborhood apprentices to gang life went howling up and down the sidewalk, trying to lure me into their games of follow-your-leader and run-sheep-run, but I was not to be lured, for I had discovered a new realm of being and a new and powerful enchantment. What was follow-your-leader to fighting savage Canucks on the Little Magalloway river, and what was chasing imaginary sheep to shooting real meese? I was near the end of the story, with the Canucks all beaten off and two carcasses of gigantic meese hanging to trees, before the author made it clear to me that the word *moose* had no plural, but remained unchanged *ad infinitum*.

Such discoveries give a boy a considerable thrill, and augment his sense of dignity. It is no light matter, at eight, to penetrate suddenly to the difference between *to, two* and *too*, or to that between *run* in baseball and *run* in topographical science, or *cats* and *Katz*. The effect is massive and profound, and at least comparable to that which flows, in later life, out of filling a royal flush or debauching the wife of a major-general of cavalry. I must have made some effort to read *Chatterbox* at the time my Grandmother Mencken gave it to me, which was at Christmas, 1887, but for a while it was no go. I could spell out the shorter pieces at the bottoms of columns, but the longer stories were only jumbles of strange and baffling words. But then, as if by miracle, I found suddenly that I could read them, so I tackled "The Moose Hunters" at once, and stuck to it to the end. There were still, of course, many hard words, but they were no longer insurmountable obstacles. If I staggered and stumbled somewhat, I nevertheless hung on, and by the Fourth of July, 1888, I had blooded my first book.

An interval of rough hunting followed in Hollins street and the adjacent alleys, with imaginary Indians, robbers and sheep and very real tomcats as the quarry. Also, I was introduced to chewing tobacco by the garbageman, who passed me his plug as I lay on the roof of the ash-shed at the end of the backyard, watching him at his public-spirited work. If he expected me to roll off the roof, clutching at my midriff, he was fooled, for I managed to hold on until he was out of sight, and I was only faintly dizzy even then. Again, I applied myself diligently to practising leap-frog with my brother Charlie, and to mastering the rules of top-spinning, catty and one-two-three. I recall well how it impressed me to learn that, by boys' law, every new top had to have a license burned into it with a red-hot nail, and that no strange boy on the prowl for loot, however black-hearted, would venture to grab a top so marked. That discovery gave me a sense of the majesty of the law which still sustains me, and I always take off my hat when I meet a judge — if, of course, it is in any place where a judge is not afraid to have his office known.

But pretty soon I was again feeling the powerful suction of beautiful letters — so strange, so thrilling, and so curiously suggestive of the later suction of amour — , and before Christmas I was sweating through the translation of Grimms' Fairy Tales that had been bestowed upon me, " for industry and good deportment," at the closing exercises of F. Knapp's Institute on June 28. This volume had been put into lame, almost pathological English by a lady translator, and my struggles with it awoke in me the first faint gutterings of the critical faculty. Just what was wrong with it I couldn't, of course, make out, for my gifts had not yet flowered, but I was acutely and unhappily conscious that it was much harder going than " The Moose Hunters," and after a month or so of unpleasantly wrestling with it I put it on the shelf. There it remained for more than fifty years. Indeed, it was not until the appearance of " Snow White " as a movie that I took it down and tried it again, and gagged at it again.

That second experiment convinced me that the fault, back in 1888, must have been that of either the brothers Grimm or their lady translator, but I should add that there was also some apparent resistant within my own psyche. I was born, in truth, without any natural taste for fairy tales, or, indeed, for any other writing of a fanciful and unearthly character. The fact explains, I suppose, my lifelong distrust of poetry, and may help to account for my inability to memorize even a few stanzas of it at school. It probably failed to stick in my mind simply because my mind rejected it as nonsense — sometimes, to be sure, very jingly and juicy nonsense, but still only nonsense. No doubt the same infirmity was responsible for the feebleness of my appetite for the hortatory and incredible juvenile fiction fashionable in my nonage —

the endless works of Oliver Optic, Horatio Alger, Harry Castlemon and so on. I tried this fiction more than once, for some of the boys I knew admired it vastly, but I always ran aground in it. So far as I can recall, I never read a single volume of it to the end, and most of it finished me in a few pages.

What I disliked about it I couldn't have told you then, and I can account for my aversion even now only on the theory that I appear to have come into the world with a highly literal mind, geared well enough to take in overt (and usually unpleasant) facts, but very ill adapted to engulfing the pearls of the imagination. All such pearls tend to get entangled in my mental *vibrissae*, and the effort to engulf them is as disagreeable to me as listening to a sermon or reading an editorial in a second-rate (or even first-rate) newspaper. I was a grown man, and far gone in sin, before I ever brought myself to tackle " Alice in Wonderland," and even then I made some big skips, and wondered sadly how and why such feeble jocosity had got so high a reputation. I am willing to grant that it must be a masterpiece, as my betters allege — but not to *my* taste, not for *me*. To the present moment I can't tell you what is in any of the other juvenile best-sellers of my youth, of moral and sociological hallucination all compact, just as I can't tell you what is in the Bhagavad-Gita (which Will Levington Comfort urged me to read in 1912 or there-

about), or in the works of Martin Tupper, or in
the report of Vassar Female College for 1865. I
tried dime-novels once, encouraged by a boy who
aspired to be a train-robber, but they only made
me laugh. At a later time, discovering the pseudo-
scientific marvels of Jules Verne, I read his whole
canon, and I recall also sweating through a serial
in a boys' weekly called *Golden Days*, but this last
dealt likewise with *savants* and their prodigies,
and was no more a juvenile, as juveniles were then
understood, than " Ten Thousand Leagues Under
the Sea."

But before you set me down a prig, let me tell
you the rest of it. That rest of it is my discovery
of " Huckleberry Finn," probably the most stupendous event of my whole life. The time was the
early part of 1889, and I wandered into Paradise
by a kind of accident. Itching to exercise my
newly acquired art of reading, and with " The
Moose Hunters " exhausted and Grimms' Fairy
Tales playing me false, I began exploring the house
for print. The Baltimore *Sunpaper* and *Evening
News*, which came in daily, stumped me sadly, for
they were full of political diatribes in the fashion
of the time, and I knew no more about politics than
a chimpanzee. My mother's long file of *Godey's
Lady's Book* and her new but growing file of the
Ladies' Home Journal were worse, for they dealt
gloomily with cooking, etiquette, the policing of
children, and the design and construction of mil-

linery, all of them sciences that still baffle me. Nor
was there any pabulum for me in the hired girl's
dog's-eared files of *Bow Bells* and the *Fireside
Companion*, the first with its ghastly woodcuts of
English milkmaids in bustles skedaddling from
concupiscent baronets in frock-coats and cork-
screw mustaches. So I gradually oscillated, almost
in despair, toward the old-fashioned secretary in
the sitting-room, the upper works of which were
full of dismal volumes in the black cloth and gilt
stamping of the era. I had often eyed them from
afar, wondering how long it would be before I
would be ripe enough to explore them. Now I
climbed up on a chair, and began to take them
down.

They had been assembled by my father, whose
taste for literature in its purer states was of a generally low order of visibility. Had he lived into the
days of my practice as a literary critic, I daresay
he would have been affected almost as unpleasantly
as if I had turned out a clergyman, or a circus
clown, or a labor leader. He read every evening
after dinner, but it was chiefly newspapers that he
read, for the era was one of red-hot politics, and
he was convinced that the country was going to
Hell. Now and then he took up a book, but I found
out long afterward that it was usually some pamphlet on the insoluble issues of the hour, say
" Looking Backward," or " If Christ Came to Chicago," or " Life Among the Mormons." These

works disquieted him, and he naturally withheld them from his innocent first-born. Moreover, he was still unaware that I could read — that is, fluently, glibly, as a pleasure rather than a chore, in the manner of grown-ups.

Nevertheless, he had managed somehow to bring together a far from contemptible collection of books, ranging from a set of Chambers' Encyclopedia in five volumes, bound in leather like the Revised Statutes, down to " Atlantis: the Antediluvian World," by Ignatius Donnelly, and " Around the World in the Yacht *Sunbeam*." It included a two-volume folio of Shakespeare in embossed morocco, with fifty-odd steel plates, that had been taken to the field in the Civil War by " William H. Abercrombie, 1st Lieut. Company H, 6th Regiment, Md. Vol. Inftr.," and showed a corresponding dilapidation. Who this gallant officer was I don't know, or whether he survived the carnage, or how his cherished text of the Bard ever fell into my father's hands. Also, there were Dickens in three thick volumes, George Eliot in three more, and William Carleton's Irish novels in a third three. Again, there were " Our Living World," by the Rev. J. G. Wood; " A History of the War For the Union," by E. A. Duyckinck; " Our Country," by Benson J. Lossing, LL.D., and " A Pictorial History of the World's Great Nations From the Earliest Dates to the Present Time," by Charlotte M. Yonge — all of them likewise in threes, folio, with lavish illustrations on steel, stone and wood, and smelling heavily of the book-agent. Finally, there were forty or fifty miscellaneous books, among them, as I recall, "Peculiarities of American Cities," by Captain Willard Glazier; "Our Native Land," by George T. Ferris; "A Compendium of Forms," by one Glaskell; "Adventures Among Cannibals" (with horrible pictures of missionaries being roasted, boiled and fried), "Uncle Remus," "Ben Hur," "Peck's Bad Boy," "The Adventures of Baron Münchhausen," "One Thousand Proofs That the Earth Is Not a Globe" (by a forgotten Baltimore advanced thinker named Carpenter), and a deadly-looking "History of Freemasonry in Maryland," by Brother Edward T. Schultz, 32°, in five coal-black volumes.

I leave the best to the last. All of the above, on my first exploration, repelled and alarmed me; indeed, I have never read some of them to this day. But among them, thumbing round, I found a series of eight or ten volumes cheek by jowl, and it appeared on investigation that the whole lot had been written by a man named Mark Twain. I had heard my father mention this gentleman once or twice in talking to my mother, but I had no idea who he was or what he had done: he might have been, for all I knew, a bartender, a baseball-player, or one of the boozy politicoes my father was always meeting in Washington. But here was evidence that he was a man who wrote books, and I noted at once that the pictures in those books were not of the usual funereal character, but light, loose and lively. So I proceeded with my inquiry, and in a little while I had taken down one of them, a green quarto, sneaked it to my bedroom, and stretched out on my bed to look into it. It was, as smarties will have guessed by now, " Huckleberry Finn."

If I undertook to tell you the effect it had upon me my talk would sound frantic, and even delirious. Its impact was genuinely terrific. I had not gone further than the first incomparable chapter before I realized, child though I was, that I had entered a domain of new and gorgeous wonders, and thereafter I pressed on steadily to the last word. My gait, of course, was still slow, but it became steadily faster as I proceeded. As the blurbs on the slip-covers of murder mysteries say, I simply couldn't put the book down. After dinner that evening, braving a possible uproar, I took it into the family sitting-room, and resumed it while my father searched the *Evening News* hopefully for reports of the arrest, clubbing and hanging of labor leaders. Anon, he noticed what I was at, and demanded to know the name of the book I was reading. When I held up the green volume his comment was " Well, I'll be durned! "

I sensed instantly that there was no reproof in this, but a kind of shy rejoicing. Then he told me that he had once been a great reader of Mark Twain himself — in his younger days. He had got hold of all the volumes as they came out — " The Innocents " in 1869, when he was still a boy himself ; " Roughing It " in 1872, " The Gilded Age " in 1873, " Tom Sawyer " in 1876, " A Tramp Abroad " in 1880, the year of my birth, and so on down to date. (All these far from pristine firsts are still in the Biblioteca Menckeniana in Hollins street, minus a few that were lent to neighbor boys and never returned, and had to be replaced.) My father read them in the halcyon days before children, labor troubles and Grover Cleveland had begun to frazzle him, and he still got them down from the shelf on quiet evenings, after the first-named were packed off to bed. But a man of advancing years and cares had to consider also the sorrows of the world, and so he read in Mark less than aforetime.

As for me, I proceeded to take the whole canon at a gulp — and presently gagged distressfully. " Huckleberry Finn," of course, was as transparent to a boy of eight as to a man of eighty, and almost as pungent and exhilarating, but there were passages in " A Tramp Abroad " that baffled me, and many more in " The Innocents," and a whole swarm in " The Gilded Age." I well recall wrestling with the woodcut by W. F. Brown on page 113 of the " Tramp." It shows five little German girls swinging on a heavy chain stretched between two stone posts on a street in Heilbronn, and the legend under it is " Generations of Bare Feet." That legend is silly, for all the girls have shoes on, but what puzzled me about it was something quite different. It was a confusion between the word *generation* and the word *federation*, which latter was often in my father's speech in those days, for the American Federation of Labor had got under way only a few years before, and was just beginning in earnest to harass and alarm employers. Why I didn't consult the dictionary (or my mother, or my father himself) I simply can't tell you. At eight or nine, I suppose, intelligence is no more than a small spot of light on the floor of a large and murky room. So instead of seeking help I passed on, wondering idiotically what possible relation there could be between a gang of little girls in pigtails and the Haymarket anarchists, and it was six or seven years later before the " Tramp " became clear to me, and began to delight me.

It then had the curious effect of generating in me both a great interest in Germany and a vast contempt for the German language. I was already aware, of course, that the Mencken family was of German origin, for my Grandfather Mencken, in his care for me as *Stammhalter*, did not neglect to describe eloquently its past glories at the German universities, and to expound its connections to the most remote degrees. But my father, who was only half German, had no apparent interest in either the German land or its people, and when he spoke of the latter at all, which was not often, it was usually in sniffish terms. He never visited Germany, and never signified any desire to do so, though I recall my mother suggesting, more than once, that a trip there would be swell. It was " A Tramp Abroad " that made me German-conscious, and I still believe that it is the best guide-book to Germany ever written. Today, of course, it is archaic, but it was still reliable down to 1910, when I made my own first trip. The uproarious essay on " The Awful German Language," which appears at the end of it as an appendix, worked the other way. That is to say, it confirmed my growing feeling, born of my struggles with the conjugations and declensions taught at F. Knapp's Institute, that German was an irrational and even insane tongue, and not worth the sufferings of a freeborn American. These diverse impressions have continued with me ever since. I am still convinced that Germany, in the intervals of peace, is the most pleasant country to travel in ever heard of, and I am still convinced that the German language is of a generally preposterous and malignant character.

" Huck," of course, was my favorite, and I read it over and over. In fact, I read it regularly not less than annually down to my forties, and only a few months ago I hauled it out and read it once more — and found it as magnificent as ever. Only one other book, down to the beginning of my teens, ever beset me with a force even remotely comparable to its smash, and that was a volume called

" Boys' Useful Pastimes," by " Prof. Robert Griffith, A.M., principal of Newton High School." This was given to me by my Grandmother Mencken at Christmas, 1889, and it remained my constant companion for at least six years. The sub-title describes its contents: " Pleasant and profitable amusement for spare hours, comprising chapters on the use and care of tools, and detailed instructions by means of which boys can make with their own hands a large number of toys, household ornaments, scientific appliances, and many pretty, amusing and necessary articles for the playground, the house and out-of-doors." Manual training was still a novelty in those days, and I suspect that the professor was no master of it, for many of his plans and specifications were completely unintelligible to me, and also to all the neighborhood boys who dropped in to help and advise. I doubt, indeed, that any human being on earth, short of an astrophysicist, could have made anything of his directions for building boat models. But in other cases he was relatively explicit and understandable, and my brother Charlie and I, after long efforts, managed to make a steam-engine (or, more accurately, a steam-mill) according to his recipe. The boiler was a baking-powder tin, and the steam, issuing out of a small hole in the top, operated a sort of fan or mill-wheel. How we provided heat to make steam I forget, but I remember clearly that my mother considered the process dangerous, and ordered us to take the engine out of the cellar and keep it in the backyard.

I had no more mechanical skill than a cow, but I also managed to make various other things that the professor described, including a what-not for the parlor (my mother professed to admire it, but never put it into service), a rabbit-trap (set in the backyard, it never caught anything, not even a cat), and a fancy table ornamented with twigs from the pear tree arranged in more or less geometrical designs. " Boys' Useful Pastimes " was printed by A. L. Burt on stout paper, and remains extant to this day — a rather remarkable fact, for other boys often borrowed it, and sometimes they kept it on their work-benches for a long while, and thumbed it diligently. One of those boys was Johnnie Sponsler, whose father kept a store in the Frederick road, very near Hollins street. Johnnie was vastly interested in electricity, as indeed were most other boys of the time, for such things as electric lights, motors, telephones and doorbells were just coming in. He thus made hard use of Professor Griffith's Part VII, which was headed " Scientific Apparatus and Experiments," and included directions for making a static machine, and for electroplating door-keys. He later abandoned the sciences for the postal service, and is now, I believe, retired. " Boys' Useful Pastimes," and my apparent interest in it, may have been responsible for my father's decision to transfer me from F.

Knapp's Institute to the Baltimore Polytechnic in 1892. If so, it did me an evil service in the end, for my native incapacity for mechanics made my studies at the Polytechnic a sheer waste of time, though I managed somehow to pass the examinations, even in such abysmal subjects as steam engineering.

The influence of " Huck Finn " was immensely more powerful and durable. It not only reinforced my native aversion to the common run of boys' books; it also set me upon a systematic exploration of all the volumes in the old secretary, and before I finished with them I had looked into every one of them, including even Brother Schultz's sombre history of Freemasonry in Maryland. How many were actually intelligible to a boy of eight, nine, ten? I should say about a fourth. I managed to get through most of Dickens, but only by dint of hard labor, and it was not until I discovered Thackeray, at fourteen, that the English novel really began to lift me. George Eliot floored me as effectively as a text in Hittite, and to the present day I have never read " Adam Bede " or " Daniel Deronda " or " The Mill on the Floss," or developed any desire to do so. So far as I am concerned, they will remain mere names to the end of the chapter, and as hollow and insignificant as the names of Gog and Magog.

But I plowed through Chambers' Encyclopedia relentlessly, beginning with the shortest articles and gradually working my way into the longer ones. The kitchen-midden of irrelevant and incredible information that still burdens me had its origins in those pages, and I almost wore them out acquiring it. I read, too, the whole of Lossing, nearly all of Charlotte M. Yonge, and even some of Duyckinck, perhaps the dullest historian ever catalogued by faunal naturalists on this or any other earth. My brother Charlie and I enjoyed " Our Living World " chiefly because of the colored pictures, but I also read long stretches of it, and astonished my father by calling off the names of nearly all the wild beasts when the circus visited Baltimore in 1889. Finally, I recall reading both " Life Among the Mormons " and " One Thousand Proofs That the Earth Is Not a Globe."

Thus launched upon the career of a bookworm, I presently began to reach out right and left for more fodder. When the Enoch Pratt Free Library of Baltimore opened a branch in Hollins street, in March, 1886, I was still a shade too young to be excited, but I had a card before I was nine, and began an almost daily harrying of the virgins at the delivery desk. In 1888 my father subscribed to *Once-a-Week*, the predecessor of *Collier's*, and a little while later there began to come with it a long series of cheap reprints of contemporary classics, running from Tennyson's poems to Justin M'Carthy's " History of Our Own Times "; and simultaneously there appeared from parts unknown a similar series of cheap reprints of scientific papers, including some of Herbert Spencer. I read them all, sometimes with shivers of puzzlement and sometimes with delight, but always calling for more. I began to inhabit a world that was two-thirds letterpress and only one-third trees, fields, streets and people. I acquired round shoulders, spindly shanks, and a despondent view of humanity. I read everything that I could find in English, taking in some of it but boggling most of it.

This madness ran on until I reached adolescence, and began to distinguish between one necktie and another, and to notice the curiously divergent shapes, dispositions and aromas of girls. Then, gradually, I began to let up.

But to this day I am still what might be called a reader, and have a high regard for authors.

XI

FIRST STEPS IN

𝔇𝔦𝔳𝔦𝔫𝔦𝔱𝔶

In the days of my earliest memories my father had
an acquaintance named Mr. Garrigues, a highly
respectable man of French origin who operated a
men's hat-store in West Baltimore, not far from
our home in Hollins street. This hat-store of his,
though it drove an excellent trade, occupied him
only on week-days; on Sundays he threw himself,
rather curiously for a man of his race, into super-
intending the Sunday-school of a little Methodist
chapel in nearby Wilkens avenue. Early one Winter evening he dropped in while my brother Charlie
and I were playing Indians up and down the front
staircase, and proposed to my father that we be
articled to his Sunday-school. I recall, of course,
nothing of his argument, though my brother and

I naturally eavesdropped; I remember only that it lasted but a few minutes, and that the very next Sunday afternoon Mr. Garrigues came to the house in a high silk hat, and conducted us to his seminary.

It was not until years afterward that I learned why my father had succumbed so quickly, or indeed at all. I understood by that time that he was what Christendom abhors as an infidel, and I took the liberty of expressing some wonder that he had been willing, in that character, to expose his two innocent sons to the snares of the Wesleyan divinity. He hemmed and hawed a little, but finally let go the truth. What moved him, he confessed, was simply his overmastering impulse to give over the Sunday afternoons of Winter to quiet snoozing. This had been feasible so long as my brother and I were puling infants and could be packed off for naps ourselves, but as we increased in years and malicious animal magnetism and began to prefer leaping and howling up and down stairs, it became impossible for him to get any sleep. So he was a set-up for Mr. Garrigues, and succumbed without firing a shot. " The risk," he went on to explain, " was much less than you seem to think. Garrigues and his Methodists had you less than two hours a week, and I had you all the rest of the time. I'd have been a hell of a theologian to let them nail you."

I recall very little of his counter-revolutionary

propaganda, and all that little took the form of a sort of satirical cross-examination, deliberately contrived to be idiotic. " Have they got you to Jonah yet? Have you heard about him swallowing the whale? " And so on. I recall even less of the teaching in the Sunday-school itself, though I apparently picked up from it some knowledge of the *dramatis personae* of the Old Testament. At all events, I can't remember the time when I did not know that Moses wrote the Ten Commandments with a chisel and wore a long beard; that Noah built an ark like the one we had in our Christmas garden, and filled it with animals which, to this day, I always think of as wooden, with a leg or two missing; that Lot's wife was turned into a pillar (I heard it as *cellar*) of table salt; that the Tower of Babel was twice as high as the Baltimore shot-tower; that Abraham greatly pleased Jahveh by the strange device of offering to butcher and roast his own son, and that Leviticus was the father of Deuteronomy. But all this learning must have been imparted by a process resembling osmosis, for I have no recollection of any formal teaching, nor even of any teacher.

The one thing I really remember about that Sunday-school is the agreeable heartiness of the singing. It is, of course, the thing that all children enjoy most in Sunday-schools, for there they are urged to whoop their loudest in praise of God, and that license is an immense relief from the shushing

they are always hearing at home. Years later I
lived for a while beside a Christian Science establishment in which the larval scientificoes were
taught, presumably, that their occasional belly-
aches were only mortal error, but all I ever heard
of this teaching was their frequent antiphon of
cheerful song, with each singer shrilling along in
a different key. If the Bach Choir could work up
so much pressure in its pipes, the Mass in B minor
would become as popular as "·Sweet Adeline." So
far as I can make out, I attended Mr. Garrigues's
hive of hymnody but two Winters, and yet I carried away from it a répertoire of Methodist shouts
and glees that sticks to me to this day, and is turned
loose every time I let three-bottle men take me for
a ride.

My favorite then, as now, was " Are You Ready
For the Judgment Day? " — a gay and even rollicking tune with a saving hint of brimstone in the
words. I am told by Paul Patterson, who got his
vocal training in the Abraham Lincoln Belt of
Inner Illinois, that the No. 1 hymn there in the
eighties was " Showers of Blessings," but in Baltimore, though we sang it, it was pretty far down the
list. We grouped it, in fact, with such *dolce* but
unexhilarating things as " In the Sweet By-and-
By " and " God Be With You Till We Meet
Again " — pretty stuff, to be sure, but sadly lacking in bite and zowie. The runner-up for " Are
You Ready? " was " I Went Down the Rock to

Hide My Face," another hymn with a very lively swing to it, and after " the Rock " came " Stand Up, Stand Up for Jesus," " Throw Out the Life-line," " At the Cross," " Draw Me Nearer, Nearer, Nearer, Blessed Lord," " What a Friend We Have in Jesus," " Where Shall We Spend Eternity? " " The Sweet By-and-By," and " Hallelujah, Hallelujah, Revive Us Again," which last was cabbaged by the I.W.W.'s years later, and converted into proletarian ribaldry. We also learned the more somber classics — " Nearer, My God, To Thee," " Onward, Christian Soldiers," " Whiter Than Snow," " From Greenland's Icy Mountains," " Rock of Ages," " There is a Green Hill Far Away," and so on — but they were not sung often, and my brother and I had little fancy for them. It was not until I transferred to another Sunday-school that I came to know such lugubrious horrors as " There is a Fountain Filled With Blood." The Methodists avoided everything of that kind. They surely did not neglect Hell in their preaching, but when they lifted up their voices in song they liked to pretend that they were booked to escape it.

My early preference for " Are You Ready? " was no doubt supported by the fact that it was also a favorite among the Aframerican evangelists who practised in the alley behind Hollins street, alarming and shaking down the resident sinners. These evangelists did not confine themselves to Sundays, but worked seven days a week, and it seemed to me as a boy that there was always one of them in operation. They were both male and female. I recall clearly a female who wore a semi-ecclesiastical robe of violent purple, and had a voice so raucous that the white neighbors often begged the cops to chase her away. Whenever she was hustled out she kept on shouting warnings over her shoulder, always to the effect that the Day of Judgment was just round the corner. Her chief target was a low-down white man who lived in the alley with a colored woman, and had a large family of mulattoes. When he retreated into his house she howled at him through the window. So far as I know, she never made any impression on him, nor on his children, though his lady sometimes gave her a penny. This sinful white man, who never did any work, eventually disappeared, and the colored people reported that he had been killed in a brawl, and his body hustled to the University of Maryland dissecting-room. Of his children, one son was later reported to be hanged.

The evangelists always began their proceedings by lining out a hymn, and usually it was " Are You Ready? " It brought out all the colored people who happened to be at home, and in a few minutes white boys began to leap over the Hollins street back-fences to join the congregation. (In those days no self-respecting boy ever went through a gate. It was a point of honor to climb over the fence.) When the opening hymn reached its tenth and last stanza the evangelist would pray at length, mentioning salient sinners by name. Then there would be another hymn, and after that he would launch into his discourse. Its subject was always the same: the dreadful state of Aframerican morals in West Baltimore. It was delivered in a terrifying manner — indeed, it ran mainly to shrieks and howls — but it was seldom long, for the colored people preferred their theology in small and powerful doses. Then there would be another hymn, and the reverend would begin to show signs that a collection was impending. The moment those signs were detected nine-tenths of his audience vanished. Not infrequently, in fact, ten-tenths of it vanished, and all he could do, after mopping his brow and stuffing his handkerchief into his hat, was to shuffle on to some other alley.

We white boys always joined in the hymns, and listened to the sermons. From the latter we picked up a great deal of useful information about the geography, dimensions, temperature, social life and public works of Hell. To this day I probably know more about the matter than most ordained clergymen. The Hell we heard about was chiefly peopled, of course, by the colored damned; it was sometime later before I began to understand clearly that there was also accommodation for Caucasians. We seldom attempted to rough-house these services, though once in a while a boy whose people had family prayers and who thus hated religion would heave a dead cat over the fence or run down the alley yelling " Fire! " The colored communicants commonly gave ear with perfect gravity. Indeed, the only one who ever ventured to dispute the theology on tap was Old Wesley, the alley metaphysician, who reserved his caveats for the preaching of his brother, a divine who pastored a tar-paper tabernacle down in Calvert county, and showed up only to rowel and bedevil Wesley for living in adultery with our next-door neighbor's colored cook.

It was the dream of every alley evangelist to be called to a regular church, and sometimes that dream was realized. The call consisted in renting a room in a tumble-down house, putting in a couple of rows of benches, and finding two or three pious colored women to feed the pastor and pay the rent. There was always a sign outside giving the name of the establishment, the name of the pastor (followed by D.D.), and the order of services. These signs followed an invariable pattern, with all the *S*'s backward, and plenty of small *a*'s, *e*'s and *r*'s scattered through the capitals. Such signs are still plentiful in the poorer colored neighborhoods of Baltimore, and the old church names survive — the Watch Your Step Baptist Temple, the Sweet Violet Church of God, the Ananias Penecostal Tabernacle, and so on. One such basilica that I recall stood in the middle of a lot down near the Baltimore & Ohio tracks, surrounded by Jimson weeds and

piles of rusting tin-cans. The sistren of the Ladies'
Aid roved the vicinity, cadging contributions from
white passers-by. Whenever my father and his
brother passed of a Sunday morning on their way
to George Zipprian's beer-garden across the tracks
they gave up ten cents apiece to the first collector
who flagged them. They always made her jab a
hat-pin through her collection-card in their presence, professing to fear that otherwise she might
bilk the pastor.

We were not permitted to enter any of these
tabernacles, for they were supposed to swarm with
ticks, fleas, spiders, lice, thousand-legs and other
Arthropoda. But we were free to attend the street-
corner hullabaloos of the Salvation Army, which
was then a novelty in the United States, and almost as good as a circus. Here our training in
Wesleyan hymnody stood us in good stead, for the
hymns the Army howled were the same that we had
howled ourselves in Mr. Garrigues's chapel. We let
go with all brakes off, and greatly enjoyed the ensuing confessions of the saved. There was one old
man who admitted such appalling crimes that we
never got enough of him, and it was a sad day when
he failed to appear, and one of the corner loafers
intimated that he had been hauled off to a lunatic
asylum. When the beautiful Amazons of God began circulating in the crowd with their tambou-
rines we took to our heels, for we believed in conscience that salvation should be free.

Mr. Garrigues died suddenly in 1888, and my father thereupon shifted us to another and much larger Sunday-school, run by the English Lutherans in Lombard street. It met, unfortunately, on Sunday mornings, so he had to suffer some interruption of his afternoon nap, but as we grew older and more decorous that objection faded out. We liked it very much during the first few years, for the superintendent, Mr. Harman, was a Methodist at heart and often lined out the rousing hymns that we knew and esteemed. We also greatly enjoyed the cornet-playing of the treasurer, whose name I recall as Mr. Mentzer. He was an elegant fellow in a silky mustache, a white choker collar and an immaculate cutaway, and when he lifted his cornet to his lips it was with a very graceful flourish — at all events, it seemed so to us. As he let go *fortissimo* the whole Sunday-school seemed to heave, and the stained-glass rattled in the church upstairs. In the singing that went with his blasts of tone ordinary yelling was not enough; a boy of any spirit had to scream. More than once I came home hoarse, and was put to gargling with painkiller.

The pastor of the church in those days was the Rev. Sylvanus Stall, D.D., a tall, gaunt Pennsylvanian with a sandy beard and melancholy voice. I find on investigation that he was precisely forty years old in 1887, but he seemed to my brother and me to be as ancient as Abraham. He looked at first

185

glance like a standard-model Class B Protestant
ecclesiastic, but there was much more to him than
met the eye. One Sunday morning in 1889 or thereabout he showed up in Sunday-school with a
strange contraption under his arm. Rapping for
order, he announced that it was a newly invented
machine that could talk like a human being, and
not only talk but even sing. Then he instructed us
to sing his favorite hymn, which was " God Be
With You Till We Meet Again." We bawled it
dutifully, and he explained that the machine would
now bawl it back. " But not," he went on, " as
loudly as you did. Listen carefully, and you will
hear it clearly enough. The sound of the machine
is very faint, but it is also very penetrating." So he
turned it on, and we heard a phonograph for the
first time. Ah, that it had been the last!

A little while later the good doctor quit pastor-
ing to take the editorship of a church paper, with
dashes into book-writing on the side. His first two
or three books had such depressing titles as " Methods of Church Work," " Five-Minute Object
Sermons " and " Bible Selections For Daily Devotion," and appear to have scored only successes
of esteem. But in 1897, long after I had escaped his
former Sunday-school and almost forgotten him,
he brought out a little volume called " What a
Young Boy Ought to Know," and thereafter he
began rolling up money with such velocity that
when he died in 1915 he was probably the richest

Lutheran pastor, at least in the earned brackets, that the Republic has ever seen. For that little volume founded the great science of sex hygiene, which eventually developed into a major American industry, with thousands of practitioners and a technic become as complicated as that of bridge or chess.

He wrote all its official texts for male seekers — "What a Young Man Ought to Know," "What a Young Husband Ought to Know," "What a Man of Forty-five Ought to Know," and so on — and he inspired, copy-read and published all its texts for females, beginning with "What a Young Girl Ought to Know" and ending, I suppose, with "What a Decent Grandmother Ought to Forget." Indeed, he held the field unchallenged until the explosion of the Freud ammunition-dump of horrors, and by that time he was so well heeled that he could afford to laugh ha-ha. He left his money, I believe, to a college for training missionaries to the sexually misinformed and underprivileged, but where it is located I don't know and don't care.

Of the theology he radiated in his Baltimore days I retain precisely nothing. There was, in fact, little expounding of doctrine in his Sunday-school; the instruction, in so far as there was any at all, was predominantly ethical, and had as its chief apparent aim the discouragement of murder, robbery, counterfeiting, embezzlement and other such serious crimes, none of which occurred in the student body in my time. Those were the cradle days of religious pedagogy, and the teachers confined themselves mainly to expounding the week's International Sunday-school Lesson, and trying to induce their pupils to memorize the Golden Text. Inasmuch as I could never memorize anything, I failed regularly. But there was no penalty for failure, and it was hardly remarked, for virtually all the other boys in my class failed too.

Tiring of this puerile futility, I began to agitate for my release at the age of ten, and finally escaped when I went into long pants. My father, it turned out, had not underestimated the potency of his evil influence : it left me an infidel as he was, and as his father had been before him. My grandfather died too soon to have much direct influence upon me, but I must have inherited something of his attitude of mind, which was one of large tolerance in theological matters. No male of the Mencken family, within the period that my memory covers, ever took religion seriously enough to be indignant about it. There were no converts from faith among us, and hence no bigots or fanatics. To this day I have a distrust of such fallen-aways, and when one of them writes in to say that some monograph of mine has aided him in throwing off the pox of Genesis my rejoicing over the news is very mild indeed.

XII

THE RUIN OF AN

𝔄𝔯𝔱𝔦𝔰𝔱

THE PIANO that introduced me to the tone-art was a Stieff square made in Baltimore, with a shiny black case, a music-rack that was a delirium of jig-saw whorls, and legs and ankles of the sort that survive today only on lady politicians. It came into the house in Hollins street on January 13, 1888, and there it groaned and suffered for twenty years, gradually taking on the unhealthy patina and tin-can tone of age. How many hours I gave over to banging it, first and last, I don't know, but certainly they must have been enough to set loose a couple of billion decibels. When, in 1906 or there-about, I joined a music club, and we began to play occasionally in Hollins street, the infirmities of the old Stieff were remarked unpleasantly by the other members, and after a year or two of resistance I traded it in for an upright. Inasmuch as squares, by that time, had gone completely out of fashion, even on excursion boats and in houses of ill-fame, the dealer who acquired it could not find a buyer for it, and in the end he had to contribute it to a huge bonfire of unsalable instruments that the despairing piano men of the east staged at Atlantic City, to the accompaniment of considerable publicity. A few years later someone invented the trick of turning old squares into colonial desks, and there arose a sudden demand for them from antique manufacturers, with the prices soaring. The dealer spent his brief remaining days denouncing me for overreaching him, and his clamor in the saloons was largely responsible for the bad name that I still bear in Baltimore as a prince of pelf.

My first teacher was a gentleman I chiefly remember, not because of what he taught me, but because of the extraordinary luxuriance of his whiskers. Hair on the face, of course, was not unusual in the eighties; indeed, it was the rule, and I knew men with beards almost a yard long, and others who affected Burnsides, Dundrearys and even Galways. But foliage so wild and lawless as that of Mr. Maass — for such was his name — was nevertheless somewhat unusual. It was divided in the middle in such a way that it seemed to be blown apart by a gale of wind, and it swept so far to either side that it passed and concealed his narrow shoulders. He wore it, I learned, because he suffered from a weakness of the chest, and that same weakness had wrecked his career as a piano virtuoso. He was working at the time, in fact, as my father's bookkeeper, and he slipped away from his stool twice a week to fan my nascent talents and pick up an extra dollar. He was a patient and kindly man, and must have been a very fair teacher, for in hardly more than a year he got me through Ferdinand Beyer's Preliminary School for the Piano-Forte,[1] and even introduced me to some of the lesser horrors of Karl Czerny's School of Velocity.[2] But the weakness in the chest continued, and only too soon poor Mr. Maass had to give up both his teaching and his bookkeeping. A little while longer, and he was dead. I remember nothing of his funeral, and not much more of his pedagogy,

[1] I have the book yet, and lately paid a binder $7.50 to repair its dog's ears. In Grove's Dictionary of Music there is an article by the late Edward Dannreuther dismissing Beyer as "a fair pianist and tolerable musician whose reputation rests upon an enormous number of easy arrangements, transcriptions, potpourris, fantasias, divertissements, and the like, such as second-rate dilettanti and music-masters at ladies' schools are pleased to call amusing and instructive." Dannreuther's own compositions consisted, according to another writer in Grove, of "two sets of songs and one of duets." I pronounce a curse upon him in passing. He died in 1905, and is probably still in Purgatory. May he linger there for 10,000,000,000 more years!

[2] For Czerny I never developed any affection, and neither did any other male piano student of my generation. He was admired only by vinegary little girls who wore tight pigtails tied with pink ribbons, and played his infernal scales and arpeggios in a pretentious and offensive manner. So late as 1930, being in Vienna, I visited and desecrated his grave.

191

but I recall very well his gentle spirit and his stupendous whiskers.

On his departure I fell into the hands of a series of lady teachers, and they both wrecked my technic and debauched my taste. There were thousands of such damsels roving the American towns in the last century, radiating an influence for evil even worse than that of the contemporary white-slave traders, spiritualists and politicians. They charged a uniform price of twenty-five cents apiece for lessons, and derived their really living wages from the retailing of sheet music. Some of the music they taught me still exists in my library: " La Châtelaine," by A. Leduc; Dance Écossaise, by Fred T. Baker; the " Old Roman " march, by M. H. Rosenfeld (dedicated to " the Hon. Allen G. Thurman, the noblest Roman of them all ") ; " Monastery Bells," Leybach's Fifth Nocturne, the " Black Key " polka, the " Chopsticks " waltz, and other such rubbish. I achieved a considerable fluency in its performance, and at the age of ten was often put up to drive unwelcome guests out of the house.

This purpose, of course, was concealed from me, and I believed innocently that my proficiency was admired. The trick was played by my father. When some bore dropped in unexpectedly of an evening (which was no uncommon misadventure in those days, for there were no telephones) he would get out the jugs that were his tools of hospitality,

yell upstairs for me to come down, set me at the
Stieff square, and order me to play "something
lively." I thereupon launched into a programme
of marches and gallops, all of them executed with
the loud pedal held down. If I let up long enough
to attempt something soft and sneaking, he would
stop me at once, and order me to turn on the juice
again. This dreadful din went on until the guest
withdrew. I remember trying to figure out why a
rational man, entertaining his apparent friends,
should want to deafen them, but the truth did not
occur to me until long afterward. In fact, it did
not occur to me even then; I derived it from one of
my father's occasional confidences, which increased
as I grew in years and discretion.

This unwitting service as bouncer made me a
slave to the *forte* pedal, and I remain more or less
under its spell to this day, as critics have often
noted. My father was tone-deaf, and was thus not
incommoded when, in reaching for the C below the
bass clef, I hit B or D. He had been put to the fiddle in boyhood, but never got beyond the third position in Jacques-Féréol Mazas's Complete Violin
Method: the rest of the book (which is still in the
house) shows no pedagogical marks. He had two
violins, but ventured to play them only when encouraged by libation. At such times he would
tune up by performing "Yankee Doodle." If it
sounded plausible he would proceed. Some years
after his death I showed his violins to the late Al-

bert Hildebrandt, of Baltimore, a friend of mine and a renowned violin expert. He dismissed one of them as trash, but told me that the other was an excellent German imitation of a sound Cremona model. He put it in order for me, and I was later offered $200 for it. Astounded, I called a family court of inquiry, and eventually excavated the fact that my father's stepmother had bought it for him on a visit to Leipzig in the sixties. She knew no more about violins than he did, but somehow she had managed to pick up a good one.

The lady music teachers, as I have said, undermined my virtuosity and vitiated my taste, but despite their hard efforts they did not destroy either altogether. I managed somehow to become a pretty good sight-reader, and I was soon proceeding by the way of the Strauss waltzes (which still delight me) to the whole salon répertoire of the time. There was some Mozart in it, and even some Beethoven, but it ran mainly to Moskowski and his cogeners. I well recall the sensation when Paderewski's minuet in G was added to it: people lined up for the music in the music-stores as they were soon afterward lining up for the Sousa marches. My command of waltzes, polkas, schottisches, mazurkas and so on, and later on of two-steps, kept me on the piano-stool at parties, and so I managed to get through my nonage without learning to dance. I took a few belated lessons at the end of my teens, but turned out to be unteachable without recourse to complicated and costly apparatus, apparently because my center of gravity was not stable.

My real regret today, looking back over my career as a *Tonkünstler*, is that those preposterous lady Leschetizkys never gave me any instruction in elementary harmony. They avoided the subject, of course, simply because they knew nothing about it, and had, in fact, probably never heard of it. I don't recall any of them ever referring to a composition by naming its key; they always said it was " in three sharps," or " five flats," and never distinguished between major and minor. I was twelve years old before it dawned upon me that there must be ascertainable differences between chords, and it was a good while thereafter before I began to find out what those differences were. The creative frenzy of the mid-teen years prompted me to write a great many piano pieces, chiefly waltzes, but I had to harmonize them by the method of trial and error at the piano. If my inclination had run to songs this method might have made a George M. Cohan of me, or even an Irving Berlin. Perhaps fortunately, I was born with an intense distaste for vocal music, and to this day think of even the most gifted Wagnerian soprano as no more than a blimp fitted with a calliope. If a bass singer shows up at my funeral to sing " *Im tiefen Keller sitz ich hier* " it will take the whole platoon of clergy and pallbearers to hold me down.

It was not until I was passing out of my teens

that I ever opened a *Harmonielehre* and not until several years afterward that I began to associate familiarly with competent musicians. It was then too late for me to devote any serious attention to the subject, for I was in active practice as a reporter on a newspaper, and the job kept me jumping. That was long before it had occurred to anyone that reporters would be benefitted culturally by five-day weeks and time-and-a-half for overtime. I worked six days of twelve hours each, and often had to lend a hand on my day off. There was a year during which I accumulated no less than twenty full days of overtime. The city editor gave me what I thought was a handsome compensation by raising my pay $2 a week, letting me do copyreading on the side for the experience, and adding five days to my annual vacation.

If I speak of my lack of sound musical instruction lightly, please do not be deceived. I was only dimly aware of it at the time, but it was really the great deprivation of my life. My early impulse to compose was no transient storm of puberty, explicable on purely endocrine grounds. It stuck to me through the years of maturity, and is still far from dead as I slide into the serenity of senility. When I think of anything properly describable as a beautiful idea, it is always in the form of music. Alcohol has the effect of filling my head with such ideas, and I daresay hashish would do even better. I have sketched out, in my day, at least ten sonatas

THE RUIN OF AN ARTIST

for piano, and there was a time when I had accumulated fifty or sixty pounds of music-paper, all of it covered with pothooks. It ran, in the main, to waltzes, always my great delight, but it also included the score of a musical comedy put on by the boys at the Baltimore Polytechnic in 1895 or thereabout — most of it, of course, snitched from other composers. This musical comedy, despite a book that was frowned on as contumacious and even a bit salacious, made a great success, and I sat at the piano as its whole orchestra.

In those days I knew nothing about orchestra music, but when the music club I have mentioned began to function I developed an interest in fiddles and flutes, and was soon writing for them. One of our first members, now long dead, was an Irishman named Joe Callahan, a charming fellow who loved music to excess, but was of such limited skill as a violinist that he could be trusted only on the open strings. I wrote many parts for him in the safe keys of C and G major, and it gave him great delight to chime in, even though he could do it only occasionally. I also wrote violin and cello obbligatos for the songs of a lady singer who joined us for a while. Once I launched into the incredible project of arranging Dvořák's " New World " symphony for piano, violin and cello, and another time I actually made such an arrangement of Beethoven's No. 1. For years I collected orchestra scores, and what is more, studied them diligently, though I am almost as tone-deaf as my father, and could never get any more out of them than a ghostly reverberation, like the sound of a brass band heard from afar on a rainy night.

Meditating on this, my lifelong libido that has never come to anything, I become aware of the eternal tragedy of man. He is born to long for things that are beyond him, as flight through the air is beyond a poor goldfish in a globe, and stardom in Hollywood must remain forever outside the experience, though not outside the dreams, of all save a few hundred of the girls in the ten-cent stores. Not many men of my unhappily meagre equipment have ever had a better chance than I to fling their egos into the face of this world. I have, in fact, made a living for many years by thrusting myself upon the attention of strangers, most of them reluctant. I have written and printed probably 10,000,000 words of English, and continue to this day to pour out more and more. It has wrung from others, some of them my superiors, probably a million words of notice, part of it pro but most of it con. In brief, my booth has been set up on a favorable pitch, and I have never lacked hearers for my ballyhoo. But all the same I shall die an inarticulate man, for my best ideas have beset me in a language I know only vaguely and speak only like a child.

The loss to humanity, of course, is not serious enough to cause any general gloom. In truth, my real reason for failing to pursue music to a bitter

finish was probably not, as I have intimated, that
I was too busy with other things, nor even that I
was too old when my first really good chance came.
It was simply that I had no talent for it. This
dreadful fact gradually forced itself into my consciousness as the years passed, helped along by the
satirical efforts of musical friends, and today it is
so firmly embedded that though I still itch I no
longer scratch. But the underlying mystery remains. Why should a man so completely devoid of
fitness for the tone-art yet have so powerful an impulse to practise it, and get so much pleasure out
of it? I have no answer, but I suspect that my disease is more widespread than is generally assumed.
Every concert audience probably swarms with baffled Beethovens and frustrated Wagners. I used
to believe and argue that any person who had a
genuine love of music would undertake some effort,
soon or late, to make it, but even that I now doubt,
for I know men who go to concerts almost as regularly as they eat, and sit at the phonograph or the
radio by the hour, and yet have so little impulse to
raise a din themselves, and so little curiosity about
the ways and means of doing so, that they can't so
much as pick out the scale of C major at the piano.
As for me, I delight in the sound of horse-hair on
catgut as honestly and as vastly as a cop delights
in beer, and yet I am quite unable to tune a fiddle.
The mystery is only one of a thousand that bedevil
man in his swift and senseless flight through the

world. The gods, in the main, are vicious, but now and then they show an unmistakable touch of humor.

My inclination toward the graphic arts began earlier and ended earlier than my devotion to music, and was much feebler. There are, in the family files, crude drawings dated 1886 and 1887, and a little while later, sitting under Mr. Paul at F. Knapp's Institute, I copied a whole series of the drawing-books then in fashion, and picked up some pale skill at draftsmanship as that science was then understood by German pedagogues. But my natural lack of manual dexterity hindered me here, and I never got beyond the elements. At Christmas, 1888, some one gave me a box of water-colors, and during the years following I made various attempts to use them. Having learned by reading that paintings were commonly done on canvas, I made a small wooden frame, stretched it with muslin borrowed from my mother's rag-bag, and was astonished and baffled to find that when water-colors were applied to it they all ran together. This unhappy *Jugendwerk* still survives. Also, there is a water-color on paper, signed " H. L. Mencken, July, 1892," which not only survives, but is framed in a gilt frame, and hangs on my office wall. It shows a scene along Jones falls, near our Summer home at Mt. Washington, and is anything but bad for a boy less than twelve years old. The rocks are painted in a thoroughly bold and modern manner, and the water falling over them actually looks like water. I have often thought of entering this composition in some free-for-all exhibition of Modernist Art — with the date and signature, of course, discreetly painted out.

XIII

IN THE FOOTSTEPS OF

Gutenberg

On November 26, 1888 my father sent his book-keeper, Mr. Maass, to the establishment of J. F. W. Dorman, at 217 East German street, Baltimore, and there and then, by the said Maass's authorized agency, took title to a Baltimore No. 10 Self-Inker Printing Press and a font of No. 214 type. The press cost $7.50 and the font of type $1.10. These details, which I recover from the receipted bill in my father's file, are of no conceivable interest to anyone else on earth, but to me they are of a degree of concern bordering upon the super-colossal, for that press determined the whole course of my future life. If it had been a stethoscope or a copy of Dr. Ayers' Almanac I might have gone in for medicine; if it had been a Greek New Testament or a set of baptismal grappling-irons I might have pursued divinity. As it was, I got the smell of printer's ink up my nose at the tender age of eight, and it has been swirling through my sinuses ever since.

The press and type, of course, were laid in by my father against Christmas, and were concealed for the nonce in a cupboard at home, but my brother Charlie and I had a good look at them before early candlelight of November 27. We decided that they were pretty nifty, or, as the word was then, nobby. If Charlie, comparing them to the velocipede that lay in wait for him, was bemused by envy, he had only himself to blame, for he had delayed his coming into the world for twenty months after my own arrival, and was still virtually illiterate. It was barely three months, in fact, since he had begun to attend the sessions of F. Knapp's Institute, and he yet had some difficulty in distinguishing, without illustrative wood-cuts, between the words *cat* and *rat*. Compared to him, I was so far advanced in *literae humaniores* as to be almost a savant. During the previous Summer I had tackled and got down my first book, and was even then engaged in exploring the house library for another. No doubt this new and fevered interest in beautiful letters was marked in the household, and set afloat the notion that a printing-press would be to my taste. Indeed, I probably hinted as much myself.

If my mother approved, which she undoubtedly did, she must have developed a certain regret on

Christmas Day, for my father undertook to show me how to work the press, and inasmuch as he knew no more about printing than Aristotle and had so little manual dexterity that he could not even lace a shoe, he made a ghastly mess of it. Before he gave it up as a bad job all the ink that came with the outfit had been smeared and slathered away, and at least half the type had been plugged with it or broken. I recall clearly that we ran out of white cards before noon, and had to resort to the backs of his business cards. By that time all the brass gauge-pins had been crushed, one of the steel guides that held cards against the platen was bent, and the mechanism operating the ink-roller was out of order. It was a sad caricature of a printing-press that went to the cellar at midday, when my mother ordered a halt and a clean-up.

Next morning, after my father shoved off for his office, I unearthed it and set to work to scrub the ink off it and make it go. Unfortunately, I had almost as little skill with my hands as my father, so it must have been New Year's Day, at the earliest, before I succeeded. My cash takings, that Christmas, had been excellent; in fact, I had amassed something on the order of $2. With this money I went down to Dorman's, bought a new can of ink and a large bottle of benzine, and also laid in a new font of type. With the press there had come a font of Black Letter and to it, apparently on the advice of Mr. Maass, who was an aesthete, my fa-

ther had added one of Script. My own addition
was a prosaic font of Roman, with caps only. I
now had enough faces to begin printing on a commercial scale, and early in 1889 I was ready with
the following announcement:

```
┌─────────────────────────────────────┐
│                                      │
│        H.  L.  Mencken               │
│           Card Printer               │
│      1524 HOLLINS ST.                │
│      BALTIMORE, MD.                   │
│                                      │
└─────────────────────────────────────┘
```

Up to this time I had always written my name
Henry L., or Harry, which last, as I have noted,
has been my stable-name all my life. My change to
H. L. was not due to any feeling that the form better became the dignity of a business man, but simply to the fact that my father, in the course of his
Christmas morning gaucheries, had smashed all my
Black Letter lower-case *r*'s, and I had to cut my
coat to fit my cloth. During the ensuing months I
had some accidents of my own, and by the time I began to print billheads I had wrecked the penultimate cap *M* in my Roman font, and was forced to
abbreviate Baltimore to Balto. But I still had an
undamaged *&* in Black Letter and also a service-
able though somewhat mangey cap *C*, so I added
" & Co " to the style and designation of my house.
So far as I can remember, my father was my

only customer. His taste in typography, as in the other arts, was very far from finicky, and his pride in the fact that I could print at all sufficed to throttle such feeble qualms as he may have had. In February, 1889, he set off to one of the annual deliriums of the Knights Templar, and I applied for, and got, the contract for printing his fraternal *cartes de visite*. These cards were exchanged by brethren from North, East, South and West whenever two or more of them happened to be thrown together in the saloons of the convention town. They followed a rigid model. Each showed the name and home-town of the bearer, and a series of colored symbols representing his Masonic dignities.

The symbols were naturally lacking in my composing-room, and I had no idea where they were to be obtained. Moreover, my Baltimore No. 10 Self-Inker was hardly fitted for work in six or eight colors. But such impediments could not stump a really up-and-coming business man. I simply put in the symbols by hand, and colored them with the water-colors that had also been among my Christmas presents. My father professed to be delighted with the cards, and on his return from the convention told me that he had presented specimens of them to Freemasons from points as far distant as Key West, Fla., Duluth, Minn., and Ogden, Utah, and that among the recipients were some of the most puissant and austere dignitaries of the order, including two Governors and a dozen United States

Senators. This was my first attempt upon a national audience. My bill for the job survives. It shows that I charged my father 8½ cents a dozen for the cards, including the hand-painting. Of the cards themselves, two or three also survive. They will go to the Bodleian after they have made the round of the American galleries.

In a little while I was branching out. On the one hand I issued a circular offering to print advertising at what, even in the primitive West Baltimore of that remote era, must have seemed to my competitors to be cut rates. And on the other hand, I launched into the publication of a newspaper in rivalry to the celebrated Baltimore *Sunpaper*, the news Bible at 1524 Hollins street as it has always been in every other respectable Baltimore household, then, now and forever. My circular offered to produce advertisements 2 by 2 inches in area, in any quantity below the astronomical, at the uniform rate of 4 cents a hundred. For an additional 2 cents a hundred I offered to blow them up to the magnitude of 3 inches by 3¼. This was as far as I could go, for it was the full size of the chase of my press. For business cards on plain white stock, " any size," I asked 5 cents a dozen, or 2 cents a quarter of a dozen. Why I assumed that anyone would want as few as a quarter of a dozen, or even a dozen, I don't recall: there must have been some reason, but it has slipped me. The " any size," of course, was only a euphemism: as I have said, my maximum size was 3 inches by 3¼. I never got any orders for these goods. I solicited my mother's trade, but she replied coldly that she was not in any commercial business, and had no use for cards or circulars. I also solicited my brother Charlie, but he was poor in those days, and believed that it was a kind of lunacy to lay out money on printed matter. He much preferred the black licorice nigger-babies sold by Old Man Kunker in Baltimore street, and commonly went about with his face mired by their exudations.

The newspaper I set up against the *Sunpaper* also came to nothing. It was doomed from the start, for it was afflicted by every malady that a public journal can suffer from — insufficiency of capital, incomplete news service, an incompetent staff, no advertising, and a press that couldn't print it. No copy of it survives, but I remember that it consisted of four pages, and was printed on scraps of wrapping-paper filched from the hired girl's hoard in the kitchen. I had to print each page separately, and to distribute the type between pages, for I hadn't enough to set up all four at once. Having no news service whatever, and not knowing where any was to be had, I compromised by lifting all of my dispatches out of my rival. In those days the Associated Press foreign report consisted largely of a series of brief bulletins, and the *Sunpaper* printed them on its first page every morning under the standing head of "Latest Foreign News." I chose the shortest, and when there were none short enough, chopped down the longer. Thus the most important item I ever printed was this:

Berlin, March 9 — William I is dead aged 91.

This came out in my paper on March 15 or thereabout, a week after the *Sunpaper* had made it generally known in Baltimore, Washington, Virginia, West Virginia and the Carolinas. My domestic news came from the same source, and consisted wholly of telegraphed items, for they were usually short. I made no effort to cover local news, though there was then plenty of it in West Baltimore. Almost every day Murphy the cop made one of his hauls of ruffianly Aframericans in Vincent alley, and I could sit at my third-story office-and-bedroom window and see him drag them through Union Square to the watch-house at Calhoun and Pratt streets. It was common, also, for car-horses to fall dead in their tracks, for children to get lost, and for great gang-wars among the neighborhood dogs to tear up the Union Square lawns. But I never attempted to report any of these things. I remain a bad reporter, in fact, to this day. During my term of servitude as city editor of a Baltimore daily, long after my own paper blew up, I blushed inwardly every time I had to excoriate a member of the staff for failing to get the age, weight, color and address of a lady jugged for murdering her husband, or the names of the brave cops who had tracked her down.

Rather curiously, I can't recall the name of my paper, if, in fact, it had one. The chances are at least even that it didn't, for I was chronically short of what printers call sorts, and never wasted a single piece of type if I could help it. A little while later, probably during the ensuing Autumn, I discovered a perfect mine of supplies in the hell-box that stood outside the printing plant of Isaac Friedenwald & Son, in Paca street, across narrow Cider alley from my father's factory. It was Mr. Maass who directed me to this Golconda, and I began to work it diligently. From it I recovered all sorts of mangey woodcuts, many empty ink-cans with a little ink remaining in them, a great deal of scrap paper and cardboard, and an occasional piece of condemned type, always badly battered. Unfortunately, this type was of small use to my newspaper, for the Friedenwalds were printers to the Johns Hopkins University, and laid claim to having the largest stock of foreign type-faces in the Western World, so when my eye lighted upon what looked to be a likely *E* it sometimes turned out to be a Greek *sigma* or a Hebrew *lamedh*. I could make nothing of these strange characters; in fact, I didn't know that they were characters at all, but took them to be the devices of unfamiliar branches of the Freemasons.

The Friedenwalds did not stop with such relatively intelligible alphabets, but boasted that they could print any language ever heard of on earth, and often surprised and enchanted the Johns Hopkins professors by making good. They had fonts of Arabic, Sanskrit, Russian, Coptic, Armenian and Chinese, not to mention Old Norse runes and Egyptian hieroglyphs. The specimens of these types that I recovered were always cruelly damaged, but nevertheless some of them were still legible, and if I had given them due study I might have become a linguist. But I usually traded them for marbles, chewing-tobacco tags or cigarette pictures with a neighbor who made lead soldiers of them in a mold he had somehow acquired, so I made no appreciable progress in the tongues.

Despite all these griefs and burdens, I stuck to my printing press through 1889, and it remained my favorite possession for several years afterward. Why my father, seeing my interest in it, did not buy me a larger and better one I do not know ; probably it was because I wasn't aware that a larger and better one existed, and hence did not ask for it. I have found out since that Dorman had them with chases up to 6 by 8 inches, and that his catalogue listed two or three dozen different fonts of type, some of them with highly ornate faces in the rococo taste of the time. But though my press was a poor thing and my type gradually wore out to the point where all the letters printed like squashed *O*'s, my enthusiasm for printing did not die, and even when

a rage for photography and then for chemistry began to challenge it, in my early teens, it managed
to continue a sturdy undercover existence. When,
on my father's death, as I was eighteen, I was free
at last to choose my trade in the world, I chose newspaper work without any hesitation whatever, and,
save when the scent of a passing garbage-cart has
revived my chemical libido, I have never regretted
my choice. More than once I have slipped out of
daily journalism to dally in its meretricious suburbs, but I have always returned repentant and relieved, like a blackamoor coming back in Autumn
to a warm and sociable jail.

Aside from the direct and all-powerful influence
of that Baltimore No. 10 Self-Inker and the Friedenwald hell-box, I was probably edged toward
newspapers and their glorious miseries by two circumstances, both of them trivial. The first was my
discovery of a real newspaper office in the little
town of Ellicott City, where we spent the Summers
of 1889 and 1890. Ellicott City was then a very
picturesque and charming place, and indeed still
is, despite the fact that the heavy hand of progress
is on it. It is built along the two steep banks of a
ravine that runs down to the Patapsco, and many
of the old stone houses, though four stories high in
front, scarcely clear their backyards in the rear.
It is the local legend that dogs, pigs, chickens and
even children have been known to fall out of these
backyards into and down the chimneys. The Bal-

timore & Ohio Railroad's old main line to the West
runs beside the river on a viaduct spanning the
main street, and from this viaduct, in 1889, a long
balcony ran along the second story of a block of
houses, with an entrance from the railway station's
platform. I naturally explored it, and was presently rewarded by discovering the printing-office of
the weekly Ellicott City *Times*.

The *Times*, even in those days, must have been
an appreciably better paper than my own, but its
superiority was certainly not excessive. The chief
article of equipment in its gloomy second-story office was a Washington handpress that had probably been hauled in on mule-back in the twenties
or thirties, when the town was still Ellicott's Mills,
and a famous coaching-station on the road to the
Ohio. I have seen many Washington handpresses
since, but never a hoarier one. Its standards were
oaken beams, and it looked to a marvelling boy to
be as massive as a locomotive. It was operated by
a young man and a boy, and I watched enchanted
as the white paper was placed on the chase, the
platen was brought down, and the printed sheets
were lifted off. The circulation of the *Times* at
that time was probably not more than 400, but it
took the man and the boy all day to print an edition, for only one side could be printed at a time,
and yanking the huge lever was a back-breaking
job. I noted that the young man left most of the
yanking to the boy, and encouraged him from time

to time by loud incitements and expostulations. I found out that Thursday was press-day, and I managed to be on hand every time. If my mother had no commission for me in the village on a Thursday I always suggested one.

I was captivated not only by the miracle of printing, but also by the high might and consequence of the young man in charge of the press. He was genuinely Somebody in that remote and obscure village, and the fact radiated from him like heat from a stove. He never deigned to take any notice of me. He might give me a blank glance when he halted the press to take a chew of tobacco, but that was all. He became to me a living symbol of the power and dignity of the press — a walking proof of its romantic puissance. Years later I encountered him again, and got to know him very well, and to have a great affection for him. I was by then city editor of the Baltimore *Morning Herald*, now dead and forgotten, and he was the assistant foreman of its composing-room. No man in all my experience has ever met more perfectly the classical specifications for that office.

On a rush night he gave a performance that was magnificent. Arising in his pulpit, he would howl for missing takes in a voice of brass, always using the formula hallowed since Gutenberg's time: " What --- -- - ----- has got A 17? " His chief, Joe Bamberger, was also a foreman of notable talents, and knew how to holler in a way that made even

the oldest printer gasp and blanche, but Josh
Lynch — for such was his name — could outholler
Joe a hundred to one, on the flat or over the jumps.
He was a grand fellow, and he taught me a lot about
the newspaper business that was not on tap in the
Herald editorial-rooms. Above all, he taught me
that a newspaper man, in the hierarchy of earthly
fauna, ranked only below the assistant foreman of
a composing-room, and that neither had any reason or excuse in law or equity to take any lip from
any ——— in the whole ——— world. He is dead
now, but surely not forgotten. If I miss him in
Hell it will be a disappointment.

The second experience that served to cake the ink
upon me and doom me to journalism took the form
of an overheard conversation. My father's Washington agent, Mr. Cross, paid a visit to us at Ellicott City one Sunday, and he and my father and
my uncle Henry put in the afternoon drinking beer
on the veranda of our house. They fell to talking
of the illustrious personages they were constantly
meeting in Washington — Senators who had not
been sober for a generation, Congressmen who
fought bartenders and kicked the windows out of
night-hacks, Admirals in the Navy who were reputed to be four-, five- and even six-bottle men,
Justices of the Supreme and other high courts who
were said to live on whiskey and chewing tobacco
alone. They naturally admired these prodigious
men, and I crept up to hear them described and

praised. But in the end Mr. Cross, who knew
Washington far better than my father or my uncle, permitted himself a caveat of doubt. All such
eminentissimos, he allowed, were mere passing
shapes, as evanescent as the morning dew, here today and gone tomorrow. They had their efful-
gence, but then they perished, leaving no trace save
a faint aroma, usually bad. The real princes of
Washington, he said, were the newspaper correspondents. They outlasted Senators, Congressmen, judges and Presidents. In so far as the
United States had any rational and permanent government, they were its liver and its lights. To this
day, though reason may protest bitterly, I still
revere the gentlemen of the Washington corps.

Other Christmas presents came and went, but
there was never another that fetched and floored
me like Dorman's Baltimore No. 10 Self-Inker
Printing Press. The box of water-colors that set
me to painting I have mentioned, and I have also
alluded to the camera that aroused in me a passion
for photography, and then, by way of developers
and toning solutions, for chemistry. But my career
as a water-colorist was brief and not glorious, and
the camera came after the period covered by this
history. I recall a year when some one gave me a
microscope, but it, too, held me only transiently,
for one of the first things I inspected through it was
a drop of vinegar, and the revolting mass of worms
that I saw kept me off vinegar for a year after-

ward, and cured me of microscopy. Another year I received an electric battery, and for a while I had a swell time with it, but I began to neglect it when I discovered that it could not work a small arc-light that I had made of two charred matches. Yet another year I was favored with a box of carpenter's tools, but they must have been poor ones, for the saw would not saw, the plane would not plane, the hammer mashed my thumb, and the chisel cut my hand. Nor was I greatly interested in the steam-engine that appeared at Christmas 1889, or the steam railroad that followed the year after. The latter, indeed, was probably my brother Charlie's present, not mine, for he spent much more time playing with it than I did, and in later life he took to engineering, and laid many a mile of railroad line, and worked on many a bridge and tunnel.

It was the printing-press that left its marks, not only upon my hands, face and clothing, but also on my psyche. They are still there, though more than fifty years have come and gone.

XIV

FROM THE RECORDS OF

an Athlete

IT always astonishes people familiar with my present matronly figure to hear that I was a fast runner as a boy. It not only astonishes them; it also makes them laugh. Nevertheless, a fact remains a fact, no matter how much infidels may mock it, and I like to recall this one whenever a steep stairway blows me, or I begin to choke and gurgle in the act of lacing my shoes.

Toward the end of the year 1890, when I was ten years old, I made the 100 yards in $12\frac{2}{5}$ seconds, wearing heavy Winter underwear and timed by my father's Swiss repeater watch, then the great glory of his jewel casket — that is, next to the massive gold chain that anchored it to his person, the ruby-studded Shriner's button that he wore in his coat-lapel, and the diamond solitaire that screwed into the façade of his boiled shirt. To be sure, the distance for my dash was estimated by the eye, not laid off by geometers, but all the same it must have been accurate to within 15 or 20 yards. I made it in less than 13 seconds, not once but six or eight times in close succession, and would have gone on running all afternoon if my mother had not intervened on what I gathered to be hygienic grounds. I recall clearly only her suggestion that my father must be going crazy.

He himself was surely no athlete. Once, seeking to edify my brother Charlie and me, he essayed to jump over a bale of hay, but only succeeded in landing on top of it belly-down, kicking and hollering. When the mood to inspire us by boasting was on him he liked to tell us that he had been a powerful swimmer in his youth, but I never saw him in actual water save once, and he then came out very promptly, shivering and upset. When a natatorium was opened in Baltimore and I demanded to be taken to it and taught the art, he kept on postponing the visit until the place finally went bankrupt and closed. He also claimed to be gifted as an oarsman, but on the only occasion when I ever saw him enter a rowboat he upset it at the first stroke, and got a good dousing, and was upbraided by my mother for resorting to the cup on a fine Summer afternoon, better fitted for nature study and other such sensible recreation.

As I have noted in a previous chapter, he was completely devoid of all the usual small skills. Never once, to my knowledge, did he ever undertake any of the repairs that are needed so incessantly in a dwelling-house, with children running wild in it. If a plank got loose in the backyard fence he had to send for a neighborhood handy-man to nail it tight, and if a spigot needed a washer it was a job for the plumber. If my brother and I, playing in the yard, tossed a ball into a rain-gutter, he sent us to the alley to find a colored boy to recover it. If the family dog choked on a bone he hustled it to Reveille's livery-stable two blocks away, to be succored by the Aframerican barber-surgeons there in practise. The grape vines in the backyard needed tying up now and then, what with blowing winds and climbing cats, but my father never undertook the job. My mother told me years later that he had tried it once, standing on a chair, but that the chair legs had sunk into the soft ground, and tumbled him head over heels.

He and his brother often sat in the Summer-house below the arbor on warm Sunday mornings, drinking beer and discussing the infamies of Terence V. Powderly, the Chicago anarchists, and other such scamps. The beer was usually Anheuser-Busch from St. Louis, and it came in flour-barrels holding 96 bottles, packed in straw. When a new barrel arrived my uncle would sometimes suggest waggishly that my father open it. Now and then he rose to the bait, but when he began work with a hatchet he made so much noise, broke so many bottles and so inevitably cut his hand that my uncle always had to finish the job. My uncle was more or less clumsy too, following the pattern of all the Menckenii since their escape from the Teutoburgerwald, but compared to my father he was almost a prestidigitator.

I have hitherto noted his prowess with firearms. All Winter long, throughout my nonage, the side-yard between our two houses was hung with the carcasses of wild ducks that had fallen to his aim. He would turn out before dawn, proceed to the Chesapeake marshes by train, and come rolling home in the late afternoon with dozens of them, mainly canvasbacks. They often hung in the yard for weeks, for his own family revolted against them by Christmas, and my mother had them on her blacklist, mainly because picking them was a painful chore and had the effect of filling hired girls with subversive ideas. Thus I grew up unaware that wild duck was a luxury open only to millionaires. Indeed, I was amazed years later to find it priced at $3 a portion on Delmonico's bill-of-fare. It was a quite common victual in the Baltimore of my youth — not so common, to be sure, as soft-crabs or shad-fish, but still very far from something to get excited about.

My uncle's hunting trips extended much further than the shores of the Chesapeake. Whenever

he made a business journey, which was pretty often, he always took his guns along, and usually he
would come back with many souvenirs and tall tales
of the chase. He went all the way to Florida, which
was then only a wilderness, to shoot alligators, and
returned with the story that he had lured them out
of the bayous by tying Negro babies to stakes along
the bank. Whether or not this story was true I do
not know, but my brother Charlie and I believed it
firmly at the time.

On one of these Florida trips my uncle took along
one of the drummers of Aug. Mencken & Bro., by
name Christian Abner, a magnificently handsome
Rhinelander who some years later returned home,
married a wife with a substantial *dot*, and set up a
carpet-sweeper factory. Abner sent his relatives in
Cologne a glowing account of alligator-hunting in
Florida, and urged them not to be upset by the use
of Negro babies as bait. At first, he explained, he
had shrunk from it himself as incompatible with
Christian principles and German *Kultur*, but
travel had a tendency to broaden the mind, and he
had come to the view that it was bigotry to judge
the *mores* of a new and progressive country by
those of Europe, now so old and decadent. In later
letters he confessed confidentially that he had proceeded experimentally to actual nigger-shooting
in Georgia, but added in excuse and avoidance that
he did not like it. To this day there is no taste for

American ways among the bourgeoisie of Cologne, and no belief in American idealism.

Despite his brother's enthusiasm for the chase my father disliked it, and never owned a gun. The only lethal weapon I could find in his effects after his death was his Knight Templar sword, a sleazy blade that would have curled up if jabbed into a tub of butter. It has now vanished, and I suspect that my mother either had it buried in the back-yard, or gave it to the Salvation Army. A pair of dumb-bells survived in the cellar for many years, but my father never touched them to my knowl-edge. They were of cast-iron, and weighed 15 or 18 pounds apiece. My brother Charlie and I began to feel almost grown-up when we could so much as lift them, but that is as far as we ever got.

Our chief sports in those early days were run-ning, climbing backyard fences, and making long exploratory tramps to Steuart's Hill or the other open country west of Hollins street. With the boys of the neighborhood we played at least half a dozen different running games, and very often there were match races. It was in these races that I developed the speed aforesaid. The prime of my talent was reached before the age of twelve, but I remained pretty fast until I had passed twenty and began to put on blubber. Even to this day I could probably run down a horse-car if there were any left in the world, and I still had my old facility for sucking in air. All my muscles are in my legs. My biceps are puny, and my fingers are so weak that a couple of hours of playing the piano at high voltage makes them ache and itch.

This relative feebleness above-decks prevented me from shining as a boxer. Like every other boy in Hollins street I had ambitions in that direction, for Jake Kilrain opened a saloon in nearby Baltimore street after John L. Sullivan finished him in 1889, and his familiar proximity inspired us all. We were free to look at and venerate him as he stood in front of his place on balmy days, his coat off and his shirt sleeves rolled up. His forearms looked to us to be quite as massive as the hind legs of elephants. But he was a very reserved and solemn fellow, and never paid any attention to us. What little we learned of boxing we learned by pummelling one another. But this was poor sport, for there was one boy in the gang, Chauncey West by name (the Chauncey was always pronounced *Chance-y*, not *Chawnce-y*), who could lick any of the rest of us, or any two of us, or indeed all of us put together.

One Summer day, while we were in the country, my father came home with two pairs of boxing gloves, picked up at a bargain from an insolvent pugilist encountered in a saloon. They were much too big for my brother Charlie and me, but we finally managed to tie them on, and proceeded to bang each other all over the place. My mother was scandalized by these barbarities, and insisted on amending the house statutes by forbidding us (*a*) to clout each other above the neck, or (*b*) to fight at all unless my father or some other grown man was on hand to referee. Our first formal combat under these rules was our last. We staggered on for twenty rounds, with my father refereeing and keeping time, but I was in trouble after the tenth round, and in the twentieth Charlie floored me with a right hook to the neck, and I couldn't get up. After that I had no more stomach for boxing.

The one sport my father was really interested in was baseball, and for that he was a fanatic. This, of course, was before the days of the celebrated Baltimore Orioles, but nevertheless Baltimore had a very good team, and he attended its sessions at Oriole Park whenever he and it were in town together. When it was on the road, he would slip away from his office in the late afternoon to glim the score at Kelly's oyster house in Eutaw street. There were, in that era, no baseball extras of the newspapers, so the high-toned saloons of the town catered to the fans by putting in telegraph operators who wrote the scores on blackboards. Kelly's operator was supposed to be the fastest and most accurate in town. He sat in a little balcony half way up the wall of the barroom, and was so greatly respected that on a busy afternoon, with the Baltimores winning, he harvested treats running to twenty or thirty beers, and perhaps half as many cigars.

I often went with my father on his visits to Kelly's, for in those days I spent many of my free afternoons in his cigar factory in Paca street, watching and envying the stripper-boys, stealing cigarbands, cigar-box nails and other such negotiable commodities, and excavating the wastebaskets in the office for postage stamps, worn-out pens and rubber bands. When he set out he would take me with him, and while he stood at the bar with one eye on the blackboard and a beer before him, I would be parked on the brass rail, with a glass of sarsaparilla in one hand and a pretzel in the other. I figure that before I was nine years old I had put down at least 5000 bottles of sarsaparilla and the same number of pretzels. In the end I got so used to sitting on brass bar rails that I could do so without holding on.

My father had a branch of his business in Washington, at the corner of Seventh and G streets, and connected with it there was a cigar-store. This cigar-store became the baseball headquarters of Washington, and he got to know all the principal ball-players and managers of the time. Eventually, he bought an interest in the Washington club, and became its vice-president. In his papers I find a letter from its secretary, dated July 27, 1891, and running as follows:

Last time we went West rate was $30 each for 13 men. The R. R. Agents here have since formed a combination to squeeze us and now make the rate at $40.50 for each man. We understand this applies only to Washington. Won't you kindly see Barnie and see what rate he pays and see if you can't get same rate for our men from Baltimore? Route will be Balto to Cincinnati, to Columbus, to Louisville, to St. Louis, and then home.

Barnie was the manager of the Baltimore club. He and my father had frequent palavers in those days, not only about the extortions of the railroads, but also about the outrageous demands of the players, some of whom, though they were getting $1500 and even $1800 a year, had the impudence to ask for more. These palavers were usually held in the Summer-house in Hollins street on Sunday mornings, and the Bolsheviks were summoned there, and put on the mat. Many a time I have seen six or eight head of stars assembled together, drinking beer and smoking ten-cent cigars in their uncomfortable Sunday clothes, and quailing under the moral indignation of Barnie and my father. The boys of the neighborhood flocked to the back-gate to get glimpses of them, and my brother Charlie and I would open it a few inches for particular friends, and so convert friends into slaves.

The most eminent of all the stars who suffered the correction of their false thinking in the Summer-house was Matt Kilroy, a pitcher now somehow forgotten, though he was as vastly admired in

his day as Amos Rusie afterward. He was an Irishman with eight brothers who were also ball-players,
and my father toyed with the idea of organizing
them into a nine and sending them on a tour of
the country. Unfortunately, Kilroy belonged to
Barnie, and Barnie hung on to him. My father
sought surcease from this bafflement by naming a
five-cent cigar after the great man, and employed
his catcher, Sam Trott, to sell it. Sam was a novice
to *Geschäft*, but he developed a considerable gift
for it, and the Kilroy was thus a big success. When
Kilroy himself blew up the five-center went with
him, and Sam became Baltimore agent for a cigar
factory in Philadelphia. He continued in the trade
to the end of his life, and I often encountered him
on the streets in his later years.

He was a handsome, four-square fellow with
enormous shoulders, and every finger of his two
hands was as gnarled as a cypress-tree. This was
a souvenir of the days when catchers caught with
their bare paws. He adopted a glove toward the
end of his career, but it was too late either to save
his hands or to change his technic. When a ball
came zooming in from the outfield and an enemy
player tried to steal home Sam always threw aside
his glove and planted himself at the plate *au natu-
rel*. He was an amiable man, and when my brother
and I began to major in baseball he gave us a lot
of useful advice. But he never managed to make a
good player of either of us.

We could do little playing in the Winter, for the cops of West Baltimore objected to anything more serious than one-two-three in the street, and the nearest grounds were disputed by other boys, including, now and then, brigandish fellows from the vicinity of the Baltimore & Ohio railroad shops. When these ruffians were in a relatively mild mood they were content to chase us off the diamond, but when their glands were flowing freely they also cabbaged our bats, balls and gloves. In the Summers beyond the period I here embalm we had a better chance, for just behind our newly-acquired house at Mt. Washington there was a large hay-field, and the farmer who owned it was glad to rent us room enough for a diamond, once he had got in his hay. Along with the neighbor boys we paid him $15 a year for it, and had the place all to ourselves, morning, afternoon and evening, on Sundays as well as on week-days. Years ago our baseball field became part of the first golf course ever seen in Baltimore. That course is still in operation, but it now seems so far downtown that most of the members of the Baltimore Country Club, which owns it, prefer the newer links ten miles out in the country.

The four Lürssen boys, who were our next-door neighbors, were baseball fans of the first chop, and there were plenty of other enthusiasts nearby, so we had games going on all the time. In the middle of Summer we often played until eight o'clock in the evening, and when formal play had to be stopped we put in another hour catching flies from the darkening sky. Two miles nearer the city there was a little mill-town, Woodberry by name, that turned out an amazing number of first-rate ball-players, for most of the jobs in the mills were for females, which left the bucks all day to practise. One of the prodigies thus given to humanity was Frank Foreman, a pitcher who developed the widest and wickedest curves I have ever seen. He got into the big leagues, and for all I know may be still living in Baltimore, though very few Baltimoreans now recall his once immortal name.

On Sundays he would sometimes bring his nine to our field, and play a couple of games with scrub nines from Baltimore. Inspired and inflamed by his incomparable virtuosity, I set up for a pitcher, but nothing ever came of it, for I had little speed and no control at all. When I ventured on an in-shoot it was apt to be recovered, not by the catcher, but by the third baseman. So the Lürssen boys, who were older than my brother and I, retired me to the outfield, or, as it was then called, the farm, and from there I slowly worked my way back as far as the position of short-stop. One day a sizzler gave my left little finger a terrific clout, and I was out of the game for weeks. The finger remains slightly cauliflowered to this day — another reason, perhaps, why I have never made much of a shine as a piano virtuoso.

My father seldom took any part in these games,

though some of the other men of the vicinity often did so. Once he bought us an outfit of uniforms, but they didn't last long, for we younger players quickly outgrew them, and the visitors who were invited in from time to time had a habit of making off with those issued to them. My own I'll never forget. It was made of a woolen material as thick as a Scotsman's Winter underwear, and as I gradually increased in stature and bulk the breeches pulled up until their bottoms were halfway between my knees and my hips, and the shirt began to bind my chest like a surgical bandage. My brother and I used to go to Mt. Washington on Sunday afternoons early in Spring, long before the family had moved out for the Summer, and there get in a lot of hard practice. I recall that we were always stiff in the legs and arms until the Wednesday following. But all this diligent work got me nowhere, and I began slowly to grasp the humiliating fact that I was not earmarked for a career of glory on the diamond. When the Baltimore Orioles started out to astound mankind with their new prodigies, in 1894, I withdrew in despair, though I remained a fan for a few years longer. Since 1900 I have seen but two professional baseball games.

THE CAPITAL OF THE

𝕽epublic

My father, in the days when I first knew him, visited his Washington office every Friday; after I went into pants he occasionally took me along. I recall standing between his knees as the train conductor came round, and hearing him protest that I was too young to pay any fare, even half-fare. Whether these protests were serious or not I don't know, but in all probability they were not, for the conductor was always in a very affable mood, and sometimes he let me work his ticket-punch on one of my father's business cards. The candy-butcher also showed me some attention, but that had plain self-interest in it, for he carried a basket containing oval boxes of figs, little red railroad lanterns full of candy pills, gumdrops in red, white and green, and other such favorite refreshments and souvenirs of the era, and my father was always good for a sale.

At that early period Washington was hardly more than a blur to me, and I divided my four or five hours there between admiring the meerschaum pipes and cigar-holders in the cigar-store connected with the branch office of Aug. Mencken & Bro., and accompanying my father on his subsequent rounds of his customers, many of whom kept either restaurants or saloons. He disappeared into his office the moment we got to Seventh and G streets, N.W., and spent the next hour or so auditing its books, with his agent standing by to answer questions. By that time I was half starved, so a great wave of hosannahs rolled through me when we started off for lunch. We usually ate, of course, in the restaurant of some customer, and no doubt we visited, first and last, a great many, but the one I remember best was kept by Mr. Burkhardt, who had once been my father's agent himself, but had now, by dint of diligence and thrift, acquired a business of his own. He always instructed his carver, a coal-black man called Snowball, to give me extra-large portions, and I always got them down. Indeed, I commonly ate so heartily that during the subsequent tour of saloons I had relatively little stomach for the pretzels that were handed down to me at my perch on the brass rail, and even gagged at drinking more than two or three bottles of sarsaparilla.

As I emerged from the fog of infancy Washington began to take on shape and substance, and pretty soon I was wallowing delightedly in its marvels. The greatest of them, in that era, was not the Capitol at the end of Pennsylvania avenue, nor even the Washington Monument, but the asphalt streets. Asphalt was then a novelty in the United States, and Washington was the only city that could show any considerable spread of it: in Baltimore it was still thought to be dangerous to horses. What I remember of it chiefly is the dreadful heat it threw up in Summer. The cobblestones of Baltimore, with their lush interstitial crops of grass, oats and Jimson weed, were cool in the warmest weather, but in Washington the white asphalt bounced the sun back into people's faces, and every stranger was told that in July and August the inhabitants abandoned their kitchen stoves altogether and cooked their meals on the street. This tale still pops up whenever there is an extraordinarily severe spell of heat, and it has probably gone out over the wires at least forty times. It was untrue when I first heard it as a small boy, and it remains untrue to this day, but for some reason or other people like to believe it, and so it hangs on.

Of my first trip to the top of the Washington Monument, which must have been made soon after it was opened in 1888, I recall only the fact that we descended by walking down the long, dark steps, and it seemed a journey without end. There was in those days a bitter debate as to whether a baseball thrown from the top of the monument could be caught by a catcher on the ground, and my father was much interested and full of mathematical proofs that it couldn't be done. Some time later it was tried, and turned out to be very easy. He also had a hand in a long and acrimonious discussion of curve pitching, one faction holding that the path of the ball was actually a curve and the other maintaining that the whole thing was only an optical illusion. Which side he took I don't recall, but I remember him coming home with the news that the reality of curves had been proved by setting up three stakes in a straight line at the Washington baseball grounds, and putting a pitcher to work on them. After knocking them down or missing them altogether for half an hour running he finally succeeded in pitching a ball clearly to leftward of the two end ones and as clearly to rightward of the middle one. This feat attracted a large crowd and was dealt with by the newspapers as if it had been some great public calamity or first-rate murder, but I was in school that day, and so had to miss seeing it. Later on my father undertook to show me how to curve a baseball, but inasmuch as he never could do it himself I made very little progress.

Most of my visits to Washington, at least from 1886 onward, must have been made after school let out in Spring, for I remember the town as always warm, and both my father and me as always thirsty. As he proceeded from one restaurant or saloon to another, usually with his agent, Mr. Cross, and palavered amiably with their proprietors, I sat on a long succession of brass rails, munching my pretzels and drinking my sarsaparilla. This life had its moments of boredom, especially when the visit to any given place was prolonged, but on the whole I enjoyed it, and to this day I retain a friendly feeling for saloons, though I seldom stand up at their bars, for I long ago associated myself with the Chinese doctrine that it is foolish to do anything standing up that can be done sitting down, or anything sitting down that can be done lying down. In the days before Prohibition, which were also the days before air-cooling, I doted on the cool, refreshing scent of a good saloon on a hot Summer day, with its delicate overtones of mint, cloves, hops, Angostura bitters, horse-radish, *Blutwurst* and *Kartoffelsalat*. It was always somewhat dark therein, and there was an icy and comforting sweat upon the glasses. The huge, hand-painted oil painting facing the bar, nearly always of Venus stripped for her weekly tub, was covered with netting to keep off the flies, and the mirror that framed the bartender was decorated with Winter landscapes drawn in soap. I have visited in my day the barrooms of all civilized countries, but none that I ever saw came within miles of a high-toned American saloon of the Golden Age. Today the influence of the cocktail lounge has brought in blue glass, chrome fixtures, and bars of pale and puny woods, but in the time I speak of saloon architects stuck to mirrors as God first made them, to honest brass, and to noble and imperishable mahogany.

My father sometimes took an afternoon off from his calls on restauranteurs (for that is what they all liked to call themselves, including the unmistakable saloonkeepers) to show me the salient sights of the capital, or, perhaps more often, sent his office-boy with me while he struggled with accounts in his office. The majestic spectacle of the United States Senate was thus a commonplace to me before I was eight years old, and by the time I was ten I was a familiar of the Smithsonian and the National Museum. Both of the latter were even more meagre and measly then than they are now, but I was too young to know it, and hence enjoyed them immensely. There were two exhibits in the Smithsonian that fascinated me especially. The first, perhaps naturally, was the skeleton of a prehistoric monster, ten or twelve feet high at the shoulder. The second, rather curiously, was a primitive ox-cart with wheels made of solid slices of tree trunks. Why this last should have struck me so powerfully I do not know, but there is the fact. I wrote a description of it in my composition-book, and gained thereby the praise of Mr. Willie, son to the chancellor of F. Knapp's Institute. I also got his favorable notice by exhibiting a small bust of Abraham Lincoln, made of condemned and macerated paper money from the Treasury. Such busts are still obtainable in Washington, and honeymooners from the remoter villages of Virginia and Maryland often take them home. Their price runs in proportion to the face value of the deceased greenbacks in them. One containing the remains of mere $1 bills goes cheaply, but one made of $1000 bills costs a pretty penny. In my day the little hill on which the Washington Monument stands was still bestrewn with large chips of marble left by the builders. I recovered, first and last, at least a hundred pounds of them, and my brother Charlie and I hoarded them for a long while, for it was believed in Hollins street that soda-water could be made of them, though we never found out how. They disappeared eventually into a rockery that my mother made in the backyard.

At the Capitol and in the other public buildings of the town its magnificoes could be viewed only at a distance, but in the saloons they came down to earth, and laid themselves open to intimate inspection. Their principal resort was Shoomaker's oldtime groggery in Pennsylvania avenue, but my father seldom visited it, so I had to get my eyeful of them at other places, notably Mr. Burkhardt's. Mr. Burkhardt, I conclude on reflection, must have specialized in the judiciary, for I recall a great many customers who were addressed as Judge, or even as Mr. Justice. These eminent men were quiet drinkers, but assiduous. They apparently had short working-hours, for they showed up at the bar early in the afternoon, and stuck around until it was time for us to return to Baltimore. There was a very old one, in a long-tailed black coat and white chin-whiskers, who one day lifted me to speechless veneration by slipping me a quarter. But the next time I encountered him he failed to give me another, so I transferred my devotion to other gods. There were also several Senators in the Burkhardt stock company, and a great many Congressmen. I noticed, boy as I was, that Mr. Burkhardt kept his deference and solicitude for the Senators and the judiciary, and had none left for Congressmen. He addressed them familiarly as George, Jack and Bill, and once I heard him invite one of them to get the hell out of the place, and stay out. My father explained that this was because Congressmen were too numerous in Washington to be of any note; moreover, not a few of them were given to caterwauling and wrestling in barrooms, a habit that he always deprecated. They yet linger, I believe, in their lowly station, and are regarded by most Washingtonians as hardly worthy of common politeness.

Of all the eminent men I had the honor of witnessing in those days, the only one who ever showed me much personal attention, and hence the only one I remember with any vividness, was Mr. Mc-

Carthy, a member of the higher joboisie of the State Department. Mr. McCarthy was a hunchback, but his infirmity did not damp his spirits, which were naturally very gay. I can see him yet as he stood at the stately bar of Mr. Burkhardt's restaurant, with his head scarcely reaching the mahogany rail but his good right arm plenty long enough to keep a firm hold on the glass of beer that the bartender had just drawn for him. He could get down five or six in a row, and yet retain both his courtly manners and his wide knowledge of international affairs. My father relied upon him for confidential information about the filthy schemes of the chancelleries of Europe, and I relied upon him for a steady supply of foreign postage stamps. He seemed to have something to do with handling departmental mail, for his pockets were always full of stamps from the farthest and most outlandish places, many of which have long since disappeared from the stamp catalogues, at least as current producers — for example, Korea, Montenegro, and Thurn und Taxis. He never failed to hand me a handful, and I never failed, on returning home, to paste them carefully in a blue-covered stamp-album that my mother had given me. When, in the course of human events, I tired of stamp-collecting, I turned over the album to my young sister, Gertrude, and when she, in her turn, took to other concerns, its contents passed to our niece Virginia, the daughter of my brother Charlie, and she then handed it on to one of her cousins, and so on and so on. I suppose that Mr. McCarthy's stamps are still cherished somewhere by some youngster or other. As for Mr. McCarthy himself, he appears to have been absorbed into the cosmos long years ago, but in my mind his memory is still green.

Mr. Cross, who had succeeded Mr. Burkhardt as my father's Washington nuncio, was another of my favorites, for he saved up rubber-bands for me, let me inspect and handle the florid meerschaum pipes in his showcase (one of them, I recall, was priced $300), and was always good for a piece of cash money. In those days the custom of tipping boys was as widespread in the United States as it still is in England, and my brother Charlie and I derived a considerable revenue from it, especially in Summer, when visitors often came to the country for all-day visits. These visits sometimes strained my mother's housekeeping dangerously, and once or twice broke it down altogether, but they were highly agreeable to Charlie and me, for that was a scurvy fellow who did not fork up at least a quarter. One Sunday when we were still at the Vineyard Mr. Cross staggered us by slipping us a dollar each — a large sum for any boy to have in his hands in the eighties, and perhaps roughly comparable to a couple of shares of Eastman Kodak or Am. Tel. & Tel. today. What is more, Mr. Cross kept to his mark thereafter, so we were always rich dur-

ing the week following one of his visits, and regarded him at all times as a gentleman of sur-
passing elegance, which indeed he was. He was a
handsome man with a brisk coal-black mustache
and prematurely white hair, and he made a striking figure in the somewhat advanced tailoring that
he affected. One day he surprised us by bringing
along a beautiful lady in a small bonnet and large
bustle: in the course of time, I believe, they were
married. But that must have been after he retired
from the service of Aug. Mencken & Bro., and we
saw him no more.

The old office at Seventh and G streets still
stands, and when I last saw it it had changed little
since 1889. There was the same areaway beside it,
with the same pipe railing, and across the street the
old building of the Patent Office looked exactly as
I remember it as a boy. In the eighties the building
next door was occupied by Mr. Voigt, a jeweler and
one of my father's friends. On September 26,
1890, as I find by my father's bill-file, he bought
a Swiss repeater watch from Mr. Voigt, paying
$200 for it in cash — a strange transaction for
him, for he commonly preferred barter, and settled
most of his major bills in either cigars or leaf tobacco, or both. Even his tailor's bills were commonly paid that way — not directly to the tailor,
but to a curious *entrepreneur* named Mr. Butke,
who seems to have carried on a complicated series
of similar transactions with half the business men

of Baltimore. He would start out by finding someone who wanted the cigars or tobacco that he had
got from my father, and end by finding someone
who had something that the tailor wanted. The
number of his intermediate trades varied from time
to time, and often ran to many. He lived at Ellicott City, and was supposed to have mortgages on
half the farms in the circumambient county. My
father had some gifts as a trader himself, and so
did his brother, but they were always a bit wary of
Mr. Butke, for his talents began where theirs left
off. They considered him, in fact, a public menace,
but for many years they kept on dealing with him,
hoping against hope that some day he would slip
a cog and they would be able to throw him.

Mr. Voigt got cash for the Swiss repeater watch,
I suspect, simply because Mr. Butke's diocese did
not extend to Washington. The watch itself was
my father's proudest possession until his death.
It not only had a hand that made five jumps to the
second; it was also fitted with a device which could
be made to strike the hours, halves and quarters,
thus telling the time in the dark. But my father
never quite mastered the code of this device, so he
could never really find out, in the dark, just what
time it was. Moreover, it was always much easier to
strike a match. In the days after his death, when I
began to wear the watch myself, this apparatus
got out of order, and the best watchmakers in Baltimore failed to cure it, though they sent me very

large bills. In the end the rest of the works also went flooey, and I retired the piece to a safe-deposit box which houses a series of family watches running back to the year 1700. At my own exitus they will be thrown into the market. Meanwhile, I receive a bill from the bank every six months, and they thus waste my substance and help to hold me in the literary sweatshop.

I find by the bill-file that Mr. Voigt supplied many of the articles of *virtu* that engauded our house in Hollins street in my early days. There are bills for a cuckoo-clock, a music-box, and other such things, beside a gold watch for my mother, and a chain and locket for it. Mr. Eckhardt, who was our neighbor in Hollins street and operated an art works in downtown Baltimore street, was also active in this trade. His contributions included the pier-glass that still stands in the old house; a photograph album bound in plush, with a music-box inside; a pair of sombre steel engravings from paintings by Turner, showing the English seaports of Hastings and Dover, each with a heavy walnut frame; another steel engraving entitled " King Solomon and the Iron Worker," apparently of Masonic significance; and " 1 pce. statuary " billed on October 19, 1885 — unquestionably the Rogers group, " Fooling Grandpa," that stood on a rococo table in the parlor for many years, and is still cherished by my sister. The music-box that came from Mr. Voigt's emporium in 1887, at the price of $125 cash in hand, was as large as (and much resembled) a child's coffin,[1] and my father had to have a special hollow-topped table made to accommodate it. It not only played ten loud and swinging tunes — including Johann Strauss's "Rosen aus dem Süden," and selections from "Boccaccio," "The Mascot" and "The Tales of Hoffmann"; it was also outfitted with drums and bells, and when my brother Charlie and I set it going on a Sunday morning it shook the house. We employed it, boylike, to build up advantage in the neighborhood. Boys and girls who were polite to us were let in to listen to it perform, and a favored few of extraordinary amiability were permitted to wind it, and to turn the drums and bells off and on.

I always enjoyed the train ride to and from Washington, and in fact still prefer railroad travel to any other mode of conveyance by land. We used the B. & O. exclusively, not only because its ancient Baltimore station, Camden, was convenient to my father's office, but also as a matter of local pride and patriotism. The B. & O. made Baltimore, and Baltimoreans have never forgotten the fact. The company is tax exempt in Maryland to this day, and Baltimoreans going to New York would use its trains almost invariably if it had a tunnel through

---

[1] It still exists, and after writing the above I measured it. It is two feet, seven and a half inches long, fourteen inches wide, and ten inches high. It seemed much larger as I recalled it from infancy. Indeed, I'd have guessed that it was nearer four feet long.

the North river. Its once famous flyer, the Royal Blue, did not go into service until 1890, but it had fast trains running between Baltimore and Washington so long ago as 1881, and by the middle eighties they were making the forty miles in fifty minutes, including the time wasted in getting in and out of the two cities. My father began to sell cigars to the B. & O. back in the seventies, when it added the first dining-cars to its star trains, and this business, along with the accompanying station-restaurant business, helped to put his firm on its feet. He died convinced that B. & O. trains were somehow superior to all others. If it were argued in his presence that they shipped a great deal of ballast dust and locomotive ash, then he would reply that those of both the Pennsylvania and the New York Central shipped even more, and that in any case no rational man could object to a nuisance that had its origin in immutable natural laws, and was thus in accord with the will of God. My father placed, in general, very little reliance upon heavenly legislation, but in this and a few other difficult situations he resorted to it to get rid of belly-achers and casuists.

XVI

RECREATIONS OF A

𝕽eactionary

My father and his brother and partner, like most
reasonably successful American business men of
the eighties, always had plenty of time on their
hands. The business they were in had not yet been
demoralized and devoured by the large combinations of capital that were to come later on, and there
was room in their field, which was principally in
the Southeast, for all the firms in their line in Baltimore. They were thus on peaceful terms with their
competitors, and regarded at least some of them
with a kind of approval almost akin to respect.
They had a competent staff of drummers on the
road, their principal customers stuck to them
pretty faithfully, and, though they gave a great
deal of energy to excoriating labor agitators, they

RECREATIONS OF A REACTIONARY

had very little labor trouble in their own establishment.

My father's daily routine was no doubt quite typical of that of hundreds of other Baltimore employers of the period. He arose at what would be considered an early hour today, and immediately after breakfast proceeded to his office. If we were in the city he travelled by horse-car; if we were at Mt. Washington he drove his buggy, or, in impossible weather, went by train. In either case he tackled his mail the moment he reached his desk, which was a high one in the ancient mode, made for use standing up. If the mail contained enough checks and orders to content him he was in good humor all morning, and polite to the drummers who dropped in to sell him cigar-box labels, cigar bands, advertising novelties, wrapping paper, and other such minor supplies. But if the orders were light, or a letter turned up news that another deadbeat in Georgia or South Carolina had absconded, he would growl at these drummers in a most churlish way, and instruct the bookkeeper to write letters to all his own drummers, accusing them formally of wasting their time and his money on cards, dice, women and the bottle. This routine was broken only by his weekly trip to Washington.

On a normal morning all the cigars made in the factory the day before were waiting for his inspection in racks ranged in long rows. He would get to this job at about 10 a.m. and it took him probably half an hour. In theory, either he or his brother examined each and every cigar made in the place, but actually this was impossible; what they did was simply to draw out samples, feel of them critically, and set aside any plug or skipper that they discovered. A plug was a cigar so overstuffed with filler that sucking wind through it would probably be unfeasible, and a skipper was one so carelessly wrapped that the adjoining layers of wrapper did not overlap. There were plenty of days when my father found no case at all of either sort of pathology. When he encountered one he took the sick cigar upstairs, holding it at arm's length as if it had smallpox, and upbraided the offending cigar-maker. On his return he dropped it in a drawer which supplied complimentary smokes to truck-drivers, messenger boys who looked to be more than twenty-one years old, collectors for non-Masonic charities, bank runners, colored clergymen, and policemen below the rank of lieutenant.

The rest of the morning he devoted to a furious and largely useless figuring. He was immensely vain of his arithmetical capacities, and prepared elaborate cost-sheets long before they began to be whooped up at Harvard. They showed precisely what it stood the firm to produce 1000 of any one of the twenty or more brands of cigars on its list. Every time there was a ponderable change in the price of any kind of leaf tobacco, he recalculated those sheets. When the job was done he put them

249

in one of the drawers of his desk, and that was the last anyone ever heard of them. His brother, who was not much interested in mathematics, gave them only a polite glance, and no one else in the place ever saw them at all, not even the bookkeeper.

A few minutes before one o'clock he suddenly clapped on his hat and dashed out for lunch. If the house in Hollins street was open he almost always lunched there; if not, he patronized one of the saloon-restaurants in the neighborhood, all of which advertised business men's lunches at the uniform price of twenty-five cents. When he went to Hollins street he made the round trip by horse-car and invariably took a nap after his meal. The scene or instrument of this nap was a frowsy old walnut and hair-cloth lounge in the dining-room, and the clearing off of dishes had to be deferred until a couple of Cheyne-Stokes snores notified the fact that he had passed out. After half an hour or so, he awoke with a start, looked about him wildly, reached for his hat, and started back to his office. To the casual eye he seemed to be in haste, but when he got to the office there was really next to nothing for him to do, and he usually spent the afternoon reading the *Tobacco Leaf* or the *Sporting Times* (this last for baseball news), searching out the ratings of prospective customers in the big Bradstreet book, or gossiping with his brother, the bookkeeper, or any caller who happened to drift in. At five-thirty he knocked off for the day.

I never knew him to visit his bank : all his routine business with it was transacted by the bookkeeper, and he never borrowed a nickel. Indeed, he regarded all borrowing as somehow shameful, and looked confidently for the bankruptcy and probable jailing of any business man who practised it regularly. His moral system, as I try to piece it together after so many years, seems to have been predominantly Chinese. All mankind, in his sight, was divided into two great races : those who paid their bills, and those who didn't. The former were virtuous, despite any evidence that could be adduced to the contrary ; the latter were unanimously and incurably scoundrels.

He had a very tolerant view of all other torts and malfeasances. He believed that political corruption was inevitable under democracy, and even argued, out of his own experience, that it had its uses. One of his favorite anecdotes was about a huge swinging sign that used to hang outside his place of business in Paca street. When the building was built, in 1885, he simply hung out the sign, sent for the city councilman of the district, and gave him $20. This was in full settlement forevermore of all permit and privilege fees, easement taxes, and other such costs and imposts. The city councilman pocketed the money, and in return was supposed to stave off any cops, building inspectors or other functionaries who had any lawful interest in the matter, or tried to horn in for private profit.

Being an honorable man according to his lights, he kept his bargain, and the sign flapped and squeaked in the breeze for ten years. But then, in 1895, Baltimore had a reform wave, the councilman was voted out of office, and the idealists in the City Hall sent word that a license to maintain the sign would cost $62.75 *a year*. It came down the next day.

This was proof to my father that reform was mainly only a conspiracy of prehensile charlatans to mulct taxpayers. I picked up this idea from him, and entertain it to the present day. I also picked up his doctrine that private conduct had better not be inquired into too closely — with the exception, of course, of any kind involving beating a creditor. In the Breckinridge-Pollard breach of promise case, a nation-shaking scandal in 1892, rating columns of verbatim testimony in the newspapers, he sympathized openly with Breckinridge, whom he had met in the Washington saloons, and denounced La Pollard as a scheming minx. In the matter of polygamy among the Mormons, which kept all the moral theologians of the country in a dither down to 1890, he was a champion of the Saints, and argued that it was nobody's damned business how many wives they had, so long as they paid their bills, which seemed to be the case.

He had little truck with the Germans who swarmed into Baltimore during the seventies and early eighties, and regarded most of them as idiots, but, like his father, he admired the so-called Pennsylvania Dutch, with whom he had constant business, for many of them were tobacco growers. In various salient respects, he would say, they were so loutish as to be hardly human, but nevertheless they abhorred debt, and that was enough. Contrariwise, he had a low opinion of the Virginians who had flocked to Baltimore after the Civil War, for though many of them were elegant and charming fellows, and a few were even the aristocrats they all claimed to be, they were usually very hard up, and anyone who gave them credit had a hard time getting his money.

As I have said, my father's work-day was usually pretty well over by the time he got back to his office from lunch, and he had the rest of the afternoon for recreation. If the Baltimore baseball club was playing in town he would go to the game; if it were on tour he would go to Kelly's oyster-house to learn the score. In Winter he waited for a customer to drop in, or one of his own drummers, and if his hopes were realized he would propose a drink in the saloon next door. Getting it down, and the others that always chased it, would occupy the time until five-thirty, when the cigarmakers came downstairs with their day's produce, the bookkeeper locked the safe, and the day was over. In that era all American business was carried on to the accompaniment of such libations. To let a customer go without offering him a drink was an almost unheard of insult.

It was also considered unendurably boorish to refuse a drink when it was offered. There were bankers and brokers in South street, the Wall Street of Baltimore, who never got back from lunch at all. They ate in the luxurious bars of the neighborhood, and all their afternoon business, if they had any, was done in the same places.

My father preferred the saloon next to his office, not only because it was conveniently near, but also because it was kept by an old German named Ehoff, who pretended obligingly to be an extraordinarily innocent and credulous fellow. Many a time, as a small boy, I have sat on the brass rail, getting down my sarsaparilla and pretzel, and listened to my father complaining to Ehoff all over again, and perhaps for the fiftieth time, that his ice was stale, or telling him that the Brooklyn Bridge had fallen down, or that the Dutch were being driven out of Holland, or that Cardinal Gibbons had joined the A.P.A., or that Bismarck was moving to Baltimore and proposed to open a brewery. Ehoff, I suspected even then, knew better, but he always professed to be astounded. Thus he was a favorite among the business men of the vicinity, who all tried their fancy upon him. They avoided very diligently a saloon a bit up the street, kept by one William Ruth, for over its door hung a sign reading *Union Bar*. No one knew then that this Ruth, by the exercise of his generative powers a few years

254

later, was to become the father of the imperishable Babe.

On afternoons when nothing better offered, my father and his brother lolled in their office concocting hoaxes and canards. Their masterpiece was the creation of a mythical brother named Fred, who went on living in gaseous form for many years; to this day a rheumy old Baltimorean sometimes stops me on the street to ask what has become of him. Fred was supposed to be a clergyman. Everyone knew that my grandfather was an infidel, so my father and his brother represented that Fred was a cruel burden and disgrace to him, and warned all comers to avoid mentioning the clergy in his presence, lest his sorrow suddenly overwhelm and unman him. The Fred legend gradually took on elaborate embroideries. Fred had been invited to become chaplain of the United States Senate. He had converted 5,000 heathen in one week in Chicago. He had broken into the old man's house, and tried to pray him up to grace. He had bought Ehoff's saloon and Coblens's adjoining livery-stable and was planning to build a church or a Bible factory on the site. Finally, after my grandfather's death, they announced that Fred had been made a bishop, and there they let him rest.

My father's solo flights, I must say as a more or less honest historian, sometimes got perilously close to the line limiting the best of taste. When he bought the Summer home at Mt. Washington, one of the new neighbors asked him casually if he had any plans for developing the place, which was somewhat dilapidated. He replied solemnly that he proposed to give over the long slope of lawn in front of the house to the breeding of blooded hogs, a race of cattle too much neglected in Maryland. This news naturally staggered the neighbor, and he ran about the vicinity spreading it. By the time the first delegation of protest arrived my father was ready with large blue-prints of the proposed piggery, prepared by a builder friend and showing the name " Pig Hill " on a banner hung between two immense flagpoles at the main entrance. The excitement began to die down after we moved in and the long ranks of pens continued *non est*, but there was a revival of it every time workmen appeared to gravel a walk or repair a porch. Worse, the name of " Pig Hill " stuck to the place, and was gradually extended to the whole settlement. It survived, in fact, until the city of Baltimore, proliferating northward, finally obliterated both the settlement and the name.

There was something of the same barbarity, though it did much less damage, in an operation against a German friend, a gentleman who owned a wood-working factory. He was the most inoffensive man imaginable, and his only known vice was playing *Schafskopf* of an afternoon with a few friends. One day he got into a row with a Maine lumber company about a schooner load of lumber, and the company finally threatened him with a lawsuit. This alarmed him greatly, so he dropped in to consult my father. He was particularly concerned lest the noise and fumes of the dispute induce Bradstreet's, the commercial credit agency, to reduce his credit rating. My father offered at once to get a Bradstreet report on him to find out if anything of the sort had been done — and then spent the next two afternoons concocting a report that left nothing of him save a ruined name and his immortal soul.

This bogus report was typewritten on flimsy in exact imitation of a real one. It started off by saying that the old man was a once prosperous and respected *entrepreneur*, but that his gross neglect of his business had brought it down to the edge of bankruptcy. He left his office every day, it said, at 2 p.m., drove out to a notorious resort in the country (described so as to identify his own home), and there wasted what remained of his substance gambling with a gang of police characters. It added that he drank vast amounts of beer during this play, and was already showing signs of *mania à potu*. It ended by hinting that his family was considering having him put under restraint as *non compos mentis*, and that his creditors were forming a committee to join in the action.

The old man's response to all this nonsense was almost terrifying. He leaped in the air, began God-damning horribly in English and German, and talked wildly of shaking the dust of the United States from his feet and going back to his native Bremen. He laid the whole blame upon the lumber company, which was operated, so he said, by Yankee swindlers of a kind that, in any civilized country, would be looked to by the *Polizei*. He became so excited that my father grew alarmed, and began to confess in haste that the report was spurious. But by this time the victim was so wrought up that he wouldn't listen, and it was not until the bookkeeper was dispatched to Bradstreet's Baltimore office for a real one, and it turned out on inspection to be highly complimentary, that he recovered any calm. Even so, he kept on denouncing the lumber company, and it retained first place in his menagerie of monsters so long as he lived.

About this time the half-grown son of a neighbor at Mt. Washington became stage struck and began to prepare himself diligently for his chosen art. His preparations took the form of dreadful howls and shrieks in the woods behind his home, designed to improve his breathing. This noise set all the dogs for half a mile round to barking, and scared the horses, cats, nurse-maids and small children of the settlement out of their wits. My father's characteristic device for getting rid of the nuisance was to complain to the police at the county seat that a wild man was loose in the woods, devouring rabbits raw and alive, and threatening canni-

RECREATIONS OF A REACTIONARY

balism. The rural cops arrived on horseback and at a gallop, surrounded the woods, discharged their side-arms menacingly, and then rushed in and confronted the astonished actor. It took my father a couple of days and several boxes of Grade D cigars to convince them that some miscreant had played a joke on them.

But such designs and inventions were, after all, only small game. In his later years, reviewing his career as Münchhausen and Joe Cook from the serene pinnacle of the forties, my father dismissed them lightly as no more than inconsiderable impromptus. The true peak of his talent, he allowed, was reached in his successful scheme to wreck the cigarmakers' union of Baltimore, which called a strike along about 1889. In his own shop the strike lasted only a few days, but the men stayed out in some of the other shops of the town for weeks and months, and as a result large numbers of them began to fall behind in their rent and grocery-bills, and to hear unpleasantly from their wives. The union had a war fund, but it wasn't large enough to pay the strikers full benefits; the best it could offer, at least toward the end, was free tickets to Philadelphia, which then had so many shops that it was known as the Cigarmakers' Heaven. The union sent hundreds of the strikers there, and most of them got jobs, but other hundreds remained in Baltimore, and the war fund began to play out.

It was at this stage that my father formulated his

scheme to put the wounded enemy out of its misery. There were in the cellar of every cigar-shop in town a great many supernumerary cigarmakers' box-wood boards and cutting tools, left behind by tramp workmen who had come in from nowhere, worked a few weeks, got drunk and fired, and then vanished. The possession of such a board and set of tools was sufficient proof that the bearer was a cigarmaker. The union was eager to clear out all such casuals of the trade, for they were always half starved when they arrived, and it was thus easy for the bosses to induce them to work as strikebreakers.

When my father's spies reported that a dozen or more of them were being shipped to Philadelphia every day the inspiration for his museum piece seized him. If a board and a set of cutting tools made a cigarmaker, why not fashion a whole regiment of them out of the abandoned boards and tools in the cellar? To get the men was easy: there were hundreds and thousands of them in the flop-houses of Baltimore — sailors who had gone on drunks and missed their ships, farm-boys come to town to make their fortunes, old soaks not yet quite ready for the morgue, and a dozen other kinds of miserable and hopeless men. So an agent was sent down to the region of Pratt street wharf to round up a squad, and in a little while he returned with twenty-five. Each was given a cigarmaker's board, a set of cutting tools, a drink of horse-liniment, and fifty cents in cash, and instructed how to find the headquarters of the union, and what to say on reaching it. The agent then started them off, and in an hour they were all aboard a train for Philadelphia, each with a ticket in his hand that had cost the union $1.85, and a quarter for refreshments *en route.*

When the boards in the cellar of the Metropolitan Cigar Factory of Aug. Mencken & Bro. gave out those in the cellars of other factories were levied upon, and in the course of the next few weeks at least a thousand poor bums were run through the mill. They cost the union $2.10 apiece, and its remaining funds swiftly melted away. Finally, the spies brought news that it could go on for but one day more. My father always lingered over this part of the story. The union was now wrecked, but how could the fiends in human form in charge of it be made to understand clearly *how* it had been wrecked, and by whom? How could its defeat be converted into shame and vain repining? His solution, though it strained his powers to the utmost, was really very simple. He sent his agents down to Pratt street wharf to round up a dozen *one-armed* men, outfitted them with the usual boards and tools, and had them marched to union headquarters. The instant they got there the fiends tumbled to the trick that had been played on them. With low cries of dismay, they gathered up the few dollars remaining, rushed to the Baltimore & Ohio dépôt, and fled to Philadelphia themselves.

The union sneaked back into Baltimore afterward, but it was a long time afterward. While my father lived it troubled him no more. He died full of a pious faith that he had finished it.

XVII

Brief Gust of Glory

In my boyhood in the Aurignacian Epoch of Baltimore the favorite bivouac and chapel-of-ease of all healthy males of tender years was the neighborhood livery-stable. I have since learned, by a reading in the social sciences, that the American livery-stables of that era were seminaries of iniquity, with a curriculum embracing cursing and swearing, gambling, cigarette-smoking, tobacco-chewing, the classical or Abraham Lincoln repertoire of lewd anecdotes, the design and execution of dirty pictures, and even the elements of seduction, burglary and delirium tremens. It may have been true, for all I know, in the pathological small towns that all social scientists appear to hail from, but certainly it was not true in West Baltimore. I was a regular student at Reveille's stable in Stricker street from the beginning of my seventh year to the end of my nonage, and as special student at Coblens's stable in Paca street, off and on, for most of the same period, but so far as I can recall I never heard a word uttered in either of them, or beheld any human act, transaction or phenomenon, that might not have been repeated before a bench of bishops.

On the contrary, they were both schools of decorum, operated by proud and even haughty men, and staffed by blackamoors of a generally high tone. No palpably dipsomaniacal or larcenous coon could survive more than a few days in any such establishment: there were too many valuable horses and rigs in hand to be trusted to the former, and too many valuable carriage-robes, buggy-whips, hassocks, etc., to be exposed to the latter. My father's No. 1 whip, hung up by the snapper in Mr. Reveille's office, had a gold band around the handle engraved with the insigne of the Ancient Arabic Order of Nobles of the Mystic Shrine, and in Mr. Coblens's office, where he commonly kept his No. 2 whip and his dayton-wagon, there was also a buffalo robe that he set great store by, although I should add that its hair had pretty well played out, and that after his death I gave it freely to the poor.

Mr. Coblens was a man of erect bearing, reserved manner, and great dignity. He wore none of the loud checks associated with his vocation, but was always clad in plain colors, and not infrequently appeared in a black cutaway. His only concession to the public expectation was a gray derby hat, very high in the crown. If you can imagine a Jewish

colonel of a swagger cavalry regiment, then you
have got him to the life. My father had a high regard for him, and often paused to discuss horses
with him — a subject about which he knew everything and my father next to nothing. He seldom
descended from his heights to speak to my brother
or me. He knew us very well, and would indicate by
a vague flicker of his eyes that he was aware of our
presence, but it was not often that he said anything.

His cousin Felix was a far more cordial fellow.
Felix was a bachelor in those days, and apparently
a somewhat gay one, for more than once I saw him
set out of an afternoon in a buggy shining like a
$100 coffin, with sometimes a blonde lady beside
him and sometimes a brunette. My brother and I,
boylike, regarded his ease and success at gallantry
with great respect. He was, indeed, one of our
heroes, and also one of our friends. He was never
too busy to explain to us, with the use of living
models paraded by his blackamoors, the points of
a harness horse, and he also had illuminating ideas
about buggy architecture. When my father gave
my brother Charlie and me the pony Frank, it
was Mr. Felix who taught us how to handle him
— no mean art, I assure you, for Shetland ponies
not only kick like mules, but also bite like dogs,
and no doubt would scratch like cats if they had
claws. To this day I have a scar on my bosom,
often passing for a war wound, that proves how
effectively Frank could use his teeth.

In 1890 or thereabout my father traded two cases of Zimmer Spanish leaf tobacco for a gelding bearing the strange name (for a horse) of John. John was a trotter, and supposedly of some speed in harness, but my father could never get it out of him. The two did so badly together, indeed, that my father concluded that John must have rheumatism, and thereafter, for two or three months, the poor beast was the patient of a veterinarian who sent in large bottles of a fiery, suffocating liniment and even larger bills, but never did John any good. Mr. Felix, it appeared, had suspected all the while that the trouble was predominantly in the driver rather than in the horse, and eventually he volunteered to go out with my father some afternoon, and make a scientific review of his driving. He returned downcast. " Your pa," he said to me the next time I dropped in, " is hopeless. It would take him two or three hundred years to learn to drive a cart-horse, let alone a trotter. He holds the lines like a man dealing cards. If he ever got John to really stepping he would fall out of the buggy and break his neck."

A few days later, as if reminded by conscience that he may have been hasty in dismissing his duty to the family, he amazed and delighted me by offering to give *me* a few lessons. It was a colossal opportunity to a boy of eleven, for Mr. Felix was an eminent figure in the trotting world of Baltimore, and seldom condescended to pedagogy. I had, as I recall it, only four or five lessons, but when they were over Mr. Felix was so complimentary that I developed on the spot a complacency which still survives after nearly fifty years, protecting me like an undershirt of concrete from the contumely of mankind. Indeed, he said flatly, and I believe he meant it, that I had in me the makings of a really smart harness driver. " By the time you begin to shave," he concluded, " you'll be showing 'em."

By that time, alas, I had turned from equestrology to chemistry, and a little while later I abandoned chemistry for the kind of beautiful letters on tap in newspaper offices. But for a couple of years I drove John every day, and so gradually improved and mellowed my technic. On Summer afternoons, when my father and I were driving home to Mt. Washington, and the clomp-clomp of a trotter's scissoring hooves began to sound behind us on the Pimlico road speedway, he would silently hand me the reins, and settle back to be torn between parental pride and personal repining. I seemed to hear him groan now and then, but he never said anything. When John, who was really very fast, had left the other nag behind, and the brush was over, he would quietly relight his cigar and resume the reins. He never complimented me: it was too painful. Despite the unction to my vanity that flowed out of these episodes, there was also melancholy in them, and they implanted in me a lifelong conviction that children, taking one day with another, must be damned pests.

But it was not the Coblens stable but the Reveille stable that was my chief haunt in boyhood. The Coblens stable was downtown in Paca street, a few yards from my father's place of business, but the Reveille stable was only two blocks from our home in Hollins street. My brother and I spent many happy hours there, watching the blackamoors currying, feeding and watering the horses, plaiting their tails, excavating and blacking their hooves, dosing them with Glauber's salts and condition powders, and treating their lampas (pronounced *lampers*) with red-hot pokers. This last was a horrifying spectacle, for lampas is an overgrowth of tissue behind the upper incisor teeth, and burning it out involved thrusting the poker into the poor horse's gaping mouth. But I learned before long that horses have very little sense of pain, if indeed any at all; and years afterward I saw one with a leg cut off in an accident munching the grass between the cobblestones as it lay on a Baltimore street, waiting for a cop to come out of a saloon to shoot it.

Mr. Reveille was a Frenchman who seemed venerable and even ancient to my brother and me, for he wore a long beard and always had on a black coat. He had two grown sons, both stout and hearty fellows, but, like their father, very digni-

fied. There was a period when both the trotter
John and the pony Frank (whose stable at the bottom of our backyard was transiently shut down)
were quartered in the Reveille establishment, along
with two buggies, a pony cart and several other
rigs, so my brother and I had plenty of excuse for
hanging about. The Reveilles always welcomed us
gravely, and let us warm up, in Winter, in their
tiny office, which was so filled with robes that there
was scarcely room for the stove, always verging
on white-hot. We admired especially the rack of
whips, which included some virtuoso pieces by the
Baltimore master-craftsmen of the time. A good
whip might cost as much as $25, and we figured that
the whole lot must be worth at least $1000.

The colored brethren who pontificated at Reveille's have all faded, with the flight of the years, into
a brown smudge — all, that is, save Old Jim. Jim
was the carriage-washer, and a fellow of vast size
and unparalleled amiability. He was coal-black
and built like a battleship, and when he got into his
hip-high rubber boots and put on his long rubber
apron he looked like an emperor in Hell. Jim's
atelier was a skylighted space at the rear of the
carriage-house, paved with cobblestones and always flowing with water. He got to work at six in
the morning, and was sometimes still going hard at
nine at night. He had the care of fifty or more
buggies, and of perhaps as many other vehicles,
and he kept them clean and shining. His hardest

time came on Sunday morning, when he had to wash
and polish all the buggies in preparation for the
pleasure jaunts of the afternoon. For this business
he brought out his newest sponges and cleanest
chamois-skins. Also, he put on a black derby hat,
never worn on week-days.

In the intervals of his washing and polishing Jim
took out rigs to the homes of clients of the stable,
and thereby sometimes acquired quiet brannigans,
for it was the custom to reward him, not with
money, but with drinks. My father kept a special
jug for the purpose. It was shared by the ice-man,
but Jim got most of it, for in view of his great bulk
he was given a much larger drink than the ice-man.
He always downed it at a gulp, and after it was
down he would blink his eyes, rub his belly, and say
" Ah-h-h-h-h-! " This was a Baltimore custom of
the time, practised by most of the nobility and
gentry and imitated by serving folk. Sometimes
Jim also got a cigar. He would light it at once, and
stalk back to Reveille's smoking it at an angle of
forty-five degrees. When he reached the stable he
would choke it carefully and deposit it on a high
ledge in the brick wall, out of reach of his less Hi-
malayan and reliable colleagues.

My brother and I greatly admired Jim, and delighted in watching him at work. He had a way of
spinning buggy-wheels that was really magnificent, and he worked with larger sponges and
broader chamois-skins than any other carriage-

washer in West Baltimore. The buggies of those days all had carpets, and when there was nothing else to do he would get out a dozen or so of them, and beat them. Sometimes he would find a nickel or a dime under one of them. It always went into his pocket, for it was the theory among the colored proletarians of Baltimore in those days that whatever a white person lost or mislaid he really didn't want. If he wanted it, he would ask for it, and probably raise hell about it. Jim's income from this source was not large, for he found a great many more pins than nickels. He always laid them aside carefully and then threw them into the manure-pit, for a pin in the frog of a horse's hoof might bring on calamity.

One day my brother and I were astonished to find Jim missing; it seemed almost as strange as finding Mr. Reveille missing, or the stable itself. His *locum tenens*, a short, spotty colored man named Browny, ordinarily a hostler, told us the sad news. Jim's youngest son, a youth of sixteen, had been blown up by an explosion in a one-horse soda-pop factory up a nearby alley, and Jim was off for the day, arranging for the interment of the few fragments that had been recovered. We had never heard of this son, but we were full of sympathy, and when Jim returned we tried to tell him so in the shy manner of boys. He replied that it was God's deliberate act and will, and that he did not mourn beyond reason. The son, he went on judicially, was not really bad, at least as sons went in an age of moral chaos, but nevertheless there was some worry in him, for now and then, like any other high-spirited colored boy, he got into trouble with the cops, and when that wasn't going on he wasted his substance on trashy yallah gals. Now he was far, far away, riding some cloud or rainbow, and hence safe from the hangman forever. He had even escaped, by the unusual manner of his death, the body-snatchers.

Two or three days later we saw a brisk-looking white man in a short yellow overcoat talking to Jim, and the day following Jim again disappeared. We heard from Browny that the brisk-looking man had been a lawyer, and that the talk had been of damages. Another talk, he said, was now proceeding downtown. Jim was gone a week, and then suddenly reappeared, but not to resume work. He showed up one morning in a stove-pipe hat and a long-tailed black coat, carrying an ebony cane with a bone head in the shape of a horse with widely distended nostrils tinted red, and green gems for eyes. His right-hand coat pocket was bulging with at least a quarter's worth of peanuts, and he invited all his old colleagues to thrust in their paws and help themselves. In his other coat pocket he had half a dozen apples for horses he especially liked, including the pony Frank but not the trotter John, and in the hand unburdened by the cane he carried a two-pound bag of lump-sugar. In all four pockets of his white waistcoat were five-cent cigars, standing in rows like cartridges in a belt. He offered the cigars freely, and recommended them as the best in West Baltimore. He even offered one to Mr. Peter Reveille. His hip pockets were stuffed with chewing-tobacco.

Such was Jim in the full tide of his bereavement. Mr. Peter Reveille told us that the lawyer had offered him $250, but that Jim had stuck out for $300, and got it. He let it be known that he had demanded the money in $1 bills, but where he kept them we didn't know until later. Some of the hostlers were of the opinion that he had sneaked into the stable-loft by night and hidden them in the hay, and for a week or so a vain search for them went on. Browny insisted that they were in Jim's stove-pipe hat. He knew, as all of us knew, that policemen always kept their valuables in their helmets; *ergo*, why not Jim? But this theory blew up when Jim dropped in, a week or so later, without his hat, and complaining that two bad niggers from Vincent alley had knocked it off with clubs, and run away with it. The hat was gone, but Jim continued in funds for a long while afterward — indeed, for fully a month. He dropped into the stable almost daily, and never failed to distribute cigars, peanuts, and chewing tobacco, with sugar and apples for the horses. He appeared, at different times, in no less than five hats, and was often mildly in liquor. But he never brought any liquor on the

premises, so the Reveilles, who had a large experience with the darker races, tolerated him patiently.

They knew that he would be back in his long
boots and rubber apron soon or late, and he was.
One morning early they found him at work, somewhat trembly and with a cut over his left eye, but
otherwise as he had been in the days before wealth
corrupted him. He had not been seen during the
preceding week, and for a while his final adventures
were unknown, for neither then nor thereafter did
he ever mention them. But the other colored men
gradually assembled and disgorged the story, and
the cop on the beat helped out with a fact or two. It
was really very simple. Jim, a decent widower, had
been ganged and undone by the massed yallah gals
of three alleys. They had all tackled him singly
and failed, but when they tackled him in a body he
succumbed.

The ensuing party raged for four days and four
nights, with continuous music by banjos, accordi-
ons, and bones. It began in a little saloon that was
the G.H.Q. of one of the alleys, but gradually
spread over the whole block, and ended at last in
a loft over an empty stable. There was no hint
whatever of carnality; the thing was purely alcoholic. After the first few hours each of the yallah
gals sent for her regular fellow, and beginning
with the second day all sorts of gate-crashers
barged in. Thereafter there was a flow in and a
flow out. Every hour or two some guest would col-

lapse and roll home, and another would make the gate. Only Jim himself and a yallah gal named Mildred survived from beginning to end. Mildred, by that time, was in the first stages of *mania à potu*, and the cop on the beat, locking in, ordered her off the job, but Jim was still going strong.

Alas, he didn't go long, for a little while later the saloonkeeper's son Otto came in to say that time was called on the party. Otto and his brother Hermann had been hauling booze for it for four days and four nights, and both were badly used up. Hermann, in fact, had had to be put to bed. But it wasn't fatigue that made Otto call time; it was the fact that Jim's last dollar bill had been devoured. The father of Otto and Hermann was known to be a determined man, with the cops always on his side, so no one questioned the fiat. One by one, they simply faded away, leaving only Jim. He rolled himself in his long-tailed coat and lay down to a prodigal's dreams. He slept all the rest of that day, and all of the ensuing night to 5 a.m. Then he shuffled off to Reveille's stable, chased Browny away from his job, and resumed his station in life.

It was not until long afterward that my brother and I learned where Jim had kept his fortune while it oozed away. Mr. Reveille, worming the story out of the blackamoors, told my father, who told it to a neighbor, Mr. Scherer, whose boy Theodore, lurking about, overheard the telling, and brought it to us. The money had been in the care and custody of the saloonkeeper all the while. He doled it out to Jim dollar by dollar, marking the score on a blackboard behind his bar. He charged Jim a dollar a day " interest " for keeping it. When the final orgies began he charged a dollar for every day and a dollar for every night.

The Scherer boy reported that, in telling about this " interest," my father swore in a hair-raising manner. He had, in fact, a generally suspicious view of saloonkeepers. He would often say that while he knew and respected some upright men among them, only too many were disgraces to a humane and even noble profession.

XVIII

THE CAREER OF A

𝔓𝔥𝔦𝔩𝔬𝔰𝔬𝔭𝔥𝔢𝔯

THAT learning and virtue do not always run together I learned early in life from the example of Old Wesley, a man of color living in the alley behind our house in Hollins street. Wesley dwelt in illicit symbiosis with Lily, the stately *madura* cook of our next-door neighbors, and once a year his younger brother, who pastored an A.M.E. church down in Calvert county, dropped in on him to remonstrate against his evil ways. But Wesley always won the ensuing bout in moral theology, for he had packed away in his head a complete roster of all the eminent Biblical characters who had taken headers through No. 7, beginning with King David and running down to prophets of such outlandish names that, as I now suspect, many of them were probably invented on the spot. Moreover, Wesley could always floor his rev. brother with a final poser: How could he marry Lily so long as she had two other husbands, both of them united to her by impeccable Christian rites? Did the pastor propose the commission of trigamy? If so, then let him go down to the watchhouse in Calhoun street and ask the cops to show him chapter nine, verse twenty, in the big black lawbook behind the desk, a foot or two east of the water-cooler.

The pastor, I believe, never went. He had too healthy a respect for Wesley's scholarship in legal science, and indeed in all the other sciences, including especially those of an ethical or sacred nature. Thus the debate always petered out into futile logic-chopping, and the other residents of the alley, having crowded up to Wesley's open door for the show, got only headaches for their pains. Wesley would thereupon suggest that the pastor preach to them as a sort of solatium. Along with the other white boys of Hollins street, I heard more than one of those sermons, and I can testify that they were very powerful. Each had not only a subject, invariably the post-mortem dangers of sin, but also an object — one of the congregation assembled.

I remember well the day when it was Old Aunt Sophie's turn. She was the widow of a black barber from Fauquier county, Virginia, who had spent the years 1863 and 1864 caring for the whiskers of

General George H. Thomas, and since her husband's death she had lived chastely on her pension,
attending (on the sidewalk) all the funerals, white
or black, in West Baltimore, and lending a hand
whenever special orgies were staged in the colored
churches. No more innocent person lived on this
earth. She had worn the same black veil for thirty
years, and it well indicated the sombre rectitude of
her soul. But the pastor lit into her as if she were
a child-stealer or a pirate on the high seas, and
after ten minutes of his discourse she was flat on
the cobblestones, suffocated by the fumes of brimstone and howling for deliverance.

Old Wesley himself listened to all these sermons
politely, though he was known to be an infidel, and
had a long argument to prove that there was not
enough coal and wood in creation to stoke the fires
of the Methodist Hell. He was, in fact, very proud
of his brother's homiletic talents, and when the
smaller colored boys on the edge of the crowd made
whoopee he would go among them with a lath and
paddle them far from gently. We white boys,
knowing that the prevailing *mores* forbade him to
paddle *us*, were bound in honor to keep quiet, and
this we always did. At the end of the sermon we
joined in the closing hymn — usually " Whiter
Than Snow " or " Are You Ready for the Judgment Day? " Then the pastor would suggest an
offering for his tarpaper tabernacle down in Calvert county, and the assemblage would disperse in

swift silence. But Wesley always put in a nickel, and sometimes a dime, and I recall one day when his sinister eye halted so many fugitives that the total plate was nearly thirty-five cents. This would be enough, said the grateful pastor, to replace a window-pane in the tabernacle, broken by agents of Satan. For three and a half years it had been sorely missed, for the butcher paper pasted over the opening shut out the light.

The pastor's visitations always came in the Summer, and usually in the afternoon. They quite upset Wesley's routine for hot days. His Lily had to clear out at seven o'clock to get breakfast for her white folks, but Wesley himself never arose before eight. The first sign that he was astir would be the appearance of their feather bed through the second-story front window of their four-room house. They apparently slept on it all the year round. On every fair morning, Wesley would shove it out of the window to air, and there it would remain until noon, unless storms came up in the meantime. He made his own breakfast, and then busied himself with undisclosed household tasks until eleven o'clock, when he took a walk around the block.

On his return, he had an armful of newspapers and other printed matter, dredged out of trash boxes on the way, and most of the afternoon he devoted to reading them. It was said that he could read any word, however hard. Colored schoolboys sometimes tackled him with appalling specimens, got from their teachers, but he was always ready to give them names, and to explain their significances. I myself, in the year 1889, sought to floor him with *phthisic*, then all the rage at my school. He called it off without a second's hesitation, and even offered to pronounce it backward. Its meaning? " It's one of them diseases," he said, " that you catch in the Fall of the year. It's something like what you call the heaves in a horse, and then again it ain't. There was a man up in Vincent alley died of it about the time the stockyards burned down. All the pallbearers took it, but none of them had it what you would call bad. Sometimes it don't amount to much."

In Summer, Wesley always did his reading across the alley from his house, in the shade of a white neighbor's backyard fence. He would bring out a kitchen chair shortly after noon, plant it carefully on the narrow and squidgy sidewalk, with its treacherous " she " bricks, and proceed solemnly to business. Years before, he had bought a pair of spectacles from a pack peddler, but he didn't need them, and seldom used them. He would read until three or four o'clock, and then he would be ready for easy and informative conversation until eight in the evening, when Lily returned from her place with a vast pan of victuals for their evening meal. Wesley, so far as I know, never ate lunch. Like most colored folk of the old school, he preferred to gorge at night, and to proceed direct from the table to bed. He was said once to have eaten a whole ham and a whole cabbage at a sitting, but I got that at third hand, and do not take responsibility for it.

I knew him best not as a gourmet but as a metaphysician. He had ready and overwhelming answers to all the questions that have baffled such professionals as Thomas Aquinas and Immanuel Kant, F. W. Nietzsche and William James. For example, What is truth? His answer, reduced to brevity, was as follows: " Truth is something that only damned fools deny." But how are you going to detect the damned fools? By the fact that they deny it. Is there a hole in this reasoning? Perhaps. But there are also holes, according to Kant, in the reasoning of Aquinas, and, according to Nietzsche and William James, in the reasoning of Kant, and so on to the end of the murky chapter.

Wesley had answers to all the other great riddles of the universe, and most of them were equally confident. He knew, for example, the causes of each and every one of the pestilences commonly afflicting Aframericans. Rheumatism, he explained, was due to bending over and lifting weights. The backbone, it appeared, crackled like a bent cornstalk. It could be restored to its natural shape and resilience only by adopting some sedentary avocation: this, in fact, was the reason Wesley himself lived at the cost and expense of Lily. His rheumatism, acquired during his former practice as a hod-

carrier, still troubled him a bit, but sixteen years
of ease had certainly improved it. He had got rid
of the ague by carrying a horse chestnut in his
pocket. Here the rationale was absurdly transparent. Horses and mules were notoriously immune to
the ague; hence horse chestnuts would cure it. If
there had been cow chestnuts or dog chestnuts, they
would have cured it, too.

Wesley's pockets were full of many other such
specifics. He carried a quince seed to hold in check
the quinsy that beset him every Winter, some BB
shot to prevent hiccoughs (the reasoning here I
don't recall, or maybe never heard), and a small
spring, apparently from a deceased firearm, to
keep his wool in kink. This was before Aframerica
began to patronize hair-straighteners. To Wesley,
straight hair on a colored man was unearthly, and
even alarming. The kinks, he taught, held the skull
tight, and so kept the air out, and warded off headaches, blind staggers, and insanity. There had
been a yellow fellow in Vincent alley with hair that
was not only straight but also somewhat sandy.
His fate was known to all. One windy night he
went loony and cut his wife's throat, and a few
months later, on a Friday that was the thirteenth
of the month, he was hanged at the city jail.

Wesley seldom got farther than a block from his
house in the alley behind Hollins street, but twice a
year he went down into South Eutaw street near the
railroad tracks to attend the meetings of a lodge

that he belonged to. Its name I never discovered, or the character of its mysteries. Wesley always left home smoking a cigar, and, according to Lily, came back smelling of gin. The nearest route would have taken him past the University of Maryland Medical School at Lombard and Greene streets, but it was no secret that he always avoided the place by making a detour of six or eight blocks. This was not because he had any fear of the thousands of cadavers reported to be piled up like stovewood in the university deadhouse. As I shall show, he regarded the departed as beneficent presences, or, at all events, as harmless. But he held it to be manifest that medical students were indistinguishable from demons. They lay in wait in dark Greene street with their dreadful hooks, saws, lassos, and knives, and when they had roped a poor colored man they dragged him into their den with hellish shrieks, sawed off his legs and arms, scalped him, and boiled down what remained of him to make medicine. There were, of course, no witnesses to prove these obscene rites, for there were no survivors, but the facts needed no testimony, for they were admitted *quod ab omnibus, quod ubique, quod semper.*

Wesley's attitude toward the dead was one of easy confidence. He believed that the overwhelming majority of them turned into angels, and that these angels were invariably white. " Who would be black if he could he'p it? " he would ask solemnly, not without a touch of pathos. And then, as usual, he would answer himself, " Angels *can* he'p it." The non-angelic dead were simply probationers, roving the vicinity of their coffins (and hence extremely numerous in graveyards) until their cases could be adjudicated. Wesley rejected the idea of Hell, not only for the reason I have stated a while back, but also on legalistic grounds. There would be a profound irrationality, he argued, in punishing evildoers in one world for what they had done in another. Was a chicken thief in Calvert county jailed in Baltimore? Obviously not. The very cops would laugh at the idea. He had other reasons, too, but what they were I forget.

It was in the year 1891 that Wesley had a chance to test his faith in the beneficence of the departed. One day Lily came home from her place complaining of a terrible misery in the head. Wesley put her to bed at once, and sat up all night tearing towels and sheets into strips, soaking them in Dr. Jackson's Reliable Vinegar Liniment for Man and Beast, and binding them tightly to her head. But the air must have got in nevertheless, for by dawn Lily was out of her wits, and carrying on so loudly that the neighbors were all aroused, and came flocking in to assist at the bedside, and to tell one another when they had seen Lily last, and what she had said to them. Presently someone got word to Dr. Benson, the young white medico who had just opened an office in Hollins street, and he came rushing out of his back gate with his nightshirt stuffed into his trousers, and his shiny new black bag bulging reassuringly. But the science of young Dr. Benson, though it was extraordinarily fresh, and indeed came down almost to that precise moment, was insufficient to save poor Lily, and as the whistle down at the Mount Clare carshops blew for seven o'clock she gave up the ghost.

Wesley took his calamity like the philosopher that he was. Nor did he blanch when word came that the burial society to which Lily had belonged for eighteen years, dutifully paying in fifteen cents every week, was insolvent, and could not meet its liability of forty dollars. He borrowed two dollars from young Dr. Benson, produced eleven dollars and some odd cents from a mysterious cigar box, and talked the undertaker, Brother James Gadsden, into giving him credit for what was needed to make up twenty-five. Thus Lily, though she missed the gaudy Class A Nazarene funeral that she had looked forward to for so many years, was at least assured of dignified interment, and in an hour or two Brother Gadsden and his son Joe arrived with a neat black box, and she was duly laid out in the little parlor. A plate rested on her chest, and as the neighbors and the public generally filed past there was an occasional tinkle. Wesley raked in the money from time to time, not wanting to expose kindly friends to temptations beyond human endurance. By evening he had nearly a dollar and a half, and this he gave to Brother Gadsden to affix a copious but somewhat rusty crêpe to the spot on the front-door frame where a bell would have been if there had been one. A postal card was sent to the clerical brother down in Calvert county, inviting him to conduct the obsequies if his ecclesiastical and private engagements permitted. Wesley didn't expect him to show up, and he didn't. His professional view of Lily's morals was very low.

No less than two brave spirits, one of them the alley half-wit and the other a dubious-looking mulatto from the region behind Hollins Market, offered to sit up with Lily, but Wesley waved them away. There would be no death watch, he announced, and no wake. Along about nine o'clock in the evening he adjourned proceedings for the day, jammed a chair against the front door to keep it shut, made a solitary supper of cold meats, and went to bed in the little room above the chamber of death. The neighbors marveled at this fortitude. What if Lily should take to walking? What if her ghost began to moan? What if the Devil dropped in to look her over?

They listened cautiously for a while, but if they heard anything it was only Wesley's snores. His nursing duties the night before and all the excitement of the day had worn him out, and he was quickly asleep. There was no room in his philosophy for fear of the dead. If they became angels, they were, of course, harmless, and if they were put on probation, they naturally carried themselves very discreetly, in the hope of early release. It was only when those fiends, the medical students, disturbed them in their graves, dragging them out of the earth to rend and cook them, and leaving screwdrivers, broken knives, cigarette butts, and whiskey bottles in their empty coffins — it was only then that they went on in a riotous and alarming manner, and even so their worst screams were simply calls for help. Treat them with reasonable politeness, and they were no more evil than policemen, who responded in the same way to the same dose. Wesley had confidence in Lily. Living, she had paid his rent for many years, and provided him with nourishing board. Dead, she would certainly not afflict him.

But that, alas, is precisely what she did. The details are not all clear, but Wesley seems to have shown a brave and tolerant spirit. It was not until the grisly hour before dawn that he appeared at the door of his neighbors, the Perkinses, and rapped softly. Three of the seven Perkins children slept on pallets in the front room, and they let him in and called their father. Wesley was almost apologetic — not for himself but for Lily. " She don't seem to be restin'," he explained, " as well as she ought. Otherwise, I don't know *what* to call it. No sooner was I asleep than she pulled off my covers. Then I went to sleep again, and she pulled 'em off again. That went on six or seven times. Then she commenced to blow in my face. And then she buzzed like a mosquito. And then she meeowed like a cat. And then — well, I thought I'd better clear out, and maybe she could get some rest. I don't know *what's* troublin' her."

The Perkins children were scared half to death. It had been bad enough to sleep with only a thin wall between them and Lily; now that she was aprowl, the thing became appalling. But their parents, who told the whole neighborhood about it later, were not alarmed, or even surprised. They suggested that Lily, on her deathbed, had probably forgotten to tell Wesley something, and that it was still lying on her mind and driving her thoughts from celestial matters. Wesley himself had to admit the plausibility of the hypothesis. The next day he told Brother Gadsden, the undertaker, that she was most likely trying to tell him where he would find the cigar box and its hoard of nickels and pennies. In life, it appeared, she had never suspected that he knew about it all the while and had even burgled it modestly once or twice. But Brother Gadsden, though naturally a stupid fellow, came back with a series of disconcerting questions. " If she didn't know it when she was alive," he demanded, " is that any sign she didn't know it soon as she was dead? Can't a ghost *see?* And wasn't the box standing right there on the mantelpiece, plumb empty? "

So far as I know, Wesley never resolved the riddle. It seemed to bother him a great deal during the weeks following, and may have had something to do with his early demise. He was always bringing it up, and laboring it futilely. He even talked to himself about it. When the neighbors ceased to think of him as a lone and lorn widower, and so ceased to feed him, he turned anti-social, and was presently in the hands of the cops. Jailed for stealing two hams and a sack of flour from a grocer's delivery wagon, he came down with pneumonia in his damp dungeon. With the unhappy alacrity of his race, he was dead in five days, and a week later the medical students had him. I have never known a more gifted metaphysician, or one who came to a sadder end.

XIX

𝔍𝔫𝔫𝔬𝔠𝔢𝔫𝔠𝔢

IN A WICKED WORLD

BOMBAZINE is often spoken of by authors, usually in a sneering way, but the only person I ever knew to wear it was Aunt Sophie, the ancient colored woman mentioned in the last chapter. As I recall it, it was a somewhat stiff and shiny fabric, apparently black at the start, but converted by the oxygen of the air into a sinister, malarious polychrome like that of the waters of a stagnant frog pond. Aunt Sophie wore it on all public occasions, along with a long crêpe veil of the same unappetizing color. As the widow of a military barber, she was in receipt of a modest pension from the United States Treasury, and on it she lived at ease in her little four-room house, and even in a kind of opulence.

Her days were very busy. Whenever there was a funeral in West Baltimore, whether in a white street or a colored, she arrived in good time and planted herself on the sidewalk. She carried a white cambric handkerchief that, under the ravages of time, had taken on the texture of a lace curtain, and as the pallbearers emerged with the departed she always applied it politely to her eyes. If the cortege went to any church within walking distance, she hustled along beside it, and since the hack horses of those days were encouraged to move slowly, she usually beat them to the sacred edifice by at least a length, and grabbed a decorous seat near the door. There she mourned quietly in the character of an old friend, or even of a relative, if the departed happened to be colored, and in that of a family retainer if he or she were white. She was, in fact, more or less related to fully half the black folk in our neighborhood, for most of them had come from either Fauquier county, Virginia, where her husband was born, or Calvert county, Maryland, where she was born herself. And all the white folks knew and esteemed her.

This funeral-going occupied a large part of her time, and it was seldom that she got through two days running without putting on her uniform of woe. Among her own people her absence from the forefront of mortuary orgies was always remarked, and often it had a moral significance. For she was a woman of strict Christian principles, and permitted herself no compromise with sin. Thus she took her station at least five or six doors away from the house of sorrow when Lily, the consort of Wesley the metaphysician, was laid to rest, for their long association had been unblessed by any sacrament. And when the yellow fellow in Vincent alley ran amuck one night and slit his wife's weasand, and was duly hanged for it at the city jail, she refused primly to patronize the ensuing ceremonials in any way, shape or form, though they attracted all the other colored people for a mile around, and also all the white boys who could escape their mothers' vigilance. My brother and I both sneaked into the tiny parlor to see the corpse, and were haunted for many nights afterward by the marks of the rope on its gaunt, felonious neck.

Old Sophie was made welcome at funerals, for she was very well regarded throughout West Baltimore. The only time she was ever turned away, to my knowledge, was when Joe Gans, the colored pugilist, was buried. Joe was so eminent a character among his own people that his funeral had to be divided into three cantos and held successively in three different churches to accommodate the immense concourse. Even so, many more appeared than could get in to hear and see, and his heirs and assigns, at the last moment, made a rule that only those who arrived in carriages should be admitted. This barred out Aunt Sophie, for she had no carriage and was too thrifty a woman to blow in four dollars — the extortionate price for the day — on a public hack. Worse, the baffled crowds outside the three churches were so large and turbulent, despite the bellowing and scuffling of the police, that she never got within half a block of poor Joe's bones. Thus she appeared, unwittingly, to be operating her familiar moral boycott on him, but as a matter of fact she admired him vastly, and had proofs, as she said, that he had died in the bosom of the A.M.E. Church and confident of a glorious resurrection.

The one curse of Aunt Sophie's otherwise peaceful and happy life was her fear of the murderous villains she called body-snatchers. These body-snatchers were not grave-robbers, but criminals who engaged in the far worse business of manufacturing cadavers for the trade. Sophie's fear of them actually had some ground in logic, for in the early eighties one Emily Brown, another respectable old Baltimore colored woman, had been murdered by two thugs, and her remains sold to the janitor of the University of Maryland Medical School for fifteen dollars. The pursuit and trial of the assassins gave Baltimore, white and black, a show that was remembered for years afterward. They had represented to the janitor that they were undertakers trying to get rid of an insolvent client, so he was cleared of all guilt, but they themselves were hanged. The janitor was very careful after that, but most colored people believed that he still had murderers in his employ, and only the bravest or craziest ever ventured to pass the Medical School after dark.

Aunt Sophie held the view that his agents were on the prowl, not only in the immediate vicinity of his grisly den but also all over West Baltimore. Thus, when she had to be abroad by night she kept to well-lighted streets, and whenever it was possible induced someone else to go along. When she was alone her eye was alert for policemen, and after she had passed one she always looked back over her shoulder two or three times, to make sure that he was still there, and ready to protect her if necessary. Most of the cops knew her, and now and then one of them would have some fun by letting off a fearful whoop after she had gone by. In such cases it was hard for her to make up her mind whether she should rush back to him or gallop on.

One dismal Autumn night, on her way down Hollins street to her A.M.E. tabernacle in Stockton street, she was suddenly alarmed by the sound of stealthy footsteps behind her. She quickened her pace, but the steps continued close; in fact, they gradually came closer. Finally she broke into what, in spite of her rheumatism, must be described as a kind of run, but there was no speed in it, and the sinister steps still followed her. She was convinced that her last hour had come, and was preparing to die howling and scratching when suddenly she saw a policeman on the other side of the dark street.

At once she swung round, and confronted her pursuer, who turned out to be a young white man.

"I know what you is!" she screamed. "You's a body-snatcher! Begone, you wicked rapscallion! Don't you lay none o' your dirty hands on *me!*"

But the young white man only laughed, and when the cop ambled across the street to see what the uproar was about, he laughed too. It was a disconcerting dénouement, certainly, and as Aunt Sophie thought it over during the days following, she began to read very unpleasant significances into it. In the end she went about the neighborhood warning all persons of color that the police had entered into a corrupt compact with the body-snatchers, and that the streets were more unsafe by night than ever before. She became, like all other persons with grievances against the government, somewhat extravagant in her denunciations, and playful cops liked to set her off when a crowd of loafers was at hand. Before her scare wore off, she went to the length of threatening to arm herself with her late husband's sword, and to run it through anyone who approached her after nightfall, whether cop or layman. It was news to most people that colored barbers in the Union Army had been armed with swords, but so far as I can recall, no one ever raised the point. Nor did anyone ever see the sword.

The little parlor in Aunt Sophie's house remained substantially as her husband Jeems had left it. He had practised his profession intermittently, charging five cents flat for shaving either a face or a scalp, but his pension put him above worldly cares, and most of his time had been given to the art of painting in oils. There were several examples of his genius on the walls of the room — one a picture of a full-rigged ship laboring in a pea-green ocean. Jeems had to pick up his paints and brushes where he could find them, usually in trash cans, so his color schemes were sometimes very unusual. He once did a portrait of Old Wesley, using coal-black paint for the face. This greatly offended Wesley, who was of a rich chestnut color and liked to believe that he had Indian blood.

Sophie left Jeems's mirror on the wall after his death, along with the wooden shelf beneath it bearing his razor, comb, and brush. His operating chair presented no problem, for it was an ordinary cane-seat chair of the period, with the lost canes replaced by strips of wood from a soapbox. A large wooden spittoon filled with sawdust still stood under the mirror; for Jeems had chewed tobacco in the Army to relieve his frequent toothaches, and never gave up the practice afterward. Against the farther wall stood a scuffed Victorian side table with a cracked marble top, and on it were the *objets d'art* that Sophie had collected in her tours of the kitchens and backyards of the adjacent white folks.

The most striking of these ornaments was a large Dresden cupid with both wings missing and a crack across the face which gave it the appearance of a prizefighter staggering up for the twentieth round. There was also a glass bell covering a stuffed canary that had lost its tail and one of its eyes. Propped against the bell were several pieces of curved colored glass, all relics of deceased goblets or bottles. Some souvenirs of the Philadelphia Centennial of 1876 were also in the collection — one of them an oyster shell embellished with a sketch of Independence Hall in full color. Sophie had not visited the exposition herself; in fact, she had never been farther north in this world than Harlem Square in Baltimore. But as its white frequenters gradually discarded their souvenirs of it, she acquired them and, having acquired them, cherished them.

She used to make regular rounds of all the white folks' kitchens in the neighborhood — that is, of all wherein she was reasonably sure of a welcome. The cooks of her own race were glad to see her, for she knew all the gossip, both white and colored, and was full of wise advice to those having trouble with their husbands, their children, their madames, or the police. She usually appeared at mealtimes and always refused the first ten or twenty invitations to have a bite. But in the end she would sit down, and if she happened to be in good form she devoured enough to feed a longshoreman, though she couldn't have weighed much more than a hundred pounds. If anything was left over, she wrapped it in a newspaper and took it home. No one ever saw her buy anything, whether food or clothing. She ate, so to speak, on the country, and her wardrobe had been fixed and complete for years. Her pension went (*a*) for her rent, which was $1.25 a week, (*b*) to the funds of the A.M.E. Church in Stockton street, (*c*) to funeral collections, and (*d*) into a dime savings bank down in Baltimore street. When she died at last, and a young white lawyer in the neighborhood volunteered, as *amicus curiae*, to investigate her affairs, he found that she had amassed the substantial sum of $67.10.

Her visits to our kitchen were always made at about four o'clock in the afternoon, for she knew that my mother had tea at that time, and that she was sure of four or five cups of it, and a slab of whatever cake happened to be current. Her favorite was raisin bread, which she liked with plenty of powdered sugar. A whole dynasty of our hired girls, white and black, thus fed her. Sometimes, in the course of her formal refusals to have any refreshment, she would rush out of the kitchen door, but she always returned before the teapot was cold. In Summer, however, her refusal of iced tea was real, for she regarded ice as a poison almost as deadly as cucumbers. She liked her drinks very hot, and one of our hired girls once told me that she could eat a red pepper straight out of the tarragon-vinegar cruet without batting an eye.

Aunt Sophie lived to a great age, and in her last

years was somewhat shaky. One day, in my hearing, my mother asked her how old she was, precisely. She thought sombrely for a minute or two, and then answered that she must be well along toward thirty. This was in 1897 or thereabout, and she had been married to her Jeems some time before the Civil War. Another day my mother asked her why she didn't move back to Calvert county, where she had nephews to look after her, including two preachers, and her pension would make her a grand lady. Again she gave herself to meditation, and then answered simply, " They ain't never no parades in the country."

XX

STRANGE SCENES AND

𝕱𝖆𝖗 𝕻𝖑𝖆𝖈𝖊𝖘

To my brother Charlie and me our father seemed to be a tremendous traveler — indeed, almost a Marco Polo. His trips to buy tobacco ranged from New York State and Connecticut in the North to Cuba in the South, and from the wilds of the Pennsylvania Dutch in the East to Wisconsin in the West, and he also made at least one journey a year to some national potlatch of the Freemasons. In this last mysterious order he never attained to any eminent degree or held any office, but he was enrolled in both of its more sportive and expensive sub-divisions, the Knights Templar and the Shriners. At the orgies of the Knights Templar he appears to have arrayed himself in a uniform resembling that of a rear-admiral, for in the wardrobe

that he took with him there were a long-tailed blue
coat with brass buttons, a velvet chapeau with a
black feather, a silk baldric, and a sword. With
them he carried the red fez that marked him a member of the Ancient Arabic Order of the Nobles of
the Mystic Shrine. Whether or not the Shriners
and the Knights met jointly I don't know, but every time he returned from a muster of either the one
or the other or both he brought back souvenirs of
the convention and the convention town, and these
entertained Charlie and me in a very agreeable way,
and gave us considerable credit, when they were
exhibited, among the boys of the neighborhood.
Other such objects of art and instruction flowed in
from his tobacco-buying trips, so that the house
was always well supplied. I recall especially some
ornate fans from Havana, some jars of guava jelly
from the same place, a large book illustrating the
objects of interest in St. Louis, a photograph of
the bar of the Palmer House in Chicago, showing
(not very clearly) its floor of silver dollars, and a
book of views along the French Broad river in
North Carolina, apparently a souvenir of a visit
to Asheville. My father's traveler's tales were full
of thrills to Charlie and me, especially those that
had to do with bullfighting in Cuba. My mother always protested against them as horrifying and
brutalizing, but we never got enough of them. Or
of his accounts of strange victuals devoured and
enjoyed in far places. I well remember his return

from Kansas City, probably in 1889 or thereabout, with the first news that had ever reached Hollins street of a dessert called floating-island, then apparently a novelty in the world. We made him describe it over and over again, and in the end some effort was made to concoct it in the family kitchen, but that effort came to naught.

Our own travels, down to the end of the eighties, had been very meagre. I had been to Washington often, and Charlie rather less often, but neither of us had ever been far enough from home to have to stay overnight, and neither of us had ever eaten in a dining-car or slept in a sleeper. It was thus a gaudy piece of news when, in the first days of 1891, my grandfather Abhau let it be known that he had some long-neglected relatives in faraway Ohio, and was of a mind to pay them a visit, and take me along. These relatives were new to me, and even my mother had only the vaguest idea of them. They were the descendants, it appeared, of my grandfather's elder sister, who had been so much his senior that she might have been his aunt. On arriving in the United States at some undetermined time in the past, they had bought a lottery ticket on the dock, won a substantial prize (my grandfather's estimate of it ranged up to $20,000), and used the money to buy a couple of fine farms on the borders of the Western Reserve in Ohio, not far from Toledo. My grandfather now proposed to wait upon them, and to stop on the way to see some friends in Cleveland. Himself of no experience as a land traveler (though he had made some sea voyages as a youth), he wanted companionship for the journey, and as his oldest grandchild I got the nomination. It was to me as exciting a surprise as being appointed hostler to Maud S. or president of the Foos candy factory down the alley behind Hollins street.

The preparations for the journey took a couple of weeks, at least. There was, first of all, the matter of my trousseau. What was the climate of Northern Ohio in Winter? No one seemed to know, so my mother proceeded on the assumption that it must be pretty terrible. I thus drew a new and well-padded overcoat from Oehm's Acme Hall, and a new Winter cap with ear-flaps from Mr. Garrigues, the Bible-searching hatter in Baltimore street. Simultaneously, my mother began assembling a large stock of extra-heavy stockings and underclothes, and a great battery of mufflers, mittens and pulse-warmers, and to it was added a pair of massive goloshes. All these things had to be tried on, and some of them were broken in by being worn on my daily journeys to F. Knapp's Institute, for the weather in Baltimore had conveniently turned very cold. But I had no appetite in days so electric for the proceedings at F. Knapp's Institute, and for the first and last time in my school life I came home at the end of January with bad marks. Of the many sciences taught there that month, the only one that I really paid any attention to was geography, and in geography my studies were confined to the State of Ohio. I learned to my satisfaction that Toledo was very near its western frontier, and hence within handy reach of the spot where Sitting Bull had just been killed; that the village we were bound for was only a few miles from Lake Erie, which was twice as large as Chesapeake Bay and probably jammed to the brim with oysters, crabs and shad-fish; and that Cleveland was celebrated all over the world for the magnificence of its Euclid avenue, lined with the *palazzi* of Christian millionaires.

My father entered the picture in the closing days of our preparations. He came home one day with the tickets, including the Pullman tickets, and proceeded to instruct me in the technic of getting to bed at night and up again the next morning on a sleeper. He said that he would see us off at Camden Station, Baltimore, and, if there was time enough, make sure that we were properly stowed, but on the chance that the train would not halt more than a few minutes, he would also request his Washington agent, Mr. Cross, to take a look at us when we reached Washington. We were to travel, of course, by Baltimore & Ohio, and the route ran through Washington and Pittsburgh. I recall nothing of our actual departure, nor of Mr. Cross's inspection in Washington, but I remember very well my father's last-minute fears that I might not have

enough money for possible expenses. My grandfather was the treasurer of the expedition, but inasmuch as he was an ancient of sixty-four there
was always the chance that he might stray off and
get lost, or fall into the hands of bunco-steerers, or
succumb to amnesia, or lose his faculties otherwise,
so it was necessary for me to be financed on my
own. Every time my father thought of another of
these contingencies he gave me another dollar bill,
and urged me to store it safely. By the time we finally shoved off I had them secreted all over my person, and on our return two weeks later I managed
to omit a couple from my settlement of accounts.
With these, after a discreet interval, my brother
Charlie and I bought a new air-rifle. The marks of
its darts are still in the door of a cupboard on the
third floor of Hollins street.

My grandfather and I changed trains at Pittsburgh in the morning, and I had my first glimpse
of a quick-lunch counter. The appearance of a
white waiter behind it was a piquant novelty to me,
for all the restaurants I knew in Baltimore and
Washington were served by blackamoors. I remember that the white coat of this Caucasian appeared to show a certain lack of freshness, but I
forgot the fact when he shoved a huge stack of
wheat cakes before me, with a large pitcher of
syrup beside it, and then politely turned his back.
At home the syrup pitcher was rigorously policed,
and emptying it over a pancake brought a repri-

mand, if not a box of the ears, but in Pittsburgh there seemed to be no rules, so I fell to in a large and freehand way. Once or twice I noticed my grandfather looking at me uneasily, and making as if to speak, but he actually said nothing, and by the time we had to rush for our train the wheat cakes were all gone, and so was most of the syrup. There was also a plate of bread on the table, but I never touched it. As we left I saw the waiter return the slices to a pile on a shelf behind the counter. This gave me a considerable shock, and set me to wondering if the wheat cakes had also passed over some other plate before they reached mine. But I was too full of them to worry much, and after what seemed a very brief ride through country covered with snow, we reached Cleveland and were met by my grandfather's friend, Mr. Landgrebe.

Mr. Landgrebe turned out to be a very pleasant man, and when we got to his house he produced a young son, Karl, slightly older than I, who was agreeable too. How long we stayed in Cleveland I don't know, but it must have been no more than two days. But though the time was short, Mr. Landgrebe showed us all the marvels of the town, including not only the millionaires' elegantly hand-tooled castles along Euclid avenue, with every lawn peopled by a whole herd of cast-iron deers, dogs, cupids and Civil War soldiers, but also the infernal valley wherein the oil of these millionaires was processed and barreled, and a lunatic asylum in which, presumably, the victims of their free competition were confined. My grandfather, a man of tender heart, was much upset by the carryings-on of the Napoleons, George Washingtons and Pontius Pilates in the wards, and shushed me with some asperity whenever I ventured to giggle. It was my first visit to a lunatic asylum, and I enjoyed it in the innocent and thankful manner of any normal boy of ten. There was one poor maniac who entertained me particularly, for his aberration took the form of rolling up thin cylinders of paper and sticking them in his nose and ears. When I got home and told my brother Charlie about the wonderful things I had seen on my travels, he pronounced this lunatic the most wonderful of all. My own first choice, after mature reflection, was the trolley-car that ran past the Landgrebe house in Cleveland. There had been one in Baltimore for six months, but its route lay far from Hollins street, so I knew nothing about it. What struck me especially about the Cleveland car was the loud, whistling buzz that its trolley made as it came down the street. This buzz could be heard *before* the noise of the car itself was detectable — a marvelous indicator, to me, of the unearthly powers of electricity. But Charlie, who was less than nine years old, stuck to the lunatic.

When we finally got to the farms of my grandfather's kinfolk the snow had melted and the whole countryside was an ocean of mud, but by the next morning I had forgotten it, for by that time I was

on easy terms with the boys and girls of the two
houses, and thereafter they showed me what, in
those days, was called an elegant time. I had already spent two Summers at the Vineyard, and
was thus more or less familiar with rural scenes,
but the Vineyard, after all, was only ten miles as
the bird flies from Baltimore, and we were only
Summer sojourners. Here were real farms inhabited by real farming people, and in their daily life
there was something every minute that was new to
me, and full of fascination. I got to know cows and
hogs familiarly, and learned to esteem them. I
helped the younger Almroths (it was at their house
that we stayed) to crack walnuts in the barn, to
fetch up apples from the cellar, and to haul wood
for the great egg-stoves that kept us warm. The
enormous country dinners and suppers, with their
pyramids of fried chicken and their huge platters
of white home-cured hog-meat, swimming in grease,
stoked and enchanted my vast appetite, and I rolled
and wallowed at night in the huge feather-beds.
It was pleasant to go out of a morning with Mr.
Almroth, and watch him (from a safe distance)
blow out stumps with sticks of dynamite. It was
even more pleasant to go into the woods with his
two older sons, and help stack the firewood that
they cut. One day I labored so diligently at this
task that I got into a lather and picked up a sore
throat, and the next day Mrs. Almroth cured it
with a mixture of honey and horse-radish — a pre-

scription that went far beyond anything Dr. Wiley
ever ordered. The days ran by as fast as the Cleveland trolley-car, and the evenings around the
egg-stove in the parlor were trips to a new and romantic world. The youngsters and I stuffed doughnuts, tortured the house dogs and swapped riddles
out of Dr. Ayers' Almanac while my grandfather
and the elders searched the remotest reaches of
their genealogy, and the village schoolma'm (who
boarded out during the term, and was the Almroths' guest that Winter) sat by the lamp on the
table reading a book that seemed to me to be the
thickest on earth. Before we left I sneaked a look
at its title, and when we got back to Baltimore I
borrowed it from the branch of the Pratt Library
in Hollins street, but I never managed to get beyond its first chapter. It was " St. Elmo," by Mrs.
Augusta Jane Evans Wilson.

The Almroths, it appeared, were professing
Christians, and on the Sunday following our arrival they took my grandfather and me to their
church, which stood in the midst of a slough in the
village, and was, as I recall, of some branch or
other of the Lutheran communion. We got in late
and my grandfather diffidently declined to go forward to the Almroth pew, but slipped into a seat
near the door and dragged me with him. But if he
thought to escape the glare of notoriety by that
device he was badly fooled, for at the close of the
proceedings an officer arose near the pulpit and

read a report on the attendance for the day. When he came to " Number of visitors present: two " the whole congregation arose as one Christian and rubber-necked East, West, North and South until we had been located. There was indeed such a hubbub that my grandfather was induced to arise and make a bow. As we were passing out afterward he was introduced to the pastor and all the notables of the congregation, including many who welcomed him in German, for the whole Lake Erie littoral was full of Germans. The pastor eyed me speculatively and seemed about to try me out on the Catechism, but just then a female customer began to whoop up his sermon in high, astounding terms, and I escaped under cover of his grateful thanks.

But of all the incidents of that memorable journey to the Wild West the one that sticks in my recollection most firmly was the last, for it was aided in gaining lodgment by an uneasy conscience. My grandfather and I, on our return, were hardened travelers, and dealt with train conductors, Pullman porters and such-like functionaries in a casual and confident manner. We arrived at Washington very early in the morning, and my father's plenipotentiary, Mr. Cross, was there to meet us. His face, when we sighted him on the platform, was very grave, and he approached us in the manner of a man charged with an unhappy duty. It took the form of handing us a telegram. My grandfather blanched when he saw it, and passed it to me without reading it, for telegrams always alarmed him. I opened it at his nod, and then proceeded to read it to him in a chastened whisper, as follows:

Frank Cross,   Baltimore, February 26, 1891
   Aug. Mencken & Bro.,
     Seventh and G streets, N.W.,
       Washington, D.C.
               Mr. B. L. Mencken is dead.
                          Habighurst.

Mr. Habighurst was my father's bookkeeper, and Mr. B. L. Mencken was my other grandfather, the progenitor, chief justice and captain general of all the American Menckenii. My grandfather Abhau was silent on the short trip back to Baltimore, and remained silent as we boarded a horsecar at Camden Station and rode out to Hollins street, our bags piled beside the driver. We got off at Stricker and Lombard streets, and made for the house across Union Square. As we came to the fishpond in the center of the square I saw that there was a black crêpe on the handle of the doorbell, in token of filial respect to the dead patriarch. The sight made me feel creepy, for that was the first crêpe I had ever seen on a Mencken doorbell. But I was only ten years old, and the emotions of boys of that age are not those of philosophers. For a brief instant, I suppose, I mourned my grandfather, but before we had crossed the cobblestones

of Hollins street a vagrom and wicked thought ran
through my head. I recognized its enormity instantly, but simply could not throttle it. The day
was a Thursday — and they'd certainly not bury
the old man until Sunday. No school tomorrow!

NEWSPAPER

DAYS

1899-1906

H. L. MENCKEN

NOTE

Some of these chapters have appeared, either wholly or in part, in the *New Yorker*. The author offers his thanks to the editors of that magazine for permission to reprint them.

PREFACE

THE RECOLLECTIONS here embalmed, I should say
at once, have nothing in common with the high,
astounding tales of journalistic derring-do that
had a considerable run several years ago, after the
devourers of best-sellers had begun to tire of medical memoirs. In the second half of the period here
covered I became a city editor, which is to say, a
fellow of high mightiness in a newspaper office, and
at the very end I was lifted by one of fate's ironies
into even higher dignities, but the narrative has
principally to do with my days as a reporter, when
I was young, goatish and full of an innocent delight in the world. My adventures in that character, save maybe in one or two details, were hardly
extraordinary; on the contrary they seem to me
now, looking back upon them nostalgically, to have
been marked by an excess of normalcy. Nevertheless, they had their moments — in fact, they were

made up, subjectively, of one continuous, unrelent-
ing, almost delirious moment — and when I revive them now it is mainly to remind myself and
inform historians that a newspaper reporter, in
those remote days, had a grand and gaudy time of
it, and no call to envy any man.

In the long, busy years following I had experiences of a more profound and even alarming nature, and if the mood were on me I could fill a book
with inside stuff almost fit to match the high,
astounding tales aforesaid. I roamed, in the practise of my trade, from the river Jordan in the East
to Hollywood in the West, and from the Orkney
Islands in the North to Morocco and the Spanish
Main in the South, and, like every other journalist,
I met, listened to and smelled all sorts of magnificoes, including Presidents and Vice-Presidents,
generals and admirals, bishops and archbishops,
murderers and murderesses, geniuses both scientific
and literary, movie and stage stars, heavyweight
champions of the world, Class A and Class B royal-
ties, judges and hangmen, millionaires and labor
goons, and vast hordes of other notables, including
most of the recognized Cæsars and Shakespeares of
journalism. I edited both newspapers and magazines, some of them successes and some of them not,
and got a close, confidential view of the manner in
which opinion is formulated and merchanted on
this earth. My own contributions to the mess ran
to millions of words, and I came to know intimately

many of its most revered confectioners. More than
once I have staggered out of editorial conferences
dripping cold sweat, and wondering dizzily how
God got along for so many years without the *New
Republic* and the Manchester *Guardian*. And at
other times I have marvelled that the human race
did not revolt against the imposture, dig up the
carcass of Johann Gutenberg, and heave it to the
buzzards and hyenas in some convenient zoo.

A newspaper man in active practise finds it hard
to remain a mere newspaper man: he is constantly
beset by temptations to try other activities, and if
he manages to resist them it takes a kind of fortitude that less protean men, badgered only by their
hormones and their creditors, never have need of.
I was born, happily, with no more public spirit
than a cat, and have thus found it relatively easy
to throw off all the commoner lures, but there have
been times when the sirens fetched me clearly below
the belt, and I did some wobbling. In 1912, though
no one will ever believe it, I was groomed surreptitiously as a dark horse for the Democratic Vice-
Presidential nomination, and if one eminent American statesman, *X*, had not got tight at the last
minute, and another, *Y*, kept unaccountably sober,
I might have become immortal. Two years later I
was offered $30,000 cash, deposited in bank to my
order, to write anti-Prohibition speeches for the
illiterates in the two Houses of Congress. A little
further on an Episcopal bishop asked me to tackle

and try to throw a nascent convert, female and rich, who had thrice slipped out of his hands at the very brink of the font. Another time the prophet of a new religion, then very prosperous in the Middle West, offered to consecrate me as a bishop myself, with power to bind and loose; and almost simultaneously I was arrested on Boston Common on a charge of vending obscene literature to the young gentlemen of Harvard. I have seen something of the horrors of war, and much too much of the worse horrors of peace. On five several occasions I have been offered the learned degree of *legum doctor*, though few men are less learned in the law than I am, or have less respect for it; and at other times I have been invited to come in and be lynched by the citizens of three of the great Christian states of the Union.

Such prodigies and monstrosities I could pile up for hours, along with a lot of instructive blabbing about what this or that immortal once told me off the record, for I have had the honor of encountering three Presidents of the United States in their cups, not to mention sitting Governors of all the states save six. But I bear in mind Sir Thomas Overbury's sneer at the fellow who " chooseth rather to be counted a spy than not a politician, and maintains his reputation by naming great men familiarly," and so hold my peace: let some larval Ph.D. dig the dirt out of my papers marked " Strictly Private: Destroy Unread " after I shove

off for bliss eternal. In the present book my only
purpose is to try to recreate for myself, and for
any one who may care to follow me, the gaudy life
that young newspaper reporters led in the major
American cities at the turn of the century. I believed then, and still believe today, that it was the
maddest, gladdest, damndest existence ever enjoyed by mortal youth. At a time when the respectable bourgeois youngsters of my generation were
college freshmen, oppressed by simian sophomores
and affronted with balderdash daily and hourly by
chalky pedagogues, I was at large in a wicked seaport of half a million people, with a front seat at
every public show, as free of the night as of the
day, and getting earfuls and eyefuls of instruction
in a hundred giddy arcana, none of them taught in
schools. On my twenty-first birthday, by all orthodox cultural standards, I probably reached my all-
time low, for the heavy reading of my teens had
been abandoned in favor of life itself, and I did
not return seriously to the lamp until a time near
the end of this record. But it would be an exaggeration to say that I was ignorant, for if I neglected
the humanities I was meanwhile laying in all the
worldly wisdom of a police lieutenant, a bartender,
a shyster lawyer, or a midwife. And it would certainly be idiotic to say that I was not happy. The
illusion that swathes and bedizens journalism,
bringing in its endless squads of recruits, was still
full upon me, and I had yet to taste the sharp teeth

of responsibility. Life was arduous, but it was gay
and carefree. The days chased one another like
kittens chasing their tails.

Whether or not the young journalists of today
live so spaciously is a question that I am not competent to answer, for my contacts with them, of late
years, have been rather scanty. They undoubtedly
get a great deal more money than we did in 1900,
but their freedom is much less than ours was, and
they somehow give me the impression, seen at a distance, of complacency rather than intrepidity. In
my day a reporter who took an assignment was
wholly on his own until he got back to the office, and
even then he was little molested until his copy was
turned in at the desk; today he tends to become
only a homunculus at the end of a telephone wire,
and the reduction of his observations to prose is
commonly farmed out to literary castrati who
never leave the office, and hence never feel the wind
of the world in their faces or see anything with their
own eyes. I well recall my horror when I heard,
for the first time, of a journalist who had laid in
a pair of what were then called bicycle pants and
taken to golf: it was as if I had encountered a stud-
horse with his hair done up in frizzes, and pink
bowknots peeking out of them. It seemed, in some
vague way, ignominious, and even a bit indelicate.
I was shocked almost as much when I first heard of
reporters joining labor unions, and describing
themselves as wage slaves. The underlying ideol-

ogy here, of course, was anything but new, for I
doubt that there has ever been a competent reporter in history who did not regard the proprietors of his paper as sordid rascals, all dollars and
no sense. But it is one thing (a) to curl the lip
over such wretches, and quite another thing (b) to
bellow and beat the breast under their atrocities,
just as it is one thing (a^2) to sass a cruel city editor
with, so to speak, the naked hands, and another
thing (b^2) to confront him from behind a phalanx
of government agents and labor bravoes. The a
operations are easy to reconcile with the old-time
journalist's concept of himself as a free spirit and
darling of the gods, licensed by his high merits
to ride and deride the visible universe; the b's must
suggest inevitably a certain unhappy self-distrust,
perhaps not without ground.

Like its companion volume, " Happy Days "
(1940) this book is mainly true, but with occasional stretchers. I have checked my recollections
whenever possible, and found them reasonably accurate. For the rest, I must throw myself upon the
bosom of that " friendly and judicious reader " to
whom Charles Lamb dedicated the Essays of Elia
— that understanding fellow, male or female, who
refuses to take " everything perversely in the absolute and literal sense," but gives it " a fair construction, as to an after-dinner conversation."

BALTIMORE, 1941.   H. L. M.

I

ALLEGRO

CON BRIO

My father died on Friday, January 13, 1899, and was buried on the ensuing Sunday. On the Monday evening immediately following, having shaved with care and put on my best suit of clothes, I presented myself in the city-room of the old Baltimore *Morning Herald*, and applied to Max Ways, the city editor, for a job on his staff. I was eighteen years, four months and four days old, wore my hair longish and parted in the middle, had on a high stiff collar and an Ascot cravat, and weighed something on the minus side of 120 pounds. I was thus hardly a spectacle to exhilarate a city editor, but Max was an amiable fellow and that night he was in an extra-amiable mood, for (as he told me afterward) there was a good dinner under his belt, with a couple of globes of malt to wash it down, and all of his reporters, so far as he was aware, were transiently sober. So he received me very politely, and even cordially. Had I any newspaper experience? The reply, alas, had to be no. What was my education? I was a graduate of the Baltimore Polytechnic. What considerations had turned my fancy toward the newspaper business? All that I could say was that it seemed to be a sort of celestial call: I was busting with literary ardors and had been writing furiously for what, at eighteen, was almost an age — maybe four, or even five years. Writing what — prose or verse? Both. Anything published? I had to play dead here, for my bibliography, to date, was confined to a couple of anonymous poems in the Baltimore *American* — a rival paper, and hence probably not admired.

Max looked me over ruminatively — I had been standing all the while — and made the reply that city editors had been making to young aspirants since the days of the first Washington hand-press. There was, unhappily, no vacancy on the staff. He would take my name, and send for me in case some catastrophe unforeseen — and, as I gathered, almost unimaginable — made one. I must have drooped visibly, for the kindly Max at once thought of something better. Did I have a job? Yes, I was working for my Uncle Henry, now the sole heir and assign of my father's old tobacco firm of Aug. Mencken & Bro. Well, I had better keep that job, but maybe it might be an idea for me to

drop in now and then of an evening, say between
seven thirty and seven forty-five. Nothing, of
course, could be promised; in fact, the odds against
anything turning up were appalling. But if I
would present myself at appropriate intervals
there might be a chance, if it were God's will, to try
me out, soon or late, on something commensurate
with my undemonstrated talents. Such trial
flights, it was unnecessary to mention, carried no
emolument. They added a lot to a city editor's already heavy cargo of cares and anxieties, and out
of the many that were called only a few were ever
chosen.

I retired nursing a mixture of disappointment
and elation, but with the elation quickly besting
the disappointment — and the next night, precisely at seven thirty-one, I was back. Max waved
me away without parley: he was busy jawing an
office-boy. The third night he simply shook his
head, and so on the fourth, fifth, sixth and seventh.
On the eighth — or maybe it was the ninth or tenth
— he motioned me to wait while he finished thumbing through a pile of copy, and then asked suddenly: " Do you ever read the *Herald?* " When I
answered yes, he followed with " What do you think
of it? " This one had all the appearance of a trap,
and my heart missed a couple of beats, but the holy
saints were with me. " I think," I said, " that it is
much better written than the *Sunpaper.*" I was to
learn later that Max smelled something artful

here, but, as always, he held himself well, and all I could observe was the faint flutter of a smile across his face. At length he spoke. " Come back," he said, " tomorrow night."

I came back, you may be sure — and found him missing, for he had forgotten that it was his night off. The next night I was there again — and found him too busy to notice me. And so the night following, and the next, and the next. To make an end, this went on for four weeks, night in and night out, Mondays, Tuesdays, Wednesdays, Thursdays, Fridays, Saturdays and Sundays. A tremendous blizzard came down upon Baltimore, and for a couple of days the trolley-cars were stalled, but I hoofed it ever hopefully to the *Herald* office, and then hoofed it sadly home. There arrived eventually, after what seemed a geological epoch by my calendar, the evening of Thursday, February 23, 1899. I found Max reading copy, and for a few minutes he did not see me. Then his eyes lifted, and he said casually : " Go out to Govanstown, and see if anything is happening there. We are supposed to have a Govanstown correspondent, but he hasn't been heard from for six days."

The percussion must have been tremendous, for I remember nothing about getting to Govanstown. It is now a part of Baltimore, but in 1899 it was only a country village, with its own life and tribulations. No cop was in sight when I arrived, but I found the volunteer firemen playing pinochle in their engine-house. The blizzard had blockaded their front door with a drift fifteen feet high, but they had dug themselves out, and were now lathering for a fire, though all the water-plugs in the place were still frozen. They had no news save their hopes. Across the glacier of a street I saw two lights — a bright one in a drugstore and a dim one in a funeral parlor. The undertaker, like nearly all the rest of Govanstown, was preparing to go to bed, and when I routed him out and he came downstairs in his pants and undershirt it was only to say that he had no professional business in hand. The druggist, hugging a red-hot egg-stove behind his colored bottles, was more productive. The town cop, he said, had just left in a two-horse buggy to assist in a horse-stealing case at Kingsville, a long drive out the Belair pike, and the Improved Order of Red Men had postponed their oyster-supper until March 6. When I got back to the *Herald* office, along toward eleven o'clock, Max instructed me to forget the Red Men and write the horse-stealing. There was a vacant desk in a far corner, and at it, for ten minutes, I wrote and tore up, wrote and tore up. Finally there emerged the following:

A horse, a buggy and several sets of harness, valued in all at about $250, were stolen last night from the stable of Howard Quinlan, near Kingsville. The county police are at work on the case, but so far no trace of either thieves or booty has been found.

7

Max gave only a grunt to my copy, but as I was leaving the office, exhausted but exultant, he called me back, and handed me a letter to the editor demanding full and friendly publicity, on penalty of a boycott, for an exhibition of what was then called a kinetoscope or cineograph. " A couple of lines," he said, " will be enough. Nearly everybody has seen a cineograph by now." I wrote:

At Otterbein Memorial U.B. Church, Roland and Fifth avenues, Hampden, Charles H. Stanley and J. Albert Loose entertained a large audience last night with an exhibition of war scenes by the cineograph.

I was up with the milkman the next morning to search the paper, and when I found both of my pieces, exactly as written, there ran such thrills through my system as a barrel of brandy and 100,-000 volts of electricity could not have matched. Somehow or other I must have done my duty by Aug. Mencken & Bro., for my uncle apparently noticed nothing, but certainly my higher cerebral centers were not focussed on them. That night I got to the *Herald* office so early that Max had not come back from dinner. When he appeared he looked me over thoughtfully, and suggested that it might be a good plan to try my talents on a village adjacent to Govanstown, Waverly by name. It was, he observed, a poor place, full of Methodists and Baptists who seldom cut up, but now and then a horse ran away or a pastor got fired. Reaching it after a long search in the snow, and raking it

8

from end to end, I turned up two items — one an Epworth League entertainment, and the other a lecture for nearby farmers, by title (I have the clipping before me), "Considering the Present Low Price of Hay, Would It Not Be Advisable to Lessen the Acreage of Hay for Market?" Max showed no enthusiasm for either, but after I had finished writing them he handed me an amateur press-agent's handout about a new Quaker school and directed me to rewrite it. It made twenty-eight lines in the paper next morning, and lifted me beyond the moon to Orion. On the night following Max introduced me to two or three reporters, and told them that I was a youngster trying for a job. My name, he said, was Macon. They greeted me with considerable reserve.

Of the weeks following I recall definitely but one thing — that I never seemed to get enough sleep. I was expected to report at the cigar factory of Aug. Mencken & Bro. at eight o'clock every morning, which meant that I had to turn out at seven. My day there ran officially to five thirty, but not infrequently my uncle detained me to talk about family affairs, for my father had died intestate and his estate was in process of administration, with two sets of lawyers discovering mare's nests from time to time. Thus it was often six o'clock before I escaped, and in the course of the next hour or so I had to get home, change my clothes, bolt my dinner, and return downtown to the *Herald* office. For a couple of weeks Max kept me at my harrying of the remoter suburbs — a job, as I afterward learned, as distasteful to ripe reporters as covering a fashionable church-wedding or a convention of the W.C.T.U. I ranged from Catonsville in the far west to Back River in the east, and from Tuxedo Park in the north to Mt. Winans in the south. Hour after hour I rode the suburban trolleys, and one night, as I recall uncomfortably over all these years, my fares at a nickel a throw came to sixty cents, which was more than half my day's pay from Aug. Mencken & Bro. Max had said nothing about an expense account, and I was afraid to ask. Once, returning from a dismal village called Gardenville, a mile or two northeast of the last electric light, I ventured to ask him how far my diocese ran in that direction. "You are supposed to keep on out the road," he said, "until you meet the Philadelphia reporters coming in." This was an ancient Baltimore newspaper wheeze, but it was new to me, and I was to enjoy it a great deal better when I heard it worked off on my successors.

But my exploration of the fringes of Baltimore, though it came near being exhaustive, was really not long drawn out, for in a little while Max began to hand me city assignments of the kind that no one else wanted — installations of new evangelical pastors, meetings of wheelmen, interviews with bores just back from Europe, the Klondike or

Oklahoma, orgies of one sort or another at the Y.M.C.A., minor political rallies, concerts, funerals, and so on. Most of my early clippings perished in the great Baltimore fire of 1904, but a few survived, and I find from them that I covered a number of stories that would seem as antediluvian today as a fight between two brontosauri — for example, the showing of a picture-play by Alexander Black (a series of lantern-slides with a thin thread of banal recitative), and a chalk-talk by Frank Beard. When it appeared that I knew something of music, I was assigned to a long series of organ recitals in obscure churches, vocal and instrumental recitals in even more obscure halls, and miscellaneous disturbances of the peace in lodge-rooms and among the German singing societies. Within the space of two weeks I heard one violinist, then very popular in Baltimore, play Raff's Cavatina no less than eight times. The *Herald's* music critic in those days, an Englishman named W. G. Owst, was a very indolent fellow, and when he discovered that I could cover such uproars without making any noticeable bulls, he saw to it that I got more and more of them. Finally, I was entrusted with an assault upon Mendelssohn's " Elijah " by the Baltimore Oratorio Society — and suffered a spasm of stage fright that was cured by dropping into the Pratt Library before the performance, and doing a little precautionary reading.

Thus the Winter ran into Spring, and I began

to think of myself as almost a journalist. So far, to be sure, I had been entrusted with no spot news, and Max had never sent me out to help a regular member of the staff, but he was generous with his own advice, and I quickly picked up the jargon and ways of thought of the city-room. In this acclimatization I was aided by the device that had helped me to fathom Mendelssohn's " Elijah " and has always been my recourse in time of difficulty : what I couldn't learn otherwise I tried to learn by reading. Unhappily, the almost innumerable texts on journalism that now serve aspirants were then still unwritten, and I could find, in fact, only one formal treatise on the subject at the Pratt Library. It was " Steps Into Journalism," by E. L. Shuman of the Chicago *Tribune*, and though it was a primitive in its class it was very clearly and sensibly written, and I got a great deal of useful information out of it. Also, I read all of the newspaper fiction then on paper — for example, Richard Harding Davis's " Gallegher and Other Stories," Jesse Lynch Williams's " The Stolen Story and Other Stories," and Elizabeth G. Jordan's " Tales of the City-Room," the last two of which had but lately come out.[1]

How I found time for this reading I can't tell

[1] It must have been a little later that I read " With Kitchener to Khartoum," " From Capetown to Ladysmith " and the other books of George W. Steevens, of the London *Mail*. They made a powerful impression on me, and I still believe that Steevens was the greatest newspaper reporter who ever lived.

you, for I was kept jumping by my two jobs, but find it I did. One night, sitting in the city-room waiting for an assignment, I fell asleep, and the thoughtful Max suggested that I take one night off a week, and mentioned Sunday. The next Sunday I stayed in bed until noon, and returned to it at 8 p.m., and thereafter I was ready for anything. As the Spring drifted on my assignments grew better and better, and when the time came for high-school commencements I covered all of them. There were five in those days, beginning with that of the City College and ending with that of the Colored High-school, and I heard the Mayor of Baltimore unioad precisely the same speech at each. Max, who knew the man, complimented me on making his observations sound different every time, and even more or less intelligent, and I gathered the happy impression that my days as an unpaid volunteer were nearing their end. But a city editor of that costive era, at least in Baltimore, could take on a new man only by getting rid of an old one, and for a month or so longer I had to wait. Finally, some old-timer or other dropped out, and my time had come. Max made a little ceremony of my annunciation, though no one else was present. My salary, he said, would be $7 a week, with the hope of an early lift to $8 if I made good. I would have the use of a book of passes on the trolley-cars, and might turn in expense-accounts to cover any actual outlays. There was, at the moment, no typewriter available for me, but he had hopes of extracting one from Nachman, the business manager, in the near future. This was followed by some good advice. *Imprimis*, never trust a cop: whenever possible, verify his report. *Item*, always try to get in early copy: the first story to reach the city-desk has a much better chance of being printed in full than the last. *Item*, be careful about dates, names, ages, addresses, figures of every sort. *Item*, keep in mind at all times the dangers of libel. Finally, don't be surprised if you go to a house for information, and are invited to lift it from the *Sun* of the next morning. "The *Sun* is the Bible of Baltimore, and has almost a monopoly on many kinds of news. But don't let that fact discourage you. You can get it too if you dig hard enough, and always remember this: any *Herald* reporter who is worth a damn can write rings around a *Sun* reporter."

This last was very far from literally true, as I was to discover when I came to cover stories in competition with such *Sun* reporters as Dorsey Guy and Harry West, but there was nevertheless a certain plausibility in it, for the *Sun* laid immense stress upon accuracy, and thus fostered a sober, matter-of-fact style in its men. The best of them burst through those trammels, but the rank and file tended to write like bookkeepers. As for Max, he greatly favored a more imaginative and colorful manner. He had been a very good reporter himself, with not only a hand for humor but also a trick of pathos, and he tried to inspire his slaves to the same. Not many of them were equal to the business, but all of them save a few poor old automata tried, and as a result the *Herald* was rather briskly written, and its general direction was toward the New York *Sun*, then still scintillating under the impulse of Charles A. Dana, rather than toward the Baltimore *Sun* and the *Congressional Record*. It was my good fortune, during my first week on the staff, to turn up the sort of story that Max liked especially — the sudden death of a colored street preacher on the street, in the midst of a hymn. I was not present at the ringside, and had to rely on the cops for the facts, but I must have got a touch of drama into my report, for Max was much pleased, and gave me, as a reward, a pass to a performance of Rose Sydell's London Blondes.

I had gathered from the newspaper fiction mentioned a few pages back that the typical American city editor was a sort of cross between an ice-wagon driver and a fire-alarm, "full of strange oaths" and imprecations, and given to firing whole files of men at the drop of a hat. But if that monster actually existed in the Republic, it was surely not in the Baltimore *Herald* office. Max, of course, was decently equipped for his art and mystery: he could swear loudly enough on occasion and had a pretty hand for shattering invective, but most of the time, even when he was sorely tried, he kept to good humor and was polite to one and all. Whenever I made a mess of a story, which was certainly often enough, he summoned me to his desk and pointed out my blunders. When I came in with a difficult story, confused and puzzled, he gave me quick and clear directions, and they always straightened me out. Observing his operations with the sharp eyes of youth, I began to understand the curious equipment required of a city editor. He had to be an incredible amalgam of army officer and literary critic, diplomat and jail warden, psychologist and fortune-teller. If he could not see around corners and through four or five feet of brick he was virtually blind, and if he could not hear overtones audible normally only to dogs and children he was almost deaf. His knowledge of his town, as he gathered experience, combined that of a police captain, an all-night hackman, and a priest in a rowdy parish. He was supposed to know the truth about everyone and everything, even though he seldom printed it, and one of his most useful knowledges — in fact, he used it every day — was his knowledge of the most probable whereabouts of every person affected with a public interest, day or night.

Max had these skills, and many more. How he would have made out on the larger papers of a later period, with their incessant editions, I do not attempt to guess, but in his time and place he was a very competent man, and had the respect as well as the affection of his staff. In person he was of

middle height, with light hair that was beginning
to fall out, and an equator that had already begun
to bulge. What remained of his hair he wore
longish, in what was then called the football style.
He affected rolling collars, and sometimes wore a
Windsor tie. His colored shirts, in the manner of
the day, were ironed to shine like glass, and his
clothes were of somewhat advanced cut. We
younger reporters modelled ourselves upon him in
dress as in mien. The legends that played about
him were mainly not of a professional nature, but
romantic. He was a bachelor, and was supposed to
be living in sin with a beautiful creature who occasionally took a drop too much, and exposed him to
the embarrassment of her caterwauling. Whether
or not that creature had any actual existence I
can't tell you: all I can say is that I never saw her,
and that the only time I ever visited Max in his
quarters (he was laid up with pink-eye) I found
him living *a cappella* upstairs of a French restaurant, and waited on by the proprietor's well-sea-
soned and far from aphrodisiac wife.[2]

It was a pleasant office that I found myself en-

2 When he quit the *Herald* Max went into politics, and lived
to be one of the Democratic bosses of Baltimore. But the first
time he ran for elective office he was beaten, mainly, so it was reported, because many voters assumed from his name that he was
a Jew, and others suspected that he might even be a Chinaman.
He was actually of Scotch-Irish, Welsh, English and Pennsylvania German stock. He later married the charming secretary
of the Governor of Maryland, and became the father of a son
and a daughter who followed him into the newspaper business.
He died in 1923.

tering. Many of the reporters, to be sure, were
rummy old-timers who were of small ability and no
diligence, but they were all at least amiable fellows,
and working beside them were some youngsters of
superior quality. The *Herald* Building was new,
and its fifth-floor city-room was one of the most
comfortable and convenient that I have ever seen,
even to this day. But in many respects it would
seem primitive now: it had, for example, but two
telephones — one belonging to each of the two companies that then fought for subscribers in Baltimore. Both were Paleozoic instruments attached
to the wall, and no one ever used them if it could be
avoided. There was no telephone on the city
editor's desk until my own time in that office, beginning in 1903. The office library, save for a dog's-
eared encyclopedia with several volumes missing,
was made up wholly of government reports, and
the only man who ever used it was an old fellow who
had the job of compiling cattle and provision
prices. He finished work every day at about 5 p.m.
and spent an hour reading in the encyclopedia.
There was no index of the paper, and no office
morgue. The city editor kept a clipping file of his
own, and when it failed him he had to depend upon
the shaky memories of the older reporters.

The city staff, save for such early birds as the
court reporter, came to work at half an hour after
noon, and every man was responsible for his bailiwick until 11 at night. The city editor himself be-

gan work an hour earlier and worked an hour or so later. There were no bulldogs or other early editions. The first mail edition did not close until after midnight. In consequence, there was no hurry about getting stories on paper, except very late ones. Rewrite men were unheard of. Every reporter, no matter how remote the scene of his story, came back to the office and wrote it himself. If he lagged, his copy was taken from him page by page, and he was urged on by the grunting and growling of the city editor, who was his own chief copy-reader, and usually wrote the head on the leading local story of the night. A great deal of copy was still written by hand, for there were not enough typewriters in the office to go round, and every time Nachman, the business manager, was asked to buy another he went on like a man stabbed with poniards. But every reporter had a desk, and every desk was equipped with a spittoon. This was a great convenience to me, for I had acquired the sinful habit of tobacco-chewing in my father's cigar factory, and am, in fact, still more or less in its loathsome toils.

The office was kept pretty clean by Bill Christian, a barber who had got the job of building superintendent because Colonel Cunningham, the managing editor, liked his tonsorial touch. Bill was allergic to work himself, but he rode herd diligently on his staff of colored scavengers, and the whole editorial floor was strangely spick and span

for that time. Even the colonel's own den was ex-
cavated at least twice a month, and its accumulation of discarded newspapers hauled out. Bill
failed, however, to make any progress against the
army of giant cockroaches that had moved in when
the building was opened, three or four years before.
On dull nights the copy-readers would detail office-
boys to corral half a dozen of these monsters, and
then race them across the city-room floor, guiding
them with walking-sticks. The sport required some
skill, for if a jockey pressed his nag too hard he
was apt to knock off its hind legs.

II

DRILL FOR A

ROOKIE

My first regular assignment as a reporter was South Baltimore, or, to speak technically, the Southern police district. It was, as I shall remark again in Chapter XVIII, a big territory, and there was always something doing in it, but though my memories of it are copious and melodramatic, I must have spent only a few weeks in it, for by the end of the Spring, as I find by a promenade through the *Herald's* files, I was covering Aframerican razor-parties in the Northwestern, which was almost as black as Mississippi, and making occasional dips into the Western, which embraced the largest and busiest of Baltimore's five Tenderloins.

In those days a reporter who had durable legs

and was reasonably sober tended to see a varied
service, for it was not unusual for one of his elders
to succumb to the jug and do a vanishing act.
More than once during my first weeks, after turning in my own budget of assaults, fires, drownings
and other such events from the Southern, I was
sent out at eleven o'clock at night to find a lost colleague of the Eastern or Northeastern, and pump
his news out of him, if he had any. It was by the
same route, in July, that I found myself promoted
to the Central, which was the premier Baltimore
district, journalistically speaking, for it included
the busiest of the police courts, a downtown hospital, police headquarters, the city jail, and the
morgue. The regular man there had turned up at
the office one noon so far gone in rum that Max relieved him of duty, and I was gazetted to his place
as a means of shaming him, for I was still the
youngest reporter in the office. When he continued
in his cups the day following I was retained as his
locum tenens, and when he went on to a third day
he was reduced to the Northern police district, the
Siberia of Baltimore, and I found myself his heir.

This man, though we eventually became good
friends, resented his demotion so bitterly that for
weeks he refused to speak to me, but I was too busy
in my new bailiwick to pay any attention to him.
Its police court was the liveliest in town, and had
the smartest and most colorful magistrate, Gene
Grannan by name. He was always willing to help

the press by developing the dramatic content of the cases before him, and during my first week he thus watered and manured for me a couple of stories that delighted Max, and boosted my own stock. Such stories were almost a *Herald* monopoly, for *Sun* reporters were hobbled by their paper's craze for mathematical accuracy, and most *American* reporters were too stupid to recognize good stuff when they saw it. Max helped by inventing likely minor assignments for me, and one of them I still remember. It was a wedding in a shabby street given over to second-hand shops run by Polish Jews and patronized by sailors. The bride had written in demanding publicity, and I was sent to see her — partly as a means of gently hazing a freshman, but also on the chance that there might be a picturesque story in her. In the filthy shop downstairs her father directed me to the second floor, and when I climbed the stairs I found her in process of being dressed by her mother. She was standing in the middle of the floor with nothing on save a diaphanous vest and a flouncy pair of drawers. Never having seen a bride so close to the altogether before, I was somewhat upset, but she and her mother were quite calm, and loaded me with all the details of the impending ceremony. I wrote the story at length, but Max stuck it on his " If " hook, and there it died.

But such romantic interludes were not frequent. My days, like those of any other police reporter, were given over mainly to harsher matters — murders, assaults and batteries, street accidents, robberies, suicides, and so on. I well recall my first suicide, for the victim was a lovely young gal who had trusted a preacher's son too far, and then swallowed poison: she looked almost angelic lying on her parlor floor, with a couple of cops badgering her distracted mother. I remember, too, my first autopsy at the morgue — a most trying recreation for a hot Summer day — , and my first palaver with a burglar, and my first ride with the cops in a patrol-wagon, but for some reason or other my first murder has got itself forgotten. The young doctors at the City Hospital (now the Mercy Hospital) were always productive, for they did a heavy trade in street and factory accidents, and a very fair one in attempted suicides. In those days carbolic acid was the favorite drug among persons who yearned for the grave, just as bichloride of mercury was to be the favorite of a decade later, and I saw many of its customers brought in — their lips swollen horribly, and their eyes full of astonishment that they were still alive. Also, I saw people with their legs cut off, their arms torn off, their throats cut, their eyes gouged out. It was shocking for a little while, but then no more. Attached to the City Hospital was the first Pasteur Institute ever set up in America, and to it came patients from all over the South. It was in charge of an old doctor named Keirle, and usually he managed to save them, but now and then one of them reached him too late, and died of rabies in frightful agony. He let me in on several of these death scenes, with the poor patient strapped to the bed and the nurses stepping warily. When the horror became unendurable the old doctor would take over with his hypodermic. He was a humane and admirable man, one of the few actual altruists that I have ever known, and I marvel that the Baltimore which has monuments to the founder of the Odd Fellows and to the president of a third-rate railroad has never thought to honor itself by erecting one to his memory.

On July 28, 1899, when I was precisely eighteen years, ten months and sixteen days old, I saw my first hanging; more, it was a hanging of the very first chop, for no less than four poor blackamoors were stretched at once. When I was assigned to it as legman for one of the older reporters I naturally suffered certain unpleasant forebodings, but the performance itself did not shake me, though one of the condemned lost his black cap in going through the trap, and the contortions of his face made a dreadful spectacle. The affair was staged in the yard of the city jail, and there was a large gathering of journalists, some of them from other cities, for quadruple hangings, then as now, were fancy goods. I went through the big iron gate at 5 a.m., and found that at least a dozen colleagues had been on watch all night. Some of them had sustained themselves with drafts from a bottle, and were already wobbling. When, after hours of howling by relays of colored evangelists, the four candidates were taken out and hanged, two of these bibbers and six or eight other spectators fell in swoons, and had to be evacuated by the cops. The sheriff of Baltimore was required by law to spring the trap, and he had prepared himself for that office by resorting to a bottle of his own. When it was performed he was assisted out of the jail yard by his deputies, and departed at once for Atlantic City, where he dug in for a week of nightmare.

I saw a good many hangings after that, some in Baltimore and the rest in the counties of Maryland. The county sheriffs always took aboard so much liquor for the occasion that they were virtually helpless: they could, with some help, pull the trap, but they were quite unable to tie the knot, bind the candidate, or carry off the other offices of the occasion. These were commonly delegated to Joe Heine, a gloomy German who had been chief deputy sheriff in Baltimore for many years, and was such a master of all the technics of his post that no political upheaval could touch him. So far as I know, Joe never actually put a man to death in his life, for that was the duty of the sheriff, but he traveled the counties tying knots and making the condemned ready, and there was never a slip when he officiated. I missed the great day of his career, which fell in 1904 or thereabout, for I was becom-

ing bored with hangings by that time, and when a
nearby county sheriff invited me to one as his private guest and well-wisher, I gave my ticket to my
brother Charlie. This was Charlie's first experience and he saw a swell show indeed, for the candidate, a colored giant, fought Joe and the sheriff on
the scaffold, knocked out the county cops who came
to their aid, leaped down into the bellowing crowd,
broke out of the jail yard, and took to an adjacent
forest. It was an hour or more before he was run
down and brought back. By that time all the fight
had oozed out of him, and Joe and the sheriff
turned him off with quiet elegance.

But a reporter chiefly remembers, not such routine themes of his art as hangings, fires and murders, which come along with dispiriting monotony,
but the unprecedented novelties that occasionally
inspire him, some of them gorgeous and others only
odd. Perhaps the most interesting story I covered
in my first six months had to do with the purloining
of a cadaver from a medical college. The burglar
was the head *Diener* of the dissecting-room, and he
packed the body in a barrel and shipped it to a colleague in the upper Middle West, where there was
a shortage of such provisions at the time. Hot
weather coming on *en route*, it was discovered, and
for a week we had a gaudy murder mystery. When
the *Diener* shut off the uproar by confessing, it
turned out that the maximum punishment he could
be given, under the existing Maryland law, passed

in 1730, was sixty days in the House of Correction.
On his return to duty the medical students welcomed him with a beer party that lasted forty-
eight hours, and he boasted that he had been stealing and shipping bodies for years. But the cops,
discouraged, did nothing about it.

At a somewhat later time, after I had forsaken
police reporting, the moral inadequacy of the ancient Maryland statutes was revealed again. This
time the culprit was a Methodist clergyman who
operated one of the vice crusades that then afflicted
all the big cities of the East. The cops, of course,
were violently against him, for they could see nothing wrong about honest women making honest livings according to their talents. When the pastor
charged that they pooh-poohed him because they
were taking bribes from the girls they determined
to get him, and to that end sneaked a spy into the
Y.M.C.A. One night soon afterward the pastor
visited the place with a Christian young man, and
the spy, concealed in a cupboard, caught the two
in levantine deviltries. The former was collared at
once, and the State's attorney sent for. Unhappily, he had to advise the poor cops that the acts
they laid to their prisoner were not forbidden by
Maryland law, which was singularly tolerant in
sexual matters. The maximum penalty it then
provided for adultery, however brutal and deliberate, was $10 fine, with no alternative of imprison-
ment, and there was no punishment at all for forni-

cation, or for any of its non-Euclidian variations.
The cops were thus stumped, but they quickly
resolved their dilemma by concealing it from the
scared pastor, and giving him two hours to get out
of town. He departed leaving a wife and five children behind him, and has never been heard from
since. The Legislature being in session, the cops
then went to Annapolis and begged it to sharpen
the laws. It responded by forbidding, under heavy
penalties, a list of offenses so long and so bizarre
that some of them are not even recorded in Krafft-
Ebing.

I myself, while still assigned to the Central district, covered a case that well illustrated the humanity of the old Maryland statute. The accused
was a man who had run away from Pittsburgh with
another man's wife, and they had come to Baltimore in the drawing-room of a sleeper. The lady's
husband, having got wind of their flight, wired
ahead, asking the cops to arrest the pair on their
arrival. The cops refused to collar an apparently
respectable female on any such charge, but they
brought in the man, and he was arraigned before
Gene Grannan. As a matter of law, his guilt had
to be presumed, for the Court of Appeals of Maryland had decided only a little while before that
when a man and a woman went into a room together
and locked the door it would be insane to give them
the benefit of the doubt. Moreover, the prisoner,
advised by a learned police-station lawyer, ad-

mitted the charge freely, and confined his defense
to swearing that the crime had not been committed
until after the train crossed the Maryland line. If
he were sent back to Pennsylvania for trial he
would be in serious difficulties, for the penalty for
adultery there was almost as drastic as that for
arson or piracy, but in Maryland, as I have said,
it was a mere misdemeanor, comparable to breaking a window or spitting on the sidewalk. Grannan
doubted the truth of the defense, but decided that a
humane judge would have to accept it, so he fined
the culprit $2, and the pair resumed their honey-
moon with loud hosannas. When a Pennsylvania
cop showed up the next day with extradition papers he was baffled, for the man had been tried and
punished, and could not be put in jeopardy again.

Grannan held a session of his court every afternoon, and I always attended it. It was seldom, indeed, that he did not turn up something that made
good copy. He had been, before his judicial days,
chief of the Baltimore & Ohio's railroad police, and
thus had a wide acquaintance among professional
criminals, especially yeggmen, and held the professional respect of the cops. In that remote era
there was no file of finger-prints at Washington,
and even the Bertillon system was just coming into
use. The cops, in consequence, sometimes picked
up an eminent felon without knowing who he was.
But if he came before Grannan he was identified at
once, and started through a mill that commonly

landed him in the Maryland Penitentiary. That
institution, which occupied a fine new building near
the city jail, then had as its warden a reformed
politician named John Weyler. He had been a
tough baby in his day, and was even suspected of
a hand in a homicide, but when I knew him he had
said goodbye to all that, and was an excellent
officer. I dropped in on him two or three times a
week, and usually picked up something worth
printing. He had a strange peculiarity: he never
came outside the prison walls save when it was raining. Then he would wander around for hours, and
get himself soaked to the skin, for he never used an
umbrella. Once a month his board of visitors met
at the Penitentiary, and he entertained the members at dinner. These dinners gradually took on
lavishness and gaiety, and during one of them a
member of the board, searching for a place marked
" Gents," fell down the main staircase of the place
and had to be sent to hospital. After that Weyler
limited the drinks to ten or twelve a head.

Another good source of the kind of news that
Max Ways liked was an old fellow named Hackman, the superintendent of the morgue. The
morgue was housed in an ancient building at the
end of one of the city docks, and Hackman seldom
left it. There was a sort of derrick overhanging
the water, and on it the harbor cops would pull up
the floaters that they found, and let them dry.
Some of them were covered with crabs and bar-

nacles when they were brought in, and Hackman had a long pole for knocking such ornaments off. How greatly he loved his vocation was shown when a new health commissioner fired him, and he refused to give up his keys. The health commissioner thereupon called for a squad of cops, and went down to the morgue to take possession by force, followed by a trail of reporters. But Hackman was defiant, and when firemen were sent for to aid the cops, he barricaded himself among his clients, and declared that he would never be taken alive.

The ensuing battle went on all afternoon, and was full of thrills. The cops refused to resort to firearms and the firemen refused to knock down the door with their hose, so Hackman seemed destined to hold out forever. Every now and then he would open the door for a few inches, and howl fresh defiance at the health commissioner. Finally, one of the reporters, Frank R. Kent, of the *Sun*, sneaked up along the wall, and thrust in his foot the next time the door was opened. Before Hackman could hack Kent's foot off the cops rushed him, and the morgue was taken. The poor old fellow burst into tears as he was being led away. The morgue, he wailed, was his only solace, almost his only life; he had devoted years to its upkeep and improvement, and was proud of its high standing among the morgues of Christendom. Moreover, many of the sponges, cloths and other furnishings within, including the pole he used to delouse floaters, were his personal property, and he was being robbed of them. The health commissioner promised to restore them, and so Hackman faded from the scene, a victim to a Philistine society that could not fathom his peculiar ideals.

There were press-agents in those days as in these, and though they had not reached the dizzy virtuosity now on tap they nevertheless showed a considerable ingenuity and daring. One of the best I encountered in my first years remains unhappily nameless in my memory, though I well recall some of his feats. He slaved for Frank Bostock, a big, blond, tweedy, John Bullish Englishman who had leased an old cyclorama in Baltimore and put in a wild animal show. Even before the doors were open the agent bombarded the local newspapers with bulletins worthy the best tradition of Tody Hamilton, press-agent for P. T. Barnum — battles between tigers and boa constrictors, the birth of infant giraffes and kangaroos, the sayings of a baboon who could speak Swahili, and so on. When, after the opening, business turned out to be bad, he spit on his hands, and turned off some masterpieces. The one I remember best was the hanging of a rogue elephant, for I was assigned to cover it. This elephant, we were informed, had become so onery that he could be endured no longer, and it was necessary to put him to death. Ordinarily, he would be shot, but Bostock, as a patriotic and law-abiding Englishman, preferred hanging, and would serve as executioner himself.

The butchery of the poor beast — he looked very mangey and feeble — was carried out one morning in the Bolton street railroad yards. First his legs were tied together, and then a thick hawser was passed around his neck and pulled tight, and the two ends were fastened to the hook of a railroad crane. When Bostock gave the signal the crane began to grind, and in a few minutes the elephant was in the air. He took it very quietly, and was pronounced dead in half an hour. A large crowd saw the ceremony, and after that business at the Bostock zoo picked up. The press-agent got rid of the S.P.C.A. by announcing that the elephant had been given six ounces of morphine to dull his sensations. His remains were presented to the Johns Hopkins Medical School for scientific study, but no one there was interested in proboscidean anatomy, so they finally reached a glue factory.

Six months later the Bostock zoo gave the Baltimore newspapers a good story without any effort by its press-agent. On a cold Winter night, with six inches of sleet in the streets, it took fire, and in a few minutes all its major inmates were burned to death and the small fry were at large. The pursuit of the latter went on all night and all the next day, and the cops turned up an occasional frost-bitten monkey as much as a week later. No really dangerous animal got loose, but the town was in a state of terror for weeks, and many suburban dogs, mistaken for lions or tigers, were done to death by vigilantes. I recall picking up a powerful cold by wallowing around the night of the fire in the icy slush.

But the best of all the Baltimore press-agents of that age was a volunteer who worked for the sheer love of the science. His name was Frank Thomas, and he was the son of a contractor engaged in building a new courthouse. There were to be ten or twelve huge marble pillars in the façade of the building, and they had to be brought in from a quarry at Cockeysville, fourteen miles away. The hauling was done on trucks drawn by twenty horses. One day a truck lost a wheel and the pillar aboard was broken across the middle. Frank announced at once that a fossil dog had been found in the fracture, and supported the tale by having a crude dog painted on it and the whole photographed. That photograph made both the *Herald* and the *American*, though the suspicious *Sunpaper* sniffed at it. It took the geologists at the Johns Hopkins a week to convince the town that there could be no canine fossils in sedimentary rocks. A bit later Frank made it known that the new courthouse would be fitted with a contraption that would suck up all sounds coming in from the streets, and funnel them out through the sewers. In his handout he described eloquently the comfort of judges and juries protected against the noises of traffic and trade, and the dreadful roar of the accumulated sounds as they emerged from the sewers along the waterfront. Frank indulged himself in many other inventions, and I handled most of them for the *Herald*, for the courthouse was in my parish. When the building was finished at last he published an illustrated souvenir book on it, and I wrote the 8000 words of its text. My honorarium was $25.

His days, alas, were not all beer and skittles, for putting up a large building in the heart of a busy city is a job shot through with cephalalgia. While it was under way a high board fence surrounded it, and on that fence were all the usual advertising signs, most of them hideous. The *Herald* started a violent crusade against them, arguing that they disgraced the courthouse and affronted all decent people. I was assigned by Max Ways to write some of the indignant stories we printed, and thus I met Frank in the dual rôle of friend of his fancy and enemy of his fence. So far as I could make out, the *Herald's* crusade had no support whatsoever in public sentiment — in fact, it became more and more difficult to find anyone to endorse it — but it roared on for months. The fence came down at last at least three or four weeks later than it would have come down if there had been no hullabaloo, for Frank had iron in him as well as imagination, and held out defiantly as long as he could.

It was a crusading time, with uplifters of a hundred schools harrying every major American city, and every newspaper of any pretensions took a hand in the dismal game. I recall crusades against sweat-shops, against the shanghaiing of men for the Chesapeake oyster fleet, and against dance-halls that paid their female interns commissions on the drinks sold. I had a hand in all of them, and if they filled me with doubts they also gave me some exhilarating experiences. With the cops I toured the bastiles of the waterfront crimps, and examined the jails that they maintained for storing their poor bums, and with health department inspectors I saw all the worst sweat-shops of the town, including one in which a huge flock of hens was kept hard at work laying eggs in a filthy cellar. In the war upon bawdy dance-halls I became a witness, unwillingly, against the cops, for I was put on the stand to testify that I had seen two detectives in one of them, and that the detectives must have been aware of what was going on. The poor flatfeet were unquestionably guilty, for I had discussed the matter with them in the place, but I managed to sophisticate my testimony with so many ifs and buts that it went for nothing, and they were acquitted by the police board. That was my first and last experience as an active agent of moral endeavor. I made up my mind at once that my true and natural allegiance was to the Devil's party, and it has been my firm belief ever since that all persons who devote themselves to forcing virtue on their fellow men deserve nothing better than kicks in the pants. Years later I put that belief into a proposition which I ventured to call Mencken's Law, to wit:

Whenever *A* annoys or injures *B* on the pretense of saving or improving *X, A* is a scoundrel.

The moral theologians, unhappily, have paid no heed to this contribution to their science, and so Mencken's Law must wait for recognition until the dawn of a more enlightened age.

III

SERGEANT'S STRIPES

WHEN I project my mind back into space and time it gathers in more pictures from my days as a police reporter than from any other period, and they have more color in them, and a keener sense of delight. But they were actually not long, for before I had been on the *Herald* staff a year I was promoted out of the world of common or dirt felony and assigned to cover the more subtle skullduggeries of the City Hall. This promotion was surely not to be sniffed at, for the City Hall assignment was then regarded by all reporters as something choice and important, and is so regarded, in fact, to this day. Moreover, it gave me more chance to shine than I had had in police work, and so got me frequent offers from the other Baltimore papers, and jacked up my salary on the *Herald*. I find by an old account-book that my first raise from $7 to $8 a week was not lifted to $10 until the beginning of 1900, but during the ensuing Summer I was promoted to $14, in December to $16, and in February, 1901, to $18. But during my first weeks in the City Hall I was homesick for Gene Grannan and the cops, the jail and the morgue. I was still very green — indeed, much greener than I was aware of in my youthful vanity — and it took me some time to fathom the art of handling politicians. Even the ordinary routine of City Hall reporting was full of snares, and I fell into some of them.

One fetched me on my very first day in the new service. There had been a municipal election during the previous Spring, and though its results were long known and its victors in office, the official returns had not yet been published by the Board of Election Supervisors. They were now, it appeared, to be given to a waiting world. Unhappily, I was slowed down in my tour of the City Hall by my unfamiliarity with its very geography, and when I got to the office of the supervisors at last it was closed for the day. I can still remember every twinge of my terror. What if I fell down on the story? The least penalty I could imagine would be return to a police assignment — and maybe not even a good one. So I hopped a trolley-car and tracked down the secretary to the board — an amiable politico whose name was Deane. He was sitting down to supper, but I conveyed to him enough of my alarm to induce him to come down to his office at once, open his safe, and give me a copy of the returns. When I got to the *Herald* office late, and Max Ways froze me with a growl, I thought it best to tell him the truth. He received it with a tolerant smile. " If you were older," he said, " you'd have known better. Such official documents are not worth so much trouble. If you had come in without it I could have got a proof of it from Jim Doyle [city editor of the *American*] or Hallett [city editor of the *Sun*]. But don't think that I blame you. We live and learn."

My relief was stupendous, and I chalked up one more article in my long bill of debts to Max. Soon afterward he quit the *Herald* and newspaper work, and was succeeded by a new city editor who had been, only lately, a City Hall reporter himself, so I had to hustle, and hustle I did. My job was gradually made pleasant, though surely not lightened, by the fact that the Mayor then in office — he had come in but a short time before — was an extremely eccentric and rambunctious fellow, so full of surprises that he had already acquired the nickname of Thomas the Sudden. His name was Hayes, and he was at one and the same time a very shrewd lawyer, an unconstructed Confederate veteran, a pious Methodist, and a somewhat bawdy bachelor. He was a wiry little fellow with a high forehead and a gigantic black moustache, and was the precise image of the Nietzsche depicted in Hans Olde's familiar drawing. There never lived on this earth a more quarrelsome man. He never had less than

41

six feuds going at once, and some of them reached unparalleled altitudes of raucousness. When he could not fetch his enemies by any other method he sued them in the courts, and during all of his four-year term the appellate judges of Maryland were kept humping by his litigations. There was in Baltimore at the time another litigant of ferocious assiduity, to wit, Charles J. Bonaparte, who was a grand-nephew of Napoleon I and was later to become Secretary of the Navy and then Attorney General in the Cabinet of Roosevelt I. But Bonaparte usually lost his cases, and in fact frittered away on them the better part of an inherited fortune of $1,000,000, whereas Hayes invariably won.

His method of celebrating victory was to go on a grand drunk. One evening, in the course of such a drunk, he arrived home in a state of incoördination, and fell down a stairway in his house, breaking a leg. After that, for a couple of months, the City Hall reporters of Baltimore had to see him in bed, and loud and long were the snorts and screams of moral indignation that issued from it. He lived with his sister, an old maid schoolma'm, and she tried her best to police him, but with very little success. Propped up in a frayed and filthy nightshirt, he chewed tobacco all his waking hours, and spit the juice into space without stopping to aim. On a table beside his bed was a box of five-cent cigars, but I never saw him smoke one, and he never offered one to a visitor. It was his theory that his enemies in and out of the City Hall were taking advantage of his disablement to ruin his administration, reduce Baltimore to bankruptcy, and undermine civilization, and in support of that theory he was always ready with great masses of evidence, some of it more or less plausible, but most of it plainly bogus. We reporters had to sift the little that could be printed from the mass that was poisonously libellous, and sometimes the job was anything but easy. But we liked the old boy nevertheless, for good stories radiated from him like quills from the fretful portentine, and if we had to scrap two-thirds of his fulminations there was always enough left to keep us rich in copy.

He was one of the most brazen boasters I have ever encountered, but I soon learned from him the immoral but useful lesson that boasters are not necessarily liars. He was, in fact, a really first-rate public official, and he pretty well cleaned out the corruption that had burdened Baltimore for generations, and set up so rational and efficient a municipal administration that its momentum is still visible, though he has been dead many years. His chief enemy, rather curiously, was another Confederate veteran whose honesty and competence were as notable as his own. This was Major Richard M. Venable, a member of the City Council and one of the stars of the Maryland bar. Though the two were on the same side at bottom, and both served Baltimore magnificently, they always differed in detail, and inasmuch as neither could ever imagine the slightest decency in an opponent, they carried on their wars *à outrance* and kept the town in a dither. Once they landed before the Court of Appeals at Annapolis on nine separate points of law, and though Venable was the more learned lawyer, and by far, Hayes won on every point. His celebration went on for weeks, and in the course of it he issued statements sneering at Venable as a putrid pettifogger, questioning the election returns that put him in the Council, and even hinting that there was something phony about his war record. None of them were ever printed.

Venable was also a bachelor, and a personage quite as picturesque as Hayes himself. He was of great stature, had a belly so vast that his waistcoat looked like a segment of balloon, and wore a huge and bristling beard. He kept house in a sort of one-man monastery in a decayed downtown street, and was beautifully served by a staff of colored servants. One dull Sunday evening, seeking only to set him to talking, I asked him how he managed to run his establishment so well. He replied that there were two reasons. The first was that no white women were allowed in the house, and the second was that he had a standing offer to his servants to pay them half again as much as anyone else was willing to pay them. He had two great hates, one against women and the other against Christianity.

His large library was principally made up of works on theology, and he read them constantly, and damned them violently. He was, in fact, the premier town atheist of his generation, and after his death it was reported that he had left orders that his ashes were to be disposed of by throwing them into any convenient ashcan. If he actually left such orders they were disregarded; instead, his ashes were scattered in Druid Hill Park, for in his last days he had been a member of the Park Board. His loathing of women embraced the whole sex, but its worst poisons were concentrated on a lady eminent in good works. It was a common joke in Baltimore city-rooms to send a new reporter to him for verification of a presumed report that he was about to marry her. His roars usually scared the reporter out of a month's growth.

The major easily dominated both houses of the City Council, and it usually served him docilely in his gory wars on Mayor Hayes. It consisted, then as always, of a scattering of intelligent raisins in a big loaf of dunderheads. One of its members was a brewery collector, another was a writer of dime novels, and two others were operators of O.E.A. (*i.e.*, odorless excavating apparatus) companies, which is to say, they were engaged professionally in cleaning the privies that survived in thousands of Baltimore backyards until 1915 or thereabout, when the sewerage system was completed. The rest sloped down to saloonkeepers, small trucking con-

tractors, and miscellaneous ward-heelers. The
major rode these poor idiots in a bold and berserk
fashion, and whenever one of them ventured to vote
against him, which was not often, he gave a magnificent exhibition of moral indignation. They
trembled under his bellowing, but like inferior men
at all times and everywhere, ended by admiring
him vastly, and even, in their dull way, loving him.
Sometimes he would gather them together in one
of the council chambers after a meeting had adjourned, and delight them with Rabelaisian anecdotes in the manner of Abraham Lincoln. He had
a large répertoire, and his delivery was aided considerably by his commanding mien and florid
beard.

It was part of my job, of course, to cover the
sessions of the Council, and I always enjoyed them
greatly. Inasmuch as there were two houses I was
given an assistant for the duration, but I usually
managed to look in at both chambers, and never
missed the upper one when Major Venable was on
his legs. The hour of meeting was 5 p.m. and the
sessions often lasted until 8. We reporters were allowed 50 cents a head by our papers for supper
money, and usually victualled before returning to
our offices, for in those primitive days the maniacal
demand for early copy that now palsies journalism
was unheard of. Across the street from the City
Hall there was a saloon in which a dinner consisting of a coriaceous T-bone steak, a dab of fried

potatoes, a slice of rye bread and a cup of coffee could be had for a quarter, and most of the reporters patronized it, and so made a profit of the other quarter. But there was one among them of more voluptuous inclinations, and he soon convinced me that it was better to eat a more elegant dinner. He was Frank Kent, of the *Sun*. He had discovered that such a meal was on tap in a hotel in Calvert street, and thereafter he and I ate it every Council night. Sometimes we had to add ten cents to the fifty to cover our checks, but we were reckless fellows, and did not begrudge any kindness to our pyloruses.

This epicureanism rather set us apart from the other City Hall reporters, and our singularity was even more unpleasantly marked when we gave Major Venable aid and applause in his war upon what had been known for years and years as " the meritorious measure." This was an ordinance put through whenever the Council adjourned for its Summer recess, giving every reporter who had covered its proceedings a gratuity of $150. It had been passed yearly since the Civil War, and maybe since the Revolution, but the major announced that he was implacably agin it, and, what is more, that he would attack it in a taxpayer's suit if it were passed. Frank and I, having convinced ourselves virtuously that any such gratuity was an insult to journalism, let it be known that we'd refuse the money if the major came to grief, and this got us

some unpopularity among our colleagues, but
when he won hands down the matter was quickly
forgotten, and we were again on good terms with
all hands. There were so many sources of news in
the City Hall that it was impossible for one reporter to cover all of them, so we had perforce to
pool our daily accumulations. How that arrangement once broke down, and how human ingenuity
restored it, will be told in Chapter XVIII.

The examples of Hayes and Venable were proofs
enough that honest and competent men could sometimes get on the public payroll, and I soon found
many more on lower levels. Hayes's secretary, a
courtly Irishman named William A. Ryan, was one,
and another was a man named Julius Freeman,
who was deputy city register: both knew their jobs
and gave the city hard and faithful service. A
third was a curious character named McCuen, a
bachelor like Hayes and Venable, and like Venable
again, the master of a fierce set of whiskers. Mc-
Cuen's were almost as red as blood, and he wore
them parted in the middle, and drawn out into two
horns. He came from South Baltimore, and his
past was that of any other neighborhood politico,
but when Hayes made him superintendent of lamps
and lighting he took his duties with great gravity,
and was soon discharging them in a highly efficient
and even stylish manner. All day he slaved in his
office, and half the night he roved the streets, spot-
ting lights that were not working, and picking out

places to set up new ones. For the first time in its history Baltimore was decently lighted. Moreover, McCuen replaced thousands of the old rickety lamp-posts with new ones of excellent design, and in general showed an aesthetic sense that was astounding in a politician. But now and then he reverted unaccountably to more primitive canons of taste, and once he spent a lot of money putting colored lights into a fountain in one of the city reservoirs. The effect was that of an explosion of stick-candy, but more Baltimoreans admired it than laughed at it, and the lights remain in place to this day, forty years afterward.

At about the same time a Civil War veteran who was superintendent of the City Hall decided that the large bronze lamps which flanked its main entrance were too dirty to be endured, and had his men give them a coat of bright green paint. This improvement set loose an uproar, for the patina on them had been accumulating for thirty years, and was much prized by the town cognoscenti. I well recall the distress of the poor old man when he finally took in the notion that his honest effort to imitate the arty McCuen had resulted in a *faux pas*. I really felt sorry for him, but my responsibility to my own art had to be considered first, so I helped to heap ribaldry upon him. The Baltimore cartoonists had a grand time while his agony lasted. McKee Barclay of the *Evening News* did a plate showing all the principal local monuments bedizened in the new manner, including the Washington column striped like a barber's pole. It took the City Hall scavengers two weeks to scrape the paint off the lamps, and in doing so they removed the patina too.

The City Hall seemed dullish after the Central police district, but even so it had its moments. There was a battle in the war between Hayes and Venable every few weeks, and in the intervals the members of the various city boards locked horns, and gave us good shows. During the Winter smallpox broke out in Baltimore, and patients dragged out of the alleys by the cops were stored every afternoon in the City Hall annex, an old school building occupied by the Health Department, a block or so away from the Hall itself. Whenever a wagonload accumulated it was started for the pesthouse down the harbor. Visiting the Health Department every day, we reporters had to pass within a few feet of these candidates for the potter's field. To protect us the doctors vaccinated us once a week. The vaccinations produced less effect on me than so many gnat bites, for my arm had been scraped back in 1882 by our family physician, Dr. Z. K. Wiley, and when he did a job of that kind he left behind him a scar like a shell crater, good for a generation.

Hayes distrusted all his official advisers, and especially his legal staff, but he had a kitchen cabinet that had his confidence, composed mainly of third-rate politicians. One Sunday I printed in the *Herald* what purported to be a report of its latest star-chamber proceedings, and the buffoonery was so well received that I went on with it thereafter from week to week. In a little while one of the members offered to give me more or less accurate minutes of its actual sessions if I would agree to treat him politely. I agreed readily, and after that my stories were accepted in the City Hall as authentic. Hayes himself tried to worm out of me the source of my information, but the pieces were unsigned, and I refused to admit that I was writing them. His suspicions were finally fixed on a quite innocent member, and this unfortunate was expelled from the cabinet, and threatened with the loss of his city job. It is a remarkable fact that the member who really leaked was never detected, and indeed never even suspected. I kept on writing this somewhat obvious stuff until my term of servitude in the City Hall ended. Even today I occasionally meet an old-time politician who remembers it uneasily, and tries to induce me to tell him who blabbed. More than once my report of the cabinet's debates, touched up artistically, ruined some design of Hayes and his torpedoes, and covered Major Venable with soothing unguents. But the major never admitted that he read such trivia. He was essentially a serious man.

Hayes himself came to a bad end. After his four-years' term as Mayor he dropped out of politics, and resumed his law practise, which was mainly devoted to criminal business. He knew how to holler in court and was thus successful before juries, but in Maryland most criminal trials go on without juries, even in capital cases, and he made much less impression on judges. A Methodist by early training, he gradually gave over the jug and devoted himself more and more to Christian endeavor. He became the superintendent of a Methodist Sunday-school, and inveigled the *Sunday Sun* into printing his weekly observations on the International Sunday-school Lessons. These observations were of a high degree of fatuity, and when I became Sunday editor of the *Sun* myself, in 1906, I killed them. In his last years, which were lonely and unhappy, for his schoolma'm sister had died, his income was diminishing and his services to Baltimore were beginning to be forgotten, he wasted at least half his time on his theological debauchery, greatly to the distress of his former secretary, Ryan, who was a very intelligent man, and moreover, a Catholic. Ryan himself had made progress in politics, and was by now collector of customs. I dropped in on him often, and we moaned over poor Hayes's deterioration, but there was nothing that we could do about it. When he died at last his funeral orgies were on a scale fit for a bishop, or even an archangel, and the Methodists of Baltimore still remember him as a prophet comparable to Nehemiah, Habakkuk or Deuteronomy. But to all the less sanctified Baltimoreans he has grown vague, and there is no public memorial to him in the town.

He was the last of the Civil War veterans to reach high public office there, and even during his term as Mayor the old city was changing. The great fire of 1904 was to hasten its transmogrification, and today it bears little resemblance to the Baltimore of my first memories. But in my reportorial days there were still whole sections, especially along the waterfront, that still looked and smelled exactly as they must have looked and smelled in 1861. The Back Basin, which made up into the town so far that its head was only four blocks from the main crossroads, received the effluence of such sewers as existed, and emitted a stench as cadaverous and unearthly as that of the canals of Venice. In Summer it took on extra voltage, and became almost unendurable, but the old-time Baltimoreans pretended that they didn't notice it, and even professed to believe that it was good for their sinuses and a prophylactic against the ague. During the crusading era the local newspapers often set up demands that something be done about it, but it continued to afflict the town until the new sewerage system was completed, and the Back Basin was reduced to the humble status of a receptacle for rain water. Once a *Herald* editorial writer proposed in print, and quite seriously, that a dam be built across the mouth of the Basin, to the end that the water backed up at high tide might be released suddenly when the tide was low. His theory was that the resultant flood would carry off all the dead dogs, decayed bunches of bananas and multitudinous worse filth that floated on the Basin's surface. When an Old Subscriber wrote in asking what would happen to the shipping in the lower harbor when this flood roared down the Patapsco, the editorial writer was indignant, and accused various reporters of writing the letter.

My days in the City Hall, like my days as a police reporter, were not long, but by the time they were over I had begun to think of myself as a journeyman journalist, and was so accepted by the elder brethren of the craft. It was not unusual for me to be taken off the job for a day or two, or even for a week or two, and assigned to some other work. After the middle of 1900 I had a hand in nearly all the big stories that engaged the Baltimore newspapers. Even in 1899 I had been told off to do the election-day lead, and given three columns for it. It was a story of some importance, for up to that time Baltimore had never seen an election day without at least one murder. But the tide was now flowing toward peace and decorum, and though I roved the town all day, looking for dead and wounded, I had to base my lead on the surprising fact that no one had been killed, and only a few poor bums hurt. The next year I was put to writing a pre-election series of instructions to voters, for the election laws had been lately changed by taking all party emblems off the ballots, which thus became Chinese puzzles to the plain people, who had been voting for either Abraham Lincoln's beard or the Democratic rooster for years. At the time I performed this educational service I had just passed my twentieth birthday, and could not vote myself until nearly a year later.

I was used to newspaper hours by now, and liked them. On Summer nights it was always beginning to grow cool when I got home — sometimes as early as one o'clock, but usually nearer three. I got in some reading in the quiet of the house, and slept like a top. Arising at ten or thereabouts, I had a couple of hours for my literary enterprises before going to work. I lost a good many days off, but those that I got were very pleasant, for they gave me some extra time for writing, and in the evening I went to the theatre. As older men dropped out I inherited Saturday as my day off — the choice one of the whole week, for there were matinées on it, and some sort of newspaper party was always staged after work on Saturday night. I began to reflect upon my trade, and to discern some of its principal virtues and defects. Of the latter, the worst was the fact that it worked me too hard, but though I was aware of it I did not resent it, for I was still full of the eagerness of youth, and hot to see the whole show. Of the former, the greatest was that a newspaper man always saw that show from a reserved seat in the first row. The rest of humanity had to wait in line and struggle for places, but not a reporter. He was always expected, and usually welcomed. He got into places by a side door. To this day it always irritates me absurdly to have to stand in line, even for a few minutes — say at a ticket-window or on a customs pier. It seems to me to be an intolerable affront, not only to my private pomp and circumstance, but also to the honor of the Fourth Estate.

IV

APPROACH TO

LOVELY LETTERS

WHEN I told Max Ways, on applying for a job on
the *Herald*, that I had been busting with literary
ardors for four or five years I was stating a simple
fact. It must have been before 1895 that I made
my first formal attempt to do something for publication: it was an article on a chemical invention of
my own — a platinum toning bath for silver
photographic prints. All the photographic magazines of the time rejected it, and it never got into
print until 1925, when the late Isaac Goldberg
published it in a book called " The Man Mencken."
I was in those days vacillating between chemistry
and journalism, and two teachers at the Baltimore
Polytechnic, from which I was graduated in 1896
as the youngest member of my class, had something

to do with my final choice. I had got interested in chemistry through photography, and in photography through the gift of a camera at Christmas, 1892, just as I had got interested in journalism through the gift of a printing-press at Christmas, 1888.

By 1894 I had a laboratory in Hollins street, and was engaged in eager but usually inconclusive experiments. All the orthodox accidents happened to me, including four or five explosions and an inhalation of bromide gas that nearly strangled me, and no doubt had something to do with the sore throat that pestered me for years afterward. If I had encountered a competent teacher of chemistry at the Polytechnic I'd have gone on in that science, and today I'd be up to my ears in the vitamines, for it was synthetic chemistry that always interested me most. But the gogue told off to nurture me succeeded only in disheartening me, so I gradually edged over to letters, helped by another gogue who really knew his stuff, and, what is more, loved it. He was a young *Cand. jur.* named Edward S. Kines, who had but recently graduated from the Baltimore City College, and was pursuing his legal studies of an evening at the University of Maryland Law School. He taught English literature at the Polytechnic, and judged by any plausible standard must have been set down a bad teacher, but somehow or other he managed to impart to me, and to a few other boys, his honest enthusiasm for what then passed in schools for good books. My reading, up to the time he began to operate on me, had been scattered and futile, but he gave it direction, and I was soon leaping and prancing through the whole classical répertoire, and enjoying it. I even tackled such revolting doses as Butler's "Hudibras," Herbert's "The Temple," the contributions to the *Spectator* by Eustace Budgell, and Colley Cibber's Apology.

Kines, so far as I know, had no literary ambitions of his own: he was content to spout his favorite passages, and in his later years he devoted himself assiduously to his trade as a trial lawyer. Nor was there much scratching for the *cacoethes scribendi* among his pupils. Indeed, I can recall but one who ever spoke of writing. He was Arthur W. Hawks, who had a brother on the *Herald* staff, and was to join it himself a little while before I did. It may be that the example of the two Hawkses led me to the *Herald* instead of to the *Sun*, but on that point my memory is cloudy, and I am sure that they knew little about my actual attempts at writing, at any rate before 1898. I recall going out to the Baltimore baseball grounds in 1895, and doing a play-by-play report of a game between the famous Baltimore Orioles and some visiting nine, but though I was delighted the next morning to find that it coincided with the stories in the newspapers I never showed it to anyone. Nor did I solicit opinion on any of the verse that I began to do about the same time. Indeed, I have always been shy about showing my writings to other people, though it would certainly be an exaggeration to call me, generally speaking, a violet; and to this day I have never asked anyone to read a manuscript of mine, or even a printed book. My first production was a satirical poem on a baseball theme, and I sent it to the Baltimore *American* unsigned, and was amazed to see it in print. After that I favored the *American* with almost daily contributions, but only one more was ever printed. At the Polytechnic my yearning to make the staff of the school paper was thwarted by the class politicians, and when the time came to concoct a class play I was not invited to help write it, but put to banging the piano for the performance.

To a youngster of my inclinations the literary movement of the nineties was naturally a cosmic event, and I followed it as best I could, with no one to guide me, once I had departed from Kines. I remember haunting a newsdealer's shop in West Baltimore, hot to grab every new magazine as it came out, and first and last I must have waded through scores of them. The majority were idiotically eccentric: there was one, for example, in which the illustrations, printed separately, were pasted in, and another that sold pretentiously for a cent. But my critical faculties were still embryonic, and I devoured the bad with the good. The *Chap-Book* and the *Lark* went through my mill, but so did many an arty monstrosity that lasted but one number. I recall, however, enjoying *M'lle New York* better than most, for there was in it a writer named James G. Huneker whose illuminating sophistication and colorful, rapid style gave me a special thrill. Years later I was to know him well and see much of him, but in 1895 he was as far out of my world as Betelgeuse.

When I began to find my way about the *Herald* office I discovered to my delight that I was on the actual frontiers of lovely letters, for all those members of the staff who showed a mental age above thirteen were consumed by either one or the other of two then prevalent ambitions: to write the book of a comic opera, or to set up a weekly journal of literary, theatrical, musical and political opinion. The elder Hawks, Wells, was actually engaged upon the former, and though, as a young reporter, I was not admitted to his confidences, his brother Arthur sneaked some of its lyrics to show me, and we agreed that they were masterpieces. No weekly ever precipitated itself from the current dreams, but a monthly called *Dixie* was really in existence, and if the contributions of the local literati made no noise, the magazine was at least getting notice for some of its illustrations. They were done by a pen-and-ink artist named G. Alden Peirson. Turning away from the uptown prides and glories of Baltimore, he went down to the waterfront for his subjects, and there produced some very charming drawings.[1] The newspaper artists of the town were naturally miles behind him, but they, too, had their quest for an earthly Grail. It took them to a dark office in an old building under the elevated in North street, where there lurked a syndicate man who was always ready to buy a comic drawing of the sort then in fashion. Unhappily, there had to be a he-and-she joke to go with it, and inventing these jokes usually stumped the artists. When they could not find a literary reporter able to supply one, they went to the Pratt Library and dug it out of the back files of *Puck*, *Judge* or *Texas Siftings*. The market price for joke and drawing was $1.

There were some high-toned literati living in Baltimore in those days — for example, Edward Abram Uffington Valentine, who printed a book of poems in 1902 that got very good reviews — but I never met any of them, and there was little to lift me, after I got used to it, in the endless gabble that went on in the *Herald* office about the weekly that never came to birth. My own aspirations were gradually turning from poetry to prose. I had a drawer full of verse, but I was making fewer and fewer additions to it. A large part of it consisted of dreadful imitations of Kipling, who was then my god, and the rest was made up of triolets, rondeaux and other experiments in the old French forms that

[1] *Dixie* lasted from January, 1899, to April, 1900. The rest of its illustrations scarcely got above the candy-box-top level. Its literary contents were even worse.

Austin Dobson and Andrew Lang had brought in.
In the Autumn of 1900, when I was given a weekly
column on the editorial page, and invited to do my
damnedest, I unearthed a lot of these *Jugendwerke*,
and so saved the labor of writing new stuff. They
were all pretty bad, but they seemed to be well received in the office, and in December I received the
singular honor of being invited by the new managing editor, Carter, to do a poem for the first page.
It was not, to be sure, quite original, for it was
based upon ,a French piece lately published by
Edmond Rostand, roundly denouncing the Boer
leader, Oom Paul Kruger. Carter put Rostand's
French into English prose, and I turned it into
burning tetrameter, with poor old Oom reduced to
a greasepot at the end. It was blowsy stuff, God
knows, but Carter professed to like it, and, good or
bad, there it glowed and glittered in long primer
italic on page one — a glory that no other American poet, however gifted, has ever achieved, at
least to my knowledge. My column ran on until
my reserves of prosody began to be depleted. I
then diluted it with more and more prose, and
finally it became prose altogether. Beginning in
June, 1901, it took the form of a weekly tale of ancient Rome, in which all the characters were American politicians, thinly disguised. Every tale
ended with the hanging of the principal personage.
I don't recall how many such pieces I did, but it
was well beyond thirty, and toward the end of the

series I was hard put to invent something new every week, and yet keep within the formula.

My poetical contributions to the editorial page in 1900 and 1901 made up most of the contents of my first book, "Ventures Into Verse," though it did not come out until 1903. It was a typical product of the aesthetic movement of the time, then gradually subsiding. Its projectors were two young fellows named Marshall and Beek, who had formed a firm to do fine printing and taken into partnership an artist named Gordon. The three came to me asking that I suggest a likely source of copy for a small volume that would show off their advanced typography, and I naturally nominated myself. Marshall set the book by hand, and there were decorations by Gordon, and by another artist named John Siegel. The press-run was 100 copies, of which I got half and the firm got half. Some were bound à la Roycroft, in rough binders' boards with red labels, but most were issued in plain brown paper. I sent ten of my copies to the principal critical organs of the time, and presented the rest to libraries or to friends. As incredible as it may seem, the book got good notices, but only three orders for it ever reached Marshall, Beek and Gordon. My presentation copies seem to have been preserved in odd corners, for when American firsts began to bring fantastic prices, in 1925, a good many appeared in the market, and at one time a clean specimen brought as much as $225. All those

APPROACH TO LOVELY LETTERS

that had gone to public libraries were stolen. Some ass spread the story that I was buying up the copies offered by dealers, and burning them. It was, of course, not true. I can recall buying but one copy, and that one I gave to a friend. It cost me $130.

Meanwhile, I was devoting all my meagre leisure to writing. I still did an occasional poem, and some of them were published in magazines. The first to make high literary society, so far as I can recall, was a rhymed address to my hero Kipling, urging him to forget politics and go back to Mandalay. It was written in the Autumn of 1899, while I was in the midst of my apprenticeship as a police reporter, and I sent it to the *Bookman*, then edited by Harry Thurston Peck. It went in anonymously and with no return address on the manuscript, and I was both surprised and enchanted when it came out in the December issue. I wrote to Peck at once, admitting its paternity with suitable blushes, and was surprised again when one of his assistants replied politely, and enclosed a check for $10. I quote from the letter:

> As we are paying you more than we usually do for poems, you may judge from that fact that the poem appealed to us. We may add, also, that the poem has been quoted quite a little in the newspapers.

I recall a curious detail of the day the December *Bookman* appeared on the newsstands in Baltimore.

When I discovered my verses in it I was so addled that I was quite unfit for work, and decided to seek peace and recuperation in the old Odeon Theatre in Frederick street, to which I had the entrée. The Odeon was a burlesque house, and while I sat in a stage box, reading my burning lines over and over again, two comedians broke slapsticks over each other's fundaments, and the ladies of the ensemble engaged in what were then called muscle dances. But the manager of the house, James Madison, was himself a writer,[2] and when he dropped in on me and I showed him the magazine he joined in my rejoicings. On returning to the *Herald* office, I told Max Ways my purple secret, and he spread it in the office. That night Colonel Cunningham, who was presently to retire as managing editor, paused on his way through the city-room to compliment me officially.

I sold verse during the following Winter to *Life*, to *Leslie's Weekly*, to the *National Magazine* and to the *New England Magazine*, but in the main I wrote short stories, and most of them landed eventually in magazines. In an old account-book I find a record of my operations: it is interesting chiefly because it shows that the magazines I attempted are nearly all long gone and forgotten, for example, the

---

[2] He wrote vaudeville sketches and dialogues for Dutch, Irish and Jewish comedians, and had a large following. Later on he abandoned that art for the book business, and is at present (1941) the publisher of an excellent monthly for bibliophiles.

Criterion, the *Broadway, Judge, Puck,* the *Black Cat, Munsey's, Success, Ainslee's, Leslie's* (the monthly, not the weekly), *Lippincott's,* the *Youth's Companion, McClure's, Everybody's, Pearson's, Golden Days,* the *Critic,* the *World's Work,* the *Century, Hearst's, Town Topics,* the *Metropolitan,* the *Argosy, Harper's Weekly.* Eheu! it is a roll of the noble dead. The *Bookman* under Peck was the best literary monthly the United States has ever seen; *Munsey's, McClure's* and *Everybody's* had immense circulations; the *Youth's Companion* was read by every American boy; the *Black Cat* was " the story-telling hit of the century "; and a barber-shop without *Puck* and *Judge* would have seemed as nude as one without the *Police Gazette.* But now they are all in the shades, and only a few doddering oldsters recall even their names.

The *Criterion,* then edited by Emory Pottle, husband of Juliet Wilbor Tompkins, was the only solvent survivor of the literary movement of the nineties. I banged away at Pottle for a good while without shaking him, but finally he bought a short story called " The Heathen Rage," born of my trip to Jamaica (Chapter V), and after that I sold him others. For one of them, I find by my records, he paid me $51 and for another $34.35. It was a day of close prices. My steadiest customer in the long run, however, was not Pottle, but Ellery Sedgwick, then editor of *Frank Leslie's Popular Monthly* and later to be editor of the *Atlantic*

Monthly. Sometime in 1901 he bought two of my short stories, and thereafter he bought others. Moreover, he sent me criticisms of those he rejected, and then, as later on, I learned a lot from him. He also put me to work writing articles under the *nom de plume* of John F. Brownell. *Leslie's* was illustrated, and Sedgwick would first pick up a good series of photographs, and then have me write a text to fit them. One such series, as I remember, had to do with the Hagenbeck Zoo at Hamburg. I had never been to Hamburg (and, in fact, never got there until 1938), but I was by now a journeyman reporter, so I did an article that apparently pleased the readers of *Leslie's*, and Sedgwick offered me a job on his home-office staff. The salary he named was more than I was getting on the *Herald*, and he proposed to add a round-trip railroad pass to Baltimore once a month, but I declined at once, for I had already made up my mind that I didn't want to live in New York. Many other offers to move there came later, and beginning with 1914 I actually had an office in the town for twenty years on end, but I stuck to living in Baltimore, which suited me, and still suits me, precisely. While I was an editor of the *Smart Set* and then of the *American Mercury* I commuted to New York as often as weekly, but I stayed at the Algonquin, and never had any permanent quarters.

I was reasonably successful as a writer of short stories, and sold virtually every one I wrote, though not always at the first attempt. One of my good markets was *Short Stories,* and I also had a welcome from Karl Edwin Harriman, then editor of the *Red Book.* Toward the end of 1901 I sold two stories to the *Youth's Companion* that somehow got pigeon-holed in the office, and were not exhumed and published until more than thirty years later. At that time the editor sent me proofs of them, and invited me to make any changes that a generation of experience might suggest, but I passed them without changing a word. They were on the bad side as stories, but they were no worse than the general. Until I joined the staff of the *Smart Set* as its book reviewer, in 1908, I had sold it but one piece of copy — a poor little triolet — and even that never got into the magazine, for I discovered at once that I had already used it in my *Herald* column, and had to recall it. Between 1899 and 1902 I must have bombarded the *Smart Set* with at least forty other pieces of verse, always in vain.

How I managed to find time for all this writing, considering the heavy work I was doing for the *Herald,* I simply can't tell you. My output during my first years on the staff, in and out of the office, was really enormous, for in addition to my short stories and doggerels, I wrote a great many articles for other papers, and began work on a novel. The novel, happily, never got very far. Its scene was Elizabethan England, and Shakespeare was to have been one of the characters. It blew up when I discovered that I knew no more about Elizabethan England than about the M. M. III age of Crete. I was constantly turning up news and feature stories in Baltimore that were of interest in other cities, and selling them there. The first paper I thus broke into was the Philadelphia *Inquirer*, and it was soon followed by the New York *Morning Telegraph*, and then, after a while, by the New York *Sun*. My contributions to the *Sun* were mainly interviews with an imaginary Civil War colonel from the Eastern Shore of Maryland, who was supposed to be the world's greatest authority on the mint julep. Unless my memory plays me false they started that controversy about the proper compounding of the julep which still rages.

Nor did I confine myself, in my reachings out for fresh fields and lusher pastures, to this great Republic. There was in New York in those days a Rhinelander named Henry W. Fischer who made a living translating news items from the chief European papers, and selling them in the United States. The cable service of the time was much leaner than it is today, so there was room for him. It occurred to me that I might set up a similar service from the Far East, and to that end I approached various newspapers in that region, offering to send them occasional American letters in return for the right to mine their news columns. A number bit, and in a little while I was the American correspondent of the Hongkong *Press*, the Kobe *Chronicle*, the Nagasaki *Press*, and the *Ceylon Observer* of Colombo, and had letter-heads printed to prove it. Unfortunately, I soon learned that very few American newspapers were interested in Far Eastern news, and my cash takings remained scanty. Finally, I decided to go to New York to consult Fischer, with a view to an amalgamation. I found him in carpet-slippers at his home in Bensonhurst, and remember clearly his brief comment when I recited to him the list of my papers. It consisted of the single word " Jesus! " But we quickly came to terms, and the amalgamation was effected on the spot. That is to say, I gave him my business, such as it was, and he returned to Manhattan with me and took me to Lüchow's in Fourteenth street, where he bought me an excellent lunch and half a dozen horns of Würzburger.

I have said that I never met any of the recognized literati of Baltimore, but I should mention one exception. He was Jean Havez, who had been a reporter on the *Evening News* only a short time before, and was now eminent as the author of " Goodbye, Booze! ", " Everybody Works But Father," and " He Cert'n'y Was Good to Me," all of them great popular successes. Havez was of French parentage, and a fellow of huge bulk, powerful thirst, and notable amiability. Whenever he returned to Baltimore from Broadway for a visit to the home folks there was a party that lasted for days. While one of them was going on, toward the end of 1900, Lew Dockstader came to town with his minstrel company, and tried to induce Jean to write some local stanzas for his songs. But Jean was too busy to fool with such chicken feed, and for some reason that I forget turned the job over to me. I wrote the stanzas in a few hours, and went to Ford's Opera House that night to hear Lew sing them, full of agreeable anticipations. But he had got an overdose of Jean's party during the afternoon, and when he came upon the stage it was apparent to the judicious that he was not altogether himself. In consequence, he made a horrible mess of my poor jocosities, but the customers roared none the less, for a theatre audience will always laugh at the mention of a familiar name by a comedian, no matter how idiotic the joke he makes on it. Later in the week Lew pulled himself together and did better, and after the Saturday matinée he handed me $10 for my labor. A month later I collared another ten-spot by doing parodies for a Democratic mass-meeting.

But though all these extra-mural activities brought in money, and I was soon earning more outside the office than in it, I began to be conscious of a lack of direction, and tried a number of times to decide formally what I really wanted to do, and to get on with the doing of it. Such advice as I sought usually turned out to be bad, and in consequence I did a great deal of wobbling. I tried all sorts of things, including even advertising writing, but they satisfied me as little as the concoction of verse, which had begun to pall dismally. My short stories, as I have said, were doing pretty well, and I got some comfort and solace in the writing of them from another youngster in the office, Leo Crane by name and secretary to the managing editor by trade. Crane was writing short stories too, and making *Harper's* with them, which was even better than I was doing. But it gradually dawned on me that fiction was not my *forte*, and I did none after 1902. The Boston lemon-squeezer, Richard G. Badger, tried to inveigle me, in that year, into letting him bring out a volume of my stories, but when, after a considerable correspondence, I discovered that he expected me to pay for it, I fled from his blandishments. He gave me to understand that he thought me one of the coming masters of the short story in America, but I was already in grave doubt about that. For two years I let the matter lie there. Then, through the theatre, I became interested in George Bernard Shaw, and through Shaw I found my vocation at last. My first real book, begun in 1904, was a volume on his plays and the notions in them, critical in its approach. It was the first book about him ever published, and it led me to begin a larger volume on Nietzsche in 1907, and to undertake a book on Socialism two years later, in the form of a debate with a Socialist named La Monte, now recusant and forgotten. After that I was a critic of ideas, and I have remained one ever since.

In all probability, my various false starts did me no harm, though I was undoubtedly delayed in coming to fruit by trying to do too many things at once. My work for the *Herald* was enough in itself to keep one man busy, and I recall many times when I finished a day so nearly worn out that I could barely keep my eyes open. More than once I produced 5000 words of news copy between noon and midnight — not in a single continuous story, which might have been easy enough, but in a miscellany of perhaps twelve or fifteen, every one of them requiring some legging. The newspaper padrones of that era, like the steel magnates, had not yet discovered that over-long hours greatly diminish the amount of good work done. A little while ago I spent an uncomfortable afternoon going through the files of the *Herald,* reading my contributions to it in 1900 and 1901. I discovered that I had done a great deal of shabby writing, full of clichés and banalities. But it was well regarded in the office at the time, and was at its worst appreciably better than the work of many of my colleagues. Not until a somewhat later date did anything properly describable as good writing become the rule on the *Herald.* At least half the members of the staff had literary ambitions of some sort or another, but not one of them ever got anywhere as a writer in the years following. Several took to executive work and became city editors and managing editors, but more became press-agents, and still more left journalism altogether. That is its continuing tragedy: it opens all sorts of outside opportunities to its slaves, and so loses them. I have known newspaper men who have become bank presidents, judges, United States Senators, Governors, generals in the Army, and even bishops. One of the worst who ever lived, Warren Gamaliel Harding, actually became President of the United States. And in Baltimore, during the thirteen years of horror, the best bootician in service was a former newspaper artist.

V

FRUITS OF

DILIGENCE

THE ASSIDUITIES described in the preceding chapters had rewards both subjective and objective, for I not only enjoyed every minute of every day, but also got a good many friendly grunts from Max Ways, and, though I didn't know it, substantial promotion was just around the corner. Unhappily, my hustling bore rather heavily upon a constitution that had some holes in it, and so early as the Spring of 1900 I began to lose weight, and to show other symptoms of exhaustion. From my childhood I had been badgered by disorders of the upper respiratory tract. Every Autumn, on returning to school, I suffered for several weeks from a bleariness that seems, in retrospect, to have been the beginnings of hay-fever, and during my chem-

ical days I picked up a sore throat that stuck to me
more or less steadily for ten years.

In most ways, to be sure, I was a perfectly
healthy animal, for I could eat and digest anything
colorably organic, I recovered quickly from all
minor wounds and infections, and to this day I
have never had a headache. But there was always
something unpleasant going on in my nose or
throat, and it took the faculty a long while, not to
mention a considerable shedding of blood, to repair
the blunders of Yahweh there, and launch me on
the robustness that marked my thirties and forties.
How many times I went on the table I don't recall
precisely, but it must have been half a dozen at
least. My tonsils were removed no less than twice
— a complete impossibility, as I well know, but
nevertheless I was present both times. Even after
all that butchery hay-fever remained, and it was
not until I was fifty years old that it ever showed
any sign of yielding — whether to the vaccines
that I was taking by the pint or to the belated mercies of higher powers I do not know.

When, in June of 1900, the fatigues of a hard
Winter began to blossom into downright debility,
I waited on our old family physician, Dr. Z. K.
Wiley,[1] and he talked so mysteriously and so dole-
fully about tuberculosis that I got alarmed, and
rushed off at once to a specialist downtown. This
specialist was a competent journeyman of the tran-

[1] He is dealt with at length in Chapter VII of Happy Days.

sition stage between sweet spirits of nitre and the barbituric acid compounds: he was enough of a modernist to wear the first white coat I had ever seen on a doctor in private practise, but he stuck to a carpet on the floor of his surgery, and there was a huge (and rusty) static electricity machine in a corner. He listened to my chest sounds for half an hour or so, pulled down a couple of books, meditated profoundly, and then said that if I wanted to keep out of trouble I had better take a sea voyage, preferably in a sailing ship. His precise diagnosis, whatever it was, he did not mention, and I never learned it afterward, though I assumed that he had heard something upsetting in my bronchial tubes, or maybe even my lungs. There were craft sailing out of Baltimore, he went on, that offered what I needed in a very cheap and convenient form. They were the small schooners that went to the Bahamas every Spring to bring back pineapples. They were not licensed to carry passengers, but he reckoned that my newspaper connections would enable me to get rid of that difficulty.

When I brought this advice to Max Ways he was full of sympathy, and proceeded immediately to practical aid. I had two weeks vacation coming to me, and to them, he said, he would add another week to make up for the days off that I had lost. (I had actually lost at least fifteen, but let it go). Furthermore, if I wanted to add a fourth week I might take it without salary: beyond that he could not go without risking a row with the business office. This seemed fair to me, and Max added to my gratitude by ordering our shipping reporter to go down to the wharves at once, book passage for me on the next pineapple schooner to sail, and arrange the matter of the passenger license with his friend Bill Stone, the collector of customs. The shipping reporter came back presently with the news that the last schooner of the season had cleared that very morning, but he added consolingly that there was a banana boat sailing for the West Indies in two days, and that Old Man Buckman, the Baltimore banana king of the time, was willing to let me sign on it as supercargo. My duties and wages would be nothing, and if I paid $2.50 a day for my transportation and subsistence it would be enough.

I went down to Bowley's Wharf the next morning to have a look at the banana boat. It was a small British tramp of the kind that used to be rolled out along the Clyde as Fords were later to be littered along the River Rouge. Such paint as it showed was in patches of different colors, all of them hideous, and the only members of the crew in sight were a couple of Chinamen. It was the *Ely* of Cardiff, Captain Corning, and only the other day I went through a dusty old book at the Baltimore Customshouse to learn its official specifications. Its registered tonnage, I found, was 541

tons,[2] and it carried a crew of nineteen men. But as
it lay there at Bowley's Wharf on that far-off June
morning, gradually disgorging its cargo of green
bananas, it loomed high above the express wagons
on the quay, and seemed almost oceanic beside the
bumboats that clustered about it. The heady smell
of the tropics gushed from it, and as I gaped at it
a strange-looking yellow-faced man in white duck
clothes and a Panama hat came out of Old Man
Buckman's office and went aboard. Only a few
months before I had read Lafcadio Hearn's " Two
Years in the French West Indies," and now the
glamor of it rose up to enchant me all over. I had
never been to sea, and here I was making ready to
sail not only the great Atlantic but also the romantic Caribbean. In ten days or less I'd be loitering
beneath the palm trees, and plucking bananas,
cocoanuts, pineapples, oranges, lemons, limes,
coffee, chocolate, nutmegs, cinnamon and allspice
from the vine.

I recall nothing of our departure: my first recollection is of the sneaking, poisonous roll of the
Atlantic outside the Chesapeake capes. We cleared
the capes during the night, and when I came on

2 I take this from the clearance papers, but should add that
Captain Corning told me the tonnage was 800. There are, in
fact, four sorts of tonnage — the net, which is lowest; the gross,
the deadweight, and the displacement, which is highest. Inasmuch as port charges are commonly based on tonnage, the masters of tramp steamers pretend to the lowest that the customs
authorities will tolerate. The tonnage of large passenger liners,
of course, is reckoned as liberally as possible, to fetch customers.

deck next morning we were already out of sight
of land. To Captain Corning the day was fair and
the sea calm, but not to me. In brief, I was sea-
sick, and after I had refused breakfast and made a
couple of melancholy trips to the *leeward* rail (I
had read enough maritime literature to know *that*)
the good captain unearthed a dilapidated deck-
chair, had it taken up to the starboard wing of the
bridge, and invited me to use it. The air up there,
he said, was fresher than below, and I'd thus recover the quicker. I lolled in the chair all day and
all the following night, with my mouth open and
my eyes rolling, and was still full of misery the
next morning, but toward midday I began to recover, and by the second night I was on my legs
again, and very hungry. What I needed now, said
the captain, was some physic, so he got out his
medicine-chest and handed me a pill — the largest
and blackest, I believe, ever seen on earth. Its effects were almost those of siege artillery, but it did
me no harm, and I was presently sitting on the
after-deck eating a plate of clam chowder with the
captain.

It was his theory that clam chowder was the
queen of all human victuals, and he ate it in large
bowls every day. He said he bought it in cans,
which was reassuring, for I had taken a look into
the galley, and the Chinese cook, naked to the waist
and barefooted, was certainly not appetizing.
While we thus ate our first meal together (there

was nothing beyond the chowder save crackers and bananas) a strange shape suddenly appeared from the depths of the ship. It was that of a skinny old man wearing greasy dungarees and carpet slippers, and showing four or five days' growth of gray beard. His right arm was extended and from his hand hung a strip of what appeared to be bacon — held as gingerly as one might hold a dead rat by the tail. It turned out that he was the Scotch chief engineer, and that he had a complaint. " Is this the sort of meat," he croaked, " to feed a British crew? " " What's the matter with it? " demanded the captain. " There's worms in it," said the chief engineer. " How do you know? " said the captain. " I bit into one," said the chief engineer. " Well, then," said the captain, " spit it out and go to Hell. Back to your engine-room! "

The captain appeared to be glad of my company, for the commander of a British ship is a lonely man, and we ate together for the remainder of the voyage. It lasted eight days altogether — six days to Port Antonio on the north coast of Jamaica, and two days up the coast and back. The total distance covered was something under 1800 miles, but the *Ely* had been built, not for speed but for economy, and it took a brisk tail wind to lift her to nine knots. On the fourth day we passed the little island of San Salvador, where Columbus first sighted America, and the captain made a course close inshore, so that I could see the cairn on the

beach that marks the most fateful landfall in all
history. We were among the islands after that,
with great masses of yellow seaweed floating by on
the ever bluer water, and flying-fish leaping among
them, and strange birds coming out to have a look.
On a day so bright that it was blinding I caught
glimpses of both Cape Maysi, Cuba, and the western mountains of Haiti, but it was not until the
next morning, just before daylight, that we made
Port Antonio. The east began to show streaks of
pink as we entered the little harbor, and so I got
my first sight of the tropics in the vast splendors
of dawn.

It was a spectacle so superb that I stood on deck
silent and almost abashed. As the sun cleared the
horizon and its first rays broke through the palms
of Upper Titchfield they picked up a thousand
gaudy hues, and in a few minutes the whole scene
was shimmering like the image in a kaleidoscope. I
had always thought of the tropics as luxuriant, but
somehow, despite the word-painting of Hearn, I
had overlooked their magnificent color. Now I got
all that color with the light exactly right, and behind it, gradually fading into blue and gray,
stretched the immense escarpment of the Blue
Mountains, just short of a mile and a half high.
And down from the heights, borne by the land-
breeze of the dawn, came the indescribable tropical smell — half sweet and half sour, laden with
strange and lovely scents, but also with whiffs of

decay. I was brought back to the rusty and decrepit *Ely* by the clatter of oar-locks: a small boat was making out from the shadows of the shore. When it came close I saw a very impressive man standing in its stern — coal black as to complexion, but clad in immaculate white ducks and a sun helmet. He was some sort of port functionary, and he entered upon an official parley with the captain. " How many? " I heard him bellow, and the captain bawled back " Nineteen officers and hands and one passenger." Passenger? Wasn't I on the ship's papers as supercargo? The captain recalled the fact instantly and corrected his report. " I meant to say," he howled, " *twenty* officers and hands, and *no* passengers." The functionary made no reply, and I was soon preparing to go ashore.

But at the last minute the captain proposed that I stay aboard while he ran up the coast to load bananas, and in an hour we were off. How far we went I have forgotten, but I recall going ashore at a little place called Port Maria, and wandering through a village that looked precisely like an African kraal, even to the high-pitched thatched roofs and the stilts under the wicker houses. The captain went along and we palavered with the females of the settlement, and watched their naked children at play, while the bucks hauled bananas out to the *Ely* in surf-boats. When it was time for us to return to the ship there was a warning blast of its siren, and all the children dived under the

houses. We got back to Port Antonio on the second
morning following, again at dawn, and I saw the
show of light and color all over again. The *Ely* did
not enter the harbor, but only slowed down outside,
and I went ashore in a surf-boat, along with four
or five banana-checkers of the white race, and a
dozen black roustabouts. One of the checkers was
a ventriloquist, and he entertained the rest of us by
evoking sepulchral shrieks of " Help! " and
" Murder! " from the depths of the Caribbean,
and turning the livers of the poor Afro-Jamaicans
to water.

When we parted the captain and I agreed to
meet again in Baltimore on my return, and we did
so a couple of months later. I took him to lunch
and he asked for clam chowder: he was still eating
it every day. He was a Blue Nose from Nova
Scotia, and not very communicative, but on this
occasion he confided to me an aspiration that, so I
learned afterward, was shared by all the merchant
masters in the West Indies trade. It was to get a
towing line, some happy day, aboard a disabled
steamship of large tonnage, and so strike a blow
for humanity and collar the captain's share in a
juicy pot of salvage. Whether or not this chance
for Service ever came to him I never heard, but
years afterward, crossing the Atlantic in a luxurious *Doppelschraubenschnellpostdampfer*, I met
another captain of the Spanish Main to whom it
had. He was a Dane from Schleswig, and his share

of the honorarium, so he told me, ran to $30,000.
He invested it in certain mysterious speculations in
the Oriente province of Cuba, and when I encountered him he had on a Panama hat that had cost
him $125 wholesale, and was passing out Upmann
cigars at least eight inches long.

I put in a couple of weeks roving and seeing
Jamaica, and was delighted enormously by its varied but always gorgeous scenery. I crossed the
island on a train that ducked through twenty-four
tunnels in forty miles, and between them ran along
gorges thick with bamboo and brilliant with
crocuses of a hundred colors and a thousand patterns. On another train I traveled westward over
the high country, and spent a night at the very
English hill-station of Mandeville, where I dined
on a cut from a pale, bluish joint of island beef,
with two vegetables that tasted like stewed hay. I
put up at the old Myrtle Bank Hotel in Kingston
(soon to be destroyed in the great earthquake of
1907), and there became acquainted with planters'
punch, a drink that I have esteemed highly ever
since, and also with an exiled native king from the
Mosquito Coast, who lived in gloomy splendor on
an official solatium of £1 a day and spent all his
time trying to grasp the game of billiards. And I
went up to Spanish Town, the old capital of the
island, and there searched the records for vestiges
of my father's mother's people, the McClellans,
who had lived in Jamaica nearly a century before.

These records were in charge of a colored intellectual who wore the thick spectacles with Oxford
frames that still mark a learned blackamoor in the
British West Indies. He brought out a dozen elephant folios from his catacombs, and deputed a
lowly clark, a mulatto with sandy hair, to help me
explore them. All the clark and I could find was
the will of my great-great-uncle, Jeremiah, who
had died in Kingston back in the early forties. He
had left, it appeared, a small legacy to my grandmother, then still a child, but whether she ever got
it I do not know: I suppose that I must assume that
she did, for his executor was a clergyman. This
Jeremiah never married, but there was in him none
the less a strong strain of philoprogenitiveness, and
I discovered that his descendants were numerous all
over the southern parishes of the island, and that
some of the latest generation had reverted to an almost burnt cork complexion. On my return to Baltimore I spread the news, and acquired thereby a
standing in the inner Confederate circles of the
town that was very useful to me in my later newspaper work.

Kingston itself was an ancient and romantic
town, and I spent some agreeable mornings wandering along its sea-front or rambling through its
market, which swarmed with native farmers from
back in the brush. They offered all sorts of comes-
tibles that were new to me — for example, cacao
beans, plantains, mangoes, and cashew nuts, all of

them still unknown in the United States. They had heaps of pimento berries, from which allspice is made, spread out on newspapers, and here and there was a country butcher with rounds and chops of goat meat. I learned to smoke and like the dark, spicy Jamaican cigars, and I had a colored tailor sitting at his booth by the market place make me a suit of white ducks. They were ready in two hours and cost £1, then the standard price for a Class A suit in Kingston. The tailor told me that he had other and cheaper models, some as low as eight shillings, but that he never recommended them to distinguished visitors. I also made acquaintance with a Jamaican soft-drink called cola — the progenitor, I suspect, of Coca-Cola, which was yet concealed in the womb of time. And, as a fanatical Kiplingite, I was enchanted to observe Mulvaney, Learoyd and Ortheris, direct from " Soldiers Three," strutting along the streets of the town with their swagger sticks, tomcatting the more likely black gals, and taking their ease in the less refined bars.

All these studies and recreations were very pleasant, but my time was running short, so I shoved back to Port Antonio to find a ship for home. I learned at once that a Norwegian tramp of about the size and speed of the *Ely* would be clearing in a few days, and I booked passage at once. The next day was a Sunday, and I resolved to spend it sitting on the veranda of the old Titchfield Hotel, listening to the gabble of the super-cargoes, plantation overseers and English remittance men who then constituted the society of the place. They started off after breakfast with a series of magnificent tales of love, trading and carnage, for it was not often that they encountered a new listener who was really eager to listen. But suddenly, in the midst of a hair-raising anecdote about cannibalism in Haiti, two of them rose quietly and faded away, and then two more followed, and then three, and in half a minute I was alone with the raconteur, an Irishman who claimed to be the son of a Spanish duke. Finally, even *he* made off at a quick sneak, and I looked behind me anxiously, almost expecting to see a crocodile bearing down, or even a shark. But all I could find was an old man with a long white beard, buttoned up in a black frock coat of the vintage of 1880. He looked harmless enough, certainly, but I was soon to learn that he was the most dangerous carnivore on the island, for what he packed was a messianic delusion.

In brief, he was tortured by a libido to save the souls of carnal wayfarers, and in order to feed and furnish it he maintained at his own expense a Methodist chapel down in the town. The cost was no burden to him, for he had come to Jamaica back in the first days of the banana business, and picked up plenty of easy money. Now his whole time was given over to his missionarying, and every Sunday

89

morning he swooped down on the Titchfield veranda and tried to round up the damned assembled there. As I learned afterward, only strangers somewhat gone in liquor ever succumbed to him, and when they got back from his services they always reported a terrible experience. Being sober at the time, I resisted, and inasmuch as I was already something of an amateur theologian, and hence familiar with all the classical grips and grapples, I resisted to some effect. But I am glad to testify today, after so many years, that never in this life have I gone to the mat with a tougher evangelist. He beat any Christian Scientist ever heard of, or any Presbyterian, however ferocious, or any foot-wash Baptist. I have been tackled in my day by virtuosi ranging from mitred abbots to the kitchen police of the Salvation Army, but never have I had to fight harder to preserve my doctrinal chastity. Over and over again the old boy got to my chin or midriff with scriptural texts that had the impact of a mule's hoof, and when he turned from upbraiding to cajolery, and began to argue that my sufferings in Hell would be upon his head, I almost threw up the sponge. Indeed, if it had not been for the audience lying in wait (I could hear it panting behind the jalousies), I'd have gone down to his gospel mill with him, if only to get rid of him, but as it was I was in honor bound to resist, and in the end he gave up in despair, and shuffled off down the path to the town. The loafers, when they sneaked back, stood me a communal drink, and I surely needed it. Some years later, on returning to Port Antonio, I was told that the old man had got himself into a wilder and wilder lather as his years advanced, and that he finally prayed himself to death.

The Norwegian tramp that brought me home, though it was as slow as the *Ely* and little if any larger, turned out to be a great deal cleaner and more shipshape. The young captain, who told me that he owned a 3/70ths interest in it, his father an 18/70ths, and his rich Uncle Olaf a 32/70ths, had his wife with him — a handsome and charming blonde from Bergen, with enlightened ideas about eating and drinking, and a flair for interior decoration in the provincial Scandinavian mode. Every chair in the cabin had a knitted tidy on it, and there were window-boxes at all the portholes, with geraniums growing in them. We dined at 1 p.m., which is to say, we *began* to dine at 1 p.m. The meal itself, prepared by an excellent Danish cook, lasted until 3, and then the steward came in with a large Gjedser cheese, a plate of crackers, a pot of coffee and a bottle of Madeira, and we lingered over them until 4 or even 5. The captain and his wife were eager propagandists for the Norwegian *Kultur*, and they told me so much about Ibsen, then still a dubious character in America, that I became, a few years later, Baltimore's recognized authority on the subject, and even went to the

length of reading all the plays, including " The
Warriors at Helgeland," perhaps the worst play
ever written. I blush to say that I can't remember
the name of this amiable and excellent pair, though
I seem to recall that it was something on the order
of Olsen, Jensen, Hansen, Knutson, Halvorsen or
Magnussen. They were intelligent and kindly people, and the captain was a brisk and competent
mariner.

But even the briskest mariner collides now and
then with what the marine insurance policies call
an act of God, and this happened to my friend
somewhere or other off the Middle Atlantic coast.
It was a misty morning, and in consequence he
could not leave the bridge, so I climbed up to keep
him company. Suddenly there was a thinning of
the mist, and a light-ship loomed up off the *starboard* bow. In other words, we were *inside* the
light-ship — and maybe only a few yards from the
beach. The captain had yanked the wheel out of
the quartermaster's hands in a split second, and
the ship heeled over alarmingly as we made a quarter turn on the nautical equivalent of a ten-cent
piece. We continued due East for two hours at
least, and the next morning, though the sky was as
clear as crystal, the captain approached the Delaware capes as cautiously as a sheep approaching a
coyote, and, in fact, did not venture to enter at all
until another ship came along and showed the way.

That my trip to Jamaica had done me any good

did not appear immediately. I was still under-weight, and as Summer faded into Autumn I developed a cough. The specialist, however, professed to believe that his prescription had worked, and I was presently so busy that I forgot my malaises. I wrote three pieces for the *Sunday Herald* on my adventures, illustrated by halftones from photographs that I had bought on the island. I was ready and willing to write three more, or a dozen more, but Colonel Cunningham got rid of me by saying that a stringent economy order had just come up from the business office, and that he'd catch hell if he authorized any more halftones. I continued skinny until 1904, as the frontispiece to this work shows, but after that I gradually picked up weight, and by the time I was thirty I was so rotund that another specialist put me on one of the first of the reducing diets.

VI

THE GOSPEL OF

SERVICE

It was in the month of May, 1901, that I got my first really juicy out-of-town assignment — and began to develop in a large way my theory that Service is mainly only blah. The scene was the town of Jacksonville, Fla., and I had been sent there to cover the great fire of May 3, the largest blaze in American history between the burning of Chicago in 1871 and the burning of Baltimore in 1904. It destroyed, as I learn from an encyclopedia, no less than 2361 buildings, stretching over 196 city blocks and 450 acres: all I can add to these statistics is that when I arrived by train, all set to load the wires with graphic prose, there seemed to be nothing left save a fringe of houses around the municipal periphery, like the hair on a friar's head.

Only one hotel was left standing, and, so far as I could discover, not a single other public convenience of any sort, whether church, hospital, theatre, livery-stable, jail, bank, saloon, barber-shop, pants-pressing parlor, or sporting-house.

But what so powerfully reinforced my growing suspicion of Service was not this scene of desolation, but the imbecility of the public effort to aid its ostensible victims. In every American community of Christian pretensions, North, East, South and West, busy-bodies began to collect money and goods for their succor the moment the first bulletins came in, and by the time I reached what was left of the Jacksonville railroad station the first relief shipments were on their way. The *Herald* started a communal subscription at the drop of the hat, and had cabbaged half a carload of eleemosynary supplies before I left for the South. The city editor (not Max Ways, but one of his successors) favored me from hour to hour with dispatches recording the progress of this philanthropy. The first one, I recall, announced that the boys at the Pimlico race-track had contributed 100 second-hand horse-blankets, and on its heels came one reporting that the saloonkeepers of Baltimore had matched them with 100 cases of Maryland rye.

When I took these dispatches to the Mayor of Jacksonville I expected (at least officially) that he would burst into tears and bid me thank the good people of Baltimore for their generosity, but what he actually did was to laugh. I must confess that, at thought of the horse-blankets, I had to smile myself, for the temperature in Jacksonville was rising 80 degrees, and most of the dispossessed householders, white and black, were camping out gaily in their erstwhile backyards, and refreshing themselves with swims in the St. Johns river. The Mayor was amused, but not surprised, for he had telegrams on his desk showing that many other Northern cities were even more idiotic than Baltimore. St. Paul, it appeared, was sending a couple of bales of old fur coats, and Boston was loading a car with oil-stoves. Even some of the nearby towns, though they should have known better, had contributed supplies almost as insane. Thus, a large box of woolen mittens had already come in from Montgomery, Ala., and Winston-Salem, N. C., had sent a supply of the heavy, sanitary red underwear for which it was then famous.

But it was the Maryland whiskey, not the Pimlico horse-blankets, that really flabbergasted the Mayor. He was far from a Prohibitionist, but the fire had given him plenty of worries, and he did not welcome the new one provided by those hundred cases of rye. What would he do with them when they arrived — supposing they escaped the hobos and railroad men on the way? If he distributed them as medical supplies every white man in Jacksonville would be in a state of liquor within an hour, and probably half of the blackamoors. If he put

his town cops to guarding them he would lose his
police force, which was sorely needed. And if he
asked for a detail from the Florida militia, which
was flocking into town from the swamps to the
southward, there would be a military drunk of a
virulence unparalleled since Sherman's march to
the sea, with a good deal of promiscuous shooting.

I had no suggestion to offer His Honor, and left
him. I wrote a column and a half on the scene of
desolation, and then went to inquire of the railroad
men when the first car from Baltimore could be expected. They knew nothing about it, and had
never even heard of it. Indeed, it was not until
hours later that I got a bulletin from Baltimore
saying that it had just started, and in the same bulletin came news that it was now two cars instead of
one. The second, it appeared, was loaded mainly
with medical and chirurgical *matériel*, including a
bale of splints, five gallons of sulphuric ether, half
a ton of bandages, a crate of wooden legs, and
twenty Potter's Field coffins in shooks. Inasmuch
as no one had suffered anything worse than a few
singes in the fire, and all the other survivors were in
robust health and excellent spirits, this shipment
seemed somehow irrational, but figuring out what
to do with it was the Mayor's grief, not mine, and I
confined myself to trying to learn when it would
arrive.

The Mayor, when I saw him again that evening,
was not as put out about the medical supplies as I

expected, for he said that the militiamen from the Everglades would undoubtedly begin shooting one another anon, and it would be handy to have the splints and coffins, if not the wooden legs. But when I told him (as I had just been advised by a latter bulletin) that the freight of the medical car included a dozen cases of champagne, he immediately took a graver view of the situation, and, in fact, showed a considerable perturbation. This seemed unreasonable to me, for I believed the cops and militiamen, all of them unschooled in the ways of the northern Babylons, would probably take to their heels in alarm the moment the first champagne cork popped, but when I said so to the Mayor he replied that a moral question was involved — in brief, that champagne was still regarded by the decent people of Florida as a lecherous drink, and that having it on his hands might embarrass him politically almost as much as having a trunk full of tights. I could see this point of view and even sympathize with it, though I was young at the time, so I proposed to His Honor that he commandeer the champagne the instant it arrived, wrap it in the horse-blankets from Pimlico, and lock it up in the catacombs under City Hall, for such future reference as human ingenuity and the course of events might suggest. Whether or not this was actually done I do not know to the present day, as the narrative following will show.

It was now late at night, and I began to think

about a place to sleep. As I have said, there was
only one hotel left standing, and when I got to it I
found that it was swamped by guests — some of
them newspaper reporters like myself, but most of
them insurance adjusters, brick and lumber sales-
men, and agents for sprinkling systems and fire ex-
tinguishers. They were sleeping five and six in a
room, and all the upstairs corridors were full of
cots. Every one of the arm-chairs in the lobby had
been grabbed by a sleeper, and others were snoring
on the dining-room tables. The night-clerk, a very
affable fellow, received my importunities politely,
but shook his head. Finally, he had a bright idea.
Between the lobby and the dining-room there was a
small ladies' parlor, and in it was a grand piano,
with a heavily embroidered spread covering it.
Why not remove the spread, roll it up for a pillow,
and then turn in *under* the piano? I'd thus have the
whole space beneath the instrument to myself, a
larger area than anyone else had, and I'd be protected from the hooves of guests stumbling through
the parlor in the dark. The idea seemed magnificent, and in five minutes I was berthed behind the
pedals and sound asleep.

Unhappily, I was not booked for an easy night,
for before I got halfway through my first dream
a squad of moron soldiery took up post on the veranda outside the parlor window, to guard a burned
bank across the street, and their simian gabble and
guffawing made me toss and moan, dead tired

though I was. But the worst was reserved for 3 a.m. or thereabouts. The goofs had brought a primeval machine-gun with them, and one of them, thinking he saw ghouls in the ruins of the bank, suddenly turned it on. With the sounding-board of the piano directly over my head I got the full force of the reverberation — indeed, I got a great magnification of it. It took on the proportions of the explosion of a battleship, and when I fetched up with a start my head banged the hull of the piano, and I got a bump that stuck to me until I was back in Baltimore. The night-clerk patched me up with vinegar and butcher-paper from the kitchen, but I slept no more that night.

All the next day I devoted to badgering the railroad men about the two relief-cars, and all of the day following, with occasional pauses to file instalments of my thriller on the ruins. No report of them had come in. No one had any notion where they were. Meanwhile, my city editor bombarded me with demands that I get and send a statement from the Mayor, setting forth Jacksonville's gratitude. Rather curiously for so philosophical a man, he raised scruples about giving it to me. What if the cars never arrived at all? What if they were wrecked along the way, and the whole world learned that they had not got in? Inspired and goaded by my city editor, I labored with His Honor, and in the end he compromised with his conscience by requiring me to swear that if he gave me a statement

I would not send it until the cars were safe in port. I was ready, by that time, to agree to anything, and after a conference with his advisers he produced the document. It turned out, after all that backing and filling, to be only a carbon of one that had been dispatched to Savannah, Atlanta, New Orleans, and various other nearby cities, with the name of Baltmore inserted in a blank left for the purpose. It began by saying that the people of Jacksonville were completely overcome by the astounding generosity and loving-kindness of the (Baltimore) humanitarians, and would never forget it so long as the pleasant and mutually profitable business relations between Jacksonville and (Baltimore) continued. It went on in this vein for 500 or 600 words, and then closed with some sly remarks about the salubriousness of the Florida climate, and the incomparable flavor of the citrus fruits. This was before the great Florida land boom, so there was no mention of real estate opportunities, but the general tenor of it was certainly very complacent, and I heard when I got home that some of the horse-lovers of Pimlico, on reading it, said they wished they had kept their blankets.

Armed with the carbon, I spent the evening in the railroad yards searching for the two cars of relief supplies, and not finding them. Along about ten o'clock the fireman of a switching engine told me that he had seen a couple of suspicious-looking cars on a siding about a mile out of town, and I hoofed there to have a look. I got to the place all right, and even found the cars, only to learn that they were two old wrecks loaded with razor-back hog hides from Waycross, Ga. I turned sadly away, and started down the long, long trail back to stricken but contented Jacksonville. I had gone hardly a third of the distance when a yahoo militia-man jumped from behind a gondola, and jammed his bayonet into my front. He was taking his stance to shove it through me when I managed to yell. This set him to yelling too, and in a moment two more privates, a corporal, a sergeant, and finally a lieutenant rushed up. It appeared that the yahoo charged me with looting, though there was nothing within half a mile that any sensible man would loot. I demanded trial on the spot, and it was presently in progress, with the lieutenant serving as both president and judge-advocate. He was an ill-favored fellow, and if he lived to 1934 he probably got a part in " Tobacco Road," but he knew something about the rules of evidence, and so acquitted me with honor, and even offered me a chew from his plug as a solatium.

There ensued three days and three nights of fevered hunting for those cars, gladdened on the afternoon of the third day by a telegram from the Seaboard's division superintendent at Savannah saying that they had been found on a siding near a water-tank called Jones. I tried to wire to Jones, but was told that there was no operator there, nor indeed anything save the tank itself and an old man who spent his time plugging its leaks with rosin. I laid off the third night, and had a fair sleep, and then spent the next morning writing a long piece describing the grateful gloats and sobs of the starving and shivering Jacksonville populace as the cars rolled in, and the supplies were distributed. I figured on filing this palpitating stuff the instant they really arrived, or were reported anywhere below the Georgia frontier, but when they failed to turn up at 6 p.m. I filed it anyhow, and was encouraged two hours later by a complimentary telegram from the home office.

Bucked up by this appreciation, I decided to put in another night in the yards, looking for the cars. When I got there no one had seen them, or heard anything about them, but while I stood talking with the yardmaster, wondering whether I had better give up, they suddenly appeared from nowhere, directly before our eyes. They were running next to the caboose of a way-freight, and how they got there I never learned. The door of one hung by a single hinge, but when it came to a halt I could find no sign that it had been burgled, and the railroad men showed no predatory interest in its contents. On both sides of each car were muslin banners (or what was left of them) reading:

BALTIMORE MORNING HERALD
RELIEF TRAIN FOR
JACKSONVILLE FIRE SUFFERERS

The railroad men snickered quietly at the words " train " and " sufferers," and began pulling the signs down — as I gathered from their talk, to make shirts for their children. I filed the Mayor's long-delayed statement before turning in, and slept late the next morning, for my mission of mercy was over. At noon or thereabout I dropped into His Honor's office, and he promised to do something about the cars as soon as he could come round to it — that is, if the anthropoid militiamen did not seize them meanwhile, and spirit them away to the Everglades. He even suggested politely that if I would stick about a day or two longer a couple of the bottles of Maryland rye would be mine for the asking. But I needed sleep more than stimulants, and, what is more, I was lathering for a square meal, for the catering arrangements at Jacksonville, even disregarding the fire, were much less elaborate in those days than they are today, and I was tired of tough hog-meat and greasy corn-pone. That night I boarded a train for Baltimore, and the next day, at a meal-stop called Norlina, near the border between North Carolina and Virginia, I tackled a platter of country victuals that still sticks in my mind after forty years. It was, in quality, superb, for it consisted principally of chicken fried to perfection, with hominy cakes and cream gravy. In quantity, it was colossal, and the half hour allowed for devouring it was enough to dispose of only about a third of it. The rest, according to the custom of travelers in that age, I stuffed into my pockets, and I was still at work on it when we crossed the James river.

A year later I was sent back to Jacksonville to find out how the town was making out. I found, as I expected, that the fire had been the luckiest act of God in all its history. The marsh that used to lie between it and the channel of the St. Johns river, generating mosquitoes and malaria, was now filled with the debris, and dozens of new warehouses were going up. A little while later Congress ordered the 19-foot channel dredged to 24 feet, and then to 30. During the next decade the population of Jacksonville more than doubled, and today it is a metropolis comparable to Nineveh or Gomorrah in their prime, with the hottest night-clubs between Norfolk and Miami, and so many indigenous salvage-crews of humanitarians that Florida can't contain them, and they are constantly reaching out for more distant clients. When, in 1904, Baltimore itself had a big fire, they proposed to send up enough oranges (some of them almost fresh) to supply 500,000 people for 100 days, but the Baltimore authorities declined them.

My exertions on my mission seem to have been well received in the *Herald* office, for during the following year I was given a number of other interesting out-of-town assignments. I recall, for example, being sent to the battlefield of Antietam, in Western Maryland, to cover the dedication of a soldiers' monument by the immortal McKinley. He was to become an angel only a couple of months later, but he did not know it at the time, and so made a roaring speech from an open-air stand on a very hot day. There were scores of reporters present, including a large squad of Washington correspondents wearing cutaway coats and carrying doggy walking-sticks. This was the first time that I had ever come into contact with such eminent journalists, and you may be sure that I gaped at them with every show of respect. Inasmuch as McKinley's secretary, George B. Cortelyou, had brought along copies of the presidential speech, it was not necessary to risk sunstroke by listening to it, so I spent the hour of its delivery roving about the grounds. A large marquee had been erected for the accommodation of distinguished guests, and in it I found a dozen or more United States Senators loading up on fried chicken and champagne. Late in the afternoon the whole party returned to Washington on a special train provided by the Baltimore & Ohio Railroad, and I heard the same Senators go through a long programme of American folk-song, including " The Old Black Bull." There were no ladies present, for in those days the female politician had not yet begun to spoil junkets.

Various assignments took me to Washington, and there came eventually the glorious day when I sat in the Senate press-gallery for the first time.

Like all the really massive experiences of life, it turned out to be more or less disappointing. I also made a number of trips to Annapolis, to help my betters cover the Maryland Legislature, and there I sniffed for the first time the peculiar smell that radiates from all such bodies — that sickening mixture of stale beer and free lunch, contributed by the city members, and cow and sweat, contributed by the yokels. In the years since I have smelled it in six or eight other state capitals, and have never been able to detect a difference of more than two per cent. between one and the next. But the best of all the assignments that came to me in those happy days, and indeed the best of my whole career on newspapers, I had to miss. It was the Martinique volcano story of 1902. The first blow-off of Mont Pelée, of course, happened too suddenly to be covered, but when the Navy started a couple of rescue ships for the island there was room on them for a few reporters, and Carter got a place for the *Herald,* and assigned me to it. The boys on those rescue ships saw the most stupendous spectacle ever staged on earth, for when they heaved in sight of the island the volcano went off again, and with ten times the violence of the first time. The ships were rocked by the blast and covered with ashes, but no one was hurt. All the reporters vomited purple copy, and for a week afterward it filled the American newspapers. Alas, none of it was mine, for on the day before the ships sailed I was served with a summons in a lawsuit relating to my father's estate, and my lawyer warned me that if I disregarded it I might land in jail on my return, and my mother might lose a piece of property. No one else was sent.

VII

SCENT OF THE

THEATRE

THE REPORTER covering the theatres for the
Herald, during my first year on the staff, was Theodore M. Leary, a charming young Irishman who
was a graduate of the Johns Hopkins and whose
father, a general in the Army, was commandant at
Fort McHenry, the Baltimore military post. The
job, in those days, was not a full-time one, and
Leary was often given other assignments. In June,
1900, he was sent to Philadelphia to help Al Goodman, the political reporter of the paper, cover the
Republican National Convention. The importance of the job impressed him vastly, and when his
train reached Wilmington he put off a telegram
to Max Ways, announcing the fact. Half an hour

later, having got to Philadelphia, he sent another, reading:

Have arrived safely. Delegates pouring in. Prepare for at least a column and a half tonight.

The waggish Max passed these telegrams around the office, and when Leary returned he was given a heavy dose of kidding. But he threw it off by doing excellent work, and was soon ranked among the four or five best reporters on the paper. Such a youngster, when assigned to the theatres, was always marked, in those days, by the theatrical managers of New York, and in a little while he began to receive offers from this one or that one to go on the road as press-agent of a traveling company. At the beginning of the season of 1901–2 he finally succumbed, and at his suggestion I was given his place. Thus I escaped the City Hall at last, and in the intervals of covering the theatres took general assignments. In October I was made Sunday editor, but continued to do the theatres and also to write for the editorial page.

Baltimore then had two first-class playhouses, Ford's Opera House and the Academy of Music, a third that played dollar shows, a fourth that offered vaudeville, a fifth that had a stock company, a sixth that played only melodrama, and a couple of burlesque houses. There was a change of bill in each of them every week, and every change of bill had to be noticed. The theatre reporter (or, as he was called, the dramatic editor) commonly did the principal attraction of the week, but when Robert I. Carter became managing editor of the *Herald* at the end of 1900 he took over the leading notice himself, for he had formerly been a dramatic critic, was still greatly interested in the theatre, and knew more about plays than any other man I had encountered up to that time. Thus, when I succeeded Leary, it was only the second choice that fell to me, but I was very well content, for two times out of three Carter would pick the more serious plays, which left me the comedies and musical pieces. I recall, for example, that I did " Florodora " when it first came to Baltimore, and liked it so well that I dropped in at every subsequent performance of the week, usually just as the famous sextette was coming on. In the first theatre page that I got out as Sunday editor, the piano score of the sextette was reproduced as a background for a photograph of the six elegant bucks and six gorgeous wenches who danced and sang it.

On Monday evenings, after Carter had dictated his own notice and I had written mine, he would invite me to his office, and instruct me in the technic of reviewing. He believed, and taught me, that a dull notice, however profound, was not worth printing. " The first job of a reviewer," he would say, " is to write a good story — to produce something that people will enjoy reading. If he has nothing to say he simply can't do it. If he has, then it doesn't make much difference whether what he says is fundamentally sound or not. Exact and scientific criticism is not worth trying for, especially on a provincial paper. Don't hesitate to use the actors roughly: they are mainly idiots. And don't take a dramatist's pretensions too seriously: he is usually only a showman." Carter warned me against associating with theatrical people, but added that he meant performers, not authors or managers. In search of material for my daily column of theatrical gossip I tackled all members of the latter two classes who visited Baltimore, and thereby got to know many notables of the time, for example, Daniel Frohman, Victor Herbert, Clyde Fitch, Paul Armstrong, Augustus Thomas, Charles Klein and A. M. Palmer. Charles Frohman I never met. When he came to town he secreted himself mysteriously, and getting to see him was an elaborate business, almost as difficult as seeing the Pope. When, in the end, I was solemnly invited to the felicity of waiting on him, I refused, for I had seen a good many of his plays by that time, and come to the conclusion that he was a fraud.

But I naturally met all of the salient press-agents of the era, for they came to my office as soon as they got to town. Most of them were former newspaper reporters, and all that I can remember were very pleasant fellows. One of the liveliest was a Dane with the strange name of A. Toxen Worm, who stood at the head of the craft but is now forgotten. Another who was good company was a tall, slim, handsome blond young man named Herbert Bayard Swope, who interrupted a successful newspaper career to whoop up the English actor, Martin Harvey. Harvey seemed to me to be a ham, but Swope I came to terms with quickly, and we have been on a footing of mutual esteem and suspicion ever since. In 1912 he was married in Baltimore, and I was best man at his wedding. In 1906 I was drafted for the same delicate office by Channing Pollock, who then combined press-agenting and play-writing, but I had to function *in absentia,* for at the last moment he and Anna Marble decided to be married in Canada. Many other press-agents of that era were interesting and able men, among them, Paul Wilstach, who whooped up Richard Mansfield and actually believed that he was the greatest actor on earth; James Forbes, who labored for many bad stars, including Robert Edeson; Eugene Walter, who did the same, again including Edeson; Bayard Veiller, who represented, among other first-chop performers, his own excellent wife, Margaret Wycherly; and Frank J. Wilstach, who was Paul's elder brother, and served, at different times, De Wolf Hopper, E. H. Sothern, Julia Marlowe, Viola Allen, William Faversham and Mrs. Leslie Carter. These were all clever fellows, and every one of them made his mark in the years following. Paul Wilstach wrote a number of successful plays, accumulated a competence, and retired in bachelor splendor to a romantic old estate on the Potomac. Forbes, in 1906, wrote " The Chorus Lady," which broke records on Broadway; Walter, in 1908, alarmed and delighted it with " The Easiest Way "; and Veiller had two big successes in 1918 and 1928 — " Within the Law " and " The Trial of Mary Dugan." Frank Wilstach wrote no plays, but devoted all his leisure to a dictionary of similes that had a cordial reception when it came out at last, and remains the standard work in its field. He collected its contents as he toured the country ahead of his various troupes, and always carried a large ledger for recording them. I supplied him with scores, including many that I invented on the spot, with modest credit to such authors as Aristotle, Confucius and John Calvin. Frank died in 1933 and Forbes five years later, but the rest still flourish.

In 1902, coming to Baltimore ahead of Robert Edeson, Forbes confided to me that he had planted an illustrated article on his star's achievements at field sports, and asked for my help in making the photographs. Edeson, as a matter of fact, knew no more about field sports than a mother superior, but we soon borrowed an outfit of guns, fishing tackle, shooting jackets, hip boots and so on, and went out to Druid Hill Park with a photographer. The time was mid-morning, and the park was deserted. For the fishing pictures a small pond served as stream, and then Edeson changed to the shooting jacket and began to draw beads on imaginary birds. Suddenly a mounted cop came galloping over a hill, and put the whole party under arrest. He had heard, he said, several shots. Didn't we know that it was a serious offense to shoot birds in a public park? We protested that no shot had been fired, and handed over the gun to prove it. We also offered to let the cop search us for cartridges. But he insisted that he had heard at least three shots from the other side of the hill. Why, else, should he have charged us at a gallop? The mystery was never solved. We finally talked the cop out of calling the wagon, but he went away muttering. To this day his imbecile, puzzled face returns to me in my dreams, and wakes me in a sweat. Druid Hill Park, as every Afro-Baltimorean knows, is infested by witches, but who ever heard of a witch using firearms?

Paul Armstrong I met for the first time when he came to Baltimore to put on his first play, " St. Ann." He had been working for Hearst as a sports reporter specializing in pugilism, and had saved enough money to buy scenery and hire a company. All the regular managers of the time had refused the play, and Armstrong was already full of a loathing for them that continued to his death. It turned out to be a dreadful *réchauffé* of Sardou, Pinero and Augustus Thomas, and the opening performance was a nightmare to both audience and dramatist. One of the principal actors showed up drunk and had to be fired, and then another actor, though sober, undertook to beat up Armstrong for an imaginary insult to the leading woman. Armstrong, who was a tough fellow, knocked out this poor fish, so there were two vacancies in the cast, and when a girl who had a small part began to be saucy she was fired too, and there were three. The first act wobbled, the second was worse, the third became downright maniacal, and the fourth was never finished. These proceedings, and especially the bout between Armstrong and the actor, made excellent newspaper fodder, and it was my sworn duty to describe them in the *Herald*. Armstrong, as a newspaper man, understood my position and did not resent my story. Instead, he seemed grateful that I had tamed it down as much as possible, and we straightway became warm friends. A few years later he was the king of Broadway, with three big successes running at once. Having thus fallen into funds, he decided to become a landed proprietor in Maryland, where, as he used to say, there were more shades of green in Spring than anywhere else on earth. He bought an ancient and dilapidated estate below Annapolis, and moved there with his wife and three little girls, and after that I used to see a lot of him, for I spent many weekends with him and he seldom passed through Baltimore without looking me up.

One day in the Spring of 1915 I received a letter

from him, dated Atlantic City, saying that he was laid up there by a heart attack, and asking me to arrange for his treatment at the Johns Hopkins Hospital. I did so at once, and in a few days he was at the hospital under the care of Dr. Lewellys F. Barker, the successor of Osler as its chief physician. Dr. Barker found that his heart was very badly impaired, and warned him that he'd have to avoid excitement if he expected to live. Armstrong promised solemnly to go on a Mark Twain regimen — doing all his writing in bed, and leaving every sort of business to his confidential agent, Ben Piazzi. But he had hardly got back to New York before he became involved in a lawsuit, and before long he was engaged in his usual fights with actors. By the end of the Summer he was dead. He was a curious man, and had some talent. His plays, to be sure, were mainly trash, but nevertheless they were very adroitly constructed, and he made success after success, some of them record-breaking. Despite his truculent ways and fearsome makeup — he wore a Buffalo Bill goatee and a two-gallon hat, and liked striking clothes and flashy jewelry — he was a simple-minded fellow at bottom, and more than once, listening to him expound the plot of a new play at his dinner-table, I have seen tears roll down his cheeks. He probably earned more money than any other dramatist up to his time, whether here or in Europe. His revenues from a single one-acter, played by two companies in

117

vaudeville, ran, to my personal knowledge, beyond $2000 a week for two years on end. He was preparing, in his last days, to invade the movies in the grand manner, and if he had lived ten years more he'd have died a multi-millionaire, for he was already master of all the eye-popping, heartbreaking and liver-scratching devices that the movie Shakespeares were to develop only long afterward. At least five years before D. W. Griffith exacerbated the soul of humanity with "The Birth of a Nation" Armstrong was entertaining me with projects for historical films on twice its scale, with such excursions and alarms in them that they would have paled it. He died at forty-six, leaving three widows. Both of the two that I knew were beautiful and charming women.

I met a great many other dramatic authors in those days, and also most of the current composers of operettas and musical comedies. Reginald De Koven I remember mainly for the fact that he was in liquor every time I had him under my eye, and Victor Herbert because of his marked German accent. Herbert had been brought up in Stuttgart, where his mother had married for the second time, and he looked, talked and carried himself far more like a Württemberger than like the Irishman that he was. He spent a couple of Summers in Baltimore as the director of pop concerts. A man of large bulk, with a neck that required a No. 20 collar, he suffered much from the heat. I used to drop in on him between numbers, and usually found him sitting in his dressing-room in his undershirt, drinking Rhine wine and damning the thermometer. During one especially hot spell he wrecked four or five shirts of an evening, and had to put on a fresh collar after every number. Once, to make conversation, I asked him how he had got the idea for the lovely gipsy love-song in " The Fortune Teller." He replied that he didn't know. " I was aware," he said, " that Eugene Cowles would sing it, and when I sat down to write it I had his voice in mind. After that, I just wrote it." Another popular composer of the time, Willard Spenser, told me that he fetched up melodies by improvising at a church organ. This Spenser was a tall, cadaverous fellow with wispy side-whiskers, and looked more like a Presbyterian deacon than a composer for the theatre. He was, in fact, very prim and pious, and never visited back-stage if he could help it. His two operettas, " The Little Tycoon " and " The Princess Bonnie," were enormous successes, but today they are as teetotally forgotten as " Erminie " or " Fra Diavolo."

It was usual, when a new play had its first performance in Baltimore, for colleagues from New York, Philadelphia and Washington to come to town for the event, and I thus became acquainted with a number of them. One was Acton Davies, of the New York *Evening Sun*, a short, squatty fellow with a high piping voice and a somewhat effeminate

119

manner. One night he appeared for the opening of
a new Clyde Fitch play, and after the first act became engaged in a debate in the lobby of Ford's
Opera House with the author, whose voice was even
higher than his own, and whose manner was even
more girlish. Presently they were joined by a
Baltimorean who surpassed both of them in both
respects. In a few minutes the three were surrounded by an appreciative gallery, and when it
began to applaud and wise-crack Charlie Ford had
to shut off a possible riot by shooing them into the
house. The older dramatic critics, in those days,
wore opera cloaks and plug hats, and looked a good
deal like melodrama villains. They were mainly
ignoramuses, though some of them could write.
The dean of the corps was William Winter, of the
New York *Tribune*, who would sometimes take
three of the wide columns that his paper then affected to review a Shakespearean performance.
Four-fifths of his critique, of course, was written
in advance, and consisted of a pedantic discourse
on the play. He was a violent opponent of all
novelty in the theatre, and spent his last years denouncing Ibsen, Hauptmann and Shaw. He died
in 1917, aged eighty-one. If he had lived into the
Eugene O'Neill era he'd have suffered so powerfully that his death would have been a kind of capital punishment.

Winter, like most of the other dramatic critics of
the time, tried to write plays himself, but never

with any success. There were, however, a few of
the brethren who kept resolutely on their own side
of the footlights. To be precise, there were two
that I knew of — Stuffy Davis of the New York
Globe and myself. In 1903 we organized a national association called the Society of Dramatic
Critics Who Have Never Written Plays, and began to hold quarterly conventions in Brown's
Chophouse, in New York, then the chief boozing-
ken of theatrical business men. We got friendly
notice in the stage weeklies, and several other colleagues applied for membership, but it always
turned out, on investigation, that they had plays
under way in secret, and were thus frauds. Stuffy
kept the oath of the organization until his lamented
death, but soon afterward I succumbed so far as to
write a couple of one-acters. I consoled my conscience, which was still functioning more or less in
those days, by maintaining that they were unplay-
able. When they were actually played I began to
wobble, and in 1919 I had wobbled so far that I
wrote a full-length play in collaboration with
George Jean Nathan. But though Nathan thus
sinned with me, he professed to support the principles of the Davis-Mencken society, and the two
of us cleared our skirts by refusing to let the play
be done on Broadway. One manager offered us
$10,000 cash for the refusal of it, but we had gone
too far by then to turn back, and had to say no.
To this day it has never been played.

One of the most competent young dramatic editors of the early century was Will A. Page, of the Washington *Post*. In the Autumn of 1901, soon after I had taken over the job in Baltimore, he moved there to be press-agent for a new stock company organized by George Fawcett. Fawcett was an educated and intelligent man, and his company soon made a big success. His beautiful wife, Percy Haswell, was the competent leading woman, and the leading man was Frank Gillmore, a handsome young Englishman who was later to become the head of Actors' Equity. The stage manager of the company was Percy Winter, old William's son, and its youngest member was a youth named Frank Craven, afterward to be well known as both actor and dramatist. The Fawcett company opened in " The Liars " and then proceeded to a series of other plays of the same amusing and civilized sort. Almost every night I dropped in at the theatre for a palaver with Page, and he was soon reinforcing Carter's attempt to make me take the drama seriously. It was from him that I first heard of George Bernard Shaw, and he fanned my interest in Ibsen, first set going by the episode described at the end of Chapter V. One day at the beginning of the season of 1902–3 he asked me if I thought that the Baltimore public would stand for a production of Ibsen's " Ghosts," which had been recently suppressed in London and was poison to all the current William Winters. I was naturally hot for it, and

on November 12 the play was put on, with Mary
Shaw as Mrs. Alving, Frederick Lewis as Oswald,
Maurice Wilkinson as Pastor Manders, Charles A.
Gay as Engstrand, and Virginia Kline as Regina.

The first night was somewhat exciting, for the
house manager, misunderstanding the action,
jumped to the conclusion that Mrs. Alving was
trying to seduce Oswald, and rushed out of the
house exclaiming " We'll all go to jail! " The next
day the critic of the *Sun* deplored " the revolting
theme " and " the ghastly story," and the *American* and *News* lamented that such immoral and
pathological stuff should be shown in a Christian
city, but, with Carter's eager approval, I beat the
drum for it in the *Herald*, and Baltimore received
it without any further sign of moral trauma. It
had, in fact, a good week, and after that the cast
presenting it was detached from the Fawcett company and took it on the road. First and last, it was
shown for three years. Other plays of pathological
and subversive flavor were added to the little
troupe's répertoire, but " Ghosts " remained its
stand-by. Miss Shaw not only played it in scores
of remote towns, some of them deep in the Bible
Belt; she also lectured on it at many bucolic colleges, and always escaped without encountering
anything worse than a few bewildered belches.
From time to time fresh actors were thrown into
the male parts, but Virginia Kline stuck to the end.

The " Ghosts " week was the high point of the

Fawcett company. Page tried to get the American rights to the early Shaw plays, and had a brisk correspondence with Shaw on the subject, but they could not come to terms. In 1903 he left the company, and when business turned bad Fawcett resorted to such obvious boob-squeezers as " The Three Musketeers," " Monte Cristo " and " Blue Jeans." When he quit at last he was succeeded by a manager of such small experience in the theatre that he was constantly appealing to newspaper men for advice. I was promoted to city editor at about the same time, and was followed as dramatic editor by a smart young reporter named Eugene Bertram Heath, who quickly became this manager's chief confidant and fatal curse. When Heath first came to work on the *Herald* a careless city editor, remembering only that his given name was somewhat romantic, entered him on the payroll as Percy, and Percy he remained to the end of his days. He lived to do the American book of " Sari," a great musical success, and to become a considerable figure in Hollywood. His counsel to Fawcett's unhappy heir and assign was chiefly waggish. Noting that the leading woman of the company was a blonde of large curves, he suggested that she be cast as Hamlet, *à la* Sarah Bernhardt. The manager fell for it — and to everyone's astonishment the week showed good takings. Percy then proposed satirically that her talents be turned loose upon " The Two Orphans," and when it, too, showed a profit, he advised that it be followed by a different version of the same play. The result was a gay and delirious week, for the actors trying to play the second version could not forget the first, and wallowed in confusion from curtain to curtain. Percy will appear again in Chapter XV. He was a man of parts. Unhappily, he had taken on family responsibilities, and when a good offer to go on the road as a press-agent came to him he accepted it, and Baltimore knew him no more.

I naturally received such offers myself, but I always refused them, for I was determined to stay in Baltimore. One of those offers was from E. H. Sothern. It was harder to resist certain more subtle approaches. Once I got word that David Belasco, then at the height of his celebrity, desired my opinion on a play, and it was hinted that he would expect to pay a substantial honorarium for it. I declined without thanks, for I regarded Belasco as a mountebank, and knew that what he wanted was not my judgment on a play but my support for all his trashy enterprises. The attempts of local managers to fetch me sometimes almost succeeded. When Charlie Ford would call me up at home, and tell me with trembling voice that a traveling press-agent was too drunk to function, and ask me in God's name to take over his work for a couple of days, I was unpleasantly tempted, but my natural cynicism always came to my aid, and I ducked. There were also blandishments from actors, but here it was easier going, for I knew very few of them, and never had anything to do with them. Once, after I had written a somewhat tart notice of Richard Mansfield's performance in Schiller's " Don Carlos," he invited me to dine with him on his private car and favor him with my notions in more detail, but I replied that I was too busy to come. He thereupon sent me a large photograph of himself, elegantly inscribed.

My general view of the theatre, in truth, was always somewhat skeptical. I continued to do an occasional review even after I became city editor, and when the *Herald* blew up at last and I transferred to the *Sun* I became its principal reviewer, though not its dramatic editor. Not many plays of any real interest came out in those days. The favorite dramatists were such cheap jacks as Clyde Fitch and Charles Klein, and the dominant managers were such charlatans as Charles Frohman, Belasco, and Klaw and Erlanger. During the Winter of 1905–6, working for the *Sun*, I wrote twenty-three unfavorable notices in a row. Charlie Ford thereupon complained bitterly that I was ruining his business, and protested that he was not to blame, for he had to take whatever plays the Theatrical Trust sent him. On reflection, I found myself sympathizing with him, and thereupon asked to be relieved. I have never written a line of dramatic criticism since.

VIII

COMMAND

WHEN Carter appointed me Sunday editor toward the end of 1901 I was as green as grass, and made heavy weather of it for the first few weeks. It may seem strange, but I can't recall the name of the man I succeeded. Whoever he was, he must have left the office as well as the job, for I got no instruction from him, and had to find my own way. In those days, as in these, reporters were taught nothing about printing, nor even about make-up, and it was rare for one of them to so much as peep into the composing-room, the engraving department, the stereotype foundry, or the press-room. Thus when I made my appearance in the first-named I was almost helpless. But Joe Bamburger, the foreman, was a sympathetic fellow, and so was his assistant, Josh Lynch, and in a little while they had broken me in. I naturally developed a grateful affection for them, and I think they liked me too, for we remained on friendly terms until both were dead. In a little while we fell into the habit of victualling together every Saturday evening between the time the last page of the Sunday supplement closed and the time the first page of the news section was ready. We always stopped first at a saloon in Fayette street, and there laid in a couple of beers. Then we proceeded to an eating-house in Baltimore street, where the principal dish was a beef stew so nourishing and so cheap that Joe called it the Workingmen's Friend. We ate it every Saturday, to the accompaniment of butter-cakes and coffee, and then returned to the *Herald* office to search the supplement, which was just coming up from the cellar, for bulls. We always found them, and always blamed one another. Joe was a tall, slim, solemn-looking fellow with a black beard, but when the spirit moved him he could swear magnificently. He was a pious Catholic, de-nounced the new heresy of birth control as mortal sin, and had eleven or twelve children. Josh was short and stout, with a gift for profanity that was more explosive than Joe's, but perhaps fell below it in reach and endurance. Joe would often say: " Josh is an inhuman bluff." Both were first-rate printers, trained in the days before the linotype had reduced printing to the level of typewriting, and I learned more about the newspaper trade from them than I ever learned from anyone in the editorial department with the one exception of Max Ways.[1]

Save on a few metropolitan papers, the Sunday editor of today is not much concerned about his pages of colored comics, for they are supplied by syndicates, and most of them are printed by outside contractors, far from the office. But in 1901 there were no syndicates, and every paper had to prepare and print its own. This work, untrained as I was, gave me endless torment, for I quickly found that comic artists were a temperamental and nefarious class of men, that engraving departments were never on time, that pressmen had an unearthly talent for printing colors out of register, so that a blue spot intended to represent an eye usually appeared clear outside the cheek, and that plates plainly marked red were often printed as yellow, and *vice versa*. The first page of the color sheet, in those days, was seldom given over to comics, which were still regarded as somewhat *infra dig.;* its more usual adornment was a large picture of a damsel in an hour-glass corset and trailing skirts, labeled "The Summer Girl," "The Spirit of Thanksgiving," or something of the sort. The artists who drew these sugar-teats were even worse characters than the concocters of comics, and needed more policing. If one of them delivered a drawing on schedule he was sure to be *non est* when

[1] There is more about them in Chapter XIX following, and yet more on pp. 214 and 215 of my book, Happy Days.

129

the time came to block out the color plates, and if he did the color plates promptly it always turned out that he had done them wrong. There were weeks when I spent at least two-thirds of my working hours wrestling with these criminals. They were, taking one with another, very affable fellows, and they used to try to mollify me by presenting me with large colored drawings of beautiful gals without any clothes on, but my professional relations with them were usually strained, and it never gave me any pain when I heard that one of them had broken a leg or got soaked for heavy alimony by his wife. Toward the end of 1902, happily for my sanity, syndicated comics began to appear, and I need not say that I subscribed to them with cheers. The very names of the first ones are now forgotten — Simon Simple, Billy Bounce, the Teasers, the Spiegelburgers. Finally came Foxy Grandpa, and we were on our way. Even so, it was necessary to keep a comic artist or two on call, for now and then the business office sold a quarter-page ad on a comic page, and something had to be cooked up to go 'round it. I not only had to supervise the preparation of this home-made stuff, but also to supply the ideas for it. The only ideas that the comic artists of that age ever produced on their own were either too banal to be used, or too lascivious.

Some time ago I put in a gloomy afternoon in the Pratt Library in Baltimore, going through the files of the *Sunday Herald* for the period of my editorship. There was little in them to lift me. A whole page was given over every week to the dismal humors of M. Quad — Mr. Bowser, the Limekiln Club, the *Arizona Kicker*, Major Crowfoot, and so on. Quad was an old-time printer whose actual name was Charles B. Lewis. He was the last of the long line of American newspaper humorists which began with Seba Smith (Major Jack Downing), and ran through H. W. Shaw (Josh Billings), D. R. Locke (Petroleum V. Nasby) and C. F. Browne (Artemus Ward) to Bill Nye and Bob Burdette. George Ade and Finley Peter Dunne were already blazing new paths in Chicago, but as yet they were not syndicated, and I had to do without them. I paid Quad $5 a week for his page, which included the matrices for four or five illustrations. He was already an old man, and from his home in Brooklyn he farmed out his work to various bright young reporters in New York. All of his features followed precise patterns, and it was child's play to write them.

Another stand-by of the *Sunday Herald* — and of scores of other Sunday papers — was the weekly travel article of Frank G. Carpenter. He was the Marco Polo of his generation, and had been roving the world since 1881. The stuff that he sent back from such places as Tierra del Fuego, Lapland and Cochin-China was excessively dull, and the photographs that came with it made engravers weep, but there was a superstition on the

Herald that the customers liked travel articles, and
so I had to print him. One day a young man
walked into the office with the news that he was
barging into the trade in competition with Carpenter. He had with him, and exhibited, some specimens of his art: they had to do, as I recall, with
South America. They were so much better than
Carpenter's that I took on this newcomer at once.
His name was Frederic J. Haskin, and he came
from Quincy, Ill. He demanded $10 a week,
whereas Carpenter had got but $5, but I was so
glad to get rid of Carpenter that I strained my
budget to pay it. Haskin continued to do his own
traveling and writing for some years thereafter,
but then he began to give over most of his time to
selling his stuff, and hired assistants to fetch it in.
He was a superb salesman, and at his peak was
probably the most successful syndicate man in
America, with a weekly foreign letter, a daily article from Washington, and a questions-and-answers
service that still exists. He began to publish books
for the one-book-a-year trade in 1911, with such
titles as "The American Government," "The
Panama Canal" and "10,000 Answers to Questions," and ran up such sales that the regular pub-
lishers of the country were staggered. I got to
know him very well, and every time he dropped off
in Baltimore we gave over the evening to drinking
Pilsner and laughing at the human race. His journalistic bee-hive in Washington turned out some

notable graduates, for example, Louis Brownlow,
the expert on municipal government, and Harvey
Fergusson, the novelist.

My own writing for the *Sunday Herald* was
pretty well confined to the theatre pages : I had too
many troubles to do much else. Those pages, as
such things ran in that era, were not bad. I devoted them to plays rather than to actors, and
made a point of giving some account of every new
drama of any importance that reached the stage,
whether in this country or Europe. Not many that
were worth describing came along, and I was often
reduced to wasting space on trash, but now and
then a Shaw or a Hauptmann stepped up to the
bat for me, and I was happy. The frenzied encomiums on actors that poured in from press-agents
I cut down to brief paragraphs and printed literally, with a heading reading " What the Press-
Agents Say." There was a weekly letter about
stage doings in New York by Charles Henry Melt-
zer, who had been dramatic critic for the New York
Herald and *World* and one of the associates of
James Huneker on *M'lle New York*. My main effort, outside the theatre pages, was devoted to re-
forming the archaic typography of the Sunday
paper, and trying to get rid of its ancient features.
As I have said, I succeeded with Carpenter but
failed with M. Quad. One of its worst relics of a
more innocent day was a full page of fraternal
order news — supplied free by the secretaries of

the various lodges, but so badly written that copy-reading it was a heavy chore. The theory in the office was that this balderdash made circulation — that all the joiners of the town searched it every Sunday morning for their own names. This seemed to me to be bad reasoning, for any given joiner was bound to be disappointed nine Sundays out of ten. One Sunday I quietly dropped the page — and not a single protest came in.

Carter quit as managing editor at the end of 1902 and was succeeded by Lynn R. Meekins, of whom a great deal will be heard in Chapters XIX and XX. Meekins, after spending a couple of weeks surveying the office, decided that the city-room, since Max Ways's time, had been going downhill. This was something that was palpable to the meanest understanding, and no one knew it better than I, who had emerged from the place only a little while before. A good many of the more competent men of Ways's days had disappeared, and their places had been taken by third-, fourth- and fifth-raters. That they wrote bad stuff was not unnatural, but that it got into the paper was really shocking. I well recall my writhing discomfort over some of it. When, in the Autumn of 1901, the immortal McKinley was done to death by one of Hitler's agents, and his remains were dragged through Baltimore on their way to Washington, the following paragraph was actually printed in a *news* story:

COMMAND

In the silent masonry of men's souls all over this fair
land of ours you hold a place today with Washington and
Lincoln — a place no power can plead away — a place
God-given by right of honor and justice, peace and
equity, faith and hope. Vale McKinley!

This drivel, it appears, was highly esteemed by
the city editor of the time. Carter should have
killed it, but Carter was but little interested in the
news department, and seldom read the proofs that
reached his desk every night. Meekins was much
more attentive, and during his first month he got
rid of several of the worst word-painters. But a lot
of muck remained, and he decided finally to put in
a new city editor. When he offered the job to me
I was really astonished, and, what is more, considerably alarmed. It was, to be sure, a step up
that must have flattered any youngster of twenty-
three, but I knew that reorganizing the staff would
be a difficult job, and I was in fear that I'd have
special difficulties with some of the older men, several of whom, at one time or another, had been my
superiors. But Meekins was optimistic, and my
fear turned out to be without ground. With one
or two exceptions, all the old-timers gave me hearty
support, and at Meekins's suggestion I got rid of
the worst of the rag-tag and bob-tail by firing a
whole platoon of them on my first day at the city-
desk.

This was wise surgery, but it left the staff much
depleted, and my job for a while was less that of a

city editor than that of a rewrite man. In fact, I usually put in all my time from 9 p.m. onward rewriting leads, leaving my assistant, Joe Callahan, to run the desk. Meekins was pleased with the improvement in the paper, and especially with the disappearance of fustian and hooey, but when he discovered what I was doing he prohibited it, and ordered me to stick to my proper duties. My model and idol, in those days, was the New York *Sun*, and I made desperate efforts to bring the *Herald* up to its standard of good writing. This, of course, was impossible, for there were no such reporters in Baltimore as those who adorned the *Sun*, but nevertheless some progress was made, and after the staff had been strengthened with a few good men the *Herald* began to shine. To this day, in fact, no American provincial paper that I can recall has ever been so briskly written. We were often beaten on news by the Baltimore *Sunpaper*, but our bright young men wrote rings around it every day.

I soon found, as every young city editor must find, that Sunday night brings the zero hour of the week. There is, ordinarily, very little news stirring, and that little tends to be a great deal less than exhilarating. Everything really interesting and instructive falls off on Sunday, from murders to dog-fights. The courts, the City Hall, and a dozen other principal sources of news are closed, and the public orgies of the day are of a predom-

inantly chaste and diuretic character.[2] That was
a red-letter Sunday, in 1903, when news came in
that a colored lodge of Odd Fellows, excursioning
on the Chesapeake in a barge towed by a tug, had
been run down by a banana boat, and another when
a wild man was reported loose in the woods over
Baltimore's northern city-line, with every dog
barking for miles around, and all women and children locked up. I got special delight out of the
wild man, for I had invented him myself, and no
one else knew that he was imaginary save Tom
Dempsey, an old-time police lieutenant, who had
kindly helped me with the job. The other cops took
him quite seriously, and hunted him with loud
shouts and the frequent discharge of their pistols.
Before the day was over they had roped and
brought in at least a dozen poor bums, and put
them through very stiff workouts in the back room.
When Monday dawned, and Baltimore resumed its
usual carnalities, the wild man was forgotten, but
Dempsey and I revived him the next Sunday, and
so every week for a month following. The story
was spoiled at last when an alarmed magistrate, believing the bogus evidence offered by the cops
against a half-wit stranger that they had collared,

[2] In these days, of course, there is always a heavy grist of
fatal automobile accidents, but it is seldom that anyone of any
importance is killed. Politicians have learned to reserve their
radio crooning and other prophesying for Sunday nights, but
their blather commonly comes by wire, and thus does not help
city editors.

sentenced him to six months in the House of Correction.

I discovered one day that what would now be called an Open Forum was in operation on Sunday afternoons in a hall over a West Baltimore livery-stable, and assigned a reporter without too much conscience to have a look. He came back with a swell story about a riotous debate between a Single Taxer and a Socialist, with the Socialist pulling a butcher-knife and the Single Taxer leaping out of a window. The two came in the next day to protest that the matter had been exaggerated, but I nevertheless continued the same reporter on the job, and in a little while he had peopled the Open Forum with a whole stock company of fantastic characters, some of them still remembered in Baltimore. His imagination was of high octane content, but his literary style ran to long and tortured sentences. I took over the burden of reading copy on him, and usually managed to translate him into reasonably clear English. Unhappily, I eventually lost him, for his writing was so bad that it got him a job as editorial writer on another paper. His efforts, while he lasted, reduced the whole Open Forum movement in Baltimore to the level of barroom humor, and to this day no one there cares what is said or advocated by the orators who rant and roar in such quarters. They can argue for Communism all they please, or even for cannibalism, adultery or kidnaping. The very cops listen placidly.

For a while this sort of thing entertained me pleasantly, but in the end it began to bore me. I was, I suspect, a bad city editor. My interest in what is called spot news had begun to wither after I was graduated from police reporting myself, and I was now chiefly intent on making the *Herald* better written. Any reporter who could write reasonably well seemed a good one to me, and any one who couldn't a mutt. This judgment could be defended like any other, but there was also a good deal to be said against it. I took a number of long chances with stories chiefly fanciful, but curiously enough, picked up no libel suits save with those that were substantially true. The worst of these litigations (which always alarm a newspaper office, however easy their defense may look) was launched by a lady who, according to the cops, was a common prostitute. She was the widow of an Italian who had also left another widow, and this other one had later married a Chinaman. One night Widow No. 1 was jugged for street-walking, and the cops mistook her for Widow No. 2. When the *Herald* reported the next morning, relying on their dope, that she was the Chinaman's wife she instructed her solicitor to enter suit. We thought we had her, for dozens of cops volunteered to testify that she was free of both the white and black races, and hence had no reputation to lose, but the judge ruled out all this testimony on the ground that it had nothing to do with our false and foul allegation that she had married a Chinaman. Even a street-walker, he said, might object to that, at least in the eye of the law. We seemed to be lost, but at the last minute the lady's solicitor, not content to let well enough alone, rose up to address the jury. Within two minutes his eloquent description of her mental anguish had the twelve jurymen snickering, and in five minutes they were howling, along with the learned judge. Our own lawyer kept silent, and the jury gave us a verdict without leaving the box.

Not infrequently the long hours and endless vexations of my job worked me down so far that I was in a state bordering on paranoia. The *Herald* office, by this time, had a complete outfit of telephones, and mine rang an average of once a minute. I had to keep track of the comings and goings of thirty men, some of them with a high talent for disappearing. It was a formidable business, when a big fire broke out or a nice murder was announced, to round up enough of them to cover it, and once they got out of sight it was quite as harassing to recover them. Very often, at the end of a long afternoon, I'd sneak out of the office for a little peace, and let it sweat and fester on its own. Sometimes I would go to a French restaurant a few blocks away, where a slow but sound meal was to be had for sixty cents, and the proprietor (who was also the chef) turned up a new wife (who was also the cashier) every month. That refuge was spoiled one night when two of these wives had it out with crockery just as I was about to sit down to a plate of onion soup. I then took to making quiet round trips to Washington, and dining on the train. In those days every city editor had a pocketful of annual passes: I had them myself, in fact, on every railroad east of St. Louis or north of Atlanta, and also on all the coastwise steam-packets. The dining-car dinners I thus engulfed were seldom very appetizing, but it was refreshing to escape from the city-room for a while and rest my eyes on the frowsy wilderness that runs between Baltimore and Washington. When I saw a yap at a cross-roads, waiting on his mule for the train to pass, I forgot the hookworms and other parasites at work upon his liver and lights, and almost envied him.

But despite all these woes I still had a reasonably pleasant time, and my leisure, though scanty, was at least more than I had enjoyed as a reporter. One of its fruits was a sharp revival of my interest in music. Carter had given me a start in that direction, and now I was helped on by the learned conversation of our music critic, Owst, who was an abyss of thorough-bass, and set me to studying a textbook of that science; by daily contact with Lew Schaefer, one of the reporters, who devoted his own leisure to writing piano pieces for children; and, above all, by the untutored but very real enthusiasm of my assistant, Joe Callahan. Joe was perhaps the worst violinist who ever lived; in fact, his technic went but little beyond the open strings; but he knew a great many musicians, and brought me into contact with them. It was through him that I met Fred Gottlieb, a rich brewer who was also an amateur flautist, and Al Hildebrandt, a violin-dealer by trade who played the cello for the fun of it, and remained one of my warmest friends to the end of his days. There were also Isidor Goodman, the night editor, who had once played the flute in a circus band, and Emanuel Daniel, assistant sporting editor, who passed in the office under the nickname of Schmool, and was a violinist. Under Joe's conniving, Schmool, Al and I took to playing trios, and in a little while other amateurs joined us, and then a few professionals, and by 1904 we had a club meeting regularly. It exists to the present day, and I never miss one of its Saturday night sessions when I am in Baltimore. I am now the only survivor of its original members. Goodman never belonged to it, but he and I often played together, for he had a girl who was a singer, and he liked to play flute obbligatos to her singing, while I did the piano accompaniment. For these refined soirées we commonly borrowed a small studio in a piano-dealer's establishment, a block from the *Herald* office. There was never any audience, for Goodman believed that his technic had degenerated since his circus days, and was shy of criticism. As for me, I banged away innocently, and often drowned out both the poor girl's voice and her admirer's tootling.

Goodman had an elder brother named Al who was the *Herald's* political reporter. He had a bald head and a Van Dyke beard and was old enough to be my father, but we got on very well, and he taught me a great deal about the science of politics as he had observed it. It was his theory that all reformers were either frauds or idiots, and that some of them were both. He believed that practical politicians, taking one with another, made the safest and most competent public officials, if only because they were intelligent. He granted somewhat grudgingly that there were occasional thieves among them, but he argued that their worst corruptions were cheaper to the taxpayer than the insane wastes of the uplift. It was from him that I first heard all the familiar maxims of American statecraft, for example, " In politics a man must learn to rise *above* principle," and " When the water reaches the upper deck follow the rats." Al took me to my first pair of national conventions — those of 1904. In theory I was his superior officer, but I was glad to go as his legman, for he knew all the politicians, high and low, and was full of illuminating confidences about them. I recall his telling me in St. Louis that William Jennings Bryan, though a teetotaler, was a glutton, and predicting that he would eat himself to death. This

prophecy was a long time coming true, but after
twenty-two years it came true at last.

Al always wrote a long political disquisition for
the Sunday *Herald*, and usually composed it in the
city-room on Saturday afternoon, when there was
comparative quiet there. He looked upon the typewriter as a new-fangled absurdity, and always
wrote by hand. Ever and anon he would pause in
his work, slap his bald head, clear his throat, and
deliver himself of a soliloquy of his own composition. It began as follows:

> Yes, my belovéd bullpups: it was not always thus. So
> his arse hit the ceiling with great éclat, and the little birds
> sang hallelujah.

This went on for a minute or two, and then
rounded up with a quotation from " Barbara
Frietchie ":

> " Strike, if you must, this old gray head,
> But spare your country's flag," she said.

Once a female reporter, overhearing this ritual,
complained to me that it was painful to her prud-
eries. I invited her to do her work thereafter in the
press-room, for I admired Al, and greatly enjoyed
his observations, however vulgar. He and his
brother Isidor had nicknames for all the office boys,
usually borrowed from the Yiddish nomenclature,
and often indecent. They also had nicknames for
most of the reporters and editors. I daresay they

had one for me, too, and maybe a blistering one, but if so I never heard it. City editors, in those days, were addressed familiarly by their given names by all save the youngest reporters, but even in those days city editors were treated a bit tenderly.

The supreme climax and boiling point of my service in that office I reserve for Chapter XIX.

IX

THREE

MANAGING EDITORS

In the days of which I write the chief editorial dignitary on every American daily paper was called the managing editor, and his jurisdiction extended, not only over all the news departments, but also over the editorial page. He was himself, in fact, the chief editorial writer, and on most papers his only help in that line came from two or three ancient hulks who were unfit for any better duty — copy-readers promoted from the city-room to get rid of them, alcoholic writers of local histories and forgotten novels, former managing editors who had come to grief on other papers, and a miscellany of decayed lawyers, college professors and clergymen with whispered pasts. Some of these botches of God were pleasant enough fellows, and a few even showed a certain grasp of elemental English, but taking one with another they were held in disdain by the reporters, and it was almost unheard of for one of them to be promoted to a better job. Everyone believed as an axiom that they lifted four-fifths of their editorials from other papers, and most authorities held that they bitched them in the lifting. If anyone in the city-room had ever spoken of an editorial in his own paper as cogent and illuminating he would have been set down as a jackass for admiring it and as a kind of traitor to honest journalism for reading it at all. No editorial writer was ever applied to for a loan, or invited to an office booze-party.

But the managing editor, though he also wrote editorials, escaped the infamy of the caste, no doubt because he was mainly concerned with news, and usually emanated from the news department himself. He was, indeed, the chief hero of all the younger reporters, even when they denounced him for overworking and underpaying them, and they tried to model their mien and metaphysic on his — that is, provided he were not, by an office calamity, a teetotaler or an opponent of smoking. Myths about him were always in circulation, some of them based upon actual feats of professional or other derring-do, but most of them purely imaginary. Colonel A. B. Cunningham, managing editor of the *Herald* when I joined its staff in 1899, was generally depicted, by office gossip, as a very truculent and even bloodthirsty man, with a long record of carnage behind him. His career in the Confederate Army was assimilated to those of Jeb Stuart, J. S. Mosby and Joe Wheeler, and it was believed that he had refused to come in after Appomattox, but chosen rather to flee to Egypt, where he gradually cooled himself off by slaughtering dervishes. He had worked as a reporter on the St. Louis *Post-Dispatch* under the celebrated John Albert Cockerill, and out of the fact developed a legend that he had once fought a duel with Cockerill, with bowie knives as weapons.

The colonel's aspect gave a certain amount of support to his reputation, for he was tall, well-built and of military bearing, had flashing black eyes under heavy brows, and wore his wavy, coal-black hair brushed back from his forehead. His head, in fact, was a fine one, and his smooth-shaven face was not unhandsome. But he was actually a much milder man than his lieges believed, and it was only when he was in his cups that he made any noise in the office. The facts about him came out in 1906, when he reached the dignity of inclusion in "Who's Who in America." He was a native, it appeared, of Minden, a small town in northwestern Louisiana, just under the Arkansas line, and he was less than fifteen years old when the Civil War began. But despite his tender years he enlisted in the Eighteenth Louisiana Infantry, and after that, in succession, in the Fifth Texas Cavalry and Mc-Nelly's Scouts, and fought doggedly until the end of the war. After Appomattox he put in a few years at flag-stop colleges in Louisiana, and then, in 1874, he was offered a commission in the Egyptian Army, which was being reorganized on a grandiose scale by the spendthrift Ismail. Many other ex-Confederates received similar offers, and some actually went to Egypt, but Cunningham apparently never made the trip, though he kept his title of colonel (*bey*) for the rest of his life. It was, in its way, a kind of gilding of the lily, for all Southern editors in that era were colonels by brevet, and many of them, especially in the smaller towns, are so to this day. When I became managing editor of the *Herald* myself, in 1905, I was usually so addressed in communications from confrères below the Potomac.

The colonel seldom showed himself in the city-room, save to stalk through it, but he knew all the reporters by name, and sometimes joined in their extramural activities. At the time of the first election I ever helped to cover there was a dollar pool in the office on the majority of the winning candidate, and the colonel won it. It amounted to $50 or $60, and he blew in the money royally on a midnight supper to the staff. Toward the end of the party, which was large and loud, someone remembered that the annual ball of the Nonpareil Social Club was going on in a shabby hall near the waterfront, and it was resolved to look in. The Nonpareil was one of two rival organizations of Balti-

more harlots, or, perhaps more accurately, of their
male parasites and protectors, and its functions
were always attended by large delegations of whiskey drummers, brewery collectors, professional
bondsmen, minor court officials, and cops in mufti.
By the time we got to the hall it was pretty late,
and the festivities on the floor were abating, but the
colonel revived them by taking a seat in the front
row of the gallery, and heaving handfuls of small
silver overboard. No less than three times he had
$10 bills changed into dimes, and every time he
went into action all the waiters on the floor dropped
their trays and began to scramble for the money.
The third time a committee consisting of two distinguished madames and a deputy sheriff came up
to the gallery to protest. They said the honor of
his presence was appreciated, but that his largess
was incommoding the service of drinks and wrecking the ball. He professed to be offended, and
threatened to denounce the affair in a *Herald* editorial as snobbish and anti-social, but he was only
having his joke, and in a little while he gave the
signal for us to withdraw. On the street outside,
stimulated by the dawn, he lined us up along the
curbstone, and gave the signal for one of those
combats in uresis which festive males of *Homo
sapiens* have been carrying on since the days of
Abraham. It was won easily by a young reporter
with powerful reflexes, whose name sounded something like Macon.

When the rival organization, the Rogers Pleasure Social, gave a ball a few weeks later, it sent a special committee to the *Herald* office to invite the colonel and his suite, but he said he had had enough of sexual society for a while, and refused to come. The rest of us, however, went in strength, and had the pleasure of witnessing a battle with beer bottles between two madames. Both were blooded, and the cops made a great pother of dragging them apart and carting them to hospital. Many of the more nefarious political clubs of the town gave somewhat similar parties, and we were usually invited. I remember one especially, for it was arranged in layers, with the wives and daughters of the ward heelers entertained on the second floor and the fancy women on the third. The former danced to a five-piece orchestra and the latter to a hand-organ. When we reporters arrived at the street door and made ourselves known we were ushered at once to the third floor.

The colonel had only contempt for the public attentions that pursue newspaper editors. He never went to a banquet if he could help it, and never signed manifestoes or sat on committees. The only public office he ever accepted was membership on the Baltimore School Board, which was unpaid. This was in 1901 or thereabout, and an effort was being made at the time to rid the Baltimore schools of the dirt pedagogy that had prevailed in them since colonial times, and to substitute the new wizardries from Teachers College, Columbia. The president of the board was a local corporation lawyer of the highest elegance, and one of the members was Dr. Daniel Coit Gilman, president of the Johns Hopkins University. I was assigned to cover the meetings for the *Herald* and commonly returned from them with the colonel, riding on the rear platform of a trolley-car. He never made any suggestions about the way the story was to be written, but in the confidence of a smoke together he often thought aloud about his fellow-members, most of whom he put in the debased class of uplifters. One evening he asked me if I had taken notice of one who spoke habitually in despairing tones, wore a long-tailed coat, and looked the perfect Christian philanthropist. " That poor eunuch," he said, " claims to be the father of five or six children. Turn your mind to the physiology of mammalian reproduction, and see if you can imagine it." I had to confess that I couldn't.

When it came to salaries the colonel was excessively hard-boiled, for the *Herald*, in those days, was poor compared to the *Sun* and *News:* even his own pay, as I learned on becoming managing editor myself and snooping through the books, was never more than $90 a week. But he stuck to his men when they got into trouble, and it was on such occasions that his Southern fire was oftenest manifested. I well recall a case in point, for I was a

figure in it. It came in the first years of the century, when not only the public schools, but also
all the other municipal departments of Baltmore,
including even the police force, were in the clutches
of primeval New Dealers. Presently the poor cops
had a new and terrifying master — a retired Army
captain with a walrus moustache who had been sitting for years in the window of the Athenaeum
Club in Charles street, glaring at the passers-by.
His name was Hamilton, and he was the perfect
model of the *Rittmeister* of tradition — stiff, vain,
boorish and stupid. He set the cops to saluting on
all occasions, ordered the old ones to train off their
bay-windows, and put the whole unhappy outfit
to drilling in the hot sun.

These reforms made for news, but getting it was
something else again. When I was assigned to
headquarters, and made my first call at the new
chief's office, he let me stand for at least ten minutes while he busied himself with the papers on
his desk. The second day I stood for fifteen minutes, and the third day for twenty minutes, and
when the old boy looked up at last he would bark
as if I had been an insurance agent or a collector
for the orphans. After that I kept out of his office, and my information about his doings was derived from cops who were as friendly to newspaper
reporters as they were hostile to their new commander. The inevitable result was that the *Herald*
printed some stories that annoyed him, and in a

little while he wrote a letter to the colonel, complaining that I never came near his office and that my reports of his doings were faked. This was a serious charge and the colonel ordered me up for trial the next morning. My defense was brief: I simply told the truth. The colonel was not long in reaching his verdict. " Go back to that goddam son-of-a-bitch," he roared, " and tell him with my compliments that a *Herald* reporter kisses *no* man's arse." I relayed this communiqué to Hamilton through one of his stooges, and he was polite enough thereafter. Before long he had got the cops into such a mess that he had to be kicked out, and they returned joyously to Bach.

When the *Herald* was sold to Wesley M. Oler, a rich Baltimorean who had made his money in the ice business and eventually rose to be president of the American Ice Company, the colonel's position became very uncomfortable, for Oler was a Republican and wanted to use the paper to promote his political aspirations, which were wide and deep. The colonel, of course, was a Democrat. After a series of squabbles he quit his job and started an afternoon paper of his own, but it blew up quickly, and he became the Baltimore agent of the Associated Press.[1] His successor was Robert I. Carter, who had been recommended to Oler by the Tafts of Cincinnati, where he had worked on the *Times-*

[1] He died in Baltimore in 1915. Born in 1846, he was 54 years old in 1900, but to us young reporters he seemed a patriarch.

Star and assisted in launching William Howard of
that ilk as a statesman. On all imaginable counts
he was at the opposite pole from the colonel. A
native of Massachusetts and a graduate of Harvard, with a game leg, a conservative paunch and
a red Van Dyke beard, he looked the college professor far more than the newspaper editor, and in
all his tastes, methods of work, theories of journalism and habits of mind he differed abysmally from
his predecessor. At the start the boys in the *Herald*
office hardly knew what to make of him, for it was
quickly bruited about that he could speak seven
(soon lifted to seventeen) languages, and he
alarmed everybody on his second night by showing
up in a dinner coat. But it soon became apparent
that he was anything but a dilettante, and when
he fired several old-timers, ordered some raises in
salaries, and put a rambunctious female reporter
in her place, office opinion began to swing toward
him, and the usual legends about him were hatched.
One was to the effect that he had killed a man in
Cincinnati, and another accounted for his game
leg by a fall off a fire-escape leading down from the
boudoir of a rich brewer's beautiful fourth wife.
He was reputed to be wealthy himself, and there
were two theories about the origin of his hoard:
one being that he was an heir of the Carter's Ink
fortune and the other that he was an heir of the
Carter's Little Liver Pills fortune.

My own relations with him have been described

more or less in Chapter VII. He was a highly civilized and very charming man, and his influence upon me at a time when I was in some danger of yielding to the Philistinism which then dominated Baltimore journalism was powerful and all to the good. He made it plain to me, and to others, that it was quite possible to be a good newspaper man, and still cherish some pretense to decent tastes. His own eager interest in the fine arts, and especially in music and the drama, was contagious, but he was as far from being priggish as the old colonel himself. On the contrary, he was a very amiable and expansive fellow, fond of good eating and drinking, and tolerant of the so-called Bohemianism of the city-room, though he kept aloof from it himself. He fired the old-timers, not primarily because they were boozers, but because they were booze-grafters, and hence disgraceful to the paper.

The job he had taken on was not an easy one, for the departure of Cunningham, followed soon by that of Max Ways, and then by that of Nachman, the business manager, had left the *Herald* organization crippled and demoralized. Carter tried out several new city editors in succession, but they fell very far short of Ways. He was burdened with editorial writers even worse than usual, and was reduced at one time to inviting members of the city staff to contribute volunteer editorials. But his most severe headaches came from above, not below. Oler was a poor substitute for William Howard

Taft, though he had the same itch to shine in statecraft. He was a tall, thin, dour Methodist with a funereal black beard, and never got to first base in politics, though he once collared a great deal of notice (at least in his own paper) by inducing Theodore Roosevelt, then President, to ride over from Washington to visit him in his suburban mansion. Roosevelt, who made the trip on horseback, followed by a squad of sweating Army officers, let it be known that Oler was a man of astounding abilities and would make a superb United States Senator, but no one else ever believed it. To replace the smart and competent Nachman as business manager he brought in a Canadian named Peard — a majestic and singularly handsome fellow with no more capacity for the job than a police sergeant. So the *Herald* gradually got into difficulties, and Carter's hard work went for nothing. He modernized the typography of the paper, reformed some of its archaic Southern practises, and brought in a few good men, but in the end he had to confess failure. After two years and two months of it he resigned in January, 1903, and was succeeded by Lynn R. Meekins.[2]

---

[2] Carter joined the New York *Herald* after leaving Baltimore, and became editor of its Paris edition and one of the confidential men of James Gordon Bennett. He had traveled very widely as a young man and now traveled even more. I encountered him occasionally in New York after he left Baltimore, but eventually lost sight of him. He disappeared from Who's Who in America after the 1912–13 edition. He was 32 years old when he came to the *Herald* in Baltimore.

Of the three managing editors that I sat under on the *Herald* Meekins was the most competent, and by long odds, but he came into the office carrying several handicaps, and it took him some time to get rid of them; indeed, it was not until the great Baltimore fire of 1904 brought out his quick resourcefulness and high capacity for command that he was generally accepted in the office. His first handicap was that he had got most of his training on the Baltimore *American,* a rival that was not even given the flattery of fear, but simply held in contempt. His second was that he had spent most of his seventeen years there writing editorials — a trade, as I have said, that no reporter respected. His third, and heaviest, was that he was reported to be a Methodist, and what is worse, a Methodist of the so-called Methodist Protestant sub-sect, which, even in 1903, was already whooping up Prohibition. When his membership in this infamous outfit was confirmed there was something close to moral indignation in the office, and one of the artists actually announced that, provided he could find a better job elsewhere, he would resign in protest.

Nor did Meekins's first tour of inspection reassure the brethren, for he turned out to be a slight, clerical-looking fellow wearing a small gray moustache and scholarly spectacles, with a voice that never arose to the barks and snarls proper to a managing editor. But though the legend of his

anti-social heresies persisted for a year, it was
soon apparent to the more judicious that he was
anything but a milksop. On the contrary, he
turned out to be bold and even pugnacious, and in
a little while he was carrying on a revolt against
Peard's ineptitudes downstairs, and getting rid of
a lot of dead wood in the editorial rooms. My own
inclination was to see something in him, for he
had two novels behind him and was a frequent con-
tributor to *Harper's Magazine;* and that inclination was converted into an active prejudice pro
when he called me into his office one day and told
me that my salary as Sunday editor was to be increased $5 a week. This was the first time since I
had joined the *Herald* that I had ever got a raise
without first being offered a better job elsewhere,
and the miracle naturally filled me with amiable
sentiments. Nor was my delight diminished when
he told me that I needed better help in my job, and
ordered me to find a couple of likely young aides,
male or female. What he had to say about the Sunday edition, some of it favorable but most of it
critical, was searching and sensible, and I soon discovered that he knew more about such things than
anyone else in the office. This, I must confess,
seemed incredible in an editorial writer — until
presently I learned that, in the interval between
writing editorials for the *American* and coming to
the *Herald,* he had been the first managing editor
of the *Saturday Evening Post,* then just started

on its opulent career of fostering the national letters.

But the fact remained that Meekins, compared to Cunningham or even to Carter, was a subdued and highly respectable fellow, and that life in the *Herald* office began to lose something of its old wild glitter. He was not, it soon appeared, an actual Prohibitionist, but he had a low opinion of the more alcoholic journalists of the era, and began to ease them out one by one. The *Herald* office thus became much more efficient than it had ever been before, but it ceased to be as merry as it once was, and if the men got more money they enjoyed less recreation, as recreation was then understood. We had another Methodist in the office, a reporter named Stockbridge, but he was so pleasant a fellow that no one held it against him, though we showed our dissent from his superstitions by giving him the satirical title of Bishop. When, in July, 1903, Pope Leo XIII died, and the cardinals began hustling to Rome to elect his successor, an office wag put the following notice on the city-room bulletin-board:

FOR POPE:

The Right Rev. Jason Stockbridge, D.D.,
Bishop of Sodom and Gomorrah *in partibus infidelium*
Subject to the Democratic primaries

This jocosity, though it lay snugly within the traditional *Herald* pattern of office humor, outraged Meekins, and he not only ordered it removed at once but went through the forms of an investigation that lasted for two weeks. While his inquiries were going on I trembled lest he accuse some innocent member of the staff, and so force me to step up and confess the truth, which was that I had done the deed myself. But the investigation frittered out without an indictment, and it was years later, after the *Herald* had been long buried, and forgotten by all save its alumni, that Meekins told me he had recognized my literary style at once. His failure to accuse me was revelatory of his peculiar character: he was fundamentally a somewhat prissy fellow, but he always refrained from wreaking his prissiness on others. Until his professional exploits at the time of the fire of 1904 won him unanimous acceptance at last, he remained a suspicious person to most of the reporters, for it was still a cardinal article of office doctrine that a Methodist (despite the glaring contrary example of Bishop Stockbridge) was necessarily and *ipso facto* a devious, inimical and mean fellow, bent only on afflicting and injuring the human race. But Meekins was constantly doing things that made that easy formula untenable, and the ground was thus gradually preparing for his elevation to respect and esteem in 1904. If there had never been any fire it might have been delayed, and without question it would have stopped short of canonization, but certainly it would have come.

Meekins had been born in a small village on the

Eastern Shore of Maryland, where Yahweh remains a threatening character to this day, and if he kept some of the theological naïveté of his native wildwood, he also showed a good deal of country humor. He took the horrible alarms and vicissitudes of newspaper life without too much seriousness, and was full of sharp judgments of men and events. He viewed editorial writers much as reporters viewed them, though he had been one for so many years himself, and at a later period, when he resumed the shroud of the craft in the service of Hearst, he cackled over its futilities every time we met. It was his theory that no editorial that showed genuine sense was fit to print, or, indeed, could be printed without danger. He could write very good ones on occasion, for he had a clear mind and a first-rate English style, but he got more fun, I am sure, out of writing the bad ones — for example, arguments in favor of new parks and a reformed police force, and obituary encomiums of dead local worthies, nine-tenths of whom he knew personally to be either idiots or scoundrels. The Hearst paper he worked for was the heir of both his first love, the Baltimore *American,* and the Baltimore *News.* Its leading editorials were mainly canned goods from the New York headquarters of the chain; his job was simply to keep the home fires burning. A conservative by instinct, he was amused rather than outraged by the exuberance of the Hearst typography, and used to defend it wryly on the ground that it at least enabled him to fill a lot of space at small expense of labor.

As an author himself he took a great deal of interest in my own literary strivings. His advice in that department was always sound, and he was ever ready with it. He knew most of the American literati of the Howells generation, and was full of illuminating anecdotes about them. His own writings were in their manner, but he was very hospitable to the newcomers who finally unhorsed them, and he did a great deal of miscellaneous reading, even in his busiest days as managing editor of the uremic *Herald*, and, later, as its publisher. Unlike Carter, he had no appetite for music and very little for the theatre, but his knowledge of books was enormous, and he set me to reading many a tome that I might have missed otherwise. I suspect that it was largely his influence that caused me to resolve, when the *Herald* finally went down, to subordinate executive work, during the rest of my days, to writing. In all probability he lived to regret that he had not done so himself.[3]

---

[3] Meekins died in 1933 in London, where his only son was commercial attaché of the American embassy.

X

SLAVES OF

BEAUTY

I⊤ was not until I became Sunday editor that I had any official relations with the fantastic Crocodilidæ known as newspaper artists, but I had naturally encountered a number of them in my days as a reporter. The first one I ever saw in the flesh, so far as I can recall, was an Irishman wearing a seedy checked suit, a purple Windsor tie, a malacca stick, and a *boutonnière* consisting of two pink rosebuds fastened together with tinfoil. This was in a saloon near the *Herald* office in the year 1899, and I remember saying to myself that he certainly looked the part. It appeared at once that he also acted it, for when the bartender hinted that the price of beer was still five cents a glass, cash on delivery, the artist first snuffled up what remained of the foam in his schooner, and then replied calmly that it was to be charged to his account. I was still, in those days, a cub reporter, and full of an innocent delight in the wonders of the world. The decaying veteran at my side had invited me out, as he put it, to introduce me to society, and while he did the introducing I bought the beer. He now nudged me, and whispered romantically that the artist had spent his last ten cents for the *boutonnière:* it had been bought, it appeared, of a street vendor in front of police headquarters — a one-armed man who was reputed to get his stock by raiding colored graveyards by night. This vendor trusted no one below the rank of a police lieutenant, so the rosebuds had to be paid for, but bartenders showed more confidence in humanity. After the artist had filled his pockets with pretzels and stalked out grandly, flirting his malacca stick in the manner of James A. McNeill Whistler, the old-timer explained that he was honorable above the common, and always paid his reckonings in the long run. " Whenever," I was informed, " some woman with money gets stuck on him, or he sells a couple of comics to a syndicate, he goes around town settling up. Once I saw him lay out $17 in one night. He had to beat it from England in a cattle-boat. There was a rich Jewish duke packing a gun for him."

I never saw this marvel again, for a few days later he was shanghaied on the Baltimore waterfront, and when, after a couple of months of bitter Winter weather down Chesapeake Bay, he escaped from the oyster fleet by legging it over the ice, he made tracks for Canada and the protection of the Union Jack, leaving more than one bartender to mourn him. But in the course of the next half dozen years, first as Sunday editor, then as city editor, and finally in the austere misery of managing editor, I made acquaintance with many other artists, and acquired a lot of unpleasant information about their habits and customs. They ranged from presumably respectable married men with families (sometimes, indeed, with two families) down to wastrels who floated in from points South or West, remained only long enough to lift an over-coat and two or three bottles of Higgins's drawing ink, and then vanished as mysteriously as they had come. A few of them even neglected to draw their pay — always to the indignation of the office cashier, who had to carry a small and incredible overage on his books until he got up nerve enough to buy the city editor a couple of drinks, and so discharge his debt for theatre passes. But whatever the differences marking off these jitney Dürers into phyla and species, they all had certain traits in common, mostly productive of indignation in editors. Each and every one of them looked down his nose at the literati of journalism, and laughed at them as Philistines almost comparable to bartenders or policemen. One and all had an al-

most supernatural talent for getting out of the
way when fire broke out in a medical college or
orphan asylum, and there were loud yells for illustrative art. And so far as I can recall, there was
never one who failed, soon or late, to sneak something scandalous into a picture at the last moment,
to the delight the next morning of every soul in
town save what we then called the Moral Element.

I write, of course, of an era long past and by
most persons forgotten, and I have no doubt that
artists are now much changed, whether on newspapers or off. Some time ago a man in charge of
the art department of a great metropolitan daily
told me that fully a third of his men read the
Nation, and that many of the rest had joined the
C.I.O. and were actually paying their dues. He
even alleged that there were two teetotalers among
them, not to mention a theosophist. In my time
nothing of the sort was heard of. The artists of
that day were all careless and carnal fellows, with
no interest in their souls and no sense of social responsibility. Their *beau idéal* was still the Rodolfo
of " La Bohème," and if not Rodolfo, then some
salient whiskey drummer, burlesque manager or
other Elk; for the contemporaneous Roosevelts,
Willkies, Hulls, Ma Perkinses, Bishop Mannings
and John L. Lewises they had only razzberries.
Long before naked women were the commonplaces
of every rotogravure supplement — indeed, long
before rotogravure supplements were invented —

large drawings of ladies in the altogether, usually in the then fashionable sepia chalk, decorated every newspaper art department in America. It was believed by young reporters that artists spent all their leisure in the company of such salacious creatures, and had their confidence. Even the most innocent young reporter, of course, was aware that they used no living models in their work, for everyone had noted how they systematically swiped from one another, so that a new aspect of the human frame, or of a dog's, or cat's, or elephant's frame, once it had appeared in a single newspaper in the United States, quickly reappeared in all the rest. But the artists fostered the impression that they did hand-painted oil-paintings on their days off, direct from nature unadorned. They let it be known that they were free spirits and much above the general, and in that character they sniffed at righteousness, whether on the high level of political and economic theory or the low one of ordinary police regulations.

I well recall the snobbish rage of a primeval comic-strip artist whom I once rebuked for using the office photographic equipment to make counterfeit five-dollar bills. It was on a Sunday morning, and I had dropped into the office for some reason forgotten. Hearing me shuffling around, he bounced out of the darkroom with a magnificent photograph of a fiver, cut precisely to scale, and invited me to admire it. I knew it would be useless

to argue with him, but I was hardly prepared for
his screams of choler when I grabbed the phoney,
tore it up, and made off to the darkroom to smash
the plate. He apparently regarded my action, not
only as a personal insult, but also as an *attentat*
against human enlightenment. If the word *bourgeois* had been in circulation at the time he would
have flung it at me. As it was, he confined himself
to likening my antipathy to counterfeit money to
Lynn Meekins's Methodist aversion to drunkards,
and laughed derisively at all the laws on the
statute-books, from those against adultery to those
prohibiting setting fire to zoos. I fired him on the
spot, but took him back the next day, for good
comic-strip artists were even more rare in that age
than they are today.

Another that I fired — for what reason I forget
— refused to come back when I sent for him, and I
found on inquiry that he had got a job making
side-show fronts for a one-ring circus. He produced such alarming bearded ladies, two-headed
boys and wild men of Borneo that the circus went
through the Valley of Virginia like wildfire, and in
a little while he had orders from four or five of its
rivals. By the end of a year he was the principal
producer of side-show fronts south of the Mason
& Dixon Line, and had three or four other artists
working for him. Also, he had a new girl, and she
appeared in public in clothes of very advanced cut,
and presently took to drink. Undaunted, he put in

another, and when she ran away with a minstrel-show press-agent, followed with a third, a fourth, and so on. Finally, one of them opened on him with a revolver, and he departed for Scranton, Pa. When he edged back to Baltimore a month or two later, glancing over his shoulder at every step, his business had been seized by his assistants, and the last I heard of him he was working for a third-rate instalment house, making improbable line drawings of parlor lamps, overstuffed sofas, washing-machines, and so on. Many other artists of that time went the same sad route. Starting out in life as painters of voluptuous nudes in the manner of Bouguereau, they finished as cogs in the mass production of line-cuts of ladies' hosiery.

In the heyday of this fellow I had a visit one day from a sacerdotal acquaintance — a Baptist clergyman who pastored a church down in the tide-water Carolinas. His customers, he told me, had lately made a great deal of money growing peanuts, and a new brick church was approaching completion in his parish. In this church was a large concrete baptismal tank — the largest south of Cape Hatteras — and it was fitted with all the latest gadgets, including a boiler downstairs to warm the water in cold weather. What it still lacked, said the pastor, was a suitable fancy background, and he had come to see me for advice and help on that point. Would it be possible to have a scene painted showing some of the principal events of sacred history? If so, who would be a good man to paint it? I thought at once of my side-show-front friend, and in a little while I found him in a barrel-house, and persuaded him to see the pastor.

The result was probably the most splendiferous work of ecclesiastical art since the days of Michelangelo. On a canvas fifteen feet high and nearly forty feet long the artist shot the whole works, from the Creation as described in Genesis I to the revolting events set forth in Revelation XIII. Noah was there with his ark, and so was Solomon in all his glory. No less than ten New Testament miracles were depicted in detail, with the one at Cana given the natural place of honor, and there were at least a dozen battles of one sort or another, including two between David and Goliath. The Tower of Babel was made so high that it bled out of the top of the painting, and there were three separate views of Jerusalem. The sky showed a dozen rainbows, and as many flashes of lightning, and from a very red Red Sea in the foreground was thrust the maw of Jonah's whale, with Jonah himself shinning out of it to join Moses and the children of Israel on the beach. This masterpiece was completed in ten days, and brought $200 cash — the price of ten side-show fronts. When it was hung in the new Baptist church, it wrecked all the other evangelical filling-stations of the lower Atlantic littoral, and people came from as far away as Cleveland, Tenn., and Gainesville, Va., to wash out their sins in the tank, and admire the art. The artist himself was invited to submit to the process, but replied stiffly that he was forbidden in conscience, for he professed to be an infidel.

The cops of those days, in so far as they were aware of artists at all, accepted them at their own valuation, and thus regarded them with suspicion. If they were not actually on the level of water-front crimps, dope-pedlars and piano-players in houses of shame, they at least belonged somewhere south of sporty doctors, professional bondsmen and handbooks. This attitude once cost an artist of my acquaintance his liberty for three weeks, though he was innocent of any misdemeanor. On a cold Winter night he and his girl lifted four or five ash-boxes, made a roaring wood-fire in the fireplace of his fourth-floor studio, and settled down to listen to a phonograph, then a novelty in the world. The glare of the blaze, shining red through the cob-webbed windows, led a rookie cop to assume that the house was afire, and he turned in an alarm. When the firemen came roaring up, only to discover that the fire was in a fireplace, the poor cop sought to cover his chagrin by collaring the artist, and charging him with contributing to the delinquency of a minor. There was, of course, no truth in this, for the lady was nearly forty years old and had served at least two terms in a reformatory for soliciting on the street, but the lieutenant at the station-house, on learning that the culprit was an artist, ordered him locked up for investigation, and he had been in the cooler three weeks before his girl managed to round up a committee of social-minded saloonkeepers to demand his release. The cops finally let him go with a warning, and for the rest of that Winter no artist in Baltimore dared to make a fire.

But it was not only artists themselves who suffered from the harsh uncharitableness of the world; they also conveyed something of their Poësque ill fortune to all their more intimate associates. I never knew an artist's girl, however beautiful, to marry anyone above a jail warden or a third-string jockey, and most of the early photo-engravers came to bad ends, often by suicide. The engravers used various violent poisons in their work, including cyanide of potassium. It was their belief that a dose of cyanide killed instantly and was thus painless, but every time one of them rounded out a big drunk by trying it he passed away in a tumultuous fit, and made a great deal of noise. The survivors, however, no more learned by experience than any other class of men, and cyanide remained their remedy of choice for the sorrows of this world. They had in their craft a sub-craft of so-called routers, whose job it was to deepen the spaces between the lines in line-cuts. This was done with a power-driven drill that bounced like a jumping-jack and was excessively inaccurate. If the cut was a portrait the router nearly always succeeded in routing out the eyes. Failing that, he commonly fetched one of his own fingers. Many's the time I have seen a routing machine clogged to a standstill by a mixture of zinc eyes and human tissue, with the router jumping around it with his hand under his arm, yelling for a doctor or a priest.

In those days halftones were not much used in newspapers, for it was only a few years since Stephen H. Horgan, of the New York *Tribune*, had discovered that they could be stereotyped. Most provincial stereotypers still made a mess of the job, so line-cuts were preferred, and relatively more artists were employed than today. Nevertheless, photographs were needed, if only to be copied in line, and every paper of any pretensions had at least one photographer. The first I recall on the *Herald* was a high-toned German of the name of Julius Seelander, who had served his apprenticeship in his native land. He wore a beard trimmed to display the large stickpin that glowed from his Ascot necktie: it was, in fact, *two* pins, with a filigree silver chain connecting them. Julius was an excellent technician, but had a habit of aesthetic abstraction in emergencies. Once, in bitter Winter weather, I took him along when I was assigned to go down the Chesapeake on an ice-boat, to cover the succoring of a fishing village that had been frozen in for weeks. We got to the place after a bumpy struggle through the ice, and Julius took a dozen swell pictures of the provisions going ashore

and the starving oystermen fighting for them on
the wharf. But when we got back to the office, and
I was in the midst of my story, he came slinking out
of his darkroom to confess that he had made all of
the photographs on one plate. He said he was
throwing up his job, and asked me to break the
news to Max Ways: he was afraid that if he did so
himself Max would stab him with a copy hook or
throw him out of the window. But when I told Max
he was very little perturbed, for he believed that
all photographers, like all artists, were as grossly
unreliable and deceptive as so many loaded dice,
and it always surprised him when one of them carried out an assignment as ordered. The next day
Julius was back in his darkroom, and so far as I
know, nothing more was ever said about the matter.

But the most unfortunate camp-follower of art
that I ever knew was not a photographer, nor even
a photo-engraver, but a saloonkeeper named Kuno
Something-or-other, who had a great many artists
among his customers. When, in 1900, he opened a
new saloon, they waited on him in a body, and offered to decorate its bare walls without a cent of
cost to him, save only, of course, for their meals
while they were at work, and a few drinks to stoke
their aesthetic fires. Kuno, who loved everything
artistic, jumped at the chance, and in a few days
the first two of what was to be a long series of pre-
dacious frauds moved in on him. The pair daubed
away for four or five hours a day, and it seemed

to him, in the beginning, to be an excellent trade, for they not only got nothing for their services, but attracted a number of connoisseurs who watched them while they worked, and were good for an occasional flutter at the bar. But at the end of a couple of weeks, casting up accounts with his bartender, Kuno found that he was really breaking less than even, for while the credit side showed eight or ten square feet of wall embellished with beautiful girls in transparent underwear, the debit side ran to nearly 100 meals and more than 500 beers, all consumed by the artists.

Worse, the members of the succeeding teams were even hungrier and thirstier than the first pair, and by the time a fourth of one wall of the saloon was finished Kuno was in the red for more than 500 meals and nearly 7000 beers, not to mention innumerable whiskeys, absinthes and shots of bitters, and a couple of barrels of paint. The easy way out would have been to throw the artists into the street, but he respected the fine arts too much for that. Instead, he spent his days watching the Work in Progress and his nights trying to figure out how much he would be set back by the time it was finished. In the end these exercises unbalanced his mind, and he prepared to destroy himself, leaving his saloon half done, like a woman with one cheek made up and the other washed.

His exitus set an all-time high for technic, for he came from Frankfurt-an-der-Oder, and was a

Prussian for thoroughness. Going down to the Long Bridge which spanned the Patapsco below Baltimore, he climbed on the rail, fastened a long rope to it, looped the other end around his neck, swallowed a dose of arsenic, shot himself through the head, and then leaped or fell into the river. The old-time cops of Baltimore still astound rookies with his saga. He remains the most protean performer they have ever had the pleasure of handling post-mortem.

XI

THE DAYS OF THE

GIANTS

NOT infrequently I am asked by young college folk, sometimes male and sometimes female, whether there has been any significant change, in my time, in the bacchanalian virtuosity of the American people. They always expect me, of course, to say that boozing is now at an all-time high, for they are a proud generation, and have been brought up to believe that Prohibition brought in refinements unparalleled on earth since the fall of Babylon. But when I speak for that thesis it is only to please them, for I know very well that the facts run the other way. My actual belief is that Americans reached the peak of their alcoholic puissance in the closing years of the last century. Along about 1903 there was a sudden

and marked letting up — partly due, I suppose, to
the accelerating pace and hazard of life in a civilization growing more and more mechanized, but
also partly to be blamed on the lugubrious warnings of the medical men, who were then first learning how to reinforce their hocus-pocus with the
alarms of the uplift.

In my early days as a reporter they had no more
sense of civic responsibility than so many stockbrokers or policemen. A doctor of any standing
not only had nothing to say against the use of
stimulants ; he was himself, nine times out of ten, a
steady patron of them, and argued openly that
they sustained him in his arduous and irregular
life. Dr. Z. K. Wiley, our family practitioner, always took a snifter with my father when he
dropped in to dose my brother Charlie and me with
castor oil, and whenever, by some unusual accident
of his heavy practise, he had any free time afterward, he and my father gave it over to quiet wrestling with the decanters. His favorite prescription for a cold was rock-and-rye, and he believed
and taught that a shot of Maryland whiskey was
the best preventive of pneumonia in the R months.
If you object here that Dr. Wiley was a South-
erner, then I answer at once that Dr. Oliver Wen-
dell Holmes was a Yankee of the Yankees, and yet
held exactly the same views. Every schoolboy, I
suppose, has heard by this time of Dr. Holmes's
famous address before the Massachusetts Medical

Society on May 30, 1860, in which he argued that
" if the whole materia medica, as now used, could
be sunk to the bottom of the sea, it would be all the
better for mankind — and all the worse for the
fishes "; but what the pedagogues always fail to
tell their poor dupes is that he made a categorical
exception of wine, which he ranked with opium,
quinine, anesthetics and mercury among the sovereign and invaluable boons to humanity.

I was thus greatly surprised when I first heard a
medical man talk to the contrary. This was in the
Winter of 1899–1900, and the place was a saloon
near a messy downtown fire. I was helping my betters to cover the fire, and followed them into the
saloon for a prophylactic drink. The doctor, who
was a fire department surgeon, thereupon made a
speech arguing that alcohol was not a stimulant
but a depressant, and advising us to keep off it
until the fire was out and we were relaxing in preparation for bed. " You think it warms you," he
said, sipping a hot milk, " but it really cools you,
and you are seventeen point eight per cent. more
likely to catch pneumonia at the present minute
than you were when you came into this doggery."
This heresy naturally outraged the older reporters, and they became so prejudiced against the
doctor that they induced the Fire Board, shortly
afterward, to can him — as I recall it, by reporting that he was always drunk on duty. But his
words made a deep impression on my innocence,

and continue to lurk in my mind to this day. In
consequence, I am what may be called a somewhat
cagey drinker. That is to say, I never touch the
stuff by daylight if I can help it, and I employ it
of an evening, not to hooch up my faculties, but to
let them down after work. Not in years have I ever
written anything with so much as a glass of beer
in my system. My compositions, I gather, sometimes seem boozy to the nobility and gentry, but
they are actually done as soberly as those of William Dean Howells.

But this craven policy is not general among the
literati, nor was it to be noted among the journalists of my apprentice days. Between 1899 and
1904 there was only one reporter south of the
Mason & Dixon Line who did not drink at all, and
he was considered insane. In New York, so far as
I could make out, there was not even one. On my
first Christmas Eve on the *Herald* but two sober
persons were to be found in the office — one of them
a Seventh Day Adventist office-boy in the editorial
rooms, and the other a superannuated stereotyper
who sold lunches to the printers in the composing-
room. There was a printer on the payroll who was
reputed to be a teetotaler — indeed his singularity
gave him the nickname of the Moral Element — ,
but Christmas Eve happened to be his night off.
All the rest were full of what they called hand-set
whiskey. This powerful drug was sold in a saloon
next door to the *Herald* office, and was reputed to

be made in the cellar by the proprietor in person
— of wood alcohol, snuff, tabasco sauce, and coffin
varnish. The printers liked it, and got down a
great many shots of it. On the Christmas Eve I
speak of its effects were such that more than half
the linotype machines in the composing-room
broke down, and one of the apprentices ran his
shirt-tail through the proof-press. Down in the
press-room four or five pressmen got hurt, and the
city edition was nearly an hour late.

Nobody cared, for the head of the whole establishment, the revered managing editor, Colonel
Cunningham, was locked up in his office with a case
of Bourbon. At irregular intervals he would throw
a wad of copy-paper over the partition which separated him from the editorial writers, and when this
wad was smoothed out it always turned out to be
part of an interminable editorial against General
Felix Agnus, editor of the *American.* The General
was a hero of the Civil War, with so much lead in
his system that he was said to rattle as he walked,
but Colonel Cunningham always hooted at his war
record, and was fond of alleging — without any
ground whatsoever — that he had come to America
from his native France in the pussy-like character
of a barber. The editorial that he was writing that
Christmas Eve was headed, in fact, " The Barber
of Seville." It never got into the paper, for it was
running beyond three columns by press-time, and
the night editor, Isidor Goodman, killed it for fear

that its point was still to come. When the Colonel inquired about it two or three days afterward he was told that a truck had upset in the composing-room, and pied it.

The hero of the *Herald* composing-room in those days was a fat printer named Bill, who was reputed to be the champion beer-drinker of the Western Hemisphere. Bill was a first-rate linotype oper-ator, and never resorted to his avocation in work-ing-hours, but the instant his time was up he would hustle on his coat and go to a beer-house in the neighborhood, and there give what he called a setting. He made no charge for admission, but the spectators, of course, were supposed to pay for the beer. One night in 1902 I saw him get down thirty-two bottles in a row. Perhaps, in your wanderings, you have seen the same — but have you ever heard of a champion who could do it *without once retir-ing from his place at the bar?* Well, that is what Bill did, and on another occasion, when I was not present, he reached forty. Physiologists tell me that these prodigies must have been optical delu-sions, for there is not room enough in the coils and recesses of man for so much liquid, but I can only reply *Pfui* to that, for a record is a record. Bill avoided the door marked " Gents " as diligently as if he had been a débutante of the era, or the sign on it had been " For Ladies Only." He would have been humiliated beyond endurance if anyone had ever seen him slink through it.

In the year 1904, when the *Herald* office was
destroyed in the great Baltimore fire, and we had
to print the paper, for five weeks, in Philadelphia,
I was told off to find accommodation for the printers. I found it in one of those old-fashioned $1-a-
day hotels that were all bar on the first floor. The
proprietor, a German with goat whiskers, was
somewhat reluctant to come to terms, for he had
heard that printers were wild fellows who might be
expected to break up his furniture and work their
wicked will upon his chambermaids, but when I
told him that a beer-champion was among them he
showed a more friendly interest, and when I began to brag about Bill's extraordinary talents his
doubts disappeared and he proposed amiably that
some Philadelphia foam-jumpers be invited in to
make it a race. The first heat was run the very next
night, and Bill won hands down. In fact, he won so
easily that he offered grandly to go until he had
drunk *twice* as much as the next best entry. We restrained him and got him to bed, for there had been
some ominous whispering among the other starters,
and it was plain that they were planning to call in
help. The next night it appeared in the shape of a
tall, knotty man from Allentown, Pa., who was introduced as the champion of the Lehigh Valley.
He claimed to be not only a beer-drinker of high
gifts, but also a member of the Bach Choir at Bethlehem; and when he got down his first dozen mugs
— the boys were drinking from the wood — he cut

loose with an exultant yodel that he said was one
of Bach's forgotten minor works. But he might
very well have saved his wind, for Bill soon had
him, and at the end of the setting he was four or
five mugs behind, and in a state resembling suffocation. The next afternoon I saw his disconsolate
fans taking him home, a sadder and much less melo-
dious man.

On the first two nights there had been only slim
galleries, but on the third the bar was jammed, and
anyone could see that something desperate was
afoot. It turned out to be the introduction of two
super-champions, the one a short, saturnine Welshman from Wilkes-Barré, and the other a hearty
blond young fellow from one of the Philadelphia
suburbs, who said that he was half German and
half Irish. The Welshman was introduced as the
man who had twice drunk Otto the Brewery Horse
under the table, and we were supposed to know who
Otto was, though we didn't. The mongrel had a
committee with him, and the chairman thereof offered to lay $25 on him at even money. The print-
ers in Bill's corner made up the money at once, and
their stake had grown to $50 in forty minutes by
the clock, for the hybrid took only that long to
blow up. The Welshman lasted much better, and
there were some uneasy moments when he seemed
destined to make history again by adding Bill to
Otto, but in the end he succumbed so suddenly that
it seemed like a bang, and his friends laid him out

on the floor and began fanning him with bar-
towels.

Bill was very cocky after that, and talked gran-
diosely of taking on two champions at a time, in
marathon series. There were no takers for several
nights, but after that they began to filter in from
the remoter wilds of the Pennsylvania Dutch country, and the whole *Herald* staff was kept busy
guarding Bill by day, to make sure that he did not
waste any of his libido for malt liquor in the afternoons. He knocked off twenty or thirty challengers
during the ensuing weeks, including two more
Welshmen from the hard-coal country, a Scotsman with an ear missing, and a bearded Dunkard
from Lancaster county. They were mainly push-
overs, but now and then there was a tough one.
Bill did not let this heavy going interfere with the
practise of his profession. He set type every night
from 6 p.m. to midnight in the office of the *Evening
Telegraph*, where we were printing the *Herald*,
and never began his combats until 12.30. By two
o'clock he was commonly in bed, with another
wreath of laurels hanging on the gas-jet.

To ease your suspense I'll tell·you at once that
he was never beaten. Germans, Irishmen, Welshmen and Scotsmen went down before him like so
many Sunday-school superintendents, and he
bowled over everyday Americans with such facility that only two of them ever lasted more than
half an hour. But I should add in candor that he

was out of service during the last week of our stay
in Philadelphia. What fetched him is still a subject of debate among the pathologists at the Johns
Hopkins Medical School, to whom the facts were
presented officially on our return to Baltimore.
The only visible symptom was a complete loss of
speech. Bill showed up one night talking hoarsely,
the next night he could manage only whispers, and
the third night he was as mute as a shad-fish.
There was absolutely no other sign of distress. He
was all for going on with his derisive harrying of
the Pennsylvania lushers, but a young doctor who
hung about the saloon and served as surgeon at the
bouts forbade it on unstated medical grounds. The
Johns Hopkins experts in morbid anatomy have
never been able to agree about the case. Some
argue that Bill's potations must have dissolved the
gummy coating of his pharyngeal plexus, and thus
paralyzed his vocal cords; the rest laugh at this as
nonsense savoring of quackery, and lay the whole
thing to an intercurrent laryngitis, induced by insufficient bedclothes on very cold nights. I suppose
that no one will ever know the truth. Bill recovered
his voice in a couple of months, and soon afterward
left Baltimore. Of the prodigies, if any, that
marked his later career I can't tell you.

He was but one of a notable series of giants who
flourished in Baltimore at the turn of the century,
bringing the city a friendly publicity and causing
the theory to get about that life there must be de-

lightful. They appeared in all the ranks of society. The Maryland Club had its champions, and the cops had theirs. Some were drinkers pure and simple; others specialized in eating. One of the latter was an old man of easy means who lived at the Rennert Hotel, then the undisputed capital of gastronomy in the terrapin and oyster country. But for some reason that I can't tell you he never did his eating there; instead, he always took dinner at Tommy McPherson's eating-house, six or eight blocks away. He would leave the hotel every evening at seven o'clock, elegantly arrayed in a long-tailed black coat and a white waistcoat, and carrying a gold-headed cane, and would walk the whole way. Tommy's place was arranged in two layers, with tables for men only alongside the bar downstairs, and a series of small rooms upstairs to which ladies might be invited. The cops, goaded by vice crusaders, had forced him to take the doors off these rooms, but he had substituted heavy portières, and his colored waiters were instructed to make a noise as they shuffled down the hall, and to enter every room backward. The old fellow I speak of, though there were tales about his wild youth, had by now got beyond thought of sin, and all his eating was done downstairs. It consisted of the same dishes precisely every night of the week, year in and year out. First he would throw in three straight whiskeys, and then he would sit down to *two* double porterhouse steaks, with *two* large plates of peas, *two* of French fried potatoes, *two* of cole-slaw, and a mountain of rye-bread. This vast meal he would eat to the last speck, and not infrequently he called for more potatoes or bread. He washed it down with two quarts of Burgundy, and at its end threw in three more straight whiskeys. Then he would light a cigar, and amble back to the Rennert, to spend the rest of the evening conversing with the politicoes who made their headquarters in its lobby.

One day a report reached the *Herald* office that he was beginning to break up, and Max Ways sent me to take a look. He had, by then, been on his diet for no less than twelve years. When I opened the subject delicately he hooted at the notion that he was not up to par. He was, he told me, in magnificent health, and expected to live at least twenty years longer. His excellent condition, he went on to say, was due wholly to his lifelong abstemiousness. He ate only a sparing breakfast, and no lunch at all, and he had not been drunk for fifteen years — that is, in the sense of losing all control of himself. He told me that people who ate pork dug their graves with their teeth, and praised the Jews for avoiding it. He also said that he regarded all sea-food as poisonous, on the ground that it contained too much phosphorus, and that fowl was almost as bad. There was, in his view, only one perfectly safe and wholesome victual, and that was beef. It had everything. It was nourishing, palat-

able and salubrious. The last bite tasted as good
as the first. Even the bones had a pleasant flavor.
He ate peas and potatoes with it, he said, mainly
to give it some company: if he were ever cast on a
desert island he could do without them. The cole-
slaw went along as a sort of gesture of politeness
to the grass that had produced the beef, and he ate
rye-bread instead of wheat because rye was the
bone and sinew of Maryland whiskey, the most
healthful appetizer yet discovered by man. He
would not affront me by presuming to discuss the
virtues of Burgundy: they were mentioned in the
Bible, and all humanity knew them.

The old boy never made his twenty years, but
neither did he ever change his regimen. As the uplift gradually penetrated medicine various doctors
of his acquaintance began to warn him that he was
headed for a bad end, but he laughed at them in
his quiet way, and went on going to Tommy's place
every night, and devouring his two double porter-
houses. What took him off at last was not his eating, but a trifling accident. He was knocked down
by a bicycle in front of the Rennert, developed
pneumonia, and was dead in three days. The
resurrection men at both the Johns Hopkins and
the University of Maryland tried to get his body
for autopsy, and were all set to dig out of it a whole
series of pathological monstrosities of a moral tendency, but his lawyer forbade any knifeplay until
his only heir, a niece, could be consulted, and when

she roared in from Eufaula, Ala., it turned out that she was a Christian Scientist, with a hate against anatomy. So he was buried without yielding any lessons for science. If he had any real rival, in those declining years of Baltimore gastronomy, it must have been John Wilson, a cop: I have always regretted that they were never brought together in a match. Once, at a cop party, I saw John eat thirty fried hard crabs at a sitting — no mean feat, I assure you, for though the claws are pulled off a crab before it is fried, all the body-meat remains. More, he not only ate the crabs, but sucked the shells. On another occasion, on a bet, he ate a ham and a cabbage in half an hour by the clock, but I was not present at that performance. When, a little later, he dropped dead in the old Central station-house, the police surgeons laid it to a pulmonary embolus, then a recent novelty in pathology.

XII

THE

JUDICIAL ARM

My recollection of judges and my veneration for them go back a long way before my newspaper days, for I was a boy not more than eight or nine years old when my father began taking me on his tours of the more high-toned Washington saloons, and pointing out for my edification the eminent men who infested them. Not a few of those dignitaries were ornaments of the Federal judiciary, and among them were some whose names were almost household words in the Republic. But it was not their public fame that most impressed me; it was the lordly and elegant way in which they did their boozing. Before I really knew what a Congressman was I was aware that Congressmen were bad actors in barrooms, and often had to be thrown out, and years before I had heard that the United States Senate sat in trials of impeachment and formerly had a say in international treaties I had seen a Senator stricken by the first acrobatic symptoms of delirium tremens. But though I search my memory diligently, and it is especially tenacious in sociological matters, I can't recall a single judge who ever showed any sign of yielding to the influence. They all drank freely, and with a majestic spaciousness of style, but they carried their liquor like gentlemen.

Boy-like, I must have assumed that this gift for the bottle ran with their high station, and was, in fact, a part of their professional equipment, for I remember being greatly astonished years later, when I first encountered, as a young reporter, a judge definitely in his cups. There was nothing to the story save the bald fact that the poor old man, facing a hard calendar in equity on a morning when he was nursing a hangover from a Bar Association banquet, had thrown in one too many quick ones, and so got himself plastered. When he fell sound asleep in his pulpit, with his feet on the bench, there was a considerable pother, and by the time I wandered upon the scene his bailiffs had evacuated him to his chambers and doused him with ice-water, and he was rapidly resuming rationality, as his loud swearing indicated. Being still innocent, I reported the facts truthfully to Max Ways, and was somewhat puzzled when he

ordered me to write a brief piece saying that His
Honor had been floored at the post of duty by
stomach ulcers, but was happily out of danger.
Later on, as my journalistic experience widened, I
saw many judges in a more or less rocky state,
though I should add at once that I never saw another in that condition on the actual bench or
within its purlieus, and that most of those I encountered were very far from their own courts.
Indeed, I gradually picked up the impression that
judges, like police captains, never really let themselves go until they were away from home. In those
days all the police captains of the Eastern seaboard, whenever they felt that they couldn't stand
the horrors of their office another minute, went to
Atlantic City, and there soused and bellowed in-
cognito, without either public scandal or danger to
their jobs. Sometimes as many as a dozen gathered in one saloon — two or three from New York,
a couple each from Philadelphia, Baltimore and
Washington, and maybe the rest from points as
far west as Pittsburgh. In the same way judges
commonly sought a hide-away when the impulse
to cut loose was on them; in their own archdioceses
they kept their thirsts in hand, and so avoided the
prying eyes of the vulgar.

At the time I began to find my way about as a
reporter there was a rich old fellow in Baltimore
who gave a big stag dinner every year at the
Maryland Club. He was himself of no prominence,

and his dinner had no public significance: it was simply that he loved good eating and enlightened boozing himself, and delighted in getting a group of men of the same mind about him. He had begun long before with a relatively small party, but every year the grateful patients suggested that it would be nice to include this or that recruit, and in the era I speak of the feast had grown to be very large and surpassingly elaborate, with seventy or eighty head of guests at the long table, as many colored waiters toting in the oysters, wild duck and terrapin, a large staff of sommeliers at the wine-buckets, and a battery of bartenders out in the hall. One year a judge was among the delegation of stockbrokers, bank presidents, wine-agents, Tammany leaders and other dignitaries who came down from New York, and the next year he brought another, and the year following there were three, and then six, and so on. They greatly enjoyed the entertainment, and no wonder, for it was in the best Maryland Club manner; and the host, on his side, appreciated having so many men of mark at his board. But in the course of time it began to be hard on the families of some of the judges, and almost as hard on the cops and newspaper reporters of Baltimore.

For every time there was a dinner it launched a drunk in the grand manner, and every time there was such a drunk the job of rounding up the judiciary took two or three days, and was full of embarrassments and alarms. Many of the other guests, of course, also succumbed to the grape, but no one ever seemed to care what had become of them. A Tammany leader could disappear for two days, and cause no remark; even a bank president would not be posted at Lloyd's until the third day. But judges, it appeared, were missed very quickly, if not by their catchpolls then certainly by their wives and daughters, and by the late afternoon of the day after the dinner inquiries about this or that one would begin to come in from the North. Not infrequently the inquiry would be lodged in person by a frantic daughter, and when she was put off by the cops with weasel words she would tour the newspaper offices, declaring hysterically that her pa must have been murdered, and demanding the immediate production of his carcass.

The cops were indifferent for a plain reason: they always knew where the missing judges were. So, in fact, did everybody know, but it was not etiquette to say so. For aside from a few very ancient men who had gone direct from the dinner to the nervous diseases ward of the Johns Hopkins Hospital, and were there undergoing the ammonia cure, all the recreant Pontius Pilates were safely housed in the stews of Baltimore, which were then surpassed in luxury and polish only by the stews of St. Louis. Every such establishment had appropriate accommodations for just such clients. They would be lodged in comfortable rooms, watched over by trustworthy bouncers, entertained with music, dancing and easy female conversation, and supplied with booze until they seemed about to give out, whereupon they would be put on strict rations of milk and soda-water and so prepared for restoration to the world. All the chatêlaines of the Baltimore houses of sin were familiar with that kind of trade, and knew precisely how to handle it, for they got a great deal of it, year in and year out, from Washington. Having handled maniacal Senators and Ambassadors, not to mention even ' higher dignitaries, they were not daunted by a sudden rush of harmless judges.

Unhappily, it was hard to convince the daughters of the missing jurists that they were comfortable and happy, and under no hazards to either their lives or their morals. Every such inquirer refused violently to be placated with generalizations: she demanded to be taken to her father instantly, and allowed to convoy him home. Inasmuch as no one dared to tell her where he was, it became the custom to say that he had gone down to a ducking club on the Eastern Shore of Maryland, and was there engaged in shooting mallards and canvasbacks. But there were always daughters who declared that their fathers were not marksmen, and in fact had a fear of guns, and sometimes it took a good deal of blarney to convince them that duck-shooting could be learned in half an hour, and was done with air-rifles or sling-shots.

Even those who swallowed the lie often made trouble, for they usually proposed to proceed to the duck country at once, and I recall one who spent two days and nights roving the Eastern Shore, seeking some trace of a tall old man wearing a heavy white moustache, weighing 220 pounds, and dressed in a broadcloth cutaway and striped pants. It would have done no good to tell this poor lady that her father was still wearing the evening clothes that he had put on for the dinner. All the visitors, in fact, continued in their tails until the time came to wash them up and start them home. The champion in my day went on thus for four days and nights, and when the whistle was blown on him at last his judicial collar, white lawn tie and boiled shirt were in a truly scandalous state. Within the month following his return to duty, so I was told afterward, he sentenced five men to death.

How the old boys accounted for their disappearance to their daughters, once they had got back to their hotels and changed clothes for the journey home, I do not know, and never inquired. I suppose that a daughter is bound in law to believe anything her father tells her, especially if he be a judge, and I assume that judges, having been lawyers, have good imaginations and ready tongues. All I can tell you is that this annual man-hunt was a headache to the city editors of Baltimore, and to their faithful reporters. We had to keep watch on the whole gang for two or three days and nights, ever full of a pardonable hope that this one or that one would fall out of a window, brain a piano-player, drop dead of *mania à potu*, or otherwise qualify for our professional attentions. It would never do to be beaten on such a story — if such a story ever bobbed up. But it never did. The judges all got home safely, and whenever it turned out that one of them had left his watch behind, or his wallet, or his plug hat, the cops always recovered it promptly, and turned it over to the host, who saw that it was restored to its owner.

There was in those days a standard Maryland dinner for all festive occasions, and it was eaten five hundred times a year in the more polished hotels and clubs of Baltimore. It had the strange peculiarity of being wholly devoid of vegetables: every item on the bill save the salad was protein, and even the salad had slices of ham in it. It began with Chesapeake Bay oysters, proceeded to Chesapeake Bay terrapin, went on to Chesapeake Bay wild ducks, and then petered out in lettuce salad with Smithfield ham, and harlequin ice-cream. Sometimes a thin soup was served between the oysters and the terrapin, but often not. The oysters were not the rachitic dwarfs now seen on dinner tables, but fat, yellow, eunuchoid monsters at least six inches long; indeed, they were frequently nearer ten than six. A stranger to the Maryland cuisine, confronting such an oyster for the first time, usually got into a panic, but his host always bucked him up to trying it on his esophagus, and when he did so it commonly went down without choking him, for an oyster is a very pliant and yielding animal, and is also well lubricated. To cut up one would be regarded, in Maryland, as an indecency to be matched only by frying soft crabs in batter or putting cream into terrapin stew. The last two crimes against humanity obtain in New York, Philadelphia and Washington, but not in Baltimore. Soft crabs are always fried (or broiled) there in the altogether, with maybe a small jockstrap of bacon added, and nothing goes with terrapin save butter, seasoning and a jigger or two of sherry. Today a Marylander will give humble thanks to God for any kind of wild duck he can shoot, trap, beg, bootleg or steal, but in the Golden Age he offered his guests only the breasts of canvasbacks. Along with the orthodox dinner that I have outlined went an equally rigid programme of drinks. If cocktails were served before going to the table they had to be Manhattans, for no Baltimorean of condition ever drank gin: it was for blackamoors only, with a humane reservation in favor of white ladies suffering from female weakness. With the terrapin came sherry, or maybe Madeira, and with the duck, champagne, or maybe Burgundy. The rest of the dinner was washed down with champagne only, and the more of it the better.

This bill-of-fare, with all the drinks save the

cocktails included, cost $10 a plate in any good Baltimore hotel. In that age of low living costs it was a high price, and the persons who paid it tried to get the worth of their money by guzzling all the champagne they could hold. As a young reporter I covered many such dinners, and saw some drinking bouts of very high amperage. The annual banquet of the Merchants and Manufacturers Association, then the chief organization of the local Babbitti, always ended in one of them. The chief speaker was usually either the Governor of some Southern state or a United States Senator, but it was seldom that his remarks were heard by anyone save the reporters and a few old Presbyterian misers, for all the rest of the guests were far gone by the time he got up, and not infrequently he was pretty well smeared himself. As I have noted, it was nothing to me to see a Senator in his cups, but it always shocked the Presbyterians, and after every dinner they proposed that the next one be dry. This proposal, when it got into the newspapers, set off a debate that went on for weeks and invariably ended in one way, with Colonel Cunningham and General Agnus joined in brotherly amity on the triumphant wet side. No M. & M. party was ever even ostensibly dry until the Prohibition murrain came down upon the country. The classical Maryland dinner was one of that great curse's first victims, and has never been revived, for when Prohibition went out at last new game laws came in, and it would be impossible today to assemble enough canvasback ducks to feed 500 men, or even fifty. In the midst of the thirteen doleful years the M. & M. itself gave up the ghost, and was absorbed by a new organization which devotes itself mainly to shipping and manufacturing statistics, and is not interested in the good living which once made Baltimore the envy of every other American city save New Orleans.

XIII

RECOLLECTIONS OF

NOTABLE COPS

Some time ago I read in a New York paper that fifty or sixty college graduates had been appointed to the metropolitan police force, and were being well spoken of by their superiors. The news astonished me, for in my reportorial days there was simply no such thing in America as a book-learned cop, though I knew a good many who were very smart. The force was then recruited, not from the groves of Academe, but from the ranks of workingmen. The best police captain I ever knew in Baltimore was a meat-cutter by trade, and had lost one of his thumbs by a slip of his cleaver, and the next best was a former bartender. All the mounted cops were ex-hostlers passing as ex-cavalrymen, and all the harbor police had come up through the tugboat and garbage-scow branches of the merchant marine. It took a young reporter a little while to learn how to read and interpret the reports that cops turned in, for they were couched in a special kind of English, with a spelling peculiar to itself. If a member of what was then called " the finest " had spelled *larceny* in any way save *larsensy*, or *arson* in any way save *arsony*, or *fracture* in any way save *fraxr*, there would have been a considerable lifting of eyebrows. I well recall the horror of the Baltimore cops when the first board to examine applicants for places on the force was set up. It was a harmless body headed by a political dentist, and the hardest question in its first examination paper was " What is the plural of *ox?*," but all the cops in town predicted that it would quickly contaminate their craft with a great horde of what they called " professors," and reduce it to the level of letter-carrying or school-teaching.

But, as I have noted, their innocence of *literae humaniores* was not necessarily a sign of stupidity, and from some of them, in fact, I learned the valuable lesson that sharp wits can lurk in unpolished skulls. I knew cops who were matches for the most learned and unscrupulous lawyers at the Baltimore bar, and others who had made monkeys of the oldest and crabbedest judges on the bench, and were generally respected for it. Moreover, I knew cops who were really first-rate policemen, and loved their trade as tenderly as so many art artists

or movie actors. They were badly paid, but they
carried on their dismal work with unflagging diligence, and loved a long, hard chase almost as much
as they loved a quick, brisk clubbing. Their one
salient failing, taking them as a class, was their belief that any person who had been arrested, even on
mere suspicion, was unquestionably and *ipso facto*
guilty. But that theory, though it occasionally
colored their testimony in a garish manner, was
grounded, after all, on nothing worse than professional pride and *esprit de corps*, and I am certainly
not one to hoot at it, for my own belief in the mission of journalism has no better support than the
same partiality, and all the logic I am aware of
stands against it.

In those days that pestilence of Service which
torments the American people today was just getting under way, and many of the multifarious duties now carried out by social workers, statisticians,
truant officers, visiting nurses, psychologists, and
the vast rabble of inspectors, smellers, spies and
bogus experts of a hundred different faculties
either fell to the police or were not discharged at
all. An ordinary flatfoot in a quiet residential section had his hands full. In a single day he might
have to put out a couple of kitchen fires, arrange
for the removal of a dead mule, guard a poor epi-
leptic having a fit on the sidewalk, catch a runaway
horse, settle a combat with table knives between
husband and wife, shoot a cat for killing pigeons,

rescue a dog or a baby from a sewer, bawl out a white-wings for spilling garbage, keep order on the sidewalk at two or three funerals, and flog half a dozen bad boys for throwing horse-apples at a blind man. The cops downtown, especially along the wharves and in the red-light districts, had even more curious and complicated jobs, and some of them attained to a high degree of virtuosity.

As my memory gropes backward I think, for example, of a strange office that an old-time roundsman named Charlie had to undertake every Spring. It was to pick up enough skilled workmen to effect the annual re-decoration and refurbishing of the Baltimore City Jail. Along about May 1 the warden would telephone to police headquarters that he needed, say, ten head of painters, five plumbers, two blacksmiths, a tile-setter, a roofer, a bricklayer, a carpenter and a locksmith, and it was Charlie's duty to go out and find them. So far as I can recall, he never failed, and usually he produced two or three times as many craftsmen of each category as were needed, so that the warden had some chance to pick out good ones. His plan was simply to make a tour of the saloons and stews in the Marsh Market section of Baltimore, and look over the drunks in congress assembled. He had a trained eye, and could detect a plumber or a painter through two weeks' accumulation of beard and dirt. As he gathered in his candidates, he searched them on the spot, rejecting those who had

no union cards, for he was a firm believer in organized labor. Those who passed were put into
storage at a police-station, and there kept (less the
unfortunates who developed delirium tremens and
had to be handed over to the resurrection-men)
until the whole convoy was ready. The next
morning Gene Grannan, the police magistrate,
gave them two weeks each for vagrancy, loitering,
trespass, committing a nuisance, or some other
plausible misdemeanor, the warden had his staff of
master-workmen, and the jail presently bloomed
out in all its vernal finery.

Some of these toilers returned year after year,
and in the end Charlie recognized so many that he
could accumulate the better part of his convoy in
half an hour. Once, I remember, he was stumped
by a call for two electricians. In those remote days
there were fewer men of that craft in practise than
today, and only one could be found. When the
warden put on the heat Charlie sent him a trolley-
car motorman who had run away from his wife and
was trying to be shanghaied for the Chesapeake
oyster-fleet. This poor man, being grateful for
his security in jail, made such eager use of his
meagre electrical knowledge that the warden decided to keep him, and even requested that his sentence be extended. Unhappily, Gene Grannan was
a pretty good amateur lawyer, and knew that such
an extension would be illegal. When the warden
of the House of Correction, which was on a farm

twenty miles from Baltimore, heard how well this system was working, he put in a requisition for six experienced milkers and a choir-leader, for he had a herd of cows and his colored prisoners loved to sing spirituals. Charlie found the choir-leader in no time, but he bucked at hunting for milkers, and got rid of the nuisance by sending the warden a squad of sailors who almost pulled the poor cows to pieces.

Gene had been made a magistrate as one of the first fruits of the rising reform movement in Baltimore, and was a man of the chastest integrity, but he knew too much about reformers to admire them, and lost no chance to afflict them. When, in 1900, or thereabout, a gang of snoopers began to tour the red-light districts, seeking to harass and alarm the poor working women there denizened, he instructed the gals to empty slops on them, and acquitted all who were brought in for doing it, usually on the ground that the complaining witnesses were disreputable persons, and could not be believed on oath. One day, sitting in his frowsy courtroom, I saw him gloat in a positively indecent manner when a Methodist clergyman was led out from the cells by Mike Hogan, the turnkey. This holy man, believing that the Jews, unless they consented to be baptized, would all go to Hell, had opened a mission in what was then still called the Ghetto, and sought to save them. The adults, of course, refused to have anything to do with him, but he managed, after a while, to lure a number of *kosher* small boys into his den, chiefly by showing them magic-lantern pictures of the Buffalo Bill country and the Holy Land. When their fathers heard of this there was naturally an uproar, for it was a mortal sin in those days for an orthodox Jew to enter a *Goy Schul.* The ritual for delousing offenders was an arduous one, and cost both time and money. So the Jews came clamoring to Grannan, and he spent a couple of hours trying to figure out some charge to lay against the evangelist. Finally, he ordered him brought in, and entered him on the books for " annoying persons passing by and along a public highway, disorderly conduct, making loud and unseemly noises, and disturbing religious worship." He had to be acquitted, of course, but Gene scared him so badly with talk of the penitentiary that he shut down his mission forthwith, and left the Jews to their post-mortem sufferings.

As I have noted in Chapter II, Gene was a high favorite among us young reporters, for he was always good for copy, and did not hesitate to modify the course of justice in order to feed and edify us. One day an ancient German, obviously a highly respectable man, was brought in on the incredible charge of beating his wife. The testimony showed that they had been placidly married for more than 45 years, and seldom exchanged so much as a bitter word. But the night before, when the old man came home from the saloon where he played *Skat* every evening, the old woman accused him of having drunk more than his usual ration of eight beers, and in the course of the ensuing debate he gave her a gentle slap. Astounded, she let off an hysterical squawk, an officious neighbor rushed in, the cops came on his heels, and so the old man stood before the bar of justice, weeping copiously and with his wife weeping even more copiously beside him. Gene pondered the evidence with a frown on his face, and then announced his judgment. " The crime you are accused of committing," he said, " is a foul and desperate one, and the laws of all civilized countries prohibit it under heavy penalties. I could send you to prison for life, I could order you to the whipping-post [it still exists in Maryland, and for wife-beaters only], or I could sentence you to be hanged. [Here both parties screamed.] But inasmuch as this is your first offense I will be lenient. You will be taken hence to the House of Correction, and there confined for twenty years. In addition, you are fined $10,000." The old couple missed the fine, for at mention of the House of Correction both fainted. When the cops revived them, Gene told the prisoner that, on reflection, he had decided to strike out the sentence, and bade him go and sin no more. Husband and wife rushed out of the courtroom hand in hand, followed by a cop with the umbrella and market-basket that the old woman had forgotten. A week or two later news came in that she was ordering the old man about in a highly cavalier manner, and had cut down his evenings of *Skat* to four a week.

The cops liked and admired Gene, and when he was in good form he commonly had a gallery of them in his courtroom, guffawing at his whimsies. But despite his popularity among them he did not pal with them, for he was basically a very dignified, and even somewhat stiff fellow, and knew how to call them down sharply when their testimony before him went too far beyond the bounds of the probable. In those days, as in these, policemen led a social life almost as inbred as that of the justices of the Supreme Court of the United States, and outsiders were seldom admitted to their parties. But reporters were exceptions, and I attended a number of cop soirées of great elegance, with the tables piled mountain-high with all the delicacies of the season, and a keg of beer every few feet. The graft of these worthy men, at least in my time, was a great deal less than reformers alleged and the envious common people believed. Most of them, in my judgment, were very honest fellows, at least within the bounds of reason. Those who patrolled the fish-markets naturally had plenty of fish to eat, and those who manned the police-boats in the harbor took a certain toll from the pungy captains who brought up Baltimore's supplies of watermelons, cantaloupes, vegetables, crabs and oysters from the Eastern Shore of Maryland: indeed, this last impost amounted to a kind of *octroi,* and at one time the harbor force accumulated so much provender that they had to seize an empty warehouse on the waterfront to store it. But the pungy captains gave up uncomplainingly, for the pelagic cops protected them against the thieves and high-jackers who swarmed in the harbor, and also against the land police. I never heard of cops getting anything that the donor was not quite willing and even eager to give. Every Italian who ran a peanut stand knew that making them free of it was good institutional promotion and the girls in the red-light districts liked to crochet neckties, socks and pulse-warmers for them. It was not unheard of for a cop to get mashed on such a girl, rescue her from her life of shame, and set her up as a more or less honest woman. I knew of several cases in which holy matrimony followed. But the more ambitious girls, of course, looked higher, and some of them, in my time, made very good marriages. One actually married a banker, and another died only a few years ago as the faithful and much respected wife of a prominent physician. The cops always laughed when reformers alleged that the wages of sin were death — specifically, that women who sold their persons always ended in the gutter, full of dope and despair. They knew that the overwhelming majority ended at the altar of God, and that nearly all of them married better men than they could have had any chance of meeting and roping if they had kept their virtue.

One dismal New Year's day I saw a sergeant lose an excellent chance to pocket $138.66 in cash money: I remember it brilliantly because I lost the same chance at the same moment. There had been the usual epidemic of suicides in the waterfront flop-houses, for the dawn of a new year turns the thoughts of homeless men to peace beyond the dissecting-room, and I accompanied the sergeant and a coroner on a tour of the fatal scenes. One of the dead men was lying on the fifth floor of a decaying warehouse that had been turned into ten-cent sleeping quarters, and we climbed up the long stairs to inspect him. All the other bums had cleared out, and the hophead clerk did not offer to go with us. We found the deceased stretched out in a peaceful attitude, with the rope with which he had hanged himself still around his neck. He had been cut down, but then abandoned.

The sergeant loosed the rope, and began a search of the dead man's pockets, looking for means to identify him. He found nothing whatever of that sort, but from a pants pocket he drew out a fat wad of bills, and a hasty count showed that it contained $416. A situation worthy of Scribe, or even Victor Hugo! Evidently the poor fellow was one of the Russell Sages that are occasionally found among bums. His money, I suppose, had been diminishing, and he had bumped himself off in fear that it would soon be all gone. The sergeant looked at the coroner, the coroner

looked at me, and I looked at the sergeant. Then
the sergeant wrapped up the money in a piece of
newspaper lying nearby, and handed it to the coroner. " It goes," he said sadly, " to the State of
Maryland. The son-of-a-bitch died intestate, and
with no heirs."

The next day I met the coroner, and found him
in a low frame of mind. " It was a sin and a
shame," he said, " to turn that money over to the
State Treasury. What I could have done with
$138.67! (I noticed he made a fair split, but col-
lared one of the two odd cents.) Well, it's gone
now — damn the luck! I never *did* trust that flat-
foot."

XIV

A

GENIAL RESTAURANTEUR

I AM well aware that the word *restauranteur*, as it appears in the title of this chapter, contains an *n* that the French eschew; my plea in confession and avoidance must be that I am not writing French but American, and, specifically, the American in vogue on the newspapers of my native Baltimore in my salad days as a journalist. No reporter of that era ever thought of referring to a respectable saloonkeeper as a saloonkeeper: the term was reserved, at least in print, for such dubious characters as Bob Fosbender, whose place at Pine and Raborg streets was the very Capitol of the Western red-light district — and when I say Capitol I mean exactly that, for the representative assembly of the adjacent landladies, always called simply the Senate, met in his back room once a week. All saloonkeepers above Bob's social and moral level, with one exception, were restauranteurs, with the *n*, and all that were personally known to newspaper men, and held in reasonable esteem, rated the *genial* in front of *restauranteur*.

This large company included even Frank Junker, probably one of the least genial men, in actuality, that ever suffered from varicose veins, the occupational malady of all the old-timers of his profession. He was a stout, short, silent, suspicious German who was a Scotsman in all save the husk or rind, and he owned a modest but very profitable saloon opposite the Baltimore City Hall. Having learned by experience that municipal job-holders, as a class, were grasping and cantankerous men, he did not cater to them, but directed his lures (*a*) to the musicians, stagehands and ham actors of the old Holliday Street Theatre, which was half a block away, and (*b*) to journalists. Neither of these groups had any great amount of money, but they could be trusted to spend all they had, and, moreover, they spread their boozing over both day and night. Like any other downtown saloonkeeper Frank had plenty of business in daylight hours, but at night most of the streets near the City Hall were as dead as Herculaneum, and many of the genial restauranteurs in them actually closed at 9 p.m. But not this one, for he had learned that that was the hour when musicians and actors began to duck out for really earnest drinking, and he knew, too, that journalists hardly got under way until an hour or two later. Thus his place was crowded every night, and I have seen it so jammed at midnight that Frank and his bartender, Emil, had to call off all mixed drinks, and serve only straight whiskey and beer.

I have spoken of the actors as hams, and that, unhappily, was what they were, for the Holliday Street was one of the oldest theatres in America, and had long since descended to Theodore Kremer and Charles E. Blaney melodramas. It had a matinée every day (heavily patronized by night-shift street-car conductors and motormen, and their doxies), and before every performance, no matter what the weather, the orchestra, playing as a brass band, performed on the portico over the entrance. This was tough work in Winter, and the work indoors, Winter or no Winter, was almost as onerous, for there was continuous music while a melodrama was going on, and the musicians had to look sharply or miss their cues. The hottest spot was that of Hank Schofield, the bull-fiddler, for on his vigilance depended the success of every scene of lust, vengeance or despair. Whenever the villain was on the stage, which was nearly always, Hank had to accompany his lubricious rascalities *pizzicato*, and when the comic man split his pants the sound had to be caught and augmented *col arco*. Even the love scenes gave Hank no rest, for it was the convention in those days to signalize every kiss with a jocose *glissando*, and that *glissando* always started in the bull-fiddle.

Thus Hank was pretty dry by the time the evening performance was over, and nearly every night he sat at one of Frank's greasy tables with several other *Tonkünstler* and discussed the decay of their chosen art. By the time we journalists began to drop in some of these artists were more or less lit, and so the evening's ceremonies started off in a very friendly manner. On our side there was a fixed ritual. We were organized into a professional society known as the Stevedores' Club (the name, of course, was a subtle reference to the unloading of schooners), and as soon as a *minyan* was present Frank was elected an honorary member. He always received this distinction with modest deprecation and embarrassment, and apparently lived and died without ever figuring out why he got it so often. But he knew the rule that a new member was expected to set up the drinks, and in consequence we always got a round free. Once the experiment was tried of electing him *twice* in a night, but he failed to hear the second election, and the scheme was abandoned. But at about the same time we invented and established a rule that *guests* could treat the house, though members were forbidden to do so. The Holliday Street Theatre boys kept this rule alive by steering in a steady stream of ham actors, all of whom were welcomed with flattering speeches. The musicians were not members of the

Stevedores' Club, but when they had a ham in tow they were free to sit in.

How long the club went on I don't know, for it was in existence years before my time, and there were vestiges of it visible so late as 1915, long after I had become a managing editor and was no longer eligible. At its peak, say in 1900, it had about a dozen regular members, and a dozen more who dropped in off and on. Not only was its direct patronage valuable to Frank; it also helped him to wealth by enabling him to stay open beyond the Baltimore closing hour, which in those days was midnight. The news of this immunity getting about, he was soon catering to a large body of miscellaneous night-hawks, including printers, post-office clerks, bank watchmen, and even street cleaners. We objected to the last-named on the ground of their smell, and they were finally excluded, but the rest kept coming, and Frank wore out a cash-register a year ringing up their money. In 1904, when his place was burned in the great Baltimore fire, the insurance he received, added to his accumulations, gave him the impressive cash capital of $175,000, and with it he built a stag hotel and was quickly rolling in an income even larger than his old one. Unhappily, his dignity as host of his hotel required him to wear his Sunday suit every day, and he soon began to pine away, and was presently no more.

As I have said, it was the presence of the Steve-

dores' Club that enabled him to keep open after
hours, for we journalists naturally had some drag
with the cops, and when we represented to Ned
Schleigh, their captain in that precinct, that it was
inhuman to ask us to clear out at midnight, perhaps in the midst of a belated meal, he allowed
that the point was well taken, and instructed his
flatfeet to act accordingly. But the reform wave
that began to afflict Baltimore at the turn of the
century was especially hard on cops, and in 1901
or thereabout a new chief of police took to sending
squads of plain-clothes men from remote precincts
into the downtown areas of sin, seeking to catch
the regular watch in derelictions. One night such
a gang of shoo-flies, as they were called, bust into
Frank's, and though the members of the Stevedores' Club set up a dreadful bellow, and threatened to break and jail the sergeant in command,
Frank got a summons, and we were put to the
trouble of having it torn up next morning.

This episode greatly incensed Ned Schleigh, the
captain, not only because it revealed to the people
of Baltimore a crass violation of the liquor laws in
his bailiwick, but also and more especially because
it flouted his lawful command and authority. He
responded by stationing one of his own cops, in full
uniform, at the back door·we used for getting in
and out of the place, and that cop stood on guard
there every night for something on the order of six
months, for it took that long for the reform move-

ment to subside. His instructions were to inform
any raiders who showed up that the place was already in the custody of Schleigh himself, who had
raided it only half an hour before. No more appeared, but the six months included a hard February, and the poor cop on duty at the back door,
whose name was Joe, suffered painful frostbites
until his native intelligence suggested that he come
in now and again, and thaw out behind Frank's
stove. Every time he came in he got a shot of Class
C rye, so the arrangement was satisfactory to all
hands. When the reformers were thrown off at
last, and Christian peace and order were restored
in Baltimore, we persuaded the Police Board to
promote Joe to a sergeancy.

Frank, as I have remarked, was a man without
social graces, and it was rare for him to say more
than *Wie geht's* to a customer, whether journalistic or other. But he was highly skilled at his social-
minded craft, and thus enjoyed a kind of esteem
that, in a more responsive man, would have passed
for popularity. He understood very well the principle that a glass of beer running to less than sixteen ounces or costing more than five cents is an
economic atrocity. He also had the acumen to
charge only ten cents for deviled crabs, with an inside rate of five cents to members of the press.
Thus his customers ate well and drank freely, and
in his nightly election to honorary membership in
the Stevedores' Club there was really almost as

much good will as self-interest. When he opened
his stag hotel the club followed him, but the place
was rather too elegant for the literary trade, and
most of the members presently deserted it for the
establishment of a compatriot with goat whiskers,
known to everyone as Weber and Fields. Weber
and Fields was only one man, but no one could
make out which of the two comedians he resembled
most, so he was named for both. His place was in a
dark alley behind the Baltimore *Sun* office, and his
small bar was packed every night. He was himself
a beer-drinker of great gifts, and was reputed to
get down fifty shells a day. The shell he used had
a false bottom, but even so his daily ration sounded
impressive, and he enjoyed a high degree of public
respect.

Those members of the Stevedores' Club who
stuck to the splendors of Frank's stag hotel had a
somewhat quiet time of it, for the roomers at the
place went to bed early, and there was little outside
trade in the bar. The bartender, in fact, knocked
off every night at midnight, and Frank himself
withdrew soon afterward, worn out by the abra-
sions of his boiled shirt and Sunday suit. This left
the main deck in charge of a night-clerk nearly
eighty years old, with a young fellow named Rudolph as his only aide. Rudolph served as bell-hop,
house dick, and night bartender and oyster-
shucker. The night-clerk's faculties were so far
clouded by age that he could be disregarded, which

reduced the problem before the club to this : how to
get rid of Rudolph long enough to pillage the bar
and oyster-bar? It was solved night after night by
tipping him off that some member not present had
just sneaked in with a female, and disappeared up
the stairway behind the elevator. This set him to
searching the house, and while he was so engaged a
leisurely burglary was effected. After the fraud
had been worked on him forty or fifty times he began to show signs of tumbling, so the club withdrew. The stag hotel, in fact, was never very popular with the brethren.

But Frank's old place opposite the City Hall
had been their favorite for years, and so long as it
survived it was the home port of all Baltimore
journalists of the malt-liquor moiety. They used,
of course, other saloons — or, as the cops of the
era preferred to call them, kaifs — , but Frank always got them in the end. When his bartender,
Emil, set up business on his own the boys attended
the opening, and some of them dropped in occasionally afterward, but inasmuch as the new establishment was in a remote suburb, half a mile
beyond the rail-head of the nearest trolley line,
getting to it was a fatiguing business. Once, when
Emil threw a party to celebrate the fifth anniversary of the death of Bismarck, the full strength of
the club waited on him, taking along the band of
the Holliday Street Theatre. But when the band
marched up the road from the trolley, playing

brisk Sousa marches, the whole suburb turned out
of bed to hoot and holler, for it was after midnight,
and in those pre-radio days decent people in such
neighborhoods were in the hay by 9:30. The cops
who were summoned joined the party and became
such life as it had, but it never had much, and it was
not repeated.

There were other restauranteurs in the Baltimore of that time who will get friendly notice if
the true history of the town is ever written, which
is, alas, improbable. I remember, for example,
John Roth, who kept a swell place in Fayette street,
next door to the *Herald* office, with a pool parlor
upstairs. He was the *beau idéal* of an old-time
saloonkeeper, with a walrus moustache, a large
paunch, and the manners of an ambassador. He
never went behind his own bar, but always stood in
front of it, near the entrance, so that he could greet
incoming clients. On the wall opposite was the
largest hand-painted oil-painting of Venus rising
from her bath in all the Baltimores. His free lunch
was very well spoken of, and he offered a business
men's lunch at midday that was worth twice its
prix fixe of twenty-five cents. But the best free
lunch of the era was to be had at the Diamond in
Howard street, kept by Muggsy McGraw and Wil-
bert Robinson, two heroes of the old Baltimore
Orioles. Muggsy was too contentious a man to
make a good saloonkeeper, and in a little while he
vanished from the place, but the fat and amiable

Robinson continued on duty for several years, always standing in front of the bar like John Roth.
The free lunch at the Diamond was based on an
immense chafing-dish of hot dogs, always bubbling,
but it also included roast beef, *Schwartenmagen*,
and a superior brand of rat-trap cheese. There
was a high-toned colored man behind the counter,
and any customer of reasonably neat appearance
was free to eat all he could hold. The only persons who were barred out as a class, so far as I
can recall, were newspaper artists. Robbie had a
very low opinion of them, and when one of them
wandered in and had to be bounced, he always did
it personally.

The most austere restauranteur in Baltimore,
and perhaps in the United States, was one Kepler,
who kept a place in North street near the City
Hall. He was a grave, even sombre man who smiled
only once or twice a week. I seldom entered his
door, but one snowy night in the Winter of 1900–
01 I came near having the honor of being assassinated in front of his bar. The assassin was a minor
labor leader who had developed a hate for me because I had written a story revealing him as the
caitiff of a fight in a bawdy-house, and he came into
the place looking for me, apparently on the mistaken theory that I frequented it. Pulling out two
pistols he laid them on the bar, and announced his
purpose, naming me by name. Kepler was for trying moral suasion on him, but one of my *Herald*

colleagues, who happened to be drinking in the place, preferred more direct action. Seizing a quart bottle of Maryland rye that was on the bar, he brought it down on the labor leader's head, knocking him out at one crack. He then dragged the poor fellow's carcass out into the street, and shoved it into a snow drift. There it lay until the cops came along and sent it to hospital. When, a little while later, I ran into its owner on the street, he seemed to be completely restored, but had no more murder in his heart. The whole thing, he assured me, was a mistake. He was only trying to scare Kepler.

The most hated saloonkeeper in Baltimore in those days — that is, among journalists — was Mike Ganzhorn, who kept a small stag hotel in Baltimore street, with an ornate bar and eating-room downstairs. He was the only member of the whole fraternity who was never, under any circumstances, mentioned in print as a genial restauranteur. Indeed, he never got any mention at all, save only when there was a fight in his bar, or a guest committed suicide upstairs. Mike's crime was that he had once told someone who had told someone who had told someone that he could buy any newspaper man in Baltimore for a drink. This libel rankled for years. It rankled mainly because there was so much truth in it. Mike had taken in slightly too much territory, but there was certainly enough sound ground in the middle to sustain him.

XV

A GIRL FROM

RED LION, P.A.

SOMEWHERE in his lush, magenta prose Oscar Wilde speaks of the tendency of nature to imitate art — a phenomenon often observed by persons who keep their eyes open. I first became aware of it, not through the pages of Wilde, but at the hands of an old-time hack-driver named Peebles, who flourished in Baltimore in the days of this history. Peebles was a Scotsman of a generally unfriendly and retiring character, but nevertheless he was something of a public figure in the town. Perhaps that was partly due to the fact that he had served twelve years in the Maryland Penitentiary for killing his wife, but I think he owed much more of his eminence to his adamantine rectitude in money matters, so rare in his profession. The very cops, indeed, regarded him as an honest man, and said so freely. They knew about his blanket refusal to take more than three or four times the legal fare from drunks, they knew how many lost watches, wallets, stick-pins and walking-sticks he turned in every year, and they admired as Christians, though deploring as cops, his absolute refusal to work for them in the capacity of stool-pigeon.

Moreover, he was industrious as well as honest, and it was the common belief that he had money in five banks. He appeared on the hack-stand in front of the old Eutaw House every evening at nine o'clock, and put in the next five or six hours shuttling merrymakers and sociologists to and from the red-light districts. When this trade began to languish he drove to Union Station, and there kept watch until his two old horses fell asleep. Most of the strangers who got off the early morning trains wanted to go to the nearest hotel, which was only two blocks away, so there was not a great deal of money in their patronage, but unlike the other hackers Peebles never resorted to the device of driving them swiftly in the wrong direction and then working back by a circuitous route.

A little after dawn one morning in the early Autumn of 1903, just as his off horse began to snore gently, a milk-train got in from lower Pennsylvania, and out of it issued a rosy-cheeked young woman carrying a pasteboard suitcase and a pink parasol. Squired up from the train-level by a

car-greaser with an eye for country beauty, she
emerged into the sunlight shyly and ran her eye
down the line of hacks. The other drivers seemed
to scare her, and no wonder, for they were all
grasping men whose evil propensities glowed from
them like heat from a stove. But when she saw
Peebles her feminine intuition must have told her
that he could be trusted, for she shook off the car-
greaser without further ado, and came up to the
Peebles hack with a pretty show of confidence.

"Say, mister," she said, "how much will you
charge to take me to a house of ill fame?"

In telling of it afterward Peebles probably exaggerated his astonishment a bit, but certainly he
must have suffered something rationally describable as a shock. He laid great stress upon her air
of blooming innocence, almost like that of a cavorting lamb. He said her two cheeks glowed like
apples, and that she smelled like a load of hay. By
his own account he stared at her for a full minute
without answering her question, with a wild stream
of confused surmises racing through his mind.
What imaginable business could a creature so obviously guileless have in the sort of establishment she
had mentioned? Could it be that her tongue had
slipped — that she actually meant an employment
office, the Y.W.C.A., or what not? Peebles, as he
later elaborated the story, insisted that he had
cross-examined her at length, and that she had not
only reiterated her question in precise terms, but

explained that she was fully determined to abandon herself to sin and looked forward confidently to dying in the gutter. But in his first version he reported simply that he had stared at her dumbly until his amazement began to wear off, and then motioned to her to climb into his hack. After all, he was a common carrier, and obliged by law to haul all comers, regardless of their private projects and intentions. If he yielded anything to his Caledonian moral sense it took the form of choosing her destination with some prudence. He might have dumped her into one of the third-rate bagnios that crowded a street not three blocks from Union Station, and then gone on about his business. Instead, he drove half way across town to the high-toned studio of Miss Nellie d'Alembert, at that time one of the leaders of her profession in Baltimore, and a woman who, though she lacked the polish of Vassar, had sound sense, a pawky humor, and progressive ideas.

I had become, only a little while before, city editor of the *Herald*, and in that capacity received frequent confidential communications from her. She was, in fact, the source of a great many useful news tips. She knew everything about everyone that no one was supposed to know, and had accurate advance information, in particular, about Page 1 divorces, for nearly all the big law firms of the town used her facilities for the manufacture of evidence. There were no Walter Winchells in that

era, and the city editors of the land had to depend
on volunteers for inside stuff. Such volunteers
were moved (*a*) by a sense of public duty grace-
fully performed, and (*b*) by an enlightened desire
to keep on the good side of newspapers. Not infrequently they cashed in on this last. I well remember the night when two visiting Congressmen from
Washington got into a debate in Miss Nellie's
music-room, and one of them dented the skull of
the other with a spittoon. At my suggestion the
other city editors of Baltimore joined me in straining journalistic ethics far enough to remove the
accident to Mt. Vernon place, the most respectable
neighborhood in town, and to lay the fracture to a
fall on the ice.

My chance leadership in this public work made
Miss Nellie my partisan, and now and then she
gave me a nice tip and forgot to include the other
city editors. Thus I was alert when she called up
during the early afternoon of Peebles' strange adventure, and told me that something swell was on
ice. She explained that it was not really what you
could call important news, but simply a sort of hu-
man-interest story, so I asked Percy Heath to go to
see her, for though he was now my successor as Sunday editor, he still did an occasional news story, and
I knew what kind he enjoyed especially. He called
up in half an hour, and asked me to join him. " If
you don't hear it yourself," he said," you will say
I am pulling a fake."

When I got to Miss Nellie's house I found her sitting with Percy in a basement room that she used as a sort of office, and at once she plunged into the story.

"I'll tell you first," she began, "before you see the poor thing herself. When Peebles yanked the bell this morning I was sound asleep, and so was all the girls, and Sadie the coon had gone home. I stuck my head out of the window, and there was Peebles on the front steps. I said: 'Get the hell away from here! What do you mean by bringing in a drunk at this time of the morning? Don't you know us poor working people gotta get some rest?' But he hollered back that he didn't have no drunk in his hack, but something he didn't know what to make of, and needed my help on, so I slipped on my kimono and went down to the door, and by that time he had the girl out of the hack, and before I could say 'scat' he had shoved her in the parlor, and she was unloading what she had to say.

"Well, to make a long story short, she said she come from somewheres near a burg they call Red Lion, P.A., and lived on a farm. She said her father was one of them old rubes with whiskers they call Dunkards, and very strict. She said she had a beau in York, P.A., of the name of Elmer, and whenever he could get away he would come out to the farm and set in the parlor with her, and they would do a little hugging and kissing. She said Elmer was educated and a great reader, and he would

bring her books that he got from his brother, who
was a train butcher on the Northern Central, and
him and her would read them. She said the books
was all about love, and that most of them was sad.
Her and Elmer would talk about them while they
set in the parlor, and the more they talked about
them the sadder they would get, and sometimes she
would have to cry.

"Well, to make a long story short, this went on
once a week or so, and night before last Elmer come
down from York with some more books, and they
set in the parlor, and talked about love. Her old
man usually stuck his nose in the door now and
then, to see that there wasn't no foolishness, but
night before last he had a bilious attack and went
to bed early, so her and Elmer had it all to their-
self in the parlor. So they quit talking about the
books, and Elmer began to love her up, and in a
little while they was hugging and kissing to beat
the band. Well, to make a long story short, Elmer
went too far, and when she come to herself and
kicked him out she realized she had lost her honest
name.

"She laid awake all night thinking about it, and
the more she thought about it the more scared she
got. In every one of the books her and Elmer read
there was something on the subject, and all of
the books said the same thing. When a girl lost
her honest name there was nothing for her to do
excepting to run away from home and lead a life

of shame. No girl that she ever read about ever done anything else. They all rushed off to the nearest city, started this life of shame, and then took to booze and dope and died in the gutter. Their family never knew what had became of them. Maybe they landed finally in a medical college, or maybe the Salvation Army buried them, but their people never heard no more of them, and their name was rubbed out of the family Bible. Sometimes their beau tried to find them, but he never could do it, and in the end he usually married the judge's homely daughter, and moved into the big house when the judge died.

" Well, to make a long story short, this poor girl lay awake all night thinking of such sad things, and when she got up at four thirty a.m. and went out to milk the cows her eyes was so full of tears that she could hardly find their spigots. Her father, who was still bilious, give her hell, and told her she was getting her just punishment for setting up until ten and eleven o'clock at night, when all decent people ought to be in bed. So she began to suspect that he may have snuck down during the evening, and caught her, and was getting ready to turn her out of the house and wash his hands of her, and maybe even curse her. So she decided to have it over and done with as soon as possible, and last night, the minute he hit the hay again, she hoofed in to York, P.A., and caught the milk-train for Baltimore, and that is how Peebles

found her at Union Station and brought her here.
When I asked her what in hell she wanted all she
had to say was ' Ain't this a house of ill fame?', and
it took me an hour or two to pump her story out of
her. So now I have got her upstairs under lock and
key, and as soon as I can get word to Peebles I'll
tell him to take her back to Union Station, and
start her back for Red Lion, P.A. Can you beat
it? "

Percy and I, of course, demanded to see the girl,
and presently Miss Nellie fetched her in. She was
by no means the bucolic Lillian Russell that Peebles' tall tales afterward made her out, but she was
certainly far from unappetizing. Despite her loss
of sleep, the dreadful gnawings of her conscience
and the menace of an appalling retribution, her
cheeks were still rosy, and there remained a considerable sparkle in her troubled blue eyes. I never
heard her name, but it was plain that she was of
four-square Pennsylvania Dutch stock, and as
sturdy as the cows she serviced. She had on her
Sunday clothes, and appeared to be somewhat uncomfortable in them, but Miss Nellie set her at ease,
and soon she was retelling her story to two strange
and, in her sight, probably highly dubious men.
We listened without interrupting her, and when she
finished Percy was the first to speak.

" My dear young lady," he said, " you have been
grossly misinformed. I don't know what these
works of fiction are that you and Elmer read, but

they are as far out of date as Joe Miller's Jest-Book. The stuff that seems to be in them would make even a newspaper editorial writer cough and scratch himself. It may be true that, in the remote era when they appear to have been written, the penalty of a slight and venial slip was as drastic as you say, but I assure you that it is no longer the case. The world is much more humane than it used to be, and much more rational. Just as it no longer burns men for heresy or women for witchcraft, so it has ceased to condemn girls to lives of shame and death in the gutter for the trivial dereliction you acknowledge. If there were time I'd get you some of the more recent books, and point out passages showing how moral principles have changed. The only thing that is frowned on now seems to be getting caught. Otherwise, justice is virtually silent on the subject.

" Inasmuch as your story indicates that no one knows of your crime save your beau, who, if he has learned of your disappearance, is probably scared half to death, I advise you to go home, make some plausible excuse to your pa for lighting out, and resume your care of his cows. At the proper opportunity take your beau to the pastor, and join him in indissoluble love. It is the safe, respectable and hygienic course. Everyone agrees that it is moral, even moralists. Meanwhile, don't forget to thank Miss Nellie. She might have helped you down the primrose way; instead, she has restored

you to virtue and happiness, no worse for an interesting experience."

The girl, of course, took in only a small part of
this, for Percy's voluptuous style and vocabulary
were beyond the grasp of a simple milkmaid. But
Miss Nellie, who understood English much better
than she spoke it, translated freely, and in a little
while the troubled look departed from those blue
eyes, and large tears of joy welled from them.
Miss Nellie shed a couple herself, and so did all
the ladies of the resident faculty, for they had
drifted downstairs during the interview, sleepy but
curious. The practical Miss Nellie inevitably
thought of money, and it turned out that the trip
down by milk-train and Peebles' lawful freight of
$1 had about exhausted the poor girl's savings,
and she had only some odd change left. Percy
threw in a dollar and I threw in a dollar, and Miss
Nellie not only threw in a third, but ordered one
of the ladies to go to the kitchen and prepare a
box-lunch for the return to Red Lion.

Sadie the coon had not yet come to work, but
Peebles presently bobbed up without being sent
for, and toward the end of the afternoon he started
off for Union Station with his most amazing passenger, now as full of innocent jubilation as a
martyr saved at the stake. As I have said, he embellished the story considerably during the days
following, especially in the direction of touching
up the girl's pulchritude. The cops, because of

their general confidence in him, swallowed his ex-
aggerations, and I heard more than one of them
lament that they had missed the chance to handle
the case professionally. Percy, in his later years,
made two or three attempts to put it into a movie
scenario, but the Hays office always vetoed it.

How the girl managed to account to her father
for her mysterious flight and quick return I don't
know, for she was never heard from afterward.
She promised to send Miss Nellie a picture post-
card of Red Lion, showing the new hall of the
Knights of Pythias, but if it was ever actually
mailed it must have been misaddressed, for it never
arrived.

XVI

SCIONS OF THE

BOGUS NOBILITY

Of late years, as I have noted in my Preface, American newspaper reporters have come to think of themselves as proletarians, and reach out for communion with coal-miners, truck-drivers, pipe-fitters, bricklayers, and other such wage slaves. It was certainly not so in my early days in the craft. We young journalists, to be sure, were far from snobbish, and in the saloons we frequented we had very amicable relations with various classes of workingmen, notably printers, policemen, musicians and hackmen; nevertheless, we always kept a little distance, and our eyes, when they rolled at all, rolled in the other direction. The hero of our dreams was not Sam Gompers or Gene Debs, but Richard Harding Davis, who was reputed to own twenty suits of clothes, or James Creelman, who had interviewed the Pope. And we were always susceptible to the glamor of less eminent colleagues who had any claim, however false, to high connections, however mysterious. That was a shabby newspaper staff, at least in the big cities, which could not show at least one son of a Civil War general, or nephew of an archbishop, or French count.

In the *Herald* office we had two of the last named, though I should add that neither called himself an actual count. Both were content to let it be known that they were cadets of French families running back to Charlemagne, and would be eating very high on the hog if they could only get their rights. One, when in his cups, spoke of himself as Jean-Baptiste du Plessis de Savines, and the other allowed that he was Jacques de Corbigny. Naturally enough, du Plessis de Savines could not hope to rate his full style and appellation in the turmoil of a newspaper office, so he did not object seriously when Max Ways renamed him Jones. It was a plebeian name — but so, he believed, were all British names. As for Jacques de Corbigny, he was Jake to everyone from Colonel Cunningham down to the office boys, and also to all the functionaries in the Baltimore sties of justice, where he served the *Herald* as court reporter.

Jones oscillated through various jobs in my day, but all of them were of the desk variety, and usually he was telegraph editor. The night report of the Associated Press was then very meagre and in consequence he had a good deal of time on his hands, especially after midnight. In such hours of relaxation he liked to gather a group of young reporters about him, and astonish them with tales of his high doings in a dozen fields of enterprise. He had fought the ten duels that all French counts of his generation had to ring up, and one of them, as the custom provided, was with M. de Blowitz, Paris correspondent of the London *Times.* In addition, he had served his orthodox six years in the Foreign Legion, had escaped in nothing save his pants and hat from an intrigue with a Spanish infanta, had stolen two girls from the Prince of Wales (afterward Edward VII), had climbed the Matterhorn, and had blacked the eyes of both Jake Kilrain and James Gordon Bennett. So far he only ran true to type. But in addition he claimed to be the most adept church organist since Johann Sebastian Bach, and it was in that unusual character that he appeared in some of his most edifying anecdotes.

I well recall one that had to do with his appearance as guest organist at Trinity Church in New York. The news that he was to perform, so he said, brought in such a mob of fans from all over the East that the church was packed. Unhappily, it was discovered at the last minute, just as he was taking off his shoes to fall to, that something was wrong with the organ, and the sexton who usually looked after it not only could not remedy the trouble but even failed to find out what it was. Jones said that his own extraordinarily acute ear solved the mystery at once, though he let the sexton sweat a while in malice: there was something ailing the huge pedal pipe that sounded eighteen octaves below middle C. This pipe was at least two feet in diameter, and its length was such that it ran half way up the steeple. There should have been a manhole in it at the bottom, but Jones could not find one, so while the expectant audience buzzed, scratched itself and blew spitballs, he climbed up to the steeple to look down the open top, as a laryngologist looks down the trachea of a radio crooner.

I shall not detain you with the details: suffice it to say that he lost his balance and plunged headlong down the tube. Fortunately, he was a close fit, so the air was compressed as he went along, and when he landed at last in the conical war-nose of the pipe the jar was no greater than that of a fall on the ice. Nor was there any danger of suffocation, for the organ-pump was still working, and it was easy to turn a stiff breeze into the pipe. But how to get out? Jones confessed that, for a while, he was baffled. He could hear what was going on outside, and he soon picked up the news that the sexton proposed to attempt his rescue with an ax. The rector, it appeared, objected to this, and so did Jones, for he knew the crude technic of sextons, and feared that the ax which liberated him might also decapitate him. In the end he hit on a better scheme, and shouted a command that it be executed. It consisted in sending for riggers, hoisting the pipe out of the steeple, turning it up-side down, and then bouncing out Jones on a leap-tick of pew-cushions heaped up on the sidewalk.

There were sassy young reporters who refused to believe this story, and some of them asked search-ing and embarrassing questions, with diagrams de-signed to show its impossibility, but Jones always stuck to it, and many who doubted when they first heard it came to believe afterward. It was only one chapter in a long saga of his adventures as a per-former of sacred music. One of his favorite tricks, he said, was to search out a pipe whose sound made the stained-glass windows of the church vibrate in unison, and then pop them off in the midst of a solemn anthem, to the alarm of the clergy, choir and congregation. He said he had learned how to do this trick with an ordinary parlor, or reed-or-gan, and once utilized his skill to liberate a baby in arms from a bank vault. The baby's mother, it ap-peared, had put it in the vault without notifying the bank personnel, and as a result it had been im-prisoned when the time-lock clamped down. When Jones was sent for he borrowed an organ from a nearby Sailors' Bethel, found a note in it that would vibrate steel, and so shook the time-lock to pieces. Why the mother had chosen a bank vault for storing her baby, and how she managed to stow it away without being noticed, he did not say.

Toward the end of his life Jones forgot his noble French ancestry, and began shopping around the world for forefathers, and even for fathers. Whenever a bulletin would come in announcing the death of some eminent man he would stagger out into the city room with the Associated Press flimsy, apply his handkerchief to his eyes, and sob piteously. The city editor was then expected to engage him in the following dialogue:

> *City Editor* — What are you blubbering about?
> *Jones* — So-and-so is dead.
> *City Editor* — Well, what of it? What do you care for that ————?
> *Jones* (in a sepulchral whisper) — He — was — my — father.

Everyone would then offer him formal condolences, and he would return to his desk much comforted. Sometimes he would have to be comforted two or three times a week. These raids upon the Christian sympathies of the city editor became so frequent that they irked him, and he terminated them with a bang on the night of November 7, 1901, when news came in of the death of Li Hung Chang. He was aided by a gang of ruffianly copyreaders, organized for the purpose. When Jones appeared with his flimsy and his tears they let fly with ink- and paste-pots, copy-hooks and spittoons. One of them even let go an old typewriter. Jones quit a little while later, and everyone was amazed when word drifted in that he was actually working as organist in a Presbyterian church in a poor suburb — and claiming to be a son of both John Calvin and John Knox.

Jake was a man of more modest pretensions: the most he ever alleged was that his father had been, at one and the same time, a Confederate general, a French nobleman, and a graduate of both Oxford and Cambridge. Unlike Jones, who was very abstemious, Jake was a lusher; indeed, there was a period, say from 1899 to 1902, when he was probably the ranking lusher of the whole region between the Mason & Dixon Line and the James river. He was magnificently ombibulous, drinking anything that contained ethyl alcohol, whatever its flavor or provenance. By day he would sustain himself as court reporter mainly by resorting to the handset whiskey that the printers guzzled at night, and in the evening he would always drop in at Frank Junker's saloon for the session of the Stevedores' Club, with its diligent unloading of schooners of beer. But whenever anything else offered, he got it down, giving thanks to God. Once I saw him drink a quart of apricot brandy at a sitting, and at other times I watched him as he dispatched Angostura, Fernet Branca and Boonekamp bitters by the goblet, all without chasers.

Jake was a tall, sturdy and even herculean fellow, with the wide, confident mouth of a carp or orator, but there came eventually a time when his heroic physique went back on him, and the young doctors at the City Hospital took him on as an out-patient and laboratory animal. So far as I could make out they could never agree on a diagnosis. One held that there was nothing wrong with him save a gastritis so acute that the lining of his stomach had turned to a kind of asphalt, and another that he was in the last stages of cirrhosis of the liver. There were others who voted for Bright's disease, cholelithiasis and scurvy, and a larval psychiatrist held out for paresis, for in those days that malady was still ascribed to drink. Jake himself also favored paresis, for he had noted in his court work that it frequently afflicted distinguished members of the bar. One night he was reciting his symptoms in Junker's when Joe, the cop on the beat, dropped in for his hourly shot of rye, and stood listening in uncomfortable fascination. Finally Joe gave a shiver, and burst out with " Goddam if I don't believe I got the same goddam thing." Jake glared at him for half a minute with singeing scorn, and then replied:

" So you have got paresis, too, have you? A *cop* with paresis? Well, of all the infernal impertinence ever heard of on earth! What ails you, Joe, is *jim-jams*. In order to have paresis you have to have *brains*."

Whatever it was that afflicted Jake, it presently threw him, and he had to be sent to St. Agnes' Hospital, which then specialized in treating the

wounded garrison-troops of the Baltimore barrooms. The lower floor of the institution, called
Hogan's Alley, was always full of them, and Jake
found many old friends there, including a rich
theatre manager who came down with *mania à potu*
twice a year, and always celebrated his cure by
giving the good sisters who ran the place some elegant present — one year a *porte cochère*, the next
year a new boiler for their heating plant, the third
a stained-glass window for their chapel, and so on.
There were iron bars on the windows of Hogan's
Alley and the inmates lived under rigid discipline,
which included complete abstention from alcohol,
but they were allowed visitors, were fed upon
hearty victuals, and in general led a very easy life.

Jake had a girl known to the boys as the Battleship — a vast, rangy creature built on his own
scale, with the broad shoulders and billowing bos-
oms of a Wagnerian contralto. She came to see
him one evening as in duty bound — and an hour
later the gentlemen of Hogan's Alley were all full
of liquor and cutting wild capers. The sisters,
after quieting them, made a search for the source
of their supply, but could not find it. Two days
later the Battleship made another call — and Hogan's Alley had another too-cheerful night. When
it happened a third time the sisters put two and
two together, the Battleship was barred from the
place, and Jake himself was requested to find some
other asylum. They never learned the technic of

the smuggling, but Jake himself later revealed it. The Battleship, on each visit, had stowed two quarts of rye between the huge hemispheres of her bosom, and then slipped them quietly to the idol of her dreams, who disposed of them at a dollar a big drink.

Jake's expulsion turned out to be a great stroke of luck for him. The institution he transferred to was a suburban drink-cure run by an enlightened medico who, after curing him, put him to work as a capper in the downtown saloons. All Jake had to do was to keep a sharp lookout for gentlemen showing the first signs of delirium tremens, and report their names to the medico, who thereupon alarmed their families, and usually got them as patients. Jake had comfortable quarters over the dead-house of the drink-cure, and a liberal expense-account. For two or three years he led the life of Riley, and was much envied by all the other boozers of Baltimore. Then, one morning, he dropped dead in a barroom, and was given a neat Odd Fellows funeral by the medico. Some time later a *Herald* reporter digging up a story at the Health Department happened upon Jake's death certificate. It showed that he was born in Philadelphia, that his father's name was something on the order of Schultz, Schmidt or Kraus, and that he had been baptized Emil.

XVII

ALIENS, BUT NOT YET

ENEMIES

THE CURRENT American concept of the German as an excessively sly, bellicose and sinister fellow, apt at any moment to panic the radio audience with false news or blow up a gas-works, was undreamed of in my early days in journalism. We thought of him then as predominantly benignant and not too smart, and that view was fostered by the German reporters who swarmed in all the big cities of the East and Middle West. In every such city there was at least one German daily, with a staff like any other newspaper and not infrequently of considerable importance in local politics. In Baltimore there were two, not to mention four or five weeklies, and on these sheets were some of the most eminent and popular reporters of the town. They covered spot news, to be sure, only sketchily, for a four-alarm fire was nothing to them unless the owner of the burned premises happened to be a German, or, at worst, an Austrian or a Swiss; but ever and anon they had a complicated and hair-raising German suicide to trade for a colored murder, or a riot at a *Gesangverein* rehearsal for a City Hall story, and at all times they were salient figures in what may be called the social life of the Fourth Estate.

If there was any member of our Stevedores' Club who stood out head and shoulders above all the rest of the members, as Ward McAllister rose above the sea-level of the New York 400, then it was certainly John Gfeller of the *Deutsche Correspondent*, a Züricher with a flowing yellow moustache, and a full-dress outfit of frock coat, plug hat and ivory-headed walking-stick that set him off magnificently. Save when he had to cover the wedding of a brewer's daughter or some other such overshadowing and interminable shambles, he showed up at Junker's saloon every night at midnight, and there he led all the other Stevedores in their unloading of schooners. He was the first man of whom I ever heard it said that his legs were hollow, and the last of whom I ever believed it. Malt liquor seemed to have no more effect upon him than so much sarsaparilla, and in all my acquaintance with him I saw him flustered but once, and that was after he had been induced to drink eight or ten mint juleps on a hot July afternoon.

A drinking club always develops a ritual, and the Stevedores' followed the pattern. The basic design of its evening program was simply to shake poor Junker down for free beers, but there was also singing, and in this John naturally led, for he not only had the highest tenor voice in the club, but also a large repertory of robustious songs, most of them relics of his student days in Switzerland. With one or two exceptions the other members knew no more German than so many Irish cops; nevertheless, they learned many of John's songs by rote, as the Welsh and Slovak miners in the Bach Choir at Bethlehem, Pa., learn the Bach cantatas. And even when they were vaguest about the rest of the words they could at least chime in on the choruses, and this they did in voices of brass, always to Junker's alarm, for he lived in fear that, in spite of the immunity the presence of newspaper men was supposed to give him, the cops would clamp down on him for keeping open after hours.

One of the favorites of the club was a song by the celebrated Viktor von Scheffel, whooping up the victory of the primeval Nazis over the Romans under P. Q. Varus in the year 9 A.D. — a victory that threw the Romans over the Rhine for keeps, and made its scene, the Teutoburger Forest, sacred ground in German history. It is now nearly forty years since I last joined in singing this composition, but I remember its opening as clearly as if

John were still uprisen before me, beating time
with a foam-scraper:

> Als die Römer frech geworden,
> Zum, ze rum zum, zum, zum, zum;
> Zogen sie nach Deutschland's Norden,
> Zum, ze, rum zum, zum, zum, zum.

All the students' *Liederbücher* indicate that
every *zum* should have been a *sim*, but in our ig-
norance we followed John without question, and
when we came to the imitation of trumpets in the
next strophe we converted them into calliopes,
Junker or no Junker, *Polizeistunden* or no *Polizeistunden*. John knew all the seven stanzas, and
would sing them with voluptuous gusto, especially
the one telling how Varus, in departing swiftly
through a swamp, left both of his boots and one
of his socks behind, but the rest of us confined ourselves to the choruses, and did not stop to question
this somewhat strange account of Roman military
costume.

The German reporters led lives that were the admiration of many of their American colleagues,
for, as I have said, their papers were not much interested in ordinary news, and there was no court-
martial if one of them missed a bank robbery or
even a murder, provided, of course, no German
were involved. Their main business was to cover
the purely German doings of the town — weddings, funerals, concerts, picnics, birthday parties,
and so on. This kept them jumping pleasantly,

for there were then 30,000 of their compatriots in
Baltimore, and most of the 30,000 seemed to be
getting on in the world, and were full of social enterprise. It was not sufficient for a German reporter to report their weddings as news: he also had
to dance with the bride, drink with her father, and
carry off a piece of the wedding cake, presumably
for his wife. At a funeral of any consequence —
say, that of a saloonkeeper, a pastor, or the head
basso of a singing society — his duties were almost
as onerous as those of a *Totsäufer* for a brewery,[1]
and if he quit before the last clod hit the coffin it
was an indecorum. When there were speeches,
which was usually, he had to make one, whether at
a birthday party, a banquet of the German Freemasons, Knights of Pythias or Odd Fellows, or the
opening of a new picnic-grounds, saloon, or Lutheran church. Whenever refreshments were offered, which was always, he had to eat and drink
in a hearty and demonstrative manner, and he was
remiss in his duties if he failed to sneak in a nice
notice for the lady who had prepared the *Sauer-
braten* or the *Häringsalat*. In his reports all malt
liquor had to be superultra, and all potato salad
the best yet seen on earth.

The fattest regular story of the German brethren in my time was the monthly arrival of the
North German Lloyd immigrant ship at Locust

---

[1] A *Totsäufer* is a brewery's customers' man. One of his
jobs is to weep and beat his breast at the funeral of a saloonkeeper.

Point. All leaves were canceled on that day, and the instant the ship tied up at the Baltimore & Ohio pier its decks swarmed with journalists. Even at the turn of the century, of course, most of the actual immigrants aboard were Slavs or Jews, but there were still some Germans, and among them there were bound to be a number of characters worth embalming in print — say, a barber who had once shaved Bismarck, or a man with nineteen children, or a Prussian lieutenant whose foot had slipped in one way or other, forcing him, as the Germans say, to go 'round the corner. The captain of the ship always spread a buffet luncheon for the reporters, and they always got down a couple of barrels of Munich beer. During his stay in port the captain would be entertained extensively by the German societies, for the commander of a North German Lloyd liner was a notable in all respectable German circles, and even a young third officer was a social lion and a swell catch. The German reporters attended all such functions officially, and stayed until the band went home.

But the story that came nearest to straining their powers in the days when I knew them best was the opening of the Anheuser-Busch Brewery's Baltimore branch in 1900. To cover that historic event the *Deutsche Correspondent* threw in its whole local staff, and with them came the chief editor, an editorial writer, and the circulation manager. How much space the affair got the next morning I forget, but it must have been many, many columns, despite the fact that several of the older reporters blew up in the course of the evening, and had to be laid out in the cold-storage room to recover. The rival *Journal* not only sent its whole staff but also a photographer. The photographer went down for a count of two or three hundred before he had so much as unlimbered his camera, and was fired on the spot, but when he recovered he rejoined the festivities, and did prodigies with his second wind. A great many reporters from the American papers of Baltimore were also present, and to this day the old-time journalists of the town recall the Anheuser-Busch party as indubitably tops in its class. No other brewery ever came within miles of it.

The lordly life of the German colleagues spread the rest of us with the sickly green of envy, but the gods seem to have become envious also, for the great Baltimore fire of 1904 dealt heavy licks to their papers, and World War I finished them. One of the two German dailies succumbed to the first of these calamities, and the other to the second, and all save one of the weeklies went down the chute with the latter. As a result, a great many merry fellows were out of jobs. A few were slipped upon the public payroll by friendly politicians, and a few more managed to make the grade on English newspapers, but the rest had a hard time of it, for their labors, though delightful, had not been lucrative. Indeed, I can recall but one German reporter who ever accumulated any considerable capital, and that one was such a marvel that he was generally regarded as almost inhuman. He was a tall, sallow Oldenburger of the name of Delmenhorst, and in the course of four years' service, at a salary of $15 a week, he saved the neat sum of $16,500. With this he returned to Germany, bought a brickyard in a county town of Brandenburg, and survived into quite modern times — opulent, comfortable, and universally respected.

His wealth, of course, did not flow from his salary: a schoolboy could figure *that*, or even a schoolma'm. He gathered it in simply by turning all the other usufructs of his calling into quick assets. When he went to a German birthday party, and there was on the table a round of *Rinderbrust mit Meerrettig* that met his notions, he not only gobbled down 10,000 or 20,000 calories of it, but lamented loudly that his wife was not present to enjoy it. The hostess, flattered by the encomium of an expert, thereupon always insisted that he take a couple of thick slabs home with him, and in the course of packing them she usually added a bowl of *Bohnensalat*, a chocolate *Torte*, and maybe a bottle of Liebfraumilch or a dozen bottles of beer. Similarly, if paprika chicken was the main dish, he departed with a whole fowl, and if there was

roast goose with red cabbage he got enough of each
to feed his wife for two or three days.

At the start, so I was told by his fellow-Germans,
he confined himself to her actual victualling, but in
a little while he began to arrive home with so much
provender that she could not get it all down, or
even the half of it, so it occurred to him that it
might be a good idea for her to take a boarder.
The first boarder, a bookkeeper in a sauerkraut
factory, put on weight so fast that everyone remarked it, and soon there were eager applications
for the second spot. Within a month there were
six highly appreciative paying guests at the table,
and soon afterward the Delmenhorsts moved to a
larger house, put in a colored maid, and increased
their clientèle to ten, and then finally to twelve.
Simultaneously, they began weeding out such poor
fellows as bookkeepers, and substituting bachelors
and widowers who could pay better, for example,
assistant brewmasters, secretaries of building associations, and interpreters for the North German
Lloyd.

Delmenhorst had to sweat hard to round up
enough chow for a dozen men. Sometimes he covered eight or ten weddings, birthday parties and
other such orgies in an evening, and had a dreadful
time promoting a sufficiency of handouts without
eating himself to death. But he gradually developed a technic that saved his life, and after a

while he hired a colored boy to accompany him from feast to feast with a toy wagon, to haul the loot home. Whenever, by some unhappy accident, there were not enough parties of a night to load the wagon Mrs. Delmenhorst put her boarders on bologna, rat-trap cheese and rye-bread, but that happened very seldom, for the Germans of Baltimore, as I have said, were very social in those days, and loved to stuff their friends. Such wines and beers as he accumulated Delmenhorst sold to the boarders at a discount of twenty per cent., and when his stock began to go beyond their capacity he disposed of the beer to private friends at the same rate, and the wine to the proprietor of a wine-room in East Baltimore.

Nor was it only food and drink that he accumulated. Once a rich baker, celebrating not too quietly the bankruptcy of a rival, gave him a hand-painted oil-painting of the castle at Heidelberg, and he sold it within a week for $17, and another time he wangled a barrel of chinaware from a china-dealer in Gay street. That he ever collected cash was not established to public knowledge, for the matter was naturally kept confidential, but after his return to Germany his old colleagues used to declare that he did, and even professed to know his prices. For an ordinary wedding story, they said, he expected (and usually got) $5, but if it was in moneyed circles, and the bride was so homely that it took some straining of conscience to call her

ravishing, he raised the ante to $10, $15, or $25.
A pious Lutheran, he never charged anything for
funerals, but he would take $5 for a christening,
and when he dealt with a silver or golden wedding
in the upper brackets the sky was the limit. All
saloonkeepers had to pay double, and all brewers
quadruple. Thus, for four years, Delmenhorst
held up the banner of the foreign-language press
in Baltimore, and then, his wife having taken on
such weight that her health broke down, he and she
departed for fresh fields in Brandenburg. They
sailed from Baltimore by the North German
Lloyd, traveling on passes. There was a gaudy
farewell party on the ship — paid for by the line.
For the first time in the four years Delmenhorst
took nothing home from the table.

XVIII

THE SYNTHESIS OF

NEWS

ONE of the first enemy reporters I came to terms with in the days of my beginnings was an amiable, ribald fellow with a pot belly and a pointed beard, by name Leander J. de Bekker. He hailed from Kentucky by way of Cincinnati and Chicago, and was proud of the fact that he was of Dutch descent. The Dutch, he told me at our first meeting, were the champion beer-drinkers of Christendom, and had invented not only free lunch but also the growler, which got its name, so he said, from the Dutch word *grauw*, signifying the great masses of the plain people. This de Bekker and I made many long and laborious treks together, for he was doing South Baltimore for the *American* when Max Ways sent me there to break in for the *Herald*, and South Baltimore was a vast area of indefinite boundaries and poor communications, with five or six miles of waterfront. At its upper end were the wharves used by the Chesapeake Bay packets, and at its lower end the great peninsula of Locust Point, given over mainly to railroad-yards and grain elevators, but adorned at its nose by Fort McHenry, the bombardment of which in 1814, allegedly by a B——h fleet, inspired Francis Scott Key to write " The Star-Spangled Banner."

There was always something doing in that expansive territory, especially for a young reporter to whom all the major catastrophes and imbecilities of mankind were still more or less novel, and hence delightful. If there was not a powder explosion at Fort McHenry, which was armed with smooth-bore muzzle-loaders dating from 1794, there was sure to be a collision between two Bay packets, and if the cops had nothing in the way of a homicide it was safe to reckon on a three-alarm fire. The blackamoors of South Baltimore were above the common in virulence, and the main streets of their ghetto — York street, Hughsie street and Elbow lane — always ran blood on Saturday nights. It was in Hughsie street, one lovely Summer evening in 1899, that I saw my first murderee — a nearly decapitated colored lady who had been caught by her beau in treason to her vows. And it was in the jungle of warehouses and railroad tracks on Locust Point that I covered my first fire.

De Bekker and I and the reporter for the *Sun-paper* (I forget his name) attended all these public events together, and since de Bekker was the eldest of the trio, and had a beard to prove it, he set the tone and tempo of our endeavors. If, on an expedition to the iron wilds of Locust Point, he decided suddenly that it was time for a hiatus and a beer, we downed tools at once and made for the nearest saloon, which was never more than a block away. Unhappily, the beers of those days, especially along the waterfront, ran only a dozen or so to the keg, and it was thus sometimes difficult for us youngsters, after two or three of them, to throw ourselves into gear again. At such times de Bek-ker's professional virtuosity and gift for leader-ship were demonstrated most beautifully.

" Why in hell," he would say, " should we walk our legs off trying to find out the name of a Polack stevedore kicked overboard by a mule? The cops are too busy dragging for the body to ask it, and when they turn it in at last, maybe tomorrow or the day after, it will be so improbable that no union printer in Baltimore will be able to set it up. Even so, they will only guess at it, as they guess at three-fourths of all the names on their books. Moreover, who gives a damn *what* it was? The fact that another poor man has given his life to engorge the Interests is not news: it happens every ten minutes. The important thing here, the one thing that brings us vultures of the press down into this god-forsaken wilderness is that the manner of his death was unusual — that men are not kicked overboard by mules every day. I move you, my esteemed contemporaries, that the name of the deceased be Ignaz Karpinski, that the name of his widow be Marie, that his age was thirty-six, that he lived at 1777 Fort avenue, and that he leaves eleven minor children."

It seemed so reasonable to the *Sun* reporter and me that we could think of no objection, and so the sad facts were reported in all three Baltimore morning papers the next day, along with various lively details that occurred to de Bekker after he had got down another beer. This labor-saving device was in use the whole time I covered South Baltimore for the *Herald*, and I never heard any complaint against it. Every one of the three city editors, comparing his paper to the other two, was surprised and pleased to discover that his reporter always got names and addresses right, and all three of us were sometimes commended for our unusual accuracy. De Bekker, I should add, was a fellow of conscience, and never stooped to what he called faking. That is to say, he never manufactured a story out of the whole cloth. If, under his inspiration, we reported that a mad dog had run amok down the Point and bitten twenty children, there was always an actual dog somewhere in the background, and our count of the victims was at least as authentic as any the cops would make. And if, when an immigrant ship tied up at the North German Lloyd pier, we made it known that fifteen sets of twins had been born during the voyage from Bremen, there were always some genuine twins aboard to support us.

Thus, in my tenderest years, I became familiar with the great art of synthesizing news, and gradually took in the massive fact that journalism is not an exact science. Later, as I advanced up the ladder of the press, I encountered synthesists less conscientious than de Bekker,[1] and indeed became one myself. It was well for me that I showed some talent, else my career might have come to disaster a year or so later, when I was promoted to the City Hall. There I found myself set against two enemy reporters of polished technic and great industry — Frank Kent of the *Sunpaper* and Walter Alexander of the *American*. Kent was a youngster only a little older than I was, but he was a smart fellow, and Alec was already covering his third or fourth city administration, and knew every rat-hole in the City Hall. He remained there for years afterward, and became, in the end, a bottomless abyss of municipal case and precedent. Mayors, comptrollers, health commissioners, city councilmen and other such transient jobholders consulted him as dili-

[1] He left Baltimore in 1901 to join the staff of the Brooklyn *Standard-Union,* and afterward worked for the New York *Tribune* and *Evening Post.* In 1908 he published a dictionary of music, and in 1921 a work on words and phrases in collaboration with Dr. Frank H. Vizetelly, editor of the Standard Dictionary. He died in 1931.

gently as they consulted the daily racing dope. Even in 1900 he knew more than any of them, and was thus a formidable competitor.

Once I had got my legs, Kent and I tried to rope him into a camorra such as de Bekker operated in South Baltimore, but he knew very well that he would contribute a great deal more to its assets than we would, so he played coy, and there was seldom a day that he didn't beat us. One week he let us have it daily with both barrels, and we got into trouble with our city editors. There was, of course, only one remedy, and we were forced into it in haste. Thereafter, we met every afternoon in Reilly's ale-house opposite the City Hall, and concocted a fake to bounce him. That fake appeared the next morning in both the *Sun* and the *Herald*, with refinements of detail that coincided perfectly, so all the city editors of the town, including Alec's, accepted it as gospel. For a week or two Alec tried to blitz and baffle us with real news beats, but when we proceeded from one fake a day to two, and then to three, four, and even more, he came in asking for terms, and thereafter the three of us lived in brotherly concord, with Alec turning up most of the news and Kent and I embellishing it. Our flames of fancy having been fanned, we couldn't shut them off at once, but whenever we thought of a prime fake we let Alec have it also. If it was so improbable that his somewhat literal mind gagged at it we refrained from printing it ourselves, but in such cases we always saved it from going to waste by giving it to the City Hall man of the *Deutsche Correspondent*, a Mannheimer who was ready to believe anything, provided only it was incredible. Once we planted on him an outbreak of yellow fever in the City Jail, but inasmuch as his account of it was printed in German, and buried in columns of gaudy stuff about German weddings, funerals, bowling contests, and other such orgies, our city editors never discovered it.

Kent and I remained in the City Hall about a year, and until the end of that time our relations with Alec were kindly and even loving; in fact, we continued on good terms with him until his lamented death many years afterward. Unhappily, our successors never got next to him as we had, and in consequence he beat them almost every day, and often in a dramatic and paralyzing manner. In the end it was impossible for any rival reporter to stand up to him, and the rich *Sun* had to shanghai him from the poor *American* to avoid disgrace and ruin. More than once Baltimoreans of public spirit, even in the City Hall, proposed that he be elected Mayor himself, and in perpetuity, but like nearly every other good newspaper man, he looked on political office as ignominious, and preferred to remain a reporter. When he died at last the City Hall flag was at half-mast for a week.

The failure of the post-Kent-Mencken flight of City Hall reporters to bring him to a stand as the

Old Masters had done was probably due not only
to the natural recession of talent among them, but
also to a curious episode that had made a dreadful
pother on the *Herald* and was still remembered uneasily by all the journalists of Baltimore. The central figure of that episode was a reporter whose
name I shall suppress, for he was unhappily an
addict to the hand-set whiskey of the Baltimore
printers, and spent a large part of his time sleeping it off in police-stations. Let there be a murder, a fire or even an earthquake, and he would
snore through it in one of the roomy barroom
chairs that were then provided for the use of professional witnesses, straw bondsmen, and cops on
reserve. Max Ways was a man of enlarged views,
and had no objection to alcoholism as such, but a
narcolept was of little more use to him than a dead
man, and one rainy Sunday in the early Winter
of 1898–99, being somewhat exacerbated by drink
himself, he had the culprit before him, and gave
him such a bawling out that even the office boys
were aghast.

Moreover, that bawling out was reinforced by
an ultimatum. If, by 6 p.m. of that same day, the
culprit did not appear in the office with a story
worth at least two sticks [2] he was to consider himself fired for the nth and last time, with no hope of
appeal, pardon, commutation or reprieve, whether
in this world or the next. The poor fish, alarmed,

[2] A stick is about two inches of type.

shuffled off to police headquarters and begged the cops to help him, but they reported that the bleak, filthy weather had adjourned all human endeavor in the town, and that they had nothing in hand save two lost colored children and a runaway horse. He then proceeded to such other public offices as were open, but always he met with the same response. Somewhere or other he picked up the death of a saloonkeeper, but the saloonkeeper was obscure, and thus worth, at most, only a few lines. It began to look hopeless, and he slogged on despairingly, soaked by the rain and scarcely knowing where he was going.

This woeful tramp took him at last to the shopping district, and he started to plod it just as dusk was coming down. Simultaneously, the arc-lights which, in that era, hung outside every store of any pretensions began to splutter on, and in his gloomy contemplation of them he was suddenly seized with an idea — the first, in all likelihood, that had occurred to him for long months, and maybe even years. Those arc-lights were above the range of pedestrians on the sidewalks, but it would be easy to reach any of them with an umbrella. Suppose a passer-by carrying a steel-rodded umbrella should lift it high enough to clear another passer-by's umbrella, and its ferrule should touch the steel socket that held the lower carbon of one of the lights, and suppose there should be some leakage of electricity, and it should shoot down the umbrella rod, and into the umbrella's owner's arm, and then, facilitated by his wet clothes, down his legs and into the sidewalk — what would be the effect upon the man? The speculation was an interesting one, and the poor fish paused awhile to revolve it in his deteriorated mind.

The next morning the *Herald* printed a story saying that a man named William T. Benson, aged forty-one, a visitor from Washington, had made the experiment accidentally in West Baltimore street, and had been knocked, figuratively speaking, into a cocked hat. There was a neat description of the way the current had thrown him half way across the street, and a statement from him detailing his sensations *en route*. He had not, he said, lost consciousness, but gigantic pinwheels in all the colors of the rainbow whirled before his eyes, and in the palm of his right hand was a scarlet burn such as one might pick up by grasping a red-hot poker. Moreover, his celluloid collar had been set to smoking, and might have burst into flames and burned his neck if a stranger had not rushed up and quenched it with his handkerchief. The young doctors at the University Hospital, so it appeared, regarded Mr. Benson's escape alive as almost miraculous, and laid it to the fact that he had rubber heels on his shoes. Fortunately, their science was equal to the emergency, and they predicted that their patient would be as good as new, save for his burned hand, by morning. But they trembled to think of the possible fate of the next victim.

This story, which ran well beyond two sticks and rated a display head, saved the narcolept's job — but only temporarily. By ten o'clock the next morning more than 200 Baltimore merchants had called up the electric company and ordered the lights in front of their stores taken away at once. By noon the number was close to a thousand, and by 3 p.m. the lawyers of the electric company were closeted with Nachman, the business manager of the *Herald*, and his veins were running ice-water at their notice of a libel suit for $500,000. They were ready to prove in court, they said, that it was as impossible to get a shock from one of their lights as from a child's rattle. The whole apparatus was fool, drunk, boy, idiot, suicide, and even giraffe proof. It had been tested by every expert in the nation, and pronounced perfect.

What became of the poor fish no one ever learned, for he got wind of the uproar before coming to the office the next day, and in fact never came at all, but vanished into space. The check-up that went on, with half the staff thrown into it, produced only misery of a very high voltage. The cops knew nothing of any such accident, the doctors at the University Hospital had no record of it, and the only William T. Benson who could be found in Washington had not been in Baltimore for nine years. Nor was there any lifting of the

gloom when the *Herald's* own lawyer was consulted. This gentleman (he afterward reached the
eminence of a Federal circuit judge) was one of
those old-fashioned attorneys who saw every case
as lost, and liked to wring their clients' hearts. If
the *Herald* went into court, he said, he would have
to stand mute, for there was no conceivable defense, and if it offered a compromise the electric
company would be insane to take anything less
than $499,999.99. The most that could be hoped
for was that a couple of implacable utilities-haters
would sneak past the company's fixers and get on
the jury, and there scale down the damages to
something less brutal — say $250,000 or $300,-
000.

During the month following the *Herald* printed
twenty or thirty news stories acknowledging and
denouncing the fake, and at least a dozen editorials
apologizing for it, but many of the merchants had
become immovably convinced that what could be
imagined might some day actually happen, so the
revenues of the electric company continued depleted, and the bellowing of its lawyers broke all
records. When the case was finally set down for an
early trial every *Herald* man felt relieved, for it
was clearly best to get the agony over, go through
a receivership, and start anew. On the day before
the day of fate there was really a kind of gaiety in
the office. Once more it was raining dismally, but
everyone was almost cheerful. That afternoon a

man carrying a steel-rodded umbrella lifted it to clear another pedestrian's umbrella in West Baltimore street, and the ferrule touched the lower carbon-socket of one of the few surviving arc-lights. When the cops got him to hospital he was dead.

I tell the tale as it was told to me : it all happened before I joined the staff. My own talent for faking fell into abeyance after I left the City Hall, and especially after I became city editor. In that office, in fact, I spent a large part of my energy trying to stamp it out in other men. But after I was promoted to managing editor, it enjoyed a curious recrudescence, and my masterpiece of all time, with the sole exception of my bogus history of the bathtub, printed in the New York *Evening Mail* on December 28, 1917, was a synthetic war dispatch printed in the *Herald* on May 30, 1905. The war that it had to do with was the gory bout between Japan and Russia, and its special theme was the Battle of Tsushimi or Korea Straits, fought on May 27 and 28. Every managing editor on earth knew for weeks in advance that a great naval battle was impending, and nearly all of them had a pretty accurate notion of where it would be fought. Moreover, they all began to get bulletins, on May 27, indicating that it was on, and these bulletins were followed by others on the day following. They came from Shanghai, Hongkong, Foochow and all the other ports of the China coast. They were set in large type and printed under what were

then called stud-horse heads, but they really offered nothing better than rumors of rumors.
Everyone knew that a battle was being fought, and
everyone assumed that the Japanese would win,
but no one had anything further to say on the subject. The Japs kept mum, and so did the Russians.

Like any other managing editor of normal appetites I was thrown into a sweat by this uncertainty.
With the able aid of George Worsham, who was
then news editor of the *Herald*, I had assembled a
great array of cuts and follow stuff to adorn the
story when it came, and though the *Herald* had
changed to an evening paper by that time, he and
I remained at our posts until late in the evenings
of May 27 and 28, hoping against hope that the
story would begin to flow at any minute, and give
us a chance to bring out a hot extra. But nothing
came in, and neither did anything come in on May
29 — that is, nothing save more of the brief and
tantalizing bulletins from the China coast. On the
evening of this third day of waiting and lathering
I retired to my cubby-hole of an office — and wrote
the story in detail. The date-line I put on it was
the plausible one of Seoul, and this is how it began:

From Chinese boatmen landing upon the Korean coast
comes the first connected story of the great naval battle
in the Straits of Korea on Saturday and Sunday.

After that I laid it on, as they used to say in
those days, with a shovel. Worsham read copy on

me, and contributed many illuminating details. Both of us, by hard poring over maps, had accumulated a knowledge of the terrain that was almost fit to be put beside that of a China coast pilot, and both of us had by heart the names of all the craft in both fleets, along with the names of their commanders. Worsham and I worked on the story until midnight, and the next morning we had it set in time for our noon edition. It began on Page 1 under a head like a fire-alarm, jumped double-leaded to Page 2, and there filled two and three-quarters columns. It described in throbbing phrases the arrival of the Russians, the onslaught of the Japs, the smoke and roar of the encounter, and then the gradual rolling up of the Jap victory. No one really knew, as yet, which side had won, but we took that chance. And to give verisimilitude to our otherwise bald and unconvincing narrative, we mentioned every ship by name, and described its fate, sending most of the Russians to the bottom and leaving the field to Admiral Count Heihachiro Togo. With it we printed our largest, latest and most fierce portrait of the admiral, a smaller one of his unhappy antagonist, Admiral Zinivy Petrovitch Rozhdestvensky, and a whole series of pictures of the contending ships, with all the Russian marked either " damaged " or "sunk."

Thus the *Evening Herald* scored a beat on the world, and, what is more, a beat that lasted for nearly two weeks, for it took that long for any authentic details of the battle to reach civilization. By that time, alas, our feat was forgotten — but not by its perpetrators. Worsham and I searched the cables from Tokyo, when they began to come in at last, with sharp eyes, for we lived in fear that we might have pulled some very sour ones. But there were no such sour ones. We had guessed precisely right in every particular of the slightest importance, and on many fine points we had even beaten the Japs themselves. Years later, reading an astonishing vivid first-hand account of the battle by an actual participant, Aleksei Silych Novikov,[3] I was gratified to note that we were still right.

[3] Translated as Tsushima; New York, 1937.

XIX

FIRE ALARM

At midnight or thereabout on Saturday, February 6, 1904, I did my share as city editor to put the *Sunday Herald* to bed, and then proceeded to Junker's saloon to join in the exercises of the Stevedores' Club. Its members, having already got down a good many schooners, were in a frolicsome mood, and I was so pleasantly edified that I stayed until 3:30. Then I caught a night-hawk trolley-car, and by four o'clock was snoring on my celibate couch in Hollins street, with every hope and prospect of continuing there until noon of the next day. But at 11 a.m. there was a telephone call from the *Herald* office, saying that a big fire had broken out in Hopkins Place, the heart of downtown Baltimore, and fifteen minutes later a reporter dashed up to the house behind a sweating hack horse, and rushed in with the news that the fire looked to be a humdinger, and promised swell pickings for a

dull Winter Sunday. So I hoisted my still malty
bones from my couch and got into my clothes, and
ten minutes later I was on my way to the office with
the reporter. That was at about 11:30 a.m. of
Sunday, February 7. It was not until 4 a.m. of
Wednesday, February 10, that my pants and shoes,
or even my collar, came off again. And it was not
until 11:30 a.m. of Sunday, February 14 — precisely a week to the hour since I set off — that I got
home for a bath and a change of linen.

For what I had walked into was the great Baltimore fire of 1904, which burned a square mile out
of the heart of the town and went howling and
spluttering on for ten days. I give the exact schedule of my movements simply because it delights
me, in my autumnal years, to dwell upon it, for it
reminds me how full of steam and malicious animal
magnetism I was when I was young. During the
week following the outbreak of the fire the *Herald*
was printed in three different cities, and I was present at all its accouchements, herding dispersed and
bewildered reporters at long distance and cavorting gloriously in strange composing-rooms. My
opening burst of work without a stop ran to sixty-
four and a half hours, and then I got only six hours
of nightmare sleep, and resumed on a working
schedule of from twelve to fourteen hours a day,
with no days off and no time for meals until work
was over. It was brain-fagging and back-breaking, but it was grand beyond compare — an adven-

ture of the first chop, a razzle-dazzle superb and
elegant, a circus in forty rings. When I came out
of it at last I was a settled and indeed almost a
middle-aged man, spavined by responsibility and
aching in every sinew, but I went into it a boy, and
it was the hot gas of youth that kept me going.
The uproar over, and the *Herald* on an even keel
again, I picked up one day a volume of stories by
a new writer named Joseph Conrad, and therein
found a tale of a young sailor that struck home to
me as the history of Judas must strike home to
many a bloated bishop, though the sailor naturally
made his odyssey in a ship, not on a newspaper, and
its scene was not a provincial town in America, but
the South Seas. Today, so long afterward, I too
" remember my youth and the feeling that will
never come back any more — the feeling that I
could last forever, outlast the sea, the earth, and
all men . . . Youth! All youth! The silly,
charming, beautiful youth ! "

Herald reporters, like all other reporters of the
last generation, were usually late in coming to work
on Sundays, but *that* Sunday they had begun to
drift in even before I got to the office, and by one
o'clock we were in full blast. The fire was then
raging through a whole block, and from our fifth-
floor city-room windows it made a gaudy show, full
of catnip for a young city editor. But the Baltimore firemen had a hundred streams on it, and
their chief, an old man named Horton, reported

that they would knock it off presently. They might have done so, in fact, if the wind had not changed suddenly at three o'clock, and begun to roar from the West. In ten minutes the fire had routed Horton and his men and leaped to a second block, and in half an hour to a third and a fourth, and by dark the whole of downtown Baltimore was under a hail of sparks and flying brands, and a dozen outlying fires had started to eastward. We had a story, I am here to tell you! There have been bigger ones, of course, and plenty of them, but when and where, between the Chicago fire of 1871 and the San Francisco earthquake of 1906, was there ever one that was fatter, juicier, more exhilarating to the journalists on the actual ground? Every newspaper in Baltimore save one was burned out, and every considerable hotel save three, and every office building without exception. The fire raged for a full week, helped by that bitter Winter wind, and when it fizzled out at last the burned area looked like Pompeii, and up from its ashes rose the pathetic skeletons of no less than twenty overtaken and cremated fire-engines — some of them from Washington, Philadelphia, Pittsburgh and New York. Old Horton, the Baltimore fire chief, was in hospital, and so were several hundred of his men.

My labors as city editor during that electric week were onerous and various, but for once they did not include urging lethargic reporters to step into it. The whole staff went to work with the enthusiasm of crusaders shinning up the walls of Antioch, and all sorts of volunteers swarmed in, including three or four forgotten veterans who had been fired years before, and were thought to have long since reached the dissecting-room. Also, there were as many young aspirants from the waiting-list, each hoping for his chance at last, and one of these, John Lee Blecker by name, I remember brilliantly, for when I told him to his delight that he had a job and invited him to prove it he leaped out with exultant gloats — and did not show up again for five days. But getting lost in so vast a story did not wreck his career, for he lived to become, in fact, an excellent reporter, and not a few old-timers were lost, too. One of the best of them, sometime that afternoon, was caught in a blast when the firemen began dynamiting buildings, and got so coagulated that it was three days before he was fit for anything save writing editorials. The rest not only attacked the fire in a fine frenzy, but also returned promptly and safely, and by four o'clock thirty typewriters were going in the city-room, and my desk was beginning to pile high with red-hot copy.

Lynn Meekins, the managing editor, decided against wasting time and energy on extras: we got out one, but the story was too big for such banalities: it seemed like a toy balloon in a hurricane. " Let us close the first city edition," he said,

" at nine o'clock. Make it as complete as you can. If you need twenty pages, take them. If you need fifty, take them." So we began heaving copy to the composing-room, and by seven o'clock there were columns and columns of type on the stones, and picture after picture was coming up from the engraving department. Alas, not much of that quivering stuff ever got into the *Herald*, for a little before nine o'clock, just as the front page was being made up, a couple of excited cops rushed in, howling that the buildings across the street were to be blown up in ten minutes, and ordering us to clear out at once. By this time there was a fire on the roof of the *Herald* Building itself, and another was starting in the press-room, which had plate-glass windows reaching above the street level, all of them long ago smashed by flying brands. We tried to parley with the cops, but they were too eager to be on their way to listen to us, and when a terrific blast went off up the street Meekins ordered that the building be abandoned.

There was a hotel three or four blocks away, out of the apparent path of the fire, and there we went in a dismal procession — editors, reporters, printers and pressmen. Our lovely first edition was adjourned for the moment, but every man-jack in the outfit believed that we'd be back anon, once the proposed dynamiting had been done — every man-jack, that is, save two. One was Joe Bamberger, the foreman of the composing-room, and the other was Joe Callahan, my assistant as city editor. The first Joe was carrying page-proofs of all the pages already made up, and galley-proofs of all the remaining type-matter, and all the copy not yet set. In his left overcoat pocket was the front-page logotype of the paper, and in his left pocket were ten or twelve halftones. The other Joe had on him what copy had remained in the city-room, a wad of Associated Press flimsy about the Russian-Japanese war, a copy-hook, a pot of paste, two boxes of copy-readers' pencils — and the assignment-book!

But Meekins and I refused to believe that we were shipwrecked, and in a little while he sent me back to the *Herald* Building to have a look, leaving Joe No. 2 to round up such reporters as were missing. I got there safely enough, but did not stay long. The proposed dynamiting, for some reason unknown, had apparently been abandoned, but the fire on our roof was blazing violently, and the press-room was vomiting smoke. As I stood gaping at this dispiriting spectacle a couple of large plate-glass windows cracked in the composing-room under the roof, and a flying brand — some of them seemed to be six feet long! — fetched a window on the editorial floor just below it. Nearly opposite, in Fayette street, a sixteen-story office building had caught fire, and I paused a moment more to watch it. The flames leaped through it as if it had been made of matchwood and drenched with gasoline, and in half a minute they were roaring in the air at least 500 feet. It was, I suppose, the most melodramatic detail of the whole fire, but I was too busy to enjoy it, and as I made off hastily I fully expected the whole structure to come crashing down behind me. But when I returned a week later I found that the steel frame and brick skin had both held out, though all the interior was gone, and during the following Summer the burned parts were replaced, and the building remains in service to this day, as solid as the Himalayas.

At the hotel Meekins was trying to telephone to Washington, but long-distance calls still took time in 1904, and it was fifteen minutes before he raised Scott C. Bone, managing editor of the Washington *Post*. Bone was having a busy and crowded night himself, for the story was worth pages to the *Post*, but he promised to do what he could for us, and presently we were hoofing for Camden Station, a good mile away — Meekins and I, Joe Bamberger with his salvage, a copy-reader with the salvage of the other Joe, half a dozen other desk men, fifteen or twenty printers, and small squads of pressmen and circulation men. We were off to Washington to print the paper there — that is, if the gods were kind. They frowned at the start, for the only Baltimore & Ohio train for an hour was an accommodation, but we poured into it, and by midnight we were in the *Post* office, and the hospitable Bone and his men were clearing a place for

us in their frenzied composing-room, and ordering
the press-room to be ready for us.[1]

Just how we managed to get out the *Herald* that
night I can't tell you, for I remember only trifling
details. One was that I was the principal financier
of the expedition, for when we pooled our money
at Camden Station it turned out that I had $40 in
my pocket, whereas Meekins had only $5, and the
rest of the editorial boys not more than $20 among
them. Another is that the moon broke out of the
Winter sky just as we reached the old B. & O. Station in Washington, and shined down sentimen-
tally on the dome of the Capitol. The Capitol was
nothing new to Baltimore journalists, but we had
with us a new copy-reader who had lately come in
from Pittsburgh, and as he saw the matronly dome
for the first time, bathed in spooky moonlight, he
was so overcome by patriotic and aesthetic sentiments that he took off his hat and exclaimed " My
God, how beautiful! " And a third is that we all
paused a second to look at the red glow over Baltimore, thirty-five miles away as the crow flies. The
fire had really got going by now, and for four
nights afterward the people of Washington could
see its glare from their streets.

Bone was a highly competent managing editor,
and contrived somehow to squeeze us into the tu-

1 Bone was an Indianan, and had a long and honorable
career in journalism, stretching from 1881 to 1918. In 1919 he
became publicity chief of the Republican National Committee,
and in 1921 he was appointed Governor of Alaska. He died in
1936.

multous *Post* office. All of his linotypes were already working to capacity, so our operators were useless, but they lent a hand with the make-up, and our pressmen went to the cellar to reinforce their *Post* colleagues. It was a sheer impossibility to set up all the copy we had with us, or even the half of it, or a third of it, but we nevertheless got eight or ten columns into type, and the *Post* lent us enough of its own matter to piece out a four-page paper. In return we lent the hospitable *Post* our halftones, and they adorned its first city edition next morning. Unhappily, the night was half gone before Bone could spare us any press time, but when we got it at last the presses did prodigies, and at precisely 6.30 the next morning we reached Camden Station, Baltimore, on a milk-train, with 30,-000 four-page *Heralds* in the baggage-car. By 8 o'clock they were all sold. Our circulation hustlers had no difficulty in getting rid of them. We had scarcely arrived before the news of our coming began to circulate around the periphery of the fire, and in a few minutes newsboys swarmed in, some of them regulars but the majority volunteers. Very few boys in Baltimore had been to bed that night: the show was altogether too gaudy. And now there was a chance to make some easy money out of it.

Some time ago I unearthed one of these orphan *Heralds* from the catacombs of the Pratt Library in Baltimore, and gave it a looking-over. It turned out to be far from bad, all things considered. The story of the fire was certainly not complete, but it was at least coherent, and three of our halftones adorned Page 1. The eight-column streamer-head that ran across its top was as follows:

HEART OF BALTIMORE WRECKED BY
    GREATEST FIRE IN CITY'S HISTORY

Well, brethren, what was wrong about that? I submit that many worse heads have been written by pampered copy-readers sitting at luxurious desks, with vassals and serfs at their side. It was simple; it was direct; there was no fustian in it; and yet it told the story perfectly. I wrote it on a make-up table in the *Post* composing-room, with Meekins standing beside me writing a box for the lower right-hand corner of the first page, thanking the *Post* for its " proverbial courtesy to its contemporaries " and promising formally that the *Herald* would be "published daily by the best means it can command under the circumstances."

Those means turned out, that next day, to be a great deal short of ideal. Leaving Joe Callahan, who had kept the staff going all night, to move to another and safer hotel, for the one where we had found refuge was now in the path of the fire, Meekins and I returned to Washington during the morning to make arrangements for bringing out a larger paper. We were not ashamed of our four pages, for even the *Sunpaper*, printed by the Washington *Evening Star,* had done no better, but what were four pages in the face of so vast a story? The boys had produced enough copy to fill at least ten on the first day of the fire, and today they might turn out enough to fill twenty. It would wring our gizzards intolerably to see so much good stuff going to waste. Moreover, there was art to consider, for our two photographers had piled up dozens of gorgeous pictures, and if there was no engraving plant left in Baltimore there were certainly plenty in Washington.

But Bone, when we routed him out, could not promise us any more accommodation than he had so kindly given us the first night. There was, it appeared, a long-standing agreement between the *Post* and the Baltimore *Evening News,* whereby each engaged to take care of the other in times of calamity, and the *News* staff was already in Washington cashing in on it, and would keep the *Post* equipment busy whenever it was not needed by the *Post* itself. Newspapers in those days had no such plants as they now boast: if I remember rightly, the *Post* had not more than a dozen linotypes, and none of them could chew up copy like the modern monsters. The prospect seemed depressing, indeed, but Bone himself gave us a shot of hope by mentioning casually that the Baltimore *World* appeared to have escaped the fire. The *World?* It was a small, ill-fed sheet of the kind then still flourishing in most big American cities, and its own

daily editions seldom ran beyond four pages, but it
was an *afternoon* paper, and we might hire its
equipment for the night. What if it had only four
linotypes? We might help them out with hand-set
matter. And what if its Goss press could print but
5,000 six- or eight-page papers an hour? We
might run it steadily from 6 p.m. to the middle of
the next morning, bringing out edition after edition.

We got back to Baltimore as fast as the B. & O.
could carry us, and found the *World* really unscathed, and, what is more, its management willing
to help us, and as soon as its own last edition was off
that afternoon Callahan and the gentlemen of the
Herald staff came swarming down on its little office
in Calvert street. The ensuing night gave me the
grand migraine of my life, with throbs like the
blows of an ax and continuous pinwheels. Every
conceivable accident rained down on us. One of the
linotypes got out of order at once, and when, after
maddening delays, Joe Bamberger rounded up a
machinist, it took him two hours to repair it, and
even then he refused to promise that it would work.
Meekins thereupon turned to his desperate plan to
go back to Gutenberg and set matter by hand —
only to find that the *World* had insufficient type in
its cases to fill more than a few columns. Worse,
most of this type appeared to be in the wrong
boxes, and such of it as was standing on the stones

had been picked for sorts by careless printers, and
was pretty well pied.[2]

Meekins sent me out to find more, but all the
larger printers of Baltimore had been burned out,
and the only supply of any size that I could discover was in the office of the *Catholic Mirror*, a
weekly. Arrangements with it were made quickly,
and Joe Bamberger and his gallant lads of the
union rushed the place and proceeded to do or die,
but setting type by hand turned out to be a slow
and vexatious business, especially to linotype operators who had almost forgotten the case. Nor did
it soothe us to discover that the *Mirror's* stock of
type (most of it old and worn) was in three or four
different faces, with each face in two or three sizes,
and that there was not enough of any given face

[2] Perhaps I should explain some printers' terms here. The
stones are flat tables (once of actual stone, but now usually of
steel) on which printers do much of their work. Type is kept
in wooden cases divided into boxes, one for a character. As it
is set up by the compositor it is placed in galleys, which are
brass frames, and then the galleys are taken to the stone and
there made up. Sometimes, after the printing has been done,
the type is returned to a stone, and left there until a convenient
time to return it to the cases. To pick sorts is to go to such
standing type and pick out characters that are exhausted in the
cases. Pied type is type in such confusion that it cannot be returned to the cases by the usual method of following the words,
but must be identified letter by letter. To forget the case, mentioned below, is to lose the art of picking up types from the
boxes without looking at them. The boxes are not arranged al-
phabetically, and a printer learns the case as one learns the
typewriter keyboard. A face of type is a series of sizes of one
design. The face in which this line is set is called Scotch Modern and the size is eight point. The text above is in eleven and
one-half point Scotch Modern.

and size to set more than a few columns. But it was
now too late to balk, so Joe's goons went to work,
and by dark we had ten or twelve columns of copy
in type, some of it in eight-point, some in ten-
point and some in twelve-point. That night I rode
with Joe's chief of staff, Josh Lynch, on a comman-
deered express-wagon as these galleys of motley
were hauled from the *Mirror* office to the *World*
office. I recall of the journey only that it led down
a steep hill, and that the hill was covered with ice.
Josh howled whenever the horse slipped, but somehow or other we got all the galleys to the *World*
office without disaster, and the next morning, after
six or eight breakdowns in the pressroom, we came
out with a paper that at least had some news in it,
though it looked as if it had been printed by country printers locked up in a distillery.

When the first copy came off the *World's* rickety
Goss press Meekins professed to be delighted with
it. In the face of almost hopeless difficulties, he
said, we had shown the resourcefulness of Robinson
Crusoe, and for ages to come this piebald issue of
the *Herald* would be preserved in museums under
glass, and shown to young printers and reporters
with appropriate remarks. The more, however, he
looked at it the less his enthusiasm soared, and
toward the middle of the morning he decided suddenly that another one like it would disgrace us
forever, and announced at once that we'd return to
Washington. But we knew before we started that

the generous Bone could do no more for us than he had already done, and, with the *Star* monopolized by the Baltimore *Sun,* there was not much chance of finding other accommodation in Washington that would be better than the *World's* in Baltimore. The pressure for space was now doubled, for not only was hot editorial copy piling up endlessly, but also advertising copy. Hundreds of Baltimore business firms were either burned out already or standing in the direct path of the fire, and all of them were opening temporary offices uptown, and trying to notify their customers where they could be found. Even in the ghastly parody printed in the *World* office we had made room for nearly three columns of such notices, and before ten o'clock Tuesday morning we had copy for ten more.

But where to turn? Wilmington in Delaware? It was nearly seventy miles away, and had only small papers. We wanted accommodation for printing ten, twelve, sixteen, twenty pages, for the *Herald* had suffered a crippling loss, and needed that volunteer advertising desperately. Philadelphia? It seemed fantastic, for Philadelphia was nearly a *hundred* miles away. To be sure, it had plenty of big newspaper plants, but could we bring our papers back to Baltimore in time to distribute them? The circulation men, consulted, were optimistic. " Give us 50,000 papers at 5 a.m.," they said, " and we'll sell them." So Meekins, at noon or thereabout, set off for Philadelphia, and before

dark he was heard from. He had made an arrangement with Barclay H. Warburton, owner of the
Philadelphia *Evening Telegraph.* The *Telegraph*
plant would be ours from 6 p.m., beginning tomorrow, and it was big enough to print any conceivable paper. Meekins was asking the Associated Press to transfer our report from Baltimore
to Philadelphia, and the International Typographical Union to let our printers work there.
I was to get out one more edition in Washington,
and then come to Philadelphia, leaving Callahan
in charge of our temporary office in Baltimore.
But first I was to see Oscar G. Murray, president
of the B. & O. Railroad, and induce him to give us
a special train from Philadelphia to Baltimore, to
run every night until further notice.

The B. & O.'s headquarters building in Baltimore had been burned out like the *Herald* office,
but I soon found Murray at Camden Station, functioning grandly at a table in a storage warehouse.
A bachelor of luxurious and even levantine tastes,
he was in those days one of the salient characters
of Baltimore, and his lavender-and-white striped
automobile was later to become a major sight of
the town. When he gave a party for his lady
friends at the Stafford Hotel, where he lived and
had his being, it had to be covered as cautiously as
the judicial orgies described in Chapter XII. He
looked, that dreadful afternoon, as if he had just
come from his barber, tailor and haberdasher. He

was shaved so closely that his round face glowed like a rose, and an actual rose was in the buttonhole of his elegant but not too gaudy checked coat. In three minutes I had stated my problem and come to terms with him. At two o'clock, precisely, every morning a train consisting of a locomotive, a baggage-car and a coach would be waiting at Chestnut Street Station in Philadelphia, with orders to shove off for Baltimore the instant our *Heralds* were loaded. It would come through to Camden Station, Baltimore, without stop, and we could have our circulation hustlers waiting for it there.

That was all. When I asked what this train would cost, the magnificent Murray waved me away. "Let us discuss that," he said, "when we are all back home." We did discuss it two months later — and the bill turned out to be nothing at all. "We had some fun together," Murray said, "and we don't want to spoil it now by talking about money." That fun consisted, at least in part, of some very exuberant railroading. If we happened to start from Philadelphia a bit late, which was not infrequent as we accumulated circulation, the special train made the trip to Baltimore at hair-raising speed, with the piles of *Heralds* in the baggage-car thrown helter-skelter on the curves, and the passengers in the coach scared half to death. All known records between Philadelphia and Baltimore were broken during the ensuing five weeks. Finally the racing went so far beyond the seemly that the proper authorities gave one of the engineers ten days lay-off without pay for wild and dangerous malpractice. He spent most of his vacation as the guest of our printers in Philadelphia, and they entertained him handsomely.

But there was still a paper to get out in Washington, and I went there late in the afternoon to tackle the dismal job. The best Bone could do for us, with the Baltimore *News* cluttering the *Post* office all day and the *Post* itself printing endless columns about the fire still raging, was four pages, and of their thirty-two columns nearly thirteen were occupied by the advertisements I have mentioned. I got the business over as soon as possible, and returned to Baltimore eager for a few winks of sleep, for I had not closed my eyes since Sunday morning, and it was now Wednesday. In the *Herald's* temporary office I found Isidor Goodman, the night editor. He reported that every bed in downtown Baltimore was occupied two or three deep, and that if we sought to go home there were no trolley-cars or night-hacks to haul us. In the office itself there was a table used as a desk, but Joe Callahan was snoring on it. A dozen other men were on the floor.

Finally, Isidor allowed that he was acquainted with a lady who kept a surreptitious house of assignation in nearby Paca street, and suggested that business was probably bad with her in view of the competing excitement of the fire, and that she might be able in consequence to give us a bed. But when we plodded to her establishment, which was in a very quiet neighborhood, Isidor, who was as nearly dead as I was, pulled the wrong door-bell, and a bass voice coming cut of a nightshirt at a second-story window threatened us with the police if we didn't make off. We were too tired to resist this outrage, but shuffled down the street, silent and despairing. Presently we came to the Rennert Hotel, and went in hoping to find a couple of vacant spots, however hard, on a billiard-table, or the bar, or in chairs in the lobby. Inside, it seemed hopeless, for every chair in sight was occupied, and a dozen men were asleep on the floor. But there was a night-clerk on duty whom we knew, and after some mysterious hocus-pocus he whispered to us to follow him, and we trailed along up the stairs to the fourth floor. There he unlocked a door and pointed dramatically to a vacant bed, looking beautifully white, wide and deep. We did not wait to learn how it had come to be so miraculously vacant, but peeled off our coats and collars, kicked off our shoes, stepped out of our pants, and leaped in. Before the night-clerk left us we were as dead to this world and its sorrows as Gog and Magog. It was 4 a.m. and we slept until ten. When we got back to the *Herald's* quarters we let it be known that we had passed the night in the house of Isidor's friend in Paca street, along with two rich society women from Perth Amboy, N.J.

That night we got out our first paper in Philadelphia — a gorgeous thing of fourteen pages, with twenty columns of advertising. It would knock the eyes out of the *Sun* and *Evening News*, and we rejoiced and flapped our wings accordingly. In particular, we were delighted with the *Evening Telegraph's* neat and graceful head-type, and when we got back to Baltimore we imitated it. Barclay Warburton, the owner of the *Telegraph*, came down to the office to see us through — elegantly invested in a tail coat and a white tie. Despite this unprofessional garb, he turned out to be a smart fellow in the pressroom, and it was largely due to his aid that we made good time. I returned to Baltimore early in the morning on the first of Oscar Murray's special trains, and got a dreadful bumping on the curves and crossings. The circulation boys fell on our paper with exultant gurgles, and the next night we lifted the press-run by 10,000 copies.

We stayed in Philadelphia for five weeks, and gradually came to feel almost at home there — that is, if anybody not born in the town can ever feel at home in Philadelphia. The attitude of the local colleagues at first puzzled us, and then made us snicker in a superior way. Save for Warburton himself, not one of them ever offered us the slightest assistance, or, indeed, even spoke to us. We were printing a daily newspaper 100 miles from base — a feat that remains unparalleled in Amer-

ican journalism, so far as I know, to this day —
and it seemed only natural that some of the Philadelphia brethren should drop in on us, if only out
of curiosity. But the only one who ever appeared
was the managing editor of one of the morning
papers, and he came to propose graciously that we
save him a few dollars by lending him our halftones of the fire. Inasmuch as we were paying his
paper a substantial sum every day for setting ads
for us — the *Evening Telegraph* composing-room
could not handle all that crowded in — we replied
with a chilly nix, and he retired in a huff.

There was a press club in Philadelphia in those
days, and its quarters downtown offered a convenient roosting-place for the hour or two after the
night's work was done. In any other American
city we'd have been offered cards on it instantly
and automatically, but not in Philadelphia. At the
end of a week a telegraph operator working for us
got cards for us in some unknown manner, and a
few of us began using the place. During the time
we did so only one member ever so much as spoke to
us, and he was a drunken Englishman whose conversation consisted entirely of encomiums of Barclay Warburton. Whenever he saw us he would
approach amiably and begin chanting "Good ol'
Bahclay! Good ol' Bahclay! Bahclay's a good
sawt," with *sawt* rhyming with *caught*, and apparently meaning *sort*. We agreed heartily, but suffered under the iteration, and presently we forsook

the place for the saloon patronized by the *Herald*
printers, where there was the refined entertainment
described in Chapter XI.

Meekins's arrangements for getting out the
Herald so far from home were made with skill and
worked perfectly. Callahan remained in Baltimore in charge of our field quarters outside the
burned area, and on every train bound for Philadelphia during the afternoon he had an office-boy
with such copy as had accumulated. At six o'clock,
when the *Evening Telegraph* men cleared out of
their office, we opened a couple of private wires,
and they kept us supplied with later matter. Even
after the fire burned out at last Baltimore was in
an appalling state, and there were plenty of old
Baltimoreans who wagged their heads despairingly and predicted that it would never be rebuilt.
One such pessimist was the Mayor of the town: a
little while later, yielding to his vapors, he committed suicide. But there were optimists enough
to offset these glooms, and before we left Philadelphia the debris was being cleared away, many ancient and narrow streets were being widened, and
scores of new buildings were started. All these debates and doings made for juicy news, and the men
of the local staff, ably bossed by Callahan, poured
it out daily. Meekins would come to Philadelphia
two or three times a week to look over his faculty
in exile, and I would drop down to Baltimore about
as often to aid and encourage Joe. We had our

own printers in Philadelphia and our own pressmen. Our circulation department performed marvels, and the advertising department gobbled up
all the advertising in sight, which, as I have said,
was plenty. The *Herald* had been on short commons for some time before the fire, but during the
two or three months afterward it rolled in money.

Once I had caught up on lost sleep I prepared
to do a narrative of the fire as I had seen it, with
whatever help I could get from the other *Herald*
men, but the project got itself postponed so often
that I finally abandoned it, and to this day no connected story has ever been printed. The truth is
that, while I was soon getting sleep enough, at least
for a youngster of twenty-four, I had been depleted by the first cruel week more than I thought,
and it was months before I returned to anything
properly describable as normalcy. So with the rest
of the staff, young and old. Surveying them when
the hubbub was over, I found confirmation for my
distrust, mentioned in Chapter XI, of alcohol as a
fuel for literary endeavor. They divided themselves sharply into three classes. Those who had
kept off the stuff until work was done and it was
time to relax — there were, of course, no all-out teetotalers in the outfit — needed only brief holidays
to be substantially as good as new. Those who had
drunk during working hours, though in modera-
tion, showed a considerable fraying, and some of
them had spells of sickness. Those who had boozed

in the classical manner were useless before the end of the second week, and three of them were floored by serious illnesses, one of which ended, months later, in complete physical and mental collapse. I pass on this record for what it is worth.

XX

SOLD DOWN THE

RIVER

AFTER five weeks in Philadelphia we moved back
to Baltimore. The steel skeleton of the *Herald*
Building was still standing, and it might have been
furnished with a new skin and viscera as the other
burned office-buildings of Baltimore were furnished, but the city had seized it to widen a street,
and the place where it stood soon became the Courthouse Plaza, which is today given over to parked
automobiles. I had visited its ruins a number of
times during the month after the fire, and once
shinned up its shell to the fifth floor, and investigated the mortal remains of the editorial rooms.
It was easy to find the place where my desk had
stood, though the desk itself was only a heap of
white dust, for its hardware survived and so did the

301

frame of the goose-neck light that had stood upon
it. I also found my old copy-hook, twisted as if it
had died in agony, and I have it yet. But all the
clippings and other records that had stuffed the
drawers of the desk were gone, and I thus lost many
souvenirs of my earliest days, including a collection of pieces of hangmen's ropes. In that era the
sheriff pontificating at a Maryland hanging always cut up the rope afterwards to give to his fans,
and the reporters on hand were included. If my
collection had survived I suppose I'd have presented it, soon or late, to the Smithsonian, but it is
no more, and I do not repine.

The indefatigable Meekins, with such help as he
could squeeze out of Peard, the general manager,
had leased an old car-barn in South Charles street,
just outside the area of the fire, and there he set up
fifteen or twenty linotypes, and a second-hand Hoe
press that he had found in New York. I have seen
much worse newspaper offices in my time. At the
start the editorial rooms were in a little three-story
building across an alley from the barn, but that
turned out to be an inconvenient arrangement, and
we soon moved into the barn itself, which was wide
and deep. This put the whole operation of the
paper, from the writing and editing of copy to the
printing and delivery, on one floor — a scheme
that has been adopted deliberately, in recent years,
by a number of mid-Western dailies that happened
to have room enough for it. We got out a pretty

good paper, and circulation showed some gains, but the post-fire burst of advertising did not last, and by the beginning of Summer the *Herald* was in difficulties. The advertising trend, even in those days, was away from morning papers, and it was especially marked in Baltimore, where the *Evening News*, published by Charles H. Grasty, was making inroads on the morning *Sun.* In the morning field we had not only the *Sun* to face, but also the *American;* in the evening field there was nothing beside the *News* save the *World,* which had hardly any advertising at all.

So Peard decided to switch from morning to evening — and then, at the last moment, had an attack of caution, and ordered Meekins to keep the morning going until we could make out how the evening was doing. It was characteristic of that well-meaning but highly unjournalistic man that he never stopped to figure out how one staff could produce two papers. Not a single extra man was hired. Meekins was managing editor of both, and I was city editor of both. This preposterous arrangement went on for a single week, and then we all blew up. During that week I never got home at all, but slept, when I slept at all, on a couch in the office — usually from 2 a.m. to 6 or 7. It was the end of August, 1904, in sticky Summer weather, and the car-barn was only a block from the water-front, in the hottest part of Baltimore. Changes of clothes were sent to me from home, but the only baths I got were from a fire-hose in the press-room.

Launched under such disadvantages, the *Evening Herald* was naturally something of a scarecrow, and its reception by the gentry and commonalty of Baltimore was far from enthusiastic. Grasty's *Evening News* was then, as always, a bad newspaper, but it was not quite as bad as the *Evening Herald,* and the advertisers of the town showed no sign of deserting him to fatten us. Peard and his men in the business office tried to put all the blame on the editorial department, but we bit and scratched back, and after an insane week of his noble experiment the morning *Herald* was abandoned, and we began to get out an evening edition that looked more or less like a newspaper. But the Sunday morning paper was continued, and so my work-day on Saturday ran from 7 a.m. to 1 or 2 a.m. Sometimes I was able to snatch a nap in the afternoon, but more often I was not, and the thing I principally remember about the time is that I always slept so late on Sunday morning that I was unable to sleep Sunday night, and that it commonly took me until Wednesday to oscillate back to my normal hours. We all sweated and schemed, but it gradually became plain that without fresh money and new and wonder-working management the *Herald* was doomed. Natural forces were also in operation against us, for the great reduction in the number of American daily papers that marked the 20's and 30's was already beginning. Baltimore had five in 1904, and in 1903 it had had six, but today it has but three.

In the midst of these dismal struggles, at some time or other in 1905, Meekins's title was changed to that of editor-in-chief, and I was made managing editor in his place, with Joe Callahan succeeding me as city editor. It was a step that must have caressed inevitably the gills of any youngster of twenty-five, for though I was well aware of the *Herald's* gloomy prospects, it was nevertheless a daily newspaper, and in a city of more than 500,-000 people. Most of my fellow-freshmen of 1899 were still reporters, and some were out of jobs, but here was I, by the sheer power of a singular virtue, rising to great and puissant dignities, and ready to become (as I suspected) the Ajax of a new crop of legends as astonishing as those which swathed Cunningham, Carter and Meekins himself. It was a great day when I overheard an office-boy speak of me, to a colleague, as the Old Man, and another when the office stationery came back from the printers with Meekins's name blacked out and mine printed above it. But as the duties of my new office took me deeper and deeper into the affairs of the paper I became better and better aware of its parlous state. Meekins told me daily of his palavers with Peard and with Oler, the iceman who owned the paper, and what he had to report was predominantly depressing. On those rare days when news came down from the business office uptown that a new 300-line ad had been snared he and I would go to Joyce's Hotel opposite Camden Station and blow ourselves to a swell dinner.

It would be an error, however, to say that I was ever despondent, or anything remotely resembling it. I was still only twenty-five — and at twenty-five the hot ichor of youth is still roaring in the veins. I argued, even against the wise Meekins, that the paper could still be saved, and both of us certainly shirked no blood and sweat to that end. Having no responsibility for the editorial page, I leaped from crag to crag in the news department, and kept a constant eye on composing-room and press-room. If a desk man was out of service I took over his duties for the day; if there was a rush of business in the city-room I sat in as an extra copy-reader; once, for a month running, I got out the woman's page; and whenever Meekins was off the job I lent a hand with the editorial page. It was a busy and exhilarating life, despite all the lugubrious bulletins from the front office, and I enjoyed it immensely. But all the while, I am sure, I was accumulating a conviction that executive posts were not for Henry, and formulating plans, if only unconsciously, to avoid them in the still dim future. Meekins himself, as I have said in Chapter IX, probably contributed more to that determination than either he or I realized at the time.

I recall, in point, the day when the proofs of my first real book, " George Bernard Shaw: His

Plays," came in. It was a small volume, else I could not have found the time to write it at all, but it was nevertheless a book, set up and to be published by a real publisher, and I was so enchanted that I could not resist taking the proofs to the office and showing them to Meekins — on the pretense, as I recall, of consulting him about a doubtful passage. He seemed almost as happy about it as I was. " If you live to be two hundred years old," he said, " you will never forget this day. It is one of the great days of your life, and maybe the greatest. You will write other books, but none of them will ever give you half the thrill of this one. Go to your office, lock the door, and sit down to read your proofs. Nothing going on in the office can be as important. Take the whole day off, and enjoy yourself." I naturally protested, saying that this or that had to be looked to. " Nonsense! " replied Meekins. " Let all those things take care of them-selves. I *order* you to do nothing whatsoever until you have finished with the proofs. If anything pops up I'll have it sent to *me*." So I locked my-self in as he commanded, and had a shining day indeed, and I can still remember its unparalleled glow after all these years.

On January 20, 1906, there was a mysterious confab in the business office uptown, and the next day the *Herald* announced that " at a meeting of the board of directors of the *Herald* Publishing Company the resignation of Mr. Frank F. Peard as president and general manager was received with regret." On the same day Meekins appeared on the flagstaff of the paper as president and publisher, and under his name was this:

Henry L. Mencken, *Secretary and Editor*

The details of Peard's exitus I never heard, and in fact I never inquired about them. He was always extremely polite to me, but my communion with him had early convinced me that his talents, however distinguished, did not lie in the newspaper field. He had many other irons in the fire, and at one time made a weekly trip to New York to function as secretary of a typewriter company. The only part of the paper that he showed any genuine interest in was the financial page. To embellish it he saddled us with a stock tipster who used the *nom de plume* of G. de Baldevinus — an amiable old fellow who was well liked in the office, but guessed wrong almost as often as our racing tipster. Baldevinus did all his work in the composing-room, where he used one of the stones as a desk, and in the course of an average afternoon he would receive six or eight telephone calls from Peard, who played the stock market steadily, and lost nine times out of ten.

Both Peard and Oler were naturally fertile in editorial ideas, all of them bad. Whenever Oler sent in a request that something be printed about himself or one of his friends the resultant copy was

marked " Ice," which was our ground-rules equivalent of the usual newspaper " Must." I can recall
forlorn days when the city-room copy-hook was
almost choked with " Ice " stuff. Peard's orders
were quite as numerous, and even more demoraliz-
ing. Once, at Christmas time, he let the advertising manager of a Baltimore department-store sell
him the notion that it would be fine propaganda for
the *Herald* if we could induce every trolley passenger to add a penny to his nickel fare, as a Christmas offering to the conductors. A smart reporter
was assigned to work up the idea, and he did it in
a series of stories full of sly satire that Peard swallowed without suspicion. Some of the conductors
threw the pennies in the passengers' faces, for that
was before effective fare-registers had been invented, and any conductor with his wits about him
was a man of means, for he could easily knock down
five times his wages. Others got into rows with their
motormen, who tried to muscle in on the swag —
which never, I believe, amounted to anything. We
received hundreds of letters denouncing us as
rogues and imbeciles, mainly on the ground that
giving money to the conductors would only incite
the trolley monopoly to cut their wages.

Peard was always an easy mark for press-
agents, and especially for those representing what
he regarded as prospective advertisers. It would
be unjust to blame him here, for we were desperately in need of more lineage, but his seductions

were often very embarrassing to the editorial department. More than once a good reporter, assigned to write some extravagant piece of balderdash, bucked violently and threatened to resign. Inasmuch as I always sympathized with him heartily, I was debarred from putting any pressure on him, and had to resort to cajolery. Even nonadvertisers found Peard willing and eager — for example, the Christian Scientists. That was in the days before the late Charles Scribner had given them a salutary trouncing in the matter of the E. F. Dakin book on Ma Eddy, which they tried in vain to suppress. In every American city they had a committee on publication which roved the newspaper offices, confidently demanding space for the lectures of their traveling exegetes. When they first appeared in the *Herald* office I threw them out, but they soon came back with a chit from Peard, and for a couple of years we had to make room for their nonsense. The copy-desk struck back by converting it into even worse nonsense, and by writing idiotic heads on it, so I had to watch it carefully.

But now Peard had faded out at last,[1] and Meekins was in full charge of the paper, with only Oler over him. I was secretary of the company, but so far as I can recall there was never any meeting of the board; in fact, I never heard the names of the members thereof, if any. Meekins's prin-

---

1 In his later years he made a considerable success in the insurance business in California, and died there in 1925.

cipal job was to blackjack money out of the reluctant and now terrified Oler. He was successful for
a few months, but after that Oler began to dry up,
for he had become convinced at last that his political career was under the curse of God. In the early
Spring of 1906 a number of the larger advertisers
of Baltimore, concluding that it might be good
Geschäft to keep the *Evening Herald* alive, if only
for use as a club against Grasty and his *Evening
News*, appeared with an offer to chip in enough to
meet our weekly deficits. Meekins and I added a
bottle of claret to our dinner at Joyce's that night,
but when the advertisers began to mention actual
money it appeared that the best they were willing
to do was far short of our needs, and after some
vain gabble they took to the woods. From that
time onward it was only a matter of standing the
death-watch. Finally, on June 17, we printed the
following on the editorial page:

NOTICE

Tomorrow the property of the *Herald* Publishing Company will pass into new hands, and there will be no
further publication of the *Sunday Herald,* the *Evening
Herald,* or the *Weekly Herald.*

" New hands " was something of a euphemism.
We had virtually nothing to sell, for all our mechanical equipment was mortgaged, and our morning Associated Press membership, save for the Sunday edition, had been forfeited by our switch to

the evening field. Nevertheless, the other Baltimore papers seem to have put up a nominal sum to
get rid of the wreck, for I discovered years later,
on searching the corporation records of the Baltimore *Sun*, that its share had been $3,125. The
staff, during the last year, had gradually reduced
itself, for everyone suspected what was coming,
and at the time of the final crack no one was much
perturbed, at any event in the editorial department. Nearly all the boys found new jobs without
difficulty, some in Baltimore and the rest in other
cities, and those who didn't went into other trades.
Joe Callahan, the city editor, started a weekly
paper for builders and contractors that still survives and is still prosperous, though Joe himself is
long dead.

As for me, I was, like Meekins, in apparent difficulties, for it is a newspaper maxim that when a
paper blows up the chances of its hirelings landing
new jobs run in inverse proportion to their rank.
The office-boys are at work again the next day, and
good reporters are snapped up quickly, but managing editors are out on a limb, for vacancies in
their gloomy trade come rarely and are usually
filled by promotion, and if they look for lesser posts
they encounter the same prejudice that afflicts ex-
managers in the theatre. But I was lucky, for all
three of the larger dailies of Baltimore offered me
jobs, and I took the first offer that reached me. It
came from Grasty of the *Evening News:* he wanted

me to be his news editor. But after a couple of weeks in the job I decided finally that executive work was not to my taste, and in a little while I transferred to the *Sunpaper* as Sunday editor, a more leisurely and literary job. Soon I was set to writing editorials, and after that my contributions to the various *Sunpapers* — morning, evening and Sunday — were destined to go on with only an occasional break until the early days of 1941. Since 1910, save for a brief and unhappy interlude in 1938, I have never had a newspaper job which involved the control of other men's work, or any responsibility for it.

HEATHEN

DAYS

1890-1936

H. L. MENCKEN

NOTE

Some of these chapters have appeared, either wholly or in part, in the *New Yorker*. The author offers his thanks to the editors of that magazine for permission to reprint them.

PREFACE

WHEN I finished " Happy Days " in August, 1939,
anchored to an Underwood Noiseless Portable in
the lovely Summer home of Dr. and Mrs. Frederic
M. Hanes, high up in the North Carolina mountains, it would have astonished me unfeignedly if
one of the native necromancers had dropped in
from a neighboring Alp and told me that two similar volumes would follow it. I had had a grand
time doing the book, but it seemed to me that one
dose of my *curriculum vitae* was enough for poster-
ity, and with the troubles of the teens peeping
round the corner in my memory, I was rather glad
to be shet of the subject. It soon appeared, however, that I was in the hands of higher powers, some
of them supernatural but most of them merely human. The latter were customers who began writing
in suggesting that I do a companion volume on my
early newspaper adventures, and in a little while I

v

had so far succumbed to their blarney that a couple of chapters thereof were sketched out. This was in 1940. The project occupied me off and on during the year, but in the main I worked on my " New Dictionary of Quotations," and when 1941 dawned " Newspaper Days " was still only a fragment. I thereupon decided, heroically but idiotically, to jam through both books together, and the result was that I landed in hospital in April, with the dictionary finished but " Newspaper Days " yet very far short of it. After I got out of their animalhouse the resurrection men ordered me to take a holiday, and I went to Cuba by sea — probably my last ocean trip on this earth. I spent a couple of lazy weeks in Havana and its environs, hearing some excellent music, watching (and getting converted to) the cavortings of a Russian ballet company, and putting away large quantities of the nourishing Cuban victuals. When I got back to Baltimore I had so far recovered that I had a sudden burst of energy, and was soon knocking off what remained of " Newspaper Days " at the rate of 3,000 words a day — my all-time high for sustained writing. The MS. was in the hands of the Knopfs by June 18, and on June 24 I was writing to Blanche: " I note your acceptance of ' Newspaper Days.' It is naturally gratifying to a young author."

The present volume is a kind of by-product of the burst of energy just mentioned. When I came to the end of the period marked off for " Newspaper Days," I simply could not stop, but kept on going until I had accumulated four or five redundant chapters. When wind of these reached Harold W. Ross, the alert editor of the *New Yorker*, he collared them for his instructive weekly, and urged me to go on to more. When " Newspaper Days " came out in the Autumn of 1941 there was further heat from customers, and even a few whiffs from reviewers, so the present volume gradually and inevitably took form. It covers a wider range of time than either of its predecessors, for in it I have included a couple of chapters that belong to my *Erinnerungen aus dem fröhlichen Bubenleben* but somehow failed to fit into " Happy Days," and on the other end I bring it down to 1936. But there is no continuity in it, and none was attempted. It is simply a series of random reminiscences, not always photographically precise, of a life that, on the whole, has been very busy and excessively pleasant. Like any other man I have had my disasters and my miseries, and like any other author I have suffered from recurrent depressions and despairs, but taking one year with another I have had a fine time of it in this vale of sorrow, and no call to envy any man. Indeed, I seem to have been born without any capacity for envy, and to the fact, no doubt, is due a large part of my habitual tranquility, not to say complacency. But in part that contentment of spirit is due also to a kind of caginess that has dis-

PREFACE

suaded me, at all stages of my life, from attempt-
ing enterprises clearly beyond my power. Sticking
always to what I could do with reasonable comfort,
I have escaped the pains of complete bafflement,
and thus have no motive, whether Freudian or
other, for begrudging the other fellow his competence. Indeed, I simply can't imagine competence
as anything save admirable, for it is very rare in
this world, and especially in this great Republic,
and those who have it in some measure, in any art
or craft from adultery to zoölogy, are the only human beings I can think of who will be worth the oil
it will take to fry them in Hell.

Despite my two previous miscalculations, this
third volume of my more or less accurate memories
will probably be my last, for I begin to be impressed, at sixty-two, with the cogency of the Chinese warning that " it is later than you think " ; and
if I actually do any more dredging out of the past
it will undoubtedly be in a more chastened and scientific mood. The hereditary pedant in me has
made me a diligent conservator of records, and in
the files in my cellar are enough of them to entertain a whole herd of nascent Ph.D.'s — records of
forty-three years on newspapers, of forty as a
writer of books, of twenty-five as a reviewer, of
twenty as a magazine editor. These vocations have
overlapped, but they have also intermingled, and
some of my chronicles are thus rather complicated.
When I was engaged a little while back in trying

to get some order into them, I was struck by the
thought that every man given over professionally
to hearing and seeing things ought to be allowed
two lives — one to hear and see and the other to set
down what he has heard and seen. But inasmuch as
no such thought seems to have occurred to the Cre-
ator of the species, I am doomed to an inevitable
but sorry compromise. Having now done three volumes of my recollections, I shall turn away from the
past for a while and devote myself to hearing and
seeing some more. I can only say of the present volume, as I said of its two predecessors, that it is not
sober history but yarning, and is thus devoid of
any purpose save to entertain. If it fails there it is
a flop indeed. The title, alas, comes a good deal
short of satisfying me. In its provisional or studio
form I thought of the book as " Miscellaneous
Days," for it covers a long period and shows me at
ages ranging from the agonies of nonage to the beginnings of senility. But there were objections to
" Miscellaneous Days " that need not be gone into
here, so I began concocting various other titles, all
of them bad — " Busy Days," " Gaudy Days,"
" Red-Letter Days," " Assiduous Days," and so on.
Finally, I hit on " Heathen Days," which is probably worse than any of them. The precisely right title
would be " Happy Days III," just as the precisely
right title for " Newspaper Days " was " Happy
Days II," but it is now too late to undo the mistake
I made in 1941.

PREFACE

In my efforts to keep down my errors in names, dates and other facts to a reasonable minimum I have thrown myself on the kindness of several friends with better memories than my own — especially, George Jean Nathan, my former associate in many a gay enterprise; A. H. McDannald, my companion in one that is herein described at some length; Dr. Paul de Kruif, a partner in another; and Richard J. Beamish, now a member of the Public Utility Commission of Pennsylvania, but formerly a reporter as I was, and a much better one. Most of all I owe thanks to another old colleague and friend — Edgar Ellis, librarian of the Baltimore *Sunpapers*. Mr. Ellis has not only built up a newspaper morgue of the first class; he has also learned how to find his way about in it, so that its veriest scrap of information is immediately at his hand. I called on him for help at least two dozen times while the pages following were in progress, and not once did he fail me. Without his aid, always generously given, my record would show a great many more stretchers than now adorn it.

BALTIMORE, 1942.   H. L. M.

I

DOWNFALL

OF A REVOLUTIONARY

[*1890*]

OF all the eminent characters who flourished in the
West Baltimore of my infancy, the one most venerated by the boys of my generation was Hoggie
Unglebower, an uncouth youth whose empire and
influence, radiating out from an humble stable in
the alley which ran behind our house in Hollins
street, covered altogether an area of at least half a
square mile. No storekeeper of that time and place
was better known, whether for good or for evil, nor
any cop, however heinous, nor any ma'am in the
public school up Hollins street hill, nor bad nigger
in Vincent alley, nor blind man in practice at Hollins market. Between the longitude of the market
and the wilderness of Steuart's Hill, all through
a chunk of territory four or five blocks thick, he

was a hero to every boy above the age of seven.

The reader of today, soaked in the Freudian sewage for so many years, will assume at once, I suppose, that Hoggie must have been a Lothario, and his headquarters a seraglio. Nothing could have been further from the truth. He was actually almost a Trappist in his glandular life, and his hormones never gave him any visible trouble until much later on, as I shall show in due course. In the days of his greatest glory his view of all human females was predominantly disdainful, but it never led him to use them wickedly, or even impolitely. When a hired girl issued into the alley to flag a rag-and-bone man or hunt for a lost garbage box he would whistle at her satirically and shout " Ah, there! " but at the same time he always took off his hat. To women of greater age and station he was courteous to an extreme degree, and when he visited a neighboring dwelling with his terriers to purge it of rats he always wiped his feet at the back door, and never failed to address the lady of the house as Ma'am.

No, Hoggie was not carnal in the Catechism sense, and I incline to think that that was one of the reasons all the boys so greatly respected him. The male infantry of today, debauched by Progressive Education and the sex hygiene quackery, are said to be adepts at the arts of love before they are more than half house-broken, but that was certainly not true in my time. The boys of that Mous-

terian generation, until adolescence came down
upon them, regarded girls with frank aversion, and
had as little truck with them as with cats or cops.
It is, of course, a fact that the probable delights of
amour were occasionally discussed, but it was always vaguely and with a considerable uneasiness,
for any move to put a concrete project into effect
would have involved a close approach to females,
and that was never done if it could be helped. What
made Hoggie a personage was nothing in that line;
it was mainly, and perhaps even only, his successful and notorious resistance to the doctrine that
cleanliness is next to godliness.

In his father's stable he led the life dreamed of
as ideal by all normal boys, then, now, and forever.
No one, it appeared, had any authority (at all
events any authority that he recognized) to make
him comb his hair, or brush his clothes, or shine his
shoes, or wash behind the ears. He wallowed there
day in and day out, including especially Sundays,
in such slops as every normal boy longs to own, but
is seldom permitted to have. Preferring the society
of horses and dogs to that of men, he lived among
them freely and unashamedly, sleeping with them,
eating with them, and sharing his confidences with
them. He got his hair cut when he damned well
pleased, and it wasn't often. Hating neckties, he
never wore them. When he thirsted, he drank from
the end of the stable hose, and if anyone stopped to
gape at him he squeezed the hose (which was old,

5

soft and full of holes) and sent a fine stream into the gaper's eye.

In brief, a magnificent specimen of Natural Man, somehow surviving unscathed every corruption of an effete and pusillanimous civilization. He came of a bourgeois family and had been to school, but had fought off successfully every effort to denaturize him. His days were busy, and full of enterprises that, to us boys, were important, difficult and romantic. He was the architect, builder and navigator of the largest and fastest double-decker sleds known in West Baltimore, and probably the best repairer of boys' wagons ever seen in Christendom. He knew how to knock a barrel to pieces without splitting any of the staves, and how to put it together again. He could teach tricks to horses, and had so far mastered their vocabulary of whinnies and pawings that he carried on long conversations with them, often laughing at their pawky humor. He was a dog doctor of great gifts, and kept a large stock of medicines for his patients on a shelf in the stable. To cops, despite all their clubs, handcuffs and sidearms, he presented a calm and unflickering eye, and they had a high respect for him, for when he went to the aid of one who was overwhelmed by a passel of bad niggers, the bad niggers lost consciousness almost instantly, and awoke in the watchhouse with huge bumps on their heads. Hoggie, disdaining firearms, did his fighting with clubs, and

had an arsenal of them ready to hand — little ones
for light jobs, and thick, warty shillalahs for really
earnest work. When he came down upon a skull
something gave way, and it was never Hoggie or
his weapon.

He was the best dog-trainer for miles around,
and could transfer even the sorriest mutt into a
competent ratter. For this purpose he liked to have
them young; indeed, he preferred to begin on them
as soon as their eyes were open. At that age, of
course, they were no match for actual rats, and
even the more active sort of mice had the edge on
them. To equalize the odds, Hoggie would catch
infant rats in a trap, pull their teeth with a pair
of pliers, and then throw them into a barrel with a
couple of his pupils. As the latter gained in strength
and technique, he would test them with rats of
gradually larger growth, retaining at first one
tooth each, and then two, and then four or five, and
finally a whole set, upper and lower. Now and then
a freshman was badly mauled in these exercises, but
Hoggie did not despair, for he knew that any sort
of educational process was bound to be painful, and
he preferred the hard way for dogs as for men. His
graduates were all recognized virtuosi. One day he
let me go along as he took one to a hay-and-feed
warehouse for a final examination. The candidate
was only a spindly black-and-tan, but within three
minutes by the watch he had unearthed, run down

7

and killed a whole bucket of rats, some of them of the fearsome sewer variety, with fangs two inches long.

Hoggie admired dogs, and was admired by them in turn, though his medicating of them ran to heroic measures. His usual prescription for the common run of canine malaises was the better part of half a pound of Glauber's salts. The colored quacks who practised a Dahomeyan farriery in Reveille's livery stable down the street hesitated to give so large a dose to anything short of a cart horse, but Hoggie believed that it was foolish to temporize with disease, and proved it by curing most of his patients. He was also adept at surgery, and could point to at least a dozen dogs that he had treated successfully for broken bones. He sutured the lacerations that followed dog-fights with the thick, black thread used by shoemakers, and always waxed it carefully before setting to work. He was, I believe, the first canine dentist ever in practice in Baltimore; to this day, in fact, they are rare. He pulled the damaged teeth of his patients with the same pair of pliers that he employed to prepare rats for his academy, and sometimes he had to pull very hard. I heard him say once that most dogs, like most human beings, were born with too many teeth, and that getting rid of half a dozen or so toned up their systems and improved their dispositions.

No one that I ever heard of approached him in the delicate art of trimming puppies' tails. His technique was of the whirlwind variety: the tail was off before the puppy had a chance to be alarmed. In my earliest days he had a formidable rival in old Julius, an Aframerican *mohel* with headquarters in Reveille's stable, but as the years passed he gobbled all of Julius's practice, and in the end his mastery was admitted by everyone. In that era the different breeds of dogs in vogue nearly all wore their tails clipped, so Hoggie was kept busy. I have seen him knock off six or eight of an afternoon, with the whole Hollins-street gang for a gallery. Our own dogs, from the early eighties onward to the middle nineties, all passed through his hands, and every one of them was friendly to him afterward, and wagged its stump whenever it encountered him. He also treated dogs when they took to nibbling grass in the yard or showed other signs of indisposition — always with that massive dose of Glauber's salts as a starter. He had plenty of other medicines, and used them freely on occasion, but he depended mainly on the Glauber's salts, just as Dr. Wiley, our family doctor, depended on castor oil.

Hoggie's incurable boyishness was shown by the fact that, for all his fondness for horses and dogs, he hated cats with a blind and implacable hatred, and spent a great deal of his time tracking them down and executing them. There was a time, indeed, when his chronic war upon them aroused some ill-will in the neighborhood — but not, of course, among the boys. What was done about it I forget, but for a while he locked himself in his stable, and refused to have any truck with human society. Even the cops were given to understand that their room was preferred to their company. But then a stray cat scratched a baby down the block, and under cover of the ensuing uproar Hoggie emerged from his solitude, and resumed his crusade. I well recall the day when, as a gesture of triumph, he threw eight dead cats into the alley in one lot, and got into a row with the street cleaner who had to haul them away. The street cleaner, it appeared, held that a person engaged in such wholesale slaughters should dispose of his own dead, and not dump them on public officials. He cited the example of the hotels which carted off their own garbage, and that of the candy factory down the alley which kept a wagon to handle its own boiler ashes, but Hoggie refused to allow any weight to the argument. So far as he was concerned, he said, the cats could lie in the alley until the Judgment Day, along with the rats that he heaved out almost daily — the melancholy refuse of his college for puppies. The street cleaner muttered a while longer and threatened several times to submit the whole matter to Murphy the cop, but in the end he loaded the cats upon his cart, and during the weeks that followed he loaded many others. Until a fresh generation of kittens worked its way in from Hollins market, the Union Square neighborhood was almost as bare of *Felidae* as Greenland. A few, of course, survived in houses, but

DOWNFALL OF A REVOLUTIONARY

they were kept as closely penned as canary birds.

The boys of the Hollins-street gang believed, like well-educated American boys everywhere else, that cats had nine lives, but Hoggie dissented. He admitted freely that no cat within his experience ever had so little as one life, but he insisted that his researches indicated that five was the limit. Indeed, it was only battle-scarred old Toms who went even that far: the average free-lance cat, depleted by its wandering, precarious life, was disposed of finally after being killed three or four times. One day the alley metaphysician, Old Wesley, undertook to point out a possible statistical fallacy in this doctrine. What evidence was there, he demanded, that the Toms which Hoggie killed five times had not been killed four times before by other executioners, thus making up the classical nine? This argument, rather to the astonishment of his listening admirers, floored Hoggie completely. The louder he howled against it, the more he became confused and out of temper, and in the end he was reduced to the sorry expedient of denouncing Wesley as a sassy nigger, and threatening to set the medical students on him. His failure in the debate, and above all his resort to what amounted to forensic blackmail, lowered his stock with the boys of Hollins street, but not for long. In a little while he recovered face gloriously by staging, in the privacy of his stable, a dog-fight that went down into history as the most gory ever seen in West Baltimore.

11

Despite his unhappy encounter with Old Wesley, he was commonly on good terms with the colored people who lived in the alley, and exercised a general jurisdiction over them, milder and more understanding than that of the cops. They had a high respect for him, and went to him in their troubles, though in his practice as dog-doctor and cat-and-rat exterminator he was uncomfortably close to a medical student. He did not hold himself out as skilled at human medicine, but the bottles he kept for dosing dogs were at the disposal of any blackamoor who wanted to try them, and many professed to be benefited. In particular, the liniment he used on dogs run over by carts was said to be very efficacious against rheumatoid afflictions in *Anthropoidea*. Once he scared off all his Aframerican patients by stuffing a dead cat with oats, and using black shoe-buttons for its eyes. This gruesome object, while it remained on exhibition, kept all the colored people out of his stable, though we white boys thought it was very nobby. It didn't last long, for the huge, ferocious rats of Hollins market quickly heard of it, and one night they rushed the stable and devoured it, eyes and all. All that remained of it the next morning was a carriage-bolt that Hoggie had employed to counteract the flaccidity of the oats.

His downfall I can place with reasonable accuracy in the year 1890, when I was ten years old and he must have been about twenty-two or three. One afternoon in Summer, on my way to Reveille's livery stable to visit my father's horse, John, who was laid up with epizootic, I encountered Hoggie at the corner of Baltimore street in such vestments that I stopped dead in my tracks, and gaped at him as if he had been a cop in motley or a two-headed boy. He had on a brand-new suit of store clothes, golden brown in color, and wore a pair of the immense yellow shoes then in fashion — as wide, almost, as a street-car at the ball of the foot, but stretched out to a long point at the toe. On his head was a cart-wheel straw hat with a brim at least six inches deep, and a gorgeous red-and-white ribbon. His collar, which was of fresh celluloid, rose above a boiled shirt that gleamed like snow on the Alps, and around it he wore a bright green four-in-hand tie, with the ends tucked over to expose a stud that glittered like a diamond, but was no doubt something else. He was shaved so closely that his neck and chin were criss-crossed with red gashes, and the rest of his face was a brilliant vermilion. Finally, and most amazing of all, his hair — at least such of it as I could see below his hat — was cropped to its roots according to the best technique of Barber Lehnert. As I passed him, I caught a gust of Jockey Club scent, familiar to me as the special favorite of our current hired girl. I was so astounded that I passed him without greeting him, staring foolishly. He paid no attention to me, but stalked along painfully, like a man in a barrel. I spread the news over

the neighborhood, and Hoggie's secret quickly
leaked out.

He had succumbed at last, after all his years of
outlawry, to one of the most conventional of human
weaknesses: he had fallen in love. The ancient psy-
chosis that had floored and made a mock of Marc
Antony, Dante and Goethe — but *not* Shakespeare, Napoleon Bonaparte or George Washington — had now fetched him too. Some inconsiderable and probably pie-faced slip of a girl, name
unknown, had collared him, tamed him, and made
of him the dreadful popinjay that I had seen. The
rest of the pathetic story follows classical lines, and
is soon told. Hoggie disappeared from his stable,
and was reported to be occupying a bedroom in the
Unglebower family home, and actually eating at
table. In a little while he vanished altogether, and
reports came in that he was married to the lady, living in far Northwest Baltimore, and at work as a
horse-car driver. That was the last I ever heard of
him.

II

MEMOIRS OF THE

STABLE

[1891]

HORSES, taking one with another, are supposed to
be the stupidest creatures (forgetting, of course,
horse-lovers) within the confines of our Christian
civilization, but there are naturally some exceptions, and they probably include the whole race of
Shetland ponies. During the interminable epoch
stretching from my eleventh year to my fourteenth
I was on confidential terms with such a pony, and
came to have a very high opinion of his sagacity. As
the phrase ran in those days, he was as sharp as a
trap, and also excessively immoral. The last word,
I should say at once, I do not use in the Puritan or
Freudian sense, for Frank was a gelding; what I
seek to convey is simply the idea that he was also a
cheat, a rogue and a scoundrel. Nearly all his wak-

15

ing hours were given over to deceiving and afflicting my brother Charlie and me. He bit us, he kicked us, he stepped on our toes, he crowded us against the walls of his stall, and he sneezed in our faces, and in the intervals he tried to alarm us by running away, or by playing sick or dead. Nevertheless, we loved him, and mixed with our affection there was a great deal of sincere admiration.

Where he was bred we never heard, and, boy-like, did not inquire. One day in the Autumn of 1891 a couple of carpenters appeared in Hollins street and began to throw up a miniature stable at the end of the long backyard, and by the time they got the roof on Frank was in it, along with a yellow go-cart, a tabloid buggy with fringe around its top, a couple of sets of harness, and a saddle. It soon turned out that there was not room enough in the stable for both the go-cart and the buggy, so the buggy was moved to Reveille's livery-stable two blocks away, where my father's horse John was in residence. Simultaneously, a colored intern was brought in from the same place to instruct Charlie and me in the principles of his art, for we were told that we were to have the honor of caring for Frank. Inasmuch as we had been hanging about stables since infancy, watching the blackamoors at their work, this hint that we needed tutelage rather affronted us, but we were so delighted by the privilege of becoming hostlers — the dream of every American boy in that horsy age — that we let it pass, and

only too soon we learned that there was a great deal
more to servicing a Shetland pony than could be
picked up by watching blackamoors service full-
grown horses.

Charlie, I believe, got the first kick, but I got the
first bite. It was delivered with sly suddenness on
the second morning after the intern from Reveille's
had graduated me *cum laude* and gone back to his
regular job. He had cautioned me that, in currying any sort of horse it was necessary to pay particular heed to the belly, for it tended to pick up
contamination from the stall litter, and he had
added the warning that the belly was a sensitive
area, and must be tackled gently. I was gentle
enough, goodness knows, but Frank, as I was soon
to learn, objected to any sort of currying whatsoever, top or bottom, and so, when I stooped down to
reach under his hull — he was only nine hands high
at the withers — he fetched me a good nip in the
seat of my pants. My reaction was that of a coiled
spring of high tension, and it was thus hardly more
than a split second before I was out in the yard,
rubbing my backside with both hands. When I tell
you that Frank laughed you will, of course, set me
down a nature-faker; all the same, I tell you that
Frank laughed. I could see him through the window
above his feed-trough, and there were all the in-
dubitable signs — the head thrown back, the mouth
open, the lips retracted, the teeth shining, the tears
running down both cheeks. I could even hear a

17

sound like a chuckle. Thereafter I never consciously exposed my caboose to him, but time and again he caught me unawares, and once he gave me a nip so severe that the scar remains to this day. Whenever I get to hospital — which is only too often in these later years — the sportive young doctors enter it upon their chart as a war wound.

Frank quickly developed a really marvelous technic of escape. He had a box-stall that, considering his size, was roomy, and Charlie and I kept it so clean that the hostlers from all the other stables in the alley would drop in to admire it. There was a frame of soft red clay to ease his forefeet, and a large piece of rock-salt to entertain him on lazy afternoons. He got hearty meals of substantial horse-victuals three times a day, and in cold weather the water used to mix his mill-feed was always warm. Through the window above his trough he could look out into the yard, and a section of it about twenty feet square was fenced off to give him a paddock. In this paddock he was free to disport a couple of hours every day, save only when there was snow on the ground. But when he was in it he devoted most of his time to hanging his head over the paling-fence, lusting for the regions beyond. Just out of his reach was a peach tree, and beyond it a pear tree, both still young and tender. One fine Spring day, with both trees burgeoning, he somehow cracked the puzzle of the catch on the paddock gate, and by the time he was discovered he

had eaten all the bark off the peach tree, from the
ground to a height of four feet. Charlie and I
found it hard to blame him, for we liked the peach
gum ourselves and often chewed it, flies and all, but
my mother wept when the tree died, and the paddock gate was outfitted with an iron bar and two
chains.

Frank never got through it again — that is, by
his own effort. But one day, when a feeble-minded
hired girl left it open, he was in the yard instantly
and made a killing that still lives in the family tradition. Rather curiously, he did not molest the pear
tree, but by the time he was chased back to his own
ground he had devoured a bed of petunias, all my
mother's best dahlias, the better part of a grape
vine, and the whole of my father's mint patch. I
have been told by eminent horse-lovers that horses
never touch mint, but I am here dealing, not with
a horse, but with a Shetland pony. Frank gradually acquired many other strange appetites — for
example, for ice cream. Every time it was on tap
in the house he would smell it and begin to stamp
and whinny, and in the end it became the custom to
give him whatever happened to be left. Once, when
the hired girl got salt into it and the whole batch
was spoiled, he devoured all of it — probably a gallon and a half — and then drank two buckets of
water. He also ate oranges (skin and all), bananas
(spitting out the skin), grapes, asparagus and
sauerkraut. One day Charlie tried him with a slab

19

of rat-trap cheese, but he refused it. Another day Charlie gave him a piece of plug tobacco wrapped in a cabbage leaf, but again without success. This last trick, in fact, offended him and he sought revenge at once. When he bit through the cabbage into the tobacco he gave a sudden and violent cough, and the plug hit Charlie in the eye.

When we were in the country in Summer Frank had my father's horse John for a stable-mate, and they got on together well enough, though it was plain to see that Frank regarded John as an idiot. This was a reasonable judgment, for John, who was a trotter, was actually very backward mentally, and could be easily scared. Whenever the two were in pasture together Frank would alarm John by bearing down upon him at a gallop, as if about to leap over him. This would set John to running away, and Frank would pursue him all over the pasture, whinnying and laughing. John himself could no more laugh than he could read and write. He was a tall, slim sorrel with a long, narrow head, and was so stupid that he even showed no pride in his speed, which was considerable. Life to him was a gloomy business, and he was often in the hands of horse-doctors. If there was a stone on the road he always picked it up, and when we were in the country and Charlie and I had charge of him we never bedded him down for the night without investigating his frogs. In the course of an average Summer we recovered at least twenty nails from them, not to mention burrs and splinters. Like most valetudinarians he lived to a great age. After my father's death we sold him to an animal show that had Winter quarters in Baltimore, and he spent his last years as a sort of companion to a herd of trained zebras. The zebras, I heard, had a lot of fun with him.

One night, an hour or so after midnight, there was a dreadful kicking and grunting in our stable in the country, and my father and Charlie and I turned out to inquire into it. We found John standing in the middle of his box-stall in a pitiable state of mind, his coat ruffled and his eyes staring. Frank, next door, was apparently sleeping soundly. We examined John from head to foot, but could find nothing wrong, so we contented ourselves with giving him a couple of random doses from his enormous armamentarium of medicine bottles, and talking to him in soothing tones. He seemed quite all right in the morning, and my father drove him to and from town, but that night there was another hullabaloo in the stable, and we had to turn out again. On the day following John was put to grass and Charlie and I went for a colored horse-doctor in Cross Keys, a nearby village. He advised us to throw away all of John's medicines, and prescribed instead a mild course of condition powders, with a handful of flaxseed once a day. This was begun instantly, but that night the same dreadful noises came from the stable, and again the night follow-

ing, and again the night after that, and so on for a
week. Two or three other horse-doctors were called
in during that time, but they were all baffled, and
John took to looking seedy and even mangy. Meanwhile, my father began to suffer seriously from the
interruptions to his sleep, and talked wildly of having the poor horse shot and his carcass sent to a
glue-factory. Also, he began to discover unpleasant
weaknesses in his old friend Herman Ellis, from
whom John had been bought. Ellis, hitherto, had
been held up to Charlie and me as a model, but now
it appeared that he drank too much, kept two sets
of books, was a Methodist, and ought to be expelled
from the Freemasons.

Charlie and I, talking the business over at length,
came to the conclusion eventually that there must
be more to it than met the eye, and so decided to
keep watch at the stable. There was already floating through our minds, I think, some suspicion of
Frank, for we were at pains to prevent him learning what we were up to. At our bedtime we sneaked
into the carriage-house on tiptoe, and there made
ourselves bunks in the family dayton-wagon. We
were soon sound asleep, but at the usual time we
were aroused by a great clomping and banging in
the stalls adjoining, and turned out to take a
stealthy look. It was a moonlight night, and enough
of the gentle glare was filtering into the stable to
give us an excellent view. What we saw scarcely
surprised us. All the uproar, we discovered, was

being made by Frank, not by John. Frank was having a whale of a time flinging his heels against the sides of his stall. The noise plainly delighted him, and he was laughing gaily. Presently poor John, waking in alarm, leaped to his feet and began to tremble. At this Frank gave a couple of final clouts, and then lay down calmly and went to sleep — or, at all events, appeared to. But John, trying with his limp mind to make out what was afoot, kept on trembling, and was, in fact, still half scared to death when we announced our presence and tried to comfort him.

My father had arrived by this time, his slippers flapping, his suspenders hanging loose and blood in his eye, and we soon made him understand what had happened. His only comment was " Well, I'll be durned! " repeated twenty or thirty times. We soon had a bridle on Frank, with a strap rigged from it to his left hind leg, and if he tried any more kicking that night he knocked himself down, which was certainly no more than he deserved. But we heard no more noise, nor was there any the next night, or the next, or the next. After a week we removed the strap, and then sat up again to see what would happen. But nothing happened, for Frank had learned his lesson. At some time or other while the strap was on, I suppose, he had tried a kick — and gone head over heels in his stall. He was, as I have said, a smart fellow, and there was never any need to teach him the same thing twice. Thereafter, until the end of the Summer, he let poor John sleep in peace. My father fired all the horse-doctors, white and black, and threw out all their remedies. John recovered quickly, and a little while later did a mile on the Pimlico road in 2.17½ — not a bad record, for he was pulling a steel-tired buggy with my father and me in it, and the road was far from level.

In that same stable, the next Summer, Frank indulged himself in a jape which came near costing him his life. To recount it I must describe briefly the lay-out of the place. He inhabited a box-stall with a low wall, and in that wall was a door fastened by a movable wooden cleat. He was in the habit of hanging his head over the door, and drooling lubriciously, while Charlie and I were preparing his feed. This feed came down from the hayloft through a chute that emptied into a large wooden trough, and he often saw us start the feed by pulling out a paddle in the chute. One night either Charlie or I neglected to fasten the door of his stall, and he was presently at large. To his bright mind, of course, the paddle was easy. Out it came, and down poured an avalanche of oats — a bushel, two bushels, and so on to eight or ten. It filled the trough and spilled over to the floor, but Frank was still young and full of ambition, and he buckled down to eat it all.

When Charlie and I found him in the morning he was swelled to the diameter of a wash-tub, his eyes were leaden, and his tongue was hanging out dismally, peppered with oats that he had failed to get down. " The staggers! " exclaimed Charlie, who had become, by that time, an eager but bad amateur horse-doctor. " He is about to bust! There is only one cure. We must run him until it works off." So we squeezed poor Frank between the shafts of the go-cart. leaped in, gave him the whip, and were off. Twice, getting down our hilly road to the pike, he sank to his fore-knees, but both times we got him up, and thereafter, for three hours, we flogged him on. It was a laborious and painful business, and for once in his life Frank failed to laugh at his own joke. Instead, he heaved and panted as if every next breath were to be his last. We could hear his liver and lights rumbling as we forced him on. We were so full of sympathy for him that we quite forgot his burglary, but Charlie insisted that we had to be relentless, and so we were. It was nearing noon when we got back to the stable, and decided to call it a day. Frank drank a bucket of water, stumbled into his stall, and fell headlong in the straw. We let him lie there all afternoon, and all of the night following, and for three days thereafter we kept him on a strict diet of condition powders and Glauber's salt.

The bloating that disfigured him, when it began to go down at last, did not stop at normalcy, but continued until he was as thin as a dying mule, and that thinness persisted for weeks. There came with it, perhaps not unnaturally, a marked distaste for oats. His old voluptuous delight in them was simply gone. He would eat them if nothing else offered, but he never really enjoyed them again. For a year, at least, we might have made him free of a feed-trough full of them without tempting him. What John thought of the episode we could never find out. My guess is that he was too dumb to make anything of it.

III

ADVENTURES OF A

Y.M.C.A. LAD

[1894]

WHEN I reach the shades at last it will no doubt astonish Satan to discover, on thumbing my *dossier*, that I was once a member of the Y.M.C.A. Yet a fact is a fact. What is more remarkable, I was not recruited by a missionary to the heathen, but joined at the suggestion of my father, who enjoyed and deserved the name of an infidel. I was then a little beyond fourteen years old, and a new neighborhood branch of the Y, housed in a nobby pressed-brick building, had just been opened in West Baltimore, only a few blocks from our home in Hollins street. The whole upper floor was given over to a gymnasium, and it was this bait, I gathered, that fetched my father, for I was already a bookworm and beginning to be a bit round-shouldered, and he often exhorted me to throw back my shoulders and stick out my chest.

Apparently he was convinced that exercise on the wooden horse and flying rings would cure my scholarly stoop, and make a kind of grenadier of me. If so, he was in error, for I remain more or less Bible-backed to this day, and am often mistaken for a Talmudist. All that the Y.M.C.A.'s horse and rings really accomplished was to fill me with an ineradicable distaste, not only for Christian endeavor in all its forms, but also for every variety of callisthenics, so that I still begrudge the trifling exertion needed to climb in and out of a bathtub, and hate all sports as rabidly as a person who likes sports hates common sense. If I had my way no man guilty of golf would be eligible to any office of trust or profit under the United States, and all female athletes would be shipped to the white-slave corrals of the Argentine.

Indeed, I disliked that gymnasium so earnestly that I never got beyond its baby-class, which was devoted to teaching freshmen how to hang their clothes in the lockers, get into their work-suits, and run round the track. I was in those days a fast runner and could do the 100 yards, with a fair wind, in something better than fourteen seconds, but how anyone could run on a quadrangular track with sides no more than fifty feet long was quite beyond me. The first time I tried it I slipped and slid at all four corners, and the second time I came down with a thump that somehow contrived to skin both my shins. The man in charge of the establishment — the boys all called him Professor — thereupon put me to the punching-bag, but at my fourth or fifth wallop it struck back, and I was floored again. After that I tried all the other insane apparatus in the place, including the horizontal bars, but I always got into trouble very quickly, and never made enough progress to hurt myself seriously, which might have been some comfort, at least on the psychological side. There were other boys who fell from the highest trapezes, and had to be sent home in hacks, and yet others who broke their arms or legs and were heroic figures about the building for months afterward, but the best I ever managed was a bloody nose, and that was caused, not by my own enterprise, but by another boy falling on me from somewhere near the roof. If he had landed six inches farther inshore he might have fractured my skull or broken my neck, but all he achieved was to scrape my nose. It hurt a-plenty, I can tell you, and it hurt still worse when the Professor doused it with arnica, and splashed a couple of drops into each of my eyes.

Looking back over the years, I see that that ghastly gymnasium, if I had continued to frequent it, might have given me an inferiority complex, and bred me up a foe of privilege. I was saved, fortunately, by a congenital complacency that has been a godsend to me, more than once, in other and graver situations. Within a few weeks I was classifying all the boys in the place in the inverse order of their diligence and prowess, and that classification, as I have intimated, I adhere to at the present moment. The youngsters who could leap from bar to bar without slipping and were facile on the trapeze I equated with simians of the genus *Hylobates*, and convinced myself that I was surprised when they showed a capacity for articulate speech. As for the weight-lifters, chinners, somersaulters, leapers and other such virtuosi of striated muscle, I dismissed them as *Anthropoidea* far inferior, in all situations calling for taste or judgment, to schoolteachers or mules.

I should add that my low view of these prizemen was unaccompanied by personal venom; on the contrary, I got on with them very well, and even had a kind of liking for some of them — that is, in their private capacities. Very few, I discovered, were professing Christians, though the Y.M.C.A., in those days even more than now, was a furnace of Protestant divinity. They swore when they stubbed their toes, and the older of them entertained us youngsters in the locker-room with their adventures in amour. The chief free-and-easy trysting-place in West Baltimore, at the time, was a Baptist church specializing in what was called " young people's work." It put on gaudy entertainments, predominantly secular in character, on Sunday nights, and scores of the poor working girls of the section dropped in to help with the singing and lasso beaux. I gathered from the locker-room talk that some of those beaux demanded dreadful prices for their consent to the lassoing. Whether this boasting was true or not I did not know, for I never attended the Sabbath evening orgies myself, but at all events it showed that those who did so were of an antinomian tendency, and far from ideal Y.M.C.A. fodder. When the secretaries came to the gymnasium to drum up customers for prayer-meetings downstairs the Lotharios always sounded razzberries and cleared out.

On one point all hands were agreed, and that was on the point that the Professor was what, in those days, was called a pain in the neck. When he mounted a bench and yelled " Fellows! " my own blood always ran cold, and his subsequent remarks gave me a touch of homicidal mania. Not until many years afterward, when a certain eminent politician in Washington took to radio crooning, did I ever hear a more offensive voice. There were tones in it like the sound of molasses dripping from a barrel. It was not at all effeminate, but simply saccharine. Had I been older in worldly wisdom it would have suggested to me a suburban curate gargling over the carcass of a usurer who had just left the parish its richest and stupidest widow. As I was, an innocent boy, I could only compare it to the official chirping of a Sunday-school superintendent. What the Professor had to say was usually sensible enough, and I don't recall him ever mentioning either Heaven or Hell; it was simply his tone and manner that offended me. He is now dead, I take it, for many years, and I only hope that he has had good luck *post mortem*, but while he lived his harangues to his students gave me a great deal of unnecessary pain, and definitely slanted my mind against the Y.M.C.A. Even when, many years later, I discovered as a newspaper correspondent that the Berlin outpost thereof, under the name of the *christliche Verein junger Männer*, was so enlightened that it served beer in its lamissary, I declined to change my attitude.

But I was driven out of the Y.M.C.A. at last, not by the Professor nor even by his pupils in the odoriferous gymnasium — what a foul smell, indeed, a gymnasium has! how it suggests a mixture of Salvation Army, elephant house, and county jail! — but by a young member who, so far as I observed, never entered the Professor's domain at all. He was a pimply, officious fellow of seventeen or eighteen, and to me, of course, he seemed virtually a grown man. The scene of his operations was the reading-room, whither I often resorted in self-defense when the Professor let go with " Fellows! " and began one of his hortations. It was quiet there, and though most of the literature on tap was pietistic I enjoyed going through it, for my long interest in the sacred sciences had already begun. One evening, while engaged upon a pamphlet detailing devices

for catching boys and girls who knocked down part
of their Sunday-school money, I became aware of
the pimply one, and presently saw him go to a book-
case and select a book. Dropping into a chair, he
turned its pages feverishly, and presently he found
what he seemed to be looking for, and cleared his
throat to attract attention. The four or five of us
at the long table all looked up.

" See here, fellows," he began — again that
ghastly " fellows! " — " let me have your ears for
just a moment. Here is a book " — holding it up
— " that is worth all the other books ever written
by mortal man. There is nothing like it on earth except the One Book that our Heavenly Father Himself gave us. It is pure gold, pure meat. There is
not a wasted word in it. Every syllable is a perfect
gem. For example, listen to this — "

What it was he read I don't recall precisely, but
I remember that it was some thumping and appalling platitude or other — something on the order of
" Honesty is the best policy," " A guilty conscience
needs no accuser," or " It is never too late to mend."
I guessed at first that he was trying to be ironical,
but it quickly appeared that he was quite serious,
and before his audience managed to escape he had
read forty or fifty such specimens of otiose rubbish, and following nearly every one of them he indulged himself in a little homily, pointing up its
loveliness and rubbing in its lesson. The poor ass,
it appeared, was actually enchanted, and wanted

to spread his joy. It was easy to recognize in him the anti-social animus of a born evangelist, but there was also something else — a kind of voluptuous delight in the shabby and preposterous, a perverted aestheticism like that of a latter-day movie or radio fan, a wild will to roll in and snuffle balderdash as a cat rolls in and snuffles catnip. I was, as I have said, less than fifteen years old, but I had already got an overdose of such blah in the McGuffey Readers and penmanship copybooks of the time, so I withdrew as quickly as possible, unhappily aware that even the Professor was easier to take than this jitney Dwight L. Moody. I got home all tuckered out, and told my father (who was sitting up reading for the tenth or twentieth time a newspaper account of the hanging of two labor leaders) that the Y.M.C.A. fell a good deal short of what it was cracked up to be.

He bade me go back the next evening and try again, and I did so in filial duty. Indeed, I did so a dozen or more nights running, omitting Sundays, when the place was given over to spiritual exercises exclusively. But each and every night that imbecile was in the reading-room, and each and every night he read from that revolting book to all within ear-shot. I gathered gradually that it was having a great run in devotional circles, and was, in fact, a sort of moral best-seller. The author, it appeared, was a Methodist bishop, and a great hand at inculcating righteousness. He not only knew by heart all the immemorial platitudes, stretching back to the days of Gog and Magog; he had also invented many more or less new ones, and it was these novelties that especially aroused the enthusiasm of his disciple. I wish I could recall some of them, but my memory has always had a humane faculty for obliterating the intolerable, and so I can't. But you may take my word for it that nothing in the subsequent writings of Dr. Orison Swett Marden or Dr. Frank Crane was worse.

In a little while my deliverance was at hand, for though my father had shown only irritation when I described to him the pulpit manner of the Professor, he was immediately sympathetic when I told him about the bishop's book, and the papuliferous exegete's laboring of it. " You had better quit," he said, " before you hit him with a spittoon, or go crazy. There ought to be a law against such roosters." *Rooster* was then his counter-word, and might signify anything from the most high-toned and elegant Shriner, bank cashier or bartender to the most scurvy and abandoned Socialist. This time he used it in its most opprobrious sense, and so my career in the Y.M.C.A. came to an end. I carried away from it, not only an indelible distrust of every sort of athlete, but also a loathing of Methodist bishops, and it was many years afterward before I could bring myself to admit any such right rev. father in God to my friendship. I have since learned that some of them are very pleasant and amusing fellows, despite their professional enmity to the human race, but the one who wrote that book was certainly nothing of the sort. If, at his decease, he escaped Hell, then moral theology is as full of false alarms as secular law.

IV

THE

EDUCATIONAL PROCESS

[1896]

WHY my father sent me to the Baltimore Polytechnic I have never been able to make out, though from time to time I have fetched up various more or less colorable theories — and seen them go to pot when confronted with the known facts. I had, as a boy, the usual boyish interest in making things, but I soon discovered that I had no talent for it, and so my interest gradually died down. My mother was full of stories of my striking incapacity for the constructive chores of the household; indeed, she depicted me as only a little less incompetent than my father, who could not mount a ladder without falling off or drive a nail without mashing his thumb. One Summer, when we were at our country

place, she gave me the job of making a table for a
storeroom and I fell to work reluctantly but violently, using a pile of old joists and flooring as materials. When the thing was done it was so massive
and clumsy that I could not move it into the corner
where it was to stand, and the hired girl had to be
called in to help. It stood in that corner until the
house was sold after my father's death, and I heard
later from the buyer that he had a dreadful time
getting rid of it. Since it would not go through either of the doors of the room, it had to be knocked
to pieces on the spot, and this turned out to be a
laborious job, for I had put it together with fifty-
penny iron nails running fourteen to the pound,
and had not been stingy with them. These nails
had rusted, and the only way to get them out was
to split the wood, which was anything but easy, for
the joists were of yellow pine of irregular grain and
very knotty. By the time the buyer poured this tale
into my ear I had passed through the Polytechnic
and held its diploma, but if I had been put to making another such table I'd have made it just as
badly, for I don't recall learning anything of a mechanical nature while I was a student. I enjoyed
some of the shop work, especially the wood-turning
and blacksmithing, but that was mainly because it
was a rather hazardous kind of play; it left no
more sediment of profit in my mind than the
prayers the president of the school used to let go
in the assembly-room every morning.

My actual interests, in those days, lay far from tools and machinery. I was fascinated, on the one hand, by the art of writing and on the other by the science of chemistry, and both obsessions had been set going by Christmas presents — the first by that of a printing-press and the second by that of a camera. The two fought it out in my psyche all the while I was in the Polytechnic, and it was only in my last year that the writing insanity won. My first effort to write for publication was a sort of compromise between them, for it took the form of a report on a platinum solution that I had devised for toning silver prints. This was during the Summer of 1894, when I was still less than fourteen years old. Writing won in the end largely if not principally because the brethren who expounded *literae humaniores* at the Polytechnic were both enthusiasts, whereas the brother who taught chemistry knew very little about it and appeared to have only mild interest in it. Of the former, there were two, and both of them, by the ordinary academic standards of the time, were bad teachers. Moreover, they failed as moral exemplars, for one chewed tobacco incessantly and the other often showed up in class of a morning with bleary eyes and a breath like a sailor home from the sea. But they had in common an ardent and almost pious delight in good writing, and in their catch-as-catch-can way they managed somehow to convey it to such of the boys as were susceptible to such infections. Neither taught composition *qua* composition, but they knew where the best models of it were to be found, and I recall brilliantly over all these years what delights shot through me when one of them set me to reading the *Spectator* and the other introduced me to Thackeray. No other gogues in the place matched them in fanning my private fires, so I got more out of them than from all the rest, and what I got was better lasting. Between them they converted me into one of the most assiduous customers that the Enoch Pratt Free Library in Baltimore has had in its whole history. There were Winters when I visited it almost every week-day, and before I began to be fetched by the literary movement of the nineties I had read at least half of the classical English répertoire.

But I don't want to say that the other gogues at the Polytechnic were all hams, for some of them were clearly not, especially two teachers of mathematics, a subject in which I had little interest. To one of these obscure Bernoullis I owe a massive debt, and it is a pleasant privilege to acknowledge it gratefully after fifty years. He was a man named Uhrbrock, an eccentric bachelor of unknown provenance and training, and his learning in his chosen art probably went but little beyond the algebra that he taught. But he had the great merit of believing in all seriousness that algebra was a discipline of stupendous importance to civilization, and in consequence he imparted it with a degree of zeal amounting almost to frenzy. When I proceeded to the Polytechnic from F. Knapp's Institute in 1892, I was quite innocent of it, for old Professor Knapp had different ideas, and the idiot gogues who sorted out incoming boys thus put me in the lowest class. In all other respects I was ready to enter the next higher class, but the idiots stuck to the letter of their rules. In some way or other Uhrbrock heard of this, and at once offered to tutor me privately — that is, if I were willing to stay an hour after school every day until he judged that I knew enough to be promoted. I was willing, and he fell on me in his most furious manner. For a few days my head swam, but after that I began to take in algebra by the eye, the ear and the pores of my skin, and by the middle of the second week I knew everything that the boys were supposed to learn that first year. Uhrbrock thereupon took me before the committee of idiots, demanded that I be examined, stood by menacingly while they questioned me, and terrorized them into passing me with a mark of 100. The next day I was promoted, and ever since that time, down to the present glorious day, I have been a year ahead of schedule on my progress through life. I say this because, on age alone, I really belonged in the lowest class. But Professor Knapp and his goons had done such a good job of teaching me all the branches save algebra that I had almost accumulated the extra year, and it needed only Uhrbrock's philanthropy to give it to me.

I call it philanthropy advisedly, though in general philanthropy seems to me to be a purely imaginary quantity, like demi-virginity or one glass of beer. Even here, I suppose, I am forgetting the lust to teach — a passion apparently analogous to concupiscence or dipsomania, and, in the more extreme varieties of pedagogues, maybe quite as strong. I daresay that Uhrbrock was full of it, but I must point out in fairness that his yielding to it went a good deal further than has ever been usual in his order. If he merely lusted to teach he might have worked out his libido within the ordinary patterns of the place; as it was, he stepped outside them, and put himself to purely gratuitous trouble. If I had to stay after school every day, in hot September weather, then so did he. Moreover, his willingness to do this for a perfect stranger certainly had some sort of altruism in it, at least to the extent that you will find altruism in the operations of the F.B.I. or the Boy Scouts. He had never seen or heard of me before, and in fact had to ask my name ten or twenty times before he remembered it. Nor was I the bright and shining sort of youngster who may be expected to attract adult notice and favor; on the contrary, I was more unprepossessing than otherwise, with a bulging cranium, round shoulders, bow legs, and very little show of the prancing masculine gorgeousness that developed later. Thus I was very grateful to Uhrbrock for what he did for me, and shall go on thinking of it as philanthropy. In the years following, I should add in candor, he made some efforts to cash in on it. I was by that time the city editor of a newspaper in Baltimore, and he was involved in a row with his superiors — a row that went on for a long, long while. Whenever it rose to special venom he would visit me at my office and try to induce me to print his diatribes against his opponents. Inasmuch as those diatribes had but slight support in any facts known to me and many of them were packed with libel *per se*, I had to put him off, but I was always very polite to him, and whenever the chance offered to give him a little sneaking aid I seized it. In the end his enemies got him and he was drummed out of the public school system, and soon afterward he died.

He was a competent teacher, and rammed the mysteries of algebra into his boys with great success. Some of them actually became so proficient that they could solve the problems he set to them without any sort of cheating. His colleagues of the mathematical faculty were generally less proficient, and it was therefore the custom of the school to use cribs against them. One of these colleagues, an old fellow who had been a pedagogue for many years, and showed all the traditional stigmata of the craft — a pasty complexion, chalky fingers, and a preference for white neckties and black alpaca coats — eventually gave great delight to his pupils by going crazy. His infirmity crept upon him slowly, and in its earlier stages all that was noticed was that he was more crabbed than usual. When a boy went to the blackboard to solve a problem in geometry or trigonometry he would fall upon the poor fellow like a cat playing a mouse, and try to rattle him with frequent cries of " Nonsense! ", always pronounced with the two syllables equally stressed. Nine times out of ten the boy had a copy of the solution in his hand, lifted from the textbook, and had simply transferred it to the board, but the old man nevertheless found plenty to object to. In the end he began to question and deride the book itself, and it dawned upon the boys that he had gone *mashuggah*. Proof positive followed almost instantly, for he took to felicitating and whooping up the occasional boys who were too stupid to use the book solutions, or maybe even too honest. In a little while some smartie tried him out with a solution so fantastically imbecile that the dullest boys laughed at it. When he praised it as a masterpiece everyone knew for sure that his mind had happily given way, and thereafter all of his students were magnificently at ease in his classroom. My own class, which visited him twice a week, had a rollicking time. The more fatuous the solution offered, the better he liked it, so we gave him what he wanted, and got high marks day after day. Now and then, to test the progress of his malady, we put up controls armed with cribs from the textbook. Each and every time he drove them from the blackboard with yells of "Nonsense!" and we thus established the fact that he was not recovering. The boys of all his classes naturally kept his lunacy to themselves, and it was weeks before any of the other gogues noticed it. The poor old fellow was then relieved of his duties, and his successor gave us a really savage working out. At the end of that year more than half the boys in my class were plucked in mathematics, but the administration let them go on the ground that we had all suffered through no fault of our own. No boy, of course, was conscious of any actual suffering.

This unhappy gogue was a pretty good teacher in his days of normalcy, though not as good as Uhrbrock. Most of the other members of the faculty, with the shining exception of the two who professed English literature, ranged downward from indifferent to unspeakable. The great sciences of anatomy and physiology, naturally extremely interesting to adolescent boys, were in charge of a superannuated homeopath armed with a textbook in which all the abdomen south of the umbilicus was represented by a smooth and quite uneventful surface, exactly like the figleaf section of a female acrobat's pink tights. The homeopath, who must have gone through some sort of medical college in his time, was apparently convinced that he could never arouse any interest in his subject with such reticent materials, for he made no effort whatsoever to teach it. Instead, he devoted his lecture periods to ram-

bling harangues on all sorts of non-anatomical subjects, and every boy knew that all who listened with
any show of attention would get high passing marks
at the end of the year. His principal business was
really not teaching at all, but the coopering of boys
injured in the shops. This happened very frequently, and he seldom got through one of his harangues without having to stop to sew up a cut or
pull out a splinter. His assembled students always
watched these manipulations with fascination, and
some of them, called on for occasional help, became
skillful operating-room orderlies. It was not often
that a boy was hurt seriously, but once it happened
in my presence. The victim was a handsome young
fellow who was so well liked that he had been made
president of my class. Like all the rest of us, he had
been warned against the extreme dangers of using a
power plane to dress thin pieces of wood, but one
day he chose to disregard them, his piece of wood
gave way, the fingers of his right hand were sucked
into the revolving blades, and he lost every finger
save the thumb. I was standing not six feet away
from him, and the bloody spectacle shocked me
even more than it did the victim, who bore it very
bravely. We did not take him to the homeopath, but
rushed him to the City Hospital, which was separated from the Polytechnic only by an alley. There
the surgical interns stopped the hemorrhage and
sewed up the stumps, but his fingers were gone forever — a cruel calamity to an ambitious youngster.

One of the boys retrieved them from the pile of shavings under the plane, and brought them to the hospital, hoping that they could be sewed on, but the interns said that in the then state of surgery it could not be done.

There was a medical school attached to the hospital, and its students loafed and skylarked in the alley separating them from the Polytechnic. We were on friendly terms with them, and they entertained us by showing off their horrors. Also, they were of assistance to us in our wars with unpopular teachers. After we had bombarded one such unfortunate with all the classical weapons, including live rats and hydrogen sulphide, the medical students gave us an ear from an Aframerican cadaver, and we stuffed it into his inkwell. But this *attentat*, despite its boldness and ingenuity, was a failure, for the gogue, a very stupid fellow, fished the ear out of his ink and dropped it into his wastebasket without a word, and we spent the next week trying to figure out whether he had really recognized it for what it was. There was a faction that proposed to give him another and surer shock by getting a whole Aframerican head from the medical students and propping it up on his desk, but the students refused to supply it. The disappearance of an ear, they said, would pass unnoticed, but if they made off with a head there would be an inquiry and maybe a good deal of unpleasantness. Some years after this it was discovered that the *Diener* in the dissecting-room

of the college had been carrying on for years a
brisk trade in entire cadavers. He filched them from
the morgue in the basement, crammed them into
barrels, and shipped them to fly-by-night medical
colleges in the West. By the time he was taken I
was already out of the Polytechnic and working as
a newspaper reporter, and it fell to me to cover the
story of his arrest, trial and jugging.

The shop-work at the Polytechnic, as I have said,
interested me very little, save for that in the wood-
turning and blacksmith shops. For some reason or
other I got pleasure out of making the puerile gim-
cracks that were the chief product of the former,
and there was always the stimulating possibility
that one of the pointed tools we used would dig into
the wood — we called it catching a crab — and
make a kind of explosion. Such accidents always
brought the gogue in charge of the shop at a run,
and he would stop all work and deliver himself of
a long monitory lecture. He was an old fellow in a
skullcap that made him look like a rabbi and his lectures were heavy going. We took his warnings
lightly, but once I saw a block of maple, caught in
a crab, fly from the lathe with such force that when
it hit the guilty boy in the forehead he went out like
a pug caught in the jaw. By the time he revived
and we took him to the homeopath he had a bump
on his forehead as big as an egg. Another time, in
the same shop, a power-operated bandsaw broke,
and the boy using it was wound up in the blade. His

injuries, however, consisted only of a few minor cuts, and the homeopath soon had him patched up and on his way home. I liked the blacksmith shop because it was full of sparks and noise, and also, I suppose, because it was dirty. In it, after four or five months of hard struggle, I made a small iron hook that I still use as a paperweight. In it I also received the only injury I suffered in four years at the Polytechnic. It was, naturally enough, a burn, and I got it by picking up a piece of iron that looked cold to the eye but was actually still very hot. Having got hold of it, I couldn't let go, and in consequence my hand was burned badly enough to give me three or four days' holiday. I often worked in the chemical laboratory after school hours, but was never hurt there, though I had several narrow escapes. One day a boy working next to me filled a test-tube with nitric acid, plugged it with a cork, and proceeded in all innocence to heat it over a Bunsen burner. When it went off I managed to duck the murderous spatter, but the boy responsible got a big splash down one of his bare arms, and before I could douse him with an alkali a sizable groove was burned into his flesh.

It was the custom at the school for the boys of the senior class to make an ambitious piece of machinery, and my class undertook a 100-horsepower triple-expansion marine engine. The plans came from the Naval Academy at Annapolis and the castings were made outside, but we did all the ma-

chining. I say we, but my own share was confined
to finishing the crosshead brasses, for my talents
were too modest for me to be entrusted with anything more vital. I worked on those brasses all year,
and ruined two or three sets of castings before I
produced a finished set that fit. The best machinist
in my class, a really competent fellow, got the
lordly job of boring the cylinders, and was a hero
in consequence. He and the instructor, who knew
his subject as few other teachers in the place knew
theirs, spent a lot of time counselling and helping
me, but my congenital incapacity for mechanical
operations kept me in the baby class. My diligence,
however, got its reward, for at the end of the year,
though I must have been a headache to him, the instructor gave me a good mark.

The president of the Polytechnic, in those remote days, was a retired naval lieutenant — a tall,
slim, elegant fellow wearing the mustache and
goatee of Admiral Winfield Scott Schley, then a
common make-up among naval officers. He was supposed to teach us the higher arcana of steam engineering, but he was so bad a teacher that we had
to get whatever we actually learned of the subject
from the instructor in the machine-shop. I well recall my difficulties in trying to puzzle out the mysteries of an indicator diagram — a sort of chart
showing the performance of a steam-engine. After
listening to the lieutenant for a month or two I
gave it up as hopeless, but a little while later the

machine-shop instructor made it plain to me in ten minutes. I forgot it, of course, within twenty-four hours after the Polytechnic's diploma was in my hands, as I forgot virtually everything else that I had, at least in theory, learned there. At the present moment I am probably as far from a mechanical genius as it is possible for the free white American to get, and still maintain any degree of public veneration. A gasoline engine is as completely mysterious to me as the way of a serpent upon a rock, and when a fuse blows out in my house and I have to replace it the job takes me the better part of an hour.

The naval lieutenant had the easy ways of a sailor and was very popular with the boys. When they started an insurrection in the room of some numskull gogue he would let them roar on for five or ten minutes before coming in to put it down. Such events were commonly followed by mass trials, with himself as judge, but he seldom found anyone guilty and when he did so his punishments were so trivial as to be almost rewards. He had, like any other man of service on the high seas, an eye for female pulchritude, and was known to receive visits from the fair in his office after school hours. Inasmuch as the boys who observed this always reported that his visitors were beauties on the order of the loveliest actresses portrayed on the cigarette-cards of the time, the news only increased his popularity. But not with the gogues who were his subordinates. They were, in the main, creatures so unattractive

to either sex that it would be impossible to imagine even Lydia Pinkham calling on them, so they
viewed his gallantries with bilious eyes, and in the
end one of them laid charges against him with
the school board. Those charges, as reported in the
newspapers, were rather vague, but it was easy to
gather that they accused the old boy of levantine
carnalities. By the time they came out I had left the
Polytechnic, but I was interested enough to inquire
how the surviving boys had taken the business, and
got an answer that pleased me greatly. The day
after the outcry, as the lieutenant entered the assembly-room to lead in morning prayers, the whole
student body rose as one boy and launched into
such a riot of cheers that the cop on the beat came
rushing in. A little later, apparently fearing that
the names of definite ladies might be brought into
the case, he resigned without standing trial, and on
his departure got another deafening round of huzzahs. He was succeeded by another naval lieutenant, and this one, after a while, was also beset by
the school wowsers. They charged him with resorting to the jug during school hours, and he demanded and received a public trial. Acquitted
triumphantly, he got a reception from the boys almost but not quite equalling the deafening approbation of his predecessor. The latter remains to this
day the greatest hero the Baltimore Polytechnic
has ever produced. The boys, I am told, still cheer
him at football games, though they were not born

at the time of his troubles, and many of them are the sons of men who were not then born.

If I had encountered a good teacher of chemistry at the Polytechnic, it is very probable that I'd be a chemist at this moment, with a swell job on the staff of the du Ponts and maybe a couple of new synthetic rubbers or super-cellophanes to my credit. My chief interest was always in organic chemistry, but the best that was offered by the gogue aforesaid was a childish high-school course in inorganic analysis, so I began, in a kind of despair, to work off my steam in literary endeavor. My early compositions, of course, were mainly in verse, for poetry is much easier to write than prose. During my last year in school I turned out many a fair set of dithyrambs, most of them in imitation of Rudyard Kipling, who had become my adoration, and the rest in the old French forms that were favored by the literary movement of the nineties. I recall that at one time, probably during my last year at the Polytechnic, I resolved solemnly to write at least one poem a day, and that I kept it up for several weeks. But it was more than a year after my graduation before anything of mine ever got into print. During my school days I nursed a flaming ambition to be admitted to the staff of the school paper, but I kept it to myself, and was never asked to join by the politicoes who bossed such things. As a sort of final blast at the gogues the boys of my class concocted a satirical musical comedy, but though I wrote a couple of lyrics for it I had no hand in the prose scurrilities which made it a great success, and at the one performance I was told off to play the piano. Some of the more tender gogues were so outraged by the sneers at them that they talked boldly of holding up several diplomas, but the old lieutenant with the stable of lovely sweeties was still president, and he put down his heavy quarter-deck foot upon the project.

I made a pretty good scholastic record during my four years at the Polytechnic, despite my lack of interest in most of the subjects it presumed to teach. In the literary branches I really shined, and I found mathematics easy, though I disliked it. At the end of my term of servitude there was a general examination for the purpose of awarding a gold medal offered by the Alumni Association to the master scholar of the whole herd. This award was made on the basis of the examination alone, and classroom marks were not taken into account. The first day was devoted to English, and I was passed at the head of my class. The next day there was an examination in something else that happened to be easy for me, and I passed first again. When I got home with this news my father went into a state of mystical exaltation, and then stepped out of it with an offer to give me $100 in cash if I remained in first place at the end of the examinations. This seemed a hard order, for there were subjects ahead — for example, electricity — of which I knew precisely nothing, but a hundred dollars, in those days, was a fabulous fortune to a boy, and I resolved to make the attempt. My experience with Uhrbrock, four years before, had taught me something, to wit, that with hard application a subject that engaged a class a whole year could be wolfed in a few days. Favored by the fact that there was a free day between adjoining examinations, I gave it over to relentless boning up on the subject just ahead, and the result was, to make a long and painful story short, that I passed all the examinations and came out at the head of my class; indeed, I came out with a general average that has not been surpassed at the Polytechnic, so far as I know, to this day. Fortune, of course, gave me a good deal of assistance, for I was born lucky. When I came, for example, to the examination in electricity I discovered to my enchantment that the twelve questions on the paper all covered ground that I had traversed the night before, my nose in the book and the midnight oil burning. In consequence, my answers were perfect, and the amazed and disgusted gogue in charge of the examination had to give me a mark of 100. In addition to the alumni medal there was a special medal for the ranking scholar in electricity — and I had won it!

But giving it to me was something else again. The poor gogue, justifiably horrified, came out the next day with an announcement that monthly marks would be taken into account in awarding the medal, which would hand it over to a boy who really knew something about the subject. This seemed to me to be reasonable and fair, and I was glad to see him get it, but my father professed to be outraged and talked wildly of going into court for an injunction against the school board. It took me some time to argue him out of this, but in the end he calmed down, and when I brought him the news that I was to be allowed to make a speech at the commencement he forgot the matter. That speech must have been a dreadful thing, indeed, for I was still very young in those days, and had not yet acquired my present facility for rabble-rousing. But my father listened to it very politely, and he and his agents applauded it loudly when it was over. I was myself too elevated to be conscious of its badness, for his check for $100 was in the inside pocket of my tailcoat. It was not until I was approaching twenty-five that I ever earned $100 in one lump again.

V

FINALE

TO THE ROGUE'S MARCH

[1900]

WHEN I was disgorged by the Polytechnic I went to work in my father's cigar factory, theoretically to learn the tobacco business, but *Geschäft* was not to my taste, and when my father died in 1899 I quit at once and got myself a job as a cub reporter on the old Baltimore *Morning Herald*, now extinct and almost forgotten. At the start, of course, I was not entrusted with news stories of any importance, but simply served as a leg man for my elders and betters. One of the first big stories I thus helped to cover was the hanging of four blackamoors at the Baltimore City Jail. It was worth, by the standards of the time, two or three columns of space, so the reporter assigned to it was a fellow of some esteem in the office, despite an unhappy weakness for drink.

57

As for me, I had no responsibility beyond getting
the correct spelling of the attending ecclesiastics'
names, taking down the last words (if any) of the
condemned, and inquiring into the undertaking arrangements. But that programme was quickly
blown up by the fact of my senior's addiction to the
so-called hand-set whiskey of the Baltimore printers, which kept him sound asleep in the warden's office all the while the hanging was going on, got him
fired when we returned to our own office, and set me
to writing the story. The taste of the period, in all
such branches of composition, was for prose so colorful as to be virtually purple, and I must have laid
on my pigments with a shovel, for the city editor
gave me a very kind look when the proofs came
down, and I had first call on every similar assignment afterward.

I found the work light and instructive, and there
was plenty of it to do, for a movement was afoot in
my native Maryland at the time to " hang out," as
the phrase went, the whole criminal population of
the state, at all events in the higher brackets. The
notion that murderers, rapists and other such
fiends in human form were simply unfortunates suffering from mental croups and catarrhs, and that
the sensible way to deal with them was to send them
to luxurious sanatoria, and there ply them with
nourishing victuals, moral suasion and personality
tests — that notion was still hidden in the womb of
the future. The prevailing therapy was a great deal

harsher: in fact, it came down from the rough-and-
ready days of Leviticus and Deuteronomy, and its
only recent improvements had been developed during the California gold rush. It consisted, in brief,
in pursuing the erring with cops, posses and bloodhounds, putting them on trial before hanging
judges, and then dispatching them as promptly as
possible. As a young reporter I observed and recorded all branches of this *régimen,* and enjoyed
them all. But I enjoyed especially the terminal
part, for my lifelong interest in theology was already well developed, and it gave me a great kick
to hobnob and palaver with the divines who comforted the doomed.

These divines, of course, were mainly Aframericans, for the great majority of culprits hanged
below the Mason and Dixon Line were of that great
race, but though it is usually thought of down there
as somewhat backward I never saw any sign of professional incompetence in its pastors. On the contrary, they were almost invariably smart and
snappy fellows, well grounded in the Sacred Scriptures and the masters of an adroit and effective
homiletic technic. The job they had on their hands,
in the normal case, was certainly no easy one. What
they had to do was to convince a blackamoor taken
red-handed in some brutal and deliberate atrocity,
usually freely admitted, that he would nevertheless
get a free pardon for it post-mortem, and in fact
become an angel in Heaven, white in color and of

the highest repute, within ten minutes of his exitus from this earth. There were, to be sure, parts of this that needed no arguing, for they were not disputed. Every colored brother in the death-house, like every colored person of his class outside, believed in Heaven and Hell, looked forward to a drum-head trial for his sins after death, and had an unshakable faith that, in case of acquittal, he would be turned into a Caucasian angel. But that was only the half of it, and what remained must have been a great deal harder to inculcate, for it collided with everything that the candidate had been taught by other clergymen his whole life long. One and all they had concentrated on the pains and penalties of Hell, and had warned him *appassionata* and *con amore* that he would be inevitably fried in its fires if he did not curb his evil propensities. But now, having yielded the last measure of devotion to those propensities, he was asked to believe that he would escape Hell altogether, and even meet with what amounted to special handling in Heaven.

It seeemd irrational, surely, and not a few of the colored boys wrestled with it dismally for weeks and months. If things would actually be so facile and comfortable beyond the grave, then why all the horrible talk about the boiling sulphur and steaming geysers of Hell? And if Hell was a myth, then why ever be good at all, even in intent? Such were the questions the death-house divines had to answer,

and how they answered them I can't tell you with
any definiteness, though I often listened to their
explanations for hours. They must have been experts at suggestion and virtuosi at untangling complexes, though both suggestion and complexes were
unheard of at the time. All I can say is that, when
the job was done at last, the client still retained his
full faith in Hell, along with the utmost confidence
in its system of justice, and yet was completely
convinced that he would escape its fires. In his
terminal days, in fact, he usually gloated openly
over his approaching apotheosis, and not infrequently showed a certain smugness. Let the sheriff
do his damndest: he might hang a poor coon, but
out of that coon, like a butterfly from a caterpil-
lar, would emerge a celestial creature with large,
snowy wings and a complexion to match that of
any white lady in the land, however rich and beautiful.

Such ideas naturally take away the sting of
death, and it was not uncommon for the postulants
to go to the gallows as jauntily as if they were going to a barber shop. I saw some who actually
pranced — that is, to the extent that it was possible in their long black gowns, and with their arms
tied behind them. When they had anything to say
in their last minutes, which was usually, it was always of an extremely optimistic nature, and whenever they mentioned individuals by name — say the
sheriff, the warden, the pastor, or a guard of the

death-watch — it was in terms of praise. I recall
one — it was on the Eastern Shore of Maryland —
who devoted most of his farewell remarks to whooping up the jail cook, for the whole time since his
trial had been eased by fried chicken and hominy
cakes three times a day. Another even had a kind
word for the Governor who had refused to reprieve
him, and expressed regret that his approaching
translation would make it impossible for him to
vote at the coming election, in which the Governor
would be running for a second term. But mostly, of
course, they talked of themselves, for the glories
that awaited them naturally engrossed them. I have
never heard more eloquent descriptions of the geography, social life and public improvements of
Heaven than some of those that were thus loosed by
uneducated but not untutored Aframericans upon
audiences of newspaper reporters, professional
jurymen, country constables and courthouse loafers.

There was, however, one exception to the general
rule I have set forth, and him I encountered in the
city jail of Baltimore — an ancient granite structure in the feudal style of architecture, with crenel-
lated battlements along the tops of its walls, and
accommodation in its death-house, in those days,
for a dozen head of condemned. It was a gloomy
place, God knows, and not all the colored theologians of Baltimore, working in eight-hour shifts
for weeks on end, could lift its darkness for the un-

happy blackamoor I speak of. For he had been, in his time, a preacher himself, and though he had later turned apostate and was now awaiting hanging for murdering a whole family, he still retained his old talent for the sacred sciences, and especially for theological disputation. Thus he sassed back when the death-house clergy began to operate on him, and in a little while he had them completely flabbergasted. Unhappily, his success against them was his undoing, for he retained, like any other sane colored man, his full belief in Hell, and the more he proved that their talk of his becoming an angel was hooey, the more he convinced himself (and them) that he was headed for the brimstone. This naturally upset him considerably, and as the day of his departure approached he became more and more alarmed. On the morning thereof he was in a really appalling state. All he had to do, if he wanted to see a swarm of devils with their pitchforks, was to shut his eyes. Even his appetite left him, and he actually refused the magnificent breakfast that was brought to him. He was to be hanged, if the sheriff was not diverted by some other duty, at 10 a.m., and by 9.45 he was making such heavy weather of it that the jail doctor, a very humane man, decided to give him a shot of morphine.

I was present when this shot went into his arm, and noted the dose — three grains. Inasmuch as a quarter of a grain is ordinarily enough to quiet a patient, and two grains enough to quiet him for-

ever, it was apparent that the doctor was taking
no chances. He watched with satisfaction, and I
watched with him, the rapidly gathering effects of
the drug. First the candidate ceased to moan and
bellow, then his speech became thick, then his eyes
began to roll, then he sat down on his bed, and then
he looked at us blankly, apparently not recogniz-
ing us. The minutes, meanwhile, were ticking on,
and the doctor himself grew uneasy. In fifteen more
of them his patient would be blotto, and hanging
him might present serious technical difficulties.
Where was the sheriff? Why the delay? Just then
a deputy came galloping from the warden's office
with the news that the sheriff was on the telephone
— an arduous business in those days — , trying to
track down a rumor that the Governor had decided to grant the condemned a five-days' reprieve.

The doctor lost no time. He was in the warden's
office in ten seconds, and back with the sheriff in
half a minute. "Either you hang this coon at
once," he roared, " or he'll die in your face! He has
got enough morphine aboard to knock off an archbishop. Look at him! He doesn't know whether he
is here or in Indianapolis, Indiana. In an hour he'll
be dead. Get a hump on! Get a hump on! You were
supposed to hang him at ten o'clock, and it's now
ten six. Do you want to go to jail for contempt of
court? Get a hump on! Get a hump on! "

The sheriff, in a panic, got it on instanter, and
in two minutes the condemned was being half led

and half carried down the corridor, his eyes rolling more and more and his head beginning to roll too. There was some difficulty about getting him up the steps of the scaffold, but a dozen jail guards leaped forward to help, and at ten o'clock, sixteen minutes and twenty seconds a.m. he went through the trap. His eyes were closed in his last moments and his knees were buckling, but not from fear. He had forgotten all about the Christian Heaven and Hell, and was neck-deep in the poppy Paradise of the Chinese.

After a colored undertaker had made off with the remains the sheriff finally got the Governor's office by telephone, and learned that the report of a reprieve had been a canard. The next day, encountering the jail doctor in a saloon, I asked him what he would have done if it had turned out to be true.

" I'd have made out a death-certificate," he replied calmly, blowing the foam off a schooner, " saying that he died of fright."

" But," I persisted, " you couldn't have signed it. You know the law: it provides that there must be a coroner's inquest after every death in jail, and that the coroner must sign the death-certificate."

" As for that," he replied, still calm, " the coroner and I have an understanding. We always co-operate professionally."

NOTES

ON PALAEOZOIC PUBLICISTS

[1902]

IT is the fashion today, in newspaper circles, to sniff at press-agents, and even to spit at them: in the *Editor and Publisher*, the trade journal of the daily press, they are treated as if they were lepers, or even infidels. That was certainly not my own feeling about them in the days when I had most to do with them, *circa* 1902. I had by then become what was called the dramatic editor of the *Morning Herald* in Baltimore, and one of my jobs was to receive the press-agents who traveled ahead of itinerant theatrical troupes, whooping up the genius of their stars. Nine-tenths of these brethren seemed to me to be very pleasant fellows, and some of them were so smart that they afterward made considerable splashes in the world, whether inside the bounds

of the theatre or out — for example, Eugene Walter, Channing Pollock, the Wilstach brothers,
Charles Emerson Cook, Bayard Veiller and Herbert Bayard Swope. Nearly all had been newspaper
men in their time, and good ones. I cannot say that
I was very generous about giving them space; on
the contrary, I held them down to short commons,
and often spoiled the little matter I printed by adding clownish glosses to it; nevertheless, I got on
with them very well, and made some friendships
among them that endure to this day.

In that remote era some of the primeval press-
agents of the post-Civil War period still survived,
and still wore the long-tailed coats, loud waistcoats
and plug hats that had then gone with their art and
mystery. The first agent who ever called on me,
in fact, was of that already archaic company. He
was at least sixty years old, and looked to me to be
a hundred. His talk was all about Lotta, Maggie
Mitchell, Charlotte Cushman, Mary Anderson and
other such old-timers, though he was actually working for a young female star who, according to his
story, had but lately escaped from a convent in
Mauch Chunk, Pa. All his purple prose about her
was done with a lead-pencil on large sheets of ruled
yellow paper, for he regarded the typewriter as
effeminate. Another elderly visitor who made a
great impression on me was a splendid creature of
the name of Marcus B. Mayer. He had been an
opera manager in his day, and had carried over into

press-agentry the uniform of that calling — a fur overcoat, a white waistcoat elegantly embroidered, and a gold-headed walking stick. What star he represented I forget, but I remember that he offered me no handout at all, but unloaded his encomiums of him (or her) *viva voce*, and left me to write my own advance notice. In it I limited the star to a few lines, and devoted the rest of my space to Marcus himself. The local theatre manager protested against this, but Marcus was rather pleased, and sent me a signed photograph of himself in token of the fact.

Of a different type was Punch Wheeler, who had come into the theatre from the circus, and affected the make-up of a Mississippi river gambler of 1875 or thereabout — a loud checked suit, a yellow waistcoat embroidered with roses, and a red satin cravat run through a diamond ring. A little while before this time Punch had been a manager on his own account, operating a fly-by-night opera company in what is now called the Drought Bowl. The star thereof was a Baltimorean named Jerome Sykes, who was later to become a favorite on Broadway. (His best rôle there was that of Foxy Quiller in the musical comedy of the same name: I can still hear his sonorous reading of its tag-line: " ' Aha,' said Foxy Quiller, with a crafty leer ! ") When the company started out from New York for the Western steppes there was not enough money in the till to hire a chorus, so Punch had a dozen sightly kickers

painted on the back-drop. Anon and anon he would
duck ahead of the troupe to arrange its bookings,
and in every town he would let the local Frohman
name the opera to be played. If the Frohman said
" Carmen " or " Il Trovatore " or " The Chimes
of Normandy " he would bill the town accordingly,
for he had picked up a stock of miscellaneous lithographs in Cincinnati, and was his own billsticker as
well as his own advance agent. But no matter what
opera was billed, Jerome and his four or five associates, when they got to the town, would sing " The
Mascot," for that was the only opera all of them
knew.

The audiences out in the sticks seldom protested,
for most of them were hearing their first opera, and
the brisk, voluptuous tunes of " The Mascot " were
very ingratiating. Nor did they object to the fact
that the chorus was painted on the scenery, for
they assumed that such was the custom in opera.
Jerome had a loud voice, and made enough noise
to give solid support to the female singers, who
shrieked their damndest. The company thus did
very well in the cow country, and Punch accumulated so much money that on one or two occasions
he actually paid salaries. But when, having got to
El Paso, he decided to dip over the Rio Grande into
Mexico, he and his poor troupers came suddenly
and dramatically to grief, for there was a law in
Mexico in those days, passed to fetch phony one-
ring circuses, making it a criminal offense to ad-

vertise an attraction and then not give it. Punch
found out about it when Jerome and the company
began to warble " The Mascot," for the Frohman
at Juarez had asked for " Carmen," and that is
what Punch had billed. In the middle of the first
act the Mexican cops closed in, the audience (which
knew every note of " Carmen ") demanded its
money back, and Punch, Jerome and the others
were locked up in an adobe jug full of scorpions.
Jerome, who knew " Carmen," got out the next day
by singing the whole score, including the overture,
the choruses, and even the soprano and contralto
solos, to the chief of police, and a little while later
the chief also turned loose the other singers, as innocent victims of the wicked Punch, but it took
Punch himself a week or more to beat the rap, and
cost him not only all his cash in hand, but also the
costumes and scenery of the company, including
the back-drop with the chorus painted on it.

I enjoyed his visit to Baltimore immensely, and
gave him a good deal more space than his attraction — an " Uncle Tom " company working its way
back to New York from the Deep South — was
worth. There was nothing intellectual about him,
but he was a very amusing fellow, with an endless
saga of adventures in the cause of art. When I
asked him, on getting acquainted with him, why he
continued to wear his fire-alarm make-up, he said
that he had got so used to it that he felt almost
naked in ordinary clothes. Sometimes, when he hit

a town where he wasn't known, the cops would take him for a three-card monte operator, and set a watch on him. Whenever he noticed a couple of dicks trailing him, he would lead them to the main street of the town, pull out a Bible, and begin preaching salvation to the passersby. He was not, of course, in earnest, but he told me that this satirical whooping of the gospel often made converts, and that he figured he had saved at least two hundred head of rubes from Hell. Once he actually converted one of the dicks tailing him. Another time, somewhere in Tennessee, a committee waited on him to offer him the pastorate of a new Baptist church. He got out of it by saying that he was under a vow to wear his checked coat and embroidered vest all the rest of his life, which wouldn't do, of course, for an ecclesiastic, even in Tennessee.

The undisputed king of theatrical press-agents, in my time, was A. Toxen Worm, a Dane of circular cross-section, immense appetite, and low humor. He usually dined alone, mainly because it was impossible to find anyone who could keep up with his eating, or even watch it without swooning. One Sunday evening, happening to be in Philadelphia, I encountered him in the main dining-room of the Bellevue-Stratford just as he was finishing dinner. In those days a dinner-check running beyond $2 was almost unheard of in America, but I noticed that Toxen's was for $6.70. Moreover, it included no charges for drinks, for, as he told me, his kidneys were acting badly, and he was transiently on the wagon. His last course, as I could see by the debris, was a gigantic ice-cream sculpture covered with spun sugar, of the kind served at wedding breakfasts. Three waiters hung about him, panting. It was one of his quiet Sunday evenings.

But if eating was his principal business in life, practical joking was his recreation, and in his time he pulled off some masterpieces. In his own view, so he once told me, he reached his all-time high in a joke at the expense of an English theatrical manager named Hubert Something-or-other. Hubert was a pleasant fellow, but not too bright: in appearance and manner he came close to realizing what was then the average American's notion of a London clubman. He wore cutaway coats, high Piccadilly collars and pants with bold stripes, and from his neck hung a monocle on a wide black ribbon. His mind leaned toward the literal side, and its operations tended to be deliberate. He was married for a time to a well-known American actress, and accompanied her on the road as her company manager. One night, while she was playing at the Academy of Music in Baltimore, I met him in the lobby, and he began telling me an interminable anecdote about some friend of his — a man he described as one of nature's noblemen. But despite his admiration for the fellow, and their intimacy, he could not recall his name. Finally, he appealed to me for help. " You *must* have met him," he said. " Everybody knows him. He was Miss ——'s second husband, the one just before me."

One day Toxen met him in St. Louis, and found him in a low state of mind. He was homesick, it appeared, for London, and especially for its tranquil society. He tired of the wild boozing of America, and longed for the quiet stimulation of afternoon tea. " Don't worry any more," said Toxen. " I can fix it. How would you like to have tea tomorrow afternoon with a lovely lady and her five beautiful daughters — just the two of us — no mob? " Hubert thought it would be perfect, and the next day he arrayed himself in his best cutaway, bought a gardenia for his buttonhole, and, with Toxen steering, took a hack for the house. It turned out to be a fine old mansion in a quiet side street — somewhat decayed outwardly, to be sure, but very ornate inside. The parlor furniture was massive gilt, and there was a thick red carpet on the floor. Hubert liked his hostess instantly, and was delighted by her five daughters, all of whom seemed, rather curiously, to be of an age. Soon tea was served, and Hubert stood up to drink it, his cup and saucer in hand. The prettiest of the five daughters was in front of him, and he turned upon her his best tea-party chit-chat. She professed to be charmed, and moved closer and closer to him. Finally, she was so close that he took an involuntary step backward — and collided with the stern of her Mamma. " See here, you goddam son-of-a-bitch," roared Mamma, "what in hell do you think this is — a whore house?"

In telling the story, Toxen used to say that Hubert dropped cup and saucer, leaped into the hall, grabbed his hat and stick, and ran all the way back to the hotel. Toxen said that he had had to give the madame and the girls $20 for their entertainment, but declared that it would have been cheap at twice the price. Hubert, of course, said nothing, and after a while skeptics began to allege that Toxen had invented the whole story — that nothing of the sort had ever happened. In order to lay this doubt he reenacted the show in Philadelphia, with a couple of witnesses invited. The witnesses swore that Hubert actually fell for it all over, and in a large way. This time the madame not only bawled him out, but also cracked a saucer over his head, and the girls ganged on him with loud screams, and gave him the bum's rush.

Toxen indulged himself in many other such jocosities as he traveled the country ahead of theatrical troupes, and as time passed, and his technic improved, they tended to become more and more cruel. Once, in Louisville, he tipped the cops that a fellow agent named Charlie Connolly was an absconding bank cashier from Seattle, and Charlie spent a couple of days in a very uncomfortable jail. Another time he hired a loose girl in Buffalo to swear out a warrant against the most respectable agent on the road, alleging seduction under promise of marriage, though everyone knew that the accused was completely innocent. He did a heavy trade in bogus telegrams, most of them of an alarming character. The Frohman brothers, Charles and Daniel, had a brother named Gus who often went on the road for them, and Toxen sent them frequent messages announcing that Gus was locked up for jumping a board bill, or had married a chorus girl, or broken his leg, or committed suicide. His schemes often showed a macabre flavor. He would call up the cops, and tell them that there had been a murder in some theatre, or he would recruit pallbearers for a man who was still alive, or he would spread the story that a fellow agent had been rushed to hospital with smallpox or delirium tremens.

All this went on for years, and there was naturally a considerable accumulation of soreness. In the end the boys combined against Toxen, and resolved to give him a massive dose out of his own bottle. The scene was Denver, and he fell quite easily, for one of his weaknesses was vanity. Thus, when the manager of a local theatre told him in confidence that a rich widow of the town, observing him in the lobby, had got mashed on him he saw nothing impossible in it, and when a note arrived the next day, inviting him to call on her, he not only accepted, but began to throw out hints about a conquest. It was quickly arranged that he should wait upon her at her swell apartment on the top floor of Denver's newest and most elegant apartment-house, and he presented himself at the time fixed wearing his best party clothes, elegantly shaved and perfumed, and carrying a bouquet of orchids. When he rang the bell it was opened by a swarthy maid of gigantic size, and he was invited to enter. The instant he did so one of the boys, previously concealed in the hallway, rushed up and locked the door on him.

Toxen remained in that apartment for three days and three nights. It consisted of one small room, a bath and a kitchenette. The maid was an Indian of a mental age of six or seven years and knew only that she was to keep him from escaping, and dole out to him an occasional ham sandwich. There was no fire-escape, and the telephone wires had been cut. During the long watches of the night Toxen slept on the floor, and the maid snored in the kitchen. By day he spent his time trying to devise some means of escape, but he never managed it, for he was afraid to yell for help and the maid grabbed him and threw him every time he tried to pick the lock of the door. As a practical joke it was almost as successful as his own masterpieces, but as a lesson to him it was a complete failure. Two days after the boys liberated him he was busy once more with his bogus telegrams and his phony tips to the cops.

VII

THE TONE ART

[*1903*]

WHEN it was discovered by the music critic of the *Morning Herald*, a little while after I went to work as a cub reporter, that I could play the piano from the printed music and knew how many sharps were in the key of C major, he began borrowing me from the city editor to cover his third-, fourth- and fifth-string concerts, for he was not only a lazy dog but also had a sensitive ear, and it pained him to have to listen to the false notes so often struck at such affairs. As for me, I did not mind them, for my own playing, like Beethoven's, was pretty inaccurate, and my general taste in music was still somewhat low. I got no extra pay for this service, and indeed no allowance of time: all my regular work had to be done before I could go to a concert, and as a result I often arrived late, and heard only the terminal or Cheyne-Stokes tumults of the performers. But when a Summer opera company was in town, or

Sousa's band, or anything else of that loud and
hearty order, I usually managed to get, as the
phrase then went, a larger load of it, even at the expense of missing two-thirds of a colored murder, or
the whole of a Democratic ward. meeting. During
my first Summer I thus heard the whole répertoire
of bad opera from " Cavalleria Rusticana " to
" The Chimes of Normandy," not once but three or
four times, and in the intervals of this caterwauling
I dropped in now and again on half a dozen Italian
bands.

These bands were then at the height of their popularity in the United States, and every trolley park
had one. They all put on substantially the same
programme every night, beginning with one of the
more deafening Rossini overtures and ending invariably with " The Star-Spangled Banner," played
a couple of tones above the usual key of B flat to
show off the trumpets, for the Spanish-American
War was only a few years in the past, and patriotism was still bubbling in the national heart. There
were two great set pieces that were never missed:
indeed, the audiences of the day would have set
down an Italian band leader as a fraud if he failed
to play them. One was the sextette from " Lucia di
Lammermoor," done with all the trumpets and
trombones lined up on the apron of the platform,
and the other was the anvil chorus from " Il Trovatore," with a row of real anvils in the same place,
and a series of electric wires so arranged that big

blue sparks were struck off as the gentlemen of the percussion section clouted the anvils with real hammers. For this last effect, of course, the lights were always turned out. It had been invented years before, so I learned long afterward, by the celebrated Patrick Sarsfield Gilmore, the greatest of all American bandmasters, but by the turn of the century he was dead and forgotten, and the wops who worked his masterpiece all claimed credit for it.

They were, in fact, assiduous copy-cats, and whenever one of them hit on anything really new the rest imitated it at once. As a result it was hard to tell one Italian band from another. They not only played the same programme every night; they also wore the same florid uniforms, and their leaders all exhibited the same frantic gestures and the same barbaric hair-cuts. Any leader who, on coming to the coda of a Rossini overture, with its forty or fifty measures of tonic and dominant chords, did not throw his arms about like a maniac and contrive to make his back hair (it was always long and coal black) flap up and down like a loose hatch in a storm, would have seemed extremely strange. As a matter of record, no such leader was known to musical zoölogists — that is, not until I invented one myself.

This was in 1903 or thereabout, after I had been promoted to the office of dramatic editor. In that rôle, as I have said, I was in charge of all advance notices of musical and theatrical shows, and spent a part of every day receiving press-agents. One day a member of the corps dropped in to introduce, according to the custom then prevailing, a band leader who had just come to town, and the leader informed me, as usual, that he had written a Baltimore *Morning Herald* march and proposed to dedicate it to me as a tribute to my national and even international celebrity as a friend of sound music. This, of course, was an old gag, and it made no impression on me. Every Italian leader had a portfolio of dog's-eared marches that he renamed after the principal papers of whatever city he happened to be playing in, and dedicated to such members of the staffs thereof as handled advance notices. I was thus not interested, for at least six other *Morning Herald* marches had been dedicated to me during my first few months in office. But there was something unusually attractive about this last imitator of imitators of imitators, and after the formal ritual was over I invited him to sit down, and asked him how the world was using him.

He was very young, and, as I could quickly see, not too sure of himself. He had come to the United States, he said, in the hope of getting a desk as a clarinetist in a first-rate symphony orchestra, but he found that it was the prevailing theory among the Germans who then conducted all American orchestras that the only good clarinetists were either Frenchmen or Belgians, and so he had been refused even an audition. He had thereupon joined an Ital-

ian band at $14.50 a week, and after a little while
the *padrone* who owned it, and a dozen others exactly like it, had offered him the baton of one of
them, at an advance, I gathered, to not more than
$25. It was with this outfit that he had come to
Baltimore, and as we got on easy terms he confessed
to me that he greatly feared the competition of the
six or eight other bands then playing in town, for
his own was made up mainly of riffraff.

One of his tuba players, he said, could play only
by ear, and was in fact not a musician at all but a
barber, and that very morning at rehearsal it had
been necessary to fire the second snare-drummer, a
Black Hander from Palermo, for trying to disem-
bowel a piccolo player with one of his drum-sticks.
This snare-drummer was now threatening to throw
a bomb at the opening concert. The only oboist in
the band, who had to double in the English horn,
was naturally insane, for mental aberration is almost normal among oboists, but he was worse than
the common run, for his lunacy took the form of trying to blow the oboe and the English horn at once
— a preposterous feat, of no practical use or sense.
As for the six trumpet players — the very sinew
and substance of a brass band —, three were red-
ink drunkards, two were grappo addicts, and the
sixth had to wear a false moustache to throw off the
police, who suspected him of a trunk murder in Ak-
ron, O., and wanted to sweat him.

The woes of this earnest young Italian aroused

my sympathy, for I was young myself in those days
and had many tribulations of my own. Unhappily,
I could think of no way to help him against that
crew of scalawags, for my experience of musicians
had already gone far enough to convince me that
there was no cure for their eccentricities. Every
band leader in America had the same troubles, and
also every orchestra conductor, even the most emi-
inent. There was boozing in the Boston Symphony,
and gang-wars were not unheard of at the rehearsals of the New York Philharmonic. He would have
to take his band as he found it, and content himself
with doing his level damndest: the Good Book itself
said that angels could do no more. But there was
still some chance of giving him help in the field of
public relations, and I let my mind play upon the
subject while he talked. Eventually I fished up an
idea.

Why, I asked him, go on leading an *Italian* band?
There were hundreds, and maybe even thousands of
them, in the country, and they were all precisely
alike, at least in the eyes of their public. Why not
start out from the reasonable assumption that that
public was more or less fed up with them, and proceed to give it something different? The professor
pricked up his ears, and so did the press-agent, and
my fancy began to flow freely. Why not have at the
fortissimo fans with a *Spanish* band? Why not,
indeed? The Spaniards, who had been fiends in human form only a few years ago, were now fast gath-

ering popularity in the United States — a phenomenon that follows all American wars. Nothing
had been too evil to say of them while they were
butchering Cubans and Filipinos, but the moment
Uncle Sam had to take over the job himself they
began, in retrospect, to seem innocent and even humane. Spanish singers were returning to the Metropolitan Opera House, and American women were
again wearing red and yellow, the Spanish colors.

The leader and his press-agent concurred after
only brief hesitation, and soon we were engaged in
preparing an announcement. The name of the
band, it appeared, was to be the Royal Palace Band
and Drum Corps of Madrid. Its leader was Lieut.
José de la Vega of the Spanish Army, a son to the
commander of the battleship *Vizcaya*, sunk by
Schley at Santiago. The lieutenant himself had
been present at that engagement as chief bugler of
the battleship *Infanta Maria Teresa*, and had been
blown overboard by one of Schley's shells, and then
rescued by Schley's gallant jackies, and brought to
Tampa and nursed back to normalcy by a beautiful
American nurse named Miss Mary Smith, and had
fallen in love with her and was about to marry her.
The press-agent, a competent craftsman, thought
of many interesting details, and even the leader, as
he heated up, made some useful contributions.
When the question of language was adverted to he
relieved the press-agent and me by saying that he
knew a few words of Spanish — *Cuanto? De quien*

es esta sombrero? Siento! La cerveza no es buena,
and so on — enough to fool Americans. So far as I
was aware, there was only one actual Spaniard in
Baltimore, and he was a man of eighty, floored by
rheumatism. There were, of course, plenty of Cubans and Porto Ricans, but none of them would
speak to a Spanish officer.

The scheme was launched the next week, and to
the tune of considerable friendly réclame in the local press. No one, to my knowledge, detected the
imposture, not even the critic of the Baltimore *Sunpapers,* who was not let in on the secret. The leader
and his men wore the same uniforms that they had
been wearing all the while, and played the orthodox
programme, with the addition of the *habanera* from
" Carmen " and " La Paloma." The only real concession to verisimilitude was offered by the press-
agent, who had a large Spanish flag made and hung
it behind the band. At the end of the first half of
the first concert the large audience leaped to its feet
and cheered, and when the last note of the evening
was played there was so vociferous a demand for en-
cores that Lieut. de la Vega did " La Paloma "
twice more, the second time *pianissimo* with the
lights dimmed. During the intermission I encountered one of the professors at the Peabody Con-
servatory of Music, and he told me that he was
greatly enjoying the evening. Italian bands, he
said, drove him wild, but the Spaniards at least
knew how to get decent sounds out of the wood-

wind. " If this fellow," he said, " would sneak in
four or five Italian trumpet players he would have
a really good band."

Unhappily, the innovation, though an artistic
success, was killed in its infancy by the Italian
padrone who owned the band. When he heard that
it had gone Spanish he raised a considerable pother,
mainly on prudential grounds. If the news ever got
to Italy, he said, he would be disgraced forever,
and the Black Hand would probably murder his old
mother. Moreover, he was presently reinforced by
the members of the band, and especially by the
gorilla moiety thereof. They demanded an immediate raise of $2 a week as compensation for the in-
famy of being turned into Spaniards, and when it
was refused they took to sabotage. On the opening
night of the second week, when the time came to
launch the first dose of " La Paloma," the whole
band began to play " Funiculi-Funicula " instead,
greatly to Lieut. de la Vega's astonishment and
chagrin. There was, of course, nothing for him to
. do save go along, but during the intermission he
gave the performers a piece of his mind, and they
responded by threatening to plant a bomb under
his podium. Before the end of that second week the
band was demanding a raise of $4, and the *padrone*
came to Baltimore to make peace. The upshot was
that in return for a solemn promise to let his old
mother in Naples live he burned the Spanish flag,
fired the press-agent, and ordered Lieut. de la Vega

to resume the style and appelation of Antonio Brac-
ciolini, which he had been before. A little while later
the band gave place to another from the same stable, and in the course of time, I suppose, it succumbed to the holocaust which engulfed all the Italian bands in America. I never heard from Lieut. de
la Vega-Bracciolini again. But now and then I got
news of the press-agent. He was going about the
country telling newspaper colleagues that I was a
smartie who deserved a kick in the pants.

I got to know a good many other musicians in
those days, and found many of them pleasant fellows, though their ways of life were strange. I well
recall a talented lady pianist who came to Baltimore for six seasons running, and each time brought
a new husband, always of a new nationality. The
last that I saw was a Turk, and afterward, so I
have heard, she proceeded to a Venezuelan, a South
African Dutchman and a native of Monte Carlo,
but on that point I can't speak from personal
knowledge. I also remember a French tenor who
traveled with no less than three wives, but that was
before the passage of the Mann Act. Two of them
sang in the chorus of his company, and while they
were on the stage the third took care of their and
her own infants in the baggage-room. This company had come up from South America, and carried on its affairs according to provincial Italian
principles. Everything was sung in the fashion of
the sextette in " Lucia " — that is, with the singers

in a long row at the footlights. This was done even in the final agonies of " Traviata," with *Violette* dying of tuberculosis. As the curtain fell the lady playing the rôle — she weighed at least 200 pounds — was lined up with *Alfred, Annina, Germont* and *Dr. Grenvil,* howling *Gran Dio! morir si giovane!* (Great God! to die so young!) in a voice of brass. One warm evening, approaching the opera-house somewhat late, I could hear the screams of the polygamous tenor two blocks away. He was throwing a lot of violent and supernumerary high C's, many of them *sforzando,* into *Deserto sulla terra.*

I soon found that, among the instrumental players, the register of the instrument apparently had some effect upon the temperament of the artist. The bull-fiddle players were solid men who played the notes set before them, however difficult, in a dogged and uncomplaining manner, and seldom gave a conductor any trouble, whether by alcoholism or Bolshevism. The cellists were also pretty reliable fellows, but in the viola section one began to encounter boozers, communists and even spiritualists, and when one came to the fiddlers it was reasonable to expect anything, including even a lust to maim and kill. So, also, in the brass and woodwind. No one ever heard of a bassoon or tuba player saying or doing anything subversive, but the trumpeters were vain and quarrelsome, the flautists and clarinetists were often heavy drinkers, and the oboists, as I have noted, were predominantly *meshug-*

gah. Learning these instructive facts, I began to have some sympathy with orchestra conductors, a class of men I had hitherto dismissed as mere athletes, comparable to high-jumpers, circus acrobats and belly-dancers. I now realized that their lives were full of misery, and when, a few years later, I became well acquainted with a number of them, it seemed only natural to learn that they were steady readers of Schopenhauer and Nietzsche and heavy consumers of aspirin, mineral oil and bicarbonate of soda.

Indeed, my gradually growing familiarity with musicians taught me many interesting things about them, and also helped my comprehension of the general mystery of man. It did not surprise me to discover that a great many of them, in their professional capacity, hated music, for I was already aware that most bartenders of any sense were teetotalers and that some of the most eminent medical men at the Johns Hopkins Hospital took patent medicines when they were ill, but it *did* surprise me to find that this animosity to the tone art as a trade was often accompanied by a deep love of it as a recreation. I well recall my delight when I was invited by a Baltimore brewer to a party at his brewery in honor of a dozen members of the Boston Symphony Orchestra, and saw them strip off their coats and fall upon a stack of chamber music that kept them going until 4 a.m. These men, all of whom were first-rate performers, had put in the early part of the evening playing a heavy concert, with a new tone-poem by Richard Strauss, bristling with technical snares, as its principal ingredient. They agreed unanimously that Strauss was a scoundrel, that his music was an outrage upon humanity, and that anyone who paid good money to hear it was insane. Yet these same men, after nearly two hours of professional suffering, now spent four more hours playing for the pleasure of it, and one of the things they played with the greatest gusto was Strauss's serenade in E flat for wind instruments, opus 7. All they got for their labor, save for a keg of beer to each man and the applause of the brewer and of the customers he had invited to meet them, was a hot inner glow, obviously extremely grateful. As I sat listening to them I could not help pondering upon the occult satisfaction that arises from the free and perfect performance of a function, as when a cow gives milk or a dog chases a cat. If the stars were sentient they would no doubt get the same kick out of their enormous revolutions, otherwise so pointless. These reflections, in some way or other, induced me to resume music myself, abandoned since my boyhood, and I was presently playing trios and quartettes with an outfit that devoted four hours of every week to the job — that is, two hours to actual playing and the other two to the twin and inseparable art of beer-drinking.

The members of this little club were all very

much better performers than I was, and it puzzled me at the start to find them so tolerant of my inferiority. I discovered the secret when, after a little while, they took in a recruit even worse, for I was a good deal less pained by the dreadful sounds he made than cheered by his pious enthusiasm. In brief, he really loved music, and that was enough to excuse a great many false entrances and sour notes. I could stand him, at least up to a point, just as the rest could stand me, again up to a point. That club goes on to the present day, though I am the only survivor of the era of my own admission. It has included through the years some first-rate professionals and it has also included some amateurs hardly worth shooting, but they have got on together very amicably, and though they are now mainly elderly men, with kidneys like sieves, they still meet once a week, Winter or Summer, in wartime or peace-time, rain or shine. From end to end of World War I an Englishman sat between two Germans at every meeting, and in World War II a Czech has his place, and two Jews flank the Germans. What this signifies I refrain, on the advice of counsel, from venturing to suggest: in all probability it is downright unlawful. But there it is.

The club, in its day, has had some men of more or less note among its members, and there were times during its earlier stages when the question of honorifics presented a certain difficulty. Should a distinguished university, governmental or ecclesias-

tical dignitary be addressed by his simple surname
or given his title? In the case of those who sat regularly the problem was soon solved in the Rotarian
fashion by calling him Julius or Charlie, but when
he came only occasionally it was got round by giving him a satirical lift. Thus a plain Mister became
Doctor, a Doctor became Professor, and a Professor became *Geheimrat*. If there had ever been a colonel in the club we'd have made him a general, and
if there had ever been an archbishop we'd have addressed him as Your Eminence or perhaps even
Your Holiness. Once, when a baron sat in for a few
sessions, we called him Count, and another time we
promoted a judge to Mr. Chief Justice. The club
has always had a few non-performing members, but
they have been suffered only on condition that they
never make any suggestions about programmes or
offer any criticism of performances. The same rule
has applied to occasional guests: they are welcome
if they keep their mouths shut and do not sweat visibly when the flute is half a tone higher than the
first violin, but not otherwise. The club has never
gone on the air or had its disturbances recorded on
wax, but nevertheless it has done more than one
humble service to the tone art, and in the dark forward and abysm of the future those services may
be acknowledged and even rewarded. For one thing,
it has produced, from its composers' section, at
least one peerless patriotic hymn, to wit, " I Am a
100% American," by William W. Woollcott. This

magnificent composition has everything. It is both chaste and voluptuous. It radiates woof and it reeks with brrrrrrr. I am frankly tender toward it, for when the inspiration for it seized the composer I had the honor of taking it down at the piano: he was, at the moment, suffering from a sprained arm, and moreover, he plays no instrument save the triangle, and that only in a dilettante fashion. A print of it exists and may be found in libraries, but so far it has not got its deserts from the public. Perhaps it will take a third World War or even a fourth to bring it out. National hymns, as everyone knows, sometimes linger a long while in the dog-house before they win universal acceptance and acclaim. Even " The Star-Spangled Banner " was formally adopted by Congress only a few years ago; indeed, it outran " God Bless America " by hardly more than a neck.

But the greatest of all of Willie Woollcott's inspirations was his plan to play the first eight Beethoven symphonies seriatim, with only brief halts for refreshments between them. He omitted the Ninth only because the club's singing section, at that time, lacked castrati, and in fact consisted of but two men, both of them low, growling basses. We had excellent arrangements of the first eight symphonies, and after debating the project for two or three years resolved at last to give Willie's bold project a whirl. This must have been in 1922 or thereabout, when the club had the largest membership in its history, including a great many bold and reckless men, some of them aviators or ex-marines. Willie not only supplied the idea; he also proposed to supply the scene — his house in a dense woods near Baltimore, with no neighbors within earshot — and the refreshments. It seemed a reasonable arrangement, and so we fell to — at 4 o'clock of a Summer afternoon.

The First Symphony was child's play to us, and we turned it off in record time, with a pause of only ten minutes afterward. By six o'clock we had also finished the Second, and then we stopped for cocktails and dinner. After dinner there was some relaxation, and we dallied a bit with some excellent malt liquor, so that it was eight o'clock before we tackled the Eroica. It began so badly that we played the first movement twice, but after that it picked up momentum, and by 9.30 we had finished it. Then we paused again, this time for sandwiches, a walk in the woods — it was a lovely moonlit night — and another resort to the malt, but at 11.30 or maybe a little later we were back in the trenches, and the Fourth was begun. For some reason or other it went even worse than the Eroica, though it actually makes much less demand on technic, and the clock must have been near to 1 a.m. when we decided finally that it had been done well enough. Our struggles with it had naturally tired us, so we decided to knock off for an hour and find out what the malt had to offer in the way of encouragement.

This hiatus, unhappily, was a fatal one, for when
the time came to resume the hullabaloo it was discovered that two of the members had sneaked off for
home, and that two more were so sound asleep that
we could not arouse them without risk of hurting
them. Thus the C minor was begun under unfavorable circumstances, and by the time it was over
the band was reduced to what amounted to a mere
fragment, and the four-hand piano was making so
much noise that the other surviving instruments
were barely audible. The Pastoral followed at once,
but how it was done I can't say, for I fell asleep myself somewhere in the *scherzo*, and by the time Willie got me back on the piano bench the end had been
reached and there was a debate going on about No.
7. It was now nearly 5 a.m., and the east was rosy
with the dawn. One faction, it appeared, was in favor of giving up and going home; another insisted
that a round of ham and eggs and a few beers
would revive us enough to take us to the end. As to
what actually happened there are two legends. The
official story, inscribed by Willie upon the scrolls of
the club, is that we tackled the Seventh, banged
through it in circus time, and then dispatched the
Eighth. A rump account says that we blew up in
the middle of the Seventh, leaped to the Eighth,
blew up again, and were chased out by our host,
assisted by his hunting dogs. According to this
rump account, but three performers were left at the

end — the *primo* pianist, one fiddler and a man trying to play a basset-horn.

My own feeling is that in such bizarre matters precise facts are only intrusions. If we actually played the eight symphonies, then no other group of *Tonkünstler* has ever done it, on this or any other earth. And if we only tried, then no one else has ever tried.

VIII

A MASTER OF

GLADIATORS

[1907]

It always amazes me how easily men of the highest talents and eminence can be forgotten in this careless world — for example, the late Abraham Lincoln Herford, manager of the incomparable Joe Gans, lightweight champion of the world. Even Joe himself, though he was probably the greatest boxer who ever lived and unquestionably one of the gamest, is mentioned only rarely by the sporting writers, and in his native Baltimore there is no memorial to him save a modest stone in an Aframerican graveyard, far off the usual lines of tourist travel. It may be that pilgrims occasionally visit it, but if so they have to use large-scale maps, showing every culvert and hot-dog stand. Joe's funeral was a stupendous event, with services running seriatim in three different churches, ten or twelve choirs moaning sad music, and no colored Baltimorean absent who could get the afternoon off and squeeze in, but since then the dead gladiator's fellow blackamoors have let his memory fade, and gone flocking after newer and lesser heroes. There is no Gans boulevard, avenue, street or even alley in the Harlem of Baltimore, and no Gans park. Some years ago I heard talk of raising a monument to Joe in Perkins Square, hard by his humble birthplace, with a marble effigy of him in ring costume on top of it, but the scheme faded out as all plans and projects among the colored people have a way of doing. If it is ever revived I hope to be invited to participate, for my admiration for Joe was high while he lived and has not abated since his decease. Specifically, I offer herewith to contribute $100 in cash money whenever a sufficiently reliable committee opens subscription books. By reliable, of course, I do not mean one certified by the S.E.C. or by a gang of colored pastors or gamblers, but one certified by the Baltimore cops.

But if Joe was great, then Al Herford must have been great also, for he grasped Joe's genius when it was still occult to other men, and nursed it to flower with both skill and tenderness. Of Al's origins I know nothing, for I did not become acquainted with him until he was already well up in the world, and president *and* treasurer of the Eureka Athletic and Social Club. Under the laws prevailing in Maryland in those days, it was forbidden to give boxing exhibitions for hire, but any group of fans was free to form a club to stage them in private, and that is what the Eureka brethren did, with Al acting as their agent and adviser. Their meetings were held every Friday evening at the old Germania Maennerchor hall in Lombard street, and ran about three hours, with a fifteen-round bout at the end, usually between heavyweights. According to the by-laws of the club each member paid his weekly dues as he came in, and the rate for those who wanted seats near the ring was considerably higher than for those who were content to sit in the gallery. Al always opened the proceedings by reading the minutes of the last meeting. They described briefly the bouts that had entertained the members, and then went on to a technical commentary upon them, frequently of great acuteness. If there had been any distinguished new members present, say a party of Congressmen from Washington, Al recited their names, and bade them welcome to the club. At the end of the minutes he called for motions from the floor, and some member always moved that the club make up a purse and buy the president *and* treasurer a diamond ring or stick-pin. Al handed over the gavel, at this point, to Ernie Gephart, who was secretary and time-keeper of the club, but after the motion had been put and carried (as it was invariably, and unanimously) he returned long enough to announce that subscriptions might be paid to the doorkeeper on the way out.

Al never bored the members with financial statements, though he always stressed the *and* in " president *and* treasurer," for the by-laws made them virtually supererogatory. According to Article II all the money collected in dues went into a pot in the custody of the president *and* treasurer, and out of it he paid all the necessary expenses of the meetings — for example, for hall rent, announcements in the newspapers, stationery and postage, the fees of the sporty young doctor who served as the club's surgeon, and the honoraria of the pugs invited to exhibit their art. If anything was left over, which was usually the case, it was given to the president *and* treasurer, as a small return for his services. This simple system worked beautifully, and had the approval of the Baltimore cops. They came to the meetings in large numbers, and were so well appreciated by the other members that the doorkeeper, by a tacit but general understanding, always forgot to collect their dues. Sometimes, when a couple of extra-fat captains were present at the ringside, Al would have a little fun with them by announcing that they would go on for six rounds at the next meeting. He also had a line of spoofing for visitors from Washington, and did not hesitate to refer to the most puissant Senators, and even judges, by their Christian names. The other members were delighted to belong to a club which in-

cluded so many illustrious men. More than once I
have sat at the ringside with a Senator or Governor to either side of me, and two or three stars
of the Federal judiciary just behind.

Al was not only president *and* treasurer of the
club, but also its announcer, and his introductions
always showed an exuberant fancy. When two colored flyweights were brought on for a preliminary
he presented them as Young Terry McGovern of
San Francisco and Young Joe Gans of Australia.
Nearly everyone knew, of course, that they were
actually water-boys from the Pimlico racetrack,
but the members liked Al's style, and always professed to believe him. His humor was protean, and
never flagged. When two boys sailed into each other
with unusual vehemence and the members began to
howl, he would signal Ernie Gephart to let the
rounds run on, and whenever, on the contrary, a
bout was tame, he would cut them short. Once I
saw a set-to between two ferocious colored youths,
Young Corbett, of Yarmouth, England, and the
Zulu Whirlwind, of Cape Town, South Africa, in
which the average length of the five rounds, by actual timing, was twelve and a half minutes, and
another time I saw Ernie put through a flabby six-
round bout in ten minutes flat, with the pauses for
wind, massage and hemostasis included.

Al was very inventive, and many of his innovations stuck. He was, I believe, the first announcer
in Europe or America to call the penultimate

bout of an evening the semi-windup. I recall that
some of the more literate members of the Eureka
Club snickered at the neologism, and that I was
brought up by it myself. But in a little while it had
swept the boxing world, and it is now used without
any thought of vulgarity by such purists as John F.
Kieran and Grantland Rice. Al, a little later, began
to call the second from the last bout the semi-semi-
windup, and the third from the last the semi-semi-
semi-windup, but these innovations never took, and
he proceeded no further. He did not invent the bat-
tle-royal, but I believe it is only just to say that he
greatly developed it. One of his contributions was
the scheme of dividing the four boys into three very
small ones and one very tall one: this favored a
brisk entertainment, for the dwarfs always ganged
on the giant and knocked him out, usually by blows
behind the ear. Another of Al's improvements was
the device of dressing the colored boys who fought
in battles-royal, not in ordinary trunks, but in the
billowy white drawers that women then wore. The
blacker the boy, the more striking the effect. In all
such massacres, of course, the scheme of holding
back time on a good round was carried out. So long
as the members kept on guffawing and hollering Al
let the boys clout away.

Al, in his private life, was a very generous fellow, but in his character of president *and* treasurer
of the club he kept a sharp eye on its funds. The
standard fee for preliminary boys of no experience

was $4, win or lose, but he seldom paid it without a struggle, which meant that he seldom paid it at all. Once, after a long evening marked by extraordinary carnage, I sat with him in his bureau under the stage while the boys came in to collect their money. I recall a pair of young featherweights who could barely stand up — Young Jeffries, of Honolulu, and Young Fitzsimmons, of Yale University. Both of Jeffries' eyes were blacked, his nose was only a squash, and he claimed that he had broken all five fingers of his right hand. The Yale boy had been used even worse, and when I entered the bureau the club surgeon was giving him a ticket to the free surgical clinic at the University of Maryland Hospital. They had fought six really terrific rounds, and the club referee, Jim O'Hara, had let them go on after the fourth only because he could not make out which was getting the worse beating. But Al conceived it to be his duty as treasurer of the club to challenge them, and challenge them he did. " What! " he roared. " Have you bastards the nerve to come down here and talk of money after doing a *brother* act? Do you think this place is a dancing-school? Back to the Y.M.C.A., and fight with feather-pillows! I could sue you in the courts. I could sick the cops on you. Never let me see you again. Here [to Jeffries] is two dollars, and here [to Fitzsimmons de Yale] is a dollar and a half. Now scram before I get mad and kick you to hell out of here."

On this occasion, unhappily, Al went a shade too far, for the next day he was waited on by Lawyer Melville W. Fuller Fineblatt, secretary of the Central Police Court Bar Association, and forced to disgorge. Lawyer Fineblatt not only collected the balance of the four dollars that was due to each boy under the rules, but also three dollars a head for medical expenses, and a fee of twenty dollars for himself. The alternative to coughing up, he said firmly, would be a prosecution for violating the laws against giving public boxing exhibitions, allowing smoking in a theatre, maintaining a nuisance, embezzling trust funds, and contributing to the delinquency of minors. Al entered a long and indignant account of the episode in the minutes, and read it at the next meeting of the club, but when he came to the statement that the boys had put on a fake some of the members began to laugh, and he pursued the matter no further. But he continued to labor it *in petto*, and nine or ten years later, after public boxing exhibitions had become lawful in Maryland and the Eureka Athletic and Social Club had withered away, he was still talking darkly of having Lawyer Fineblatt disbarred.

How much he made out of Joe Gans, first and last, I can't tell you, for he kept his books in his hat, but I knew the man, and am morally certain that he never collared more than fifty percent, or maybe sixty percent, of Joe's earnings. If this seems a large cut, then don't forget that many of the other pug managers of the time took seventy percent, and even eighty; indeed, there were some who took all, less enough, of course, to victual their boys, and keep them housed and clothed. Joe's own share was surely considerable, for when he retired from the ring for the first of his fifteen times he had saved enough to open a gaudy night-club in Baltimore — the first black-and-tan resort the town had ever seen. To be sure, it blew up quickly, and Joe died in a low state, financially speaking, but nevertheless the money he lost had passed through his hands.

Al taught him a lot, not only about the business of boxing, but also about the carriage and conduct of a professional man, and Joe became widely known as the most gentlemanly pugilist then on earth. His manners were those of a lieutenant of the guards in old Vienna, and many managers sent their white boys to him to observe and learn. When he was shoveled away at last, Al undertook the tutelage of a colored boxer named Young Peter Jackson, a heavyweight. Peter was an apt pupil, and soon became famous for his elegance. Unhappily, he lacked Joe's natural grace, and was in fact a squat, clumsy fellow with a coal-black hide and a shaven head. Once he made a tour of England under the eye of an English manager named Jolly Jumbo, and the sports were so delighted by his suave ways that, on his return to America, they chipped in money for a farewell present. Jolly

Jumbo was deputed to select it. Forgetting Peter's depilated poll, he chose a set of gold-mounted military brushes.

Another of Al's protégés (in his announcements and harangues to the club he always pronounced the word pro-teege) was a heavyweight who shined for a brief season, but then took to heavy eating and lost his wind, and eventually got so dreadful a beating from Philadelphia Jack O'Brien that he retired from the ring and opened a saloon. I was present at his Waterloo, sitting with my knees touching the ropes, and remember it because of the poor fellow's extraordinary loss of blood, chiefly from his nose. Directly beside me sat Judge John H. Anderson, sporting editor of the *Morning Herald* and the first Harvard Phi Beta Kappa man ever to occupy such a position. The judge, who had got his title, not on the bench but at the race-track, wore a round beard *à la* James A. Garfield, and was extremely dignified and even formal in appearance and manner. I well recall his profane protests when the unhappy heavyweight's gore began to sprinkle his beard. He did not object to the rosin dust that overspread it at every meeting of the club, nor even to an occasional drop of blood, but when great gouts began to hit his foliage he set up a hell of an uproar, and if the heavyweight had not gone to the mat a little while later I have no doubt that he would have forced Al to stop the bout. When the Prohibition infamy hit the country in 1920 the heavyweight converted his saloon into a speak-easy, and was soon raided by Federal agents. The first jury acquitted him, for it was made up largely of members of Al's old club, and so did the second, third, fourth, fifth, sixth, seventh and eighth. But on his ninth appearance the district attorney took precautions, and he was duly found guilty and sentenced to three months in jail. While he was cooped there he was allowed to have his meals sent in from outside, and in a couple of weeks his gluttony had reduced him to such a state that he needed medical advice. He thereupon asked and was given permission to send for one of the visiting physicians of the Johns Hopkins Hospital — a very skillful and high-toned consultant. Simultaneously, he read in the Baltimore *Sunpaper* that his favorite niece, a pretty girl then in the foolish stage of her life, had been nabbed as a witness to a roughhouse in a rowdy suburban night-club. This smudge upon the honor of his house affected him deeply, and when the doctor waited upon him at the jail he was actually in tears. " My God, doctor," he moaned, " just think of it, just think of it! I been so ashamed to look anybody in the eye that for two days I áin't been out of my cell."

IX

A DIP INTO

STATECRAFT

[1912]

SOME time ago, in writing a book for the edification of the young, I let fall the remark that, in the now forgotten year of 1912, I was a candidate for the Democratic nomination for Vice-President of the United States. It is almost incredible that an author of my experience should have made such a slip. I must have been very well aware, even in the cachexia of composition, that the only effect of my statement would be to provoke a storm of snorts, and get me classed among the damndest liars on earth. That, indeed, is exactly what happened, and during the month after the book came out (it had a very fair sale) I received 30,000 or 40,000 letters full of hoots and sneers. Nevertheless, my statement was true in the most precise and literal sense,

and I hereby reiterate it with my hand upon the
Holy Scriptures. I was actually a candidate as I
said, but I should add at once, before historians
begin to rush up with their proofs, that I did not
get the nomination.

Perhaps the best way to tell the story, which is
mercifully brief, will be to start out with a cast of
characters. Here it is:

The Hon. J. Harry Preston, mayor of Baltimore, and
a man of aggressive and relentless bellicosity.

Charles H. Grasty, editor of the Baltimore *Sunpapers,*
an enemy to Preston, and a sly and contriving fellow.

H. L. Mencken, a young journalist in the employ of
Grasty as columnist and trigger-man.

Scene: Baltimore.

Time: The weeks preceding the Democratic National
Convention of 1912.

That was the year when the late Woodrow Wilson was nominated and so began his dizzy rise to
immortality. Grasty was for him, but Preston was
against him and in favor of Champ Clark of Missouri. This difference was only one of hundreds that
lay between them. They quarreled all the time, and
over any proposition that could be dissected into al-
ternatives. If Preston, as mayor, proposed to en-
large the town dog-pound, Grasty denounced it in
both morning and evening *Sunpapers* as an assault
upon the solvency of Baltimore, the comity of nations, and the Ten Commandments, and if Grasty
argued in the *Sunpapers* that the town alleys ought

to be cleaned oftener Preston went about the ward clubs warning his heelers that the proposal was only the opening wedge for anarchy, atheism and cannibalism. It was impossible to unearth anything against Preston's private character, though every *Sun* reporter, under Grasty's urging, made desperate efforts to do so, for he was a respectable family man, a vestryman in an Episcopal church with a watchful rector, and a lawyer of high standing at the bar. But in his rôle of politician, of course, he was an easier target, and so his doings in the City Hall were gradually assimilated (at least in the *Sunpapers*) to those of Tweed in New York, the *ancien régime* in France, and the carpetbaggers in the South.

Grasty, on his side, was vulnerable in the reverse order. That is to say, he could not be accused of political corruption, for it was notorious that he had no political ambitions, but in his private life there was more encouraging material, for several times, in the past, he had forgotten himself. The dirt thus dredged up was gradually amalgamated into the master charge that he had been run out of Kansas City (where he formerly lived) for a series of adulteries of a grossly levantine and brutal nature. This charge Preston not only labored at great length in his harangues to the ward clubs; he also included it in his commencement addresses to the graduates of the Baltimore high-schools and his speeches of welcome to visiting Elks, Shriners,

Christian Endeavorers and plumbers' supply dealers; moreover, he reduced it to writing, signed his
name to it with a bold flourish, and printed it as
paid advertising in the *Sunpapers* themselves.

The revenues from this advertising were gratefully received by Grasty, for the *Sunpapers*, in
those days, were using up almost as much red ink
in the business office as printer's ink in the press-
room. But against that pleasant flow of the wages
of sin there had to be set off the loss from the municipal advertising, which Preston, though a Democrat, diverted to a Republican paper. It took him
a long while to clear it out of the *Sunpapers*, but
clear it out he did at last. Any City Hall functionary who, by force of old habit, sent in an announcement of a tax sale or a notice of an application to
.pen a hat-cleaning parlor was fired forthwith and
to the tune of loud screams of indignation. To meet
this devastating attack the whole staff of the two
Sunpapers spent half its time in concocting reprisals. No story against Preston was too incredible to be printed, and no criticism too trivial or ir-
responsible. If the blackamoors in the death-house
at the Baltimore City Jail had signed a round robin
accusing him of sending them poison in cornpone
or snuff, it would have gone into type at once.

My own share in this campaign of defamation
was large and assiduous. In my daily column on the
editorial page of the *Evening Sun* I accused Preston of each and every article in my private cata-

logue of infamies. Once I even alleged that he was
a Sunday-school superintendent — and was amazed
to discover that it was true. I had nothing against
him personally; on the contrary, I was fond of him,
thought he was doing well as mayor, and often met
him amicably at beer-parties. But in his character
of enemy of Grasty, and hence of the *Sunpapers*,
I was bound by the journalistic code of the time to
deal him a lick whenever I could, and this I did every day. On some days, in fact, my whole column
was devoted to reviling him. Why he never hit back
by accusing me of adultery, or, at all events, of
fornication, I do not know, but no doubt it was
because he was too busy amassing and embellishing
his case against Grasty.

The plain people of Baltimore naturally took
his side against the *Sunpapers*. They are always,
in fact, against newspapers, and they are always
in favor of what reformers call political corruption. They believe that it keeps money in circulation, and makes for a spacious and stimulating
communal life. Thus they cheered Preston every
time he appeared in public, and especially did they
cheer him every time the *Sunpapers* published
fresh allegations that he and his goons, having
made off with everything movable in the City Hall,
were beginning on the slate roof and the doorknobs.
This popularity had a powerful effect on the man
himself, for he was not without the vanity that afflicts the rest of us. He began to see himself as a

great tribune of the people, ordained by God to rescue them from the entrapments of a dissolute journalism, by libel out of crim. con. More, he began to wonder if the job of mayor of Baltimore was really large enough for his talents. Wasn't there something grander and juicier ahead? Didn't the Bible itself guarantee that a good and faithful servant should have a reward? What if the people of Maryland should decide to draft the man who had saved the people of Baltimore, and make him their Governor and Captain-General? What if the people of the whole United —

But this last wayward thought had to wait until, early in 1912, the Democrats of the nation decided that Baltimore should be their convention city. Preston, as mayor, had a large hand in bringing the party national committee to that decision. He not only made eloquent representations about the traditional delights of the town, especially in the way of eating and drinking; he also agreed to raise a fund of $100,000 to pay the costs of the show, and made a big contribution to it himself, for he was a man of means. During the Spring the wild fancies and surmises that were devouring him began to emerge. One day the Republican paper getting the city advertising suggested that he would make a magnificent candidate for the Vice-Presidency, the next day he received hundreds of spontaneous letters and telephone calls from his jobholders, urging him to accept the plain call of his

country, and the third day his campaign was in the
open, and throwing out dense clouds of sparks and
smoke. It soon appeared that he had an understanding with Champ Clark. Clark had already rounded
up a majority of the delegates to the coming convention, but he needed more, for the two-thirds rule
still prevailed. Why couldn't the Baltimore gallery, packed and fomented by Preston, panic
enough waverers to give Clark the nomination? It
seemed an enlightened trade, and it was made. If
Preston delivered the goods and Clark became the
standard-bearer, Preston would have second place.

It was at this point that Grasty conceived his
hellish plot, and the rest of the story is soon told.
Under the presidential primary law then on the
books in Maryland every candidate for the Presidency who itched for the votes of the state's delegates had to file his name " before the first Monday
in May " preceding the convention, and with it deposit $270 in cash money. Under the same law can-
didates for the Vice-Presidency lay under the same
mulct. If no candidate submitted to it, the state
convention was free to instruct the delegates to the
national convention to vote for anyone it fancied,
but if there were two who had paid up it had to
make its choice between them, and if there was but
one it had to instruct the delegates to vote for him.
The agents of Wilson, Clark and all the other con-
tenders for first place on the ticket had entered
their appearances and paid their fees, but no can-

didate for the Vice-Presidency had been heard from.
Preston, of course, knew the law, but he was a
thrifty fellow and saw no reason why he should
waste $270, for he figured with perfect plausibil-
ity that he would be the only aspirant for second
place before the state convention.

Grasty's sinister mind grasped this point a day
or two before I was sailing for Europe on a holiday.
Summoned to his office, I sat enchanted while he
unfolded his plan. It was to wait until the very last
minute for filing names of Vice-Presidential candidates, and then rush an agent to Annapolis, properly equipped with $270 in cash, to file *mine*. " Go
back to your office," he instructed me, " and write
a letter of acceptance. Say in it that you are sac-
rificing yourself to save the country from the menace of Preston. Lay it on with a shovel, and take all
the space you want. To be sure, you'll be in the
middle of the Atlantic when the time comes, but
I'll send you a wireless, so you'll know what to say
when the New York *Herald* reporter meets you at
Cherbourg. The joke will wreck Preston, and the
shock may even kill him. If he actually shoots himself I'll tone down your statement a bit, but write
it as if he were still alive and howling. Imagine the
scene when the state convention is forced to instruct
the delegates to the national convention to vote for
you! Here is the law: read it and laugh. It is really
too rich, especially this point: the delegates to the
national convention will have to vote for you *as a*

unit until ' in their conscientious judgment ' you
are out of the running. That may not come until
days and even weeks after the convention starts. All
the Wilson men will throw you votes to annoy
Clark. Now get busy with your letter of acceptance
before I laugh myself to death."

On the fatal evening I was aboard ship in lat.
50 N, long. 15 W, gulping down beer with my traveling companion, A. H. McDannald, another *Sunpaper* man, and keeping a sharp lookout for a page-
boy with a radio envelope. McDannald was in on
the plot, and helped me to itch and pant. We got
through beer after beer — one, two, three, six, ten,
n. We wolfed plate after plate of sandwiches. We
returned to beer. We ordered more sandwiches. The
hours moved on leaden feet; the minutes seemed to
be gummy and half dead. Finally, we were the only
passengers left in the smokeroom, and the bartender and waiters began to shuffle about pointedly
and to douse the lights. Just as darkness closed in
on us the page-boy came at last. He had two messages for McDannald and three for me. Both of
McDannald's read " Sorry to have missed you ; bon
voyage," and so did two of mine. The third read :
" Everything is off. Say nothing to anyone."

It was not until I got home, four weeks later, that
I found out what had happened. Grasty, it appeared, had been so taken by the ingenuity and
villainy of his scheme that when he went to the
Maryland Club the next afternoon for his daily

ration of Manhattan cocktails he couldn't resist revealing it — in strict confidence, of course — to one of the bibuli there assembled. I should say that the bibulus was normally a very reliable man, and carried in his breast a great many anecdotes of Grasty that Preston would have given gold and frankincense to hear, but this time he was so overcome by the gorgeousness of the secret that he took a drop too much, and so blabbed. This blabbing was done in the sanctity of the club, but Preston had his spies even there. Thus, when Grasty's agent appeared at the office of the Secretary of State at Annapolis, at the very last minute for filing names, with $270 in greenbacks held tightly in his fist, it was only to find that Preston's agent had got there two minutes before him, and was engaged with snickers and grimaces in counting out the same sum.

I thereby missed my purple moment, and maybe even immortality. Now that the facts are before a candid world, let the publicists of the *Nation*, the *New Masses* and the *New Republic* speculate upon the probable effects upon history — nay, upon the very security and salvation of humanity — if Grasty's scheme had worked. I offer them the job without prejudice, for no matter how powerfully their minds play upon it their verdict will be only moot. It was not until years later that I discovered that the Constitution of the United States, Article II, Section 1, provides that no person shall be eli-

gible for the Presidency, and *pari passu* for the
Vice-Presidency, " who shall not have attained to
the age of thirty-five years." On that July day of
1912 when the Hon. Thomas R. Marshall of Indiana got my job I was precisely thirty-one years,
ten months and twenty-three days old — and the
Constitution was still in force.

X

COURT OF HONOR

[1913]

ONE of the oldest of legal wheezes is to the effect
that no man should sit as judge in his own case.
You will find it in the " Sententiae " of Publilius
Syrus, written in the First Century B.C., and it
must have been ancient when Publilius lifted it —
as he lifted everything else — from some forgotten
Greek. In all the years since his time no one, so far
as I can discover, has ever ventured to dispute it.
It is one of the few propositions that Leftists and
Rightists agree on, and even judges on the bench
— or, at all events, those among them who give
their dismal trade any thought at all — speak well
of it. But is it really true? Sometimes I find myself
in doubt, just as I sometimes find myself in doubt
that two and two are four, or that Jonah actually
swallowed the whale. Especially do these wayward
misgivings beset me when my memory plays with a
case of extra-legal adultery that I became privy to

in New York City in the year 1912. In that case
one and the same man was not only both judge and
complainant, but also prosecuting attorney, yet
the verdict that he handed down was fair, equitable
and just, and the sentence that he pronounced was
notably humane.

Needless to say, he was not a common or dirt
judge, deteriorated and debauched by years of listening to lying witnesses and nefarious lawyers. He
was not even, in fact, a man of any learning in the
law: he was simply a theatrical manager, and even
more ignorant than most of them are. He kept an
office in the heart of the theatrical district, but
most of his revenues came from what was then
called the sticks. If he had a success on Broadway
he thought of it only as a means of extracting
money from the people beyond the two rivers. Any
run of more than forty nights was enough to start
him off. He would flood the provinces with propaganda whooping up the play as the greatest hit
since " The Two Orphans," and in a few weeks he
would follow that propaganda with a series of road
companies, all of them outfitted with frantic press-
agents and inflammatory billing. The press-agents
he selected with care, mainly from among men who
had had circus or bicycle-race experience, and the
billing he wrote and designed himself, but to the
casting of his companies he gave only casual attention, for it was his firm conviction that the provinces could not distinguish between geniuses and

hams, and indeed were more apt to be pleased by
hams than by geniuses. Whenever he was preparing a fresh assault upon them he would send in an
order to a theatrical agency for so many head of
bucks and so many head of wenches (this is how he
always spoke of his hirelings) and in a little while
rehearsals would be under way. But now and then,
of course, he picked up a performer in some other
manner — say through a letter of introduction
from a theatre manager in Anniston, Ala., or Xe-
nia, O., or a rare crash of his office trenches and
pill-boxes.

This last happened in the case of the lady who
was the culprit in the trial I am about to describe.
She hailed from Nebraska, and had got her early
training in a company playing " The Fatal Wedding " under canvas. When the rough travel and
bad eating in the Western wilderness began to tell
on her, she threw up her job and headed for New
York. She had $375 in her stocking — the savings
of two years of hard work — , and with this to sustain her she took a modest room in the forties and
began a siege of the Broadway agents and managers. My friend's office was on her daily route, but
it was a long while before he ever saw her, or even
heard of her, for his office boy chased her out every
time she showed up. This happened in all the other
offices also, and she began to be uneasy, for her
money was fast disappearing. One morning, after
my friend's office boy — a gigantic lout who, in

these days, would be called a gorilla — had been especially unkind to her, she burst into tears and dropped into a chair by the door to have her cry out. My friend, happening to come in at that moment, was struck by something or other in her appearance, and, being in a benignant mood, invited her into his private office to talk it over. The net result was not only a job, but also a love affair. In brief, my friend got mashed on her, and within a week she had moved from her meagre lodgings in the forties to a comfortable apartment in the fifties, and had a large outfit of new clothes, with a fur coat to top it off.

But though she was properly grateful, and told everyone she met (including me) that my friend was a prince and had a heart of gold, she still itched for the stimulation of the footlights, and in a little while she began agitating for a part in one of the road companies. My friend was not averse to giving her a chance, for he believed that she was probably bad enough, professionally, to please the provinces, but his feelings toward her were still very tender, and he was loath to be separated from her, maybe for four or five months. Presently he solved the problem by organizing a company to play one of his recent forty-night sensations in towns close to New York. The farthest it would get, according to the route laid out, would be Scranton, Pa., and during a large part of its tour, so he hoped, it would be playing at a dollar-top neighborhood the-

atre in Brooklyn. The girl was accordingly given
the job of leading woman, and after two weeks in
Pennsylvania and New Jersey, was safely anchored
in Brooklyn for the run. This arrangement, for a
while, was satisfactory to all parties at interest.
The girl spent her days, save when there were matinées, on Manhattan Island, kept her clothes at the
apartment in the fifties, and usually, though not
always, returned there after the evening's performance in Brooklyn.

My friend, after the opening, never looked in on
the company, for he was a very busy man, but he
had a spy who visited it at intervals and reported
on anything amiss — say, too much boozing by the
company manager or some unusual butchery of the
lines by the actors. One day, during the fourth or
fifth week of the Brooklyn run, this spy came in
with very unpleasant news. It was to the effect that
the leading lady was carrying on injudiciously,
not to say feloniously, with the leading man. They
visited each other's dressing-rooms far more than
they had any need for, and several times they had
been detected in prolonged strangle-holds behind
the back-drop. On the evenings following matinée
days, when the girl, on the score of fatigue, remained in Brooklyn overnight, they disappeared
together and were never seen by the other members
of the company. The spy, as in duty bound, shad-
owed them on such an evening, and found them
ducking into the leading man's quarters at a third-

rate hotel. My friend was naturally upset by this report, but he had some suspicion of his spy, and so borrowed another one from a brother manager, and sent him to Brooklyn to check up. This second spy made the same report precisely. The girl was thereupon ordered to report in New York at 11 o'clock the next morning to stand her trial.

I was not, of course, present at this proceeding, but my friend described it to me at great length the next time I was in New York, and I am sure that he gave me a reasonably accurate account of it, for he was a truthful fellow, despite his business, and he had a special confidence in and kindness for me, for I was the only dramatic reviewer in America, save only Stuffy Davis of the New York *Globe*, who had never tried to sell him a play. He said that the girl appeared at his office promptly, and declined his offer to let her have counsel. Instead, she made a complete confession, instantly and without urging, and in it went much further than either of the spies had alleged. It was quite true, she said, that she and the leading man were carrying on as alleged. It had begun, in fact, before the end of the first week in Brooklyn, and it was still in progress. Moreover, she refused flatly to make any promise of an abatement, either then or thereafter, though she admitted freely that her conduct was clearly immoral.

My friend told me that this confession not only shocked him, but also greatly astonished him. He had, of course, heard " Rigoletto " and hence knew that women were mobile, but here, it seemed to him, mobility had quite run amuck. The insult to his vanity he could bear, for he was a philosopher, but the puzzle that went with it really racked him. Why on earth should a girl apparently sane engage in any such degrading and irrational malpractises with an obscure and ignominious actor, a cheap clown in a No. 5 road company, a mere ham? Why should she turn from a salient and even (in her world) distinguished man and take up with so grotesque a nonentity? My friend, who had no false modesty, told me that he put the question to her plainly. On the one side, he reminded her, was himself — a fellow of large means and generous impulses, a figure of consequence on Broadway, her tried friend and benefactor, and last but not least, a man who wore expensive and well-cut clothes and was commonly conceded to be of imposing presence. On the other was that wretched ham — a poor fish who would never get beyond the lowest rounds of his profession and was doomed to penury all his life long; moreover, a grotesque figure in his cheap and flashy garments, with a hair-cut that no he-man would tolerate, a ring on his finger set with a bogus diamond, a preposterous walking-stick, and a complexion that inevitably suggested (when his make-up was washed off) both inebriety and malnutrition. What had become of the boasted sagacity of the female sex? How could any woman abandon and betray so upstanding and admirable a man as my friend and make off with that hideous caricature?

She had, it appeared, an answer ready. She had pleaded guilty, but nevertheless she was not without a defense. She did not deny the tremendous disparity between my friend and the actor. On the contrary, she admitted it freely, and even added that it was greater than had been represented. " I am here to tell you honestly," she said to my friend, " that you are the most elegant man I have ever met. No one could be more attractive to a sensible woman. You are rich, generous, smart, celebrated and handsome. I love to hear you talk, and I even like to see you eat. You have treated me better than a queen. When I put you beside that ham it really makes me laugh: compared to you he is a rat beside a hippopotamus. But " — and she paused a bit, as an actress would, to drive the point home — " but you are here in New York, rolling in your glory — and I am out there in the wilds of Brooklyn, alone and forlorn, trying to get that terrible play over to great gangs of smelly idiots.

" Have you ever tried to figure out what that means to a refined woman? Can you imagine yourself making up in a damp, drafty dressing-room night after night, and then going out on that creaky stage and speaking the same lines over and over again to those blockheads? No; I thought not. But that is what I have to do, and, believe me, it is no easy job. Sometimes I make such a mess of my performance that I burst into tears at every exit. Well, every time I do that there is that ham standing in the wings. He comes up to me, puts his arms around me, and says 'You are wonderful tonight, darling! I watched you fascinated. You really moved me.' Do I swallow it? Naturally not. I know that I have been lousy,[1] but there he is waiting for me, to tell me that I haven't. Let me say to you that such words are music to the ear of a woman. They fetch us every time. Maybe, if it had been anywhere else but Brooklyn I might have pulled myself together and given that ham a clout over the ear, but the first time he tried me it was pouring down rain outside and the audience smelled like a cat-show, and so I fell for it. After that he had me. I knew it was crazy, but I simply couldn't resist. He never had anything to say about himself: it was always *me, me, me*. He had me acting rings around Nazimova. He got me so that when I looked in my dressing-room mirror I saw Lillian Russell. So that is my story, and you can take it or leave it."

My friend told me that it took him no more than a minute to reach his decision; he had formulated it, in fact, before the girl finished her speech. As friend, as philanthropist, as man, he was injured, outraged — but as psychologist he was hooked and landed. What answer, indeed, could he make to the

[1] This term was still a novelty in 1912, even on Broadway. It came in toward the end of 1911.

girl's argument? He could think of none whatsoever. His verdict simply had to be self-defense, and his sentence was so mild that it amounted to a parole: he bade her return to Brooklyn and try to avoid the ham as much as possible. He even let her keep the apartment in the fifties, though in view of the circumstances he had his own belongings moved out by his spy the next morning.

XI

A ROMAN HOLIDAY

[*1914*]

Most of my traveling, whether by land or by sea, has been done on business, and in consequence there has usually been a good deal more hard labor in it than *dolce far niente.* For twenty years on end I had jobs as a magazine editor in New York but kept my home in Baltimore, which meant that I had to make the round trip every couple of weeks, and sometimes oftener. These journeys, if I had been able to look out of the train windows, would have made me minutely familiar with all the scenery along the two hundred miles, but as it was I always had to keep my nose buried in manuscripts, and seldom saw anything save an occasional sash-weight factory or cow, glimpsed vaguely out of the corner of my eye. When this servitude ended, at the beginning of 1934, I employed a statistician to figure out how many words I had read during the twenty years, but when his report came in it was so full of plus and minus signs and unintelligible gabble about skew distributions and coefficients of correlation that I threw it away in disgust, and fell back on my own bare-hand guess, which was 50,000,000 words. My longer journeys, before, during and after the same time, were made principally for newspapers, and save when I contrived to get myself lost were even worse, for they were punctuated day and night by telegrams from managing editors reading " Where is your second follow lead? ", " Please call in between 11.30 p.m. and 11.40 Eastern Standard Daylight Time," or " Your story differs from the A.P. in the following particulars. . . . Please confirm or correct." All the reporters that I traveled with got the same telegrams, and not infrequently, when I received an especially outrageous one, I would change the address on it and pass it to one of my colleagues. Unhappily, the other boys and gals resorted to the same trick, with the effect that on a bad night I was bombarded with remonstrances from managing editors stretching from San Diego to Boston. No one, of course, save a greenhorn or a lunatic ever answered such messages, but nevertheless they were irritating, and after reading them for a couple of weeks I was almost in a mood for the plunge into delirium tremens that they had been accusing me of, usually only covertly but sometimes in plain English, all the while.

But there were a number of times when I threw

off such chains, and traveled for the pure deviltry of it, and it is such trips that I always remember most vividly when I am laid up with rheumatism and try to forget it in memories of my dead life. Of all those unofficial or illicit journeys, the one that I recall with the most pleasure is a jaunt in reverse along the route of the classical Grand Tour of Europe, made in the Spring of 1914 in the company of two Baltimore friends, W. Edwin Moffett and A. H. McDannald, the latter my companion on a previous pilgrimage, already mentioned in Chapter IX. Moffett is now a bull-fiddle virtuoso of such wizardry that I have actually seen and heard a symphony concert audience rise up and cheer him, and McDannald has gone so far in learning that he is the editor-in-chief of an encyclopedia, but in 1914 they were both simple fellows out for a gaudy time, as I was myself, and we unquestionably had it in Italy, Switzerland, Germany and France, not to mention the Atlantic Ocean and the Mediterranean Sea. We made the eastward ocean trip in a second-string Cunarder called the *Laconia*, one of the first of the so-called tour-ships. It was slow but very comfortable, and when we left New York we looked forward to nine lazy days to Gibraltar. We planned to spend them in the smokeroom, for all three of us believed that the glare of the sun on deck was deleterious, and had tried to put away temptation by making a pact to hire no deck-chairs. This, of course, got the deck-stewards down on us, but the bar-stewards were very polite and assiduous, and it was generally understood before we reached Nantucket light that one of the best corners in the smokeroom was ours. But our dream of crossing the ocean in peace and comfort did not last much longer, for on the first day out the usual pests got together to form the usual committees, and thereafter we were beset day and night by women selling tickets to concerts, chances on raffles, or knitted neckties made by inmates of the Sailors' Orphans' Home at Liverpool, or worse still, trying to wheedle us into going to mask balls, joining in folk-song festivals, or making speeches. Moffett put off these harpies for a few days by pointing to his right ear and bellowing " Deef! Deef! " and Mac pretended that I was a homicidal maniac and he my keeper, but the gals quickly got on to these subterfuges, and settled down in brutal earnest to fetch us.

We were, however, tough guys in those days, and as incredible as it may seem we actually came into sight of the coast of Portugal without going to a single dance, concert, raffle, spelling-bee, debate, sing-song or mass-meeting, and without contributing a single nickel to any home for decrepit sailors, or their (probably illegitimate) offspring, or their deserted wives, or their sorrowing old fathers and mothers, from the Orkney islands to Capetown. Every time the smokeroom stewards saw us throw off another solicitor they set up the drinks on the house, for, as they told us, it was unprecedented for a male passenger in the Cunard to escape his inevitable doom for such a stretch of time. Many, of course, held out for a day or two, and a few extraordinarily recalcitrant curmudgeons stood it for three days, or even four, but never since the *Britannia* sailed from Liverpool on July 4, 1840 had anyone ever survived so long as a week. This happy state of affairs prevailed until the night before we made Gibraltar, and we attained to such eminence aboard that not a few other passengers, escaping momentarily from whatever horror was afoot, came to the smokeroom door to gape at us and admire us. But after dinner that evening the massed committees of the ship's company combined to assault and rout us, and after an all-too-brief and far from glorious struggle we were had.

I need not add, I hope, that it was not argument that took us, nor anything properly describable as an appeal to our better nature: it was simply the use of female pulchritude, and in the rawest and most unsportsmanlike fashion. Hitherto all the ladies who had tackled us had been mature and even more or less overripe damsels of the sort who naturally take to good works, whether on land or sea. The worst of them came close to looking like members of the W.C.T.U., and even the best, when they were not plainly retired opera singers or cashiered stock-company actresses, carried about them a faint, sickening suggestion of Christian endeavor. But now all that orthodox but puerile technic was

out of the window, and the master-minds of the
committees, laying their heads together, were trying us with a new and far sharper excalibur. In
brief, they rounded up the three rosiest, sweetest,
triggest, archest, sauciest and all-round charming-
est cuties in the ship, and set them on us as a pot-
hunter might turn a pack of bloodhounds upon a
poor fieldmouse. We had never seen these cuties
before, for they had spent all their time dancing in
the social hall, and our own station, as I have said,
had been in the smokeroom, but now, as they bore
down upon us with pretty giggles, we got a massive
eyeful, and in ten seconds we were undone. Nor did
we recover when they began unloading the selling-
talk that the committeemen had prepared for them.
What they wanted us to do, they explained ever so
alluringly, was to squire them to a mock wedding
that was presently to be staged in the dining-room,
which had been cleared for the occasion. They were
to appear at this mock wedding in the character of
bridesmaids, and we were to be ushers. No rehearsal, they assured us, would be necessary. So far as
our own participation was concerned, it would be a
wedding like any other, and if occasional prompt-
ing turned out to be necessary they would supply
it, at the same time hanging on to our arms. All the
speaking parts were in other hands. *Allons*, com-
rades, the audience waits! Moffett, with a faint
blush for the smokeroom stewards who glared re-
proachfully from behind their bar, offered his arm

to a blonde who looked like Lillian Russell at the age of seventeen, Mac grabbed a little brunette who seemed to be of mixed Russian, French, Spanish, Algonquin and angel blood, and I was left with a red-haired girl so lovely that when I looked at her I saw only an explosion of rubies and amethysts.

Thus we were bagged, and thus we marched ignominiously to the dining-room, each hanging on to his Delilah. A large company of poor fish was already assembled, and the chief bore of the ship, a loud, officious, Rotarian-sort of fellow, was planted under an arch of British flags in the low comedy rôle of the officiating clergyman. Presently the ship's bugler blew five or six measures of the " Lohengrin " wedding march, the bride and groom marched in from the pantry, the best man and chief bridesmaid fell in behind them, and Moffett, Mac and I, with our trio of palpitating pretties, took up the rear. Of the bride I can only recall that she was a fair specimen of run-of-the-mine goods, and of the bridegroom only that he looked considerably alarmed. Later on I heard that the bride actually had her eye on him, and that they became engaged while visiting the grave of Percy Bysshe Shelley at Rome. But on that point I have only rumor, and moreover, it is irrelevant. What I remember most clearly, and indeed with a sort of dizzy dazzle, is the marriage service that the Rotarian began to read. It opened as follows:

Dearly beloved, we are gathered here together in the face of this company to join together this man and woman in asceptic matrimony, which is commended by Mendel, Ehrlich, Metchnikoff and others to be honorable among men, and therefore is not to be entered into inadvisedly or carelessly, or without due surgical precautions, but reverently, cleanly, sterilely, soberly, scientifically, and with the nearest practicable approach to chemical purity.

And so on, and so on. The audience, at first, was astonished into silence, but in a little while a few women began to titter, and soon there were snorts all over the room. The three cuties took it very merrily, and mine gave me more than one dig in the ribs with her incomparable elbow. Meanwhile, the Rotarian boomed on in roaring tones, calling upon the bridegroom to say so plainly if he were suffering from any " lesion, infection, malaise, congenital defect, hereditary taint or other impediment," and finally commanding him to produce medical certificates or forever hold his peace. At this, the bridegroom took a long envelope from his inside pocket and handed it to the Rotarian, who broke its seal in a very ceremonious manner, withdrew a paper fluttering a red ribbon, and proceeded to read from it as follows:

We, and each of us, having subjected the bearer to a rigid clinical and laboratory examination, do hereby certify that, to the best of our knowledge and belief, he is free from all disease, taint, defect, deformity or hereditary blemish. Temperature *per ora:* 98.6. Pulse: 76, strong. Respiration: 28.5. Wassermann: minus two. Phthalein: first hour, 46 per cent; second hour, 21 per cent. White blood corpuscle count: 8,925. Free gastric hydrochloric acid: 11.5 per cent. No stasis. No lactic acid.

By this time the dining-room was in an uproar, and the three cuties seemed to be on the point of busting with laughter. I was somewhat amused myself, and, in secret, delighted, but I was even more astounded, for *I had written that wedding service myself.* Yea, I had not only written it, but printed it, to wit, in the *Smart Set* for October 1913, pp. 63 *ff.*[1] Thus I listened to the Rotarian's somewhat sketchy and ruffianly version of it with all the fascination that enthralls any dramatic author when he sees his own play on the stage, and while the thing was going on I gave scarcely a thought to the throbbing virgin at my side. Nor did Mac pay any attention to his delectable brunette, for he had read the piece in the magazine and knew that I had written it. When the show was over, to great salvos of huzzahs at the end, the three cuties deserted us for their regular platoons of beaux, and we resumed our pews in the smokeroom. It may be that the Rotarian, in one of his innumerable bulletins and speeches to his suffering fellow-passengers, had given proper credit to the author, but if so we

1 It was entitled A Eugenic Wedding and was signed Owen Hatteras, a *nom de plume* I used in those days whenever my monthly contributions to the *Smart Set* were so numerous that they could not all be published under my own name. With the title changed to Asepsis: A Deduction in *Scherzo* Form, it was reprinted in my Book of Burlesques; New York, 1916.

heard nothing of it, and Mac, who was a *legum baccalaureus* of the University of Virginia and full of lingering Confederate war-lust, was all for suing him in the courts for infringement of copyright. This seemed a bad idea to me, for the copyright had been taken out, not in my name, but in that of the *Smart Set*, and anything we recovered from the Rotarian would go to John Adams Thayer, then the proprietor of the magazine. Inasmuch as Thayer was already very well heeled, I could see no sense in engorging him further, but Mac insisted that important principles were at stake, and also conjured up a number of interesting questions of law. Could we sue the Rotarian in Gibraltar, where we were due to land the next morning, or would we have to wait until we got back to New York? Furthermore, wasn't the Cunard Steamship Company responsible, as *particeps criminis*, and if so couldn't we proceed against it in admiralty, libel the *Laconia*, hang up the tour, and expose the ship to hundreds of claims for damages to the other passengers? Mac had no law-books with him, and in fact had not looked into one since he took his degree in 1898, but he kept on laboring the matter until the smokeroom stewards turned out the lights on us at 3 a.m. and we had to go to bed. The next morning, after we had landed on the Rock and were getting down *Humpen* of bicarbonate of soda in its only drug-store, he resumed the subject, but as the bicarbonate began to open the pores of his mind he forgot it, and after that I heard no more from him about it. Whether or not the Rotarian really lifted my play without credit I do not know to this day. If he did, then I forgive him belatedly and wish him good luck in his chosen career, whatever it may be.

A few days later the *Laconia* reached Naples and we went ashore through the barrage of bumboats, broken-down steam-launches and other such crazy craft that once made a riot of that lovely port. The depth of water at the docks was then insufficient to float an ocean steamer, and passengers had to be ferried in row-boats. These row-boats were operated by members of the Black Hand, and they hated one another almost as much as they hated humanity in general. Thus getting to land was a more or less hazardous business, for the instant a passenger appeared at the gangway all the Black Handers for a block around began to fight for his business. Nor was the battle over when one of them got him, for the rest proceeded to ram the victorious boat, and to prod both its operator and its passenger with their oars. It was very uncommon for a passenger to get ashore without being doused, and not infrequently he lost his baggage. On the quay he went through another similar mauling, for the customs-house red-caps, all of them gorillas brought in from the penitentiaries of Sicily, fought for him just as the boatmen had fought for him. It is a literal fact that it took Ed, Mac and me two hours to

get through the customs, though we had nothing
to declare and the actual officials were very polite.
All the delay was caused by our porters, who had
to fight for us from the moment they collared us
until they finally landed us on the street. This fighting, of course, was not done in silence. The screaming and howling, in fact, were even worse than the
jostling, and by the time the three of us got to our
hotel in the Via Caracciolo we were pretty well worn
out.

This, of course, was before the days of Mussolini, and Italy was still innocent of efficiency engineering. Exactly twenty years later, in 1934, I
returned to Naples, again by sea. I was aboard a
German liner of at least twice the tonnage of the
Laconia, but it tied up at a dock with the greatest
ease and even elegance. Looking ashore, I could see
nothing of the frantic Black Handers of 1914. At
the far end of the dock a long row of taxicabs was
lined up, and between them and the ship stood four
or five men in uniform. Whenever a passenger went
ashore one of these functionaries approached him
politely, asked him if he required a taxi, whistled
for one if he said yes, and then put him aboard it
with a deep bow. There was no more uproar than
you will hear in the middle of the Mojave Desert,
and not the slightest sign of excitement. Going
ashore for a little walk, I seemed to be in a city that
had died and been embalmed. Where were the sell-
ers of dirty postcards that had swarmed over Ed,

Mac and me in 1914? Where were the loud and urgent guides to Pompeii, to the art galleries, to the bawdy-houses? Where were the hawkers plastered with lottery-tickets? Where was all the old-time hullabaloo? Alas, it had gone with the wind, and a Fascist calm prevailed. After walking for a while I came to a little square, and there, across the grass, I saw an evil-looking youth who took me back twenty years. He saw me too, and began to approach me in a stealthy, furtive way, pausing anon to glance back over his shoulder. If any human being ever had seller of dirty postcards written on his face it was that unappetizing young wop, and I halted to give him a chance to make his sales approach. I was not, of course, in the market for his wares, but I yearned to hear him for old time's sake. But when he was not more than fifteen feet from me he stopped suddenly, stared over my shoulder like a pointer become aware of a quail, turned white with an unearthly greenish cast, and then made off to starboard with long, nervous, skulking strides, and vanished into the shadows of an alley. As he disappeared I about-faced to find out what had alarmed him. Half a block away I saw a perfect simulacrum of Benito Himself — an obvious plain-clothes man in the Fascist béret, his legs planted firmly, his arms folded in authoritative challenge, an imitation of the Mussolini frown upon his face. Such were the hazards of an innocent and industrious dirty-postcard vendor under the New Order

in Italy. Such was life in sterilized and dephlogisti-
cated Naples, once so gay with iniquities and stinks.
Such, I reflected sadly, was human progress.

But in 1914 Naples was still as free and natural
as it had been in the days when its bristling walls
scared off Hannibal. Its main streets had not been
swept since the Sixteenth Century, and in many of
its alleys there was an accumulation of garbage
going back to Roman times. Ed, Mac and I had a
grand time exploring its marvels and devouring its
garlicky and excellent victuals. One day we went
out to Capri and got lost among its vineyards, and
another day we hoofed the ruins of Pompeii and
were introduced by a friendly guide to an antique
factory adjacent, where we saw the workmen turning out Roman bronzes by the gross, all plainly
marked 200 B.C., to reassure tourists. At night we
would resort to the Galleria Umberto and listen to
the singing contests going on there all the time.
We had two large rooms at our hotel, with a magnificent bathroom adjoining, including a shower.
On the morning after our arrival I arose before the
others, and went to this bathroom to take a bath.
First I soaped myself from head to foot and then I
got under the shower and turned the handle. But
no water came out. Seeing a small stool in a corner,
I mounted it to investigate, but I could not solve
the mystery, and soon the soap got into my eyes
and blinded me, and I had to call for help. Mac responded by beating on all the pipes with the heel of

one of his shoes, but the more practical Ed went to
the telephone and called up the office. The clerk below, it appeared, could not understand English,
and Ed's Italian was far from perfect. While I tried
to mop off the soap with a towel ten feet long I
could hear him roaring into the 'phone: " Da wat'
no come in da pipe! Da dam machina no worka!
Senda da chief engineer dam quicka! "

In a few minutes there was a rap at the door,
and Mac admitted a chambermaid. She was armed
with a broom, a bucket, a mop and various other
apparatus, and turned out, fortunately, to have a
a few words of German, so I soon explained to her,
clad in that mainsail of a towel, what was wrong.
She was an efficient woman, as efficiency ran in Italy in those days, and instantly fell to work. First,
she turned on the water full tilt — but it still refused to flow. Then she put the stool into the tub,
mounted it, withdrew a large hairpin from her hair,
and proceeded to investigate the sprinkler. The
first hole she tackled turned out to be solid with
rust, but she managed by hard gouging to coax a
drop of water out of it. Encouraged, she turned to
a hole in the center of the sprinkler, and gave it a
sudden and powerful jab. There was a large scab
of rust inside, apparently covering half a dozen
holes. When this scab gave way it gave way all over,
and as a result she got a rush of water squarely in
the eye, and went over backward, yelling blue murder. The scene followed the most austere lines of

classical farce; in fact, it was worthy of Billy Watson's Beef Trust. Ed, Mac and I whooped and roared in our vulgar mirth, but when the lady became bellicose we threw her out, and I resumed my bath. When we shoved off for Rome the hotel's bill showed an item of two lire for repairing the shower, but Mac threatened suit and we got away without paying it.

We arrived in Rome late at night, and after taking a walk and a couple of drinks rolled into the hay. The next morning we were up bright and early, and on our way to St. Peter's. There we put in two or three hours admiring its wonders, especially the immense *pissoir* on the roof — the largest in Europe — , and by noon we found ourselves in the alley between the cathedral and the Vatican, thumbing through postcards at a stand there set up. While we were so engaged an American we had met on the ship strolled up, and the four of us decided to lunch together. But before we could set off for an eating-house we noticed a group of people gathered about a priest a little farther up the alley, with the priest haranguing them violently. It seemed worth looking into, so we approached the group and I noted that the priest was talking German. From his remarks it quickly appeared that his customers were pious pilgrims from Vienna, that they had been forty-eight hours in day-coaches on the way — I could well believe it by their smell — , that they had an appointment to be received by the Pope, that the time set was only a few minutes hence, and that their pastor was giving them a last-minute refresher course in Vatican etiquette. Over and over again he explained to them the stage management of a papal audience, and cautioned them to behave in a seemly and Christian manner. They would be lined up on their knees, he said, and His Holiness would walk down the line, blessing them as he went and offering them his ring to kiss. Under no circumstances were they to attempt to kiss his hand, but only the ring. " Nicht die Hand! " he kept on repeating. " Küsst den Ring! " Nor did he stop with this brief, almost military order: he also went into the considerations lying behind it. What a scandal it would be, he said, if the illustrious Pope of Rome, the spiritual father of the whole universe, were exposed in his own almost sacred person to the lewd osculation of the vulgar! What an insult to His Holiness, and what a source of obscene joy to the vast hordes of infidels! His ring was provided as a means of warding off any such calamity. It, and not his hand, was to be kissed. " Nicht die Hand, Kinder! Küsst den Ring! "

So saying, he signaled the pilgrims to follow him. As they moved over toward a door making into the Vatican I looked at Mac, Mac looked at Ed, Ed looked at the stranger from the *Laconia*, and the stranger looked at me. Why not, indeed? The group was large enough for us to be lost in it, and the pilgrims seemed to be of very low mental visibility. As for the priest, he was marching ahead of them, with his back to them and us. We therefore ducked among them, and in a minute we were marching down one of the long corridors of the Vatican, headed for the audience chamber. I expected to see a large hall elegantly turned out, with maybe a couple of pictures by Raphael or Leonardo on its walls, but the priest actually led us into a series of modest rooms that looked like parlors in a bourgeois home. They were arranged *en suite*, and the Pope, I gathered, would traverse them one after another. The priest was in the room nearest His Holiness's entrance, but when he issued a command that we fall on our knees it was relayed down the line, and we all obeyed. Mac kneeled to my left and Ed to my right and beyond Ed was the stranger. We waited patiently, but in some uneasiness. What if we were detected? Would the Swiss guards who stood at every door simply throw us out, or would it be a matter for the police? We had not long to suffer, for in a minute there was a murmur in the room beyond us and in another minute the Pope was passing before us, holding out his ring to be kissed.

He was Pius X, born Sarto, already an ancient man and beginning to break up. From the floor where we kneeled he looked tall, but I doubt that he was so in fact. His skin was of a startling whiteness, and he stooped from the effects of a large swelling at the back of his neck — not, of course, a goitre, but of the same general dimensions and aspect. As he came into our room, preceded by a chamberlain and followed by two guards, an ormolu clock on the marble mantelpiece struck twelve. He moved slowly and with effort, and appeared to be almost unaware of his visitors, though he held out his hand for the kissing of his ring, and smiled wanly. Save for the whispered words of his blessing he said nothing, and neither did any of the pilgrims. He had been Pope, by now, for eleven years, and was close to eighty years old. A man of deep piety and simple tastes, he had resisted, back in 1880, an effort to make him Bishop of Treviso, but a few years later he had been caught by the cogs of the Roman escalator and by 1893 he was the Cardinal Patriarch of Venice and ten years later he was Pope. His reign, alas, had not been any too peaceful: there had been struggles with France, turmoils among the Italian bishops, and all sorts of vexatious disputes — about the powers and jurisdictions of the Papal courts, the text of canon law, the nomination of bishops, the reform of the breviary and of church music, and so on without ceasing. He looked immensely old as he passed so slowly before us, and pretty well worn out. But he walked without help, and in less than two minutes he was gone. This was in May, 1914. Two months later a shot was fired at Sarajevo in faraway Bosnia, and on August 2 World War I began. His Holiness survived that blasting of all his hopes of peace on earth by less than three weeks. On August 20 he was dead.

Once he vanished, Mac, Ed, the stranger and I
made tracks out of the room, for we feared that the
priest might come back and discover us. Without
anyone to guide us, we got lost at once, and were
presently astonished to find ourselves in the Sistine
Chapel. It was quite empty, and we hid there for
ten minutes — long enough to throw off the scent.
Then we tried the first long corridor that offered,
and at its end found a door which took us out into
the glare of noontime Rome. A horse-hack was
waiting nearby, and in it we rode grandly to our
hotel. There was a large assemblage of *Laconia*
passengers in the dining-room, and some of them
asked us where we had been. When we replied that
we had been undergoing the honor of an audience
with the Pope there were sniffs of incredulity, and
mingled with that incredulity there was not a little hostility. Some of those other passengers were
pious Catholics come to Rome for the express purpose of paying their respects to His Holiness, but
when they had gone to the American College that
morning to apply for an audience they had been
told that it would involve a great many onerous
formalities and probably a long wait. So many applications were piled up, in fact, that the best the
clergy at the college could promise, even to a ninth-
degree Knight of Columbus and his lady, was a
possible look-in some time in July. Actual bishops,
it appeared, were hanging about for weeks before
their numbers turned up. Moreover, all the lay ap-

plicants were warned that their appointments, if, when and as obtained at all, would be for designated weeks, not for specific days, and that they might have to stand by from end to end of those weeks, the men in boiled shirts and tail coats and the ladies in black gowns with long sleeves. If, at the moment of their summons, they were not so arrayed, they would miss their turns, and maybe have to wait three months before they were called again.

All of this, naturally enough, had filled the pilgrims with unpleasant sentiments, and they were in no mood to listen with any appreciation to the tale of our own exploit. It was already very hot in Rome, and they could well imagine what it would be like in July or August to sit in unventilated hotel rooms for a week on end, clad in boiled shirts and long sleeves. At the start, they eased their minds by denouncing us as liars of unparalleled effrontery, but as we added various details in support of our narrative, they had to admit that we were probably telling something more or less resembling the truth, and thereupon they took refuge in the theory that our uninvited visit was not only an insult to the Pope, but also a carnal and blasphemous attack upon Holy Church itself, and upon the True Faith that it inculcated. The Knights of Columbus present were all too old and bulky to hope to beat us up, but they talked darkly of employing Black Handers for the purpose, and even hinted that they knew a Jesuit who could supply the Black Handers. We replied primly that there was a lawyer in our outfit, and that if any such threats were carried out he would know how to launch the secular law upon all persons responsible. This seemed to daunt the knights, who had a high reverence for the police of all nations, and they gradually subsided into mutterings about the impertinence of Protestants, and, even worse, of infidels, and the need of laws barring them from the capital of Christendom. All we could reply to that was that Teddy Roosevelt and William Jennings Bryan were both Protestants, and that Thomas Jefferson had been an infidel. It was a somewhat feeble argument, and we did not press it. In consequence, the debate gradually petered out, and when we left at last the knights and their ladies had gone back to discussing the discomforts of boiled shirts and long sleeves in hot weather.

Having now seen both St. Peter's and the Vatican and enjoyed the distinction — whether honorable or infamous — of having been received by the Pope in private audience, we decided that we had given enough time to Rome and its environs, and the next day we set out for Munich by the Brenner Express. We had an instructive and somewhat noisy time in that beautiful city, but for the purposes of the present narrative what we saw, heard and did during our visit is neither here nor there.

XII

WINTER VOYAGE

[*1916*]

IN the closing days of 1916, having been hired by
a newspaper to investigate the war raging in Europe, I sailed from New York in a Danish ship,
and seventeen days later found myself in Copenhagen. It was a slow trip, even for war time, but
my recollections of it do not have to do with its
duration, but with two relatively minor details:
(*a*) the excessively mixed and belligerent nature of
the ship's company, and (*b*) the stupendous eating
and drinking that went on aboard. Nearly every
nationality that I had heard of up to that time was
represented among the passengers, and each *bloc*
hated and reviled all the others. It did not surprise
me, of course, to find the Germans and French on
somewhat distant terms, or the Poles and Austrians, but I was certainly amazed when it turned out
that the Danes, Norwegians, Swedes and Finns
were bitter enemies, each to the other three, that the

only Scotsman refused to speak to the Englishmen, and that the French actually joined the Germans in contemning and excoriating the Italians.

At meals I sat at the doctor's table, with a Russian general in the place of honor at the other end. This general, who wore stupendous Hindenburg mustaches, glared at his trough-fellows through breakfast, lunch and dinner, and refused either to speak to them or to answer them when they spoke to him. The theory arose that he probably knew no language save Russian, so a Czech who spoke it was brought up from the second cabin to tackle him. The general, for perhaps five minutes, took no notice whatever, but the Czech was a persistent fellow, and finally dredged a single sentence out of those fearful mustaches. He reported that it was a profane declaration, *in Russian*, that the general could not speak Russian. How he talked to his adjutant, who sat beside him, I do not know, for they exchanged only grunts at meals, and between meals they disappeared.

All during those intervals, I suppose, the general slept in his cabin, for it is hard to imagine anyone keeping awake after the gargantuan feeds he got down. Certainly they never ran to less than 45,000 calories apiece, not counting bread, butter and the sugar in the coffee. Well do I recall his breakfast on the first day out, for it was a rough morning, and most of the other passengers at our table confined themselves to toast and tea. But not

151

the general. He began with three oranges *au na-turel,* followed them with a large plate of oatmeal swimming in cream, topped it with a double order of ham and eggs, and then proceeded to run through all the Danish delicacies on the table — six or eight kinds of smoked fish, as many of sausage, a bowl of pickled pigs' ears, another of spiced lambs' tongues, a large slab of Gjedser cheese, and five or six slices of toasted rye-bread spread with red caviare. To wash down this mammoth *frokost* he drank four cups of coffee and two of tea. When he finished at last a couple of waiters rushed up to help him to his feet, but he shook them off, arose with the dignity of Neptune emerging from the sea, and stalked away in his best parade-ground manner. His adjutant, following at a respectful six paces, wobbled precariously, for the ship was doing a forty-degree roll, but the general was still as perpendicular as a meridian of longitude when he disappeared down the corridor to his quarters.

By lunchtime the weather had moderated considerably, and all hands at the table were ready for earnest eating, but the general was in full form by now and managed to grab so much of everything that there was little left for the rest of us. He was aided in this enterprise by the fact that the rules of the Danish merchant marine in those days — and, for all I know, the constitution of Denmark — ordained that everything after the soup should be brought to the table on large platters and passed round. This passing round, of course, should have started with the ship's doctor at the head of the table — an old man in a long beard, and himself, as it soon appeared, no contemptible glutton — but the waiters had to come in through a door that was just behind the general's chair, and he thus got first whack at them — no doubt illegally, but none the less effectively, for he grabbed their arms if they tried to pass him. The pièce de résistance at that first lunch was a pair of gigantic cabbages stuffed with sausage meat and decorated with potato balls, beets and turnips cut into fancy designs, and hard-boiled eggs. The general nabbed the larger of the two cabbages, and had got half of it down before the other one could be carved by the doctor and served to the remaining fourteen men at the table. The doctor, incensed, instructed the waiters to make a detour around the general thereafter, but he turned out to have a reach like a gorilla, and when one of them presently staggered in with a huge plate of spare ribs and sauerkraut he had nailed two-thirds of the spare ribs and nearly all the sauerkraut before you could say Jack Robinson. And so with every other dish that followed — maybe six or eight in all, for the Danes fed their customers as if fattening them for slaughter. But it was not until the end of lunch that the general let go the last link of his virtuosity. By that time, though we had got only his meagre leavings, we were all pretty well filled, and hence hardly fit to do justice to the gigantic board of Danish pastry that ended the meal. But not the general. There were twelve separate and distinct kinds of pastry on it — and he grabbed two of each. When, having got them down, he began work on six cups of coffee, his mustaches glittered like a Christmas tree with the accumulated marmalade, powdered sugar and whipped cream.

The ship's doctor, during the two or three days following, tried various schemes to curb and baffle the old boy, but they all failed, and the only remedy remaining was to order double rations for the table. This was done, and an extra waiter was added to help rassle them, but the general improved as the service improved, and at the end of the first week the double rations had to be lifted to treble. Rather curiously, we never saw him take a drink of anything alcoholic. For a couple of days after this abstemiousness was remarked a theory floated about that he was off the stuff in compliment to King George V of England, who had gone on the waterwagon at the beginning of the war, but in the end most of the other men at the table chose to believe rather that he knocked off a quart or so of vodka before every meal, in the quiet of his quarters. We discussed him constantly despite his presence, for it was assumed as a matter of course that he knew no English, which was the common language of the table. Because of his mustaches the boys gave him the name of the Walrus. He never took any no-

tice of these debates about him, nor did he show
any resentment when all hands downed tools to
watch him snare a whole leg of veal, or wolf another
double dozen of Danish pastries. These pastries
changed at every meal: it was the boast of the line
that the same one was never served twice. The Walrus ate two of each variety at lunch and three at
dinner. At the end of the long voyage, as we were
all shivering in the customs shed at Copenhagen,
he addressed a fellow passenger for the first time
— and in excellent English. " I knew," he said,
" that you called me the Walrus, but I didn't give
a damn." Then he made off in the car of the Russian minister to Denmark, and was seen no more.

His avoidance of alcohol would have made him a
marked man on that ship, even if he had confined
himself to ordinary eating, for he was the only teetotaler, whether actual or apparent, among the
passengers. The rest guzzled day and night, full of
a resigned belief that a German submarine might
fetch them all at any minute. We were at sea on
New Year's Eve, somewhere off the coast of Greenland. It was too cold to go on deck, so the whole
ship's company gathered in the smokeroom in the
early afternoon, and gradually worked up a party
of the very highest amperage. It appeared that it
was the custom of the line for the ship's band, on
such gala occasions, to play the national airs of all
the countries represented among the passengers,
but this time the captain forbade it, for he feared

riots. Along toward midnight one of the Americans aboard played a joke on the band (and the captain) by digging up a *potpourri* of harmless German folk-songs (it began with " O Tannenbaum ") and asking the leader to put it on. The leader, who was also the bull fiddler, was so far gone in liquor by now that he could hardly stand up to his instrument, so he agreed amiably and at once plunged into the music. He either did not know, or had forgotten in his cups, that it ended with " Die Wacht am Rhein." Before he could pull up he was down to " Lieb' Vaterland, magst ruhig sein," and a Class A rough-house was in the making.

The Germans aboard (they were on their way home from Mexico and points South under a sort of flag of truce) were all either septuagenarians or cripples, but they leaped to their feet as one man, and began to *hoch* and howl in loud, exultant tones. This, of course, brought forth hoots and hisses from the English, Scotch, Canadians, French, Belgians, Russians, Japs, Italians and Rumanians, with encouragement from most of the Americans, Scandinavians, Hollanders and Latin Americans. When the first beer glass smashed a window the waiters and musicians took to flight, and in half a minute the master-at-arms was on the job with a squad of sailors, and on his heels came the captain. " Die Wacht am Rhein " having been played, the captain now had to admit that, in common equity, all the other national anthems should be played also, and when the musicians were rounded up and brought back it was solemnly done, with the master-at-arms and his goons mounting guard. At the end of the ceremonial two Swedes sitting in a corner rose up to protest that the anthem of Sweden had been forgotten. It was then that the enmity between the various Scandinavian nations became most painfully apparent, for the Danish leader of the band, half sober after his scare, replied sneeringly that Sweden *had* no anthem. The Norwegians and Danes cheered this insult, whereupon the two Swedes climbed up on their table and announced that they would *sing* their anthem, band or no band. This they did in indifferent voices, while the master-at-arms and his men kept order with drawn clubs and knives.

The party lasted for three days and nights; in fact, it was still going on, at least in spots, when we were hauled into Kirkwall and the English came out to search the ship and investigate its passengers. During this business, which went on intermittently for two days and ended with a dozen passengers being taken off for internment, the Danes denounced all the Swedes and Norwegians as German spies, the Swedes denounced all the Danes and Norwegians, and the Norwegians denounced all the Danes and Swedes. The only Finn was jugged at Kirkwall, and most of the Britons of various factions went ashore there, but the Walrus and his adjutant remained aboard, and during the trip across the

North Sea to what was then Christiania, the first
stop on the final lap to Copenhagen, he gave one of
his most impressive exhibitions. The principal dish
at lunch that day was a so-called suckling pig large
enough to have grandchildren: it was garnished
with links of sausages, stuffed with bread crumbs
and fine herbs, and had in its maw an apple so large
that it seemed to have choked to death. The Walrus
sawed off both its head and tail, and with the tail
got its whole left hind leg, including the ham. This
herculean helping he tamped down with a dozen
sausages and about two quarts of the stuffing.
While he was gobbling away a steward rushed in
with the news that a German submarine was in
sight, and we all ran on deck to get a look at it, and
make our peace with our Maker. Somewhat to our
disappointment it merely circled round us twice,
and then made off politely. When we got back to
the dining-room the Walrus was helping himself
to the forequarters of the pig, and excavating another quart of stuffing.

We got to Christiania (now Oslo) the next evening immediately after dinner, and the three waiters at the doctor's table went ashore at once,
leaving the Walrus only half way through his
mountain of Danish pastry. The rest of us followed
soon afterward, eager for a tilt at the night life of
Henrik Ibsen's old home-town, but it turned out to
be under four feet of snow, and pretty dismal.
Worse, something on the order of Prohibition had

been clamped down a week or so before, and the only spot we could find that was open and functioning was the main dining-room of the Grand Hotel, a huge chamber with a plush carpet and tarnished gilt lighting fixtures, about as cheering as the slumber-room of a mortician. After we had swallowed some bad beer and looked at the favorite chair of Ibsen we took to plodding about in the snow, hoping against hope that we would hear the sound of revelry somewhere else. We never did, but twice we caught sight of our three waiters and judged enviously that they must have been more lucky. They were crowded into a decrepit taxicab with three girls who had certainly not come from the Y.W.C.A., and as they passed us they gave us loud and boozy greetings, but did not invite us to join them. The next morning, when the ship cast off for Copenhagen and we came down for breakfast, we heard the story of their evening's adventures. This was before the German inflation, but Mexico, always forward-looking, had already gone off the gold standard, and in New York the boys had picked up a couple of hatsful of fifty-peso Mexican greenbacks at a quarter of a cent on the dollar. Two of these greenbacks, we learned, had paid for their whole entertainment in Christiania, though it included wine, women and song. The girls, not knowing about Mexico's forehandedness and assuming that a peso was still worth half a Norwegian crown, had provided all the drinks of the evening, the taxi hire, square meals for six, and the room rent — and even returned $3 change in sound crowns, then still worth 25 cents apiece.

This news got about before the three waiters themselves showed up. When they marched in with their trays, and the Walrus stretched out his mighty hooks to grab them, all the other men at the doctor's table leaped up and gave them three cheers, such being the natural hatred of men for women. And at lunch that day the three Danes and two Swedes at the table opened a couple of magnums of champagne in their honor, such being the natural hatred of all other Scandinavians for Norwegians.

XIII

GORE

IN THE CARIBBEES

[*1917*]

No reporter of my generation, whatever his genius, ever really rated spats and a walking-stick until he had covered both a lynching and a revolution. The first, by the ill-favor of the gods, I always missed, usually by an inch. How often, alas, alas, did I strain and puff my way to some Christian hamlet of the Chesapeake Bay littoral, by buggy, farm-wagon or pack-mule, only to discover that an anti-social sheriff had spirited the blackamoor away, leaving nothing but a seething vacuum behind. Once, as I was on my travels, the same thing happened in the charming town of Springfield, Mo., the Paris and Gomorrah of the Ozarks. I was at dinner at the time with the late Edson K. Bixby, editor of the Springfield *Leader*, along with Paul Pat-

terson and Henry M. Hyde, my colleagues of the
Baltimore *Sunpapers.* When the alarm reached us
we abandoned our victuals instantly, and leaped
and galloped downtown to the jail. By the time we
got there, though it was in less than three minutes,
the cops had loaded the candidate — he was a white
man — into their hurry-wagon and made off for
Kansas City, and the lynching mob had been reduced to a hundred or so half-grown youths, a couple of pedlars selling hot-dogs and American flags,
and a squawking herd of fascinated but disappointed children.

I had rather better luck with revolutions, though
I covered only one, and that one I walked into by a
sort of accident. The year was 1917 and I was returning from a whiff of World War I in a Spanish
ship that had sailed from La Coruña, Spain, ten
days before and was hoping, eventually, to get to
Havana. It was, at the moment, somewhat in the
maze of the Bahamas, but a wireless reached it nevertheless, and that wireless was directed to me and
came from the *Sunpaper* office in Baltimore. It
said, in brief, that a revolution had broken out in
Cuba, that both sides were doing such rough lying
that no one north of the Straits of Florida could
make out what it was about, and that a series of
succinct and illuminating dispatches describing its
issues and personalities would be appreciated. I
wirelessed back that the wishes of my superiors
were commands, and then sent another wireless to

a friend in Havana, Captain Asmus Leonhard, marine superintendent of the Munson Line, saying
that I itched to see him the instant my ship made
port. Captain Leonhard was a Dane of enormous
knowledge but parsimonious speech, and I had a
high opinion of his sagacity. He knew everyone
worth knowing in Latin America, and thousands
who were not, and his estimates of them seldom took
more than three words. " A burglar," he would say,
characterizing a general played up by all the North
American newspapers as the greatest trans-Rio
Grande hero since Bolívar, or " a goddam fraud,"
alluding to a new president of Colombia, San Salvador or Santo Domingo, and that was all. His reply to my wireless was in his usual manner. It said:
" Sure."

When the Spanish ship, after groping about for
two or three days in Exuma Sound, the North-East
Providence Channel, the Tongue of Ocean and various other strangely-named Bahaman waterways,
finally made Havana and passed the Morro, a
smart young mulatto in Captain Leonhard's launch
put out from shore, took me aboard his craft, and
whisked me through the customs. The captain himself was waiting in front of the Pasaje Hotel in the
Prado, eating a plate of Spanish bean-soup and
simultaneously smoking a Romeo y Julietta cigar.
" The issues in the revolution," he said, tackling
the business in hand at once, " are simple. Menocal,
who calls himself a Conservative, is president, and

José Miguel Gomez, who used to be president and
calls himself a Liberal, wants to make a come-back.
That is the whole story. José Miguel says that when
Menocal was reëlected last year the so-called Lib-
erals were chased away from the so-called polls by
the so-called army. On the other hand, Menocal
says that José Miguel is a porch-climber and ought
to be chased out of the island. Both are right."

It seemed clear enough, and I prepared to write
a dispatch at once, but Captain Leonhard suggested that perhaps it might be a good idea for me
to see Menocal first, and hear the official version in
full. We were at the palace in three minutes, and
found it swarming with dignitaries. Half of them
were army officers in uniform, with swords, and
the other half were functionaries of the secreta-
riat. They pranced and roared all over the place,
and at intervals of a few seconds more officers would
dash up in motor-cars and muscle and whoop their
way into the president's office. These last, explained Captain Leonhard, were couriers from the
front, for José Miguel, having taken to the bush,
was even now surrounded down in Santa Clara
province, and there were high hopes that he would
be nabbed anon. Despite all the hurly-burly it took
only ten minutes for the captain to get me an audience with *el presidente*. I found His Excellency
calm and amiable. He spoke English fluently, and
was far from reticent. José Miguel, he said, was a
fiend in human form who hoped by his treasons

to provoke American intervention, and so upset the
current freely-chosen and impeccably virtuous government. This foul plot would fail. The gallant Cuban army, which had never lost either a battle or a
war, had the traitor cornered, and within a few days
he would be chained up among the lizards in the
fortress of La Cabaña, waiting for the firing-squad
and trying in vain to make his peace with God.

So saying, *el presidente* bowed me out, at the
same time offering to put a motor-car and a secretary at my disposal. It seemed a favorable time to
write my dispatch, but Captain Leonhard stayed
me. " First," he said, " you had better hear what
the revolutionists have to say." " The revolutionists! " I exclaimed. " I thought they were out in
Santa Clara, surrounded by the army." " Some
are," said the captain, " but some ain't. Let us take
a hack." So we took a hack and were presently
worming our way down the narrow street called
Obispo. The captain called a halt in front of a
bank, and we got out. " I'll wait here in the bank,"
he said, " and you go upstairs to Room 309. Ask
for Dr. ——— " and he whispered a name. " Who is
this Dr. ———? " I whispered back. " He is the head
of the revolutionary junta," replied the captain.
" Mention my name, and he will tell you all about
it."

I followed orders, and was soon closeted with the
doctor — a very tall, very slim old man with a
straggling beard and skin the color of cement.

While we gabbled various persons rushed in and out
of his office, most of them carrying papers which
they slapped upon his desk. In a corner a young
Cuban girl of considerable sightliness banged away
at a typewriter. The doctor, like *el presidente*,
spoke excellent English, and appeared to be in
ebullient spirits. He had trustworthy agents, he
gave me to understand, in the palace, some of them
in high office. He knew what was going on in the
American embassy. He got carbons of all official
telegrams from the front. The progress of events
there, he said, was extremely favorable to the cause
of reform. José Miguel, though somewhat bulky
for field service, was a military genius comparable
to Joffre or Hindenburg, or even to Hannibal or
Alexander, and would soon be making monkeys of
the generals of the army. As for Menocal, he was a
fiend in human form who hoped to provoke American intervention, and thereby make his corrupt and
abominable régime secure.

All this naturally struck me as somewhat unusual, though as a newspaper reporter I was supposed to be incapable of surprise. Here, in the very
heart and gizzard of Havana, within sight and
hearing of thousands, the revolutionists were maintaining what amounted to open headquarters, and
their boss wizard was talking freely, and indeed
in a loud voice, to a stranger whose only introduction had been, so to speak, to ask for Joe. I ventured to inquire of the doctor if there were not some

danger that his gold-fish globe of a hideaway would be discovered. " Not much," he said. " The army is hunting for us, but the army is so stupid as to be virtually idiotic. The police know where we are, but they believe we are going to win, and want to keep their jobs afterward." From this confidence the doctor proceeded to boasting. " In ten days," he said, " we'll have Menocal jugged in La Cabaña. Shoot him? No; it would be too expensive. The New York banks that run him have plenty of money. If we let him live they will come across."

When I rejoined the captain downstairs I suggested again that it was high time for me to begin composing my dispatch, and this time he agreed. More, he hauled me down to the cable office, only a block or two away, and there left me. " If you get into trouble," he said, " call me up at the Pasaje. I'll be taking my nap, but the clerk will wake me if you need me." I found the cable office very comfortable and even luxurious. There were plenty of desks and typewriters, and when I announced myself I was invited to make myself free of them. Moreover, as I sat down and began to unlimber my prose a large brass spittoon was wheeled up beside me, apparently as a friendly concession to my nationality. At other desks a number of other gentlemen were in labor, and I recognized them at once as colleagues, for a newspaper reporter can always spot another, just as a Freemason can spot a Freemason, or a detective a detective. But I didn't know any of them, and fell to work without speaking to them. When my dispatch was finished I took it to the window, and was informed politely that it would have to be submitted to the censor, who occupied, it appeared, a room in the rear.

The censor turned out to be a young Cuban whose English was quite as good as Menocal's or the doctor's, but unhappily he had rules to follow, and I soon found that they were very onerous. While I palavered with him several of the colleagues came up with copy in their hands, and in two minutes an enormous debate was in progress. He was sworn, I soon gathered, to cut out everything even remotely resembling a fact. No names. No dates. Worse, no conjectures, prognostications, divinations. The colleagues, thus robbed of their habitual provender and full of outrage, put up a dreadful uproar, but the censor stood his ground, and presently I slipped away and called up Captain Leonhard. My respect for his influence was higher than ever now, and it had occurred to me that the revolutionists up the street might have a private cable, and that if they had he would undoubtedly be free of it. But when, in response to his order, I met him in front of the Pasaje, he said nothing about a cable, but heaved me instead into a hack. In ten minutes we were aboard an American ship just about to cast off from a wharf down in the region of the customs-house, and he was introducing me to one of the mates. " Tell him what to do," he said,

" and he will do it." I told the mate to file my dispatch the instant his ship docked at Key West, he nodded silently and put the copy into an inside pocket, and that was that. Then the siren sounded and the captain and I returned to the pier.

It all seemed so facile that I became somewhat uneasy. Could the mate be trusted? The captain assured me that he could. But what of the ship? Certainly it did not look fit for wrestling with the notorious swells of the Straits of Florida. Its lines suggested that it had started out in life as an excursion boat on the Hudson, and it was plainly in the last stages of decrepitude. I knew that the run to Key West was rather more than a hundred miles, and my guess, imparted to the captain, was that no such craft could make it in less than forty-eight hours. But the captain only laughed. " That old hulk," he said, " is the fastest ship in the Caribbean. If it doesn't hit a log or break in two it will make Key West in five and a half hours." He was right as usual, for that night, just as I was turning in at the Pasaje I received a cable from the *Sunpaper* saying that my treatise on the revolution had begun to run, and was very illuminating and high-toned stuff.

Thereafter, I unloaded all my dissertations in the same manner. Every afternoon I would divert attention by waiting on the censor and filing a dispatch so full of contraband that I knew he would never send it, and then I would go down to the wharf and look up the mate. On the fourth day he was *non est* and I was in a panic, for the captain had gone on a business trip into Pinar del Rio and no one else could help me. But just as the lines were being cast off I caught sight of a likely-looking Americano standing at the gangway and decided to throw myself upon his Christian charity. He responded readily, and my dispatch went through as usual. Thereafter, though the mate never showed up again — I heard later that he was sick in Key West — I always managed to find an accommodating passenger. Meanwhile, the censor's copy-hook accumulated a fine crop of my rejected cablegrams, and mixed with them were scores by the colleagues. Every time I went to the cable office I found the whole corps raising hell, and threatening all sorts of reprisals and revenges. But they seldom got anything through save the official communiqués that issued from the palace at hourly intervals.

These communiqués were prepared by a large staff of press-agents, and were not only couched in extremely florid words but ran to great lengths. I had just come from Berlin, where all that the German General Staff had to say every day, though war was raging on two fronts, was commonly put into no more than 300 words, so this Latin exuberance rather astonished me. But the stuff made gaudy reading, and I sent a lot of it to the *Sunpaper* by mail, for the entertainment and instruc-

tion of the gentlemen of the copy-desk. The Cuban
mails, of course, were censored like the cable, but
the same Americano who carried my afternoon dispatch to Key West was always willing to mail a few
long envelopes at the same place. Meanwhile, I
hung about the palace, and picked up enough off-
record gossip to give my dispatches a pleasant air
of verisimilitude, soothing to editors if not to readers. Also, I made daily visits to the headquarters of
the revolutionists, and there got a lot of information, some of it sound, to the same end. In three
days, such is the quick grasp of the reportorial
mind, I knew all the ins and outs of the revolution,
and in a week I was fit to write a history of Cuban
politics from the days of Diego Velazquez. I was,
of course, younger then than I am now, and reporters today are not what they used to be, but into
that we need not go.

After a week it began to be plain, even on the
evidence supplied by the revolutionists, that the uprising was making heavy weather of it, and when,
a day or two later, the palace press-agents announced, in a communiqué running to 8,000 words,
that José Miguel Gomez was about to be taken, I
joined the colleagues in believing it. We all demanded, of course, to be let in on the final scene,
and after a long series of conferences, with speeches
by Menocal, half a dozen high army officers, all the
press-agents and most of the correspondents, it was
so ordered. According to both the palace and the

171

revolutionists, the front was down at Placetas in
Santa Clara, 180 miles away, but even in those days
there were plenty of Fords in Havana, and it was
arranged that a fleet of them should start out the
next morning, loaded with correspondents, typewriters and bottled beer. Unhappily, the trip was
never made, for at the precise moment the order for
it was being issued a dashing colonel in Santa Clara
was leading his men in a grand assault upon José
Miguel, and after ten minutes of terrific fire and
deafening yells the Cuban Hindenburg hoisted his
shirt upon the tip of his sword and surrendered.
He did not have to take his shirt off for the purpose: it was already hanging upon a guava bush,
for he had been preparing for a siesta in his ham-
mock. Why he did not know of the projected attack
I could never find out, for he was held incommuni-
cado in La Cabaña until I left Cuba, and neither
the palace nor the revolutionists seemed willing to
discuss the subject.

The palace press-agents, you may be sure, spit
on their hands when they heard the news, and
turned out a series of communiqués perhaps unsurpassed in the history of war. Their hot, lascivious
rhetoric was still flowing three or four days later,
long after poor José Miguel was safely jugged
among the lizards and scorpions. I recall one canto
of five or six thousand words that included a minute
autopsy on the strategy and tactics of the final battle, written by a gifted military pathologist on the

staff of the victorious colonel. He described every move in the stealthy approach to José Miguel in the minutest detail, and pitched his analysis in highly graphic and even blood-curdling terms. More than once, it appeared, the whole operation was in dire peril, and a false step might have wrecked it, and thereby delivered Cuba to the wolves. Indeed, it might have been baffled at its very apex and apogee if only José Miguel had had his shirt on. As it was, he could not, according to Latin notions of decorum, lead his men, and in consequence they skedaddled, and he himself was forced to yield his sword to the agents of the New York banks.

The night of the victory was a great night in Havana, and especially at the palace. President Menocal kept open house in the most literal sense: his office door was wide open and anyone was free to rush in and hug him. Thousands did so, including scores of officers arriving home from the front. Some of these officers were indubitably Caucasians, but a great many were of darker shades, including saddle-brown and coffin-black. As they leaped out of their Fords in front of the palace the bystanders fell upon them with patriotic gloats and gurgles, and kissed them on both cheeks. Then they struggled up the grand staircase to *el presidente's* reception-room, and were kissed again by the superior public there assembled. Finally, they leaped into the inner office, and fell to kissing His Excellency and to being kissed by him. It was an exhilarating show, but full of strangeness to a Nordic. I observed two things especially. The first was that, for all the uproar, no one was drunk. The other was that the cops beat up no one.

José Miguel was brought to Havana the next morning, chained up in a hearse, and the palace press-agents announced in a series of ten or fifteen communiqués that he would be tried during the afternoon, and shot at sunrise the day following. The colleagues, robbed of their chance to see his capture, now applied for permission to see him put to death, and somewhat to their surprise it was granted readily. He was to be turned off, it appeared, at 6 a.m. promptly, so they were asked to be at the gate of La Cabaña an hour earlier. Most of them were on hand, but the sentry on watch refused to let them in, and after half an hour's wrangle a young officer came out and said that the execution had been postponed until the next day. But the next day it was put off again, and again the next, and after three or four days no more colleagues showed up at the gate. It was then announced by the palace literati that President Menocal had commuted the sentence to solitary confinement for life in a dungeon on the Cayos de la Doce Leguas off the south coast, where the mosquitoes were as large as bullfrogs, along with confiscation of all the culprit's property, whether real, personal or mixed, and the perpetual loss of his civil rights, such as they were.

174

But even this turned out to be only tall talk, for President Menocal was a very humane man, and pretty soon he reduced José Miguel's sentence to fifty years, and then to fifteen, and then to six, and then to two. Soon after that he wiped out the jugging altogether, and substituted a fine — first of $1,000,000, then of $250,000, and then of $50,-000. The common belief was that José Miguel was enormously rich, but this was found to be an exaggeration. When I left Cuba he was still protesting that the last and lowest fine was far beyond his means, and in the end, I believe, he was let off with the confiscation of his yacht, a small craft then laid up with engine trouble. When he died in 1921 he had resumed his old place among the acknowledged heroes of his country. Twenty years later Menocal joined him in Valhalla.

XIV

ROMANTIC

INTERMEZZO

[*1920*]

T<small>AKE</small> wine, women and song, add plenty of A-No. 1 victuals, the belch and bellow of oratory, a balmy but stimulating climate and a whiff of patriotism, and it must be obvious that you have a dose with a very powerful kick in it. This, precisely, was the dose that made the Democratic national convention of 1920, holden in San Francisco, the most charming in American annals. No one who was present at its sessions will ever forget it. It made history for its voluptuous loveliness, just as the Baltimore convention of 1912 made history for its infernal heat, and the New York convention of 1924 for its 103 ballots and its unparalleled din. Whenever I meet an old-timer who took part in it we fall into maudlin reminiscences of it, and tears drop off the ends of our noses. It came within an inch of being perfect. It was San Francisco's brave answer to the Nazi-inspired earthquake of April 18, 1906.

The whole population shared in the credit for it, and even the powers and principalities of the air had a hand, for they provided the magnificent weather, but chief praise went justly to the Hon. James Rolph, Jr., then and for eleven years afterward mayor of the town. In 1920, indeed, he had already been mayor for nine years, and in 1931, after five terms of four years each in that office, he was promoted to the dignity of Governor of California. He was a man of bold imagination and spacious ideas. More than anyone else he was responsible for the superb hall in which the convention was held, and more than any other he deserved thanks for the humane and enlightened entertainment of the delegates and alternates. The heart of that entertainment was a carload of Bourbon whiskey, old, mellow and full of pungent but delicate tangs — in brief, the best that money could buy.

The persons who go to Democratic national conventions seldom see such wet goods; in truth, they had never seen any before, and they have never seen any since. The general rule is to feed them the worst obtainable, and at the highest prices they can be cajoled and swindled into paying. Inasmuch as large numbers of them are Southerners, and most of the rest have Southern sympathies, it is assumed that they will drink anything, however revolting, provided only it have enough kick. In preparation for their quadrennial gathering to nominate a candidate for the Presidency the wholesale booze-sellers of the country ship in the dregs of their cellars — rye whiskey in which rats have drowned, Bourbon contaminated with arsenic and ptomaines, corn fresh from the still, gin that is three-fourths turpentine, and rum rejected as too corrosive by the West Indian embalmers. This stuff the Democrats put away with loud hosannas — but only for a few days. After that their livers give out, they lose their tempers, and the country is entertained with a rough-house in the grand manner. There has been such a rough-house at every Democratic national convention since Jackson's day, save only the *Ja-* convention at Chicago in 1940 and the incomparable gathering at San Francisco in 1920. The scene at the latter was one of universal peace and lovey-dovey, and every Democrat went home on his own legs, with his soul exultant and both his ears intact and functioning.

The beauty of this miracle was greatly enhanced by the fact that it was unexpected. Prohibition had gone into force only five months before the convention was scheduled to meet, and the Democrats arrived in San Francisco full of miserable forebodings. Judging by what they had already experienced at home, they assumed that the convention booze would be even worse than usual; indeed, most of them were so uneasy about it that they brought along supplies of their own. During the five months they had got used to hair oil, Jamaica ginger and sweet spirits of nitre, but they feared that the San Francisco booticians, abandoning all reason, would proceed to paint remover and sheep dip. What a surprise awaited them! What a deliverance was at hand! The moment they got to their hotels they were waited upon by small committees of refined and well-dressed ladies, and asked to state their desires. The majority, at the start, were so suspicious that they kicked the ladies out; they feared entrapment by what were then still called revenuers. But the bolder fellows took a chance — and a few hours later the glad word was everywhere. No matter what a delegate ordered he got Bourbon — but it was Bourbon of the very first chop, Bourbon aged in contented barrels of the finest white oak, Bourbon of really ultra and super quality. It came in quart bottles on the very heels of the committee of ladies — and there was no bill attached. It was offered to the visitors with the compliments of Mayor James Rolph, Jr.

The effects of that Bourbon were so wondrous that it is easy to exaggerate them in retrospect. There were, of course, other links in the chain of causation behind the phenomena I am about to describe. One, as I have hinted, was the weather — a series of days so sunshiny and caressing, so cool and exhilarating that living through them was like rolling on meads of asphodel. Another was the hall in which the convention was held — a new city auditorium so spacious, so clean, so luxurious in its comforts and so beautiful in its decorations that the assembled politicoes felt like sailors turned loose in the most gorgeous bordellos of Paris. I had just come from the Republican national convention in Chicago, and was thus keen to the contrast. The hall in Chicago was an old armory that had been used but lately for prize fights, dog shows and a third-rate circus, and it still smelled of pugs, kennels and elephants. Its walls and gallery railings were covered to the last inch with shabby flags and bunting that seemed to have come straight from a bankrupt street carnival. Down in the catacombs beneath it the victualling accommodations were of a grab-it-and-run, eat-it-if-you-can character, and the rooms marked " Gents " followed the primordial design of Sir John Harington as given in his " Metamorphosis of Ajax," published in 1596. To police this foul pen there was a mob of ward heelers from the Chicago slums, wearing huge badges, armed with clubs, and bent on packing both the gallery and the floor with their simian friends.

The contrast presented by the San Francisco hall was so vast as to be astounding. It was as clean as an operating room, or even a brewery, and its decorations were all of a chaste and restful character. The walls were hung, not with garish bunting, but with fabrics in low tones of gray and green,

180

and in the whole place only one flag was visible. Downstairs, in the spacious basement, there were lunch-counters served by lovely young creatures in white uniforms, and offering the whole repertory of West Coast delicacies at cut-rate prices. The Johns were lined with mirrors, and each was staffed with shoe-shiners, suit-pressers and hat-cleaners, and outfitted with automatic weighing-machines, cigar-lighters, devices releasing a squirt of Jockey Club perfume for a cent, and recent files of all the principal newspapers of the United States. The police arrangements almost deserved the epithet of dainty. There were no ward heelers armed with clubs, and even the uniformed city police were confined to a few garrison posts, concealed behind marble pillars. All ordinary ushering and trouble-shooting was done by a force of cuties dressed like the waitresses in the basement, and each and every one of them was well worth a straining of the neck. They were armed with little white wands, and every wand was tied with a blue ribbon, signifying law and order. When one of these babies glided into a jam of delegates with her wand upraised they melted as if she had been a man-eating tiger, but with this difference: that instead of making off with screams of terror they yielded as if to soft music, their eyes rolling ecstatically and their hearts going pitter-pat.

But under it all, of course, lay the soothing pharmacological effect of Jim Rolph's incomparable

Bourbon. Delegates who, at all previous Democratic conventions, had come down with stone in the liver on the second day were here in the full tide of health and optimism on the fifth. There was not a single case of mania à potu from end to end of the gathering, though the place swarmed with men who were subject to it. Not a delegate took home gastritis. The Bourbon was so pure that it not only did not etch and burn them out like the horrible hooches they were used to; it had a positively therapeutic effect, and cured them of whatever they were suffering from when they got to town. Day by day they swam in delight. The sessions of the convention, rid for once of the usual quarreling and caterwauling, went on like a conference of ambassadors, and in the evenings the delegates gave themselves over to amicable conversation and the orderly drinking of healths. The climax came on June 30, the day set apart for putting candidates for the Presidency in nomination. It was, in its way, the loveliest day of the whole fortnight, with a cloudless sky, the softest whisper of a breeze from the Pacific, and a sun that warmed without heating. As the delegates sat in their places listening to the speeches and the music they could look out of the open doors of the hall to the Golden Gate, and there see a fleet of warships that had been sent in by the Hon. Josephus Daniels, then Secretary of the Navy, to entertain them with salutes and manoeuvres.

There was an excellent band in the hall, and its leader had been instructed to dress in every speaker with appropriate music. If a gentleman from Kentucky arose, then the band played " My Old Kentucky Home "; if he was followed by one from Indiana, then it played " On the Banks of the Wabash." Only once during the memorable day did the leader make a slip, and that was when he greeted a Georgia delegate with " Marching Through Georgia," but even then he quickly recovered himself and slid into " At a Georgia Campmeeting." An entirely new problem confronted him as the morning wore on, for it was at San Francisco in 1920 that the first lady delegates appeared at a Democratic national convention. His test came when the earliest bird among these stateswomen got the chairman's eye. What she arose to say I do not recall, but I remember that she was a Mrs. FitzGerald of Massachusetts, a very handsome woman. As she appeared on the platform, the leader let go with " Oh, You Beautiful Doll! " The delegates and alternates, struck by the artful patness of the selection, leaped to their legs and cheered, and La Fitz-Gerald's remarks, whatever they were, were received with almost delirious enthusiasm. The next female up was Mrs. Izetta Jewel Brown of West Virginia, a former actress who knew precisely how to walk across a stage and what clothes were for. When the delegates and alternates saw her they were stricken dumb with admiration, but when the

band leader gave her " Oh, What a Pal Was
Mary," they cut loose with yells that must have
been heard half way to San José.

It was not these ladies, however, who made top
score on that memorable day, but the Hon. Al
Smith of New York. Al, in those days, was by no
means the national celebrity that he was to become
later. He had already, to be sure, served a year of
his first term as Governor of New York, but not
many people west of Erie, Pa., had ever heard of
him, and to most of the delegates at San Francisco
he was no more than a vague name. Thus there was
little sign of interest when the Hon. W. Bourke
Cockran arose to put him in nomination — the first
of his three attempts upon the White House. Cockran made a good speech, but it fell flat, nor did the
band leader help things when he played " Tammany " at its close, for Tammany Hall suggested
only Romish villainies to the delegates from the
Bible country. But when, as if seeing his error, the
leader quickly swung into " The Sidewalks of New
York " a murmur of appreciation ran through the
hall, and by the time the band got to the second
stanza someone in a gallery began to sing. The effect of that singing, as the old-time reporters used
to say, was electrical. In ten seconds a hundred
other voices had joined in, and in a minute the
whole audience was bellowing the familiar words.
The band played six or eight stanzas, and then
switched to " Little Annie Rooney," and then to

"The Bowery," and then to "A Bicycle Built For Two," and then to "Maggie Murphy's Home," and so on down the long line of ancient waltz-songs. Here the leader showed brilliantly his subtle mastery of his art. Not once did he change to four-four time: it would have broken the spell. But three-four time, the sempiternal measure of amour, caught them all where they were tenderest, and for a solid hour the delegates and alternates sang and danced.

The scene was unprecedented in national conventions and has never been repeated since, though many another band leader has tried to put it on: what he lacked was always the aid of Jim Rolph's Bourbon. The first delegate who grabbed a lady politico and began to prance up the aisle was full of it, and so, for all I know, was the lady politico. They were joined quickly by others, and in ten minutes Al was forgotten, the convention was in recess, and a ball was in progress. Not many of the delegates, of course, were equal to actual waltzing, but in next to no time a ground rule was evolved which admitted any kind of cavorting that would fit into the music, so the shindig gradually gathered force and momentum, and by the end of the first half hour the only persons on the floor who were not dancing were a few antisocial Hardshell Baptists from Mississippi, and a one-legged war veteran from Ohio. For a while the chairman, old Joe Robinson, made formal attempts to restore order, but after that he let it run, and run it did until the last hoofer was exhausted. Then a young man named Franklin D. Roosevelt got up to second Al's nomination. He made a long and earnest speech on the heroic achievements of the Navy in the late war, and killed Al's boom then and there.

That great and singular day was a Wednesday, and the bosses of the convention made plans the next morning to bring its proceedings to a close on Saturday. But the delegates and alternates simply refused to agree. The romantic tunes of " East Side, West Side " and " A Bicycle Built For Two " were still sounding in their ears, and their veins still bulged and glowed with Jim Rolph's Bourbon. The supply of it seemed to be unlimited. Day by day, almost hour by hour, the ladies' committee produced more. Thus Thursday passed in happy abandon, and then Friday. On Saturday someone proposed boldly that the convention adjourn over the week-end, and the motion was carried by a vote of 998 to 26. That afternoon the delegates and alternates, each packing a liberal supply of the Bourbon, entered into taxicabs and set out to see what was over the horizon. San Francisco was perfect, but they sweated for new worlds, new marvels, new adventures. On the Monday following some of them were roped by the police in places more than a hundred miles away, and started back to their duties in charge of trained nurses. One taxicab actually reached Carson City, Nev., and another was reported, probably apocryphally, in San Diego. I myself, though I am an abstemious man, awoke on Sunday morning on the beach at Half Moon Bay, which is as far from San Francisco as Peekskill is from New York. But that was caused, not by Jim Rolph's Bourbon, but by George Sterling's grappo, a kind of brandy distilled from California grape skins, with the addition of strychnine.

After the delegates went home at last the Methodists of San Francisco got wind of the Bourbon and started a noisy public inquiry into its provenance. Jim Rolph, who was a very dignified man, let them roar on without deigning to notice them, even when they alleged that it had been charged to the town smallpox hospital, and offered to prove that there had not been a case of smallpox there since 1897. In due time he came up for reëlection, and they renewed their lying and unChristian attack. As a result he was reëlected almost unanimously, and remained in office, as I have noted, until 1931. In that year, as I have also noted, he was promoted by the appreciative people of all California to the highest place within their gift, and there he remained, to the satisfaction of the whole human race, until his lamented death in 1934.

XV

OLD HOME DAY

[*1922*]

In the Autumn of 1922, being at large in Europe, I was assigned by the Baltimore *Sunpaper* to go to the island of Wieringen in the Zuider Zee to have a look at the German Crown Prince, then interned there. I recall that I had a pleasant day with him, but what he had to say I forget. Indeed, my only clear memory of the trip has to do with its difficulties, not with its object. On the map Wieringen looks to be almost as conveniently located as Staten Island, and its airline distance from Amsterdam can't be more than forty miles, but it took me two whole days and nights to get there and back, and I had to use every common means of conveyance save wheelbarrows and camels. Most of all, I remember that one of the two nights *en route* was spent in a little town called Den Helder, at the northernmost tip of the Holland mainland — the most depressing place, not excepting Waycross, Ga., and El-wood, Ind., that I have ever encountered.

Den Helder lies just under the dike that keeps the North Sea off the flat farmlands behind it, and serves in Summer as a bathing place for the inferior bourgeoisie of the North Holland towns. How these customers manage to bathe there I do not know and can't figure out, for the seaward side of the dike slopes down at an angle of at least 40 degrees and is paved with jagged and enormous cobblestones, brought in from Norway to turn the teeth of the sea. But that is neither here nor there, for when I saw the place it was well along in September, and all the Summer visitors had gone home. There was only one hotel open, and in it I was given a room on the top floor, just high enough in the air for me to see over the crest of the dike. As I glanced out of my window to get my bearings a wave was coming in from the northwest, which is to say, from the very bowels of the North Sea. It looked, to my unpractised eye, to be at least 200 feet high, and when it struck the dike and was busted and baffled by the cobblestones it made a roar like a whole herd of Niagaras. The hotel trembled so violently that I was knocked off my feet, and the ensuing reverberations must have shaken the villages as far south as Alkmaar.

Obviously, it would be impossible to sleep in that room without the use of drugs, and inasmuch as I had no opium or chloroform on me I returned downstairs to the coffee-room to find out what offered there. To my astonishment I found that none of the waiters on duty could speak English, nor, indeed, any other language that I was acquainted with, even by hearsay. I tried them with bad German, worse French, downright pathological Spanish, and even snatches of Danish, Russian, Czech, Turkish and Swahili, but they kept on spreading their hands and shaking their heads. Finally, I opened my mouth, pointed into it, made a show of swallowing, and indicated my stomach, whereupon they rushed off in a body — and returned anon with a cup of coffee! I must have lost consciousness momentarily, for by the time I found myself jawing them again there was a new man among them and he was addressing me in German so atrocious that I understood it perfectly. He was, he said, a waiter also, but he had been on duty since 6 a.m. and was preparing to go to bed when his colleagues called him. I thanked him for his kindness, asked him to bring me three large glasses of the best beer in the house, and when he returned with them invited him to sit down and drink one of them with me. He accepted politely, and turned out to be a very entertaining and even instructive fellow. We sat there together, in fact, for four hours, and during the first of them he gave me an account of his life in considerable detail. I forget most of it, but I recall that he said he was a native of a village that was half in Holland and half in Germany, and that

he had had to clear out of it because of a difficulty
with the German *Polizei*. At that very moment, he
went on, there was a reward of fifty marks outstand-
ing against him, dead or alive. He said he had come
to Den Helder because it was the most remote spot
in the settled parts of Europe, and a rival, almost,
to Spitsbergen and Archangel. No stranger had
been seen in it between the Napoleonic wars and the
arrival of the Crown Prince at Wieringen.

From such matters he went on to consider larger
affairs, and was presently discoursing upon a
theme that has always interested me — the differences between races. There was a good deal of public talk at the time about Leagues of Nations,
international peace treaties, and such like halluci-
nations, and on them he brought to bear a blistering scorn and what seemed to me to be excellent
sense. They would always and inevitably run
aground, he said, on the rocks of inter-racial enmity — a thing as natural to mankind, and almost
as hard to get rid of, as thirst or lying. The Germans and the Dutch, he said, though they had to
live side by side, hated each other with a hatred that
was fathomless and implacable, and he himself, as
a sort of neutral or mongrel, hated both. This enmity, he continued, had little basis in logic. It was
simply a matter of taste, and its springs lay in
trifles — tones of voice, ways of trimming the hair,
the cut of clothes, table manners, and so on. Nor
did it rage only between definitely different races;

it also split every race into an endless series of hostile factions. " Holland," he said, " is a small country, but the people of one part dislike those of another almost as violently as a Bavarian dislikes a Prussian. And when a Hollander goes abroad — say to the Dutch East Indies or to America — and then comes home for a visit, he finds that he dislikes them all." In witness whereof he told me a curious story, substantially as follows.

There was living down in the *Polder* near Den Helder — the *Polder* is the flat farmland, crisscrossed with tiny canals, that lies below the dikes — an old farm-wife whose only son had long ago emigrated to America, and there done very well by himself in the Dutch colony of Michigan. He never forgot his old mother, but sent her money constantly, and she lived very well on the ancestral farm — a place of eight or ten acres — , with the daughter of a neighbor to wait on her. Her house, indeed, was a kind of show-place, for it was furnished with all the swellest goods of the Amsterdam department-stores. She had a parlor so jammed with marble-topped and mahoganized furniture that it was impossible to get into it, and in her garret were scores of feather-beds — still the touchstones of wealth in all parts of rural Europe north of the Alps. When she gave a coffee-party to her buddies among the other farm wives of the neighborhood, there was so much on the table that fifty per cent. of the guests were laid up the next day.

She was Heaven's gift to the pastor of the village church. Whenever he developed a brisk appetite, which was often, she would set him a banquet that bulged him like a pouter-pigeon, and she kept him supplied with American Bull Durham for his pipe, sent to her by her loving and dutiful son.

This son, however, had not been home for years. For one thing, he had been busy building up a lime and cement business in a town near Grand Rapids, for another thing he had gone into politics, and for a third thing he had got married. His bride was a girl of Dutch ancestry, but born in Kalamazoo — a high-school graduate of aesthetic leanings, with some talent for interior decoration and the violoncello. Their affectionate coöperation had blessed them with a daughter, and the child was now four years old. The war having prospered both politics and the lime and cement business in Michigan, the son decided, in 1921, to make a long-overdue visit to his aged mother, and to take his wife and daughter along. They arrived at Rotterdam in November of that year, and early the next morning proceeded northward by train. It was a fast train, as such things go in Holland — in fact, it was known as the Kanonskogel, or Cannonball — but it took all day to make the trip from Rotterdam to the nose of North Holland, and by the time the pilgrims got to the farm it was pitch dark.

The old lady, of course, was ready with a big welcome, and had put on her best Sunday clothes for the purpose. Moreover, she and her slavey had prepared a stupendous meal to refresh the visitors after their long journey. Yet more, she had asked her friend, the pastor, to grace and bedizen the occasion, and he was present in his full ecclesiastical habiliments, with his beard beautifully curry-combed. As the visitors were set down at the door the old lady rushed out, grabbed her precious grandchild, and gave it a tremendous hug. Unhappily, the child was worn out by the long train-trip, and became alarmed by its grandma's strange costume, so it set up a shrill squawk, and by the time the party got into the house it was howling in a wild and deafening manner. Its father and mother combined to quiet it, first trying soothing and then clouting its bottom, but it took them ten minutes to shut off its caterwauling, and meanwhile the victuals had to wait.

When the party finally got to the table the pastor arose and let go with a prayer that was of truly appalling range and length. He not only prayed earnestly for all the persons present; he also prayed for the Dutch royal family, for Woodrow Wilson, for Clemenceau, for Lloyd-George, for the Dutch colonists in Michigan, for the lime and cement business, and for the heathen everywhere. And then, having got over all that ground, he prayed *against* the ex-Kaiser, the Crown Prince at Wieringen, Hindenburg, Ludendorff and all the other German generals, with occasional flings at the Austrians,

the Bulgarians and the Turks. The bride from
Kalamazoo, knowing little Dutch, could barely get
the drift of it, so she devoted herself to a sly examination of the room they sat in. Unfortunately,
there was only a single oil-lamp on the table, and
in consequence the ceiling, upper walls and far corners were in shadow, but on the wall opposite she
could see no less than five lithographs of Queen
Wilhelmina — apparently a series showing her
gradual increase in bulk from 175 pounds to 250.

The table itself was sufficiently lighted for a
more minute survey. She counted six hams, a huge
pile of black, red, gray and green sausages, a bowl
containing at least 200 boiled eggs, a fish so large
that it looked to be a dolphin, a loaf of rye
bread two feet long and a foot thick, and no less
than ten cheeses, some of them of the size of suitcases. She had been hungry when she arrived, but
now her appetite oozed out of her. Her husband ate
diligently, urged on by his loving old mother, but
after he had sampled five of the cheeses he began to
look faint, and begged for air. As for the child, it
remained quiet enough until the old lady, having
stoked the pastor, sawed off a slab of rye bread two
inches thick, added a huge stratum of ham, and
bade it eat. Its response was to resume its caterwauling, with the addition of loud demands for a
plate of shredded wheat and prunes, its usual supper in Michigan.

The conversation at table, of course, was somewhat labored. The son tried to translate his mother's remarks, and the much longer observations of the pastor, but his wife's mind kept straying from the subjects they treated, and the child went on whining and whimpering. After the meal was got down at last and the pastor had prayed again — this time at less length, for he was pretty well gorged — the old lady suggested sensibly that the little girl must be tired out, and had better be put to bed. Its mother agreed joyfully, and a march to the upper regions of the farmhouse began. It led up a stairway as dark as the family entrance to an old-time Raines law hotel. The grandmother went ahead with a lamp fetched from the kitchen, but its light was hidden by her body, and the child began yowling again in a frantic manner, the while her mother tried to quiet her, and her father, who brought up the rear, began swearing dismally in English and Dutch. The yowling continued while the undressing was going on, but the grand climax of the evening did not come until it was finished. Once the little girl was in her nightie her poor grandmother claimed the privilege of laying her in the bed awaiting her — the most sumptuous between Haarlem and the island of Texel. It was stuffed with at least a hundred pounds of the finest goose feathers known to science — not the common ones that go into ordinary feather-beds, but fine pin-feathers from the most delicate and sanitary areas of adolescent geese specially bred and fed for the service. The old lady lifted the child fondly, and then let it drop ever so gently. It gave a single blood-curdling yell — and straightway disappeared!

The waiter told me that such phenomena were not uncommon in the feather-bed country. A really good bed, made of the super-colossal feathers I have described, was as soft as a powder-puff. Getting into it required a complicated technic, and getting out was even more difficult. Why the old lady did not remember this he did not say and I do not know: no doubt she was somewhat addled by the sad failure of her party and the general uproar. Whatever the fact, the child vanished like a stone thrown into water, and at once both its father and its mother leaped in after it, seeking to bring it to the surface and drag it ashore. When it came up at last its little face was purple, its psyche was aflame with complexes, and it was in the full tide of hysterics. So, indeed, was its mother. Grasping her rescued offspring to her breast, she shooed the heart-broken grandmother downstairs, and then sat down to calm it. She remained at that labor, according to the waiter, until nearly 6 a.m. The dawn was reddening when the child finally fell asleep, and the mother fixed it a pallet on the floor. When she got to her own bedroom, and found only the nose of her husband showing, she broke into whoops of her own, and it took him another half hour to get her to bed herself. Even so, she refused to undress, but went

197

into the feathers with all her clothes on, including her shoes.

The waiter said that the rest of the story was brief but melancholy. The poor old grandmother spent a miserable night herself, wondering why her welcome to her son and his family had been such a flop, and trying to puzzle out the strange ways of American-born children. She determined to make amends by setting a breakfast in the most lavish North Holland style — the sort of thing that had brought her son down with grateful bellyaches when he was a boy. To that end she got her slavey out before dawn, and the two of them fell upon the job of preparing it. When her guests came down at last the table was spread even more royally than the evening before. On it stood a jar of every kind of preserves or pickle in her storeroom, and in the center of them was a huge platter covered with forty or fifty fried eggs, sizzling. At one end was a ham to end all hams — it apparently came from a hippopotamus — with a *Blutwurst* and a *Leberwurst* to flank it, and at the other end was a cheese as big as *two* suitcases. The daughter-in-law took one look, and then rushed out into the yard: something analogous to *mal de mer* had fetched her. The child, seeing her flee, ran after her, shrieking piteously, and the son made after the child.

At 9 a.m., continued the waiter, the three boarded the south-bound Cannonball at the nearest flagstop, with the child still carrying on in a frenzied manner, and ten or twelve hours later they were in Rotterdam. The next day they started back for America — in the same ship that had brought them in only three days before. "The poor old woman," he concluded, "never got over it. She had been blowing about her rich son and his family for months, and now they had walked out on her. Who's fault was it? Nobody's. The pastor laid the whole thing to God, and I believe he was right."

XVI

THE NOBLE

EXPERIMENT

[1924]

PROHIBITION went into effect on January 16, 1920, and blew up at last on December 5, 1933 — an elapsed time of twelve years, ten months and nineteen days. It seemed almost a geological epoch while it was going on, and the human suffering that it entailed must have been a fair match for that of the Black Death or the Thirty Years' War, but I should say at once that my own share of the blood, sweat and tears was extremely meagre. I was, so far as I have been able to discover, the first man south of the Mason and Dixon line to brew a drinkable home-brew, and as a result my native Baltimore smelled powerfully of malt and hops during the whole horror, for I did not keep my art to myself, but imparted it to anyone who could be trusted

— which meant anyone save a few abandoned Methodists, Baptists and Presbyterians, most of them already far gone in glycosuria, cholelithiasis or gastrohydrorrhea, and all of them soon so low in mind and body that they could be ignored.

My seminary was run on a sort of chain-letter plan. That is to say, I took ten pupils, and then each of the ten took ten, and so on *ad infinitum*. There were dull dogs in Baltimore who went through the course forty or fifty times, under as many different holders of my degrees, and even then never got beyond a nauseous *Malzsuppe*, fit only for policemen and Sunday-school superintendents. But there were others of a much more shining talent, and I put in a great deal of my time in 1921 and 1922 visiting their laboratories, to pass judgment on their brews. They received me with all the deference due to a master, and I was greatly bucked up by their attentions. In fact, those attentions probably saved me from melancholia, for during the whole of the twelve years, ten months and nineteen days I was a magazine editor, and a magazine editor is a man who lives on a sort of spiritual Bataan, with bombs of odium taking him incessantly from the front and torpedoes of obloquy harrying him astern.

But I would not have you think that I was anything like dependent, in that abominable time, upon home-brew, or that I got down any really formidable amount of it. To be sure, I had to apply my critical powers to many thousands of specimens, but I always took them in small doses, and was careful to blow away a good deal of the substance with the foam. This home-brew, when drinkable at all, was a striking proof of the indomitable spirit of man, but in the average case it was not much more. Whenever the mood to drink purely voluptuously was on me I preferred, of course, the product of professional brewmasters, and, having been born lucky, I usually found it. Its provenance, in those days, was kept a kind of military secret, but now that the nightmare is over and jails no longer yawn I do not hesitate to say that, in so far as my own supply went, most of it came from the two lowermost tiers of Pennsylvania counties. Dotted over that smiling pastoral landscape there were groups of small breweries that managed successfully, by means that we need not go into, to stall off the Prohibition agents, and I had the privilege and honor of getting down many a carboy of their excellent product both in Baltimore, where I lived, and in New York, where I had my office.

When I say New York I mean the city in its largest sense — the whole metropolitan region. As a matter of fact, the malt liquor on tap on the actual island of Manhattan was usually bad, and often downright poisonous. When I yearned for a quaff of the real stuff I went to Union Hill, N. J., and if not to Union Hill, then to Hoboken. Both of these great outposts radiated a bouquet of malt and hops almost as pungent as Baltimore's, and in Union Hill there was a beer-house that sticks in my memory as the most comfortable I have ever encountered on this earth. Its beers were perfect, its victuals were cheap and nourishing, its chairs were designed by osteological engineers specializing in the structure of the human pelvis, and its waiters, Axel, Otto, Julius and Raymond, were experts at their science.[1] This incomparable dump was discovered by the late Philip Goodman, then transiently a theatrical manager on Broadway and all his life a fervent beer-drinker, and he and I visited it every time I was in New York, which was pretty often. We would ease into our canons' stalls in the early evening and continue in residence until Axel, Otto, Julius and Raymond began to snore in their corner and the colored maintenance engineer, Willie, turned his fire-hose into the washroom. Then back by taxi to Weehawken, from Weehawken to Forty-second street by the six-minute ferry, and from Forty-second street by taxi again to the quick, lordly sleep of quiet minds and pure hearts.

The fact that the brews on tap in that Elysium came from lower Pennsylvania naturally suggested an expedition to the place of their origin, and

---

[1] Raymond, like Axel, was from upper Schleswig-Holstein, and hence technically a Dane. I naturally assumed that his baptismal name was an Americanized form of the old Teutonic name of Reimund, signifying a sagacious councilor. But one night he told me that his father, a *Stadtpfeiffer,* had named him after the "Raymond" overture by Ambrose Thomas, a work he greatly admired.

Goodman and I laid many plans for making the trip in his car. But every time we started out we dropped in on Axel, Otto, Julius and Raymond for stirrup cups, and that was as far as we ever got. Alone, however, I once visited Harrisburg on newspaper business, and there had the felicity of drinking close to the *Urquell*. That was in the primitive days when New York still bristled with peepholes and it was impossible to get into a strange place without a letter from a judge, but in Harrisburg there were no formalities. I simply approached a traffic cop and asked him where reliable stuff was to be had. " Do you see that kaif there? " he replied, pointing to the corner. " Well, just go in and lay down your money. If you don't like it, come back and I'll give you another one." I liked it well enough, and so did not trouble him further.

I should add, however, that I once came so near going dry in Pennsylvania, and in the very midst of a huge fleet of illicit breweries, that the memory of it still makes me shiver. This was at Bethlehem in the Lehigh Valley, in 1924. I had gone to the place with my publisher, Alfred Knopf, to hear the celebrated Bach Choir, and we were astounded after the first day's sessions to discover that not a drop of malt liquor was to be had in the local pubs. This seemed strange and unfriendly, for it is well known to every musicologist that the divine music of old Johann Sebastian cannot be digested without the aid of its natural solvent. But so far as we could make out there was absolutely none on tap in the Lehigh Valley, though we searched high and low, and threw ourselves upon the mercy of cops, taxi-drivers, hotel clerks, the Elks, the rev. clergy, and half the tenors and basses of the choir. All reported that Prohibition agents had been sighted in the mountains a few days before, and that as a result hundreds of kegs had been buried and every bartender was on the alert. How we got through the second day's sessions I don't know; the music was magnificent, but our tonsils became so parched that we could barely join in the final Amen. Half an hour before our train was scheduled to leave for New York we decided to go down to the Lehigh station and telegraph to a bootician in the big city, desiring him to start westward at once and meet us at Paterson, N. J. On the way to the station we discussed this madcap scheme dismally, and the taxi-driver overheard us. He was a compassionate man, and his heart bled for us.

"Gents," he said, "I hate to horn in on what ain't none of my business, but if you feel that bad about it I think I know where some stuff is to be had. The point is, can you get it?"

We at once offered him money to introduce us, but he waived us off.

"It wouldn't do you no good," he said. "These Pennsylvania Dutch never trust a hackman."

" But where is the place? " we breathed.

" I'm taking you to it," he replied, and in a moment we were there.

It was a huge, blank building that looked like a forsaken warehouse, but over a door that appeared to be tightly locked there was the telltale sign, " Sea Food " — the universal euphemism for beer-house in Maryland and Pennsylvania throughout the thirteen awful years. We rapped on the door and presently it opened about half an inch, revealing an eye and part of a mouth. The ensuing dialogue was *sotto voce* but *staccato* and *appassionata*. The eye saw that we were famished, but the mouth hesitated.

" How do I know," it asked, " that you ain't two of them agents? "

The insinuation made us boil, but we had to be polite.

" *Agents!* " hissed Knopf. " What an idea! Can't you *see* us? Take a good look at us."

The eye looked, but the mouth made no reply.

" Can't you tell musicians when you see them? " I broke in. " Where did you ever see a Prohibition agent who looked so innocent, so moony, so dumb? We are actually fanatics. We came here to hear Bach. Is this the way Bethlehem treats its guests? We came a thousand miles, and now — "

" *Three* thousand miles," corrected Knopf.

" *Five* thousand," I added, making it round numbers.

Suddenly I bethought me that the piano score of the B minor mass had been under my arm all the while. What better introduction? What more persuasive proof of our *bona fides?* I held up the score and pointed to the title on the cover. The eye read:

J. S. Bach
Mass in B Minor

The eye flicked for an instant or two, and then the mouth spoke. " Come in, gents," it said. As the door opened our natural momentum carried us into the bar in one leap, and there we were presently immersed in two immense *Humpen.* The quality we did not pause to observe; what we mainly recalled later was the astounding modesty of the bill, which was sixty-five cents for five *Humpen* — Knopf had two and I had three — and two sandwiches. We made our train just as it was pulling out.

It was a narrow escape from death in the desert, and we do not forget all these years afterward that we owed it to Johann Sebastian Bach, that highly talented and entirely respectable man, and especially to his mass in B minor. In the great city of Cleveland, Ohio, a few months later, I had much worse luck. I went there, in my capacity of newspaper reporter, to help cover the Republican national convention which nominated Calvin Coolidge, and I assumed like everyone else that the Prohibition agents would lay off while the job was

put through, if only as a mark of respect to their
commander-in-chief. This assumption turned out
to be erroneous. The agents actually clamped down
on Cleveland with the utmost ferocity, and produced a drought that was virtually complete. Even
the local cops and newspaper reporters were dry,
and many of the latter spent a large part of their
time touring the quarters of the out-of-town correspondents, begging for succor. But the supplies
brought in by the correspondents were gone in a
few days, and by the time the convention actually
opened a glass of malt liquor was as hard to come
by in Cleveland as an honest politician.

The news of this horror quickly got about, and
one morning I received a dispatch in cipher from a
Christian friend in Detroit, saying that he was
loading a motor-launch with ten cases of bottled
beer and ale, and sending it down the Detroit river
and across Lake Erie in charge of two of his goons.
They were instructed, he said, to notify me the instant they arrived off the Cleveland breakwater.
Their notice reached me the next afternoon, but
by that time the boys were nominating Cal, so I
could not keep the rendezvous myself, but had to
send an agent. This agent was Paul de Kruif, then
a young man of thirty-four, studying the literary
art under my counsel. Paul was a fellow of high
principles and worthy of every confidence; moreover, he was dying of thirst himself. I started him
out in a rowboat, and he was gone three hours.

When he got back he was pale and trembling, and I could see at a glance that some calamity had befallen. When he got his breath he gasped out the story.

The two goons, it appeared, had broken into their cargo on the way down from Detroit, for the weather was extremely hot. By the time they anchored off the Cleveland breakwater they had got down three cases, and while they were waiting for de Kruif they knocked off two more. This left but five — and they figured that it was just enough to get them back to Detroit, for the way was uphill all the way, as a glance at a map will show. De Kruif, who was a huge and sturdy Dutchman with a neck like John L. Sullivan, protested violently and even undertook to throw them overboard and pirate the launch and cargo, but they pulled firearms on him, and the best he could do was to get six bottles. These he drank on his return in the rowboat, for the heat, as I have said, was extreme. As a result, I got nothing whatsoever; indeed, not a drop of malt touched my throat until the next night at 11.57, when the express for Washington and points East crossed the frontier of the Maryland Free State.

This was my worst adventure during Prohibition, and in many ways it remains the worst adventure of my whole life, though I have been shot at four times and my travels have taken me to Albania, Trans-Jordan and Arkansas. In Maryland there was always plenty, and when I was in New York Goodman and I made many voyages to Union Hill. One hot night in 1927, while we were lolling in the perfect beerhouse that I have mentioned, a small but excellent band was in attendance, and we learned on inquiry that it belonged to a trans-Atlantic liner of foreign registry, then berthed at one of the North river docks. Through Axel and Raymond we got acquainted with the leader, and he told us that if we cared to accompany him and his men back to the ship they would set up some real Pilsner. We naturally accepted, and at five o'clock the next morning we were still down in the stewards' dining-room on H-deck, pouring in *Seidel* after *Seidel* and victualing royally on black bread and *Leberwurst*. The stewards were scrupulous fellows and would not bootleg, but Goodman had some talent for mathematics, and it was not hard for him to figure out a tip that would cover what we had drunk of their rations, with a reasonable *Zuschlag* added.

Thereafter, we visited that lovely ship every time it was in port, which was about once every five weeks, and in a little while we began to add other ships of the same and allied lines, until in the end we had a whole fleet of them, and had access to Pilsner about three weeks out of four, and not only to Pilsner but also to Münchner, Dortmunder, Würzburger and Kulmbacher. It was a long hoof down the dark pier to the cargo port we had to use, and a long climb from the water-line down to H-

deck, but we got used to the exertion and even came
to welcome it, for we were both under medical advice to take more exercise. When we went aboard,
usually at 10 or 11 p.m., there was no one on the
dock save a customs watchman sitting on a stool at
the street entrance, chewing tobacco, and when we
debarked at 4 or 5 a.m. the same watchman was still
there, usually sound asleep.

Gradually, such being the enticements of sin, we
fell into the habit of sneaking a couple of jugs past
the watchman — most often, of Germany brandy,
or *Branntwein*. It was abominable stuff, but nevertheless it was the real McCoy, and Goodman and I
found it very useful — he for drugging his actors
and I for dishing out to the poets who infested my
magazine office. One night there was some sort of
celebration aboard ship — as I recall it, the birthday of Martin Luther — and the stewards put on a
special spread. The *pièce de résistance* was a *Wurst*
of some strange but very toothsome kind, and Goodman and I got down large rashers of it, and praised
it in high, astounding terms. The stewards were so
pleased by our appreciation that they gave us two
whole ones as we left, and so we marched up the pier
to the street, each with a bottle of *Branntwein* in
one coat pocket and a large, globulous sausage in
the other. To our surprise we found the customs
watchman awake. More, he halted us.

" What have you got there in your pockets? " he
demanded.

We turned them out, and he passed over the two bottles without a word, but the sausages set him off to an amazing snorting and baying.

"God damn me," he roared, "if I ever seen the like. Ain't you got *no* sense *whatever?* Here I try to be nice to you, and let you get something 100% safe into your system, and what do you hand me? What you hand me is that you try to do some *smuggling* on me. Yes, *smuggling*. I know the law and so do you. If I wanted to turn you in I could send you to Atlanta for the rest of your life. God damn if I ain't *ashamed* of you."

With that he grabbed the two sausages and hugged them to him. Goodman and I, conscious of guilt, stood silent, with flushed faces and downcast eyes. What was there to say? Nothing that we could think of. We had been taken red-handed in a deliberate violation of the just laws of this great Republic. We had tried with malice prepense to rob the Treasury of the duty on two valuable sausages — say, 67½ cents at 25% *ad valorem* on a valuation of $2.50 for the pair. The amount, to be sure, was small, but the principle was precious beyond price. In brief, we were common felons, dirt criminals, enemies to society, and as reprehensible, almost, as so many burglars, hijackers or Prohibition agents.

The watchman howled on for two or three minutes, seeking, apparently, to impress upon us the heinousness of our offense. We needed no such exposition. Our consciences were devouring us with red-hot fangs. There was no need for us to say a word, for we radiated repentance and regret. But finally, as the watchman dismissed us with a parting blast, Goodman ventured upon a question.

"Do you," he asked, "want the bottles too?"

"Hell, no," replied the watchman. "What *I* am trying to bust up is *smuggling*."

XVII

INQUISITION

[*1925*]

WHEN I was a *cand. jour.* in the infancy of the century, the old-timer reporters who entertained us youngsters with tales of their professional prodigies (at our expense, of course, for the drinks) always introduced anecdotes of the Johnstown Flood and the march of Coxey's Army. Those were the two great news stories of the last decades of the century just closed, and every reporter with any age and patina on him claimed to have covered them. Most of these caricatures of Richard Harding Davis, I suspect, were liars and no more, but in every considerable city, at least in the East, there must have been plenty who actually saw service on both occasions, for the Johnstown Flood (1889) attracted the largest swarm of journalists ever seen up to that time, and Coxey's Army (1894) had a camp following of them that was almost as large as the army itself. Their narratives, whether true or imaginary, were extremely amusing and instructive to their juniors in the trade, but it didn't take me long to notice that they differed radically in various details, some important and some not. For example, there was not the slightest agreement among them about the authorship of the most famous and enduring literary monument of the flood, to wit, the saying, "Don't spit; remember the Johnstown Flood" — now almost as firmly lodged among American maxims as "It will never get well if you pick it" or "Root, hog, or die." One Polonius laid it to James Creelman, another to Karl Decker, a third to a bartender in Altoona, Pa., a fourth to an office-boy on the New York *Sun*, a fifth to Lew Dockstader, and so on. Nor did they ever agree, even within wide limits, about the number of unfortunates washed into Heaven at Johnstown, or the number of hoboes, runaway boys, three-card monte operators, absconding debtors and other such advanced thinkers who marched with Coxey.

These discrepancies puzzled me at the time, for I was still young and tender, and had not yet learned that neither journalism nor history is an exact science. Since then the fact has been rammed into me by hard experience, and by nothing more effectively than by the Scopes trial at Dayton, Tenn., in 1925, which, as I can prove by both witnesses and documents, I assisted in covering myself. It was, in its way, the Twentieth Century's effort to match the Nineteenth's flood and march. As the reporters who had hands in it always agree when they meet, it had everything — and when they say everything they do not overlook its lack of what is called sex interest, for they know as old hands (they are all fast oxidizing now) that sex interest is not necessary to first-rate drama, as, indeed, the flood and the march proved before them. In another respect, also, it closely resembled those memorable events — that is, in the respect that its saga was quickly embellished with many incidents that never really happened. Before I got home from the scene I was already hearing details that I knew were not true, and more and even less credible ones have been hatching ever since. On the unveracity of one such detail, a small one, I can speak with some authority, for I am a figure in it. It is to the effect that my reports of the trial offended the resident yahoos so grievously that they formed a posse and ran me out of town. This began to get into print soon after the proceedings ended, and the clipping bureaux continue to bring me in new and elaborate forms of it at frequent intervals, even to this day. I have reason to believe that many of the yahoos themselves now accept it as true, and that there are heroes among them who claim to have been members of the posse, and to have taken pot shots at me as I ran screaming down the road.

Nothing of the sort ever happened. It is a fact that my dispatches from the courtroom were some-

what displeasing to local susceptibilities, and that
my attempts to describe the town and its people
were even more so, and it is also a fact that there
was talk among certain bolder spirits of asking me
to retire from the scene, but beyond that it did not
go. So far as I can recall, only one Daytonian
ever went to the length of opening the subject to
me, and he was extremely polite. He was one of the
catchpolls of the court, and all he had to say was
that there was some murmuring against me, and
that he thought it might be a good idea if I met a
few of the principal citizens and let them tell me
precisely what was complained of in my writings.
I could see no objection to that, and accordingly
offered to meet these notables at the drugstore —
the Acropolis and Mars' Hill of the town — the
same evening. I got there on time and so did the
catchpoll, but a heavy thunderstorm was making
up, and the rest of the committee failed to appear.
So the catchpoll and I, after waiting half an hour,
parted amicably, and that was the last I heard of
the matter. I was in Dayton for at least four or
five days longer, carrying on my work without the
slightest molestation, and when I left at last — unhappily, before the butchery of Bryan by Clarence Darrow — it was at a time chosen before I
came, and at my own sole volition. Some of the other
reporters present, hearing of the murmuring aforesaid and eager to begaud the lily of the trial with
gilding, professed to take the posse seriously, and

let it be known that they were organizing a counter-posse of their own, with Lindsay Denison of the New York *World* as its commander. Inasmuch as there were nearly 200 reporters in the place, many of them veterans of riots, lynchings, torch murders and labor wars, it may be that the Daytonians took this counter-posse seriously and were induced thereby to cool off, but if so I certainly have no evidence of it. All I can report is that they treated me with great courtesy, despite the necessary unpleasantness of my reports, and that five years later, when the William Jennings Bryan Fundamentalist " University " was set up in a cow pasture adjoining the town, I was invited to attend its consecration, and it was even hinted that I might be allowed to make a speech.

The only strangers who actually suffered any menace to their lives and limbs during the progress of the trial were Clarence Darrow, the chief lawyer for Scopes; William K. Hutchinson of the Hearst papers; an unknown Y.M.C.A. secretary who wandered in from Cincinnati, and an itinerant atheist who came to town to exhibit a mangy chimpanzee. All four were threatened, not with assassination nor even with tarring-and-feathering, but simply with confinement in the town hoosegow; but inasmuch as the hoosegow was a one-room brick pillbox set in the middle of an open field, and the average noonday temperature in the valley of the Tennessee river during July, 1925 was at least 100

degrees, this amounted virtually to capital punishment. Only the atheist and the Y.M.C.A. brother
ever got into that dreadful cooler, but the other
two made narrow escapes. Hutchinson, in fact, appeared to be doomed, but at the last minute he was
rescued by the magnificent forensic powers of Richard J. Beamish, then of the Philadelphia *Inquirer*
and now a high dignitary in the Pennsylvania
State government, with the rank and pay of a lieu-
tenant-general. The crime of Hutch, a very competent and resourceful reporter, was that he had out-
smarted the learned judge on the bench, a village
Hampden named Raulston. The lawyers for Scopes
— Darrow, Arthur Garfield Hays, Dudley Field
Malone and John T. Neal — had made the usual
formal motion to quash the indictment, and the
judge, with a great show of judicial dog, announced that he would ponder his decision. He kept
on pondering it so long that everyone ran out of
patience, and various efforts were made to pump
him, but it remained for Hutch to do the trick. He
worked it by the simple device of asking the judge
if, after the decision was given, the court would adjourn until the next day. The judge replied that it
would, and Hutch had his secret, for if the decision
sustained the motion to quash, the trial would be at
an end and there would be no next day. Within ten
minutes the Hearst papers had a flash saying that
the indictment would be sustained, and so they beat
the country. And within half an hour the represen-

tatives of all the super- and infra-Hearst papers began to receive remonstrances from their home offices, and were clustered around the judge like bees in full fermentation, demanding to know why he had given the beat to Hutch.

This upbraiding greatly upset His Honor, and also puzzled him sorely. He realized in his dim, judicial way that he had been had, but he couldn't make out how. He tried to solve the problem by a two-headed device. First, he ordered the whole corps of correspondents herded into his courtroom for an inquiry *en masse*, and second, he cited Hutch for contempt of court. Many of the non-Hearst correspondents were inflamed against Hutch for beating them so neatly, but when they began to think of the possible consequences of the charge he faced — say, thirty days in that red-hot coop of a can in the field behind the courthouse — their sense of brotherhood overcame their ire, and they tried to devise ways and means to save him. In this Christian work the leadership was soon taken by Dick Beamish. Rising in court in his most impressive manner, he made a speech saying that the matter at issue was full of vexation, and had given all the more seasoned correspondents great perturbation. Not only were grave questions of law involved, but also questions of journalistic ethics. It might very well be — who could say offhand? — that Hutch was guilty not only of violating the statutes of Tennessee but also of shaming the great profes-

sion he theoretically adorned. There was, in Maître
Beamish's judgment, but one way to get to the bottom of the matter, and that was to appoint a committee of distinguished reporters to consider all its
bearings and report upon them at length. The
judge fell for this, and at once appointed a committee with Beamish as its chairman. The other
members were Phil Kinsley of the Chicago *Tribune*,
Forrest Davis of the New York *Herald Tribune*,
Earl Shaub of the Universal Service, and Tony
Muto, a free lance weighing 260 pounds.

This committee was in session all night in Beamish's quarters over the town hay, feed, lime and cement store. It appointed Lindsay Denison its sheriff, and from time to time he dragged in some elder
correspondent to act as *amicus curiae*. I was the
only reporter on hand who had any public standing
as a moral theologian, but Beamish categorically
forbade Denison to summon me — a lamentable evidence that the old feud between the civil and
the canon law, running back to the Eleventh Century, was still running. The deliberations of the
committee, of course, were secret, but with so many
outsiders going in and coming out some notion of
their drift reached the gallery. At the precise stroke
of midnight, it appeared, Tony Muto drew a royal
flush, and half an hour later Phil Kinsley, a great
believer in bold experiment, drew four aces to a
nine. As the laboring of legal and ethical points
grew more and more animated even greater mar-

vels were witnessed. There was, so we were told, one hand of five kings and another of six (some said seven) queens. Beamish was broke and in hock for $7 by 2.30 a.m., but toward dawn he made a glorious recovery, partly due to luck and partly to science, and when the committee, having finished its deliberations, rose at 6 a.m. he was solvent again. So, in fact, were all the others. Only one of them, Muto, was appreciably ahead of the game, and he was ahead to the extent of no more than $3 or $4. Their work done, the committeemen shaved with Beamish's razor, bathed in a washtub, and entered the hay for a brief snooze before reporting to Raulston, J. When His Honor rapped for order at 10 a.m. they were lined up respectfully before his bar, headed by their chairman and spokesman.

The whole course of the trial of Scopes was marked by gorgeous oratory, and I shall make note of another specimen of it anon, but from end to end I heard nothing more magnificent than Beamish's report. He was then at the height of his powers as a rhetorician, and in addition he was a very fine figure of a man, with broad shoulders, an attention-compelling but symmetrical paunch, and a very cocky way of carrying his head. It was the fashion of the time to wear shirts of somewhat loud design, and he had the loudest in Dayton. They were of printed silk, and ran to all the colors of the rainbow, along with many aniline inventions that no rainbow since Noah's time had ever boasted. The public admired them and Beamish loved them so tenderly that he had affectionate names for some of them — the Garden of Allah, Who is Sylvia?, the Dark-Brown Taste, I'm Called Little Buttercup, the Apotheosis of the Rose, and so on. For his effort in behalf of poor Hutch he chose the queen of his sartorial harem — a superb polychrome creation called Everybody's Sweetheart. Nobody wore coats in Dayton, so the crowd in the courtroom got a sizzling eyeful when he arose. But in half a minute the roll of his sonorous periods made everyone forget his splendors, and the whole audience, including the lawyers and the learned judge, was bedazzled and enchanted by the surge and thunder of his words.

So far as I know, no stenographic report of his speech was made, and I shall not attempt to recall it in any detail, for its effectiveness depended quite as much on manner as on content. It included, I remember clearly enough, a review of the struggle for free speech in the Anglo-Saxon countries since Beowulf's time, with extracts from the Areopagitica, the evidence and arguments in the trial of John Peter Zenger, and the writings of John Stuart Mill. There were citations, first and last, of at least a hundred cases — some of them from the standard English and American reports, but a number dredged up from obscure proceedings before county judges and police magistrates in such States as Arkansas, Idaho and Vermont — most of them unknown to the books and maybe also to history. The judge listened eagerly, and no wonder, for it is highly improbable that any argument of the same scope, punch and profundity had ever been offered in his court, or indeed in any other court of Tennessee. At length the sough of words ceased, and Beamish paused to mop his brow, hitch up his pants, fleck a horse-fly off the left arm of Everybody's Sweetheart, and intone the recommendation of the committee. His voice was now low and caressing, and as he came to the end he took a statuesque stance, adjusted his Oxford *pince-nez* on the end of his nose, threw back his head, and looked *under* the horn-rimmed lenses at the judge. " And therefore, Your Honor," he concluded, " your committee, having considered all the facts in a fair and impartial spirit, and given deep and prolonged thought to the questions of journalistic ethics that appear to be involved, now recommends most respectfully that no further proceedings be had." " It is so ordered! " exclaimed the judge, with a loud bang of his gavel, and thus Bill Hutchinson escaped the cooler, and the trial of the infidel Scopes was resumed.

Scopes himself, a modest and good-looking young man, was quickly overshadowed by the eminent characters who heaved and howled in the courtroom — Bryan, Darrow, Hays, Malone and so on. Once, after he had been unseen and unheard for two or three days, the judge stopped the proceedings to inquire what had become of him. He was found — in his shirtsleeves like everyone else — sitting in the middle of a dense mass of lawyers, infidels, theologians, biologists and reporters, and after he had risen and identified himself the uproar was resumed. Darrow, who wore wide firemen's suspenders and had a trick of running his arms under them as he spoke, was threatened with the hoosegow out in the field for a chance remark during one of his interminable arguments. The judge, sweating under his logic, which was couched in somewhat bellicose terms, stopped him and observed: " I hope counsel does not intend any offense to this court." Darrow thereupon paused, yawned ostentatiously, flapped his suspenders a couple of times, and answered: " Your Honor is at least entitled to hope." This brought down the judicial gavel with a thwack that shook the courtroom, and ten seconds later the trial was suspended and Darrow was before the bar to answer a charge of contempt of court. He naturally asked for a chance to consult his associates, and there was a wait while they put their heads together. In the end they decided that the easiest way out was for him to apologize, and this he did in extremely grudging words, with his voice full of stealthy sneers. But the letter of the apology was there, and the judge accepted it without further ado.

The atheist who suffered in the town calaboose was a traveling showman who had wandered in with

his chimpanzee to make propaganda for Darwin.
He parked it at the railroad station, which was near
the jail, and went through the town distributing
inflammatory circulars. Their purport was that his
chimpanzee proved to the eye, and with irrefutable
force, that man and the higher apes were identical,
and that a peek at it for the small sum of ten cents,
along with the accompanying lecture by the atheist
himself, would convince any reasonable customer,
however pious. The days of Genesis, according to
the circular, were pretty well over. As soon as every man, woman and child had seen the chimpanzee
and noted its striking resemblance to a United
States Senator, the American people would rise in
a body and chase all their ordained pastors from
their settlements. The atheist was a mild man, and
his chimpanzee appeared to be at the point of
death, but his selling talk aroused the local Funda-
mentalists, and in a little while he was clapped into
jail. When Denison and I heard of this we went to
the proper authorities, and demanded to see the
chapter and verse of the Tennessee statute under
which he was held. There was, of course, no such
statute. The law that Scopes had run afoul of prohibited teaching Darwinism to children in the public schools, not to adults outside. But the authorities argued that they had general powers to put
down any and every act in contempt of the revelation of God, and we had a dreadful time convincing
them that caging the atheist in that furnace out in

the field was cruel and unusual punishment. Finally, they compromised by agreeing to transfer him to a small hotel down at the railroad station, on condition that he would leave by the first outbound train, taking his obscene and sclerotic ape with him. There was a wait of three hours until the next train left, and the atheist gave them over to throwing copies of his circulars out of his second-floor window. A sort of vigilance committee was formed to gather up these circulars as they fluttered down, and burn them before they could fall into the hands of the young. But a number escaped, and they are still preserved, I hear, in the less pious sort of Tennessee Valley homes, in secret cupboards which also house jugs of forty-rod, pictures of naked women, and birth-control apparatus.

The Y.M.C.A. brother got into trouble as a result of an oafish pleasantry by my colleague, Henry M. Hyde, and myself, no doubt in bad taste. On our first day in Dayton we had gone about scraping acquaintance with the country evangelists who were swarming into town, and among them we were especially delighted by an old man named T. T. Martin, hailing from Blue Mountain, Miss. This Brother Martin, a white haired commissar of Yahweh in a clerical black coat and a collar so wide that he could pull his head through it, was a fellow full of Christian juices, and amiable to believer and infidel alike. He was one of the recognized stars of his profession, and had accumulated enough " plant," as he called it, to load two trucks. It consisted of a large stock of dog's-eared Bibles, another of hymnbooks, a reed organ of powerful voice, a portable pulpit, and a set of knock-down bleachers like those used by a one-ring circus. These bleachers he set up on the courthouse lawn, and there he not only used them at his own services but also lent them freely to rival John Baptists. He made a gallant effort to save the abandoned souls of Hyde and me, and would take a hack at us every time he met us on the streets, which was ten or twenty times a day. Indeed, he continued these efforts by mail long after the Scopes trial was over, and when he died at last, only a few years ago, he was full of friendly hopes that the seed he had jabbed into us would fructify soon or late, and that he would thus have the pleasure of meeting us in Heaven with his rings in our ears.

One morning, on meeting him in front of the town drugstore, we sought to get rid of his solicitations by hinting that important news was astir. What was it? We hemmed and hawed a bit, and then told him that it was a report from Cincinnati that a gang of Bolsheviki there were planning to come down to Dayton and butcher Bryan. At that time the Red scare following World War I was still in full blast, and in consequence Brother Martin was considerably perturbed. We warned him to keep his mouth shut, but when we left him he rushed off to the house where Bryan was staying and gave the alarm. The result was that the town constables got into a panic, and sent a hurry call for help to Chattanooga. An hour later thirty or forty Chattanooga cops got in, and the lieutenant in charge of them threw them in a cordon around Dayton, to challenge all suspicious persons as they approached. An extra heavy force was posted at the railroad station, where the afternoon express from Cincinnati was due in a little while. When it arrived only one passenger alighted — the Y.M.C.A. brother aforesaid. He looked innocent enough, God knows, for he wore a black cutaway coat and (despite the infernal heat) a high choker collar, and carried a Bible under his arm. But the Chattanooga cops were taking no chances, so they grabbed him as he alighted and rushed him to the hoosegow. There he sweated and bellowed for an hour while Hyde and I (whose consciences had begun to fever us) joined Brother Martin in trying to convince the cops that he was really what he said he was, and not a Russian trigger-man of democracy. In the end the cops let him go, but not until his choker collar was a ring of mush. He got another one somewhere, and that night he delivered a vociferous tirade against Bolshevism, boozing, atheism and their allied infamies from Brother Martin's collapsible tabernacle on the courthouse lawn. Brother Martin had forgotten where he got the tip about the attempt on Bryan even before he reached Bryan's quarters, panting and half scared

229

to death. An hour later, in fact, when Hyde and I
met him again, he imparted it to us as news, and we
thanked him very politely.

Bryan, of course, was the star of the show, and
when he appeared upon the streets, always in his
shirtsleeves and wearing a curious deep-collared
shirt made for him by his wife, he was followed by a
large gallery of the local Bible searchers. Many
tackled him with problems of exegesis that had
floored them in their studies, but he never lacked
a prompt and convincing answer. Now and then a
Holy Roller, a Dunkard, a Unitarian or even a
downright infidel had at him with a trick question,
but he always turned them off facilely, for he was
as thoroughly soaked in the Holy Scriptures as
many another aspirant to the Presidency has been
in alcohol. Bryan liked country people, and was at
ease among them. Whenever he encountered a
mountain family from the Pamirs behind Dayton,
the husband and father in his go-to-meeting over-
alls, the wife and mother giving titty (as the local
phrase had it) to her youngest child, and the rest
peeking from behind her skirts, he would stop his
parade long enough to greet them with the courtly
deportment he had picked up from the Spanish
ambassador during his days as Secretary of State.
This ceremonious greeting always made a powerful
impression upon the assembled hinds. There were
many among them who believed that Bryan was no

longer merely human, but had lifted himself to
some level or other of the celestial angels, archan-
gels, principalities, powers, virtues, dominations,
thrones, cherubim and seraphim. It would have
surprised no one if he had suddenly begun to perform miracles — say, curing a mule of heaves or a
yokel of kidney weakness, or striking oil in the field
behind the courthouse. I saw plenty of his customers approach him stealthily to touch his garments,
to wit, his shirt and pants. Those with whom he
shook hands were made men, and not a few of them,
I daresay, are showing the marks on their palms to
this day. If the Protestant theologies prevailing in
Appalachia did not prohibit relics as heathenish,
every church in the whole region would have some
souvenir of him under its high altar, if only a lock
of hair, a lead pencil or a page from one of his battery of Bibles.

That the Tennessee of 1925 was still in the Age
of Miracles was proved to me by a curious personal
experience. Before I left for the Scopes trial I had
a session in New York with Edgar Lee Masters, a
merry fellow who delights in poking fun at the
common faiths and superstitions of the country,
often by means of burlesque handbills. He told
me that, if I would agree to distribute it at Dayton, he'd prepare such a handbill in the name of one
of his favorite stooges, an imaginary evangelist
named the Rev. Elmer Chubb, LL.D., D.D. I

agreed of course, and a day or two before I set out I received about 1,000 copies of the following:

COMING!   COMING!
To Dayton, Tennessee
During the Trial of the Infidel Scopes
ELMER CHUBB, LL.D., D.D.
FUNDAMENTALIST AND MIRACLE WORKER
MIRACLES PERFORMED ON THE PUBLIC SQUARE!

Dr. Chubb will allow himself to be bitten by any poisonous snake, scorpion, gila monster, or other reptile. He will also drink any poison brought to him. . . . In demonstration of the words of our Lord and Saviour Jesus Christ, as found in the 16th Chapter of the Gospel of St. Mark:

> " *And these signs shall follow them that believe: in my name shall they cast out devils, they shall speak with new tongues; they shall take up serpents, and if they drink any deadly thing it shall in no wise hurt them; they shall lay hands on the sick and they shall recover.*"

PUBLIC DEMONSTRATION of healing, casting out devils, and prophesying. Dr. Chubb will also preach in Aramaic, Hebrew, Greek, Latin, Coptic, Egyptian, and in the lost languages of the Etruscans and the Hittites.

TESTIMONIALS — *all favorable but one:*
With my own eyes I saw Dr. Chubb swallow cyanide of potassium. WILLIAM JENNINGS BRYAN, CHRISTIAN STATESMAN

Dr. Chubb simply believes the word of God, and his power follows. REV. J. FRANK NORRIS

I was possessed of devils, and Dr. Chubb cast them out of me. Glory to God. MAGDALENA RAYBACK, R.F.D. 3, DUNCAN GROVE, MICH.

When under the spell of divine inspiration Dr. Chubb speaks Coptic as fluently as if it were his mother tongue. As to Etruscan, I cannot say. PROF. ADDISON BLAKESLEY.

Chubb is a fake. I can mix a cyanide cocktail that will make him turn up his toes in thirty seconds. H. L. MENCKEN

SPECIAL NOTICE: Dr. Chubb has never pretended that he had power to raise the dead. The Bible shows that only the Saviour and Twelve Apostles had that power.

Free will offering, dedicated to the enforcement of the anti-evolution laws.

When the trial got under way I hired a couple
of boys to distribute these circulars, and that night
Henry Hyde and I went to the courthouse green to
see what would turn up. Precisely nothing turned
up. Hundreds of copies of the circulars were flying about the grass, and dozens of yokels had them
in their hands, but no one showed any interest in
Dr. Elmer Chubb. A few discreet inquiries told us
why. It was that the miracles he offered were old
stuff in upland Tennessee. Nearly every one of the
evangelists roaring at that moment was ready to
undertake at least some of them, and there were
other evangelists back in the hills who offered to do
them all. A few nights later we saw and heard some
of the latter at a Holy Roller camp five or six miles
from Dayton: it was patronized by yahoos who believed that Dayton itself was so full of sin that they
refused to enter it, even to see Bryan. To be sure,
the performers we saw confined themselves mainly
to speaking in the tongues, and did not venture to
drink poison or to let snakes bite them, but only a
little while later they proceeded to both operations,
and after half a dozen of them had been floored the
State police closed in on them, Mark or no Mark.
But they resisted stoutly, and their customers with
them, and during the eight or ten years following
the infidel Northern newspapers reported a great
many unhappy failures of the magic, some of them
fatal. The question whether the effort to put them
down was or was not in contempt of Divine Revela-

tion became a political issue in Tennessee, with all the principal statesmen of the State sweating to take up a safe middle position, as they had at the time of the Scopes trial.

So far as I can recall, Bryan never expressed any public opinion on the subject, but his frequent declaration that every word in the King James Bible was literally true, including the typographical errors, ranged him on the side of the wonder-workers, and they were all hot for him. For Darrow they naturally had no taste, not only because he derided the Good Book, but also and principally because they really believed in miracles, and were confident that Jahveh would fetch him soon or late. Thus they kept away from him, for they didn't want to be present when the lightnings from Heaven began to fall. Their customers shared this fear, and it went so far that whenever a thunderstorm blew up, which was very often in that tropical weather, everyone save a few atheists began to edge away from Darrow in the courtroom. On the street, when the skies were clear, he had followers like Bryan, but they were by no means so numerous and most of them kept at a prudent distance. Once a mule ran away on the main street, and the whole crowd took to its heels, convinced by the clatter that Darrow's time had come. Bryan was gorged and stuffed at colossal country meals by all the surrounding gentry and illuminati, but old Clarence had to mess miserably with Hays and Malone.

Both of these juniors were also regarded as doomed, but it was generally believed that Darrow would be knocked off first, so the bolder spirits sometimes approached them quite closely, especially when no thunderstorm was in prospect. Here Malone's Irish blarney also came into effect, for he could talk even a Tennessee Baptist into smiling on him. On one horrible occasion, in fact, he came near talking the yokel jury into acquitting Scopes.

This, of course, was not to the taste of Darrow, for he was shrewd enough to see that if the prisoner in the box were acquitted the case would soon be forgotten, including even Bryan's part in it. Inasmuch as his main aim in defending Scopes was to plaster Bryan before the country as a jackass, he hoped that his ostensible client would be condemned to the hulks, for that would enable him to appeal to the Supreme Court of Tennessee, and maybe even to the Supreme Court of the United States, and so keep the searing spotlight upon Bryan. Thus he was dreadfully disconcerted one afternoon when Malone launched into a speech so eloquent that in five minutes the jurymen were visibly wobbling, and in ten minutes even the learned judge was beginning to gulp, pant and scratch himself. The subject of the speech was some formal motion of no importance, and after sending in Malone to do the job Darrow relaxed into his firemen's suspenders and prepared for a quiet little snooze. But he got no snooze that day, for Malone leaped into it with all the fervor of an Irishman pulling the British lion's tail. As I have said, the Daytonians were (and, I suppose, still are) great fans for rhetoric, and they were presently getting a horse-doctor's dose of it. Malone began no louder than an auctioneer crying a sale, but in a few minutes he let his larynx have the gas, and thereafter he produced such blasts and hurricanes of sound that I never heard the like of them until I encountered Gerald L. K. Smith eleven years later. Let him come to the end of a sentence on an open vowel, and it sounded like the roar of a thousand massed lions. Let him stop upon a consonant, and the effect was that of smashing a hundred tons of crockery. There was no loud-speaker in the courtroom, but Dudley did not need it. With his own naked voice he filled the big room with so vast and terrifying a din that it seemed almost to bulge the walls. The yaps could not make out the drift of his remarks, but they were charmed by his execution. Sitting beside Darrow in the lawyers' pen, I watched them as the poison ran through them. First they sat up, then their eyes began to sparkle, and then they half rose from their chairs and fell to breathing heavily. In a little while they were breaking into cheers at the end of every sentence, and some of the more ebullient of them were leaping up and howling. The jurymen went the same way, and even the learned judge, as I have said, began to show signs of succumbing.

All this, of course, was very disturbing to Dar-

row. " Great God! " he whispered to me; " the
scoundrel will hang the jury! " Thereupon he began to make frantic signals to Malone, commanding him to desist, but Malone, like any other orator,
was so intoxicated by the exuberance of his own
verbosity that he was deaf, dumb and blind. Indeed, if lightning had struck Darrow at that minute he'd have missed it. The one hope was that he
would run out of breath soon or late, but for a
while he seemed to be fetching up all that he needed,
and more. But in the end, of course, his lungs began to creak and splatter, and finally, after a series
of cyclonic gasps that first made his face a bright
red and then left it dead white, he shut down at
last and staggered out for air. One of his hearers
had been his charming wife, Doris Stevens; she was
standing in a corner of the courtroom surrounded
by a group of Army officers who had come up from
a nearby camp for the day's show. Dudley made for
her with the sure instinct of any husband, and she
proceeded to mop and soothe him as in wifely duty
bound. I left Darrow and followed along, eager to
offer my felicitations on what was undoubtedly the
loudest speech ever delivered by mortal man since
Apostolic times. The Army officers crowded up to
be introduced to the orator and his wife, and it fell
to me to present them. Doris, in those days, was a
violent Lucy Stoner, and had been denouncing the
reporters every time they addressed her or wrote of
her as Mrs. Malone. But while the delighted an-

thropoids still roared their applause I bethought
me of the first eight verses of Ecclesiastes III, so I
approached the lady's ear and whispered: "What
is it to be, Doris? Miss Stevens or Mrs. Malone?"
Stroking her husband's glistening bald head, she
blushed prettily and answered: "Let it be Mrs.
Malone — this time." So when I presented the
Army officers to her it was in the character of a
bourgeois wife. Her husband, under her ministra-
tions, recovered quickly, and that evening after
dinner he took Hays for $17 with four nines.

XVIII

VANISHING ACT

[*1934*]

TAKING one day with another I have but little hankering to see ruins, but when, in the early part of 1934, I found myself aboard a ship approaching the French port of Tunis, in the Mediterranean, and a Catholic bishop who was a fellow-passenger proposed that we go ashore the next day and have a look at the remains of Carthage I agreed at once, for the Carthaginians have always fascinated me, if only because they made so thorough a job of disappearing from the earth. His Excellency, it appeared, was but little interested in them himself, for they were heathens as I was, and hence outside his ordinary jurisdiction; what made him want to see their capital was simply the fact that the Roman city built upon its site had been the stamping-ground of the celebrated Tertullian, who wrote his " Apologeticus " there, and a frequent resort of the even more renowned and much less dubious St.

Augustine. The actual see of Augustine, however, was not Carthage but Hippo, and the bishop and I put in a couple of hours trying to find out where Hippo was, for if it was nearby we might very well make a side trip to it. Unhappily, none of the guide-books in the ship's library threw any light on the question, and we had about given it up as unanswerable when we happened upon a dog's-eared German encyclopedia and learned from it that there were actually two Hippos, both of them to the west of Carthage. The first, it appeared, was still carried on the books of the Vatican as Hippo Diarrhytus and the second as Hippo Regius, but now they were only the theoretical cathedral towns of titular dioceses, without anything in them even remotely resembling cathedrals. If they actually had bishops then those bishops had probably never seen them, nor made any serious inquiries into their spiritual condition, but were engaged instead upon paper work at Rome. Which Hippo was Augustine's? The encyclopedia was not altogether clear on the point, but we concluded after some speculation (as it turned out, rightly) that it must be Hippo Regius, and dug up an atlas to find out where it lay. There was no such town in the atlas, and it was not until we landed at Tunis the next day that we learned that Hippo Regius had changed its name to Bône, and was so far from Tunis that getting there and back would take us three or four days. So we gave up the idea of vis-

iting the see of Augustine, and contented ourselves
with taking a look at Carthage.

What is left of it, we found, lies about ten miles
northeast of the city of Tunis, on the brow of a
little hill now called Byrsa, jutting out into the
Gulf of Tunis, with the blue of the Mediterranean
fading off into the distance beyond. The slope of
the hill is steep in front, and the pea-green inshore
waters of the gulf come quite close to the site, but
on the landward side the descent is gradual, and
vague farms that seem almost level show themselves now and again through the dust of the Tunisian plain. There is an automobile road up from
Tunis, and also a trolley line that stops at the foot
of the hill. Down on the beach a few fishermen haul
in their nets, and in the other direction balls of
denser dust show where some laborious husband-
man is plowing with donkey or camel. The landscape looks almost as peaceful as that of Iowa.
There is no quick movement in it, not even from
birds, and the ear catches no sound. Yet it has seen
some of the wildest fighting ever recorded, and the
climaxes of that fighting were almost always massacres. The earliest navigators of the Mediterranean, coming probably from Crete, fought for a
toe-hold on the shore against the primeval anthro-
pophagi, and then against one another for the trade
that, even in those remote days, flowed up to the
gulf from the black abysm of Africa. By the Ninth
Century B.C. the Phoenicians, who were the Eng-

lish of the ancient world, had driven out all the rest
and built a handsome *cart hadash*, or new town, on
the bluff, and by the Third Century it was greater
than Tyre, their capital, and its sailors and traders roved all the waters from Syria to the Pillars of
Hercules, and even beyond. There is, indeed, every
reason to believe that they circumnavigated Africa at least 1,800 years before Vasco da Gama.
The chief port of this Western trade was always
Carthage. From it radiated routes that reached to
the farthest frontiers of the known world. The Carthaginians controlled the sea-borne carrying trade
of that world, and were its greatest jobbers and
bankers, and whenever they found a good harbor
they set up a colony, and reached out from it for
the business of the back country. One of those colonies, Tarshish in Spain, was so prosperous that
it became, in Biblical times, a sort of common symbol of opulence. Also, it became a refuge for the
broken and outlawed men of the whole Mediterranean littoral, and it was there that Jonah tried to
hide himself when he got into trouble with Jahveh,
as your pastor will tell you. But today Tarshish is
only a measly fishing village at the mouth of the
Guadalquiver, bearing about the same relation to
Cadiz that Sagaponack, L. I., does to New York. As
for Carthage itself, it is not even a village, but only
a spot.

Certainly there must be few parallels in history
to the completeness of its destruction. The Romans,

like all the other Japs and Nazis of antiquity, threw
their hearts into the job when they undertook to
pull an enemy town to pieces, but there is no record that they ever went so far anywhere else as at
Carthage. Consider, for example, the kindred case
of Jerusalem, destroyed in the year 70 A.D. That
was an earnest and comprehensive piece of work,
as such things go, and the Jews still wail it as their
worst disaster since the Babylonian Captivity; but
let us not forget that the wall before which they
do their wailing survived the Roman mortars and
torpedo-bombs almost undamaged, and remains in
excellent repair to this day. Nor is it the only
healthy relic of the days before Jerusalem was
hypothetically wiped out, to rise no more; the
town, in fact, is full of odds and ends that are
ascribed, at least by the guides, to the ages of Solomon, Moses, Abraham and even Adam. But at
Carthage the Romans really spit on their hands,
and in consequence the remains of the city, once so
rich and so puissant, are no greater in bulk and
hardly greater in significance than the remains of
a barn struck by lightning. The French fathers
settled in the place have raked up everything they
could find and stored it in what they call a museum, but you could get the whole contents of that
museum into a couple of boxcars, and most of them
are mere scraps and potsherds, unidentified and
unidentifiable. For when the Romans demolished
Carthage they not only tore down and removed all

its buildings, and plowed up its streets, and filled its wells, and emptied its graves; they also devoured and annihilated all its records, so that what is known about it today, save for the major outlines of its history, is next to nothing. Of its people we have only a few names — Hannibal, Hamilcar and so on, nearly all of them of military men. The one Carthaginian author who is remembered is San-chuniathon, and he is remembered only because a fifth-rate Greek once mentioned him, and probably also invented him.

The bishop and I were through with the relics in half an hour, and when we had finished we were no wiser than we had been before. What use did the Carthaginians make of the little stone boxes that were stretched out in a meagre row? The prevailing theory is that they were coffins for the ashes of children sacrificed to the national god, who is assumed to have been the Phoenician Moloch, but that is only a guess, and for all anyone knows to the contrary the name of the god may have been Goldberg or McGinnis, and the creatures sacrificed to him may have been, not children at all, but dogs, cats or goats. If he had a temple that temple is now less than dust, and if it had priests then all the gold, silver, myrrh and frankincense accumulated by those priests is now the same. Even the new town that the Romans built on the site long after the old one was destroyed is far along the road to annihilation and forgetfulness. Its best preserved relic is the shell of a theatre — now greatly resembling a stone quarry in the last stages of bankruptcy and decay. While His Excellency and I contemplated what is left of it, some boys who were passengers in our ship recreated themselves by leaping up and down its moldering tiers. Presently one of these boys missed his step and skinned his shins, and under cover of his caterwauling we withdrew. There was an Englishman nearby engaged upon a lecture to such visitors as cared to hear him. We listened for a while and found his patter far superior to that of the average guide, but what he had to say was, after all, precisely nothing, and that was what we already knew.

So we moved away to a quiet place overlooking the dusty Tunisian plain, and fell into silent pondering, each on his own. I can't tell you what form the bishop's meditations took, for high ecclesiastics are not given to confidences in that field, but my own, I recall, dwelt altogether on the complete obliteration, not only of Carthage the town, but also of its people. They were, I have no doubt, divided into groups and moieties as we are today, and showed all the sharp differences of fortune, virtue, capacity and opinion that have marked human societies at all times and everywhere. There must have been Carthaginians who were admired and envied by the rest, and other Carthaginians who were envied and disliked. Whenever a new source of cocoanuts, ivory or ebony was discovered along the Af-

rican coast, or a new tin mine in Cornwall, or a new
fishing bank in the waters to the North, there must
have been a heavy inflow of fresh money, and a
large part of that fresh money, you may be sure,
was collared by individual Carthaginians of superior smartness, and laid out in ostentations of
the sort that win public respect and lay the founda-
tions of doggy families. It is not hard to imagine
what followed, for the same thing is going on today, not only in all the great nations of Christendom, but also in the black kingdoms of the African
jungle and the barbarisms of Inner Asia. Once Father had the money the rest followed almost automatically. If there were any daughters in the family the general estimation of their pulchritude went
up by 200 or 300%, and all save the one who fell
in love with a lieutenant in the army made elegant
and even gaudy marriages — maybe with the sons
of old families that traced their ancestry back to
the motherland of Phoenicia and claimed descent
from a Duke of Byblus or Zarephath; maybe even
with some actual member of the Phoenician nobility, sent out to the colonies to recoup the failing
fortunes of his house. As for the sons of the new
plutocrat, they went through the Harvard of the
time (first missing Groton, but making Lawrence-
ville), put in five or six years playing polo and
keeping dancing women, and then married soberly
and settled down to sitting on boards of directors,
serving as vestrymen of the temple of Moloch (or

Goldberg, or McGinnis), and waiting patiently for the exitus of their now venerable pa.

By the time he shuffled off at last, leaving doctors' bills to the amount of at least a ton of gold, they were fathers themselves, with wives growing bulky and pious, daughters who never had enough clothes, and sons who broke the legs of the family elephants playing polo and had to be ransomed ever and anon from the clutches of designing wenches from Crete, Sicily and Spain. The grandchildren continued the sempiternal and inevitable round, familiar in Sumer and still familiar in this great free republic. Some of them, born idiots, became philosophers and refused to bathe. Others went in for gambling and were soon in hock to their brothers and cousins. Others succumbed to the evangelists of new religions who were constantly coming in from the eastward, and went about arguing that Moloch (or Goldberg, or McGinnis) was really not a god at all, but only the emanation of a god, and that his parent divinity was someone of the same name, or some other name, in Mesopotamia, the Hittite country, or elsewhere. Yet others laid out their heritage backing schemers who claimed to have discovered tin mines in Carthage itself, not twenty miles from the City Hall; or assembled vast collections of unintelligible papyri from the upper Nile, and employed Greeks with long whiskers to catalogue them; or bought large ranches in the hinterland and undertook to raise

elephants, camels or giraffes; or organized gangs
of gladiators and took them along the North African coast, challenging all comers; or drove chariots
down the main street to the peril of the cops, street-
sweeps, blind men and school children, and landed
finally in the sanitarium on the mountain over behind what is now Tunis. The fourth generation
produced a high percentage of whores and drunkards, and began to slip back to the primordial nonentity. Some of the cadets of the younger lines enlisted in the army, or in the Phoenician Foreign
Legion, and were killed fighting Assyrians, Persians, Greeks or Romans. Others became policemen,
bookkeepers, sailors, collectors for the orphans,
schochets or *mohels* (for the Carthaginians were
Semitic), school teachers, fortune tellers, barbers,
priests, stone masons or horse doctors, or even garbage haulers, fish pedlars or jail wardens. But not
infrequently there was at least one line that kept
its money and held up its collective head, and after
a century or two it came to be accepted as ancient
and eminent, and began to look down its nose at
the rest of the people. The gradual accumulation
of such lines produced an aristocracy — an inevitable phenomenon in human society, then as now.
That aristocracy had arisen from the trading class,
but in the end it was clearly and admittedly superior to the trading class. Its members were regarded
with deference by the commonalty, and had a long
list of special opportunities and privileges. One of

its constituent families, in the later days of Carthage, was that of Hannibal and Hamilcar.

But that it actually ruled the country is not very probable, for aristocracies, taking one century with another, are hardly more than false-faces. They sit in the parlor, so to speak, but down in the boiler-room quite different gangs are at work. Those gangs, whatever the form of government, are composed of professional governors, which is to say, of politicians, orators, intriguers, demagogues. They commonly occupy, in the hierarchy of caste, a place below the salt, and it is unusual for them to transmit their talents and power to their descendants, but while they last all real power is in their hands, whether the country they infest be a monarchy, an oligarchy or a free republic. As I have said, we know next to nothing of the internal history of Carthage, but the little we know indicates that it went through the same upheavals that periodically wrack all the great states of today. Every now and then the parliament, or grand council, or steering committee or whatever the governing body was called suffered a wholesale purging, and as the old gang took to the hills a new gang came in. We know nothing of the issues involved, or of the personalities participating, but it is not unreasonable to assume that what happened then was substantially what happens now. Let us not be deceived by recalling that in Carthage, so far as the meagre record shows, the proletariat had no voice in the government, and that demagogy in our sense was thus impossible. Let us recall, rather, that demagogues do not operate on the proletariat only, but also on aristocracies, plutocracies and even kings and emperors. Nay, I have seen them, with my own eyes, operating upon bishops, university presidents and newspaper editors. They are the most adept practical psychologists of the race, and when they rise to their full gifts it is impossible to prevail against them by any means whatsoever, save only by the sorry means of setting another and worse gang of demagogues upon them.

Thus Carthage lived and had its being for 668 glorious years, constantly reaching out for new trade, setting up new bridgeheads on ever remoter and remoter coasts, and piling up wealth as no other nation had ever piled it up before. Its liners and tramp freighters went everywhere, and its ships of war controlled all the seas. Now and then, to be sure, some other nation objected to this relentless penetration, and especially to the monopoly that usually followed it, and there were bloody wars, but the Carthaginians took such unpleasantnesses in their stride, for they were well aware that blood was the price of admiralty. One of their wars lasted a hundred years, but they drew profits out of it all the while it was going on, and came out of it richer than ever. Every savage tribe from the Congo to the Baltic got a taste of their steel, and they did not hesitate to

tackle the greatest empires. Even mighty Rome, at
the apex of its power, found them formidable an-
tagonists, and on several occasions they came within
an ace of sacking the Imperial City itself. Altogether, it took the Romans 119 years to knock them
off, and when it was accomplished at last it was
made possible only by the fact that the blackamoors of Africa, tired at last of Carthaginian rule,
joined Rome against them. As I looked out over
the scene of what must have been the decisive battle of the war, I could not help wondering what
these blackamoors had got out of the victory. Perhaps the Romans let them carry off a few women,
and maybe a share of the lesser bric-a-brac. Otherwise, they got nothing, for the Romans grabbed
everything really valuable for themselves, and a little while later they were running the blackamoors
precisely as prisoners are run in an efficient house
of correction, which is to say, precisely as the Carthaginians had been running them before the war.

The descendants of those poor people were before me as I pondered — laboriously plodding the
Tunisian plain behind their archaic plows and spavined donkeys and camels, each surrounded by his
ball of dust. It seemed a bleak and miserable life
that they were leading, but I couldn't help adding
to myself that they had at least survived. Of their
old masters, the Carthaginians, there was nothing
left save a Valhalla of blurred and incredible
ghosts. I tried, though cold sober, to conjure up

some of them as I contemplated their jumping-off
place, but it was a vain undertaking, for even con-
juring needs materials, and I had next to none.
Who was the chief poet of Carthage in, say, the
year 500 B.C., and what sort of poetry did he write?
I asked myself the question, but that is as far as I
got, for I was not too sure that Carthage had any
poets, and if they existed no specimens of their
work have come down to us. Well, then, what of the
executive secretary of the Carthage Chamber of
Commerce in the year 400? Here I got a little further, for a people as excessively commercial as the
Carthaginians must have had a chamber of commerce, and it is impossible to imagine one without
an executive secretary. I therefore imagined him,
but having gone so far I was stalled again, for I
could not figure out what he must have looked like,
or what sort of office he did his work in, or how
much of his time he devoted to port statistics and
how much to writing speeches for the shipping
magnates, grain exporters and bringers in of ivory,
apes and peacocks who were his employers.

It was easier, somehow, to contrive plausible
phantoms of lesser folk — for example, the stevedores down at the docks, the rowers of galleys, the
cops patrolling their beats, the wine-sellers behind
their bars, the hawkers of charms and images, the
farmers in from the country with their loads of
turnips and cabbages, the soldiers sparking the
housemaids, the barbers with their sharp razors and

clattering tongues. But even the barbers, when I
got to them, hauled me up, for I was not sure that
the Carthaginians shaved. Did the other Semites
of that era? The portraits of Moses, Abraham and
company in the art galleries of the world seem to
indicate that they didn't, and I recalled that even
the orthodox Jews of New York, up to the time
they moved to the Bronx, still wore their beards. In
the end the old gentry of Carthage gave me less
trouble than any of the other folks, for the gentry
are much the same everywhere. As the motorman of
the Tunis trolley began to bang his gong and the
bishop and I climbed aboard his car I was thinking
of the ancient families that saw at one stroke the
ruin of their nation and the annihilation of their
own lines. Some of them, by 146 B.C., had been settled in Carthage for five or six hundred years, and
their position in its society must have been quite
the equal of that of the Percys in England. Whenever there was a public procession they marched at
its head. No one ever dared to flout them, not even
the politicoes in whose puppet-show they served as
glittering dummies. They were the living symbols
of half a millennium of Carthaginian power and
glory, pomp and circumstance, and each of them
was a living repository of honor, dignity, *noblesse
oblige*. Not a few of them, I daresay, were so finely
bred that they had lost the calves of their legs and
were more or less hollow in the head, but they would
not lie and they could not be bought. So they stood

as the third Punic War came to its catastrophic end, and the ruffianly Romans closed in. By the time the burning and slaying, the raping and looting were over they had all vanished — and this is the first friendly mention that they have had in print, I suppose, for 2,088 years.

The bishop and I were silent as we were hauled back to Tunis, each sunk in his own thoughts. When the trolley-car finally stopped at the Tunis four corners we debarked from it and looked for a hack to haul us down to the wharf where a launch from our ship was waiting. At that moment a brisk and handsome young man, obviously an American, emerged from the assembled crowd, approached me politely, and asked me if I were not Mr. Mencken from Baltimore. When I replied that I was he introduced himself as a Baltimorean who had come out to the North African coast some years before, and was at present living in Tunis. I naturally asked him what he was doing there, and his reply was so astounding that I could only stare at him like an idiot. He was, he said, the manager of a baseball league stretching all along the coast, from Casablanca in the west to Cairo in the east, with a couple of outlying clubs in Syria and the Holy Land and another at Gibraltar. But where, I faltered, did he get his pitchers and catchers, his batters and fielders? What did the Moroccans, Berbers, Copts, Syrians, Arabs, Jews and the rest know about the national game of the United States?

His reply was that they knew a lot, for he had
taught them. They were young fellows with plenty
of enthusiasm in them, and hence quick to learn.
Baseball, he said, was now the favorite sport along
the whole south shore of the Mediterranean, and
when two good teams met for an important game a
large crowd turned out and there was a great deal
of loud rooting. There was to be one the next day,
and if I were free he would be delighted to have
me see it as his guest. He had lived in Tunis so long,
he said, that he was now almost a native, but his
thoughts still turned to old Baltimore, and whenever he heard that a Baltimorean was in town he
looked him up.

There was no time to cross-examine this amazing
stranger, for the bishop and I had to get back to
our ship, but he was a very well-appearing fellow,
so I swallowed his tale without too much resistance.
When I got back to Baltimore I found that it had
been true in every detail. There was, in fact, a thick
envelope of clippings about him in the morgue of
the Baltimore *Sunpapers.* I went through those
clippings with great interest, and was not surprised
to discover that not one of them mentioned the fact
that the home grounds of his Tunis club were on
the site of what had once been Carthage.

XIX

PILGRIMAGE

[1934]

I was fifty-three years, five months and sixteen days old before ever I saw Jerusalem, and by that time, with Heaven itself beginning to loom menacingly on the skyline, my itch to sob at the holy places was naturally something less than frantic. I had not, in fact, gone to Palestine for the purpose of touring them, and had no intention of doing so; the only aim that I formulated to myself, in so far as I had any at all, was to visit and investigate the ruins of Gomorrah, the Hollywood of antiquity and the only rival of Sodom in the long and brilliant chronicles of sin. What attracted me to it, of course, was simply this almost unparalleled reputation for wickedness, for my experience of mankind had taught me that ill fame was commonly very much exaggerated, just as good fame was exaggerated. Hadn't I been to Hollywood itself, and found it to be almost if not quite as respectable as Newport

News, Va., or Natchez-under-the-Hill? What if I should discover evidence, on turning over the débris of Gomorrah, that it had been maligned by history, and even by Divine Revelation? In all this, I confess, there was a certain amount of attitudinizing, but I do not apologize for it, for it was attitudinizing more than anything else that led Columbus to discover America, as you will learn by reading Dr. Samuel E. Morison's excellent work, " Admiral of the Ocean Sea." In any case, I was willing to pay my own way, which was a good deal more than could be said for Columbus. If it cost me $250 to establish my thesis I'd be glad to meet the bills out of my own pocket and call it a day, and even if it ran to $500 or $1,000 I'd not be importuning the Queen of Spain for assistance or otherwise passing the hat.

Unhappily, I quickly learned, on inquiry in Jerusalem, that the brimstone and fire described in Genesis XIX, 24 had been so effective that nothing remained of Gomorrah save a name to scare Sunday-schools. Even on the elementary question of its site all the local authorities seemed to be at odds. One of Cook's agents, a young Welshman speaking five languages, told me that it was somewhere in a swamp south of the Dead Sea, and offered to get me there in a Buick, with a chauffeur, an interpreter and three meals a day included, at a flat rate of $18.75 *per diem;* but while I was negotiating with him a Syrian employed by the Palestine Exploration Fund, and speaking seven languages, horned in with a noisy declaration that the true location was fifty miles away, on the *north* shore of the sea. Leaving these experts snorting at each other, I returned to the King David Hotel outside the walls and there consulted the *portier*, an intelligent Swiss speaking nine languages. He told me that what remained of the town was really in the bed of the sea, and offered in proof the fact that the workmen of the English company engaged in dredging the bottom for potash often brought up bones, musical instruments and bogus jewelry. This shook me, and I devoted the next morning to looking into the matter more particularly. Before noon I had accumulated six more opinions, all of them positive and authoritative, but each differing from the rest. By that time I was in a considerable sweat, for it is warmish in Jerusalem even in Winter, so I finally adopted the escapist theory that Jahveh had made a really all-out job of Gomorrah, as the Romans had of Carthage, and abandoned my plan to explore its ruins.

My decision left me with some unexpected leisure on my hands, and I employed it in moseying about Jerusalem, the glory of Israel as Ireland is of God. It turned out to be a town of about the size of Savannah, Ga., or South Bend, Ind., but differing radically from both. There had been, a short while before, some gang fights between Jews and Arabs, and they were destined, a little while later, to fall upon one another in the grand manner, but at the time of my visit, which was in 1934, there was a hiatus in these hostilities and I was not molested, though I was warned by an English cop that some sassy Arab might have at me with a camel flop as an infidel or some super-orthodox Jew might hoot me as a *chazirfresser*. Most of the so-called streets I traversed were not more than ten feet wide and a good many of them ended in dead walls. Nearly all were lined with so-called *suks*, or bazaars — a series of holes in the wall not much larger than kitchenettes. In each *suk* lurked a merchant sitting cross-legged, and in front of each merchant were spread his wares — most often, only sleazy looking rugs, tarnished brass vessels full of dents, crude pottery of the thunder-mug species, and other such gimcrackery. Having just come from Cairo, where some of the *suks* approximate the glitter of Fifth avenue specialty shops, and Algiers, where many of them offer wines and liquors and there is a bawdy-house every block or so, I was not impressed by those of Jerusalem.

There was a good deal of crowding and jostling in the streets, but what made walking really unpleasant was the paving. It was kept in reasonable repair, but it consisted predominantly of cobbles, and they were made of a soft native limestone that became as smooth as glass under foot traffic, and quite as slippery. Having come down a couple of times, I paused in a little plaza to take stock of my

injuries, and there saw a British soldier in full
equipment land on his *tochos* with a fearful clatter. When I helped him to his feet he told me that
he had served in H. M. Army for twelve years, in
posts ranging from Gibraltar to Ceylon and including such hells as Aden and Rangoon, but that
Jerusalem, in his judgment, was the bloodiest goddam place of them all. It was a lucky day, he said,
when the cobbles fetched him less than five times,
and there were bad days when he got back to barracks with his caboose as badly macerated as a
pug's nose and ears. He spoke in favorable terms of
the destruction of the city by the Romans in the
year 70 A.D., though he apparently thought that
the date of the job was as recent as Napoleonic
times. A man of speculative mind, he tried to figure
out how long it would take a smart battery of artillery posted on the Mount of Olives to knock the
whole bloody settlement to pieces, and his guess
was that it could be bloody well done in half an
hour. He was, he said, bloody hot for trying it,
and he hoped that it would be done in some bloody
future war.

This soldier told me, somewhat to my surprise,
that I was standing directly in front of the Church
of the Holy Sepulchre, and advised me with a derisive wink to have a look at the interior. A few
weeks before, he said, the walls had cracked and
the building threatened to tumble in, but since then
it had been shored up by the British authorities

and was now reasonably safe. Entering by a small door at a cost of an American quarter, collected by an Armenian clergyman in long whiskers, I found myself in what appeared, at first glance, to be the midway of a small carnival. The whole roof was hung with shabby banners and streamers, and pendent from them were almost innumerable lamps and lanterns, some lighted and smoking but the majority out of service. The floor was divided by low railings into four or five sections, and I learned from a sort of map that had been handed to me at the door that each belonged to one or another branch of the Christian Church — the Roman, the Greek Orthodox, the Armenian, the Nestorian, and so on. Each section was manned by ecclesiastics of the branch in charge of it. The actual Sepulchre, it appeared, was in charge of the Copts — whether by a permanent arrangement or by some sort of rotation I was not informed. It cost me another quarter to see it, and the priest in charge threw a good deal of hocus-pocus into showing it. What he finally had to offer, after cautioning me in half a dozen languages to keep my hat off, was simply a hole probably ten feet wide, twenty feet long and twelve feet deep, hollowed out of the solid rock and reached by a stone stairway. Obviously enough, at least to anyone familiar with John xix, 41, as I was, it was bogus; indeed it was bogus by the Synoptic Gospels also, for unless Joseph of Arimathea was a reincarnation of Samson no one could imagine him

rolling a stone large enough to close it. But I kept
my doubts to myself, bowed politely to the rev.
Copt, and shoved off to see what the Jews and Moslems had to offer, for Jerusalem is a holy city to
both of them just as it is to Christians.

The Moslems, I found, put on nothing describable as a first-rate attraction, and in fact discouraged visits to their sacred stands by unbelievers,
and the best Jewish show currently playing was
that at the famous Wailing Wall. A British cop
showing me a short cut by way of the old city ramparts, I found the place without any difficulty. It
was a huge excavation in the rock recalling those
that laborious Italians used to make in the Archean
underpinnings of Manhattan island in the days
when men of vision were still building sky-scrapers.
It was lined with masonry, and one of the walls was
considerably higher than the others. At the bottom
of this high wall was the wailing place, and as I
came down the long stairway to the bottom of the
great pit perhaps twenty-five Jews were lined up,
all of them with their faces to the wall. I naturally
expected to hear some hubbub, but save for an occasional mild shriek or groan the wailing was carried on *pianissimo*, and one had to come close to a
given Jew to hear him at all. Their operations were
apparently ritualistic in character, for each had a
book in front of him, held up against the wall, and
some of them followed the text with their forefin-
gers. At one end of the pit stood a camp-stool and a

little camp-table, and on the stool sat a British sergeant in his shirt-sleeves, intent upon a copy of the
News of the World spread out upon the table. I assumed that he was there to protect the Jews against
the Arabs, who might have bombarded them very
easily from the tops of the walls, but when I tackled him he said not.

" I have my men up there," he explained, " and
they keep all suspicious characters moving. Before
an Arab could let go with a dead cat they would
have nippers on him, and he would be on his way to
three months hard. What I am down in this bloody
hole for is to keep the peace among the Jews. They
are all very religious fellows, and so they tend to
hate each other. Suppose a Jew from Baghdad
comes down in the morning and finds that the place
he used yesterday has been grabbed by a Jew from
Salonika. Does he say, ' Excuse me, Mister, but
you have my pitch. Would you mind shoving over a
bit? ' Not at all. In the first place, the Baghdad
lingo is as different from Salonikan as English is
from French, and both speak Hebrew with thick
accents, the one, let us say, like an Irishman and
the other like a Welshman. So they simply screech
at each other, and in two minutes, if I didn't jump
into the ring and make them break, they would be
pulling whiskers, and then their friends would join
in, and we'd have a couple of jobs for the ambu-
lance. But it's not hard to handle them if you know
how. All I have to do is to let go with my fists, and

it is all over. I have been sitting here for six months, and I know most of the steady customers. Some of them, I hear, have been at it off and on for years. It is a kind of trade with them. Nine out of ten are as peaceable as so many blind men. When a shindy is going on at one end of the wall the old fellows at the other end keep on wailing. I have been told that it has been going on since Adam's time. What they are wailing about I don't know, though I have heard two or three different stories. You can never believe anything you hear in Jerusalem. The place is full of liars."

Slipping the instructive sergeant a five-cent American cigar and wishing him many happy returns of the day, I went back to the King David Hotel, and there hired a car to take me to Bethlehem, five miles out of town. The driver, a Soudanese Negro who had been a dragoman in Cairo and spoke very fair English, pointed out the places of interest along the road. The only one that I remember was the Y.M.C.A., a huge structure not far from the King David, resembling in a way a country-club in Florida and in another way the General Motors building at a world's fair. I asked the driver how so large an establishment could be supported in Jerusalem, for Protestants are almost as rare there as in South Boston or the Bronx. He replied that the money came from America, and that the actual patrons were Moslems and Jews. The Moslems, he said, went in for track work in the gymnasium, and the Jews patronized the free classes in double-entry bookkeeping, foreign exchange and scientific salesmanship. On the common ground of their dislike of Christians they met amicably, and there had never been any rough stuff at the Y, even when riots were going on at its very door. I ventured to suggest that maybe this was due to the calming influence of the Y.M.C.A. secretaries, and asked the Soudanese if they had converted any of the Moslems or Jews to their Rotarian theology. His only reply was to laugh. He said that the Salvation Army, a much more powerful theological engine than the Y.M.C.A., had been banging away in Jerusalem for years, but that its only converts to date were a few soldiers drummed out of the British Army, a few drink-crazed Scandinavian sailors wandering in from Haifa and Jaffa, and a meagre haul of other such poor fish. It was just as unlikely for a Moslem to turn Methodist, he said, as it would be for a Methodist to turn Moslem. Protestantism had no more chance in Palestine, he went on, than cannibalism would have in England. Not only were the Moslems and Jews unanimously against it; the Latin, Greek, Abyssinian, Armenian, Coptic and other old-fashioned dirt Christians were even more against it, and spent a great deal of time talking against it. The Holy Land, he said, did not have any taste for novelty, and was generally hostile to strangers. Nearly everything in sight was at least ten thousand years old, and the people distrusted anything newer. The great majority of them, including most of the Jews who were there before Zionism got afoot, preferred Turkish rule to that of the English, who were constantly shoring up tumbledown churches and mosques, arresting poor folk for clubbing donkeys or committing nuisances up alleys, issuing insane regulations for the disposal of garbage, and otherwise making pests of themselves. The Turks believed in living and letting live, and were thus esteemed. To be sure, they had laid on heavy taxes, but it was always possible to get out of paying more than a small part by seeing the right persons, and no tax they ever laid on was as heavy as those laid on by the incorruptible English.

The Soudanese told me that the only thing worth seeing at Bethlehem was the Church of the Nativity — for the rest, he said, the town consisted only of souvenir shoppes full of relics made in Japan — , so I proceeded to take a look at the sacred edifice as soon as we got to the town. It was managed jointly, the Soudanese explained, by monks of the Armenian, Greek and Latin rites, and not infrequently they got into lamentable disputes over nuances of dogma, and had been known, historically, to back up revelation with a certain amount of eye-gouging, nose-biting and whiskers-yanking. I was amazed to discover, when I got to the place, that its builders back in the Ages of Faith had appar-

ently forgotten to give it a front door, just as
Thomas Jefferson, centuries later, was to forget to
provide a stairway in his mansion at Monticello.
The entrance, in fact, was a mere hole in the wall,
and in order to get through it I had to bend almost
double. Arriving inside, I was even more amazed to
discover that there was a large and even huge door
in the rear wall — one big enough, in fact, to let
in a Fifth avenue bus. Why wasn't it used instead
of the hole in front? I asked the question of everyone I encountered in Bethlehem who could speak
English, but never got a satisfactory answer. On
my return to Jerusalem I renewed my inquiries,
and was told by the Swiss *portier* at the King
David that the hole was used simply because the
monks believed that putting customers to a little
discomfort threw them into a mortified frame of
mind, and so promoted their fear of God and made
them generous with contributions. They had read
in some quackish forerunner of " How to Make
Friends and Influence People " that it was sound
psychology to make the pious sweat a bit, lest pride
consume them. If that was actually their theory,
then it certainly failed to work in my own case, for
I emerged from the hole in the front wall, after a
scant fifteen minutes inside, full of wayward doubts
and cholers. I even began to suspect that the whole
establishment was a fake, just as the Church of the
Holy Sepulchre was a fake. How, indeed, could any

rational person reconcile the elaborate marble grotto that the monks had shown me with the manger described in Luke ii, 7, 12 and 16?

Back in Jerusalem, I took a walk that evening to work off my dubieties, and, on encountering a sort of information bureau run by the Jewish Agency, dropped in to pick up some of its literature. One of the young Jews in attendance asked me to sign the visitors' book and I did so. By the time I got back to the hotel a couple of smart agents of the Agency, both speaking fluent English, were waiting for me. It appeared that they had recognized my name as that of a man connected with the press, and had dropped in to say that if I cared to make a tour of the Jewish colonies to the north of Jerusalem they were at my service. This friendly invitation sounded so attractive that I accepted at once. As a result, one of the agents and I started out in a car very early the next morning, and by nightfall had accomplished one of the most charming trips I have ever made in this life. The day was fine, the roads were good, the car was fast, and the agent who steered me, Mr. A. L. Fellman, was an intelligent young man speaking English, Yiddish, Arabic and Hebrew, with family connections in my native Baltimore. Nearly everything worth seeing in Palestine, he told me, was north of Jerusalem, and we covered virtually all of it in the one day, for the distance from Jerusalem to the line of the Sea of Galilee, Nazareth and

Mount Carmel is less than seventy-five miles. The road northward runs almost straight, but we debouched from it often, and at the end of the day our speedometer showed a run of 350 kilometers. At one time we ran along the Jordan for a dozen or more miles and made a foray across it into Trans-Jordan, which looked a good deal like the worst parts of Arizona. Stopping at noon for a hearty *kosher* lunch at Tiberias, on the Sea of Galilee — I recall that there were two soups, three kinds of meat, and four kinds of pastry — , we struck westward over the Galilean highlands, and after seeing the place where the Gadarene swine were possessed by devils and leaped into the water, the birthplace of Mary Magdalene, the scene of the miracle at Cana — often mentioned favorably in the American newspapers of the days of Prohibition — , the town of Nazareth, and the ancient battlefield of Armageddon, we landed finally at Haifa on the sea coast. On the long way we stopped at half a dozen of the Jewish colonies, and had friendly palavers with their public relations agents, most of whom, I found, could speak either English or German, and often both.

These colonies interested me greatly, if only because of the startling contrast they presented to the adjacent Arab farms. The Arabs of the Holy Land, like those of the other Mediterranean countries, are probably the dirtiest, orneriest and most shiftless people who regularly make the first pages of the world's press. To find a match for them one must resort to the oakies now translated from Oklahoma to suffering California, or to the half-simian hill-billies of the Appalachian chain. Though they have been in contact with civilization for centuries, and are credited by many fantoddish professors with having introduced it into Europe, they still plow their miserable fields with the tool of Abraham, to wit, a bent stick. In the morning, as Fellman and I spun up the highroad to the north, I saw them going to work, each with his preposterous plow over his back, and in the evening, as we went westward across Galilee, I saw them returning home in the same way. Their draft animals consisted of anything and everything — a milch cow, a camel, a donkey, a wife, a stallion, a boy, an ox, a mule, or some combination thereof. Never, even in northwestern Arkansas or the high valleys of Tennessee, have I seen more abject and anemic farms. Nine-tenths of them were too poor even to grow weeds : they were simply reverting to the gray dust into which the land of Moab to the eastward has long since fallen. As for the towns in which the Arabs lived, they resembled nothing so much as cemeteries in an advanced state of ruin. The houses were built of fieldstone laid without mortar, and all the roofs were lopsided and full of holes. From these forlorn hovels ragged women peeped at us from behind their greasy veils, and naked children popped out to steal a scared look and then pop back. Of edible fauna there was scarcely a trace. Now and then I saw a sad cow, transiently reprieved from the plow, and in one village there was a small flock of chickens, but the cows always seemed to be dying of pellagra or beri-beri, and the chickens were small, skinny and mangy.

These Arab villages were scattered all about, but most of them were on hilltops, as if the sites had been chosen for defense. Sweeping down from them into the valleys below were the lands of the immigrant Jews. The contrast was so striking as to be almost melodramatic. It was as if a series of Ozark corn-patches had been lifted out of their native wallows and set down amidst the lush plantations of the Pennsylvania Dutch. On one side of a staggering stone hedge were the bleak, miserable fields of the Arabs, and on the other side were the almost tropical demesnes of the Jews, with long straight rows of green field crops, neat orchards of oranges, lemons and pomegranates, and frequent wood-lots of young but flourishing eucalyptus. Fat cows grazed in the meadows, there were herds of goats eating weeds, and every barnyard swarmed with white Leghorn chickens. In place of the bent sticks of the Arabs, the Jews operated gang-plows drawn by tractors, and nearly every colony had a machine-shop, a saw-mill and a cannery. The contrast between the buildings on the two sides of the hedges was as remarkable as that between the fields. The Arabs, as I have said, lived in squalid huts letting in wind, rain and flying things, and their barns were hardly more than corrals, but the Jews lived in glistening new stucco houses recalling the more delirious suburbs of Los Angeles, and their animals were housed quite as elegantly as themselves. The architecture on display, I should add, caused me to cough sadly behind my hand, but it had at least some relevance to history and the terrain, for the general effect was genuinely oriental, as indeed it is in Los Angeles. The Jews appeared to be very proud of their habitations, for every time Fellman and I stopped at one and found the householder at home he insisted on showing us through it, and almost always pointed with swelling emotion to its tiled floors, its screened doors and its running water in the kitchen.

These Jews, however, appeared to spend but a small part of their time admiring their quarters: virtually all their waking hours were given to hard labor in the fields. In the larger colonies they did not even come in for meals, but were fed from a lunch-wagon working out of the central kitchen. Nor were their wives idle, for cooking was their job, and in addition they usually had to attend to the chickens and milk the cows. In some of the more advanced-thinking colonies the care of their children was taken from them to give them more time for these chores, and handed over to professionals, always including a trained nurse with a sharp eye for loose teeth and wormy tonsils. A mother, of

course, could see her offspring in the intervals of
her labors, but until they were six or seven years
old they slept in dormitories attached to the schools,
and she was not responsible for either their ali-
mentation or their indoctrination. Fellman and I
dropped in at several schools, and inspected the
young inmates. They looked as healthy and happy
as the prize babies whose pictures appear in the
rotogravure advertisements of the milk companies.

It was pleasant roving about these luxuriant
farms and palavering with the laborious and earnest men and women who ran them, but it didn't
take long to discover that their passion for a constructive idealism was accompanied by the usual
and apparently inevitable aches and pains. Much
of the land they wrestled with was fertile enough,
once the poisonous Arabs had been cleared off it,
but there were other tracts that had suffered so
badly by the misuse of centuries that getting them
back to fecundity was an appallingly onerous business. They not only needed draining and grading
and the repair of washouts; they also needed a long
course of nursing, with heavy expenditures for
fertilizers. Would this coddling ever really pay?
Would the soil thus restored ever provide sufficient
livings for the heavy work forces needed to restore
it? On that point I found a certain amount of
doubt, concealed only defectively by tall talk. So
long as there was a steady flow of money from Zion-
ists all over the earth the problem would not be

pressing, but what if that flow were ever cut off? Also, what would happen if another world war interrupted overseas trade, and left Palestine to butter its own parsnips? One of the chief customers for the excellent oranges of the country, in 1934, was Germany. Could the Jews, with such markets closed, live on vitamins alone? I suspect that many a sweating colonist, his back bent in the field, occasionally let his mind play upon such unhappy questions, and if not in the field then in his scant hours of ease of an evening, with his radio blaring music from Berlin, Vienna and Rome, and an occasional whiff of jazz from points west.

But this fear of remote and still theoretical catastrophe was much less apparent than a fear of closer and even more unpleasant possibilities. The Arabs, who had been dispossessed of some of their best (as well as of some of their worst) lands, still hung about, and there was little reassurance in their dark and envious eyes. They blamed the *effendi* landlords in Cairo and Damascus for selling them out to the Jews, but they blamed the Jews even more for trading with the *effendis*, if only because the Jews were directly under their noses. It had been assumed by the pumpers up of Zionist enthusiasm, and in fact announced confidently, that the example of the colonists would lift these degraded step-brothers out of their ancient shiftlessness and imbecility, and make competent and successful farmers of them, but the event had proved that they were as incapable of competent farming as so many Florida crackers. Some of them had tried more or less earnestly, but all save an infinitesimal minority had failed. In plain view of the broad and smiling fields of the smart and diligent Jews they were still plowing idiotically with their bent sticks, and if Allah, by any chance, sent them more than eight bushels of wheat to an acre they hustled off to Mecca to give thanks. Like all such Chandala they ascribed their congenital unfitness to the villainy of their betters, and not infrequently they tried to cure it in the ancient Chandala manner. That is to say, they took to assassination. Already in 1934 it was becoming common for a Jew at work on the slopes making down to the Jordan to be knocked off by a shot from the other side of the river. The British had built concrete blockhouses all through that lovely country and armed them with machine-guns, but those machine-guns offered no protection to Jews on outlying farms, and by the time a squad of soldiers got to the scene of a murder the Arab was lost in the wilds of Trans-Jordan. Nor could the poor Jews do anything effective in defense of themselves. I saw a number of them plowing with rifles strapped to their backs, but it was usually in the back that the brave Arabs shot them, and when that happened the rifle went down with the man. Altogether, there was an air of dread hanging over the border, and I was glad when we struck into the Galilean high country. As we mounted the first hill we looked back at the Sea of Galilee and saw a rainbow set prettily upon it, but if that rainbow was actually a promise, as recollections of Genesis IX, 16 suggested, then it was only too obviously a false one. Only a few years later the whole land was running with blood, and then came the even greater calamity of World War II. I wonder as I write what has been the fate of some of the hopeful and persevering Jews I met on that beautiful Winter day. Most of them, I trust, are still alive, but I am not too sure that those who are still alive are more fortunate than those who are dead.

Perhaps appropriately, I made my exit from the Holy Land by way of the battlefield of Armageddon, which began to soak up gore in the remotest mists of the past, and had seen its last battle so recently as 1918, when Allenby and the Turks rounded out their little war by fighting all over it. No military geographer was needed to explain its immemorial popularity among professional bloodletters. The great barrier of the Syrian mountains here ends in the promontory of Mount Carmel, and the only way for an army to move northward or southward in any comfort is by way of the narrow beach which separates Mount Carmel from the sea. By that route all the hordes of antiquity had moved or tried to move. Here the Hittites met the Egyptians, the Egyptians met the Persians, the Persians met the Greeks, and the Jews were slaugh-

tered by one and all. Below the narrow pass the
land widens out into a wide and almost flat plain,
and it was on it that the ancient battles joined.
There is probably no more likely battlefield on
earth; it seems to have been made for the marching
and counter-marching of infantry, and dashing
cavalry charges. As we rolled over it I could not
help thinking of the hundreds of thousands of miserable John Does who had watered it, over so many
ages, with their blood. More than one long forgotten captain won his bays there, and more than one
great empire came crashing down. If it were in
America it would be dotted with hideous monuments to the Fifth Pennsylvania and the Tenth
Wisconsin, and there would be guides to carry tourists over it, and plenty of hot-dog and Coca-Cola
stands to stoke them. But at Armageddon I
couldn't find so much as a marker or a flag. Over
the dust of the immemorial and innumerable dead
some Jewish colonists were driving Ford tractors
hitched to plows. It was much safer there than
along the Jordan shore, and so they looked contented and even somewhat complacent. But I noticed that the earth their plowshares were turning
up was redder than the red hills of Georgia. In the
afternoon sunshine, in fact, it was precisely the
color of blood.

XX

BEATERS
OF BREASTS

[1936]

On September 1, in the presidential campaign year
of 1936, I received an office chit from Paul Patterson, publisher of the Baltimore *Sunpapers*, pro-
posing that I go to Boston to cover the Harvard
tercentenary orgies, then just getting under way.
On September 3, after a day given over, at least in
theory, to prayer and soul-searching, I replied as
follows:

The more I think over the Harvard project, the less it
lifts me. I'd much prefer to join Alf Landon. I like
politicoes much better than I like professors. They sweat
more freely and are more amusing.

My prayer and soul-searching, of course, were
purely bogus, as such exercises only too often are.
I had actually made up my mind in favor of the
politicians a great many years before, to wit, in

1900 or thereabout, when I was still an infant at the
breast in journalism. They shocked me a little at
my first intimate contact with them, for I had never
suspected, up to then, that frauds so bold and
shameless could flourish in a society presumably
Christian, and under the eye of a putatively watchful God. But as I came to know them better and
better I began to develop a growing admiration, if
not for their virtue, then at least for their professional virtuosity, and at the same time I discovered that many of them, in their private character,
were delightful fellows, whatever their infamies *ex
officio*. This appreciation of them, in the years following, gradually extended itself into a friendly
interest in quacks of all sorts, whether theological,
economic, military, philanthropic, judicial, literary, musical or sexual, and including even the pro-
fessorial, and in the end that interest made me a
sort of expert on the science of rooking the con-
fiding, with a large acquaintance among practitioners of every species. But though I thus threw a
wide net I never hauled in any fish who seemed to
me to be the peers of the quacks political — not,
indeed, by many a glittering inch. Even the Freudians when they dawned, and the chiropractors, and
the penologists, and the social engineers, and the
pedagogical wizards of Teachers College, Columbia, fell a good deal short of many Congressmen
and Senators that I knew, not to mention Governors of sovereign American states. The Governors,

in fact, were for long my favorites, for they constituted a class of extraordinarily protean rascals, and I remember a year when, of the forty-eight then in office, four were under indictment by grand juries, and one was actually in jail. Of the rest, seven were active Ku Kluxers, three were unreformed labor leaders, two were dipsomaniacs, five were bogus war heroes, and another was an astrologer.

My high opinion of political mountebanks remains unchanged to this day, and I suspect that when the history of our era is written at last it may turn out that they have been one of America's richest gifts to humanity. On only one point do I discover any doubt, and that is on the point whether those who really believe in their hocus-pocus — for example, Woodrow Wilson — are to be put higher or lower, in entertainment value, to those who are too smart — for example, Huey Long. Perhaps the question answers itself, for very few of the second class, in the long run, are able to resist their own buncombe, and I daresay that Huey, if the Japs had not cut him down prematurely, would have ended by believing more or less in his share-the-wealth apocalypse, though not, of course, to the extent of sharing his share. After the death of William Jennings Bryan, in 1926, I printed an estimate of his life and public services which dismissed him as a quack pure and unadulterated, but in the years since I have come to wonder if that was really just. When, under the prodding of Clarence Darrow, he made his immortal declaration that man is not a mammal, it seemed to me to be a mere bravura piece by a quack sure that his customers would take anything. But I am now more than half convinced that Jennings really believed it, just as he believed that Jonah swallowed the whale. The same phenomenon is often visible in other fields of quackery, especially the theological. More than once I have seen a Baptist evangelist scare himself by his own alarming of sinners, and quite as often I have met social workers who actually swallowed at least a third of their sure-cures for all the sorrows of the world. Let us not forget that Lydia Pinkham, on her deathbed, chased out her doctors and sent for a carboy of her Vegetable Compound, and that Karl Marx (though not Engels) converted himself to Socialism in his declining years.

It amazes me that no one has ever undertaken a full-length psychological study of Bryan, in the manner of Gamaliel Bradford and Lytton Strachey, for his life was long and full of wonders. My own contacts with him, unhappily, were rather scanty, though I reported his performances, off and on, from 1904 to 1926, a period of nearly a quarter of a century. The first time I saw him show in the grand manner was at the Democratic national convention of 1904, in St. Louis. He had been the party candidate for the presidency in 1896 and 1900, and was to be the candidate again in 1908, but in 1904 the gold Democrats were on top and he was rejected in favor of Alton B. Parker, a neat and clean but bewildered judge from somewhere up the Hudson, now forgotten by all save political antiquarians. Jennings made a stupendous fight against Parker, and was beaten in the end only by a resort to gouging *a posteriori* and kneeing below the belt. On a hot, humid night, with the hall packed, he elbowed his way to the platform to deliver what he and everyone else thought would be his valedictory. He had prepared for it by announcing that he had come down with laryngitis and could scarcely speak, and as he began his speech it was in a ghostly whisper. That was long before the day of loud-speakers, so the gallery could not hear him, and in a minute it was howling to him to speak louder, and he was going through the motion of trying to do so. In his frayed alpaca coat and baggy pants he was a pathetic figure, and that, precisely, is what he wanted to appear.

But galleries are always brutal, and this one was worse than most. It kept on howling, and in a little while the proceedings had to be suspended while the sergeants-at-arms tried to restore order. How long the hiatus continued I forget, but I well remember how it ended. One of the dignitaries in attendance was the late J. Ham Lewis, then in the full splendor of his famous pink whiskers. He sat at a corner of the platform where everyone in the house could see him, and so sitting, with the fetid miasma from

15,000 Democrats rising about him, he presently became thirsty. Calling a page, he sent out for a couple of bottles of beer, and when they came in, sweating with cold, he removed the caps with a gold opener, parted his vibrissae with a lordly gesture, and proceeded to empty the beer down his esophagus. The galleries, forgetting poor Jennings, rose on their hind legs and gave Ham three loud cheers, and when they were over it was as if an electric spark had been discharged, for suddenly there was quiet, and Jennings could go on.

The uproar had nettled him, for he was a vain fellow, and when he uttered his first words it was plain that either his indignation had cured his laryngitis or he had forgotten it. His magnificent baritone voice rolled out clearly and sonorously, and in two minutes he had stilled the hostility of the crowd and was launched upon a piece of oratory of the very first chop. There were hundreds of politicians present who had heard his Cross of Gold speech in Chicago in 1896, and they were still more or less under its enchantment, but nine-tenths of them were saying the next day that this St. Louis speech was even more eloquent, even more gaudy, even more overpowering. Certainly I listened to it myself with my ears wide open, my eyes apop and my reportorial pencil palsied. It swept up on wave after wave of sound like the *finale* of the first movement of Beethoven's Eroica, and finally burst into such coruscations that the crowd first gasped and then screamed. "You *may* say," roared Jennings, "that I have not fought a good fight. [*A pause.*] You *may* say that I have not run a good race. [*A longer pause, with dead silence in the galleries.*] But *no* man [*crescendo*] shall say [*a catch in the baritone voice*] *that I have not kept the faith!!!!* "

That was long, long ago, in a hot and boozy town, in the decadent days of an American era that is now as far off as the Würm Glaciation, but I remember it as clearly as if it were last night. What a speech, my masters! What a speech! Like all really great art, it was fundamentally simple. The argument in it, so far as I can recall it at all, was feeble, and the paraphrase of II Timothy iv, 7 was obvious. But how apt, how fit and meet, how tremendously effective! If the galleries had been free to vote, Bryan would have been nominated on the spot, and to the tune of ear-splitting hallelujahs. Even as it was, there was an ominous stirring among the delegates, boughten though most of them were, and the leaders, for ten minutes, were in a state of mind not far from the panicky. I well recall how they darted through the hall, slapping down heresy here and encouraging the true faith there. Bryan, always the perfect stage manager, did not wait for this painful afterglow. He knew that he was done for, and he was too smart to be on hand for the formal immolation. Instead, he climbed down from the platform and made his slow

way out of the hall, his huge catfish mouth set in a
hard line, his great eyes glittering, his black hair
clumped in sweaty locks over his epicycloid dome.
He looked poor and shabby and battered, but he
was pathetic no more. The Money Power had
downed him, but his soul was marching on. Some
one in the galleries started to sing " John Brown's
Body " in a voice of brass, but the band leader shut
it off hastily by breaking into " The Washington
Post March." Under cover of the banal strains the
leaders managed to restore law and order in the
ranks. The next morning Parker was nominated,
and on the Tuesday following the first Monday of
the ensuing November he was laid away forever by
Roosevelt I.

I missed Bryan's come-back in 1908, but I saw
him often after that, and was present, as I have recorded, at his Gethsemane among the Bible searchers at Dayton, Tenn., though I had left town before he actually ascended into Heaven. He was
largely responsible for the nomination of Woodrow Wilson at Baltimore in 1912, and was rewarded for his services by being made Secretary of
State. In New York, in 1924, after howling against
Wall Street for nearly three weeks, he accepted the
nomination of its agent and attorney, John W.
Davis, of Piping Rock, W. Va., and took in payment the nomination of his low comedy brother,
Charlie, to second place on the ticket. During the
great war upon the Rum Demon he hung back un-

til the triumph of Prohibition began to seem inevitable, and then leaped aboard the band-wagon with loud, exultant gloats. In brief, a fraud. But I find myself convinced, nevertheless, that his support of the Good Book against Darwin and company was quite sincere — that is, as sincerity runs among politicoes. When age began to fetch him the fear of Hell burgeoned out of his unconscious, and he died a true Christian of the Hookworm Belt, full of a malignant rage against the infidel.

Bryan was essentially and incurably a yap, and never had much of a following in the big cities. At the New York convention of 1924 the Tammany galleries razzed him from end to end of his battle against the Interests, and then razzed him again, and even more cruelly, when he sold out for the honor of the family. He made speeches nearly every day, but they were heard only in part, for the moment he appeared on the platform the Al Smith firemen in the galleries began setting off their sirens and the cops on the floor began shouting orders and pushing people about. Thus the setting was not favorable for his oratory, and he made a sorry showing. But when he had a friendly audience he was magnificent. I heard all the famous rhetoricians of his generation, from Chauncey M. Depew to W. Bourke Cockran, and it is my sober judgment, standing on the brink of eternity, that he was the greatest of them all. His voice had something of the caressing richness of Julia Marlowe's, and he could think upon his feet much better than at a desk. The average impromptu speech, taken down by a stenographer, is found to be a bedlam of puerile clichés, thumping non sequiturs and limping, unfinished sentences. But Jennings emitted English that was clear, flowing and sometimes not a little elegant, in the best sense of the word. Every sentence had a beginning, a middle and an end. The argument, three times out of four, was idiotic, but it at least hung together.

I never traveled with him on his tours of the cow country, but it was my good fortune to accompany various other would-be heirs to Washington and Lincoln on theirs, and I always enjoyed the experience, though it meant heavy work for a reporter, and a certain amount of hardship. No politician can ever resist a chance to make a speech, and sometimes, in the regions where oratory is still esteemed, that chance offers twenty or thirty times a day. What he has to say is seldom worth hearing, but he roars it as if it were gospel, and in the process of wearing out his vocal chords he also wears out the reporters. More than once, accompanying such a geyser, I have been hard at it for eighteen hours out of the twenty-four, and have got nothing properly describable as a meal until 11.30 p.m. Meanwhile, unless there is an occasional lay-over in some hotel, it is hard to keep clean, and in consequence after a couple of weeks of campaigning the entourage of a candidate for the highest secular office under God begins to smell like a strike meeting of longshoremen.

Of all the hopefuls I have thus accompanied on their missionary journeys — it is perhaps only a coincidence that each and every one of them was licked — the most amusing was Al Smith. By the time he made his campaign in 1928 he was very well known to the country, and so he attracted large crowds everywhere. Sometimes, of course, those crowds were a good deal more curious than cordial, for Al passed, in the pellagra and chigger latitudes, as no more than a secret agent of the Pope, and it was generally believed that he had machineguns aboard his campaign train, and was ready to turn them loose at a word from Rome. But the only time he met with actual hostility was not in the tall grass but in the metropolis of Louisville, and the persons who tried to fetch him there were not credulous yokels but city slickers. His meeting was held in a large hall, and every inch of it was jammed. When Al and his party got to the place they found it uncomfortably warm, but that was hardly surprising, for big crowds always engender calories. But by the time the candidate rose to speak the heat was really extraordinary, and before he was half way through his speech he was sweating so copiously that he seemed half drowned. The dignitaries on the platform sweated too, and so did the vulgar on the floor and in the galleries. Minute by minute the temperature seemed to increase, until fi-

nally it became almost unbearable. When Al shut
down at last, with his collar a rag and his shirt
and pants sticking to his hide, the thermometer
must have stood at 100 degrees at least, and there
were plenty who guessed that it stood at 110. Not
until the campaign party got back to its train did
the truth reach it. There then appeared an apologetic committee with the news that the city administration of Louisville, which was currently Republican, had had its goons fire up the boilers
under the hall, deliberately and with malice prepense. The plan had been to wreck the meeting by
frying it, but the plotters had underestimated the
endurance of a politico with an audience in front
of him, and also the endurance of an American
crowd feasting its eyes upon a celebrated character. It took Al twenty-four hours to cool off, but
I had noted no falling off in his oratorical amperage. He had, in fact, hollered even louder than
usual, and his steaming customers had howled with
delight. What his speech was about I can't tell you,
and neither, I daresay, could anyone else who was
present.

The truth is that some of his most effective harangues in that campaign were probably more or
less unintelligible to himself. The common report
was that he knew nothing about national issues, and
that he had never, in fact, been across the North
river before he was nominated, or even so much as
looked across, so he carried a Brain Trust with him

to help him prove that this report was all a lie, and its members prepared the first draft of every one of his set speeches. Its chief wizard was the famous Mrs. Belle Israels Moskowitz, but she did not travel with the candidate; instead, she remained at his G.H.Q. in New York, bossing a huge staff of experts in all the known departments of human knowledge, and leaving the field work to two trusties — the Hon. Joseph M. Proskauer, a justice of the Supreme Court of New York, and the Hon. Bernard L. Shientag, then a justice of the New York City court. The two learned judges and their secretaries sweated almost as hard every day as Al sweated in that hall in Louisville. They had a car to themselves, and it was filled with files, card indexes and miscellaneous memoranda supplied from time to time by Mrs. Moskowitz. Every morning they would turn out bright and early to concoct Al's evening speech — usually on some such unhappy and unfathomable subject (at least to the candidate himself) as the tariff, the League of Nations, Farm Relief, the Alaskan fisheries, or the crimes of the Chicago Board of Trade. They would work away at this discourse until noon, then stop for lunch, and then proceed to finish it. By three or four o'clock it was ready, and after a fair copy had been sent to Al it would be mimeographed for the use of the press.

Al's struggles with it were carried on *in camera*, so I can't report upon them in any detail, but there

is reason to believe that he often made heavy weather
of mastering his evening's argument. By the time
he appeared on the platform he had reduced it to
a series of notes on cards, and from these he spoke
— often thunderously and always to the great delight of the assembled Democrats. But not infrequently his actual speech resembled the draft of the
two judges only to the extent that the ritual of the
Benevolent and Protective Order of Elks resem-
bles the Book of Mormon and the poetry of John
Donne. The general drift was there, but that was
about all — and sometimes even the drift took a
new course. The rest was a gallimaufry of Al's recollections of the issues and arguments in a dozen
New York campaigns, with improvisations suggested by the time, the place and the crowd. It was
commonly swell stuff, but I'd certainly be exagger-
ating if I said it showed any profound grasp of national issues. Al, always shrewd, knew that a Chicago crowd, or a rural Missouri crowd, or a crowd
in Tennessee, Michigan or Pennsylvania did not
differ by more than four per cent. from a New York
crowd, so he gave them all the old stuff that he had
tried with such success in his state campaigns, and
it went down again with a roar. Never in my life
have I heard louder yells than those that greeted
him at Sedalia, Mo., in the very heart of the no-
more-scrub-bulls country. His meeting was held in
the vast cattle-shed of a county fair, and among the
20,000 persons present there were some who had

come in by flivver from places as far away as Nebraska, Oklahoma, and even New Mexico. The subject of his remarks that night, as set by the two
judges, was the tariff, but he had forgotten it in
five minutes, and so had his audience. There were
stenographers present to take down what he said,
and transcripts of it were supplied to the press-
stand sheet by sheet, but only a few correspondents
actually sent it out. The rest coasted on the judges'
draft, disseminated by the press associations during the late afternoon and released at 8 p.m., as he
arose to speak. Thus all the Americans who still
depended on the newspapers for their news — and
there were plenty of them left in 1928 — were
duped into accepting what the two laborious juris-
consults had written for what Al had actually said.
I do not know, but the thought ·has often crossed
my mind, that Hoover's overwhelming victory in
November may have been due, at least in part, to
that fact.

Al bore up pretty well under the rigors of the
campaign, but now and then he needed a rest, and
it was provided by parking his train on a side-track
for a quiet night, usually in some sparsely settled
region where crowds could not congregate. After
his harrying of Tennessee, and just before he bore
down upon Louisville to be fried, there was such a
hiatus in rural Kentucky. When I turned out in
the morning I found that the train was laid up in
a lovely little valley of the Blue Grass country,

with nothing in sight save a few farmhouses and a water-tank, the latter about a mile down the track. My colleague, Henry M. Hyde, suggested that we go ashore to stretch our legs, and in a little while we were hanging over a fence some distance to the rear of the train, admiring a white-painted house set in a grove of trees. Presently two handsome young girls issued from the house, and asked us prettily to have breakfast with their mother, who was a widow, and themselves. We accepted at once, and were very charmingly entertained. In the course of the conversation it appeared that another, daughter, not present, aspired to be the postmistress of the village behind the tank down the track, and Hyde, always gallant, promised at once that he would see Al, and get her a promise of the appointment come March 4, 1929.

When we got back to the train Hyde duly saw Al, and the promise was made instantly. Unhappily, Hoover won in November, and it seemed hopeless to ask his Postmaster-General to make good on Al's pledge. Four years of horror came and went, but the daughter down in the Blue Grass kept on hugging her ambition. When Roosevelt II was elected in 1932 her mother got into communication with Hyde, suggesting that the new administration should be proud and eager to make good on the promise of the Democratic standard-bearer four years before, even though that standard-bearer had since taken his famous walk. Hyde put the question up to Jim Farley, and Farley, a man very sensitive to points of honor, decided that Roosevelt was bound to carry out the official promises of his predecessor, however revolting they might be. An order was thereupon issued that the daughter be made postmistress at the water-tank at once, and Hyde went to bed that night feeling that few other Boy Scouts had done better during the day. But alas and alas, it turned out that the tank was a fourth-class post office, that appointments to such offices were under the Civil Service, and that candidates had to be examined. Farley so advised the widow's daughter and she took the examination, but some other candidate got a higher mark, and the scrupulous Jim decided that he could not appoint her. Hyde and I often recall the lamentable episode, and especially the agreeable first canto of it. Never in all my wanderings have I seen a more idyllic spot than that secluded little valley in the Blue Grass, or had the pleasure of being entertained by pleasanter people than the widow and her daughters. The place was really Arcadian, and Hyde and I wallowed in its bucolic enchantments while Al caught up with lost sleep on his funeral train.

He was, in his day, the most attractive of all American politicoes, but it would be going too far to say that he was any great shakes as an orator. Compared to Bryan he was as a BB shot to a twelve-inch shell, and as he was passing out of public life

there was arising a rhetorician who was even greater
than Bryan, to wit, Gerald L. K. Smith. As I have
said, I have heard all the really first-chop American breast-beaters since 1900, and included among
them have been not only the statesmen but also the
divines, for example, Sam Jones, Gipsy Smith, Father Coughlin and Billy Sunday, but among them
all I have encountered none worthy of being put in
the same species, or even in the same genus, as Gerald. His own early training was gained at the sacred desk but in maturity he switched to the hus-
tings, so that he now has a double grip upon the
diaphragms and short hairs of the *Anthropoidea*.
Add to these advantages of nurture the natural
gifts of an imposing person, a flashing eye, a hairy
chest, a rubescent complexion, large fists, a voice
both loud and mellow, terrifying and reassuring,
sforzando and *pizzicato*, and finally, an unearthly
capacity for distending the superficial blood-ves-
sels of his temples and neck, as if they were biceps
— and you have the makings of a boob-bumper
worth going miles to see and hear, and then worth
writing home about. When I first heard Gerald, at
the convention of the Townsend old-age pension
fans at Cleveland in 1936, I duly wrote home about
him to the *Sunpaper*, and in the following fervent
terms :

His speech was a magnificent amalgam of each and
every American species of rabble-rousing, with embel-
lishments borrowed from the Algonquin Indians and the

Cossacks of the Don. It ran the keyboard from the softest sobs and gurgles to the most ear-splitting whoops and howls, and when it was over the 9000 delegates simply lay back in their pews and yelled.

Never in my life, in truth, have I ever heard a more effective speech. In logical content, to be sure, it was somewhat vague and even murky, but Dr. Townsend's old folks were not looking for logical content: what they had come to Cleveland for was cheer, consolation, the sweet music of harps and psalteries. Gerald had the harps and psalteries, and also a battery of trumpets, trombones and bass-drums. When he limned the delights of a civilization offering old-age pensions to all, with $200 cash a month for every gaffer and another $200 for the old woman, he lifted them up to the highest heaven, and when he excoriated the Wall Street bankers, millionaire steel magnates, Chicago wheat speculators and New Deal social engineers who sneered at the vision, he showed them the depths of the lowest hell. Nor was it only the believing and in fact already half dotty old folks who panted under his eloquence: he also fetched the minority of sophisticates in the hall, some of them porch-climbers in Dr. Townsend's entourage and the rest reporters in the press-stand. It is an ancient convention of American journalism, not yet quite outlawed by the Newspaper Guild, that the press-stand has no opinion — that its members, consecrated to fair reports, must keep their private feelings to them-

selves, and neither cheer nor hiss. But that convention went out of the window before Gerald had
been hollering five minutes. One and all, the boys
and gals of the press abandoned their jobs, leaped
upon their rickety desks, and gave themselves up
to the voluptuous enjoyment of his whooping.
When the old folks yelled, so did the reporters yell,
and just as loudly. And when Gerald, sweating like
Al at Louisville, sat down at last, and the press resumed its business of reporting his remarks, no one
could remember what he had said.

A few weeks later I saw him give an even more
impressive exhibition of his powers. At the Townsend convention just described one of the guest
speakers had been the Rev. Charles E. Coughlin,
the radio priest, who, in return for Dr. Townsend's
politeness in inviting him, invited the doctor and
Gerald to speak at his own convention, scheduled
to be held in Cleveland a few weeks later. But Gerald's immense success apparently sicklied him o'er
with a green cast of envy, and when the time came
he showed a considerable reluctance to make good.
Finally, he hit upon the device of putting Gerald
and the doctor off until the very end of his convention, by which time his assembled customers would
be so worn out by his own rabble-rousing that nothing short of an earthquake could move them. On
the last day, in fact, they were so worn out, for
Coughlin kept banging away at them from 10 a.m.
to 8 p.m., with no breaks for meals. The device was

297

thus a smart one, but his reverence, for all his smartness, was not smart enough to realize that Gerald
was actually an earthquake. First, old Townsend
was put up, and the general somnolence was only
increased, for he is one of the dullest speakers on
earth. But then, with the poor morons hardly able
to keep their eyes open, Gerald followed — and
within five minutes the Coughlin faithful had forgotten all about their fatigues, and also all about
Coughlin, and were leaping and howling like the
Townsend old folks. It was a shorter speech than
the other, for Coughlin, frowning, showed his itch
to cut it off as soon as possible and Gerald was more
or less uneasy, but it was even more remarkable.
Once more the boys and gals in the press-stand forgot their Hippocratic oath and yielded themselves
to pure enjoyment, and once more no one could recall, when it was over, what its drift had been, but
that it was a masterpiece was agreed by all. When
Gerald came to Cleveland it was in the humble rôle
of a follower of the late Huey Long, jobless since
Huey's murder on September 10, 1935. But when
he cleared out after his two speeches it was in the
lofty character of the greatest rabble-rouser since
Peter the Hermit.

Coughlin, it seems to me, is a much inferior per-
former. He has a velvet voice, and is thus very effective on the radio, but like his great rival on the
air, Roosevelt II, he is much less effective face to
face. For one thing, he is almost totally lacking in

dramatic gesture, for his long training at the mike taught him to stick firmly to one spot, lest the fans lose him in the midst of his howling. It is, of course, impossible for an orator with passion in him to remain really immovable, so Coughlin has developed a habit of enforcing his points by revolving his backside. This saves him from going off the air, but it is somewhat disconcerting, not to say indecent, in the presence of an audience. After the convention of his half-wits in Cleveland in 1936 a report was circulated that he was experimenting with a mike fixed to his shoulders by a stout framework, so that he could gesture normally without any risk of roaring futilely into space, but if he actually ever used it I was not present, and so cannot tell you about it.

THE TYPE

This book was set on the Linotype in *Scotch Modern*, a type-face that has been in continuous service for more than one hundred years. It is usually considered that the style of " modern face " followed in our present-day cuttings of Scotch was developed in the foundry of Alexander Wilson and Sons of Glasgow early in the nineteenth century. The new Wilson patterns were made to meet the requirements of the new fashion in printing that had been set going at the beginning of the century by the " modern " types of Didot in France and of Bodoni in Italy. It is to be observed that the *modern* in these matters is a modernity of the year A.D. 1800, not of today. The " modernist " type-faces of today are quite another story.